# Alternative Services

Alternative Sources

# The Book of
# Alternative Services

## of the Anglican Church of Canada

**Anglican Book Centre**
**Toronto, Canada**

Published by the Anglican Book Centre,
600 Jarvis Street. Toronto, Ontario, Canada, M4Y 2J6

Manufactured in Canada.
Typesetting: Howarth & Smith Limited
Music engraving: Musictype Limited
Text paper: E.B. Eddy Products Limited
Cover material: Columbia Finishing Mills Limited
Printing: Webcom Limited
Binding: York Book Binders Inc.

Eighth Printing 1993

**Canadian Cataloguing in Publication Data**

Anglican Church of Canada. The book of alternative services of the Anglican
Church of Canada

Authorized by the Thirtieth Session of the General Synod of the Anglican
Church of Canada, 1983. Prepared by the Doctrine and Worship Committee of
the General Synod of the Anglican Church of Canada.

ISBN 0–919891–27–6

1.   Anglican Church of Canada - Liturgy - Texts.
I.   Anglican Church of Canada. General Synod.
II.  Anglican Church of Canada. Doctrine and Worship Committee.
III. Title.

BX5616.A5 1985      264'.03      C84–099749–3

# Table of Contents

## Pastoral Offices

## Episcopal Offices

## Parish Thanksgiving and Prayers

## The Psalter

## Music

# Introduction

On 29 January 1971, the General Synod of the Anglican Church of Canada resolved to direct the National Executive Council,

> to initiate a process of revision of Church Services without delay, which will produce alternatives to services now offered by the 1959 Canadian *Book of Common Prayer;* and which will provide guidelines for their use throughout the Anglican Church of Canada.

The Synod also resolved,

> that in future revisions of our Common Prayer Book, more emphasis be given to permissive forms and less to mandatory forms of public worship, in order that in the use of one common book, we may still achieve that flexibility and variety we deem desirable. And that in the meantime General Synod be asked to give guidance to diocesan authorities in relaxing the rigid conformist notes still written into our Common Prayer Book.

By these and other resolutions the General Synod channelled and directed a movement for liturgical change which already existed, and inaugurated a period of experiment, evaluation, and change.

Between 1974 and 1978, the Doctrine and Worship Committee produced the Canadian Anglican Liturgical Series, composed of the following publications: *Christian Initiation* (1974), *The Holy Eucharist* (1974), *Institution and Induction* (1974), *Christian Initiation: Study Document* (1975), *Thanksgiving for Birth or Adoption* (1978), *Celebration and Blessing of a Marriage* (1978). This series constituted the first step in the implementation of the resolutions of the General Synod of 1971 which related to the area of liturgy.

On 23 June 1980, the Doctrine and Worship Committee submitted a new collection of liturgical texts to the General Synod, including a new form of the eucharist, *Third Canadian Eucharist* (1979). Most of these texts were approved (either explicitly or tacitly), some with the conditions of further negotiation and editing. They were subsequently published as *The Lectionary* (1980), *Calendar of the Church Year* (1981), *Holy Eucharist: Third Canadian Order* (1981), *Alternative Ordinal* (1982), and *Holy Week* (1982). A new form for the *Celebration and Blessing of a Marriage* was published in 1982.

The 1980 General Synod made two other significant decisions

regarding the liturgy of the Church. First, it rejected a proposal to proceed with the preparation of a revised Book of Common Prayer. Second, it directed the Doctrine and Worship Committee,

> to proceed with the development of a book of alternative services, comprised of the commonly used services in the present Canadian Anglican Liturgical Series, revised where necessary, together with similar other services, for presentation to the next General Synod.

By these two actions the General Synod committed the Anglican Church of Canada, for the time being at least, to a pattern found also in the Church of England and the Anglican Church of Australia, in which the traditional rites of the Church coexist with contemporary and alternative rites. This *Book of Alternative Services* is therefore *not* a new Book of Common Prayer and does not replace it.

In 1983, the Doctrine and Worship Committee returned to the General Synod with a draft *Book of Alternative Services* which required further editing and revision. The General Synod authorized the committee to complete its task and to take the book to the National Executive Council for permission to publish for use, where permitted by the diocesan bishop, at least until the thirty-second General Synod (scheduled for 1989).

It may be seen from this brief history that the *Book of Alternative Services*, now presented for use, reflects more than fourteen years of continuous research, experimentation, criticism, and evaluation. This task has involved not only a succession of committees but a vast number of worshippers, lay people as well as clergy, who have worked in the movement for liturgical change.

Liturgical change is sometimes treated as a phenomenon unique to the twentieth century, a counter-current in the flow of Anglican piety. The truth is that the distinctive ethos of Anglicanism emerged in a period of reformation which was characterized by even greater liturgical change than our own. This comparison of the present day with the Reformation era is important for an understanding of the contemporary liturgical scene. The spirit of reformation is neither anarchic nor destructive, but is rooted in the conviction that in times of great insecurity and change the centre cannot be held by a blind preservation of the forms in which tradition has been received, but only through diligent and passionate search for fresh expressions and evocations of the tradition. The wonder is not that so many twentieth century Christians are open to change but that the experiments of the Reformation era appeared to be treated as definitive for nearly four centuries. The gospel always has a reforming, reinterpreting edge to it, and the gospel is always the proper subject of the liturgy.

While there is a strong correspondence between the dynamics of the Reformation era and the present day, there is considerable difference in detail, rising from different perspectives in the Church's understanding of itself and the world around it. The Reformation of the sixteenth century occurred at a time when Church and State enjoyed a relationship of comfortable interdependence (although the very political forces that embraced the Reformation were at the same time producing new and secular forms of government, which would eventually marginalize the Church). Christianity in its totality belonged to a known world and existed, with rare exceptions, where it enjoyed the protection of Christian princes. The goal of both Church and State was a stable society in which the place of all was known and maintained.

Theological and apostolic movements in subsequent centuries track the response of the Church to its changing context. The missionary movement in the seventeenth century and the Sunday School movement a century later both reflect a new attitude in Anglicans to the notion of unchanging boundaries, whether within the structure of society or in relation to a world beyond the borders of Christendom. The evangelical revival emphasized the importance of personal and individual faith, as distinct from mere religious conformity, and released the energy of Newton and Wilberforce to attack and subdue the trade in slaves. The Tractarians and their successors rediscovered a vision of the Church as the sacrament of God's kingdom in terms that challenged the social disorders of their day. Biblical criticism has fostered a rich, subtle, and theological understanding of the holy scriptures as the repository of the Church's symbols of life and faith.

The Church of the present day is continuous with the Church of the sixteenth century, but different, just as the Church of the sixteenth century was continuous with but different from its medieval roots.

Liturgical continuity has always been maintained in tension with liturgical change. The *Book of Common Prayer* has hardly been used exactly as its original authors intended. Ceremonial subtleties have constantly reinterpreted the liturgical tradition, as indicated by Anglican controversies relating to the location of the holy table, where the priest may stand, the vesture of clergy, the use of liturgical colours, the use of flowers and candles, as well as various physical acts of reverence. The text itself has been reformed in various ways in the Prayer Books of the different provinces of the Anglican Communion. The appearance of new and alternative books throughout the Communion reflects a further reformation of the form and structure of the text.

This *Book of Alternative Services* represents but a moment in the process of reformation. The gospel is truly perennial: unchanging but ever new in its confrontation and transfiguration of the world. Liturgy is the means by which the Church is constantly invested in that gospel, in the reading of the scriptures, in proclamation, in praise, in prayer of deep concern, and in those sign-acts which wordlessly incorporate the believer in the Word. Liturgy is not the gospel but it is a principal process by which the Church and the gospel are brought together for the sake of the life of the world. It is consequently vital that its form wear the idiom, the cadence, the world-view, the imagery of the people who are engaged in that process in every generation.

It is precisely the intimate relationship of gospel, liturgy, and service that stands behind the theological principle *lex orandi: lex credendi*, i.e., the law of prayer is the law of belief. This principle, particularly treasured by Anglicans, means that theology as the statement of the Church's belief is drawn from the liturgy, i.e., from the point at which the gospel and the challenge of Christian life meet in prayer. The development of theology is not a legislative process which is imposed on liturgy; liturgy is a reflective process in which theology may be discovered. The Church must be open to liturgical change in order to maintain sensitivity to the impact of the gospel on the world and to permit the continuous development of a living theology.

There are a number of respects in which the Church of the present day differs from that of the Reformation era. One, already noted, relates to the role of the Church in today's less rigidly structured society. Christians have discovered a new responsibility for the world, that loving their neighbours as themselves demands more than compliance with the civil law. As the *Letter of James* puts it, it is not enough to say to the poor, "'Go in peace, be warmed and filled,' without giving them the things needed for the body" (2.16). This finds expression in contemporary liturgy in consciousness of the ministry of Jesus to the distressed and in prayer for the extension of that justice which is God's own work.

A second difference in the Church of the present day appears in a growing sense among Christians that they constitute a complex and varied community, with many different roles and functions. This vision of the Church, as old as the New Testament, was never entirely lost but was certainly eclipsed during a long period of Christian history. A sharp line ran between the leadership role of the priest and the relative passivity of the laity. Today there is recognition that the Church not only contains but needs many roles and functions in its administration, witness, and service as well as in its liturgy. The purpose of presiding leadership is not to dominate but to call, encourage, and support a community of people in all their work. This principle finds liturgical expression in the *Book of Alternative Services*.

A third difference appears in a contemporary desire for greater flexibility and variety in liturgy. As already noted, this desire was expressed strongly in a resolution of the General Synod as long ago as 1971; it reflects not a rejection of tradition but a return to a much older tradition which preceded the late medieval and Reformation periods.

The Churches of the Reformation were deeply influenced by the then recent invention of printing which allowed the wider dissemination of new ideas, of the Bible, and of liturgical texts. It also guaranteed a greater degree of uniformity, which became part of the spirit of the age. (The Books of Common Prayer of the Church of England were imposed by the *Acts of Uniformity* of 1549, 1552, 1559, and 1662.) Liturgical texts became unvarying scripts, leaving little if any room for deviation. Today there is recognition that texts should provide a framework and pattern for liturgy, as well as rich resources in readings, acts of praise, and prayers, which must be used with sensitivity and creativity appropriate to the context.

Worshippers will require time to become familiar with the variety of resources contained in this book. Liturgical leaders must be sensitive to their need for bulletins and other aids to guide them through new material. It is not actually more difficult to find a new canticle or eucharistic prayer than it is to find a hymn, but the experience is new for many people and they will need help and time to become familiar with it.

A major difference in these liturgical texts is the use of modern, vernacular English. The use of vernacular language was, of course, an important principle among all the Reformers and the use of archaic English is increasingly antagonistic to their teaching. The "updating" of liturgies to meet linguistic change has been a source of problems throughout Christian history. Sometimes resistance has been so great that the liturgy has continued for some centuries in a "dead" language, known only to an educated class. Change in language has always caused nostalgia, and sometimes resentment, as it did among those who clamoured for the continuation of Latin in the sixteenth century. Certainly change in language involves both loss and gain.

Scholars speculate on the secret of Cranmer's style. Some attribute it to his proximity in time to the period of Middle English, with its use of stressed lines and alliteration. Others believe the essence of his style lies in the frequency of "doubling" or compounding of subjects and objects, so that nouns are held in paradoxical tension with each other, each modifying and amplifying the other. Whatever the source of Cranmer's elegance, it is not characteristic of the English language now. The poetry of our own day tends to be spare, oblique, incisive, relying more on the sharpness of imagery than the flow of cadence. Liturgical language must attempt to speak in its own idiom. The purpose of liturgy is not to preserve a particular form of English address but to enable a community to pray, and that demands struggling with the vernacular.

This *Book of Alternative Services* assumes, but does not demand, the use of music. Liturgical celebrations are both possible and appropriate without music, when the congregation is small or in domestic or clinical situations. However, there is an intimate relationship between liturgy and music which transcends the merely decorative. Music is not brought into liturgy to enhance it but belongs by right, with words and gestures, to the central core of liturgy's own structure. Music secures the intuitive dimension of liturgy, that aspect of perception which has been associated with the right side of the brain. The Jewish sources of Christian liturgy took music for granted, in both psalms and chanted prayers. The whole of Christian tradition is rich in musical forms. This book makes new and special recognition of that tradition in the provision of some music settings in an appendix.

This *Book of Alternative Services* is intended to extend, not break, the tradition of the Church, and not least in the area of music. Musicians are encouraged to compose new settings for canticles, responsories, litanies, and other texts. At the same time, other established versions of texts may be sung so that traditional, valued compositions may remain in use.

The work of liturgical reform is not finished; in fact it is never finished. Liturgical texts cannot be tested in an armchair or at a desk, but only in use. There is bound to be room for refinement and improvement, in language, in symbolism, in theology. Constructive comments and suggestions are welcome and should be addressed to:

The Doctrine and Worship Committee
The Anglican Church of Canada
600 Jarvis Street
Toronto ON M4Y 2J6

# The Calendar of the Church Year

The liturgy of the Church celebrates but one mystery: the life, death, and resurrection of Jesus Christ.

Each Sunday is the weekly commemoration of that mystery of Christ. Christians gather each Sunday to celebrate, in word and sacrament, their participation in Christ. The Lord's Day is consequently given primacy over other commemorations.

Each year the weekly commemoration is celebrated with particular joy when the Church keeps Passover or Easter. This observance includes forty days of preparation in Lent and fifty days of celebration in the Easter season. Easter is the central festival of the Church Year.

The commemoration of the birth of Jesus Christ at Christmas provides the focus for the other seasons of the Church Year. This festival, much later in origin than Easter, is associated with the Epiphany in some parts of the Christian world. Advent is a period of preparation for this celebration.

Sundays which are not immediately related to Easter or Christmas are numbered as Sundays after Pentecost and Sundays after Epiphany.

The Church celebrates the victory of Christ in the lives of particular individuals in the commemoration of saints. The calendar of saints' days varies among the various Christian Churches and among the various Churches of the Anglican Communion. Some saints' days are of great antiquity and universal observance and take precedence of certain other days. The Calendar also includes the names of a variety of Christians who are remembered for a number of reasons: some inspired the reverent wonder of another time and place; some are associated with the heroic struggle involved in the development of the Church in this country. In addition to those whose names appear in this Calendar, it is appropriate for the Church, at regional and even local levels, to add the names of Christians whose lives have reflected the mystery of Christ.

# The Calendar

## 1  Principal Feasts

The Principal Feasts observed in this Church are the following:

Easter Day
Ascension Day
The Day of Pentecost
Trinity Sunday
All Saints' Day, 1 November
Christmas Day, 25 December
The Epiphany, 6 January

These feasts take precedence over any other day of observance. All
Saints' Day may be observed on the Sunday following 1 November, in
addition to its observance on the fixed date.

## 2  Sundays

All Sundays of the year are feasts of our Lord Jesus Christ. In addition
to the days listed above, the only feasts appointed on fixed days to
take precedence of a Sunday are

The Naming of Jesus
The Baptism of the Lord
The Presentation of the Lord
The Birth of Saint John the Baptist
Saint Peter and Saint Paul
The Transfiguration of the Lord
Saint Mary the Virgin
Holy Cross Day
Saint Michael and All Angels

The feast of the Epiphany may be observed on the Sunday before
6 January if that day is a weekday. Should that Sunday be 1 January,
either the Naming of Jesus or the Epiphany may be observed. The
Sunday after the Epiphany is always observed as the feast of the
Baptism of Christ.

The feast of the Dedication of a Church, and the feast of its patron or title, may be observed on, or be transferred to, a Sunday, except in the seasons of Advent, Lent, and Easter.

All other feasts of our Lord, and all other Major Feasts appointed on fixed days in the Calendar, when they occur on a Sunday, are normally transferred to the first convenient open day within the week.

Harvest Thanksgiving may be observed on a Sunday as determined by local custom.

### 3 Holy Days

The following Holy Days are regularly observed throughout the year. They have precedence over all other days of commemoration or of special observance.

*Other Feasts of our Lord*

   The Naming of Jesus
   The Baptism of the Lord
   The Presentation of the Lord
   The Annunciation of the Lord
   The Visit of the Blessed Virgin Mary to Elizabeth
   The Birth of Saint John the Baptist
   The Transfiguration of the Lord
   Holy Cross Day

*Other Major Feasts*

   All Feasts of Apostles
   All Feasts of Evangelists
   The Holy Innocents
   Saint Joseph
   Saint Mary Magdalene
   Saint Stephen
   Saint Mary the Virgin
   The Beheading of Saint John the Baptist
   Saint Michael and All Angels

*Fasts*

   Ash Wednesday
   Good Friday

Feasts appointed on fixed days in the Calendar are not observed on the days of Holy Week or of Easter Week. When the feasts of Saint Joseph or the Annunciation fall on a Sunday in Lent they are transferred to the preceding Saturday or to a day in the preceding week. But when the feasts of Saint Joseph and the Annunciation fall in Holy Week or Easter Week both are transferred to the week after the Second Sunday of Easter when the Annunciation is transferred to the Monday and Saint Joseph to the Tuesday, or some other convenient days during that week.

The feasts of St Stephen, St John the Evangelist, and the Holy Innocents may be observed either on 3 August, 6 May, or 11 January respectively, or on their traditional dates after Christmas. When any of these feasts falls on a Sunday, it may be observed on its alternative date that year or on the first free day.

Feasts appointed on fixed days in the Calendar do not take precedence over Ash Wednesday.

Feasts of our Lord and other Major Feasts appointed on fixed days which fall upon or are transferred to a weekday may be observed on any open day within the week. This provision does not apply to Christmas Day, the Epiphany, and All Saints' Day.

## 4 Days of Special Devotion

Days observed by special acts of discipline and self-denial:

Ash Wednesday and other weekdays of Lent and Holy Week, except the feast of the Annunciation;

Good Friday and all other Fridays of the year, in commemoration of the Lord's crucifixion, except for Fridays in the Christmas and Easter seasons, and any feasts of our Lord which occur on a Friday.

## 5 Days of Optional Observance

Subject to the rules governing Principal Feasts, Sundays, and Holy Days, the following may be observed:

Memorials listed in the Calendar (the prayers and readings from the Common of Saints may be used at the eucharist);

Commemorations listed in the Calendar (the prayers from the Common of Saints and the ferial readings may be used at the eucharist);

other Commemorations of diocesan or parochial significance;

Rogation Days and Harvest Thanksgiving at times when crops are planted and harvested;

Ember Days;

provided that there is no celebration of the eucharist for any such occasion on Ash Wednesday, Maundy Thursday, Good Friday, and Holy Saturday.

# Titles of the Seasons, Sundays, and Major Holy Days

## Observed in this Church Throughout the Year

*Advent Season*

First Sunday of Advent
Second Sunday of Advent
Third Sunday of Advent
Fourth Sunday of Advent

*Christmas Season*

The Birth of the Lord: Christmas Day, 25 December
First Sunday after Christmas
The Naming of Jesus, 1 January
Second Sunday after Christmas

*Epiphany Season*

The Epiphany of the Lord, 6 January
The Baptism of the Lord (First Sunday after the Epiphany)
Second Sunday through Eighth Sunday after the Epiphany
Last Sunday after the Epiphany

*Lenten Season*

First day of Lent, or Ash Wednesday
First Sunday in Lent
Second Sunday in Lent
Third Sunday in Lent
Fourth Sunday in Lent
Fifth Sunday in Lent

*Holy Week*

The Sunday of the Passion: Palm Sunday
Monday in Holy Week
Tuesday in Holy Week
Wednesday in Holy Week
Maundy Thursday
Good Friday
Holy Saturday

*Easter Season*

Easter Eve
The Sunday of the Resurrection, or Easter Day
Monday in Easter Week
Tuesday in Easter Week
Wednesday in Easter Week
Thursday in Easter Week
Friday in Easter Week
Saturday in Easter Week
Second Sunday of Easter
Third Sunday of Easter
Fourth Sunday of Easter
Fifth Sunday of Easter
Sixth Sunday of Easter
The Ascension of the Lord
Seventh Sunday of Easter
The Day of Pentecost

*The Season after Pentecost*

First Sunday after Pentecost: Trinity Sunday
Second Sunday through Twenty-Seventh Sunday after Pentecost
Last Sunday after Pentecost: The Reign of Christ.

*Principal Holy Days*

The Presentation of the Lord, 2 February
The Annunciation of the Lord, 25 March
The Birth of Saint John the Baptist, 24 June
Saint Peter and Saint Paul, 29 June
The Transfiguration of the Lord, 6 August
Saint Mary the Virgin, 15 August

Holy Cross Day, 14 September
Saint Michael and All Angels, 29 September
All Saints' Day, 1 November

*Other Holy Days*

The Holy Innocents, 11 January or 28 December
The Confession of Saint Peter, 18 January
The Conversion of Saint Paul, 25 January
Saint Joseph, 19 March
Saint Mark, 25 April
Saint Philip and Saint James, 1 May
Saint John the Evangelist, 6 May or 27 December
Saint Matthias, 14 May
The Visit of the Blessed Virgin Mary to Elizabeth, 31 May
Saint Barnabas, 11 June
Saint Thomas, 3 July
Saint Mary Magdalene, 22 July
Saint James the Apostle, 25 July
Saint Stephen, 3 August or 26 December
Saint Bartholomew, 24 August
The Beheading of Saint John the Baptist, 29 August
Saint Matthew, 21 September
Saint Luke, 18 October
Saint Simon and Saint Jude, 28 October
Saint Andrew, 30 November

# Memorials and Commemorations

The distinction between memorials and commemorations is of interest
primarily to communities with frequent weekday celebrations of the
eucharist.

The intention, which derives from the Lambeth Conference of 1958, is
to help communities identify the relative significance of a particular
day, just as a distinction is made between principal feasts and holy
days elsewhere in the calendar, reflecting the relative impact of certain
persons on the devotional imagination of the church.

While the observance of both memorials and commemorations is
optional, parishes with frequent weekday celebrations of the eucharist

may decide to interrupt the weekday cycle of readings for a memorial but not for a commemoration. The distinction would also help a community decide which days to observe and the choice of liturgical colour.

The following may help to make this clear:

**Memorial**

Variable prayers from the Common of Saints
Readings from the Common of Saints
(Colour appropriate to the day)

**Commemoration**

Variable prayers from the Common of Saints
Readings from the Weekday Eucharistic Lectionary
(Colour of the season)

### Signs and Abbreviations

There are seven letters to indicate the seven days of the week. Days marked with the same letter will all fall on the same day of the week throughout the year (except during leap year).

PF—*Principal Feast*
HD—*Holy Day*
Mem—*Memorial*
Com—*Commemoration*

# January

| | | |
|---|---|---|
| 1A | **The Naming of Jesus** | HD |
| 2b | Basil the Great and Gregory of Nazianzus, Bishops and Teachers of the Faith, 379, 389 | Mem |
| 3c | | |
| 4d | | |
| 5e | | |
| 6f | **The Epiphany of the Lord** † | PF |
| 7g | | |
| 8A | | |
| 9b | | |
| 10c | William Laud, Archbishop of Canterbury, 1645 | Com |
| 11d | **The Holy Innocents** (or 28 December) | HD |
| 12e | Marguerite Bourgeoys, Educator in New France, 1700 | Com |
| | John Horden, Bishop of Moosonee, Missionary, 1893 | Com |
| 13f | Hilary, Bishop of Poitiers, Teacher, 367 | Mem |
| 14g | | |
| 15A | Richard Meux Benson, Religious, Founder of the SSJE, 1915 | Com |
| 16b | | |
| 17c | Antony, Abbot in Egypt, 356 | Mem |
| 18d | **The Confession of Saint Peter the Apostle** | HD |
| 19e | | |
| 20f | | |
| 21g | Agnes, Martyr at Rome, 304 | Com |
| 22A | Vincent, Deacon of Saragossa, Martyr, 304 | Com |
| 23b | | |
| 24c | Francis de Sales, Bishop of Geneva, Teacher of the Faith, 1622 | Com |
| 25d | **The Conversion of Saint Paul the Apostle** | HD |
| 26e | Timothy and Titus, Companions of Saint Paul | Mem |
| 27f | John Chrysostom, Bishop of Constantinople, Teacher of the Faith, 407 | Mem |
| 28g | Thomas Aquinas, Teacher of the Faith, 1274 | Mem |
| 29A | | |
| 30b | Charles Stuart, King of England, 1649 | Com |
| 31c | | |

† The Sunday after the Epiphany is kept as the feast of the Baptism of the Lord.

# February

| | | |
|---|---|---|
| 1d | | |
| 2e | **The Presentation of the Lord** | HD |
| 3f | Anskar, Missionary Bishop in Sweden, 865 | Com |
| 4g | | |
| 5A | Martyrs of Japan, 1596 | Mem |
| 6b | | |
| 7c | | |
| 8d | | |
| 9e | Hannah Grier Coome, Religious, Founder of the SSJD, 1921 | Com |
| 10f | | |
| 11g | | |
| 12A | | |
| 13b | | |
| 14c | Cyril and Methodius, Missionaries to the Slavs, 869, 885 | Mem |
| 15d | Thomas Bray, Priest and Missionary, Founder of SPG and SPCK, 1730 | Mem |
| 16e | | |
| 17f | | |
| 18g | | |
| 19A | | |
| 20b | | |
| 21c | | |
| 22d | | |
| 23e | Polycarp, Bishop of Smyrna, Martyr, 156 | Mem |
| 24f | Lindel Tsen, Bishop of Honan, 1954 and Paul Sasaki, Bishop of Mid-Japan and Tokyo, 1946 | Com |
| 25g | | |
| 26A | | |
| 27b | George Herbert, Priest and Poet, 1633 | Com |
| 28c | | |
| 29 | | |

# May

| | | |
|---|---|---|
| 1b | **Saint Philip and Saint James, Apostles** | HD |
| 2c | Athanasius, Bishop of Alexandria, Teacher of the Faith, 373 | Mem |
| 3d | | |
| 4e | | |
| 5f | | |
| 6g | **Saint John, Apostle and Evangelist** (or 27 December) | HD |
| 7A | | |
| 8b | Julian of Norwich, Spiritual Teacher, c. 1417 | Com |
| 9c | | |
| 10d | | |
| 11e | | |
| 12f | Florence Nightingale, Nurse, Social Reformer, 1910 | Com |
| 13g | | |
| 14A | **Saint Matthias the Apostle** | HD |
| 15b | | |
| 16c | | |
| 17d | | |
| 18e | | |
| 19f | Dunstan, Archbishop of Canterbury, 988 | Com |
| 20g | | |
| 21A | | |
| 22b | | |
| 23c | | |
| 24d | | |
| 25e | Bede, Priest, Monk of Jarrow, Historian and Educator, 735 | Com |
| 26f | Augustine, First Archbishop of Canterbury, 605 | Mem |
| 27g | | |
| 28A | | |
| 29b | | |
| 30c | | |
| 31d | **The Visit of the Blessed Virgin Mary to Elizabeth** | HD |

# June

| | | |
|---|---|---|
| 1e | Justin, Martyr at Rome, Teacher, c. 167 | Mem |
| 2f | Martyrs of Lyons, 177 | Com |
| 3g | Martyrs of Uganda, 1886, Janani Luwum, Archbishop of Uganda, 1977 | Mem |
| 4A | John XXIII, Bishop of Rome, Reformer, 1963 | Com |
| 5b | Boniface, Archbishop of Mainz, Martyr, 754 | Mem |
| 6c | William Grant Broughton, Bishop in Australia, 1853 | Com |
| 7d | | |
| 8e | | |
| 9f | Columba, Abbot of Iona, Missionary, 597 | Mem |
| 10g | | |
| 11A | **Saint Barnabas the Apostle** | HD |
| 12b | | |
| 13c | | |
| 14d | | |
| 15e | | |
| 16f | Joseph Butler, Bishop of Durham, 1752 | Com |
| 17g | | |
| 18A | Bernard Mizeki, Catechist in Rhodesia, Martyr, 1896 | Mem |
| 19b | | |
| 20c | | |
| 21d | | |
| 22e | Alban, First Martyr of Britain, c. 304 | Mem |
| 23f | | |
| 24g | **The Birth of Saint John the Baptist** | HD |
| 25A | | |
| 26b | | |
| 27c | | |
| 28d | Irenaeus, Bishop of Lyons, c. 202 | Mem |
| 29e | **Saint Peter and Saint Paul, Apostles** | HD |
| 30f | | |

# July

| | | |
|---|---|---|
| 1g | | |
| 2A | | |
| 3b | **Saint Thomas the Apostle** | HD |
| 4c | | |
| 5d | | |
| 6e | Thomas More, 1535 | Com |
| 7f | | |
| 8g | | |
| 9A | | |
| 10b | | |
| 11c | Benedict of Nursia, Abbot, c. 540 | Mem |
| 12d | | |
| 13e | Henry, Missionary Bishop in Finland, 1150 | Com |
| 14f | | |
| 15g | | |
| 16A | | |
| 17b | | |
| 18c | | |
| 19d | | |
| 20e | | |
| 21f | | |
| 22g | **Saint Mary Magdalene** | HD |
| 23A | | |
| 24b | | |
| 25c | **Saint James the Apostle** | HD |
| 26d | Anne, Mother of the Blessed Virgin Mary | Com |
| 27e | | |
| 28f | | |
| 29g | William Wilberforce, Social Reformer, 1833 | Com |
| 30A | | |
| 31b | | |

# August

1c

2d

3e  **Saint Stephen, Deacon and Martyr** (or 26 December)                    HD

4f

5g

6A  **The Transfiguration of the Lord**                                      HD

7b  John Mason Neale, Priest, 1866                                           Com

8c  Dominic, Priest and Friar, 1221                                          Mem

9d

10e  Laurence, Deacon and Martyr at Rome, 258                                Mem

11f  Clare of Assisi, 1253                                                   Mem

12g

13A  Jeremy Taylor, Bishop of Down and Connor, Spiritual
     Teacher, 1667                                                           Mem

14b  Dietrich Bonhoeffer and Maximilien Kolbe, Martyrs,
     1945, 1940                                                              Com

15c  **Saint Mary the Virgin**                                              HD

16d  Holy Women of the Old Testament                                        Mem

17e

18f

19g

20A  Bernard, Abbot of Clairvaux, 1153                                      Mem

21b

22c

23d

24e  **Saint Bartholomew the Apostle**                                      HD

25f

26g

27A  Monnica, Mother of Augustine of Hippo, 387                             Com

28b  Augustine, Bishop of Hippo, Teacher of the Faith, 430                  Mem

29c  **The Beheading of Saint John the Baptist**                           HD

30d  Robert McDonald, Priest in the Western Arctic, 1913                    Com

31e  Aidan, Bishop of Lindisfarne, Missionary, 651                         Com

# September

1f
2g  The Martyrs of New Guinea, 1942                                      Mem
3A  Gregory the Great, Bishop of Rome, 604                               Mem
4b  First Anglican Eucharist in Canada, 1578                             Com
5c
6d
7e
8f  The Nativity of the Blessed Virgin Mary                              Mem
9g
10A  Edmund James Peck, Missionary to the Inuit, 1924                    Mem
11b
12c
13d  Cyprian, Bishop of Carthage, Martyr, 258                            Mem
14e  **Holy Cross Day**                                                  HD
15f
16g  Ninian, Bishop in Galloway, c. 430                                  Mem
17A
18b  Founders, Benefactors, and Missionaries of the Church
     of Canada                                                          Mem
19c  Theodore of Tarsus, Archbishop of Canterbury, 690                  Com
20d  John Coleridge Patteson, Bishop of Melanesia, and his
     Companions, Martyrs, 1871                                          Com
21e  **Saint Matthew, Apostle and Evangelist**                          HD
22f
23g
24A
25b  Sergius, Abbot of Holy Trinity, Moscow, Spiritual
     Teacher, 1392                                                      Com
26c  Lancelot Andrewes, Bishop of Winchester, 1626                      Com
27d
28e
29f  **Saint Michael and All Angels**                                   HD
30g  Jerome, Teacher of the Faith, 420                                  Mem

### 3   Scripture Reading

When Morning or Evening Prayer is the principal service on Sunday, the readings will normally be those found in the Proper Sentences, Prayers, and Readings for the Church Year, on pp. 266–447; the readings found in the Daily Office Lectionary may be used at other offices.

Communities and individuals using these forms of service for weekday prayer may choose their readings from a number of sources:

the Daily Office Lectionary, which is commended for those who desire systematic and relatively sequential readings of the psalms and scriptures;

weekday readings which may be used at the offices instead of the Daily Office Lectionary, or at celebrations of the eucharist on weekdays when the Daily Office Lectionary readings have been used at the offices;

a short list of psalms and readings for other occasions, as required. These are grouped for appropriate times of the day.

### 4   Psalms, Responsories, and Canticles

It is suggested in the material which follows that the psalms, which have traditionally preceded the readings, may follow the first reading as they do at the eucharist. This arrangement is particularly appropriate when the readings in the Propers are used and there is an intended relationship between the psalm and the first reading.

Although antiphons are provided for the Invitatory, they may be used with other psalms or with the biblical canticles.

The Glory to the Father may be sung at the conclusion of the entire portion of the psalter when more than one psalm is used. It may also be sung after the Invitatory, the biblical hymn Christ our Passover, or after each psalm or portion of psalm in a sequence.

Instead of the Glory to the Father silence may follow the recitation of a psalm; the period of silence may be brought to a conclusion by the recitation of a Psalm Prayer.

There are a number of possible responses to the readings (in addition to the psalm for the day when it corresponds to the first reading). The readings may be followed by silence, a canticle, a responsory, an anthem, instrumental music, or a hymn. A combination of these responses is often appropriate: e.g., silence and a canticle, instrumental music and a hymn. When there is more than one reading (as on Sunday mornings, when there should be three readings), different options are possible in relation to different readings. Responses should relate as closely as possible to the readings which precede them.

The responsories are poetic arrangements of biblical material, intended for recitation by a cantor or reader in interchange with the congregation. Responsories may be used in place of a canticle. The responsory is

> intended to throw new light on the passage just read, to put it in the context of the history of salvation, to lead from the Old Testament to the New, to turn what has been read into prayer and contemplation, or to provide pleasant variety by its poetic beauty.[1]

When a responsory is used, a cantor or reader dictates the refrain and the congregation repeats it; the congregation continues to repeat the second half of the refrain after the verses which follow. The responsory concludes with the first half of the Glory to the Father, followed by the complete refrain.

## 5 Affirmation of Faith

An affirmation of faith may follow the liturgy of the word. The Apostles' Creed has been associated with the offices since about the eighth century. The ancient creed of the synagogue, Hear, O Israel, is provided as an alternative. This creed, used increasingly as a substitute for the ten commandments in the entrance rite of the eucharist since the eighteenth century, was in danger of being lost in the process of liturgical revision. Here it is restored to something like the central dignity it enjoyed in the synagogue tradition. The Apostles' Creed and the Hear, O Israel are complementary: the first stresses faith as teaching, the second emphasizes faith as action.

## 6 Prayers

The prayers provide opportunity for both intercession and thanksgiving. One of the short litanies may be used. These may be modified as the occasion requires, or may be replaced by seasonal litanies, or by an extempore form.

Forms of general thanksgiving are provided, but other forms of thanksgiving may be used. It is important that the actual concerns of members of the congregation be expressed and that members have opportunity to articulate their cares and joys, either aloud in their own words or during a period of silence. The prayers are completed in a collect and the Lord's Prayer.

When these forms of prayer are used on weekdays by people who have attended the eucharist on the same day, the forms of intercession and thanksgiving may appropriately be shortened. However, the Lord's Prayer, at least, should be offered.

## Saturday Vigil of the Resurrection

A different and optional form of office has been provided for use on Saturday night, where desired. It is a revival of an ancient weekly welcome of Sunday as the Lord's Day. The basic Christian festival is Sunday as the commemoration of the resurrection of the Christ; the vigil, dating back to the fourth century and mentioned in both *Apostolic Constitutions* and the journal of Egeria, provides opportunity for highly-focused liturgical expression of this theme.

1   *The General Instruction on the Liturgy of the Hours*, IX. 169.

# Concerning the Services

*In the forms of service for Morning and Evening Prayer, the term* officiant *is used to denote the person, clerical or lay, who leads the office.*

*It is appropriate that other persons be assigned to read the readings, and to lead other parts of the service not assigned to the officiant.*

*A hymn may be sung and the offerings of the people received after the Affirmation of Faith at Morning Prayer and Evening Prayer.*

*If the eucharist is to be celebrated, Morning and Evening Prayer may be concluded after the intercessions (excluding the Lord's Prayer) and the eucharist may commence with (the Peace and) the Preparation of the Gifts.*

# The Penitential Rite

*The officiant may read one or more of the following sentences of scripture, or an opening sentence proper to the day.*

The sacrifice of God is a broken spirit: a broken and contrite heart, O God, you will not despise.   *Psalm 51.18*

Seek the Lord while he wills to be found, call upon him when he draws near; let the wicked forsake their ways, and the evil ones their thoughts; and let them return to the Lord, and he will have compassion, and to our God, for he will richly pardon.   *Isaiah 55.6, 7*

If we say we have no sin, we deceive ourselves, and the truth is not in us. But if we confess our sins, God is faithful and just, and will forgive our sins and cleanse us from all unrighteousness.   *1 John 1.8, 9*

**Evening**

Stay with us, Lord, for evening draws on, and the day is almost over.   *Luke 24.29*

Seek him who made the Pleiades and Orion, and turns deep darkness into the morning, and darkens the day into night; who calls for the waters of the sea, and pours them out upon the surface of the earth: the Lord is his name.   *Amos 5.8*

Jesus said, "I am the light of the world; whoever follows me will not walk in darkness, but will have the light of life."
*John 8.12*

*The officiant says to the people,*

> Dear friends in Christ,
> as we prepare to worship almighty God,
> let us with penitent and obedient hearts
> confess our sins,
> that we may obtain forgiveness
> by his infinite goodness and mercy.

*Or this:*     Let us confess our sins
                against God and our neighbour.

*Silence is kept.*

*The officiant and people say together,*

> **Most merciful God,**
> **we confess that we have sinned against you**
> **in thought, word, and deed,**
> **by what we have done**
> **and by what we have left undone.**
> **We have not loved you with our whole heart;**
> **we have not loved our neighbours as ourselves.**
> **We are truly sorry and we humbly repent.**
> **For the sake of your Son Jesus Christ,**
> **have mercy on us and forgive us,**
> **that we may delight in your will,**
> **and walk in your ways,**
> **to the glory of your name. Amen.**

*The priest says,*

> Almighty God have mercy upon you,
> pardon and deliver you from all your sins,
> confirm and strengthen you in all goodness,
> and keep you in eternal life;
> through Jesus Christ our Lord.

*People*     **Amen.**

*A deacon or lay person using the preceding form substitutes* us *for* you *and* our *for* your.

*When the Penitential Rite is used, the Invitatory for Morning or Evening Prayer may follow immediately (p. 47 or 66).*

# Morning Prayer

*All stand. If the Penitential Rite has not been used, the officiant may read an opening sentence proper to the day or time of day.*

*Either or both of the following responses may be used. One of the alternative introductory responses on pp. 96–100 may replace all that precedes the Invitatory or, on ordinary weekdays, all that precedes the psalm.*

| | |
|---|---|
| *Officiant* | Lord, open our lips, |
| *People* | **And our mouth shall proclaim your praise.** |

| | |
|---|---|
| *Officiant* | O God, make speed to save us. |
| *People* | **O Lord, make haste to help us.** |

| | |
|---|---|
| *All* | **Glory to the Father, and to the Son, and to the Holy Spirit: as it was in the beginning, is now, and will be for ever. Amen.** |

*Except in Lent, add,*

**Alleluia!**

# The Invitatory

*Then follows one of the Invitatory psalms, or the Easter canticle, or a suitable hymn.*

*One of the following antiphons may be said or sung before and after the Invitatory psalm (and between the sections of the psalm, if desired).*

1   God rules over all the earth: O come, let us worship.

2   The Lord is in his holy temple: O come, let us worship.

3   The Lord is our refuge and strength: O come, let us worship.

4    The Lord is our light and our life: O come, let us worship.

### Advent

5    The kingdom of God is at hand: O come, let us worship.

### Incarnation

6    To us a child is born: O come, let us worship.

7    The Word was made flesh and dwelt among us:
O come, let us worship.

### Lent

8    The Lord is full of compassion and mercy: O come, let us
worship.

### Passion

9    Christ became obedient unto death: O come, let us
worship.

### Easter

10    Alleluia! The Lord is risen indeed: O come, let us worship.

### Ascension

11    Alleluia! The Sun of righteousness has risen: O come, let us
worship.

### Pentecost

12    Alleluia! The Spirit of the Lord renews the face of the earth:
O come, let us worship.

### Trinity

13    Holy, holy, holy, is the Lord God almighty: O come, let us
worship.

### Saints' Days

14    The Lord is glorious in his saints: O come, let us worship.

# Venite

*Psalm 95.1–7*

Come, let us sing to the Lord; *
 let us shout for joy to the rock of our salvation.
Let us come before his presence with thanksgiving *
 and raise a loud shout to him with psalms.

For the Lord is a great God,*
 and a great king above all gods.
In his hand are the caverns of the earth,*
 and the heights of the hills are his also.
The sea is his for he made it,*
 and his hands have moulded the dry land.

Come, let us bow down, and bend the knee,*
 and kneel before the Lord our maker.
For he is our God,
and we are the people of his pasture and the
     sheep of his hand.*
 Oh, that today you would hearken to his voice!

# Jubilate

*Psalm 100*

Be joyful in the Lord, all you lands; *
 serve the Lord with gladness
 and come before his presence with a song.

Know this: The Lord himself is God; *
 he himself has made us, and we are his;
 we are his people and the sheep of his pasture.

Enter his gates with thanksgiving;
go into his courts with praise; *
 give thanks to him and call upon his name.

For the Lord is good;
his mercy is everlasting; *
 and his faithfulness endures from age to age.

*One of the following psalms may be used as the Invitatory.*

Psalm 24          Psalm 63.1–8          Psalm 145
Psalm 51.1–18     Psalm 67

*The following may be sung or said from Easter until Pentecost.*

## Christ our Passover

*1 Corinthians 5.7–8; Romans 6.9–11; 1 Corinthians 15.20–22*

Alleluia!
Christ our Passover has been sacrificed for us; *
    therefore let us keep the feast,
Not with the old leaven, the leaven of malice and evil,*
    but with the unleavened bread of sincerity and truth.
            Alleluia!

Christ being raised from the dead will never die again; *
    death no longer has dominion over him.
The death that he died, he died to sin, once for all; *
    but the life he lives, he lives to God.
So also consider yourselves dead to sin,*
    and alive to God in Jesus Christ our Lord. Alleluia!

Christ has been raised from the dead,*
    the first fruits of those who have fallen asleep.
For since by a man came death,*
    by a man has come also the resurrection of the dead.
For as in Adam all die,*
    so also in Christ shall all be made alive. Alleluia!

# The Psalms

*The psalm, or psalms, precede or follow the first reading. When the theme of the psalm is closely related to that of the reading, it is appropriate that the psalm follow the reading as a reflection.*

*At the end of the psalm or psalms, silence may be kept and a prayer may be said. The following may be said or sung, or omitted.*

Glory to the Father, and to the Son, and to the Holy Spirit:
as it was in the beginning, is now and will be for ever.
Amen.

# The Proclamation of the Word

## The Readings

*The reading, or readings, as appointed are read, the reader first saying,*

A reading from …

*After each reading the reader may say,*

The word of the Lord.

*People* **Thanks be to God.**

*The congregation may stand or sit for a Gospel reading. The reader may say,*

The Holy Gospel of our Lord Jesus Christ
according to …

*People* **Glory to you, Lord Jesus Christ.**

*Then at the conclusion of the Gospel, the reader says,*

The Gospel of Christ.

*People* **Praise to you, Lord Jesus Christ.**

*The readings may be followed by silence, a canticle, a responsory, an anthem or other music, or a hymn. A combination of these responses may be appropriate. The psalm, as appointed, may follow the first reading.*

## Sermon

*A sermon or other comment on the readings is appropriate at principal services on Sundays and at other major gatherings of the Christian community. A silence for reflection may follow.*

# Affirmation of Faith

*The Apostles' Creed or Hear, O Israel may be said.*

## The Apostles' Creed

I believe in God,
the Father almighty,
creator of heaven and earth.

I believe in Jesus Christ, his only Son, our Lord.
He was conceived by the power of the Holy Spirit
and born of the Virgin Mary.
He suffered under Pontius Pilate,
was crucified, died, and was buried.
He descended to the dead.
On the third day he rose again.
He ascended into heaven,
and is seated at the right hand of the Father.
He will come again
to judge the living and the dead.

I believe in the Holy Spirit,
the holy catholic Church,
the communion of saints,
the forgiveness of sins,
the resurrection of the body,
and the life everlasting. Amen.

*Or the following:*

## Hear, O Israel

**Hear, O Israel,
the Lord our God, the Lord is one.
Love the Lord your God
with all your heart,
with all your soul,
with all your mind,
and with all your strength.**

**This is the first and the great commandment.
The second is like it:
Love your neighbour as yourself.**

**There is no commandment greater than these.**

# Intercessions and Thanksgivings

*A deacon or lay member of the community may lead the intercessions and
thanksgivings. Intercession or thanksgiving may be offered for*

> *the Church
> the Queen and all in authority
> the world
> the local community
> those in need
> the departed.*

*A short litany may be selected from pp. 110–127. A thanksgiving litany and
the forms of General Thanksgiving are found on pp. 128–130. Other prayers
are found on pp. 675–684. These prayers and thanksgivings may be modified
in accordance with local need, or extempore forms of prayer may be used.*

## The Collect

*The Collect of the Day or a collect appropriate to the time of day may be said.*

# The Lord's Prayer

*Officiant*   Gathering our prayers and praises into one,
let us pray as our Saviour taught us,

*All*   **Our Father in heaven,
hallowed be your name,
your kingdom come,
your will be done,
on earth as in heaven.
Give us today our daily bread.
Forgive us our sins
as we forgive those who sin against us.
Save us from the time of trial,
and deliver us from evil.
For the kingdom, the power,
and the glory are yours,
now and for ever. Amen.**

*Or*

*Officiant*   And now, as our Saviour Christ has taught us,
we are bold to say,

*All*   **Our Father, who art in heaven,
hallowed be thy name,
thy kingdom come,
thy will be done,
on earth as it is in heaven.
Give us this day our daily bread.
And forgive us our trespasses,
as we forgive those who trespass against us.
And lead us not into temptation,
but deliver us from evil.
For thine is the kingdom,
the power, and the glory,
for ever and ever. Amen.**

# Dismissal

*Then may be said or sung,*

*Officiant*    Let us bless the Lord.
*People*       **Thanks be to God.**

*From Easter Day through the Day of Pentecost,* **Alleluia** *is added to the dismissal and the people's response.*

*The officiant may conclude with one of the following:*

The grace of our Lord Jesus Christ, and the love of God, and the fellowship of the Holy Spirit, be with us all evermore. **Amen.**

May the God of hope fill us with all joy and peace in believing through the power of the Holy Spirit. **Amen.**

May the God of peace enable us to do his will in every kind of goodness, working in us what pleases him, through Jesus Christ, to whom be the glory for ever and ever. **Amen.**

The Lord bless us and keep us. The Lord make his face shine on us and be gracious to us. The Lord look upon us with favour and grant us peace. **Amen.**

# Prayers at Mid-day

| | |
|---|---|
| *Officiant* | O God, make speed to save us. |
| *People* | **O Lord, make haste to help us.** |
| | |
| *All* | **Glory to the Father, and to the Son, and to the Holy Spirit: as it was in the beginning, is now, and will be for ever. Amen.** |

*Except in Lent, add,*

> **Alleluia!**

*A hymn may be sung.*

*The following portion of Psalm 19 may be sung or said, or one or more portions of Psalm 119. Other suitable selections include Psalms 120 to 133. A table of psalms suitable for use at mid-day may be found on p. 524. At the end of the psalm or psalms silence may be kept and a prayer may be said. Glory to the Father may be said or sung or omitted.*

## Psalm 19  *1–6*

The heavens declare the glory of God,*
    and the firmament shows his handiwork.
One day tells its tale to another,*
    and one night imparts its knowledge to another.

Although they have no words or language,*
    and their voices are not heard,
Their sound has gone out into all lands,*
    and their message to the ends of the world.

In the deep has he set a pavilion for the sun; *
    it comes forth like a bridegroom out of his chamber;
    it rejoices like a champion to run its course.
It goes forth from the uttermost edge of the heavens
    and runs about to the end of it again; *
    nothing is hidden from its burning heat.

**Psalm Prayer**

*Officiant*    O God, the source of all life, you have filled the earth with beauty. Open our eyes to see your gracious hand in all your works, that rejoicing in your whole creation we may learn to serve you with gladness, for the sake of him through whom all things were made, your Son Jesus Christ our Lord. **Amen.**

*One of the following, or some other suitable passage of scripture, is read. A table of readings suitable for use at mid-day may be found on p. 524.*

The fruit of the Spirit is love, joy, peace, patience, kindness, goodness, faithfulness, gentleness, self-control. If we live by the Spirit, let us also walk by the Spirit.   *Galatians 5.22, 23a, 25*

*Reader*    The word of the Lord.
*People*    **Thanks be to God.**

*Or the following:*

For anyone who is in Christ, there is a new creation; the old creation has gone, and now the new one is here. It is all God's work. It was God who reconciled us to himself through Christ and gave us the work of handing on this reconciliation.
*2 Corinthians 5.17–18*

*Reader*    The word of the Lord.
*People*    **Thanks be to God.**

*Or the following:*

From the rising of the sun to its setting my name shall be great among the nations, and in every place incense shall be offered to my name, and a pure offering; for my name shall be great among the nations, says the Lord of hosts.   *Malachi 1.11*

| Reader | The word of the Lord. |
|---|---|
| People | **Thanks be to God.** |

*A period of silence may follow.*

| Officiant | Let us pray. |
|---|---|

Lord, have mercy.
**Christ, have mercy.**
Lord, have mercy.

*Intercessions and Thanksgivings may be offered.*

*The officiant then says one of the following collects or the Collect of the Day.*

Heavenly Father, send your Holy Spirit into our hearts to comfort us in all our afflictions, to defend us from all error, and to lead us into all truth, through Jesus Christ our Lord. **Amen.**

Blessed Saviour, at this hour you hung upon the cross, stretching out your loving arms. Grant that all the peoples of the earth may look to you and be saved; for your tender mercies' sake. **Amen.**

Almighty Saviour, at mid-day you called your servant Saint Paul to be an apostle to the Gentiles. Fill the world with the radiance of your glory, that all nations may come and worship you, for you live and reign for ever. **Amen.**

## The Lord's Prayer

| Officiant | Lord, remember us in your kingdom, and teach us to pray, |
|---|---|
| All | **Our Father in heaven,** |
| | **hallowed be your name,** |
| | **your kingdom come,** |
| | **your will be done,** |
| | **on earth as in heaven.** |
| | **Give us today our daily bread.** |

Forgive us our sins
as we forgive those who sin against us.
Save us from the time of trial,
and deliver us from evil.
For the kingdom, the power,
and the glory are yours,
now and for ever. Amen.

*Or*

*Officiant*  And now, as our Saviour Christ has taught us,
we are bold to say,

*All*  Our Father, who art in heaven,
hallowed be thy name,
thy kingdom come,
thy will be done,
on earth as it is in heaven.
Give us this day our daily bread.
And forgive us our trespasses,
as we forgive those who trespass against us.
And lead us not into temptation,
but deliver us from evil.
For thine is the kingdom,
the power, and the glory,
for ever and ever. Amen.

*Then may be said,*

*Officiant*  Let us bless the Lord.
*People*  Thanks be to God.

# Evening Prayer

*Evening Prayer may begin with the Service of Light or with the Penitential Rite on p. 45 or as on p. 66. The Service of Light is not used when the Penitential Rite is used or during Holy Week.*

*When Evening Prayer occurs in the late evening, the office may begin with Introductory Response No. 10 on p. 100, followed by Psalm 134. Psalms suitable to the late evening are 4, 31.1–5, and 91. Suitable readings may be found on p. 524. The Song of Simeon, (No. 20 on p. 90), is a traditional late evening canticle. Litany No. 11 on p. 118 is appropriate to the late evening.*

# The Service of Light

*Before the Service of Light begins there should be as little artificial light as possible. When the ministers have entered, the paschal candle, or another large candle is lit; or the ministers may carry one or more candles as they enter and place them before the congregation. An Advent wreath may be the focus of the service during Advent. Before or during the singing of the hymn Phos Hilaron, other candles and lights may be lit. If incense is to be used, it is appropriate during the singing of Phos Hilaron or during the singing of Psalm 141.*

*When the Service of Light is used in private houses, candles may be lit at the dining table, or at some other customary place. When a meal follows, a blessing over food may conclude the service.*

# Evening Prayer

## The Service of Light

*Deacon, other assistant, or the officiant:*

        Light and peace in Jesus Christ our Lord.

*People*     **Thanks be to God.**

*Or*

*Officiant*     Jesus Christ is the light of the world.

*People*     **A light no darkness can extinguish.**

*The following hymn is sung. Another translation of the text may be used, such as "O Gracious Light, Lord Jesus Christ" on p. 690, or "O Gladsome light, O grace" or "Hail gladdening Light, of his pure glory poured." On occasion, other hymns on the same theme may be substituted.*

### O Gracious Light    *Phos Hilaron*

O gracious Light,
pure brightness of the everliving Father in heaven,
O Jesus Christ, holy and blessed!

Now as we come to the setting of the sun,
and our eyes behold the vesper light,
we sing your praises, O God: Father, Son, and Holy Spirit.

You are worthy at all times to be sung by happy voices,
O Son of God, O Giver of life,
and to be glorified through all the worlds.

## Thanksgiving

*A deacon, or other assistant, or the officiant sings or says,*

        Let us give thanks to the Lord our God.

*People*     **It is right to give our thanks and praise.**

*One of the following thanksgivings is sung or said.*

**1** †

Blessed are you, O Lord our God, ruler of the universe!
You led your people Israel by a pillar of cloud by day
and a pillar of fire by night.
Enlighten our darkness by the light of your Christ.
May his word be a lamp to our feet
and a light to our path;
for you are full of loving kindness for your whole creation,
and we, your creatures, glorify you,
Father, Son, and Holy Spirit, now and for ever. **Amen.**

**2** †

We praise and thank you, O God,
for you are without beginning and without end.
Through Christ you are the creator and preserver
of the whole world;
but, above all, you are his God and Father,
the giver of the Spirit,
and the ruler of all that is, seen and unseen.
You made the day for the works of light
and the night for the refreshment of our minds and bodies.
O loving Lord and source of all that is good,
accept our evening sacrifice of praise.
As you have conducted us through the day
and brought us to night's beginning,
keep us now in Christ;
grant us a peaceful evening
and a night free from sin;
and, at the end, bring us to everlasting life.
Through Christ and in the Holy Spirit,
we offer you all glory, honour, and worship,
now and for ever. **Amen.**

---

† From *Praise God in Song*. Copyright © 1979 by G.I.A. Publications, Inc.,
Chicago, Illinois. All rights reserved.

**3** †

Blessed are you, O Lord our God, ruler of the universe!
Your word brings on the dusk of evening,
your wisdom creates both night and day.
You determine the cycles of time,
arrange the succession of seasons,
and establish the stars in their heavenly courses.
Lord of the starry hosts is your name.
Living and eternal God, rule over us always.
Blessed be the Lord, whose word makes evening fall. **Amen.**

**4   Advent** †

Blessed are you, O Lord our God, ruler of the universe,
creator of light and darkness.
In this holy season,
when the sun's light is swallowed up
by the growing darkness of the night,
you renew your promise to reveal among us
the splendour of your glory,
enfleshed and visible to us in Jesus Christ your Son.
Through the prophets
you teach us to hope for his reign of peace.
Through the outpouring of his Spirit,
you open our blindness to the glory of his presence.
Strengthen us in our weakness.
Support us in our stumbling efforts to do your will
and free our tongues to sing your praise.
For to you all honour and blessing are due,
now and for ever. **Amen.**

## 5 Christmas and Epiphany †

Blessed are you, Lord our God,
our eternal Father and David's king.
You have made our gladness greater and increased our joy
by sending to dwell among us
the Wonderful Counsellor, the Prince of Peace.
Born of Mary,
proclaimed to the shepherds,
and acknowledged to the ends of the earth,
your unconquered Sun of righteousness
destroys our darkness and establishes us in freedom.
All glory in the highest be to you,
through Christ, the Son of your favour,
in the anointing love of his Spirit,
this night and for ever and ever. **Amen.**

## 6 Lent †

Blessed are you, O Lord our God,
the shepherd of Israel,
their pillar of cloud by day,
their pillar of fire by night.
In these forty days you lead us
into the desert of repentance
that in this pilgrimage of prayer
we might learn to be your people once more.
In fasting and service
you bring us back to your heart.
You open our eyes to your presence in the world
and you free our hands to lead others
to the radiant splendour of your mercy.
Be with us in these journey days
for without you we are lost and will perish.
To you alone be dominion and glory,
for ever and ever. **Amen.**

† From *Praise God in Song*. Copyright © 1979 by G.I.A. Publications, Inc., Chicago, Illinois. All rights reserved.

### 7  Resurrection †

We praise and thank you, O God our Father,
through your Son, Jesus Christ our Lord.
Through him you have enlightened us
by revealing the light that never fades,
for dark death has been destroyed
and radiant life is everywhere restored.
What was promised is fulfilled:
we have been joined to God,
through renewed life in the Spirit of the risen Lord.
Glory and praise to you, our Father,
through Jesus your Son,
who lives and reigns with you and the Spirit,
in the kingdom of light eternal,
for ever and ever. **Amen.**

*Where desired, in places where incense is customary, incense may be offered
while all or part of Psalm 141 is sung or said, with a refrain such as*

**Let my prayer be set forth in your sight as incense.**

*After the service of light, Evening Prayer may continue with the psalm or
first reading as appropriate.*

# Evening Prayer

*All stand. If the Penitential Rite has not been used, the officiant may say one of the sentences proper to the day or time of day.*

*Either the following responses or one of the alternative introductory responses on pp. 96–100 may be used.*

Officiant    O Lord, I call to you; come to me quickly;
People       **Hear my voice when I cry to you.**

Officiant    Let my prayer be set forth in your sight as
            incense,
People       **The lifting up of my hands as the evening
            sacrifice.**

All          **Glory to the Father, and to the Son, and to the
            Holy Spirit: as it was in the beginning, is now,
            and will be for ever. Amen.**

*Except in Lent, add,*
            **Alleluia!**

# The Invitatory

*If the Service of Light has not been celebrated, the Invitatory hymn or psalm follows.*

## O Gracious Light   *Phos Hilaron*

O gracious Light,
pure brightness of the everliving Father in heaven,
O Jesus Christ, holy and blessed!

Now as we come to the setting of the sun,
and our eyes behold the vesper light,
we sing your praises, O God: Father, Son, and Holy Spirit.

You are worthy at all times to be praised by happy voices,
O Son of God, O Giver of life,
and to be glorified through all the worlds.

*Or*

## Psalm 134

Behold now, bless the Lord, all you servants of the Lord,*
   you that stand by night in the house of the Lord.
Lift up your hands in the holy place and bless the Lord; *
   the Lord who made heaven and earth bless you out of Zion.

*Or the Easter canticle (p. 50) may follow between Easter and Pentecost, if it
has not been said or sung at Morning Prayer.*

# The Psalms

*The psalm, or psalms, precede or follow the first reading. When the theme of
the psalm is closely related to that of the reading, it is appropriate that the
psalm follow the reading as a reflection.*

*At the end of the psalm or psalms, silence may be kept and a prayer may be
said. The following may be said or sung, or omitted.*

Glory to the Father, and to the Son, and to the Holy Spirit:
   as it was in the beginning, is now, and will be for ever.
              Amen.

# The Proclamation of the Word

## The Readings

*The reading, or readings, as appointed are read, the reader first saying,*

      A reading from . . .

*After each lesson the reader may say,*

The word of the Lord.

*People*  **Thanks be to God.**


*The congregation may stand or sit for a Gospel reading. The reader may say,*

The Holy Gospel of our Lord Jesus Christ
according to . . .

*People*  **Glory to you, Lord Jesus Christ.**

*Then at the conclusion of the Gospel, the reader says,*

The Gospel of Christ.

*People*  **Praise to you, Lord Jesus Christ.**

*The readings may be followed by silence, a canticle, a responsory, an anthem
or other music, or a hymn. A combination of these responses may be
appropriate. The psalm, as appointed, may follow the first reading.*


## Sermon

*A sermon or other comment on the readings is appropriate at principal
services on Sundays and at other major gatherings of the Christian
community. A silence for reflection may follow.*


# Affirmation of Faith

*The Apostles' Creed or Hear, O Israel may be said.*


## The Apostles' Creed

**I believe in God,
the Father almighty,
creator of heaven and earth.**

I believe in Jesus Christ, his only Son, our Lord.
He was conceived by the power of the Holy Spirit
and born of the Virgin Mary.
He suffered under Pontius Pilate,
was crucified, died, and was buried.
He descended to the dead.
On the third day he rose again.
He ascended into heaven,
and is seated at the right hand of the Father.
He will come again
to judge the living and the dead.

I believe in the Holy Spirit,
the holy catholic Church,
the communion of saints,
the forgiveness of sins,
the resurrection of the body,
and the life everlasting. Amen.

*Or the following:*

## Hear, O Israel

Hear, O Israel,
the Lord our God, the Lord is one.

Love the Lord your God
with all your heart,
with all your soul,
with all your mind,
and with all your strength.

This is the first and the great commandment.
The second is like it:
Love your neighbour as yourself.

There is no commandment greater than these.

# Intercessions and Thanksgivings

*A deacon or lay member of the community may lead the intercessions and
thanksgivings. Intercession or thanksgiving may be offered for*

> the Church
> the Queen and all in authority
> the world
> the local community
> those in need
> the departed.

*A short litany may be selected from pp. 110–127. A thanksgiving litany and
the forms of General Thanksgiving are found on pp. 128–130. Other prayers
are found on pp. 675–684. These prayers and thanksgivings may be modified
in accordance with local need, or extempore forms of prayer may be used.*

## The Collect

*The Collect of the Day or a collect appropriate to the time of day may be said.*

## The Lord's Prayer

*Officiant* Gathering our prayers and praises into one,
    let us pray as our Saviour taught us,

*All*   **Our Father in heaven,
    hallowed be your name,
    your kingdom come,
    your will be done,
    on earth as in heaven.
    Give us today our daily bread.
    Forgive us our sins
    as we forgive those who sin against us.
    Save us from the time of trial,
    and deliver us from evil.
    For the kingdom, the power,
    and the glory are yours,
    now and for ever. Amen.**

*Or*

| Officiant | And now, as our Saviour Christ has taught us, we are bold to say, |
| All | **Our Father, who art in heaven,** |
| | **hallowed be thy name,** |
| | **thy kingdom come,** |
| | **thy will be done,** |
| | **on earth as it is in heaven.** |
| | **Give us this day our daily bread.** |
| | **And forgive us our trespasses,** |
| | **as we forgive those who trespass against us.** |
| | **And lead us not into temptation,** |
| | **but deliver us from evil.** |
| | **For thine is the kingdom,** |
| | **the power, and the glory,** |
| | **for ever and ever. Amen.** |

## Dismissal

*Then may be said or sung,*

| Officiant | Let us bless the Lord. |
| People | **Thanks be to God.** |

*From Easter Day through the Day of Pentecost,* **Alleluia** *is added to the dismissal and the people's response.*

*The officiant may conclude with one of the following:*

The Lord almighty grant us a quiet night and peace at the last.
**Amen.**

May the God of hope fill us with all joy and peace in believing through the power of the Holy Spirit. **Amen.**

The grace of our Lord Jesus Christ, and the love of God, and the fellowship of the Holy Spirit, be with us all evermore.
**Amen.**

May the peace of God, which passes all understanding, keep our hearts and minds in Christ Jesus. **Amen.**

May the Lord of peace give us peace in all ways and at all times. **Amen.**

# Canticles

## Tables of Suggested Canticles

The following tables provide suggestions for groups and individuals who pray the Divine Office. A choice of several canticles is given for Sundays. Two canticles are given for each weekday; they may be used in several ways.

a   One canticle may be used in the morning and the other in the evening.

b   Both canticles may be used in the morning and the Song of Mary or the Song of Simeon in the evening.

c   One of the canticles may be used with the Song of Zechariah in the morning, and the other in the evening.

d   They may be spread over twice as many weeks, using one with the Song of Zechariah in the morning, and the Song of Mary or the Song of Simeon in the evening.

e   They may be combined with the use of the Responsories on pp. 101–109.

## Canticles Through the Year

**Week 1**

| Sun | 19 | Song of Zechariah, | 26 | You are God; |
|-----|----|--------------------|----|----|
|  | 18 | Song of Mary, | 20 | Song of Simeon. |

| Mon | 13 | Song of Praise | * | 7 | The New Jerusalem |
|-----|----|----------------|---|----|----|
| Tue | 2 | Song of Peace | * | 17 | The Beatitudes |
| Wed | 14 | Song of Creation 1 | * | 10 | The Souls of the Righteous |
| Thu | 12 | The Bread of Heaven | * | 21 | God's Plan of Salvation |
| Fri | 5 | The Lord's Servant | * | 23 | Song of the First-Born |
| Sat | 11 | Song of Wisdom | * | 25 | Song of the Multitude in Heaven |

**Week 2**

| | | | | |
|---|---|---|---|---|
| *Sun* | 19 | Song of Zechariah, | 26 | You are God; |
| | 18 | Song of Mary, | 20 | Song of Simeon. |

| | | | | |
|---|---|---|---|---|
| *Mon* | 15 | Song of Creation 2 | * 4 | Song of Good News |
| *Tue* | 3 | Song of Thanksgiving | * 24 | Song to the Lamb |
| *Wed* | 16 | Song of Creation 3 | * 9 | Song from Ezekiel |
| *Thu* | 8 | Song from Jeremiah | * 27 | Glory to God |
| *Fri* | 6 | Seek the Lord | * 22 | Jesus Christ is Lord |
| *Sat* | 1 | Song of Moses | * 25 | Song of the Multitude in Heaven |

# Canticles for Advent

| | | | | |
|---|---|---|---|---|
| *Sun* | 7 | The New Jerusalem, | 19 | Song of Zechariah; |
| | 18 | Song of Mary, | 20 | Song of Simeon. |

| | | | | |
|---|---|---|---|---|
| *Mon* | 4 | Song of Good News | * 24 | Song to the Lamb |
| *Tue* | 2 | Song of Peace | * 17 | The Beatitudes |
| *Wed* | 6 | Seek the Lord | * 21 | God's Plan of Salvation |
| *Thu* | 7 | The New Jerusalem | * 23 | Song of the First-Born |
| *Fri* | 8 | Song from Jeremiah | * 22 | Jesus Christ is Lord |
| *Sat* | 3 | Song of Thanksgiving | * 25 | Song of the Multitude in Heaven |

# Canticles for Lent

| | | | | |
|---|---|---|---|---|
| *Sun* | 6 | Seek the Lord, | 17 | The Beatitudes; |
| | 9 | Song from Ezekiel, | 19 | Song of Zechariah; |
| | 18 | Song of Mary, | 20 | Song of Simeon. |

| | | | | |
|---|---|---|---|---|
| *Mon* | 6 | Seek the Lord | * 23 | Song of the First-Born |
| *Tue* | 2 | Song of Peace | * 9 | Song from Ezekiel |
| *Wed* | 3 | Song of Thanksgiving | * 10 | The Souls of the Righteous |
| *Thu* | 8 | Song from Jeremiah | * 22 | Jesus Christ is Lord |
| *Fri* | 5 | The Lord's Servant | * 17 | The Beatitudes |
| *Sat* | 4 | Song of Good News | * 21 | God's Plan of Salvation |

# Canticles for Eastertide

| Sun | 1 | Song of Moses, | 26 | You are God; |
|-----|-----|-----|-----|-----|
|     | 19 | Song of Zechariah, | 27 | Glory to God; |
|     | 18 | Song of Mary, | 20 | Song of Simeon. |

| Mon | 11 | Song of Wisdom | * | 23 | Song of the First-Born |
|-----|-----|-----|-----|-----|-----|
| Tue | 7 | The New Jerusalem | * | 21 | God's Plan of Salvation |
| Wed | 8 | Song from Jeremiah | * | 24 | Song to the Lamb |
| Thu | 12 | The Bread of Heaven | * | 27 | Glory to God |
| Fri | 9 | Song from Ezekiel | * | 22 | Jesus Christ is Lord |
| Sat | 1 | Song of Moses | * | 25 | Song of the Multitude in Heaven |

# Canticles for Festivals

## Feasts of Our Lord

7   The New Jerusalem
18  Song of Mary
19  Song of Zechariah
20  Song of Simeon
21  God's Plan of Salvation
22  Jesus Christ is Lord
23  Song of the First-Born
24  Song to the Lamb
25  Song of the Multitude in Heaven
26  You are God
27  Glory to God

## Major Saints' Days

10  The Souls of the Righteous
16  Song of Creation 3
17  The Beatitudes
18  Song of Mary
19  Song of Zechariah
20  Song of Simeon
24  Song to the Lamb
25  Song of the Multitude in Heaven
26  You are God
27  Glory to God

*Other translations of these canticles may be used.*

# 1   The Song of Moses

*Exodus 15.1–3, 6, 11, 13, 17–18*

I will sing to the Lord for his glorious triumph; *
   the horse and the rider he has hurled into the sea.
The Lord has become my strength and refuge; *
   the Lord himself has become my saviour.

He is my God and I will praise him; *
   my father's God and I will exalt him.
The Lord himself is a mighty warrior; *
   the Lord, the Lord is his name.

Your right hand, O Lord, is majestic in power; *
   your right hand, O Lord, shatters the enemy.
Who is like you, O Lord, among the gods,*
   holy, awesome, worker of wonders?

In steadfast love you led your people,*
   you guided your redeemed with your great strength.
You brought them in safety to your holy place,*
   and planted them firm on your own mountain.
You brought them into your own house.*
   The Lord shall reign for ever and ever.

# 2   Song of Peace

*Isaiah 2.2–5*

In the days to come *
   the mountain of the house of the Lord
shall tower as the highest of mountains *
   and be raised above the hills.

There shall all the nations flow; *
   many peoples shall come and say,
"Let us go up to the mountain of the Lord,*
   to the house of the God of Jacob,
that he may teach us his ways *
   that we may walk in his paths."

For the law shall go out from Zion,*
  from Jerusalem the word of the Lord.
He shall judge between the nations *
  and decide for many peoples.

They shall beat their swords into ploughshares,*
  their spears into pruning-knives;
nation shall not lift sword against nation; *
  they shall never train for war again.

O people of Jacob, come,*
  let us walk in the light of the Lord.

# 3   Song of Thanksgiving

*Isaiah 12.2–6*

Surely, it is God who saves me; *
  I will trust in him and not be afraid.
For the Lord is my stronghold and my sure defence,*
  and he will be my Saviour.
Therefore you shall draw water with rejoicing *
  from the springs of salvation.
And on that day you shall say,*
  Give thanks to the Lord and call upon his name;
make his deeds known among the peoples; *
  see that they remember that his name is exalted.
Sing the praises of the Lord, for he has done great things,*
  and this is known in all the world.
Cry aloud, inhabitants of Zion, ring out your joy,*
  for the great one in the midst of you is the Holy One of Israel.

# 4   Song of Good News

*Isaiah 40.9–11*

Go up to a high mountain,*
  O Zion, herald of joy;
lift up your voice in strength,*
  Jerusalem, herald of joy;

Lift it up, fear not; *
    say to the cities of Judah:
  "Behold your God!

Behold, the Lord comes in might,*
    comes to rule with his mighty arm;
behold, his reward is with him,*
    his recompense before him.

Like a shepherd will he feed his flock,*
    gathering the lambs in his arms;
he will hold them to his breast *
    and gently lead those with young."

## 5 The Lord's Servant

*Isaiah 53.3–6*

He was despised; he was rejected,*
    a man of sorrows, acquainted with grief.
As one from whom people hide their faces,*
    he was despised, and we esteemed him not.

Ours were the sufferings he bore,*
    ours the torments he endured,
while we thought he was being punished,*
    struck by God and brought low.

He was pierced for our sins,*
    bruised for no fault but ours.
His punishment has won our peace,*
    and by his wounds we are healed.

We had all strayed like sheep,*
    all taking our own way;
but the Lord laid on him *
    the guilt of us all.

## 6   Seek the Lord

*Isaiah 55.6–11*

Seek the Lord while he wills to be found; *
    call upon him when he draws near.
Let the wicked forsake their ways *
    and the evil ones their thoughts;
And let them turn to the Lord, and he will have compassion,*
    and to our God, for he will richly pardon.
For my thoughts are not your thoughts,*
    nor your ways my ways, says the Lord.
For as the heavens are higher than the earth,*
    so are my ways higher than your ways,
    and my thoughts than your thoughts.

For as rain and snow fall from the heavens *
    and return not again, but water the earth,
Bringing forth life and giving growth,*
    seed for sowing and bread for eating,
So is my word that goes forth from my mouth; *
    it will not return to me empty;
But it will accomplish that which I have purposed,*
    and prosper in that for which I sent it.

## 7   The New Jerusalem

*Isaiah 60.1–3, 11ab, 14cd, 18–19*

Arise, shine, for your light has come; *
    the glory of the Lord has risen upon you.
Though night still covers the earth *
    and darkness covers the nations,

Over you will the Lord arise,*
    over you will his glory appear.
Nations will stream to your light *
    and kings to your dawning brightness.

Your gates will always be open; *
    day or night, they will never be shut.
They will call you, The City of the Lord,*
    The Zion of the Holy One of Israel.

Violence will no more be heard in your land,*
    ruin or destruction within your borders;
you will name your walls, Salvation,*
    you will call your gates, Praise.

No longer will the sun be your light by day,*
    no longer the moon give you light by night;
the Lord will be your eternal light; *
    your God will be your glory.

## 8   Song from Jeremiah

*Jeremiah 31.10–14*

Hear the word of the Lord, O nations; *
    tell it on the far-off shores:
"He who scattered Israel will gather *
    and guard them as a shepherd his flock."
For the Lord has ransomed Jacob,*
    redeemed them from a foe too strong.

They will come and sing for joy on Zion's height,*
    radiant at the bounty of the Lord:
the grain, the new wine, the oil,*
    the young of flock and herd.
Their life like a watered garden,*
    they will never want again.

Then will maidens show their joy in the dance; *
    men, young and old, will rejoice.
I shall turn their mourning into gladness,*
    give comfort and joy for their sorrow.
I shall satisfy the priests with abundance,*
    and fill my people with my bounty.

# 9   A Song from Ezekiel

*Ezekiel 36.24–28*

I will take you from the nations,
and gather you from every country,
and bring you home to your own land.

I will pour clean water upon you,
purify you from all defilement,
and cleanse you from all your idols.

A new heart I will give you,
and put a new spirit within you;
I will take from your body the heart of stone
and give you a heart of flesh.

I will put my spirit within you,
make you walk in my ways
and observe my decrees.

You shall dwell in the land
I gave to your forebears;
you shall be my people
and I will be your God.

# 10   The Souls of the Righteous

*Wisdom 3.1–8*

The souls of the righteous are in the hand of God; *
  no torment shall ever touch them.

In the eyes of the unwise they seemed to be dead,*
  their departure was taken for defeat,
their going from us to be disaster; *
  but they are in peace.

Though they appeared to be punished *
  their hope is rich in immortality.
Small their affliction, great their blessing; *
  God proved and found them worthy of himself.

Like gold in a furnace he tried them,*
    and accepted them as an oblation.

In the moment of God's coming
they shall kindle into flame *
    and run like sparks through the stubble.
They shall govern nations and peoples,*
    and the Lord shall be their ruler for ever.

## 11    A Song of Wisdom

*Wisdom 10.15–19, 20b–21*

Wisdom freed from a nation of oppressors *
    a holy people and blameless race.
She entered the soul of a servant of the Lord,*
    withstood dread kings with wonders and signs.

To the saints she gave the reward of their labours,*
    and led them by a marvellous way;
she was their shelter by day *
    and their starlight through the night.

She brought them across the Red Sea,*
    led them through mighty waters,
but their enemies she swallowed in the waves *
    and spat them out from the depths of the abyss.

Lord, the righteous sang hymns to your name,*
    and praised with one voice your protecting hand,
for Wisdom opened the mouths of the dumb,*
    and gave speech to the tongues of babes.

## 12    The Bread of Heaven

*Wisdom 16.20–21, 26*

You gave your people angels' food *
    and sent them bread from heaven,
ready to eat, though they did no work,*
    rich in delights, and suiting every taste.

The food which you gave *
   showed your sweetness toward your children.
It served the desire of those who ate,*
   was changed to the flavour each one wished;

That the children you love might learn, O God,*
   that not by various crops are they fed,
but it is your word which sustains *
   all those who trust in you.

## 13   A Song of Praise

*Song of the Three 29–34*

Glory to you, Lord God of our fathers; *
   you are worthy of praise, glory to you.
Glory to you for the radiance of your holy name; *
   we will praise you and highly exalt you for ever.

Glory to you in the splendour of your temple; *
   on the throne of your majesty, glory to you.
Glory to you, seated between the Cherubim; *
   we will praise you and highly exalt you for ever.

Glory to you, beholding the depths; *
   in the high vault of heaven, glory to you.
Glory to you, Father, Son, and Holy Spirit; *
   we will praise you and highly exalt you for ever.

## 14   A Song of Creation 1

*Song of the Three 35–51*

*Invocation*

Glorify the Lord, all you works of the Lord,*
   praise him and highly exalt him for ever.
In the firmament of his power, glorify the Lord,*
   praise him and highly exalt him for ever.

*The Cosmic Order*

Glorify the Lord, you angels and all powers of the Lord,*
    O heavens and all waters above the heavens.
Sun and moon and stars of the sky, glorify the Lord,*
    praise him and highly exalt him for ever.

Glorify the Lord, every shower of rain and fall of dew,*
    all winds and fire and heat.
Winter and summer, glorify the Lord,*
    praise him and highly exalt him for ever.

Glorify the Lord, O chill and cold,*
    drops of dew and flakes of snow.
Frost and cold, ice and sleet, glorify the Lord,*
    praise him and highly exalt him for ever.

Glorify the Lord, O nights and days,*
    O shining light and enfolding dark.
Storm clouds and thunderbolts, glorify the Lord,*
    praise him and highly exalt him for ever.

*Doxology*

Let us glorify the Lord: Father, Son, and Holy Spirit; *
    praise him and highly exalt him for ever.
In the firmament of his power, glorify the Lord,*
    praise him and highly exalt him for ever.


## 15   A Song of Creation 2

*Song of the Three 35–36, 52–60*

*Invocation*

Glorify the Lord, all you works of the Lord,*
    praise him and highly exalt him for ever.
In the firmament of his power, glorify the Lord,*
    praise him and highly exalt him for ever.

*The Earth and its Creatures*

Let the earth glorify the Lord.*
    Glorify the Lord, O mountains and hills,
and all that grows upon the earth,*
    praise him and highly exalt him for ever.

Glorify the Lord, O springs of water, seas, and streams,*
    O whales and all that move in the waters.
All birds of the air, glorify the Lord,*
    praise him and highly exalt him for ever.

Glorify the Lord, O beasts of the wild,*
    and all you flocks and herds.
O men and women everywhere, glorify the Lord,*
    praise him and highly exalt him for ever.

*Doxology*

Let us glorify the Lord: Father, Son, and Holy Spirit; *
    praise him and highly exalt him for ever.
In the firmament of his power, glorify the Lord,*
    praise him and highly exalt him for ever.

# 16  A Song of Creation 3

*Song of the Three 35–36, 61–65*

*Invocation*

Glorify the Lord, all you works of the Lord,*
    praise him and highly exalt him for ever.
In the firmament of his power, glorify the Lord,*
    praise him and highly exalt him for ever.

*The People of God*

Let the people of God glorify the Lord,*
    praise him and highly exalt him for ever.
Glorify the Lord, O priests and servants of the Lord,*
    praise him and highly exalt him for ever.

Glorify the Lord, O spirits and souls of the righteous,*
    praise him and highly exalt him for ever.

You that are holy and humble of heart, glorify the Lord,*
 praise him and highly exalt him for ever.

*Doxology*

Let us glorify the Lord: Father, Son, and Holy Spirit; *
 praise him and highly exalt him for ever.
In the firmament of his power, glorify the Lord,*
 praise him and highly exalt him for ever.

# 17   The Beatitudes

*Matthew 5.3–12*

Blessed are the poor in spirit,*
 for theirs is the kingdom of heaven.

Blessed are those who mourn,*
 for they shall be comforted.

Blessed are the gentle,*
 for they shall inherit the earth.

Blessed are those who hunger and thirst for what is right,*
 for they shall be satisfied.

Blessed are the merciful,*
 for mercy shall be shown to them.

Blessed are the pure in heart,*
 for they shall see God.

Blessed are the peacemakers,*
 for they shall be called children of God.

Blessed are those who are persecuted in the cause of right,*
 for theirs is the kingdom of heaven.

Blessed are you when others revile you and persecute you *
 and utter all kinds of evil against you falsely for my sake.

Rejoice and be glad,*
 for your reward is great in heaven.

## 18a    The Song of Mary

*Luke 1.46–55*

My soul proclaims the greatness of the Lord,
my spirit rejoices in God my Saviour; *
   for he has looked with favour on his lowly servant.

From this day all generations will call me blessed: *
   the Almighty has done great things for me,
   and holy is his name.

He has mercy on those who fear him *
   in every generation.

He has shown the strength of his arm,*
   he has scattered the proud in their conceit.

He has cast down the mighty from their thrones,*
   and has lifted up the lowly.

He has filled the hungry with good things,*
   and the rich he has sent away empty.

He has come to the help of his servant Israel,*
   for he has remembered his promise of mercy,
the promise he made to our fathers,*
   to Abraham and his children for ever.

Glory to the Father, and to the Son, and to the Holy Spirit: *
   as it was in the beginning, is now, and will be for ever.
              Amen.

## 18b  †                              *Metre:   10  10  10  10*

Tell out, my soul, the greatness of the Lord!
Unnumbered blessings, give my spirit voice;
tender to me the promise of his word;
to God my Saviour shall my heart rejoice.

Tell out, my soul, the greatness of his name!
Make known his might, the deeds his arm has done;
his mercy sure, from age to age the same;
his holy name—the Lord, the mighty one.

Tell out, my soul, the greatness of his might!
Powers and dominions lay their glory by;
proud hearts and stubborn wills are put to flight,
the hungry fed, the humble lifted high.

Tell out, my soul, the glories of his word!
Firm is his promise, and his mercy sure.
Tell out, my soul, the greatness of the Lord
to children's children and for evermore!


**18c** †                                    *Metre:  8 8 8 8*

My soul gives glory to the Lord,
in God my Saviour I rejoice.
My lowliness he did regard,
exalting me by his own choice.

From this day all shall call me blest,
for he has done great things for me.
Of all great names his is the best.
For it is holy; strong is he!

His mercy goes to all who fear
from age to age and to all parts.
His arm of strength to all is near;
he scatters those who have proud hearts.

He casts the mighty from their throne
and raises those of low degree;
he feeds the hungry as his own,
the rich depart in poverty.

† From *Praise God in Song*. Copyright © 1979 by G.I.A. Publications, Inc.,
  Chicago, Illinois. All rights reserved.

He raised his servant, Israel,
remember'ring his eternal grace.
As from of old he did foretell
to Abraham and to his race.

O Father, Son, and Spirit blest,
in three-fold name are you adored;
to you be ev'ry prayer addressed,
from age to age the only Lord.

## 19a    The Song of Zechariah

*Luke 1.68–79*

Blessed be the Lord, the God of Israel; *
    he has come to his people and set them free.

He has raised up for us a mighty Saviour,*
    born of the house of his servant David.

Through his holy prophets he promised of old,
that he would save us from our enemies,*
    from the hands of all who hate us.

He promised to show mercy to our fathers *
    and to remember his holy covenant.

This was the oath he swore to our father Abraham,*
    to set us free from the hands of our enemies,
free to worship him without fear,*
    holy and righteous in his sight
    all the days of our life.

You, my child, shall be called the prophet
                of the Most High,*
    for you will go before the Lord to prepare his way,
to give his people knowledge of salvation *
    by the forgiveness of their sins.

In the tender compassion of our God *
    the dawn from on high shall break upon us,
to shine on those who dwell in darkness and the shadow
                of death,*
    and to guide our feet into the way of peace.

Glory to the Father, and to the Son, and to the Holy Spirit: *
    as it was in the beginning, is now, and will be for ever.
                Amen.

## 19b
*Metre:  8 6 8 6 D*

Bless'd be the God of Israel,
the ever-living Lord,
who comes in pow'r to save his own,
his people Israel.
For Israel he raises up
salvation's tow'r on high
in David's house who reigned as king
and servant of the Lord.

Through holy prophets did he speak
his word in days of old,
that he would save us from our foes
and all who bear us ill.
To our ancestors did he give
his covenant of love;
so with us all he keeps his word
in love that knows no end.

Of old he gave his solemn oath
to Father Abraham;
his seed a mighty race should be
and bless'd for evermore.
He vowed to set his people free
from fear of ev'ry foe
that we might serve him all our days
in goodness, love, and peace.

O tiny child, your name shall be
the prophet of the Lord;
the way of God you shall prepare
to make his coming known.
You shall proclaim to Israel
salvation's dawning day
when God shall wipe away all sins
in his redeeming love.

The rising sun shall shine on us
to bring the light of day
to all who sit in darkest night
and shadow of the grave.
Our footsteps God shall safely guide
to walk the ways of peace.
His name for evermore be bless'd
who lives and loves and saves.

## 20   The Song of Simeon

*Luke 2.29–32*

Lord, now you let your servant go in peace; *
   your word has been fulfilled.

My own eyes have seen the salvation *
   which you have prepared in the sight of every people;

a light to reveal you to the nations *
   and the glory of your people Israel.

Glory to the Father, and to the Son, and to the Holy Spirit: *
   as it was in the beginning, is now, and will be for ever.
               Amen.

## 21  God's Plan of Salvation

*Ephesians 1.3–7*

Blessed be the God and Father
    of our Lord Jesus Christ,*
who has blessed us in Christ
    with all the spiritual blessings of heaven.

God chose us in Christ
    before the world was made *
to be holy and blameless,
    and to live by his love in his presence.

God planned through Jesus Christ *
    to bring us to himself as his children,
that we might praise the glory of his grace,*
    his free gift to us in the Beloved.

In Christ we gain redemption;
    through his blood our sins are forgiven.*
How rich is the grace of God!

## 22a  Jesus Christ is Lord

*Philippians 2.6–11*

Christ Jesus, by nature divine,
did not grasp for himself
a rank as equal with God.

He chose to empty himself,
becoming a humble slave,
and living the life of a man.

And human in every way,
he abased himself still more,
obedient to death on a cross.

So God has exalted him on high,
and given to him the name,
the greatest of all the names;

So that at Jesus' name
every knee should bend low
in heaven, on earth, in the depths,

And every tongue proclaim:
Jesus Christ is Lord,
to the glory of God the Father!


## 22b                                    *Metre:  10 10 10 4*

All praise to thee, for thou, O King divine,
didst yield the glory that of right was thine,
that in our darkened hearts thy grace might shine:
alleluia!

Thou cam'st to us in lowliness of thought;
by thee the outcast and the poor were sought,
and by thy death was God's salvation wrought:
alleluia!

Let this mind be in us which was in thee,
who wast a servant that we might be free,
humbling thyself to death on Calvary:
alleluia!

Wherefore, by God's eternal purpose, thou
art high exalted o'er all creatures now,
and given the name to which all knees shall bow:
alleluia!

Let every tongue confess with one accord
in heaven and earth that Jesus Christ is Lord;
and God the Father be by all adored:
alleluia!

## 23 Song of the First-Born

*Colossians 1.15–20*

Christ is the image of the unseen God,*
   the first-born of all creation,
for in him were all things made,*
   in heaven and on earth.

Through him and for him were all things made,
   before all he exists, holds all things in one.*
The Church is his body, and he is its head.

He is the beginning, the first-born from the dead; *
   in all things he alone is supreme.
God made all his fullness to dwell in him,*
   to reconcile through him all creation to himself,
everything on earth and everything in heaven,*
   all gathered into peace by his death on the cross.

## 24 A Song to the Lamb

*Revelation 4.11; 5.9–10, 13*

Splendour and honour and kingly power *
   are yours by right, O Lord our God,
For you created everything that is,*
   and by your will they were created and have their being;

And yours by right, O Lamb that was slain,*
   for with your blood you have redeemed for God,
From every family, language, people, and nation,*
   a kingdom of priests to serve our God on earth.

And so, to him who sits upon the throne,*
   and to Christ the Lamb,
Be worship and praise, dominion and splendour,*
   for ever and for evermore.

## 25   Song of the Multitude in Heaven

*Revelation 19.1, 2, 5–7*

Alleluia!
To our God belong victory, glory, and power,*
   for right and just are his judgements.
Praise our God, all you who serve him,*
   you who fear him, great and small.

Alleluia!
The Lord God almighty has claimed his kingdom.*
   Let us rejoice and triumph and give him praise:
   the time has come for the wedding-feast of the Lamb.

## 26   You are God

You are God: we praise you;
you are the Lord: we acclaim you;
you are the eternal Father:
all creation worships you.

To you all angels, all the powers of heaven,
Cherubim and Seraphim, sing in endless praise:
Holy, holy, holy Lord, God of power and might,
heaven and earth are full of your glory.

The glorious company of apostles praise you.
The noble fellowship of prophets praise you.
The white-robed army of martyrs praise you.

Throughout the world the holy Church acclaims you:
Father, of majesty unbounded,
your true and only Son, worthy of all worship,
and the Holy Spirit, advocate and guide.

You, Christ, are the King of Glory,
the eternal Son of the Father.

When you became man to set us free
you did not shun the Virgin's womb.

You overcame the sting of death
and opened the kingdom of heaven to all believers.

You are seated at God's right hand in glory.
We believe that you will come, and be our judge.

Come then, Lord, and help your people,
bought with the price of your own blood,
and bring us with your saints
to glory everlasting.

## 27   Glory to God

Glory to God in the highest,
and peace to his people on earth.

Lord God, heavenly king,
almighty God and Father,
we worship you, we give you thanks,
we praise you for your glory.

Lord Jesus Christ, only Son of the Father,
Lord God, Lamb of God,
you take away the sin of the world:
have mercy on us;
you are seated at the right hand of the Father:
receive our prayer.

For you alone are the Holy One,
you alone are the Lord,
you alone are the Most High,
Jesus Christ,
with the Holy Spirit,
in the glory of God the Father. Amen.

# Introductory Responses

*These alternative introductory responses may be used at the beginning of*
*Morning Prayer and Evening Prayer instead of* O God, make speed to
save us,*etc., and* O Lord, I call to you,*etc. On weekdays they may*
*replace all that precedes the Psalm.*

## 1 Advent

Restore us, O Lord God of hosts;
   **Show the light of your countenance, and we shall be saved.**

Will you not give us life again,
   **That your people may rejoice in you?**

Show us your mercy, O Lord,
   **And grant us your salvation.**

Blessed is the King who comes in the name of the Lord!
   **Peace in heaven and glory in the highest.**

## 2 Incarnation

Blessed be the Lord, the God of Israel,
   **May all the earth be filled with his glory.**

Light has sprung up for the righteous,
   **And joyful gladness for those who are true-hearted.**

Glory to God in the highest,
   **And peace to his people on earth.**

## 3 Christmas and Epiphany

*The first paragraph or the second paragraph may be omitted.*
Blessed are you, O Christ, Son of God,
you were before time began
and came into the world to save us.
Blessed are you, Sun of righteousness;

you shine with the Father's love
and illumine the whole universe.
Blessed are you, Son of Mary;
born a child, you shared our humanity.
**Let heaven and earth shout their praise.**

Blessed are you, Son of David;
born to rule,
you received gifts from the wise men.
Blessed are you, Son of Man;
baptized by John,
you saved us from ourselves.
Blessed are you, heavenly King;
teaching and preaching, healing and comforting,
you proclaimed the kingdom.
**Let heaven and earth shout their praise.**

With all the voices of heaven
we celebrate the coming of our Saviour.
**Let heaven and earth shout their praise.**

With all the creatures on earth
we sing and dance at his birth.
**Praise and honour and glory to you, O Lord most high.**

## 4   Repentance

Cast your burden upon the Lord,
   **And he will sustain you.**

Create in me a clean heart, O God,
   **And renew a right spirit within me.**

Cast me not away from your presence
   **And take not your Holy Spirit from me.**

Give me the joy of your saving help again
   **And sustain me with your bountiful Spirit.**

Blessed be the Lord day by day,
   **The God of our salvation, who bears our burdens.**

## 5   The Cross

Christ became obedient unto death for us,
  **Even death upon a cross.**

He was pierced for our sins,
  **Bruised for no fault but ours.**

His punishment has won our peace,
  **And by his wounds we are healed.**

Worthy is the Lamb that was slain
to receive power and riches and wisdom,
  **Strength, honour, glory, and praise. Amen.**

## 6   Resurrection

Alleluia! Christ is risen.
  **The Lord is risen indeed. Alleluia!**

Praise the God and Father of our Lord Jesus Christ.
  **He gave us new life and hope
  by raising Jesus from the dead.**

Rejoice, then, even in your distress.
  **We shall be counted worthy when Christ appears.**

God has claimed us as his own.
  **He called us from our darkness into the light of his day.**

Alleluia! Christ is risen.
  **The Lord is risen indeed. Alleluia!**

## 7   Pentecost   *and other times as appropriate*

God's love has been poured into our hearts.
  **We dwell in him and he in us.**

Give thanks to the Lord and call upon his name;
  **Make known his deeds among the peoples.**

Sing to him, sing praises to him,
**And speak of all his marvellous works.**

Holy, holy, holy, is the Lord God almighty,
**Who was and is and is to come!**

## 8   Major Saints' Days

Great is the Lord and greatly to be praised;
**There is no end of his greatness.**

One generation shall praise your works to another
**And shall declare your power.**

All your works praise you, O Lord,
**And your faithful servants bless you.**

They make known the glory of your kingdom
**And speak of your power.**

My mouth shall speak the praise of the Lord;
**Let all flesh bless his holy name for ever and ever.**

## 9   General

Blessed be God: Father, Son, and Holy Spirit.
**And blessed be his kingdom, now and for ever. Amen.**

Come, let us worship God our King.
**Come, let us worship Christ, our King and our God.**
Come, let us worship Christ among us, our King and our God.
**Holy God,**
**holy and mighty,**
**holy immortal one,**
**have mercy upon us.**

*When it is sung,* **Holy God,***etc., may be repeated three times.*

# 10   Late Evening

Into your hands, O Lord, I commend my spirit;
**For you have redeemed me, O Lord, O God of truth.**

**Glory to the Father, and to the Son, and to the Holy Spirit:
as it was in the beginning, is now, and will be for ever.
Amen.**

*Except in Lent, add,*
**Alleluia!**

# Responsories

## 1

In the evening tears;
* in the morning shouts of joy.

**In the evening tears;**
**\* in the morning shouts of joy.**

I will exalt you, O Lord, because you have lifted me up
and have not let my enemies triumph over me.
**In the morning shouts of joy.**

Sing to the Lord, you servants of his;
give thanks for the remembrance of his holiness.
**In the morning shouts of joy.**

You have turned my wailing into dancing;
you have put off my sack-cloth and clothed me with joy.
**In the morning shouts of joy.**

My heart sings to you without ceasing;
O Lord my God, I will give you thanks for ever.
**In the morning shouts of joy.**

Glory to the Father, and to the Son, and to the Holy Spirit.
**In the evening tears;**
**\* in the morning shouts of joy.**

## 2

My life is in your hand, deliver me;
* shine on your servant with the light of your love.

**My life is in your hand, deliver me;**
**\* shine on your servant with the light of your love.**

In you, O Lord, have I taken refuge;
let me never be put to shame.
**Shine on your servant with the light of your love.**

Incline your ear to me;
make haste to deliver me.
**Shine on your servant with the light of your love.**

Be my strong rock, a castle to keep me safe;
for the sake of your name, lead me and guide me.
**Shine on your servant with the light of your love.**

I put my trust in the Lord;
I will rejoice and be glad because of your mercy.
**Shine on your servant with the light of your love.**

Glory to the Father, and to the Son, and to the Holy Spirit.
**My life is in your hand, deliver me;**
**\* shine on your servant with the light of your love.**


## 3

The eyes of the Lord are upon the righteous;
\* to the brokenhearted the Lord is near.

**The eyes of the Lord are upon the righteous;**
**\* to the brokenhearted the Lord is near.**

I will bless the Lord at all times;
his praise shall ever be in my mouth.
**To the brokenhearted the Lord is near.**

Look upon him and be radiant,
and let your faces not be ashamed.
**To the brokenhearted the Lord is near.**

The righteous cry, and the Lord hears them
and delivers them from all their troubles.
**To the brokenhearted the Lord is near.**

The Lord ransoms the life of his servants,
and none will be punished who trust in him.
**To the brokenhearted the Lord is near.**

Glory to the Father, and to the Son, and to the Holy Spirit.
**The eyes of the Lord are upon the righteous;**
**\* to the brokenhearted the Lord is near.**

# 4

In my mouth he has put a new song:
\* praise to our God!

> **In my mouth he has put a new song:**
> **\* praise to our God!**

I waited patiently upon the Lord;
he stooped to me and heard my cry.
**Praise to our God!**

Many shall see, and stand in awe,
and put their trust in the Lord.
**Praise to our God!**

I love to do your will, O my God;
your law is deep in my heart.
**Praise to our God!**

I proclaimed righteousness in the great congregation;
behold, I did not restrain my lips.
**Praise to our God!**

Glory to the Father, and to the Son, and to the Holy Spirit.
**In my mouth he has put a new song:**
**\* praise to our God!**

# 5

The Lord is with us, he is our stronghold;
\* God will help at the break of day.

> **The Lord is with us, he is our stronghold;**
> **\* God will help at the break of day.**

God is our refuge and strength,
a very present help in trouble.
   **God will help at the break of day.**

We will not fear, though the earth be moved,
and though the mountains be toppled into the depths
                        of the sea.
   **God will help at the break of day.**

Come now and look upon the works of the Lord,
what awesome things he has done on earth.
   **God will help at the break of day.**

"Be still and know that I am God;
I will be exalted among the nations;
I will be exalted in the earth."
   **God will help at the break of day.**

Glory to the Father, and to the Son, and to the Holy Spirit.
   **The Lord is with us, he is our stronghold;**
   **\* God will help at the break of day.**

## 6

From age to age my mouth will proclaim your faithfulness;
\* your love, O Lord, for ever will I sing.

   **From age to age my mouth will proclaim your faithfulness;**
   **\* your love, O Lord, for ever will I sing.**

I am persuaded that your love is established for ever;
you have set your faithfulness firmly in the heavens.
   **Your love, O Lord, for ever will I sing.**

The heavens bear witness to your wonders, O Lord,
and to your faithfulness in the assembly of the holy ones.
   **Your love, O Lord, for ever will I sing.**

Who is like you, Lord God of hosts?
O mighty Lord, your faithfulness is all around you.
   **Your love, O Lord, for ever will I sing.**

Righteousness and justice are the foundations
                            of your throne;
love and truth go before your face.
**Your love, O Lord, for ever will I sing.**

Glory to the Father, and to the Son, and to the Holy Spirit.
**From age to age my mouth will proclaim your faithfulness;**
**\* your love, O Lord, for ever will I sing.**


## 7    Advent

My soul waits for the Lord;
\* in his word is my hope.

**My soul waits for the Lord;**
**\* in his word is my hope.**

Out of the depths have I called to you, O Lord;
Lord, hear my voice.
**In his word is my hope.**

There is forgiveness with you;
therefore you shall be feared.
**In his word is my hope.**

My soul waits for the Lord,
more than watchmen for the morning.
**In his word is my hope.**

O Israel, wait for the Lord,
for with the Lord there is mercy.
**In his word is my hope.**

Glory to the Father, and to the Son, and to the Holy Spirit.
**My soul waits for the Lord;**
**\* in his word is my hope.**


## 8    Incarnation

His salvation is near to those who fear him:
\* his glory shall dwell in our land.

**His salvation is near to those who fear him:**
**\* his glory shall dwell in our land.**

I will listen to what the Lord God is saying,
for he is speaking peace to his faithful people
and to those who turn their hearts to him.
**His glory shall dwell in our land.**

Mercy and truth have met together;
righteousness and peace have kissed each other.
**His glory shall dwell in our land.**

Truth shall spring up from the earth,
and righteousness shall look down from heaven.
**His glory shall dwell in our land.**

Righteousness shall go before him,
and peace shall be a pathway for his feet.
**His glory shall dwell in our land.**

Glory to the Father, and to the Son, and to the Holy Spirit.
**His salvation is near to those who fear him;**
**\* his glory shall dwell in our land.**

## 9 Lent

Incline your ear to me;
\* make haste to answer when I call.

**Incline your ear to me;**
**\* make haste to answer when I call.**

Lord, hear my prayer,
and let my cry come before you.
**Make haste to answer when I call.**

Hide not your face from me
in the day of my trouble.
**Make haste to answer when I call.**

You, O Lord, endure for ever,
and your name from age to age.
**Make haste to answer when I call.**

You will arise and have compassion on Zion,
for it is time to have pity upon her.
**Make haste to answer when I call.**

Glory to the Father, and to the Son, and to the Holy Spirit.
**Incline your ear to me;**
**\* make haste to answer when I call.**


## 10   The Cross

Surely he has borne our griefs;
\* he has carried our sorrows.

**Surely he has borne our griefs;**
**\* he has carried our sorrows.**

He was despised; he was rejected,
a man of sorrows and acquainted with grief.
**He has carried our sorrows.**

He was pierced for our sins,
bruised for no fault but ours.
**He has carried our sorrows.**

His punishment has won our peace,
and by his wounds we are healed.
**He has carried our sorrows.**

We had all strayed like sheep,
but the Lord has laid on him the guilt of us all.
**He has carried our sorrows.**

Glory to the Father, and to the Son, and to the Holy Spirit.
**Surely he has borne our griefs;**
**\* he has carried our sorrows.**

## 11  Resurrection

Let the voice of God's praise resound;
* he gives life to our souls.

> **Let the voice of God's praise resound;**
> **\* he gives life to our souls.**

Be joyful in God, all you lands;
sing the glory of his name.
> **He gives life to our souls.**

Come now and see the work of God,
how wonderful he is toward all people.
> **He gives life to our souls.**

He turned the sea into dry land,
so that they went through the water on foot.
> **He gives life to our souls.**

There we rejoiced in him.
In his might he rules for ever.
> **He gives life to our souls.**

Glory to the Father, and to the Son, and to the Holy Spirit.
> **Let the voice of God's praise resound;**
> **\* he gives life to our souls.**

## 12  The Holy Spirit—Thanksgiving

You send forth your Spirit, O Lord;
* you renew the face of the earth.

> **You send forth your Spirit, O Lord;**
> **\* you renew the face of the earth.**

O Lord, how manifold are your works!
in wisdom you have made them all;
the earth is full of your creatures.
> **You renew the face of the earth.**

All of them look to you
to give them their food in due season.
**You renew the face of the earth.**

You give it to them; they gather it;
you open your hand, and they are filled with good things.
**You renew the face of the earth.**

May the glory of the Lord endure for ever;
may the Lord rejoice in all his works.
**You renew the face of the earth.**

Glory to the Father, and to the Son, and to the Holy Spirit.
**You send forth your Spirit, O Lord;**
**\* you renew the face of the earth.**

## 13   Major Saints' Days

The Lord is righteous and delights in righteous deeds;
\* the just shall see his face.

**The Lord is righteous and delights in righteous deeds;**
**\* the just shall see his face.**

When foundations are being destroyed,
what can the righteous do?
**The just shall see his face.**

His eyes behold the inhabited world;
his piercing eye weighs our worth.
**The just shall see his face.**

The Lord weighs the righteous as well as the wicked,
but those who delight in violence he abhors.
**The just shall see his face.**

Glory to the Father, and to the Son, and to the Holy Spirit.
**The Lord is righteous and delights in righteous deeds;**
**\* the just shall see his face.**

# Litanies

*In the following litanies, petitions may be altered or omitted according to circumstances. Other petitions may be added.*

*For musical or other reasons, the response may be changed to a similar appropriate expression, such as* **Lord, have mercy; Lord, hear and have mercy; Lord, hear our prayer; Kyrie eleison.** *The suffrages may also be changed to make them fit with another response. For instance, the opening petition and response in Litany No. 6 might be changed to:*

Let us pray for the whole People of God, that each one may be a true and faithful servant of Christ.
**Lord, hear our prayer.**

*When litanies are sung, they may be introduced by a cantor singing the response, which is then repeated by all before the first petition. When they are said, they may be introduced by an expression like* **Let us pray with confidence to the Lord, saying . . .**

## 1

(In peace let us pray to the Lord, saying, "Lord, have mercy.")

For peace from on high and for our salvation, let us pray to the Lord.
**Lord, have mercy.**

For the peace of the whole world, for the welfare of the holy Church of God, and for the unity of all, let us pray to the Lord.
**Lord, have mercy.**

For our bishops, and for all the clergy and people, let us pray to the Lord.
**Lord, have mercy.**

For Elizabeth our Queen, for the leaders of the nations, and for all in authority, let us pray to the Lord.
**Lord, have mercy.**

For *this city* (*town, village, etc.*), for every city and community, and for those who live in them in faith, let us pray to the Lord.
**Lord, have mercy.**

For good weather, and for abundant harvests for all to share, let us pray to the Lord.
**Lord, have mercy.**

For those who travel by land, water, or air, for the sick and the suffering (especially . . . ), for prisoners and captives, and for their safety, health, and salvation, let us pray to the Lord.
**Lord, have mercy.**

For our deliverance from all affliction, strife, and need, let us pray to the Lord.
**Lord, have mercy.**

For the absolution and remission of our sins and offences, let us pray to the Lord.
**Lord, have mercy.**

For all who have died (especially . . . ), let us pray to the Lord.
**Lord, have mercy.**

Remembering ( . . . and) all the saints, we commit ourselves, one another, and our whole life to Christ our God.
**To you, O Lord.**

Almighty God, you have given us grace at this time with one accord to make our common supplications to you, and you have promised through your well-beloved Son that when two or three are gathered together you will hear their requests. Fulfil now our desires and petitions, as may be best for us, granting us in this world knowledge of your truth, and in the age to come eternal life; for you, Father, are good and loving, and we glorify you through your Son Jesus Christ our Lord, in the Holy Spirit, now and for ever. **Amen.**

**2**

(Let us pray with confidence to the Lord, saying, "Lord hear
our prayer.")

O Lord, guard and direct your Church in the way of unity,
service, and praise.
  **Lord, hear our prayer.**

Give to all nations an awareness of the unity of the human
family.
  **Lord, hear our prayer.**

Cleanse our hearts of prejudice and selfishness, and inspire us
to hunger and thirst for what is right.
  **Lord, hear our prayer.**

Teach us to use your creation for your greater praise, that all
may share the good things you provide.
  **Lord, hear our prayer.**

Strengthen all who give their energy or skill for the healing of
those who are sick in body or in mind.
  **Lord, hear our prayer.**

Set free all who are bound by fear and despair.
  **Lord, hear our prayer.**

Grant a peaceful end and eternal rest to all who are dying, and
your comfort to those who mourn.
  **Lord, hear our prayer.**

**3**

(Let us offer our prayers to the source of all love and all life,
saying, "Lord, hear our prayer.")

Merciful Lord, we pray for all who call themselves Christians:
that we may become a royal priesthood, a holy nation, to the
praise of Christ Jesus our Saviour.
  **Lord, hear our prayer.**

We pray for *N* our bishop, and for all bishops and other ministers: that they may remain faithful to their calling and rightly proclaim the word of truth.
**Lord, hear our prayer.**

We pray for Elizabeth our Queen, for the leaders of the nations, and all in authority: that your people may lead quiet and peaceable lives.
**Lord, hear our prayer.**

We pray for *this city* and those who live here, the poor and the rich, the elderly and the young, men and women: that you will show your goodwill to all.
**Lord, hear our prayer.**

We pray for the victims of our society and those who minister to them: that you will be their help and defence.
**Lord, hear our prayer.**

We pray for those preparing for baptism, (for those recently baptized): that they may be strengthened in the faith.
**Lord, hear our prayer.**

We give thanks for all the saints who have found favour in your sight from earliest times, prophets, apostles, martyrs, and those whose names are known to you alone: and we pray that we too may be counted among your faithful witnesses.
**Lord, hear our prayer.**

**4**

(In peace let us pray to the Lord, saying, "Lord, hear and have mercy.")

We pray for all who confess the name of Christ: fill us with the power of your Holy Spirit.
**Lord, hear and have mercy.**

We pray for those whose lives are bound in mutual love, and for those who live in celibacy: be their joy and their strength.
**Lord, hear and have mercy.**

For all in danger, for those who are far from home, prisoners, exiles, victims of oppression: grant them your salvation.
**Lord, hear and have mercy.**

For all who are facing trials and difficulties, for those who are sick, and those who are dying: show them your kindness and mercy.
**Lord, hear and have mercy.**

We pray for one another: may we always be united in service and love.
**Lord, hear and have mercy.**

We pray to be forgiven our sins and set free from all hardship, distress, want, war, and injustice.
**Lord, hear and have mercy.**

May we discover new and just ways of sharing the goods of the earth, struggling against exploitation, greed, or lack of concern: may we all live by the abundance of your mercies and find joy together.
**Lord, hear and have mercy.**

May we be strengthened by our communion with all Christ's saints.
**Lord, hear and have mercy.**

## 5

(Let us pray to the Lord, saying, "Lord, hear our prayer.")

Let us pray for the peace of the world: the Lord grant that we may live together in justice and faith.
**Lord, hear our prayer.**

Let us pray for this country, and especially for Queen Elizabeth, the Governor General, the Prime Minister, and all in authority: the Lord help them to serve this people according to his holy will.
**Lord, hear our prayer.**

Let us pray for children and young people: the Lord guide their growth and development.
**Lord, hear our prayer.**

Let us pray for the sick: the Lord deliver them and keep them in his love.
**Lord, hear our prayer.**

Let us pray for all who are condemned to exile, prison, harsh treatment, or hard labour, for the sake of justice and truth: the Lord support them and keep them steadfast.
**Lord, hear our prayer.**

We remember the prophets, apostles, martyrs, and all who have borne witness to the gospel: the Lord direct our lives in the same spirit of service and sacrifice.
**Lord, hear our prayer.**

## 6

(As we stand in God's presence, let us pray to the Lord, saying, "Lord, have mercy.")

For the whole People of God, that each one may be a true and faithful servant of Christ, let us pray to the Lord.
**Lord, have mercy.**

For those drawing near to the light of faith, that the Lord will bring them to true knowledge of himself, let us pray to the Lord.
**Lord, have mercy.**

For our families and friends, that the Lord will give them joy and satisfaction in all that they do, let us pray to the Lord.
**Lord, have mercy.**

For those who are lonely, sick, hungry, persecuted, or ignored, that the Lord will comfort and sustain them, let us pray to the Lord.
**Lord, have mercy.**

For our country, that the Lord will help us to contribute to its true growth and well-being, let us pray to the Lord.
**Lord, have mercy.**

For the whole human family, that we may live together in justice and peace, let us pray to the Lord.
**Lord, have mercy.**

# 7

(Let us pray in faith to God our Father, to his Son Jesus Christ, and to the Holy Spirit, saying, "Lord, hear and have mercy.")

For the Church of the living God throughout the world, let us ask the riches of his grace.
**Lord, hear and have mercy.**

For all who proclaim the word of truth, let us ask the infinite wisdom of Christ.
**Lord, hear and have mercy.**

For all who have consecrated their lives to the kingdom of God, and for all struggling to follow the way of Christ, let us ask the gifts of the Spirit.
**Lord, hear and have mercy.**

For Elizabeth our Queen, for the Prime Minister of this country, and for all who govern the nations, that they may strive for justice and peace, let us ask the strength of God.
**Lord, hear and have mercy.**

For scholars and research-workers, that their studies may benefit humanity, let us ask the light of the Lord.
**Lord, hear and have mercy.**

For all who have passed from this life in faith and obedience, let us ask the peace of Christ.
**Lord, hear and have mercy.**

**8**

By your incarnation and your birth in poverty, by your
baptism, your fasting, and your trials in the desert, O Lord,
hear our prayer;
**Kyrie eleison** *or* **Lord, have mercy.**

By your agony in the garden, by your cross and passion, by
your death and burial, by your resurrection and ascension, and
by the gift of your Holy Spirit, O Lord, hear our prayer;
**Kyrie eleison.**

In times of trouble and in times of well-being, at the hour we
die and on the day of your glory, O Lord, hear our prayer;
**Kyrie eleison.**

Deliver us from war and violence, from hardness of heart and
from contempt of your love and your promises; O Lord, hear
our prayer;
**Kyrie eleison.**

Enlighten our lives with your word, that in it we may find our
way and our hope; O Lord, hear our prayer;
**Kyrie eleison.**

Assist your people in every land, govern them in peace and
justice, defend them from the enemies of life; O Lord, hear our
prayer;
**Kyrie eleison.**

## 9   Morning

(Let us pray to the Lord, saying, "Lord, have mercy.")

Let us ask the Lord for a day of fulfilment and peace.
**Lord, have mercy.**

Let us ask the Lord to teach us to love others as he has
loved us.
**Lord, have mercy.**

Let us ask the Lord for peace and justice in the world.
**Lord, have mercy.**

Let us ask the Lord to strengthen and relieve those who are in need.
**Lord, have mercy.**

Let us ask the Lord to renew the Church through the power of his life-giving Spirit.
**Lord, have mercy.**

## 10   Evening

(In peace let us pray to the Lord, saying, "We pray to you, Lord.")

That this evening may be holy, good, and peaceful,
**We pray to you, Lord.**

That the work we have done this day and the people we have met may bring us closer to you,
**We pray to you, Lord.**

That we may be forgiven our sins and offences,
**We pray to you, Lord.**

That we may hear and respond to your call to peace and justice,
**We pray to you, Lord.**

That you will sustain the faith and hope of the weary, the lonely, and the oppressed,
**We pray to you, Lord.**

That you will strengthen us in your service, and fill our hearts with longing for your kingdom,
**We pray to you, Lord.**

## 11   Late Evening

Keep us, O Lord, as the apple of your eye.
**Hide us under the shadow of your wings.**

For the peace of the whole world, we pray to you, Lord.
**Lord, have mercy.**

For those who are weary, sleepless, and depressed, we pray to you, Lord,
**Lord, have mercy.**

For those who are hungry, sick, and frightened, we pray to you, Lord,
**Lord, have mercy.**

For rest and refreshment, we pray to you, Lord,
**Lord, have mercy.**

Guide us waking, O Lord, and guard us sleeping, that awake we may watch with Christ, and asleep we may rest in peace.
**Amen.**


## 12   Advent

(In joyful expectation let us pray to our Saviour and Redeemer, saying, "Lord Jesus, come soon!")

O Wisdom, from the mouth of the Most High, you reign over all things to the ends of the earth: come and teach us how to live.
**Lord Jesus, come soon!**

O Lord, and head of the house of Israel, you appeared to Moses in the fire of the burning bush and you gave the law on Sinai: come with outstretched arm and ransom us.
**Lord Jesus, come soon!**

O Branch of Jesse, standing as a sign among the nations, all kings will keep silence before you and all peoples will summon you to their aid: come, set us free and delay no more.
**Lord Jesus, come soon!**

O Key of David and sceptre of the house of Israel, you open and none can shut; you shut and none can open: come and free the captives from prison.
**Lord Jesus, come soon!**

O Morning Star, splendour of the light eternal and bright Sun of righteousness: come and enlighten all who dwell in darkness and in the shadow of death.
**Lord Jesus, come soon!**

O King of the nations, you alone can fulfil their desires: Cornerstone, you make opposing nations one: come and save the creature you fashioned from clay.
**Lord Jesus, come soon!**

O Emmanuel, hope of the nations and their Saviour: come and save us, Lord our God.
**Lord Jesus, come soon!**

## 13   Incarnation

(In joy and humility let us pray to the creator of the universe, saying, "Lord, grant us peace.")

By the good news of our salvation brought to Mary by the angel, hear us, O Lord.
**Lord, grant us peace.**

By the mystery of the Word made flesh, hear us, O Lord.
**Lord, grant us peace.**

By the birth in time of the timeless Son of God, hear us, O Lord.
**Lord, grant us peace.**

By the manifestation of the King of glory to the shepherds and magi, hear us, O Lord.
**Lord, grant us peace.**

By the submission of the maker of the world to Mary and Joseph of Nazareth, hear us, O Lord.
**Lord, grant us peace.**

By the baptism of the Son of God in the river Jordan, hear us, O Lord.
**Lord, grant us peace.**

Grant that the kingdoms of this world may become the kingdom of our Lord and Saviour Jesus Christ; hear us, O Lord.
**Lord, grant us peace.**

## 14 Lent

(With confidence and trust let us pray to the Lord, saying, "Lord, have mercy.")

For the one holy catholic and apostolic Church throughout the world, we pray to you, Lord.
**Lord, have mercy.**

For the mission of the Church, that in faithful witness it may preach the gospel to the ends of the earth, we pray to you, Lord.
**Lord, have mercy.**

For those preparing for baptism and for their teachers and sponsors, we pray to you, Lord.
**Lord, have mercy.**

For peace in the world, that a spirit of respect and reconciliation may grow among nations and peoples, we pray to you, Lord.
**Lord, have mercy.**

For the poor, the persecuted, the sick, and all who suffer; for refugees, prisoners, and all in danger; that they may be relieved and protected, we pray to you, Lord.
**Lord, have mercy.**

For all whom we have injured or offended, we pray to you,
Lord.
**Lord, have mercy.**

For grace to amend our lives and to further the reign of God,
we pray to you, Lord.
**Lord, have mercy.**

## 15   Easter

(In joy and hope let us pray to the source of all life, saying,
"Hear us, Lord of glory!")

That our risen Saviour may fill us with the joy of his holy and
life-giving resurrection, let us pray to the Lord.
**Hear us, Lord of glory!**

That isolated and persecuted churches may find fresh strength
in the Easter gospel, let us pray to the Lord.
**Hear us, Lord of glory!**

That he may grant us humility to be subject to one another in
Christian love, let us pray to the Lord.
**Hear us, Lord of glory!**

That he may provide for those who lack food, work, or shelter,
let us pray to the Lord.
**Hear us, Lord of glory!**

That by his power wars and famine may cease through all the
earth, let us pray to the Lord.
**Hear us, Lord of glory!**

That he may reveal the light of his presence to the sick, the
weak, and the dying, that they may be comforted and
strengthened, let us pray to the Lord.
**Hear us, Lord of glory!**

That he may send the fire of the Holy Spirit upon his people,
that we may bear faithful witness to his resurrection, let us
pray to the Lord.
**Hear us, Lord of glory!**

## 16   The Holy Spirit

(Let us pray to God the Holy Spirit, saying, "Come, Holy
Spirit, come.")

Come, Holy Spirit, creator, and renew the face of the earth.
**Come, Holy Spirit, come.**

Come, Holy Spirit, counsellor, and touch our lips that we may
proclaim your word.
**Come, Holy Spirit, come.**

Come, Holy Spirit, power from on high: make us agents of
peace and ministers of wholeness.
**Come, Holy Spirit, come.**

Come, Holy Spirit, breath of God, give life to the dry bones of
this exiled age, and make us a living people, holy and free.
**Come, Holy Spirit, come.**

Come, Holy Spirit, wisdom and truth: strengthen us in the risk
of faith.
**Come, Holy Spirit, come.**

## 17   A Bidding Intercession

*The leader should add particular intentions to each bidding. In the course of
the silence after each bidding, the people offer their own prayers, either
silently or aloud.*

I ask your prayers for God's people throughout the world,
for this gathering, for our bishop *N*,
and for all ministers and people.
Pray for the Church.

*Silence*

Almighty and everlasting God,
by your Spirit the whole body of your faithful people
is governed and sanctified.
Receive our supplications and prayers,
which we offer before you
for all members of your holy Church,
that in our vocation and ministry
we may truly and devoutly serve you;
through our Lord and Saviour Jesus Christ. **Amen.**

I ask your prayers for peace,
for goodwill among nations,
and for the well-being of all people.

*Silence*

Almighty God,
kindle, we pray, in every heart the true love of peace,
and guide with your wisdom
those who take counsel for the nations of the earth,
that justice and peace may increase,
until the earth is filled with the knowledge of your love;
through Jesus Christ our Lord. **Amen.**

I ask your prayers for the poor, the sick, the hungry,
the oppressed, and those in prison.
Pray for those in any need or trouble.

*Silence*

Gracious God,
the comfort of all who sorrow,
the strength of all who suffer,
hear the cry of those in misery and need.
In their afflictions show them your mercy,
and give us, we pray, the strength to serve them,
for the sake of him who suffered for us,
your Son Jesus Christ our Lord. **Amen.**

I ask your prayers for the mission of the Church.
Pray for the coming of God's kingdom
among all nations and peoples.

*Silence*

O Lord our God,
you have made all races and nations to be one family,
and you sent your Son Jesus Christ
to proclaim the good news of salvation to all people.
Pour out your Spirit on the whole creation,
bring the nations of the world into your fellowship,
and hasten the coming of your kingdom.
We ask this through the same Jesus Christ our Lord. **Amen.**

I ask your prayers for those who have died
in the peace of Christ,
and for those whose faith is known to God alone.
Pray that God may be glorified in all his saints.

*Silence*

O God, the giver of eternal life,
we give you thanks and praise
for the wonderful grace and virtue
declared in all your saints.
Grant to us, and to all who have died
in the hope of the resurrection,
a share in the victory of our Lord Jesus Christ
and fulness of joy in the fellowship of all your saints.
All this we ask in the name of Jesus Christ our Lord.
**Amen.**

Let us give thanks to almighty God for all his goodness.

*Silence*

You are worthy, O Lord our God,
to receive glory and honour and power.
   **You are worthy to receive blessing and praise,
   now and for ever.**

For yours is the majesty, O Father, Son, and Holy Spirit;
yours is the kingdom and the power and the glory,
now and for ever. **Amen.**

## 18   A Responsive Intercession

*The penitential section may be omitted.*

In peace, we pray to you, Lord God.

*Silence*

For all people in their daily life and work;
   **For our families, friends, and neighbours, and for all those
   who are alone.**

For this community, our country, and the world;
   **For all who work for justice, freedom, and peace.**

For the just and proper use of your creation;
   **For the victims of hunger, fear, injustice, and oppression.**

For all who are in danger, sorrow, or any kind of trouble;
   **For those who minister to the sick, the friendless, and the
   needy.**

For the peace and unity of the Church of God;
   **For all who proclaim the gospel, and all who seek the truth.**

For N our bishop, and for all bishops and other ministers;
   **For all who serve God in his Church.**

For our own needs and those of others.

*Silence. The people may add their own petitions.*

Hear us, Lord;
   **For your mercy is great.**

We thank you, Lord, for all the blessings of this life.

*Silence. The people may add their own thanksgivings.*

We will exalt you, O God our king;
**And praise your name for ever and ever.**


We pray for all those who have died in the peace of Christ,
and for those whose faith is known to you alone,
that they may have a place in your eternal kingdom.

*Silence. The people may add their own petitions.*

Lord, let your loving kindness be upon them;
**Who put their trust in you.**


We pray to you also for the forgiveness of our sins.

*Silence may be kept.*

Have mercy upon us, most merciful Father;
**in your compassion, forgive us our sins,**
**known and unknown,**
**things done and left undone;**
**and so uphold us by your Spirit**
**that we may live and serve you in newness of life,**
**to the honour and glory of your name;**
**through Jesus Christ our Lord. Amen.**


*The celebrant concludes with an absolution, or the following (or other suitable) collect.*

Gracious God,
you have heard the prayers of your faithful people;
you know our needs before we ask,
and our ignorance in asking.
Grant our requests as may be best for us.
This we ask in the name of your Son
Jesus Christ our Lord. **Amen.**

## 19   Thanksgiving Litany

(Let us give thanks to God our Father, always and for everything, saying, "We thank you, Lord.")

For the beauty and wonder of creation,
   **We thank you, Lord.**

For all that is gracious in the lives of men and women, revealing the image of Christ,
   **We thank you, Lord.**

For our daily food, for our homes and families and friends,
   **We thank you, Lord.**

For minds to think and hearts to love,
   **We thank you, Lord.**

For health, strength, and skill to work, and for leisure to rest and play,
   **We thank you, Lord.**

For those who are brave and courageous, patient in suffering and faithful in adversity,
   **We thank you, Lord.**

For all who pursue peace, justice, and truth,
   **We thank you, Lord.**

[Today we give thanks especially for . . .
   **We thank you, Lord.**]

For (. . . and) all the saints whose lives have reflected the light of Christ,
   **We thank you, Lord.**

# General Thanksgiving Prayers

Almighty God, Father of all mercies,
we your unworthy servants give you humble thanks
for all your goodness and loving-kindness
to us and all whom you have made.
We bless you for our creation, preservation,
and all the blessings of this life;
but above all for your immeasurable love
in the redemption of the world by our Lord Jesus Christ;
for the means of grace, and for the hope of glory.
And, we pray, give us such an awareness of your mercies,
that with truly thankful hearts
we may show forth your praise,
not only with our lips, but in our lives,
by giving up ourselves to your service,
and by walking before you
in holiness and righteousness all our days;
through Jesus Christ our Lord,
to whom with you and the Holy Spirit,
be honour and glory throughout all ages. **Amen.**


Accept, O Lord, our thanks and praise
for all you have done for us.
We thank you for the splendour of the whole creation,
for the beauty of this world, for the wonder of life,
and for the mystery of love.
We thank you for the blessing of family and friends,
and for the loving care
which surrounds us on every side.
We thank you for setting us tasks
which demand our best efforts,
and for leading us to accomplishments
which satisfy and delight us.
We thank you also for those disappointments and failures
that lead us to acknowledge our dependence on you alone.
Above all, we thank you for your Son Jesus Christ;
for the truth of his word and the example of his life;

for his steadfast obedience,
by which he overcame temptation;
for his dying, through which he overcame death;
for his rising to life again,
in which we are raised to the life of your kingdom.
Grant us the gift of your Spirit,
that we may know Christ and make him known;
and through him, at all times and in all places,
may give thanks to you in all things. **Amen.**

## Collects for Morning

### 1   A Prayer for Strength

Eternal God, you create us by your power and redeem us by
your love. Guide and strengthen us by your Spirit, that we may
give ourselves today in love and service to one another and to
you; through Jesus Christ our Lord. **Amen.**

### 2   A Prayer for Guidance

Heavenly Father, in you we live and move and have our being.
Guide and govern us by your Holy Spirit, that in all the cares
and occupations of our life we may not forget you, but may
remember that we are ever walking in your sight; through
Jesus Christ our Lord. **Amen.**

### 3   A Prayer for Peace

O God, the author of peace and lover of concord, to know you
is eternal life, to serve you is perfect freedom. Defend us your
servants from the assaults of our enemies, that we may trust in
your defence, and not fear the power of any adversaries;
through Jesus Christ our Lord. **Amen.**

#### 4  A Prayer for Guidance

Creator of the universe, the light of your glory shines in the
darkness of our lives. Make us attentive to your presence,
prompt to serve you, and ever eager to follow in the steps of
the one who is our true light, Jesus Christ your Son our Lord.
**Amen.**

#### 5  A Prayer for Grace and Faith

Lord God, the well-spring of life, pour into our hearts the living
water of your grace. By your light we see light. Increase our
faith, and grant that we may walk in the brightness of your
presence; through Jesus Christ our Lord. **Amen.**

#### 6  A Prayer for Grace

Lord God, almighty and everlasting Father, you have brought
us in safety to this new day. Preserve us with your mighty
power, that we may not fall into sin, or be overcome by
adversity; and in all we do, direct us to the fulfilling of your
purpose; through Jesus Christ our Lord. **Amen.**

#### 7  A Prayer for Sundays

Father of light, yours is the morning and yours is the evening.
Let Christ, the Sun of righteousness, shine for ever in our
hearts and draw us to that light where you live in radiant glory.
We ask this for the sake of Jesus Christ our Lord. **Amen.**

#### 8  A Prayer for Fridays

Almighty God and Father, your beloved Son willingly endured
the agony and shame of the cross for our redemption. Give us
the courage to take up our cross and follow him in newness of
life and hope. He lives and reigns with you and the Holy Spirit,
one God, now and for ever. **Amen.**

# Collects for Evening

### 9   A Prayer for Aid against Perils

Be our light in the darkness, O Lord, and in your great mercy
defend us from all perils and dangers of this night; for the love
of your only Son our Saviour Jesus Christ. **Amen.**

### 10   A Prayer for Peace

Most holy God, the source of all good desires, all right
judgements, and all just works, give to us your servants that
peace which the world cannot give, so that our minds may be
fixed on doing your will, and that, freed from fear of our
enemies, we may pass our time in rest and quietness; through
Jesus Christ our Lord. **Amen.**

### 11   A Prayer for Protection and Rest

Be present, O merciful God, and protect us through the hours
of this night, so that we who are wearied by the changes and
chances of this life may rest in your eternal changelessness;
through Jesus Christ our Lord. **Amen.**

### 12   A Prayer for God's Presence

Creator of the universe, watch over us and keep us in the light
of your presence. May our praise continually blend with that of
all creation, until we come together to the eternal joys which
you promise in your love; through Jesus Christ our Lord.
**Amen.**

### 13   A Prayer for the Presence of Christ

Remain with us, Lord, for the day is far spent and evening is at
hand. Kindle our hearts on our way that we may recognize you
in the scriptures and the breaking of bread. Grant this for the
sake of your love. **Amen.**

# Vigil of the Resurrection

**for Saturday Evenings**

*This vigil office may be used after the Service of Light (pp. 60–65) instead of the usual form of Evening Prayer.*

*After the Thanksgiving, Psalm 118.1–4, 14–29 is said or sung.*

Give thanks to the Lord, for he is good; *
  his mercy endures for ever.
Let Israel now proclaim,*
  "His mercy endures for ever."
Let the house of Aaron now proclaim,*
  "His mercy endures for ever."
Let those who fear the Lord now proclaim,*
  "His mercy endures for ever."

The Lord is my strength and my song,*
  and he has become my salvation.
There is a sound of exultation and victory *
  in the tents of the righteous:
"The right hand of the Lord has triumphed! *
  the right hand of the Lord is exalted!
  the right hand of the Lord has triumphed!"
I shall not die, but live,*
  and declare the works of the Lord.
The Lord has punished me sorely,*
  but he did not hand me over to death.

Open for me the gates of righteousness; *
  I will enter them;
  I will offer thanks to the Lord.
"This is the gate of the Lord; *
  he who is righteous may enter."
I will give thanks to you, for you answered me *
  and have become my salvation.

The same stone which the builders rejected *
   has become the chief cornerstone.
This is the Lord's doing,*
   and it is marvellous in our eyes.
On this day the Lord has acted; *
   we will rejoice and be glad in it.

Hosannah, Lord, hosannah! *
   Lord, send us now success.
Blessed is he who comes in the name of the Lord; *
   we bless you from the house of the Lord.
God is the Lord; he has shined upon us; *
   form a procession with branches up to the horns of the altar.
"You are my God, and I will thank you; *
   you are my God, and I will exalt you."
Give thanks to the Lord, for he is good; *
   his mercy endures for ever.

Glory to the Father, and to the Son, and to the Holy Spirit: *
   as it was in the beginning, is now, and will be for ever.
               Amen.

*The officiant invites everyone to pray in silence for a moment.*

Let us pray.

*Then the officiant offers the following prayer.*

God our Father,
by raising Christ your Son,
you conquered the power of death
and opened for us the way to eternal life.
Let our celebration this night
raise us up and renew our lives
by the Spirit who lives within us.
Grant this through our Lord Jesus Christ, your Son,
who lives and reigns with you and the Holy Spirit,
one God, for ever and ever. **Amen.** †

# The Resurrection Gospel

*All stand to say or sing Psalm 150, followed by the reading of a Gospel account of the resurrection.*

Hallelujah!
Praise God in his holy temple; *
   praise him in the firmament of his power.
Praise him for his mighty acts; *
   praise him for his excellent greatness.
Praise him with the blast of the ram's horn; *
   praise him with lyre and harp.
Praise him with timbrel and dance; *
   praise him with strings and pipe.
Praise him with resounding cymbals; *
   praise him with loud-clanging cymbals.
Let everything that has breath *
   praise the Lord.
   Hallelujah!

*One of the following accounts of the resurrection is read.*

| | | |
|---|---|---|
| *Matthew 28.1–10, 16–20* | *Luke 23.55—24.9* | *John 20.11–18* |
| *Mark 16.1–7* | *Luke 24.13–35* | *John 20.19–31* |
| *Mark 16.9–20* | *John 20.1–10* | *John 21.1–14* |

# Thanksgiving for Water

*The congregation may gather at the font or around a container of water where thanks may be offered in these or similar words.*

We thank you, Almighty God, for the gift of water. Over water the Holy Spirit moved in the beginning of creation. Through water you led the children of Israel out of their bondage in Egypt into the land of promise. In water your Son Jesus received the baptism of John and was anointed by the Holy Spirit as the Messiah, the Christ, to lead us, through his death and resurrection, from the bondage of sin into everlasting life.

We thank you, Father, for the water of baptism. In it we are buried with Christ in his death. By it we share in his resurrection. Through it we are reborn by the Holy Spirit. Therefore in joyful obedience to your Son, we celebrate our fellowship in him in faith.

We pray that all who have passed through the water of baptism may continue for ever in the risen life of Jesus Christ our Saviour.

To him, to you, and to the Holy Spirit, be all honour and glory, now and for ever. **Amen.**

*Then this canticle may be sung.*

## The Song of Moses

*Exodus 15.1–3, 6, 11, 13, 17–18*

I will sing to the Lord for his glorious triumph; *
   the horse and the rider he has hurled into the sea.
The Lord has become my strength and refuge; *
   the Lord himself has become my saviour.

He is my God and I will praise him; *
   my father's God and I will exalt him.
The Lord himself is a mighty warrior; *
   the Lord, the Lord is his name.

Your right hand, O Lord, is majestic in power; *
   your right hand, O Lord, shatters the enemy.
Who is like you, O Lord, among the gods, *
   holy, awesome, worker of wonders?

In steadfast love you led your people, *
   you guided your redeemed with your great strength.
You brought them in safety to your holy place, *
   and planted them firm on your own mountain.
You brought them into your own house. *
   The Lord shall reign for ever and ever.

| | |
|---|---|
| *Leader* | To our God belong victory, glory, and power. |
| *All* | **For right and just are his judgements.** |
| *Leader* | Praise our God, all you who serve him. |
| *All* | **You who fear him, great and small.** |
| *Leader* | Let us rejoice and triumph and give him praise. |
| *All* | **The time has come for the wedding feast of the Lamb!** |

*Leader*  O God who brought your people out of slavery
with a mighty hand,
strengthen us to take our stand with you
beside the oppressed of the world,
that in the victory of Christ
every fetter of body, mind, and spirit
may be broken,
and the whole human family,
restored to your image,
may sing your praise in joy, freedom, and peace;
through the same Jesus Christ our Lord.

*All*  **Amen. Alleluia!**

*Leader*  May God the Father, who raised Christ Jesus from
the dead, continually show us his loving kindness.
**Amen.**

May God the Son, victor over sin and death, grant
us a share in the joy of his resurrection.
**Amen.**

May God the Spirit, giver of light and peace, renew
our hearts in his love. **Amen.**

May almighty God, the Father, the Son, and the
Holy Spirit, continue to bless us.  †

*All*  **Amen. Alleluia!**

† The concluding blessings are from *Praise God in Song*. Copyright © 1979 by G.I.A. Publications, Inc., Chicago, Illinois. All rights reserved.

# The Great Litany

## 1 Prayer of Approach to God

God the Father, creator of heaven and earth,
**Have mercy on us.**
God the Son, redeemer of the world,
**Have mercy on us.**
God the Holy Spirit, advocate and guide,
**Have mercy on us.**
Holy, blessed, and glorious Trinity,
three persons and one God,
**Have mercy on us.**

## 2 Prayers for Deliverance

Lord, remember not our offences, nor the offences of our
forebears; spare us, good Lord, spare your people whom you
have redeemed with your precious blood.
**Spare us, good Lord.**

From all evil and mischief, from sin, from the crafts and
assaults of the devil, from your wrath, and from everlasting
condemnation,
**Good Lord, deliver us.**

From all spiritual blindness, from pride, vainglory, and
hypocrisy; from envy, hatred, and malice; and from all want
of charity,
**Good Lord, deliver us.**

From all deadly sin, and from the deceits of the world, the
flesh, and the devil,
**Good Lord, deliver us.**

From all false doctrine, heresy, and schism; from hardness of
heart, and contempt of your word and commandment,
**Good Lord, deliver us.**

From earthquake and tempest; from drought, fire, and flood; from civil strife and violence; from war and murder; and from dying suddenly and unprepared,
**Good Lord, deliver us.**

## 3 Prayer Recalling Christ's Saving Work

By the mystery of your holy incarnation, by your baptism, fasting, and temptation; and by your proclamation of the kingdom,
**Good Lord, deliver us.**

By your agony and bitter grief, by your cross and passion, by your precious death and burial, by your glorious resurrection and ascension, and by the coming of the Holy Spirit,
**Good Lord, deliver us.**

In our times of trouble, in our times of prosperity, in the hour of death, and on the day of judgement,
**Good Lord, deliver us.**

## 4 Prayers of Intercession

Receive now our prayers, Lord God. May it please you to rule and govern your holy Church universal and lead it in your way.
**Hear us, good Lord.**

*For our country*

Strengthen your servant Elizabeth our Queen in true worship and holiness of life, be her defender and keeper, that she may always seek your honour and glory, and endue the leaders of this nation with wisdom and understanding.
**Hear us, good Lord.**

Bless and defend all who strive for our safety and protection, and shield them in all dangers and adversities.
**Hear us, good Lord.**

Grant wisdom and insight to those who govern us, and to
judges and magistrates the grace to execute justice with mercy.
**Hear us, good Lord.**

*For the Church*

Enlighten all bishops, priests, and deacons with true
knowledge and understanding of your word, that in their
preaching and living they may declare it clearly and show
its truth.
**Hear us, good Lord.**

Bless all your servants preparing for ministry in your Church.
Pour your grace upon them that they may serve others as
Christ himself has served us, for the building up of his Body
in love.
**Hear us, good Lord.**

Encourage and prosper your servants who spread the gospel in
all the world, and send out labourers into the harvest.
**Hear us, good Lord.**

Bless and keep your people, that all may find and follow their
true vocation and ministry.
**Hear us, good Lord.**

Give us a heart to love and reverence you, that we may
diligently live according to your commandments.
**Hear us, good Lord.**

To all your people give growth in grace to listen to your word,
to receive it gladly, and to bring forth the fruit of the Spirit.
**Hear us, good Lord.**

Strengthen those who stand firm in the faith, encourage the
faint-hearted, raise up those who fall, and finally beat down
Satan under our feet.
**Hear us, good Lord.**

*For all people*

To all nations grant unity, peace, and concord, and to all people give dignity, food, and shelter.
**Hear us, good Lord.**

Grant us abundant harvests, strength and skill to conserve the resources of the earth, and wisdom to use them well.
**Hear us, good Lord.**

Enlighten with your Spirit all who teach and all who learn.
**Hear us, good Lord.**

Come to the help of all who are in danger, necessity, and trouble; protect all who travel by land, air, or water; and show your pity on all prisoners and captives.
**Hear us, good Lord.**

Strengthen and preserve all women who are in childbirth, and all young children, and comfort the aged and lonely.
**Hear us, good Lord.**

Defend and provide for the widowed and the orphaned, the refugees and the homeless, the unemployed, and all who are desolate and oppressed.
**Hear us, good Lord.**

Heal those who are sick in body or mind, and give skill and compassion to all who care for them.
**Hear us, good Lord.**

Grant us true repentance, forgive our sins, and strengthen us by your Holy Spirit to amend our lives according to your holy word.
**Hear us, good Lord.**

*Concluding Prayers*

Son of God, we ask you to hear us.
**Son of God, we ask you to hear us.**
Lamb of God, you take away the sins of the world:
**Grant us your peace.**

Lord, have mercy.
**Christ, have mercy.**
Lord, have mercy.

*If the eucharist follows, the Litany may end here with the Collect of the Day.*

Gathering our prayers and praises into one,
let us pray as our Saviour Christ taught us,
**Our Father in heaven,**
**hallowed be your name,**
**your kingdom come,**
**your will be done,**
**on earth as in heaven.**
**Give us today our daily bread.**
**Forgive us our sins**
**as we forgive those who sin against us.**
**Save us from the time of trial,**
**and deliver us from evil.**
**For the kingdom, the power,**
**and the glory are yours,**
**now and for ever. Amen.**

*Or*

And now, as our Saviour Christ has taught us,
we are bold to say,
**Our Father, who art in heaven,**
**hallowed be thy name,**
**thy kingdom come,**
**thy will be done,**
**on earth as it is in heaven.**
**Give us this day our daily bread.**
**And forgive us our trespasses,**
**as we forgive those who trespass against us.**
**And lead us not into temptation,**
**but deliver us from evil.**
**For thine is the kingdom,**
**the power, and the glory,**
**for ever and ever. Amen.**

*The officiant may ask the prayers of the congregation for particular persons and needs. Other prayers, including the Collect of the Day, and the following concluding prayer, may be used.*

Almighty God, you have given us grace at this time with one accord to make our common supplications to you, and you have promised through your well-beloved Son that when two or three are gathered together you will hear their requests. Fulfil now our desires and petitions, as may be best for us, granting us in this world knowledge of your truth, and in the age to come eternal life; for you, Father, are good and loving, and we glorify you through your Son Jesus Christ our Lord, in the Holy Spirit, now and for ever. **Amen.**

*When the Great Litany is said or sung as a separate service, the service may be concluded with one of the forms of dismissal on pp. 55 and 71. The Great Litany may be said or sung instead of the intercessions at Morning Prayer or Evening Prayer. When the Great Litany precedes the eucharist the Prayers of the People are omitted.*

# Baptism and
# Reconciliation

# Holy Baptism

Baptism is the sign of new life in Christ. Baptism unites Christ with his people. That union is both individual and corporate. Christians are, it is true, baptized one by one, but to be a Christian is to be part of a new creation which rises from the dark waters of Christ's death into the dawn of his risen life. Christians are not just baptized individuals; they are a new humanity.

As the World Council of Churches document *Baptism, Eucharist and Ministry* has reminded Christians, the scriptures of the New Testament and the liturgy of the Church unfold the meaning of baptism in various images (often based on Old Testament water symbols) which express the mystery of salvation.

> Baptism is participation in Christ's death and resurrection (Romans 6.3–5; Colossians 2.12); a washing away of sin (1 Corinthians 6.11); a new birth (John 3.5); an enlightenment by Christ (Ephesians 5.14); a reclothing in Christ (Galatians 3.27); a renewal by the Spirit (Titus 3.5); the experience of salvation from the flood (1 Peter 3.20–21); an exodus from bondage (1 Corinthians 10.1–2) and a liberation into a new humanity in which barriers of division, whether of sex or race or social status, are transcended (Galatians 3.27–28; 1 Corinthians 12.13). The images are many but the reality is one.[1]

Several dimensions of baptism became clear as the early Church developed its practice. Initiation into the Church was a vital concern of the whole Christian community and not only of the candidates for baptism and their immediate families. Preparation for baptism was a responsibility shared among various members of the community, both ordained and lay. Becoming a Christian had as much to do with learning to live a new lifestyle within the Christian community as it did with specific beliefs. When the day of baptism finally arrived, the event took place within the context of the Sunday eucharist, when the whole community was gathered and where the newly baptized received communion for the first time.

The celebration of this rite of Holy Baptism requires careful preparation by both the community and the candidates. The service should take place when a congregation gathers for the principal Sunday eucharist, ideally on days that are particularly appropriate for baptism—Easter (especially at the Vigil), Pentecost, All Saints, the Baptism of the Lord—and with the bishop present.

# The Rite: A Rationale of the Order

the gathering of the community
the proclamation of the word
the presentation and examination of the candidates
thanksgiving over the water
the baptism
the eucharist

### 1  The Gathering of the Community

The purpose of this initial part of the rite is the same as at any celebration of the eucharist: to unite the assembled people as a community, and to prepare them to listen to God's word. In this rite, however, the structure is simpler. The celebrant greets the community and then introduces responses which conclude with the Collect of the Day.

### 2  The Proclamation of the Word

This part of the rite is the same as at any celebration of the eucharist. Normally, the readings should be those which are proper to the day.

### 3  The Presentation and Examination of the Candidates

Sponsors first present candidates who are old enough to answer for themselves. Parents and/or sponsors then present children who are unable to answer for themselves. The renunciations, in ancient threefold form, and an act of adherence to Jesus Christ as Lord and Saviour, then follow.

A litany concludes this portion of the rite. Additional petitions may be included in the litany.

### 4  Thanksgiving over the Water

The Thanksgiving over the Water, similar in structure to the Great Thanksgiving prayer of the eucharist, recalls the waters of creation, the exodus, and the baptism of Jesus in the Jordan River. The prayer asks that those who are baptized may be buried and raised with Christ, cleansed of sin, and reborn by the Holy Spirit.

The congregation then joins with those who are to be baptized in the promises of the Baptismal Covenant. The Apostles' Creed, first composed for this purpose, symbolizes this covenant-faith. Preparation of the community for the celebration of baptism may appropriately emphasize the congregation's corporate renewal in the Baptismal Covenant.

## 5   The Baptism

In the celebration of baptism the symbolic aspects of water should be emphasized, not minimized. There should be water in quantity, enough for members of the congregation to see and hear when it is poured. An act of immersion would vividly express the Christian's participation in baptism, in the death, burial, and resurrection of Christ.

When the candidates have been baptized, the celebrant signs them with the sign of the cross. The optional use of chrism at this point restores one of the most ancient baptismal practices. Chrism evokes a rich variety of biblical images: the anointing of kings (1 Samuel 16.13), the royal priesthood (1 Peter 2.9), the eschatological seal of the saints (Revelation 7). Its traditional association with the Holy Spirit interprets baptism as the new birth by water and the Spirit (John 3.5). In a similar manner it interprets the name *Christ*, the anointed one, and relates the baptism of each Christian to the baptism of Christ.

After the signing the celebrant then prays that those who have been made new in baptism may display the gifts of the Spirit in their lives.

The newly baptized persons may be presented with a lighted candle as a sign of their new life in Jesus Christ, the light of the world.

The congregation welcomes the new members of the community and urges them to confess the faith of Christ crucified, proclaim his resurrection, and share in his eternal priesthood.

The service then continues with the Peace and the preparation of the gifts for the eucharist.

## 6  Confirmation, Reception, and Reaffirmation

Confirmation, reception, and reaffirmation are various modes of response to baptism. Whether they involve making promises on one's own behalf, seeking membership within a particular branch of the Church, or reaffirming promises made long ago, each is directly related to the covenant made in baptism. The liturgy of baptism is consequently the primary context in which these renewals of the baptismal covenant take place.

1  *Baptism, Eucharist and Ministry*, Geneva, World Council of Churches, 1982, Faith and Order Paper No. 111.

# Concerning the Service

*Christian baptism is administered with water in the name of the Father, the Son, and the Holy Spirit. The bond which God establishes in baptism is indissoluble. Holy Baptism is appropriately administered within a celebration of the eucharist as the chief service on a Sunday or other feast.*

*The bishop, when present, is the celebrant, and is expected to preach the word and preside at baptism and the eucharist. At baptism, the bishop officiates at the Presentation and Examination of the Candidates; says the Thanksgiving over the Water; reads the prayer, "Heavenly Father, we thank you that by water and the Holy Spirit"; and officiates at what follows.*

*In the absence of a bishop, a priest is the celebrant and presides at the service. If chrism is to be used, it will have been consecrated by the bishop when he has blessed oils for the use of the whole diocese.*

*Each candidate for baptism is to be sponsored by one or more baptized persons.*

*Sponsors of adults and older children present their candidates, and thereby signify their endorsement of the candidates and their intention to support them by prayer and example in their Christian life. Sponsors (traditionally called godparents) of infants present their candidates, make promises in their own names, and also take vows on behalf of their candidates.*

*It is fitting that parents be included among the sponsors of their own children. Parents and sponsors are to be instructed in the meaning of baptism, in their duties to help the new Christians grow in the knowledge and love of God, and in their responsibilities as members of his Church.*

*Additional directions are on p. 163.*

# Holy Baptism

## The Gathering of the Community

*All stand. The presiding celebrant greets the community.*

Celebrant   The grace of our Lord Jesus Christ,
            and the love of God,
            and the fellowship of the Holy Spirit,
            be with you all.
People      **And also with you.**

*Or from Easter Day through the Day of Pentecost,*

Celebrant   Alleluia! Christ is risen.
People      **The Lord is risen indeed. Alleluia!**

Celebrant   May his grace and peace be with you.
People      **May he fill our hearts with joy.**

*The celebrant then continues,*

            There is one body and one Spirit,
People      **There is one hope in God's call to us;**

Celebrant   One Lord, one faith, one baptism,
People      **One God and Father of all.**

## The Collect of the Day

Celebrant   Let us pray.

*The community may pray silently. The presiding celebrant then sings or says
the collect, after which all respond,* **Amen.**

# The Proclamation of the Word

## The Readings

*The first reading as appointed.*

*Reader*      A reading from . . .

*At the conclusion of the passage, the reader says,*

        The word of the Lord.
*People*     **Thanks be to God.**

*Silence may be kept. Then shall follow a psalm as appointed.*

*A second reading as appointed is read.*

*Reader*      A reading from . . .

*At the conclusion of the passage, the reader says,*

        The word of the Lord.
*People*     **Thanks be to God.**

*Silence may be kept. A psalm, canticle, hymn, or anthem may follow.*

*All stand for the Gospel.*

*Reader*      The Lord be with you.
*People*     **And also with you.**

*Reader*      The Holy Gospel of our Lord Jesus Christ
        according to . . .
*People*     **Glory to you, Lord Jesus Christ.**

*At the conclusion of the Gospel, the reader says,*

        The Gospel of Christ.
*People*     **Praise to you, Lord Jesus Christ.**

## Sermon

*A silence for reflection may follow.*

# Presentation and Examination of the Candidates

*The celebrant says,*

> The candidate(s) for Holy Baptism will now be presented.

### Adults and Older Children

*Candidates able to answer for themselves are presented by their parents and sponsors as follows:*

*Sponsor*  I present N to receive the sacrament of baptism.

*The celebrant asks each candidate when presented,*

> Do you desire to be baptized?

*Candidate*  I do.

### Infants and Younger Children

*Then the candidates unable to answer for themselves are presented individually by their parents and sponsors as follows:*

*Parents and sponsors,*

> I present N to receive the sacrament of baptism.

*When all have been presented the celebrant asks the parents and sponsors,*

> Will you be responsible for seeing that the child you present is nurtured in the faith and life of the Christian community?

*Parents and sponsors,*

> I will, with God's help.

*Celebrant*  Will you by your prayers and witness help this child to grow into the full stature of Christ?

*Parents and sponsors,*

> I will, with God's help.

*Then the celebrant asks the following questions of the candidates who can speak for themselves, and of the parents and sponsors who speak on behalf of the infants and younger children.*

*Question*    Do you renounce Satan and all the spiritual forces of wickedness that rebel against God?

*Answer*    I renounce them.

*Question*    Do you renounce the evil powers of this world which corrupt and destroy the creatures of God?

*Answer*    I renounce them.

*Question*    Do you renounce all sinful desires that draw you from the love of God?

*Answer*    I renounce them.

*Question*    Do you turn to Jesus Christ and accept him as your Saviour?

*Answer*    I do.

*Question*    Do you put your whole trust in his grace and love?
*Answer*    I do.

*Question*    Do you promise to obey him as your Lord?
*Answer*    I do.

*When there are others to be presented, the bishop says,*

The other candidate(s) will now be presented.

*Presenters*    I present *these persons* for Confirmation.

*Or*    I present *these persons* to be received into this Communion.

*Or*    I present *these persons* who *desire* to reaffirm *their* baptismal vows.

*The bishop asks the candidates,*

Do you reaffirm your renunciation of evil?
*Candidate*    I do.

| | |
|---|---|
| *Celebrant* | Do you renew your commitment to Jesus Christ? |
| *Candidate* | I do. |

| | |
|---|---|
| *Celebrant* | Do you put your whole trust in his grace and love? |
| *Candidate* | I do, and with God's grace I will follow him as my Saviour and Lord. |

*After all have been presented, the celebrant addresses the congregation, saying,*

Will you who witness these vows do all in your power to support *these persons* in *their* life in Christ?

*People* **We will.**

## Prayers for the Candidates

*The celebrant then says to the congregation,*

Let us now pray for *these persons* who *are* to receive the sacrament of new birth.

*A person appointed leads the following litany.*

| | |
|---|---|
| *Leader* | Deliver *them*, O Lord, from the way of sin and death. |
| *People* | **Lord, hear our prayer.** |

| | |
|---|---|
| *Leader* | Open *their hearts* to your grace and truth. |
| *People* | **Lord, hear our prayer.** |

| | |
|---|---|
| *Leader* | Fill *them* with your holy and life-giving Spirit. |
| *People* | **Lord, hear our prayer.** |

| | |
|---|---|
| *Leader* | Teach *them* to love others in the power of the Spirit. |
| *People* | **Lord, hear our prayer.** |

| | |
|---|---|
| *Leader* | Send *them* into the world in witness to your love. |
| *People* | **Lord, hear our prayer.** |

| | |
|---|---|
| *Leader* | Bring *them* to the fullness of your peace and glory. |
| *People* | **Lord, hear our prayer.** |

*The leader concludes,*

Grant, O Lord,
that all who are baptized
into the death of Jesus Christ your Son
may live in the power of his resurrection
and look for him to come again in glory;
who lives and reigns now and for ever. **Amen.**

# The Celebration of Baptism

## Thanksgiving over the Water

*The celebrant blesses the water, using one of the following forms.*

|  | The Lord be with you. |
|---|---|
| *People* | **And also with you.** |
| *Celebrant* | Let us give thanks to the Lord our God. |
| *People* | **It is right to give our thanks and praise.** |
| *Celebrant* | We give you thanks, almighty God and Father, for by the gift of water you nourish and sustain all living things. |
| *All* | **Blessed be God for ever.** |
| *Celebrant* | We give you thanks that through the waters of the Red Sea, you led your people out of slavery to freedom in the promised land. |
| *All* | **Blessed be God for ever.** |
| *Celebrant* | We give you thanks for sending your Son Jesus. For us he was baptized by John in the river Jordan. For us he was anointed as Christ by your Holy Spirit. For us he suffered the baptism of his own death and resurrection, setting us free from the bondage of sin and death, and opening to us the joy and freedom of everlasting life. |
| *All* | **Blessed be God for ever.** |

| | |
|---|---|
| *Celebrant* | We give you thanks for your Holy Spirit who teaches us and leads us into all truth, filling us with his gifts so that we might proclaim the gospel to all nations and serve you as a royal priesthood. |
| *All* | **Blessed be God for ever.** |
| *Celebrant* | We give you thanks for you have called *N* to new life through the waters of baptism. |

Now sanctify this water, that your servants who are washed in it may be made one with Christ in his death and resurrection, to be cleansed and delivered from all sin. Anoint them with your Holy Spirit and bring them to new birth in the family of your Church, that they may become inheritors of your glorious kingdom.

We give you praise and honour and worship through your Son Jesus Christ our Lord, in the unity of the Holy Spirit, now and for ever.

| | |
|---|---|
| *All* | **Blessed are you, our strength and song, and our salvation.** |

*Or the following:*

| | |
|---|---|
| | The Lord be with you. |
| *People* | **And also with you.** |
| *Celebrant* | Let us give thanks to the Lord our God. |
| *People* | **It is right to give our thanks and praise.** |
| *Celebrant* | We thank you, Almighty God, for the gift of water. Over water the Holy Spirit moved in the beginning of creation. Through water you led the children of Israel out of their bondage in Egypt into the land of promise. In water your Son Jesus received the baptism of John and was anointed by the Holy Spirit as the Messiah, the Christ, to lead us, through his death and resurrection, from the bondage of sin into everlasting life. |

We thank you, Father, for the water of baptism. In it we are buried with Christ in his death. By it we share in his resurrection. Through it we are reborn by the Holy Spirit. Therefore in joyful obedience to your Son, we bring into his fellowship those who come to him in faith, baptizing them in the name of the Father, and of the Son, and of the Holy Spirit.

Now sanctify this water by the power of your Holy Spirit, that those who are here cleansed from sin and born again, may continue for ever in the risen life of Jesus Christ our Saviour.

To him, to you, and to the Holy Spirit, be all honour and glory, now and for ever. **Amen.**

*The celebrant then says these or similar words.*

Let us join with those
who are committing themselves to Christ
and renew our own baptismal covenant.

## The Baptismal Covenant

*Celebrant*   Do you believe in God the Father?
*People*      **I believe in God,
              the Father almighty,
              creator of heaven and earth.**

*Celebrant*   Do you believe in Jesus Christ, the Son of God?
*People*      **I believe in Jesus Christ,
              his only Son, our Lord.
              He was conceived by the power of the Holy Spirit
              and born of the Virgin Mary.
              He suffered under Pontius Pilate,
              was crucified, died, and was buried.**

He descended to the dead.
On the third day he rose again.
He ascended into heaven,
and is seated at the right hand of the Father.
He will come again
to judge the living and the dead.

| | |
|---|---|
| Celebrant | Do you believe in God the Holy Spirit? |
| People | **I believe in God the Holy Spirit,**<br>**the holy catholic Church,**<br>**the communion of saints,**<br>**the forgiveness of sins,**<br>**the resurrection of the body,**<br>**and the life everlasting.** |

*Celebrant* Will you continue in the apostles' teaching and fellowship, in the breaking of bread, and in the prayers?

*People* **I will, with God's help.**

*Celebrant* Will you persevere in resisting evil and, whenever you fall into sin, repent and return to the Lord?

*People* **I will, with God's help.**

*Celebrant* Will you proclaim by word and example the good news of God in Christ?

*People* **I will, with God's help.**

*Celebrant* Will you seek and serve Christ in all persons, loving your neighbour as yourself?

*People* **I will, with God's help.**

*Celebrant* Will you strive for justice and peace among all people, and respect the dignity of every human being?

*People* **I will, with God's help.**

# The Baptism

*Each candidate is presented by name to the celebrant, or to an assisting priest or deacon, who then immerses, or pours water upon, the candidates, saying,*

> N, I baptize you in the name of the Father,
> and of the Son, and of the Holy Spirit. **Amen.**

*The celebrant makes the sign of the cross on the forehead of each one (using chrism if desired) saying to each,*

> I sign you with the cross,
> and mark you as Christ's own for ever.

*The celebrant, at a place in the full sight of the congregation, prays over the newly baptized, saying,*

> Heavenly Father,
> we thank you that by water and the Holy Spirit
> you have bestowed upon *these* your *servants*
> the forgiveness of sin,
> and have raised *them* to the new life of grace.
> Sustain *them*, O Lord, in your Holy Spirit.
> Give *them* an inquiring and discerning heart,
> the courage to will and to persevere,
> a spirit to know and to love you,
> and the gift of joy and wonder
> in all your works. **Amen.**

# The Giving of the Light

*One of the ministers may then give to each of the newly baptized a lighted candle, saying,*

> Receive the light of Christ,
> to show that you have passed from darkness to light.

*When all of the newly baptized have received candles, the people say,*

> **Let your light so shine before others**
> **that they may see your good works**
> **and glorify your Father in heaven.**

| Celebrant | Let us welcome the newly baptized. |
| People | **We receive you into the household of God.** |
| | **Confess the faith of Christ crucified,** |
| | **proclaim his resurrection,** |
| | **and share with us in his eternal priesthood.** |

# At Confirmation, Reception, or Reaffirmation

*The bishop says to the congregation,*

Let us now pray for *these persons* who *have* renewed *their* commitment to Christ.

*Silence may be kept.*

*Then the bishop says,*

Almighty God, we thank you that by the death and resurrection of your Son Jesus Christ you have overcome sin and brought us to yourself, and that by the sealing of your Holy Spirit you have bound us to your service. Renew in *these* your *servants* the covenant you made with *them* at *their* baptism. Send *them* forth in the power of that Spirit to perform the service you set before *them*; through Jesus Christ your Son our Lord, who lives and reigns with you and the Holy Spirit, one God, now and for ever. **Amen.**

*The bishop lays his hand upon each one and says,*

**For Confirmation**

Strengthen, O Lord, your servant *N* with your Holy Spirit; empower *him/her* for your service; and sustain *him/her* all the days of *his/her* life. **Amen.**

*Or this:*

Defend, O Lord, your servant *N* with your heavenly grace, that *he/she* may continue yours for ever, and daily increase in your Holy Spirit more and more, until *he/she* comes to your everlasting kingdom. **Amen.**

**For Reception**

N, we recognize you as a member of the one holy catholic and apostolic Church, and we receive you into the fellowship of this Communion. God, the Father, Son, and Holy Spirit, bless, preserve, and keep you. **Amen.**

**For Reaffirmation**

N, may the Holy Spirit, who has begun a good work in you, direct and uphold you in the service of Christ and his kingdom. **Amen.**

*Then the bishop says,*

Almighty and everliving God, let your fatherly hand ever be over *these* your *servants*; let your Holy Spirit ever be with *them*; and so lead *them* in the knowledge and obedience of your word, that *they* may serve you in this life, and dwell with you in the life to come; through Jesus Christ our Lord. **Amen.**

## The Peace

*All stand, and the celebrant addresses the people.*

The peace of the Lord be always with you.
*People*    **And also with you.**

*The members of the community, ministers and people, may greet one another in the name of the Lord.*

*The service continues with the preparation of the gifts for the eucharist.*

# Additional Directions

Baptism is especially appropriate at the Easter Vigil, on the Day of Pentecost, on All Saints' Day or the Sunday after All Saints' Day, and on the feast of the Baptism of the Lord (the First Sunday after Epiphany). It is recommended that, as far as possible, baptisms be reserved for these occasions or when a bishop is present. (If for pastoral reasons baptism is celebrated between Pentecost and All Saints', the Transfiguration of the Lord and Holy Cross Day or the Sundays after them are suitable days.)

If the ministry of a bishop or priest cannot be obtained, a deacon may preside at a public baptism.

If on the four days listed above there are no candidates for baptism, the Renewal of Baptismal Vows (p. 330) may take the place of the Nicene Creed at the eucharist.

It is appropriate that the Gospel be read by a deacon.

Lay persons may act as readers, and it is appropriate for sponsors to be assigned this function. The petitions (p. 155) may also be led by one of the sponsors.

The Nicene Creed is not used at this service.

If the Presentation of the Candidates does not take place at the font, then before or during the petitions (p. 155), the ministers, candidates, and sponsors go to the font for the Thanksgiving over the Water.

If the movement to the font is a formal procession, a suitable psalm, such as Psalm 42, or a hymn or anthem, may be sung.

Where practicable, the font is to be filled with clean water immediately before the Thanksgiving over the Water.

At the Thanksgiving over the Water, and at the administration of baptism, the celebrant, whenever possible, should face the people across the font, and the sponsors should be so grouped that the people may have a clear view of the action.

The Prayers, Readings, and Preface are normally those of the day. If the Readings are inappropriate, a selection may be made from the list on p. 165 and the Preface of Easter or the Preface of Pentecost may be used.

It may be found desirable to return to the front of the church for the prayer, "Heavenly Father, we thank you that by water and the Holy Spirit," and the ceremonies that follow it. A suitable psalm, such as Psalm 23, or a hymn or anthem, may be sung during the procession.

The oblations of bread and wine at the baptismal eucharist may be presented by the newly baptized or their sponsors.

## Conditional Baptism

*If there is reasonable doubt that a person has been baptized with water, "In the name of the Father, and of the Son, and of the Holy Spirit," the person is baptized in the usual manner, but this form of words is used.*

If you are not already baptized, N, I baptize you in the name of the Father, and of the Son, and of the Holy Spirit. **Amen.**

## Emergency Baptism

*In case of emergency, any person present may administer baptism according to the following form.*

*Using the given name of the one to be baptized (if known), pour water on him or her, saying,*

I baptize you in the name of the Father, and of the Son, and of the Holy Spirit. **Amen.**

*The Lord's Prayer is then said.*

*Other prayers, such as the following, may be added.*

Heavenly Father, we thank you that by water and the Holy Spirit you have bestowed upon *this* your *servant* the forgiveness of sin and have raised *him/her* to the new life of grace. Strengthen *him/her*, O Lord, with your presence, enfold *him/her* in the arms of your mercy, and keep *him/her* safe for ever. **Amen.**

*The person who administers emergency baptism should inform the priest of the appropriate parish, so that the baptism may be properly registered.*

*If the baptized person recovers, the baptism shall be recognized at a public celebration of the sacrament. The person baptized under emergency conditions and his or her sponsors shall take part in all parts of the baptismal liturgy, except for the baptism in water itself.*

# Readings and Psalms Suitable for Baptism Liturgies

### Old Testament Readings

Ezekiel 36.24–28   (A new heart I will give you)
Isaiah 55.1–11   (Ho, everyone who thirsts, come to the waters)

### Psalms and Suitable Refrains

23   (The Lord is my shepherd; I shall not be in want)
27   (The Lord is the strength of my life)
42.1–7   (My soul is athirst for God)
84   (Happy are they who dwell in your house!)

Canticle 3, Song of Thanksgiving, may also be used.

### New Testament Readings

Romans 6.3–5   (We were buried therefore with him by baptism into death)
Romans 8.14–17   (For all who are led by the Spirit of God are sons of God)
2 Corinthians 5.17–20   (Therefore, if any one is in Christ, he is a new
    creation)

### Gospel Readings

Mark 1.9–11   (Jesus . . . was baptized by John in the Jordan)
John 3.1–6   (Unless one is born of water and the Spirit)

# The Reconciliation of a Penitent

The ministry of reconciliation, committed by Christ to his Church, is exercised through the care of Christians for each other, through the common prayer of Christians assembled for public worship, and through the priesthood of the Church and its ministers declaring absolution.

The Reconciliation of a Penitent is available for all who desire it. It is not restricted to time of sickness. Confessions may be made at any time and in any suitable place.

Originally, Christians who sinned gravely were publicly excluded from full fellowship in the Church and publicly restored after suitable penitence. Private penitence and private reconciliation appeared only after centuries of pastoral experimentation. The Reconciliation of a Penitent, although private, is a corporate action of the Church because sin affects the unity of the Body. The absolution is restoration to full fellowship: the priest declares the forgiveness which Christ has invested in his Church. The formula, "I absolve you," which became common only in the thirteenth century, does not appear in these rites: it tends to individualize and further privatize what remains a corporate action of the Church.

Two equivalent forms of service are provided here to meet the needs of penitents. The absolution in these services may be pronounced only by a bishop or priest. If a deacon or lay person hears a confession, a declaration of forgiveness may be made in the form provided.

When the penitent has confessed all serious sins troubling the conscience, counsel and encouragement may be given, at the request of the penitent. The priest may suggest appropriate devotions or actions to be performed by the penitent after the conclusion of the rite. Those who give counsel should be properly qualified.

The secrecy of a confession of sin is morally absolute for the confessor, and must under no circumstances be broken.

# The Reconciliation
# of a Penitent

Priest     **Bless the Lord who forgives all our sins.**
Penitent   **His mercy endures for ever.**

*A brief silence is kept. Then the priest and penitent say together,*

## Psalm 51    *1–2, 11–13, 16*

Have mercy on me, O God, according to your
                     loving-kindness; *
  in your great compassion blot out my offences.
Wash me through and through from my wickedness *
  and cleanse me from my sin.

Create in me a clean heart, O God,*
  and renew a right spirit within me.
Cast me not away from your presence *
  and take not your holy Spirit from me.
Give me the joy of your saving help again *
  and sustain me with your bountiful Spirit.

Open my lips, O Lord,*
  and my mouth shall proclaim your praise.

*Or this:*

## Psalm 103    *8–10, 13–14*

The Lord is full of compassion and mercy,*
  slow to anger and of great kindness.
He will not always accuse us,*
  nor will he keep his anger for ever.
He has not dealt with us according to our sins,*
  nor rewarded us according to our wickedness.

As a father cares for his children,*
  so does the Lord care for those who fear him.
For he himself knows whereof we are made: *
  he remembers that we are but dust.

*The priest then says to the penitent,*

> Dear friend in Christ, God is steadfast in love and
> infinite in mercy, healing the sick and forgiving the
> sinful. May God, who enlightens every heart, help
> you to confess your sins and trust in his mercy.

*The penitent says,*

> Most merciful God, have mercy upon me,
> in your compassion forgive my sins,
> both known and unknown,
> things done and left undone,
> (especially . . . ).
> O God, uphold me by your Spirit
> that I may live and serve you in newness of life,
> to the honour and glory of your name;
> through Jesus Christ, our Lord. Amen.

*The priest may, with the consent of the penitent, offer words of comfort and
counsel, and then says,*

> Do you turn again to Christ?

*Penitent*   I turn to Christ.

*Priest*     Do you forgive those who have sinned against you?
*Penitent*   I forgive them.

*The priest then says,*

> Our Lord Jesus Christ, who offered himself as the
> perfect sacrifice to the Father, and who conferred
> power on his Church to forgive sins, absolve you
> through my ministry by the grace of the Holy Spirit,
> and restore you in the perfect peace of the Church.
> Amen.

*A deacon or lay person says, instead of the absolution, this declaration of forgiveness.*

Our Lord Jesus Christ, who offered himself as the perfect sacrifice to the Father, forgives our sins and grants us the grace and comfort of the Holy Spirit. Amen.

*Priest*  As our Saviour Christ has taught us, let us pray.

*Both*  Our Father in heaven,
hallowed be your name,
your kingdom come,
your will be done
on earth as in heaven.
Give us today our daily bread.
Forgive us our sins
as we forgive those who sin against us.
Save us from the time of trial,
and deliver us from evil.
For the kingdom, the power,
and the glory are yours,
now and for ever. Amen.

*Or*

*Priest*  And now, as our Saviour Christ has taught us, we are bold to say,

*Both*  Our Father, who art in heaven,
hallowed be thy name.
Thy kingdom come,
thy will be done,
on earth as it is in heaven.
Give us this day our daily bread.
And forgive us our trespasses,
as we forgive those who trespass against us.
And lead us not into temptation,
but deliver us from evil.
For thine is the kingdom,
the power, and the glory,
for ever and ever. Amen.

*The priest then dismisses the penitent.*

|            | Blessed are they whose transgressions are forgiven; |
| Penitent   | And whose sin is put away. |

| Priest     | The Lord has put away all your sins. |
| Penitent   | Thanks be to God. |

*The priest then concludes,*

Go in peace, and pray for me a sinner.

# The Reconciliation of a Penitent

**A Short Form**

*Priest*     Bless the Lord who forgives all our sins.
*Penitent*   His mercy endures for ever.

*The priest invites the penitent to trust God, in these or similar words.*

> May God, who enlightens every heart, help you
> to confess your sins and trust in his mercy.

*Penitent*   Most merciful God, have mercy upon me,
> in your compassion forgive my sins,
> both known and unknown,
> things done and left undone,
> (especially . . . ).
> O God, uphold me by your Spirit
> that I may live and serve you in newness of life,
> to the honour and glory of your name;
> through Jesus Christ, our Lord. Amen.

*The priest may, with the consent of the penitent, offer words of comfort and counsel, and then says,*

> Our Lord Jesus Christ, who offered himself as the
> perfect sacrifice to the Father, and who conferred
> power on his Church to forgive sins, absolve you
> through my ministry by the grace of the Holy Spirit,
> and restore you in the perfect peace of the Church.
> Amen.

*A deacon or lay person says, instead of the absolution, this declaration of forgiveness.*

> Our Lord Jesus Christ, who offered himself as the
> perfect sacrifice to the Father, forgives our sins and
> grants us the grace and comfort of the Holy Spirit.
> Amen.

*The priest then dismisses the penitent.*

|            | Blessed are they whose transgressions are forgiven; |
| Penitent   | And whose sin is put away. |

| Priest     | The Lord has put away all your sins. |
| Penitent   | Thanks be to God. |

*The priest then concludes,*

Go in peace, and pray for me a sinner.

# The Holy Eucharist

# The Holy Eucharist

### The Rite

As a result of both liturgical study and liturgical renewal, the last ten
to fifteen years have given evidence of a considerable consensus
among the major Western churches regarding the appropriate shape
of the eucharistic liturgy. The revision of liturgical rites in these
churches has reflected this common shape. The Lambeth Conferences
of 1958 and 1968 produced guidelines for the reform of the eucharistic
liturgy in the various provinces of the Anglican communion which
recognized and commended this common shape as the basis for
liturgical revision. The present eucharistic order is built upon this
basic shape, which it shares with other Anglican revisions (United
States 1976, Australia 1978, Scotland 1977, South Africa 1975, New
Zealand 1979, England 1980, etc.).

### Common Texts

Texts for Glory to God, the Creeds, Holy, Holy, Holy, and the Lord's
Prayer are those produced by the International Consultation on
English Texts (ICET). As such, they are common to English-speaking
churches presently engaged in liturgical revision.

## A Rationale of the Order

### 1   The Gathering of the Community

*The Entrance Rite*—The purpose of this initial part of the rite is to unite
the assembled people as a community, to prepare them to listen to
God's word and to enter into the eucharistic celebration. In many
present liturgical reforms the entrance rite remains the least examined
part of the whole liturgy. In the Prayer Book it is composed of the
vestiges of no fewer than seven entrance rites from different historical
periods, which have been left standing side by side without any
coherent rationale.

An attempt is made here to produce a more cohesive entrance rite.
The basic form is a greeting and an act of praise followed by a short
silence and the Collect of the Day.

The Collect of the Day concludes the entrance rite and provides the
transition to the readings for the day. A short silence is suggested

before the opening prayer to allow the community to gather its thoughts.

The form is extremely simple. This is intentional. The aim is to set the tone for the celebration and to lead directly into the proclamation of the word and the eucharistic celebration itself. The entrance rite ought not to become a liturgy in its own right.[1]

## 2 The Proclamation of the Word

*Purpose*—The eucharistic community is the assembly of the baptized who are gathered to hear the word of God and to celebrate the eucharist. Word and sacrament stand in a dynamic relationship to each other. The readings, the psalms, the homily, and the intercession form a cohesive whole which leads into the sacramental celebration.

*The Readings*—The lectionary intended for use with this rite (pp. 266–447) is based on the Common Lectionary. A weekday lectionary, with two daily readings, has also been provided. There is also a selection of common readings for lesser saints' days.

*Silence*—Space for silence is a particular feature of this rite. The aim of the silence is to enable the congregation to become a praying community. If the eucharistic liturgy is to become the prayer of the People of God, the community needs to be given time to reflect on the word of God and the action of the liturgy, so that it can respond in prayer, repentance, and offering.

*Psalm*—The use of psalms in the eucharist is encouraged. Rich in scriptural themes, the psalms continue the proclamation of the word of God, sum up the response of the People of God, and provide the ideal vehicle for the community's reflection on the readings. In the Sunday cycle of readings in the Common Lectionary, the psalm which is provided after the first reading is intended to be an integral part of the Proclamation of the Word. The psalms should be sung whenever possible.[2]

*Sermon*—The sermon or homily is an integral part of the Proclamation of the Word. It is the application of the word of God to the pastoral needs of a particular community at a particular time and place. It is appropriate, therefore, that there be some reflection on the word of God at every eucharist, even at weekday celebrations and at early Sunday morning eucharists, so that the good news of the gospel can be heard and responded to in a living way by the congregation.

*The Creed*—It was in the eucharistic prayer rather than in the creed that the ancient Church gave primary expression to its faith when it celebrated the eucharist. Owing to the influence of the Arian controversy and the practice of the priest's saying the eucharistic prayer in an inaudible voice, in both East and West the creed tended to replace the eucharistic prayer as the means of handing on the faith of the Church in the eucharistic liturgy. In the present rite it is suggested that the Nicene Creed be used on major festivals and it or the Apostles' Creed may be used on Sundays.

Both creeds are used in their original forms. Thus the Nicene Creed begins with "We" as a conciliar creed, and the Apostles' Creed with "I" as a creed that was used in the West as part of the examination of candidates for baptism.

The words "and the son" *(filioque)* have been removed from the Nicene Creed in accordance with the Lambeth 1978 Statement:

> The Conference . . . requests that all member Churches of the Anglican Communion should consider omitting the *Filioque* from the Nicene Creed, and that the Anglican-Orthodox Joint Doctrinal Commission through the Anglican Consultative Council should assist them in presenting the theological issues to their appropriate synodical bodies and should be responsible for any necessary consultation with other Churches of the Western tradition.

General Synod meeting at Peterborough in 1980 stated that the omission of the *filioque* does not imply a change of doctrine or belief on the part of the Anglican Church.

*The Prayers of the People*—The work of the Church is not only to praise God but also to pray for the Church and for the world. The Prayers of the People are an integral part of liturgy.

Thanksgiving and intercessions may take an extempore form following the headings given, or one of the forms provided may be used. Whichever form is used, opportunity should be given to those assembled to add their own petitions and thanksgivings to the prayers of the community.

A deacon or a lay person, rather than the priest, is the appropriate minister to lead the Prayers of the People. If the penitential rite has been used before the eucharist or if the Prayers of Penitence are to follow, the penitential petition is omitted from the intercession.

Forms for the Prayers of the People are found on pp. 110–128. These forms are, however, only suggested models. They ought not to become the standard forms used in a parish, but should be adapted with imagination to meet the needs of the local Church.

*The Peace*—The Peace is an encounter, a reconciliation, and an anticipation.

As an encounter it reminds us that we meet Christ in others and without that encounter it is impossible to meet God. "If anyone says, 'I love God,' and hates his brother, he is a liar; for he who does not love his brother whom he has seen, cannot love God whom he has not seen" (1 John 4.20).

As a reconciliation it dramatizes the injunction of Matthew 5.23–24, "So if you are offering your gift at the altar, and there remember that your brother has something against you, leave your gift there before the altar and go; first be reconciled to your brother, and then come and offer your gift."

As an anticipation it dramatizes the eucharist as a foretaste of the banquet in the kingdom. The peace and unity experienced provide a glimpse of the kingdom which is yet to come.

Many parishes are now familiar with the exchange of a sign of peace. If it is being introduced in a community, it is important that the dimensions of encounter, reconciliation, and anticipation are made clear. The style of greeting encouraged should be consistent with the sensibilities of those present.

### 3   The Celebration of the Eucharist

*The Preparation of the Gifts*—The preparation of the gifts of bread and wine is essentially functional, but together with the offering of money and other gifts, it does also symbolize the offering of ourselves and of the whole creation to God. This can best be given liturgical expression by representatives of the congregation bringing the gifts to the altar.

*The Prayer over the Gifts*—The action of preparation is gathered up in the Prayer over the Gifts. This prayer reflects the themes of the liturgy of the day and focuses not only on the gifts of bread and wine, but on the whole work of the People of God which is the offering of the Church.

*The Great Thanksgiving*—The eucharistic prayer is the great prayer of blessing said over the bread and the cup on the model of the Jewish table prayers of blessing. It is a prayer of faith addressed to God the Father, an act of praise and thanksgiving for the whole work of creation and redemption. The prayer is a unity from the opening dialogue to the final doxology and Amen. In the eucharistic prayer the Church expresses the meaning of the whole eucharistic action in which the memorial of redemption is made, and the Church is united with Christ in offering and communion through the sanctifying power of the Holy Spirit.

Six eucharistic prayers have been provided. Parishes will naturally wish to choose those which meet the particular needs of their own community.

*The Person and Work of Christ in the Eucharistic Prayers*—The biblical imagery employed in the eucharistic prayers to express the meaning of Christ's life, death, and resurrection for our salvation is rich and varied. Three images in particular stand out in the biblical material:

1   the interpretation of Jesus' death as an act of vicarious suffering on behalf of the people on the analogy of the figure of the suffering servant of Isaiah 53,

2   the interpretation of Jesus' death as a sin-offering on the analogy of the expiatory sacrifices offered in the Temple, and

3   the interpretation of the death and resurrection of Christ as an act of divine deliverance from the power of sin and death.

These images are fluid and entered in this fluid form into the liturgies and writings of the early Church.

In the Middle Ages and the Reformation period these images were given more precise definition with the use of "satisfaction" and "substitutionary" language. Jesus' death was interpreted as a satisfaction for sin, or as an act of legal substitution. According to the latter idea, Jesus, although innocent, stood in the divine courtroom in the place of guilty sinners and suffered the sentence and punishment of death for our sins. As a result, Christians are acquitted of their sins and accounted righteous. In Cranmer's eucharistic prayer the language of sin-offering and satisfaction are linked in the phrase, "full, perfect, and sufficient sacrifice, oblation, and satisfaction." In the revised Canadian eucharist prayers, on the other hand, the images of vicarious suffering, sacrifice, and divine deliverance have been employed without binding them to the later medieval and Reformation themes of atonement.

Another issue closely related to the issue of atonement is that of eucharistic offering. In the early liturgies the language of offering is very fluid, but what it expresses essentially is that the gifts and the community are offered in and through the sacrifice of Christ. The close link between offering and *anamnesis* (remembrance) in the ancient liturgies makes it clear that the offering of the gifts and the community are entirely dependent upon the one sacrifice of Christ. In the Middle Ages the idea gained ground that the eucharist is a sacrifice in its own right, independent of the sacrifice of the cross. In this context, Cranmer, along with the other Reformers, rejected the idea of the sacrifice of the mass, emphasized the once-for-all character of the sacrifice of Christ, and allowed only the offering of "praise and thanksgiving" and of "ourselves, our souls, and bodies" in the eucharist. Cranmer and the Reformers were right in insisting on the once-for-all and the "full, perfect, and sufficient" character of the sacrifice of the cross, but Cranmer's liturgy failed to give adequate expression to the unity between the Church's offering and the offering of Christ expressed in the ancient liturgies and in the patristic theology of the "whole Christ," head and members. The revision of the Canadian eucharistic prayers has sought to give this latter point clearer expression.

*Eucharistic Prayer 1*—This prayer is a new composition. It is rooted in the tradition of Apostolic Constitutions VIII and aims at a rich expression of the history of salvation.

*Eucharistic Prayer 2*—The model for this prayer is that which is found in the Apostolic Tradition of Hippolytus (c. 215). This is one of the most ancient eucharistic prayers that has come down to us. It has served as the basis for a number of Anglican, Lutheran, and Methodist revisions as well as for the second of the new Roman Catholic eucharistic prayers.

*Eucharistic Prayer 3*—The model for this prayer is Prayer B in the *Book of Common Prayer* of the Episcopal Church U.S.A. This prayer requires the use of a variable preface. These prefaces are an attempt to enrich the prayer by offering a more extensive thanksgiving for the particular aspect of the mystery of salvation being celebrated on that day.

*Eucharistic Prayer 4*—The model for this prayer is Prayer C in the Episcopal Prayer Book. Its language of praise for creation and salvation, using contemporary imagery, has made it one of the most popular of the new eucharistic prayers in the Episcopal Church. The Canadian version has a common refrain in order to encourage the use of this prayer as a text to be sung.

*Eucharistic Prayer 5*—This prayer is a new composition. Its language is simple and direct. It was written for use as a sung text with a common refrain and with celebrations with children in mind.

*Eucharistic Prayer 6*—This prayer is the work of an unofficial ecumenical committee of Roman Catholic, Episcopal, Presbyterian, Lutheran, and Methodist scholars. Its source is the eucharistic prayer in the liturgy of St Basil of Caesarea.[3] It is Eucharistic Prayer D in the Episcopal Prayer Book. This prayer brings to our tradition the richness of the Eastern tradition as well as representing an ecumenical achievement.

*The Lord's Prayer*—The use of the Lord's Prayer at this point in the liturgy is particularly appropriate in view of the petition for "daily" bread which had eucharistic associations in the early Church. The petition for the coming of the kingdom also serves to remind us that the eucharist is not only a memorial of redemption, but also an anticipation of the future banquet in the kingdom of God. The petitions for forgiveness are another way in which the eucharist as an act of reconciliation is expressed.

*The Breaking of the Bread*—The breaking of the bread is the third action in the fourfold "shape" of the liturgy: taking (the offertory), blessing (the eucharistic prayer), breaking,[4] and giving (the communion).[5] Throughout the history of the Church the basic eucharistic actions have experienced greater or lesser emphasis. The early Church highlighted the action of breaking bread, to the extent that this gesture of Christ at the Last Supper gave the entire eucharistic action its name in apostolic times. The action, while essentially functional, expresses the unity of the Church which is the fruit of the eucharist. By sharing in the one loaf which is broken into many pieces the many members are made one body in Christ.

The breaking of the bread may take place in silence or else the seasonal fraction sentences may be used to highlight the action. Anthems found on pp. 226–228 may be sung while the bread is being broken for distribution.

The phrase "The gifts of God for the People of God" serves as an invitation to receive the sacrament.

The words of distribution are said to each communicant who responds in faith: "Amen." Either kneeling or standing are seen as postures appropriate for receiving communion.

*Prayer after Communion*—Following a space for silence, a final variable post-communion prayer is said by the celebrant. It is a prayer in which the Church asks God to grant the effects of the eucharist to his people. We ask to become in action what we have received in sacrament. In doing this the prayer generally recaptures the theme of the Collect and the Prayer over the Gifts used that day. It may be concluded with a doxology said by the celebrant and the congregation together.

There is also an invariable prayer provided after communion, which may be said by the entire congregation *instead* of the variable prayer and the doxology. The theological intent of the prayer is similar to that of the variable prayers but without being related to the proper of the day.

*Dismissal*—Provision has been made for the optional use of a blessing before the dismissal where it is desired. The custom of giving a blessing at the end of the eucharistic liturgy stems from a period in the Middle Ages when very few of those present at the liturgy received communion. In our time, when very few people present at the eucharist do not receive communion, the practice of giving an additional blessing to that received in the act of communion itself appears superfluous. The dismissal, in which the people are sent into the world to be the Church, is seen therefore as the normal conclusion of the rite.

*The Penitential Rite*—The place of the penitential element in the eucharistic liturgy needs some historical perspective. In the ancient Church there was no verbal confession and absolution in the eucharistic liturgy. This element was introduced into the first Prayer Book as an element of medieval piety. The ancient Church understood the eucharist as a whole to be the means by which the People of God are renewed in their baptismal covenant and reconciled to God. "That the Church is reconciled only by verbal confession and absolution is a peculiarly Western absorption that continuously causes sacramental and liturgical problems."[6]

The present rite gives expression to the penitential element in two ways: (1) by giving liturgical expression to forgiveness in the Prayers of the People or in the Confession and Absolution, in the Peace, and in the Lord's Prayer, and (2) through the provision of a separate Penitential Order which is suitable for use during Lent and on other occasions.

1   The exception is when the Penitential Order is used as a separate rite immediately preceding the eucharist during Lent or on other occasions (see below, p. 216).

2   Massey Shepherd has written two useful books on the use of the Psalter in modern eucharistic rites. They are *A Liturgical Psalter for the Christian Year* and *The Psalms in Christian Worship, A Practical Guide*, both published by The Liturgical Press, Collegeville, Minnesota, 1976.

3   Leonel Mitchell, "The Alexandrian Anaphora of St. Basil of Caesarea: Ancient Source of 'A Common Eucharistic Prayer,'" *Anglican Theological Review*, Vol. LVIII, No.2, April 1976, pp. 194–206.

4   The breaking of the bread is thus a separate action and should not take place during the eucharistic prayer.

5   Gregory Dix, *The Shape of the Liturgy*, London: Dacre Press, 1945, 1970, pp. 48–50.

6   Aidan Kavanagh, "The Draft Proposed Book of Common Prayer: A Roman Catholic's Appreciation," *Anglican Theological Review*, Vol. LVIII, No. 3, July 1976, p. 365.

# Concerning the Liturgy

*The holy table is spread with a clean (white) cloth during the celebration.*

*The celebration of the eucharist is the work of the whole People of God. However, throughout this rite the term celebrant is used to describe the bishop or priest who presides at the eucharist.*

*As chief liturgical officer it is the bishop's prerogative to preside at the Lord's table and to preach the gospel.*

*It is appropriate that other priests who may be present stand with the celebrant at the altar during the eucharistic prayer, and join in the breaking of the bread and in the ministration of communion.*

*It is the function of a deacon to read the Gospel and to make ready the table for the celebration, preparing and placing upon it the bread and cup of wine. The deacon may also lead the Prayers of the People.*

*Lay persons should normally be assigned the readings which precede the Gospel, and may lead the Prayers of the People. When authority is given by the bishop, they may also assist in the ministration of communion.*

*It is desirable that the readings be read from a lectern or pulpit, and that the Gospel be read from the same lectern or pulpit, or in the midst of the congregation. It is desirable that the readings and Gospel be read from a book or books of appropriate size and dignity.*

*The leader of the Prayers of the People should use creativity and discretion in the planning of the intercessions and thanksgivings, and scope should be provided for members of the congregation to add their own petitions. The suggested forms are examples; these may be modified as local customs and needs require. The use of silence in the intercessions is optional.*

*If there is no communion, all that is appointed through the Prayers of the People may be said. (If it is desired to include a confession of sin, the service begins with the Penitential Order.) A hymn or anthem may then be sung, and the offerings of the people received. The service may then be concluded with the Lord's Prayer, and with one of the forms of Dismissal on p. 215, or a blessing, or with the exchange of the Peace. In the absence of a priest, all that is described above, except for the absolution and blessing, may be said by a deacon or, if there is no deacon, by an authorized lay person.*

*When a certain posture is particularly appropriate, it is indicated. For the rest of the service local custom may be established and followed. The Great Thanksgiving is a single prayer, the unity of which may be obscured by changes of posture in the course of it.*

*During the Great Thanksgiving it is desirable that there be only one chalice on the altar and, if need be, a flagon, decanter, jug, or suitable container of wine from which additional chalices may be filled after the breaking of the bread.*

*Care should be taken at the time of the preparation of the gifts to place on the holy table sufficient bread and wine for the communion of the people so that supplementary consecration is unnecessary. However, if the consecrated bread or wine does not suffice for the number of communicants, the celebrant consecrates more of either or both, by saying,*

We thank you, heavenly Father, for your saving love, and we pray you to bless and sanctify this bread (wine) with your Word and Holy Spirit, that it also may be the sacrament of the precious body (blood) of your Son, our Lord Jesus Christ. **Amen.**

*Opportunity is always to be given to every communicant to receive the consecrated bread and wine separately.*

*Communion should be given at each celebration of the eucharist from bread and wine consecrated at that liturgy.*

*Any remaining consecrated bread and wine (unless reserved for the communion of persons not present) is consumed at the end of the distribution or immediately after the service. This is appropriately done at the credence table or in the sacristy.*

# The Holy Eucharist

## The Gathering of the Community

*All stand. The presiding celebrant greets the community.*

Celebrant  The grace of our Lord Jesus Christ,
and the love of God,
and the fellowship of the Holy Spirit,
be with you all.
People  **And also with you.**

*Or from Easter Day through the Day of Pentecost,*

Celebrant  Alleluia! Christ is risen.
People  **The Lord is risen indeed. Alleluia!**

Celebrant  May his grace and peace be with you.
People  **May he fill our hearts with joy.**

*The following prayer may be said.*

Celebrant  Almighty God,
All  **to you all hearts are open,
all desires known,
and from you no secrets are hidden.
Cleanse the thoughts of our hearts
by the inspiration of your Holy Spirit,
that we may perfectly love you,
and worthily magnify your holy name;
through Christ our Lord. Amen.**

*Then may follow an act of praise: one of the following hymns, or a canticle or other hymn. It is appropriate that the hymn Glory to God be used during the Christmas season and from Easter Day through the Day of Pentecost, but not during the seasons of Advent and Lent. During Lent it is appropriate that Kyrie Eleison or the Trisagion be used. Other canticles may be found on pp. 72–95.*

## Glory to God

*Celebrant*    Glory to God in the highest,
*All*    **and peace to his people on earth.**

**Lord God, heavenly king,
almighty God and Father,
we worship you, we give you thanks,
we praise you for your glory.**

**Lord Jesus Christ, only Son of the Father,
Lord God, Lamb of God,
you take away the sin of the world:
have mercy on us;
you are seated at the right hand of the Father:
receive our prayer.**

**For you alone are the Holy One,
you alone are the Lord,
you alone are the Most High,
Jesus Christ,
with the Holy Spirit,
in the glory of God the Father. Amen.**

## Kyrie Eleison

*May be sung in three-fold, six-fold, or nine-fold form.*

**Kyrie eleison.
Christe eleison.
Kyrie eleison.**

*Or*    **Lord, have mercy.
Christ, have mercy.
Lord, have mercy.**

## Trisagion

*May be sung three times or antiphonally, and may include Glory to the Father.*

> **Holy God,**
> **holy and mighty,**
> **holy immortal one,**
> **have mercy upon us.**

## The Collect of the Day

*Celebrant*     Let us pray.

*The community may pray silently. The celebrant then sings or says the collect, after which the people respond,* **Amen.**

# The Proclamation of the Word

## The Readings

*A first reading as appointed.*

*Reader*     A reading from . . .

*At the conclusion of the passage, the reader says,*

>     The word of the Lord.
> *People*     **Thanks be to God.**

*Silence may be kept. Then shall follow a psalm as appointed.*

*On Sundays and major festivals a second reading as appointed is read.*

*Reader*     A reading from . . .

*At the conclusion of the passage, the reader says,*

>     The word of the Lord.
> *People*     **Thanks be to God.**

*Silence may be kept. A psalm, canticle, hymn, or anthem may follow.*

*All stand for the Gospel.*

| Reader | The Lord be with you. |
|--------|------------------------|
| People | **And also with you.** |

| Reader | The Holy Gospel of our Lord Jesus Christ according to . . . |
|--------|------------------------|
| People | **Glory to you, Lord Jesus Christ.** |

*At the conclusion of the Gospel, the reader says,*

|  | The Gospel of Christ. |
|--------|------------------------|
| People | **Praise to you, Lord Jesus Christ.** |

## Sermon

*A silence for reflection may follow.*

*The Nicene Creed shall be said on major festivals. On Sundays either the Nicene Creed or the Apostles' Creed is appropriate.*

## The Nicene Creed

*The celebrant may invite the people, in these or similar words, to join in the recitation of the creed.*

| Celebrant | Let us confess our faith, as we say, |
|-----------|--------------------------------------|
| All | **We believe in one God,** |
|  | **the Father, the Almighty,** |
|  | **maker of heaven and earth,** |
|  | **of all that is, seen and unseen.** |

> **We believe in one Lord, Jesus Christ,**
> **the only Son of God,**
> **eternally begotten of the Father,**
> **God from God, Light from Light,**
> **true God from true God,**
> **begotten, not made,**
> **of one being with the Father.**
> **Through him all things were made.**
> **For us and for our salvation**
> **he came down from heaven:**

by the power of the Holy Spirit
he became incarnate from the Virgin Mary,
and was made man.
For our sake he was crucified
under Pontius Pilate;
he suffered death and was buried.
On the third day he rose again
in accordance with the scriptures;
he ascended into heaven
and is seated at the right hand of the Father.
He will come again in glory
to judge the living and the dead,
and his kingdom will have no end.

We believe in the Holy Spirit,
the Lord, the giver of life,
who proceeds from the Father.
With the Father and the Son
he is worshipped and glorified.
He has spoken through the prophets.
We believe in one holy catholic
and apostolic Church.
We acknowledge one baptism
for the forgiveness of sins.
We look for the resurrection of the dead,
and the life of the world to come. Amen.

## The Apostles' Creed

*The celebrant may invite the people, in these or similar words, to join in the recitation of the creed.*

Celebrant    Let us confess the faith of our baptism,
             as we say,
All          **I believe in God,**
             **the Father almighty,**
             **creator of heaven and earth.**

I believe in Jesus Christ, his only Son, our Lord.
He was conceived by the power of the Holy Spirit
and born of the Virgin Mary.
He suffered under Pontius Pilate,
was crucified, died, and was buried.
He descended to the dead.
On the third day he rose again.
He ascended into heaven,
and is seated at the right hand of the Father.
He will come again
to judge the living and the dead.

I believe in the Holy Spirit,
the holy catholic Church,
the communion of saints,
the forgiveness of sins,
the resurrection of the body,
and the life everlasting. Amen.

# The Prayers of the People

*A deacon or lay member of the community leads the Prayers of the People
after the following model. Intercession or thanksgiving may be offered for*

> *the Church*
> *the Queen and all in authority*
> *the world*
> *the local community*
> *those in need*
> *the departed.*

*A short litany may be selected from pp. 110–127. Other prayers are found on
pp. 675–684. These prayers may be modified in accordance with local need, or
extempore forms of prayer may be used.*

# Confession and Absolution

*The following prayers may be used here if the Penitential Rite was not used before the Gathering of the Community, or if penitential intercessions were not used in the Prayers of the People.*

*The people are invited to confession in these or similar words.*

Celebrant    Dear friends in Christ,
God is steadfast in love and infinite in mercy;
he welcomes sinners
and invites them to his table.
Let us confess our sins,
confident in God's forgiveness.

*Silence is kept.*

Celebrant    Most merciful God,
All    **we confess that we have sinned against you
in thought, word, and deed,
by what we have done,
and by what we have left undone.
We have not loved you with our whole heart;
we have not loved our neighbours as ourselves.
We are truly sorry and we humbly repent.
For the sake of your Son Jesus Christ,
have mercy on us and forgive us,
that we may delight in your will,
and walk in your ways,
to the glory of your name. Amen.**

Celebrant    Almighty God have mercy upon you,
pardon and deliver you from all your sins,
confirm and strengthen you in all goodness,
and keep you in eternal life;
through Jesus Christ our Lord.
People    **Amen.**

## The Peace

*All stand, and the presiding celebrant addresses the people.*

> The peace of the Lord be always with you.

*People*    **And also with you.**

*The members of the community, ministers and people, may greet one another in the name of the Lord.*

# The Celebration of the Eucharist

## The Preparation of the Gifts

*It is appropriate that a hymn be sung during the offertory. Representatives of the people may present the gifts of bread and wine for the eucharist (with money and other gifts for the needs and responsibilities of the Church) to the deacon or celebrant before the altar.*

### The Prayer over the Gifts

*When the gifts have been prepared, the celebrant may say the Prayer over the Gifts, following which the people say,* **Amen.**

## The Great Thanksgiving

*One of the following eucharistic prayers shall be used.*

# Eucharistic Prayer 1

*Celebrant*  The Lord be with you.
*People*  **And also with you.**

*Celebrant*  Lift up your hearts.
*People*  **We lift them to the Lord.**

*Celebrant*  Let us give thanks to the Lord our God.
*People*  **It is right to give our thanks and praise.**

*Celebrant*  It is indeed right that we should praise you,
gracious God,
for you created all things.
You formed us in your own image:
male and female you created us.
When we turned away from you in sin,
you did not cease to care for us,
but opened a path of salvation for all people.
You made a covenant with Israel,
and through your servants Abraham and Sarah
gave the promise of a blessing to all nations.
Through Moses you led your people
from bondage into freedom;
through the prophets
you renewed your promise of salvation.
Therefore, with them, and with all your saints
who have served you in every age,
we give thanks and raise our voices
to proclaim the glory of your name.

*All*  **Holy, holy, holy Lord,
God of power and might,
heaven and earth are full of your glory.
Hosanna in the highest.**

**Blessed is he who comes in the name of the Lord.
Hosanna in the highest.**

*Celebrant*    Holy God, source of life and goodness,
all creation rightly gives you praise.
In the fullness of time,
you sent your Son Jesus Christ,
to share our human nature,
to live and die as one of us,
to reconcile us to you,
the God and Father of all.
He healed the sick
and ate and drank with outcasts and sinners;
he opened the eyes of the blind
and proclaimed the good news of your kingdom
to the poor and to those in need.
In all things he fulfilled your gracious will.

On the night he freely gave himself to death,
our Lord Jesus Christ took bread,
and when he had given thanks to you,
he broke it, and gave it to his disciples,
and said, "Take, eat:
this is my body which is given for you.
Do this for the remembrance of me."

After supper he took the cup of wine;
and when he had given thanks,
he gave it to them,
and said, "Drink this, all of you:
this is my blood of the new covenant,
which is shed for you and for many
for the forgiveness of sins.
Whenever you drink it,
do this for the remembrance of me."

Gracious God,
his perfect sacrifice
destroys the power of sin and death;
by raising him to life
you give us life for evermore.

Therefore we proclaim the mystery of faith.

*All*  **Christ has died.**
**Christ is risen.**
**Christ will come again.**

*Or*

*Celebrant*  Therefore we proclaim our hope.
*All*  **Dying you destroyed our death,**
**rising you restored our life.**
**Lord Jesus, come in glory.**

*Celebrant*  Recalling his death,
proclaiming his resurrection,
and looking for his coming again in glory,
we offer you, Father, this bread and this cup.
Send your Holy Spirit upon us
and upon these gifts,
that all who eat and drink at this table
may be one body and one holy people,
a living sacrifice in Jesus Christ, our Lord.

Through Christ, with Christ, and in Christ,
in the unity of the Holy Spirit,
all glory is yours, almighty Father,
now and for ever.

*People*  **Amen.**

*The service continues with the Lord's Prayer on p. 211.*

# Eucharistic Prayer 2

| | |
|---|---|
| *Celebrant* | The Lord be with you. |
| *People* | **And also with you.** |
| | |
| *Celebrant* | Lift up your hearts. |
| *People* | **We lift them to the Lord.** |
| | |
| *Celebrant* | Let us give thanks to the Lord our God. |
| *People* | **It is right to give our thanks and praise.** |

*Celebrant*  We give you thanks and praise, almighty God,
through your beloved Son, Jesus Christ,
our Saviour and Redeemer.
He is your living Word,
through whom you have created all things.

By the power of the Holy Spirit
he took flesh of the Virgin Mary
and shared our human nature.
He lived and died as one of us,
to reconcile us to you,
the God and Father of all.

In fulfilment of your will
he stretched out his hands in suffering,
to bring release to those who place their hope in you;
and so he won for you a holy people.

He chose to bear our griefs and sorrows,
and to give up his life on the cross,
that he might shatter the chains of evil and death,
and banish the darkness of sin and despair.
By his resurrection
he brings us into the light of your presence.

Now with all creation we raise our voices
to proclaim the glory of your name.

*All*  **Holy, holy, holy Lord,
God of power and might,**

heaven and earth are full of your glory.
Hosanna in the highest.

Blessed is he who comes in the name of the Lord.
Hosanna in the highest.

*Celebrant*    Holy and gracious God,
accept our praise,
through your Son our Saviour Jesus Christ;
who on the night he was handed over
to suffering and death,
took bread and gave you thanks,
saying, "Take, and eat:
this is my body which is broken for you."
In the same way he took the cup,
saying, "This is my blood which is shed for you.
When you do this, you do it in memory of me."

Remembering, therefore, his death and resurrection,
we offer you this bread and this cup,
giving thanks that you have made us worthy
to stand in your presence and serve you.

We ask you to send your Holy Spirit
upon the offering of your holy Church.
Gather into one
all who share in these sacred mysteries,
filling them with the Holy Spirit
and confirming their faith in the truth,
that together we may praise you
and give you glory
through your Servant, Jesus Christ.

All glory and honour are yours,
Father and Son,
with the Holy Spirit
in the holy Church,
now and for ever.

*People*    **Amen.**

*The service continues with the Lord's Prayer on p. 211.*

# Eucharistic Prayer 3

| | |
|---|---|
| *Celebrant* | The Lord be with you. |
| *People* | **And also with you.** |

| | |
|---|---|
| *Celebrant* | Lift up your hearts. |
| *People* | **We lift them to the Lord.** |

| | |
|---|---|
| *Celebrant* | Let us give thanks to the Lord our God. |
| *People* | **It is right to give our thanks and praise.** |

*Here follows one of the proper prefaces on pp. 218–226.*

| | |
|---|---|
| *All* | **Holy, holy, holy Lord,**<br>**God of power and might,**<br>**heaven and earth are full of your glory.**<br>**Hosanna in the highest.** |
| | **Blessed is he who comes in the name of the Lord.**<br>**Hosanna in the highest.** |

| | |
|---|---|
| *Celebrant* | We give thanks to you, Lord our God,<br>for the goodness and love<br>you have made known to us in creation;<br>in calling Israel to be your people;<br>in your Word spoken through the prophets;<br>and above all in the Word made flesh,<br>Jesus your Son.<br>For in these last days you sent him<br>to be incarnate from the Virgin Mary,<br>to be the Saviour and Redeemer of the world.<br>In him, you have delivered us from evil,<br>and made us worthy to stand before you.<br>In him, you have brought us<br>out of error into truth,<br>out of sin into righteousness,<br>out of death into life.<br><br>On the night he was handed over<br>to suffering and death, |

a death he freely accepted,
our Lord Jesus Christ took bread;
and when he had given thanks to you,
he broke it, and gave it to his disciples,
and said, "Take, eat:
this is my body which is given for you.
Do this for the remembrance of me."

After supper he took the cup of wine;
and when he had given thanks,
he gave it to them,
and said, "Drink this, all of you:
this is my blood of the new covenant,
which is shed for you and for many
for the forgiveness of sins.
Whenever you drink it,
do this for the remembrance of me."

Therefore, Father, according to his command,

*All*  **we remember his death,
we proclaim his resurrection,
we await his coming in glory;**

*Celebrant*  and we offer our sacrifice
of praise and thanksgiving
to you, Lord of all;
presenting to you, from your creation,
this bread and this wine.

We pray you, gracious God,
to send your Holy Spirit upon these gifts,
that they may be the sacrament
of the body of Christ
and his blood of the new covenant.
Unite us to your Son in his sacrifice,
that we, made acceptable in him,
may be sanctified by the Holy Spirit.

In the fullness of time,
reconcile all things in Christ,
and make them new,
and bring us to that city of light
where you dwell with all your sons and daughters;
through Jesus Christ our Lord,
the firstborn of all creation,
the head of the Church,
and the author of our salvation;

by whom, and with whom, and in whom,
in the unity of the Holy Spirit,
all honour and glory are yours, almighty Father,
now and for ever.

*People*     **Amen.**

*The service continues with the Lord's Prayer on p. 211.*

# Eucharistic Prayer 4

| | |
|---|---|
| *Celebrant* | The Lord be with you. |
| *People* | **And also with you.** |

| | |
|---|---|
| *Celebrant* | Lift up your hearts. |
| *People* | **We lift them to the Lord.** |

| | |
|---|---|
| *Celebrant* | Let us give thanks to the Lord our God. |
| *People* | **It is right to give our thanks and praise.** |

*Celebrant*    It is right to give you thanks and praise,
O Lord, our God, sustainer of the universe,
you are worthy of glory and praise.

*People*    **Glory to you for ever and ever.**

*Celebrant*    At your command all things came to be:
the vast expanse of interstellar space,
galaxies, suns, the planets in their courses,
and this fragile earth, our island home;
by your will they were created and have their being.

*People*    **Glory to you for ever and ever.**

*Celebrant*    From the primal elements
you brought forth the human race,
and blessed us with memory, reason, and skill;
you made us the stewards of creation.

*People*    **Glory to you for ever and ever.**

*Celebrant*    But we turn against you, and betray your trust;
and we turn against one another.
Again and again you call us to return.
Through the prophets and sages
you reveal your righteous law.
In the fullness of time you sent your Son,
born of a woman, to be our Saviour.
He was wounded for our transgressions,
and bruised for our iniquities.
By his death he opened to us
the way of freedom and peace.

*People*    **Glory to you for ever and ever.**

| Celebrant | Therefore we praise you,
joining with the heavenly chorus,
with prophets, apostles, and martyrs,
and with those in every generation
who have looked to you in hope,
to proclaim with them your glory,
in their unending hymn: |
|---|---|

| All | **Holy, holy, holy Lord,
God of power and might,
heaven and earth are full of your glory.
Hosanna in the highest.** |
|---|---|

**Blessed is he who comes in the name of the Lord.
Hosanna in the highest.**

| Celebrant | Blessed are you, Lord our God,
for sending us Jesus, the Christ,
who on the night he was handed over
to suffering and death,
took bread, said the blessing,
broke the bread, gave it to his friends,
and said, "Take this, and eat it:
this is my body which is given for you.
Do this for the remembrance of me." |
|---|---|

In the same way, after supper,
he took the cup of wine;
he gave you thanks,
and said, "Drink this, all of you:
this is my blood of the new covenant,
which is shed for you and for many
for the forgiveness of sins.
Whenever you drink it,
do this for the remembrance of me."

| People | **Glory to you for ever and ever.** |
|---|---|

| | |
|---|---|
| Celebrant | Gracious God, |
| | we recall the death of your Son Jesus Christ, |
| | we proclaim his resurrection and ascension, |
| | and we look with expectation for his coming |
| | as Lord of all the nations. |
| | We who have been redeemed by him, |
| | and made a new people by water and the Spirit, |
| | now bring you these gifts. |
| | Send your Holy Spirit upon us |
| | and upon this offering of your Church, |
| | that we who eat and drink at this holy table |
| | may share the divine life of Christ our Lord. |
| People | **Glory to you for ever and ever.** |

| | |
|---|---|
| Celebrant | Pour out your Spirit upon the whole earth |
| | and make it your new creation. |
| | Gather your Church together |
| | from the ends of the earth into your kingdom, |
| | where peace and justice are revealed, |
| | that we, with all your people, |
| | of every language, race, and nation, |
| | may share the banquet you have promised; |
| | |
| | through Christ, with Christ, and in Christ, |
| | all honour and glory are yours, |
| | creator of all. |
| People | **Glory to you for ever and ever. Amen.** |

*The service continues with the Lord's Prayer on p. 211.*

# Eucharistic Prayer 5

*Other refrains than "Glory to you for ever and ever" may be used with this prayer, or the refrain may be omitted.*

| | |
|---|---|
| *Celebrant* | The Lord be with you. |
| *People* | **And also with you.** |

| | |
|---|---|
| *Celebrant* | Lift up your hearts. |
| *People* | **We lift them to the Lord.** |

| | |
|---|---|
| *Celebrant* | Let us give thanks to the Lord our God. |
| *People* | **It is right to give our thanks and praise.** |

*Celebrant*
We give you thanks and praise, almighty God,
for the gift of a world full of wonder,
and for our life which comes from you.
By your power you sustain the universe.

*People*
**Glory to you for ever and ever.**

*Celebrant*
You created us to love you with all our heart,
and to love each other as ourselves,
but we rebel against you by the evil that we do.

In Jesus, your Son,
you bring healing to our world
and gather us into one great family.
Therefore, with all who serve you
on earth and in heaven,
we praise your wonderful name, as we sing (say),

*All*
**Holy, holy, holy Lord,
God of power and might,
heaven and earth are full of your glory.
Hosanna in the highest.**

**Blessed is he who comes in the name of the Lord.
Hosanna in the highest.**

| | |
|---|---|
| *Celebrant* | We give you thanks and praise, loving Father, because in sending Jesus, your Son, to us you showed us how much you love us. He cares for the poor and the hungry. He suffers with the sick and the rejected. |
| | Betrayed and forsaken, he did not strike back but overcame hatred with love. On the cross he defeated the power of sin and death. By raising him from the dead you show us the power of your love to bring new life to all your people. |
| *People* | **Glory to you for ever and ever.** |
| *Celebrant* | On the night before he gave up his life for us, Jesus, at supper with his friends, took bread, gave thanks to you, broke it, and gave it to them, saying, "Take this, all of you, and eat it: this is my body which is given for you." |
| | After supper, Jesus took the cup of wine, said the blessing, gave it to his friends, and said, "Drink this, all of you: this is the cup of my blood, the blood of the new and eternal covenant, which is shed for you and for many, so that sins may be forgiven. Do this in memory of me." |
| *People* | **Glory to you for ever and ever.** |
| *Celebrant* | Gracious God, with this bread and wine we celebrate the death and resurrection of Jesus, and we offer ourselves to you in him. |

Send your Holy Spirit on us and on these gifts,
that we may know the presence of Jesus
in the breaking of bread,
and share in the life
of the family of your children.

*People*   **Glory to you for ever and ever.**

*Celebrant*   Father, you call us to be your servants;
fill us with the courage and love of Jesus,
that all the world may gather in joy
at the table of your kingdom.

We sing your praise, almighty Father,
through Jesus, our Lord,
in the power of the Holy Spirit,
now and for ever.

*People*   **Glory to you for ever and ever. Amen.**

*The service continues with the Lord's Prayer on p. 211.*

# Eucharistic Prayer 6

| | |
|---|---|
| *Celebrant* | The Lord be with you. |
| *People* | **And also with you.** |

| | |
|---|---|
| *Celebrant* | Lift up your hearts. |
| *People* | **We lift them to the Lord.** |

| | |
|---|---|
| *Celebrant* | Let us give thanks to the Lord our God. |
| *People* | **It is right to give our thanks and praise.** |

*Celebrant*  It is right to glorify you, Father,
and to give you thanks;
for you alone are God, living and true,
dwelling in light inaccessible
from before time and for ever.
Fountain of life and source of all goodness,
you made all things
and fill them with your blessing;
you created them to rejoice
in the splendour of your radiance.
Countless throngs of angels stand before you
to serve you night and day,
and, beholding your presence,
they offer you unceasing praise.
Joining with them,
and giving voice to every creature under heaven,
we acclaim you, and glorify your name,
as we sing (say),

*All*  **Holy, holy, holy Lord,
God of power and might,
heaven and earth are full of your glory.
Hosanna in the highest.**

**Blessed is he who comes in the name of the Lord.
Hosanna in the highest.**

*Celebrant*  We acclaim you, holy Lord, glorious in power;
your mighty works reveal your wisdom and love.

You formed us in your own image,
giving the whole world into our care,
so that, in obedience to you, our creator,
we might rule and serve all your creatures.
When our disobedience took us far from you,
you did not abandon us to the power of death.
In your mercy you came to our help,
so that in seeking you we might find you.
Again and again
you called us into covenant with you,
and through the prophets
you taught us to hope for salvation.

Father, you loved the world so much
that in the fullness of time
you sent your only Son to be our Saviour.
Incarnate by the Holy Spirit,
born of the Virgin Mary,
he lived as one of us, yet without sin.
To the poor
he proclaimed the good news of salvation;
to prisoners, freedom;
to the sorrowful, joy.
To fulfil your purpose
he gave himself up to death
and, rising from the grave, destroyed death
and made the whole creation new.

And that we might live no longer for ourselves,
but for him who died and rose for us,
he sent the Holy Spirit,
his own first gift for those who believe,
to complete his work in the world,
and to bring to fulfilment
the sanctification of all.

When the hour had come for him to be glorified
by you, his heavenly Father,
having loved his own who were in the world,
he loved them to the end:

at supper with them he took bread;
and when he had given thanks to you,
he broke it, and gave it to his disciples,
and said, "Take, eat:
this is my body which is given for you.
Do this for the remembrance of me."

After supper he took the cup of wine;
and when he had given thanks,
he gave it to them,
and said, "Drink this, all of you:
this is my blood of the new covenant,
which is shed for you and for many
for the forgiveness of sins.
Whenever you drink it,
do this for the remembrance of me."

Father,
we now celebrate the memorial of our redemption.
Recalling Christ's death
and descent among the dead,
proclaiming his resurrection
and ascension to your right hand,
awaiting his coming in glory;
and offering to you,
from the gifts you have given us,
this bread and this cup,
we praise you and we bless you.

*All*  **We praise you, we bless you,
we give thanks to you,
and we pray to you, Lord our God.**

*Celebrant*  Father,
we pray that in your goodness and mercy
your Holy Spirit may descend upon us,
and upon these gifts,
sanctifying them and showing them
to be holy gifts for your holy people,
the bread of life and the cup of salvation,
the body and blood of your Son Jesus Christ.

Grant that all who share this bread and this cup
may become one body and one spirit,
a living sacrifice in Christ
to the praise of your name.

Remember, Lord,
your one holy catholic and apostolic Church,
redeemed by the blood of your Christ.
Reveal its unity, guard its faith,
and preserve it in peace.

[Remember ( . . . and) all who minister
in your Church.]
[Remember all your people,
and those who seek your truth.]
[Remember . . . ]
[Remember all who have died
in the peace of Christ,
and those whose faith is known to you alone;
bring them into the place
of eternal joy and light.]

And grant that we may find our inheritance
with [the blessed Virgin Mary,
with patriarchs, prophets, apostles, and martyrs,
(with . . . ) and] all the saints
who have found favour with you in ages past.
We praise you in union with them
and give you glory
through your Son Jesus Christ our Lord.

Through Christ, and with Christ, and in Christ,
all honour and glory are yours,
almighty God and Father,
in the unity of the Holy Spirit,
for ever and ever.

*People*  **Amen.**

# The Lord's Prayer

*Celebrant*   As our Saviour taught us, let us pray,

*All*   **Our Father in heaven,
hallowed be your name,
your kingdom come,
your will be done,
on earth as in heaven.
Give us today our daily bread.
Forgive us our sins
as we forgive those who sin against us.
Save us from the time of trial,
and deliver us from evil.
For the kingdom, the power,
and the glory are yours,
now and for ever. Amen.**

*Or*

*Celebrant*   And now, as our Saviour Christ has taught us,
we are bold to say,

*All*   **Our Father, who art in heaven,
hallowed be thy name,
thy kingdom come,
thy will be done,
on earth as it is in heaven.
Give us this day our daily bread.
And forgive us our trespasses,
as we forgive those who trespass against us.
And lead us not into temptation,
but deliver us from evil.
For thine is the kingdom,
the power, and the glory,
for ever and ever. Amen.**

*Silence*

# The Breaking of the Bread

*The celebrant breaks the consecrated bread for distribution, and may say one of the following:*

Celebrant   "I am the bread of life," says the Lord.
                    "Whoever comes to me will never be hungry;
                    whoever believes in me will never thirst."

All   **Taste and see that the Lord is good;**
        **happy are they who trust in him!**

## Or 2

Celebrant   We break this bread
        to share in the body of Christ.

All   **We, being many, are one body,**
        **for we all share in the one bread.**

## Or 3

Celebrant   Creator of all,
        you gave us golden fields of wheat,
        whose many grains we have gathered
        and made into this one bread.

All   **So may your Church be gathered**
        **from the ends of the earth**
        **into your kingdom.**

## Or 4

Celebrant   "I am the bread which has come down from
        heaven," says the Lord.

All   **Give us this bread for ever.**

Celebrant   "I am the vine, you are the branches."

All   **May we dwell in him, as he lives in us.**

## 5 Advent

Celebrant   God of promise,
        you prepare a banquet for us in your kingdom.

All   **Happy are those who are called**
        **to the supper of the Lamb.**

### 6  Incarnation

*Celebrant*  We break the bread of life,
and that life is the light of the world.
*All*  **God here among us,
light in the midst of us,
bring us to light and life.**

### 7  Lent and Holy Week

*Celebrant*  We break this bread,
*All*  **Communion in Christ's body once broken.**

*Celebrant*  Let your Church be the wheat
which bears its fruit in dying.
*All*  **If we have died with him,
we shall live with him;
if we hold firm,
we shall reign with him.**

### 8  Easter Season

*Celebrant*  Lord, we died with you on the cross.
*All*  **Now we are raised to new life.**

*Celebrant*  We were buried in your tomb.
*All*  **Now we share in your resurrection.**

*Celebrant*  Live in us, that we may live in you.

## The Communion

*The celebrant invites the people to share in communion and may say,*

The gifts of God for the People of God.
*People*  **Thanks be to God.**

*The celebrant and people then receive communion. The sacrament is given
with the following words.*

The body of Christ (given for you).
The blood of Christ (shed for you).

*Or*  The body of Christ, the bread of heaven.
The blood of Christ, the cup of salvation.

*The communicant responds each time,* **Amen.**

*During the breaking of the bread and the communion, psalms, hymns, and anthems such as those on pp. 226–228 may be sung.*

*At the conclusion of the communion, silence may be kept.*

## Prayer after Communion

*Celebrant*  Let us pray.

*Standing, the community prays in silence. The celebrant may say the Prayer after Communion appointed for the day. At the conclusion of the prayer the congregation says,* **Amen.**

*Then the following doxology may be said.*

*Celebrant*  Glory to God,
*All*  **whose power, working in us,
can do infinitely more
than we can ask or imagine.
Glory to God from generation to generation,
in the Church and in Christ Jesus,
for ever and ever. Amen.**

*Or instead of the Prayer after Communion and the doxology, the following may be said.*

*Celebrant*  All your works praise you, O Lord.
*All*  **And your faithful servants bless you.**

**Gracious God
we thank you for feeding us
with the body and blood of your Son
Jesus Christ.
May we, who share his body,
live his risen life;
we, who drink his cup,
bring life to others;**

we, whom the Spirit lights,
give light to the world.
Keep us firm in the hope you have set before us,
so that we and all your children shall be free,
and the whole earth live to praise your name;
through Christ our Lord. Amen.

# Dismissal

*The celebrant may bless the people. The deacon, or other leader, dismisses the people, saying in these or similar words,*

Go forth in the name of Christ.
*People* **Thanks be to God.**

*Or the following:*

*Leader* Go in peace to love and serve the Lord.
*People* **Thanks be to God.**

*Or the following:*

*Leader* Go forth into the world,
rejoicing in the power of the Spirit.
*People* **Thanks be to God.**

*Or the following:*

*Leader* Let us bless the Lord.
*People* **Thanks be to God.**

*From Easter Day through the Day of Pentecost,* **Alleluia** *is added to the dismissal and the people's response.*

# A Penitential Order

*This rite is appropriate for use before the eucharist on Sundays during Lent. It may also be used on other occasions or as a separate service. When this order is used before the eucharist, the eucharist begins with an act of praise or the Collect of the Day. When used separately, it concludes with suitable prayers, and one of the forms of Dismissal on p. 215 or a blessing.*

## Greeting

*All stand. The presiding celebrant greets the community.*

Celebrant  The grace of our Lord Jesus Christ,
 and the love of God,
 and the fellowship of the Holy Spirit,
 be with you all.

People  **And also with you.**

Celebrant  Bless the Lord who forgives all our sins.
People  **His mercy endures for ever.**

*The following prayer may be said.*

Celebrant  Almighty God,
All  **to you all hearts are open,
 all desires known,
 and from you no secrets are hidden.
 Cleanse the thoughts of our hearts
 by the inspiration of your Holy Spirit,
 that we may perfectly love you,
 and worthily magnify your holy name;
 through Christ our Lord. Amen.**

## The Word of God

*A suitable passage of scripture, such as one of the following, may be read.*

| | | |
|---|---|---|
| *Exodus 20.1–17* | *Matthew 9.9–13* | *Luke 15.11–32* |
| *Deuteronomy 5.6–21* | *Matthew 18.15–20* | *Luke 19.1–10* |
| *Isaiah 55.6–7* | *Matthew 25.31–46* | *John 8.1–11* |
| *Ezekiel 11.19–20* | *Mark 12.28–34* | *Romans 6.3–11* |
| *Matthew 5.13–16* | *Luke 15.1–7 or 8–10* | *1 John 1.8–9* |

*Reader*        A reading from . . .

*At the conclusion of the passage, the reader says,*

        The word of the Lord.
*People*        **Thanks be to God.**

*If this order is used as a separate service, a sermon may follow.*

## Confession and Absolution

*The people are invited to confession in these or similar words.*

*Celebrant*        Dear friends in Christ,
        God is steadfast in love and infinite in mercy;
        he welcomes sinners
        and invites them to his table.
        Let us confess our sins,
        confident in God's forgiveness.

*Silence is kept.*

*Celebrant*        Most merciful God,
*People*        **we confess that we have sinned against you**
        **in thought, word, and deed,**
        **by what we have done,**
        **and by what we have left undone.**
        **We have not loved you with our whole heart;**
        **we have not loved our neighbours as ourselves.**
        **We are truly sorry and we humbly repent.**
        **For the sake of your Son Jesus Christ,**
        **have mercy on us and forgive us,**
        **that we may delight in your will,**
        **and walk in your ways,**
        **to the glory of your name. Amen.**

*The celebrant stands and says,*

        Almighty God have mercy upon you,
        pardon and deliver you from all your sins,
        confirm and strengthen you in all goodness,
        and keep you in eternal life;
        through Jesus Christ our Lord.
*People*        **Amen.**

# Proper Prefaces

## Lord's Day

Blessed are you, gracious God,
creator of heaven and earth;
you are the source of light and life for all your creation,
you made us in your own image,
and call us to new life in Jesus Christ our Saviour.
Therefore we praise you,
joining our voices to proclaim the glory of your name.

## Lord's Day

Blessed are you, gracious God,
creator of heaven and earth;
we give you thanks and praise
through Jesus Christ our Lord,
who on this first day of the week
overcame death and the grave,
and by his glorious resurrection
opened to us the way of everlasting life.
In our unending joy
we echo on earth the song of the angels in heaven
as we raise our voices
to proclaim the glory of your name.

## Lord's Day

Blessed are you, gracious God,
creator of heaven and earth;
by water and the Holy Spirit
you have made us a holy people
in Jesus Christ our Lord;
you renew that mystery in bread and wine and nourish us,
to show forth your glory in all the world.
Therefore with angels and archangels,
and with all the holy people
who have served you in every age,
we raise our voices
to proclaim the glory of your name.

Blessed are you, gracious God,
creator of heaven and earth;
today you have gathered us together
in this eucharistic feast,
that we may be renewed in love, joy, and peace.
Now with all creation we lift our voices
to proclaim the glory of your name.

### Advent

Blessed are you, gracious God,
creator of heaven and earth;
we give you thanks and praise
through Jesus Christ our Lord,
who in the fullness of time came among us in our flesh,
and opened to us the way of salvation.
Now we watch for the day when he will come again
in power and great triumph to judge this world,
that we, without shame or fear,
may rejoice to behold his appearing.
Therefore we praise you,
joining our voices with angels and archangels
and with all the company of heaven,
who for ever sing this hymn
to proclaim the glory of your name.

### Christmas

Blessed are you, gracious God,
creator of heaven and earth;
we give you thanks and praise
through Jesus Christ our Lord,
who in the mystery of his incarnation
was made perfect man
of the flesh of the Virgin Mary his mother;
in him we have seen a new and radiant vision of your glory.
Therefore with all the angels of heaven,
we lift our voices and sing our joyful hymn of praise
to proclaim the glory of your name.

### Incarnation

Blessed are you, gracious God,
creator of heaven and earth,
because in the mystery of the Word made flesh
you have caused a new light to shine in our hearts,
to give knowledge of salvation
in the face of your Son Jesus Christ our Lord.
Now with angels and archangels
and the whole company of heaven,
we lift our voices
to proclaim the glory of your name.

### Epiphany

Blessed are you, gracious God,
creator of heaven and earth;
you have revealed your eternal plan of salvation,
and have shown your Son Jesus Christ
to be the light of all peoples.
Therefore with angels and archangels
we raise our voices in joyful praise
to proclaim the glory of your name.

### Lent

Blessed are you, gracious God,
creator of heaven and earth,
because you bid your faithful people
to cleanse their hearts
and to prepare with joy for the paschal feast;
that reborn through the waters of baptism
and renewed in the eucharistic mystery,
we may be more fervent in prayer
and more generous in the works of love.
Therefore we raise our voices to you in praise
to proclaim the glory of your name.

### Lent

Blessed are you, gracious God,
creator of heaven and earth;

we give you thanks and praise
through Jesus Christ our Lord,
who was tempted in every way, yet did not sin.
By his grace we are able to triumph over every evil,
and to live no longer for ourselves alone,
but for him who died for us and rose again.
Therefore with angels and archangels
and all who have served you in every age,
we raise our voices
to proclaim the glory of your name.

**Holy Week**

Blessed are you, gracious God,
creator of heaven and earth;
we give you thanks and praise
through Jesus Christ our Lord,
who for our sins was lifted high upon the cross,
that he might draw the whole world to himself.
By his suffering and death,
he became the source of eternal salvation
for all who put their trust in him.
Therefore with all the host of heaven
who gather around your throne and the Lamb,
we raise our voices
to proclaim the glory of your name.

**Holy Week**

Blessed are you, gracious God,
creator of heaven and earth;
we give you thanks and praise
through Jesus Christ our Lord,
who for our salvation became obedient unto death.
The tree of defeat became the tree of victory:
where life was lost, life has been restored.
Therefore with angels and archangels
and all the heavenly chorus,
we cry out to proclaim the glory of your name.

### Easter

Blessed are you, gracious God,
creator of heaven and earth;
we give you thanks and praise
for the glorious resurrection of your Son
Jesus Christ our Lord;
for he is the true paschal lamb
who has taken away the sin of the world.
By his death he destroyed death,
and by his rising to life again
he has won for us eternal life.
Therefore, joining our voices
with the whole company of heaven,
we sing our joyful hymn of praise
to proclaim the glory of your name.

### Ascension

Blessed are you, gracious God,
creator of heaven and earth;
we give you thanks and praise
through Jesus Christ our Lord,
who after his glorious resurrection
appeared to his disciples,
and in their sight ascended into heaven
to prepare a place for us;
that where he is, there we might also be,
and reign with him in glory.
Therefore we praise you with angels and archangels
and with all the company of heaven,
who for ever sing this hymn
to proclaim the glory of your name.

### Pentecost

Blessed are you, gracious God,
creator of heaven and earth;
we give you thanks and praise
through Jesus Christ our Lord.

In fulfilment of your promise
you pour forth your Spirit upon us,
filling us with gifts and leading us into all truth.
You give us power to proclaim your gospel to all nations
and to serve you as a royal priesthood.
Therefore we join our voices with angels and archangels,
and with all those in whom the Spirit dwells,
to proclaim the glory of your name.

## Trinity Sunday

Blessed are you, gracious God,
creator of heaven and earth;
we give you thanks and praise,
because, in the mystery you disclose to us,
you reveal your glory
as the glory of your Son and the Holy Spirit:
three persons equal in majesty,
undivided in splendour, yet one Lord, one God,
ever to be adored in your everlasting glory.
Therefore with all the company of heaven
we raise our voices to proclaim the glory of your name.

## Last Sunday after Pentecost: The Reign of Christ

Blessed are you, gracious God,
creator of heaven and earth;
we give you thanks and praise
through Jesus Christ our Lord.
You exalted him as Lord of all creation
that he might present to you
an eternal and universal kingdom:
a kingdom of truth and life,
a kingdom of holiness and grace,
a kingdom of justice, love, and peace.
Therefore at the name of Jesus every knee shall bow
as heaven and earth proclaim the glory of your name.

## All Saints

Blessed are you, gracious God,
creator of heaven and earth;
in the multitude of your saints
you have surrounded us
with so great a cloud of witnesses,
that we, rejoicing in their fellowship,
may run with patience the race that is set before us,
and together with them receive the crown of glory
that never fades away.
Therefore with angels and archangels
and with all who have served you in every age,
we raise our voices to proclaim the glory of your name.

## Apostles

Blessed are you, gracious God,
creator of heaven and earth;
we give you thanks and praise
through Jesus Christ our Lord,
who after his resurrection sent forth apostles
to preach the gospel and to teach all nations,
and promised to be with them always,
even to the end of the ages.
Therefore with angels and archangels
and all your holy people,
we raise our voices
to proclaim the glory of your name.

## A Saint

Blessed are you, gracious God,
creator of heaven and earth;
we give you thanks and praise
through Jesus Christ our Lord,
because in the fellowship of your saints
you have given us a glorious pledge
of the hope of our calling.
Therefore we join our voices with theirs
as earth and heaven unite
to proclaim the glory of your name.

### A Martyr

Blessed are you, gracious God,
creator of heaven and earth;
you are glorified in the assembly of your saints.
All your martyrs bless you and praise you,
confessing before the powers of this world
the great name of your only Son.
Therefore we join our voices with theirs,
and with all who have served you in every age,
to proclaim the glory of your name.

### Marriage

Blessed are you, gracious God,
creator of heaven and earth;
we give you thanks and praise
in the assembly of your people.
You made us in your image:
male and female you created us.
You give us the gift of marriage,
and call us to reflect your faithfulness
as we serve one another
in the bond of covenant love.
Therefore we raise our voices
with all who have served you in every age,
to proclaim the glory of your name.

### Commemoration of the Dead

Blessed are you, gracious God,
creator of heaven and earth;
we give you thanks and praise
through Jesus Christ our Lord,
whose victorious rising from the dead
has given to us the hope of resurrection
and the promise of eternal life.
Therefore with angels and archangels
and all who have served you in every age,
we raise our voices
to proclaim the glory of your name.

### Ordination

Blessed are you, gracious God,
creator of heaven and earth;
we give you thanks and praise
through Jesus Christ our Lord,
who came not to be served, but to serve
and to give his life a ransom for many.
He calls his faithful servants
to lead your holy people in love,
nourishing them by your word and sacraments.
Now with all creation we raise our voices
to proclaim the glory of your name.


# Anthems

#### To be Sung During the Breaking of Bread and Communion

*These anthems are of varying length, and should be chosen on the basis of the
time required. Some of them may be sung responsively between cantor and
congregation or choir as indicated.*

Christ our Passover is sacrificed for us;
   **Therefore let us keep the feast.**

The bread which we break is a sharing in the body of Christ.
   **We being many are one bread, one body,
   for we all share in the one bread.**

Lamb of God, you take away the sins of the world:
have mercy on us.
Lamb of God, you take away the sins of the world:
have mercy on us.
Lamb of God, you take away the sins of the world:
grant us peace.

My flesh is food indeed, and my blood is drink indeed,
says the Lord.
   **My flesh is food indeed, and my blood is drink indeed,
   says the Lord.**

Those who eat my flesh and drink my blood dwell in me
and I in them.
**My flesh is food indeed, and my blood is drink indeed,
says the Lord.**

Whoever eats this bread will live for ever.
**Whoever eats this bread will live for ever.**
This is the true bread which comes down from heaven and
gives life to the world.
**Whoever eats this bread will live for ever.**
Whoever believes in me shall not hunger or thirst,
for the bread which I give for the life of the world is my flesh.
**Whoever eats this bread will live for ever.**

*The following anthems are not appropriate to the season of Lent.*
Alleluia! Christ our Passover is sacrificed for us;
**Therefore let us keep the feast. Alleluia!**

Alleluia!
**Alleluia!**
Christ our Passover is sacrificed for us;
**Therefore let us keep the feast. Alleluia!**

Alleluia!
**Alleluia!**
Christ our Passover is sacrificed for us;
therefore let us keep the feast.
**Alleluia!**

The disciples knew the Lord Jesus
in the breaking of the bread.
**The disciples knew the Lord Jesus
in the breaking of the bread.**
The bread which we break, alleluia,
is the communion of the body of Christ.
**The disciples knew the Lord Jesus
in the breaking of the bread.**
One body are we, alleluia,
for though many we share one bread.
**The disciples knew the Lord Jesus
in the breaking of the bread.**

Be known to us, Lord Jesus, in the breaking of the bread.
**Be known to us, Lord Jesus, in the breaking of the bread.**
The bread which we break, alleluia,
is the communion of the body of Christ.
**Be known to us, Lord Jesus, in the breaking of the bread.**
One body are we, alleluia,
for though many, we share one bread.
**Be known to us, Lord Jesus, in the breaking of the bread.**

*Any of the fraction sentences on pp. 212–213 may also be sung.*

*The following anthems may be used as separate pieces or as refrains with selected verses from the psalms. In Easter season it is appropriate to add Alleluia to the anthem or refrain.*

Blessed are those who are called to the supper of the Lamb.

Whoever comes to me shall not hunger, and whoever believes in me shall never thirst.

Those who eat my flesh and drink my blood abide in me and I in them.

You shall eat and drink at my table in my kingdom, says the Lord.

Christ our Passover is sacrificed for us; therefore let us keep the feast.

**Suggested Psalm Verses**

Advent          Psalm 85.8–11

*Christmas through the Baptism of the Lord*

                Psalm 96.8–11        Psalm 110.1–4

Lent            Psalm 106.4–5        Psalm 108.3–6

Easter          Psalm 107.1–3, 8     Psalm 116.10–11, 16–17

General         Psalm 34.3–8         Psalm 105.1–4
                Psalm 43.3–4         Psalm 117
                Psalm 103.1–4

# The Holy Eucharist

**A Form in the Language of the Book of Common Prayer 1962**

## Concerning the Service

*Notes found on pp. 183–184 apply to this service also.*

*The celebrant should pick up and hold the bread and the cup at appropriate points in the institution narrative, but the bread should be broken after the Lord's Prayer.*

*If the consecrated bread or wine is insufficient for the number of communicants, the celebrant consecrates more, saying,*

We thank thee, heavenly Father, for thy saving love, and we pray thee to bless and sanctify this bread (wine) with thy Word and Holy Spirit, that it also may be the sacrament of the precious body (blood) of thy Son, our Lord Jesus Christ. **Amen.**

# The Holy Eucharist

**A Form in the Language of the Book of Common Prayer 1962**

# The Gathering of the Community

*All stand. The presiding celebrant greets the community.*

> The grace of our Lord Jesus Christ,
> and the love of God,
> and the fellowship of the Holy Spirit,
> be with you all.

*People*  **And with thy spirit.**

*Or from Easter Day through the Day of Pentecost,*

*Celebrant*  Alleluia! Christ is risen.
*People*  **The Lord is risen indeed. Alleluia!**

*Celebrant*  May his grace and peace be with you.
*People*  **May he fill our hearts with joy.**

*Then may be said by the celebrant alone or with the people,*

> Almighty God,
> unto whom all hearts be open,
> all desires known,
> and from whom no secrets are hid:
> cleanse the thoughts of our hearts
> by the inspiration of thy Holy Spirit,
> that we may perfectly love thee,
> and worthily magnify thy holy name;
> through Christ our Lord. **Amen.**

*Then one or more of the following may be said or sung. It is appropriate that the hymn Gloria in Excelsis be used during the Christmas season and from Easter Day through the Day of Pentecost, but not during the seasons of Advent and Lent. During Lent it is appropriate that the Kyrie Eleison or the*

## 1  The Summary of the Law

*Celebrant*     Our Lord Jesus Christ said: hear, O Israel, the Lord
our God is one Lord; and thou shalt love the Lord
thy God with all thy heart, and with all thy soul,
and with all thy mind, and with all thy strength.
This is the first and great commandment. And the
second is like unto it: thou shalt love thy neighbour
as thyself. On these two commandments hang all
the law and the prophets.

*People*     **Lord, have mercy upon us, and write both these
thy laws in our hearts, we beseech thee.**

## 2  The Decalogue   *see p. 250*

## 3  Kyrie Eleison

**Lord, have mercy upon us.
Christ, have mercy upon us.
Lord, have mercy upon us.**

*Or*

**Kyrie eleison.
Christe eleison.
Kyrie eleison.**

## 4  Gloria in Excelsis

**Glory be to God on high,
and in earth peace, good will towards men.
We praise thee, we bless thee,
we worship thee,
we glorify thee,
we give thanks to thee for thy great glory,
O Lord God, heavenly king, God the Father almighty.**

O Lord, the only-begotten Son, Jesus Christ;
O Lord God, Lamb of God, Son of the Father,
that takest away the sin of the world,
have mercy upon us.
Thou that takest away the sin of the world,
receive our prayer.
Thou that sittest at the right hand of God the Father,
have mercy upon us.

For thou only art holy;
thou only art the Lord;
thou only, O Christ,
with the Holy Ghost,
art most high in the glory of God the Father. Amen.

## 5   Trisagion

Holy God,
holy and mighty,
holy immortal one,
have mercy upon us.

## The Collect of the Day

*The celebrant shall say,*

Let us pray.

*The community may pray silently. The celebrant then sings or says the collect, after which the people respond,* **Amen.**

# The Proclamation of the Word

## The Readings

*A first reading as appointed.*

*Reader*        A reading from . . .

*At the conclusion of the passage, the reader says,*

>The word of the Lord.

*People*     **Thanks be to God.**

*Silence may be kept. Then shall follow a psalm as appointed.*

*On Sundays and major festivals a second reading as appointed is read.*

*Reader*     A reading from . . .

*At the conclusion of the passage, the reader says,*

>The word of the Lord.

*People*     **Thanks be to God.**

*Silence may be kept. A psalm, canticle, hymn, or anthem may follow.*

*All stand for the Gospel.*

*Reader*     The Lord be with you.

*People*     **And with thy spirit.**

*Reader*     The Holy Gospel of our Lord Jesus Christ
             according to . . .

*People*     **Glory be to thee, O Lord.**

*At the conclusion of the Gospel, the reader says,*

>The Gospel of Christ.

*People*     **Praise be to thee, O Christ.**

# The Sermon

*A silence for reflection may follow. The Nicene Creed shall be said on major festivals. On Sundays either the Nicene Creed or the Apostles' Creed (p. 251) is appropriate.*

# The Nicene Creed

I believe in one God,
the Father almighty,
maker of heaven and earth,
and of all things visible and invisible;

And in one Lord Jesus Christ,
the only-begotten Son of God,
begotten of the Father before all worlds,
God, of God; Light, of Light;
very God, of very God;
begotten, not made;
being of one substance with the Father;
through whom all things were made:
who for us and for our salvation
came down from heaven,
and was incarnate by the Holy Ghost of the Virgin Mary,
and was made man,
and was crucified also for us under Pontius Pilate.
He suffered and was buried,
and the third day he rose again
according to the scriptures,
and ascended into heaven,
and sitteth on the right hand of the Father.
And he shall come again with glory
to judge both the quick and the dead:
whose kingdom shall have no end.

And I believe in the Holy Ghost,
the Lord, the giver of life,
who proceedeth from the Father and the Son,
who with the Father and the Son together
is worshipped and glorified,
who spake by the prophets.
And I believe one, holy, catholic, and apostolic Church.
I acknowledge one baptism for the remission of sins.
And I look for the resurrection of the dead,
and the life of the world to come. Amen.

# The Prayers of the People

*A deacon or lay member of the community may lead the Prayers of the People.*
*Intercessions and thanksgivings may be used according to local custom and*
*need. All or portions of either of the following forms may be used.*

*Leader*     Let us pray for the Church and the world.

Almighty and everliving God, who by thy holy
Apostle hast taught us to make prayers and
supplications, and to give thanks for all people:
we humbly beseech thee most mercifully to receive
these our prayers, which we offer unto thy divine
majesty; beseeching thee to inspire continually
the universal Church with the spirit of truth,
unity, and concord: and grant that all they that
do confess thy holy name may agree in the truth
of thy holy word, and live in unity and godly
love.

Give grace, O heavenly Father, to all bishops,
priests, and deacons, (and specially to thy
servant *N* our bishop), that they may both by
their life and doctrine set forth thy true and
living word, and rightly and duly administer thy
holy sacraments: prosper, we pray thee, all
those who proclaim the gospel of thy kingdom
among the nations: and to all thy people give
thy heavenly grace, and specially to this
congregation here present, that, with meek heart
and due reverence, they may hear and receive thy
holy word; truly serving thee in holiness and
righteousness all the days of their life.

We beseech thee also to lead all nations in the
way of righteousness; and so to guide and direct
their governors and rulers, that thy people may
enjoy the blessings of freedom and peace: and
grant to thy servant Elizabeth our Queen, and to

all that are put in authority under her, that
they may truly and impartially administer
justice, to the maintenance of thy true religion
and virtue.

And we most humbly beseech thee of thy
goodness, O Lord, to comfort and succour all them,
who in this transitory life are in trouble, sorrow,
need, sickness, or any other adversity, (especially
those for whom our prayers are desired).

We remember before thee, O Lord, all thy servants
departed this life in thy faith and fear: and we bless
thy holy name for all who in life and death have
glorified thee; beseeching thee to give us grace that,
rejoicing in their fellowship, we may follow their
good examples, and with them be partakers of thy
heavenly kingdom.

Grant this, O Father, for Jesus Christ's sake, our
only Mediator and Advocate, to whom, with thee
and the Holy Spirit, be all honour and glory, world
without end. **Amen.**

*Or the following:*

| | |
|---|---|
| *Leader* | In peace let us pray to the Lord. |
| *People* | **Lord, have mercy.** |
| *Leader* | For peace from on high<br>and for our salvation,<br>let us pray to the Lord. |
| *People* | **Lord, have mercy.** |
| *Leader* | For the peace of the whole world,<br>for the welfare of the holy Church of God,<br>and for the unity of all,<br>let us pray to the Lord. |
| *People* | **Lord, have mercy.** |

| | |
|---|---|
| *Leader* | For our bishops,<br>and for all the clergy and people,<br>let us pray to the Lord. |
| *People* | **Lord, have mercy.** |
| *Leader* | For Elizabeth our Queen,<br>for the leaders of the nations,<br>and for all in authority,<br>let us pray to the Lord. |
| *People* | **Lord, have mercy.** |
| *Leader* | For *this city* (*town, village, etc.*),<br>for every city and community,<br>and for those who live in them in faith,<br>let us pray to the Lord. |
| *People* | **Lord, have mercy.** |
| *Leader* | For good weather,<br>and for abundant harvests for all to share,<br>let us pray to the Lord. |
| *People* | **Lord, have mercy.** |
| *Leader* | For those who travel by land, water, or air,<br>for the sick and the suffering (especially . . . )<br>for prisoners and captives,<br>and for their safety, health, and salvation,<br>let us pray to the Lord. |
| *People* | **Lord, have mercy.** |
| *Leader* | For our deliverance from all affliction,<br>strife, and need,<br>let us pray to the Lord. |
| *People* | **Lord, have mercy.** |
| *Leader* | For the absolution and remission<br>of our sins and offences,<br>let us pray to the Lord. |
| *People* | **Lord, have mercy.** |

| Leader | For all who have died (especially . . . ) let us pray to the Lord. |
| People | **Lord, have mercy.** |

| Leader | Remembering ( . . . and) all the saints, we commit ourselves, one another, and our whole life to Christ our God. |
| People | **To thee, O Lord.** |

| Leader | Almighty God, who hast given us grace at this time with one accord to make our common supplications unto thee; and dost promise that when two or three are gathered together in thy name thou wilt hear their requests: fulfil now, O Lord, the desires and petitions of thy servants as may be most expedient for them; granting us in this world knowledge of thy truth, and in the world to come life everlasting; for thou, Father, art good and loving, and we glorify thee through thy Son Jesus Christ our Lord, in the Holy Spirit, now and for ever. |
| People | **Amen.** |

## Confession and Absolution

*A confession of sin may be made here if a penitential rite has not been used earlier, or if penitential intercessions were not used in the Prayers of the People. The celebrant or other person may say one or more of the following:*

Hear what comfortable words our Saviour Christ saith unto all that truly turn to him.

Come unto me all that labour and are heavy laden, and I will refresh you.    *Matthew 11.28*

God so loved the world, that he gave his only-begotten Son, to the end that all that believe in him should not perish, but have eternal life.    *John 3.16*

Hear also what Saint Paul saith.

This is a true saying, and worthy of all to be received, that Christ Jesus came into the world to save sinners.  *1 Timothy 1.15*

Hear also what Saint John saith.

If anyone sin, we have an Advocate with the Father, Jesus Christ the righteous; and he is the propitiation for our sins: and not for ours only, but also for the sins of the whole world.  *1 John 2.1, 2*

*Then shall be said:*

Let us humbly confess our sins to almighty God.

*Or*  Ye that do truly and earnestly repent you of your sins, and are in love and charity with your neighbours, and intend to lead the new life, following the commandments of God, and walking from henceforth in his holy ways: draw near with faith, and take this holy sacrament to your comfort; and make your humble confession to almighty God.

*Silence is kept. The celebrant and people say together,*

**Almighty God, Father of our Lord Jesus Christ, Maker of all things and judge of all people: We acknowledge and confess our manifold sins and wickedness, Which we from time to time most grievously have committed, By thought, word and deed, Against thy divine majesty. We do earnestly repent, and are heartily sorry for these our misdoings. Have mercy upon us, most merciful Father; For thy Son our Lord Jesus Christ's sake, Forgive us all that is past; And grant that we may ever hereafter Serve and please thee In newness of life, To the honour and glory of thy name; Through Jesus Christ our Lord. Amen.**

| Celebrant | Almighty God, our heavenly Father, who of his great mercy hath promised forgiveness of sins to all them that with hearty repentance and true faith turn unto him: have mercy upon you; pardon and deliver you from all your sins; confirm and strengthen you in all goodness; and bring you to everlasting life; through Jesus Christ our Lord. **Amen.** |
|---|---|

## The Peace

*All stand, and the presiding celebrant addresses the people.*

| Celebrant | The peace of the Lord be always with you. |
|---|---|
| People | **And with thy spirit.** |

*The members of the community, ministers and people, may greet one another in the name of the Lord.*

# The Celebration of the Eucharist

## The Preparation of Gifts

*During the offertory a hymn, psalm, or anthem may be sung. Representatives of the people may present the gifts of bread and wine for the eucharist (with money and other gifts for the needs and responsibilities of the Church) to the deacon or celebrant before the altar.*

### The Prayer over the Gifts

*When the gifts have been prepared, the celebrant may say the Prayer over the Gifts, following which the people say,* **Amen.**

## The Great Thanksgiving

*One of the following Eucharistic Prayers shall be used.*

# Eucharistic Prayer A

*Celebrant*  The Lord be with you.
*People*  **And with thy spirit.**

*Celebrant*  Lift up your hearts.
*People*  **We lift them up unto the Lord.**

*Celebrant*  Let us give thanks unto our Lord God.
*People*  **It is meet and right so to do.**

*Celebrant*  It is very meet, right, and our bounden duty, that we should at all times, and in all places, give thanks unto thee, O Lord, holy Father, almighty, everlasting God, creator and preserver of all things.

*Here follows one of the Proper Prefaces on pp. 252–255.*

*Celebrant*  Therefore with angels and archangels, and with all the company of heaven, we laud and magnify thy glorious name; evermore praising thee and saying:

*All*  **Holy, holy, holy, Lord God of Hosts, heaven and earth are full of thy glory. Glory be to thee, O Lord most high.**

**Blessed is he that cometh in the name of the Lord: Hosanna in the highest.**

*Celebrant*  Blessing and glory and thanksgiving be unto thee, almighty God, our heavenly Father, who of thy tender mercy didst give thine only Son Jesus Christ to take our nature upon him, and to suffer death upon the cross for our redemption; who made there, by his one oblation of himself once offered, a full, perfect, and sufficient sacrifice, oblation, and satisfaction, for the sins of the whole world; and did institute, and in his holy Gospel command us to continue, a perpetual memorial of that his precious death, until his coming again.

Hear us, O merciful Father, we most humbly beseech thee; and grant that we receiving these thy creatures of bread and wine, according to thy Son our Saviour Jesus Christ's holy institution, in remembrance of his death and passion, may be partakers of his most blessed body and blood;

who, in the same night that he was betrayed, took bread; and, when he had given thanks, he brake it; and gave it to his disciples, saying, "Take, eat; this is my body which is given for you: Do this in remembrance of me."

Likewise after supper he took the cup; and when he had given thanks, he gave it to them, saying, "Drink ye all, of this; for this is my blood of the new covenant, which is shed for you and for many for the remission of sins: Do this, as oft as ye shall drink it, in remembrance of me."

Wherefore, O Father, Lord of heaven and earth, we thy humble servants, with all thy holy Church, remembering the precious death of thy beloved Son, his mighty resurrection, and glorious ascension, and looking for his coming again in glory, do make before thee, in this sacrament of the holy bread of eternal life and the cup of everlasting salvation, the memorial which he hath commanded:

*All* **We praise thee, we bless thee, we thank thee, and we pray to thee, Lord our God.**

*Celebrant* And we entirely desire thy fatherly goodness mercifully to accept this our sacrifice of praise and thanksgiving, most humbly beseeching thee to grant, that by the merits and death of thy Son Jesus Christ, and through faith in his blood, we and all thy whole Church may obtain remission of our sins, and all other benefits of his passion; And we pray that by the power of thy Holy Spirit, all we who are

partakers of this holy communion may be fulfilled
with thy grace and heavenly benediction; through
Jesus Christ our Lord, by whom and with whom, in
the unity of the Holy Spirit, all honour and glory be
unto thee, O Father Almighty, world without end.
**Amen.**

*The service continues with the Lord's Prayer on p. 245.*

## Eucharistic Prayer B

| | |
|---|---|
| *Celebrant* | The Lord be with you. |
| *People* | **And with thy spirit.** |

| | |
|---|---|
| *Celebrant* | Lift up your hearts. |
| *People* | **We lift them up unto the Lord.** |

| | |
|---|---|
| *Celebrant* | Let us give thanks unto our Lord God. |
| *People* | **It is meet and right so to do.** |

*Celebrant*     It is very meet, right, and our bounden duty,
that we should at all times, and in all places, give
thanks unto thee, O Lord, holy Father, almighty,
everlasting God, creator and preserver of all things.

*Here follows one of the Proper Prefaces on pp. 252–255.*

*Celebrant*     Therefore with angels and archangels, and with all
the company of heaven, we laud and magnify thy
glorious name; evermore praising thee and saying:

*All*     **Holy, holy, holy, Lord God of hosts,
heaven and earth are full of thy glory.
Glory be to thee, O Lord most high.**

**Blessed is he that cometh in the name of the Lord:
Hosanna in the highest.**

*Celebrant* All glory be to thee, O Lord our God, who didst make us in thine own image; and, of thy tender mercy, didst give thine only Son Jesus Christ to take our nature upon him, and to suffer death upon the cross for our redemption. He made there a full and perfect sacrifice for the whole world; and did institute, and in his holy Gospel command us to continue, a perpetual memory of that his precious death and sacrifice, until his coming again;

who, in the same night that he was betrayed, took bread; and when he had given thanks to thee, he broke it, and gave it to his disciples, saying, "Take, eat, this is my body, which is given for you. Do this in remembrance of me."

Likewise, after supper, he took the cup; and when he had given thanks, he gave it to them, saying, "Drink this, all of you; for this is my blood of the new covenant, which is shed for you, and for many, for the remission of sins. Do this, as oft as ye shall drink it, in remembrance of me."

Wherefore, O Lord and heavenly Father, we thy people do celebrate and make, with these thy holy gifts which we now offer unto thee, the memorial thy Son hath commanded us to make; having in remembrance his blessed passion and precious death, his mighty resurrection and glorious ascension; and looking for his coming again with power and great glory.

And we most humbly beseech thee, O merciful Father, to hear us, and, with thy Word and Holy Spirit, to bless and sanctify these gifts of bread and wine, that they may be unto us the body and blood of thy dearly-beloved Son Jesus Christ.

*All* **We praise thee, we bless thee, we thank thee, and we pray to thee, Lord our God.**

And we earnestly desire thy fatherly goodness to accept this our sacrifice of praise and thanksgiving, whereby we offer and present unto thee, O Lord, ourselves, our souls and bodies. Grant, we beseech thee, that all who partake of this holy communion may worthily receive the most precious body and blood of thy Son Jesus Christ, and be filled with thy grace and heavenly benediction; and also that we and all thy whole Church may be made one body with him, that he may dwell in us, and we in him; through the same Jesus Christ our Lord;

By whom, and with whom, and in whom, in the unity of the Holy Spirit all honour and glory be unto thee, O Father Almighty, world without end. **Amen.**

## The Lord's Prayer

*Celebrant* And now, as our Saviour Christ hath taught us, we are bold to say:

*All* **Our Father, who art in heaven,**
**hallowed be thy name,**
**thy kingdom come,**
**thy will be done,**
**on earth as it is in heaven.**
**Give us this day our daily bread.**
**And forgive us our trespasses,**
**as we forgive those who trespass against us.**
**And lead us not into temptation,**
**but deliver us from evil.**
**For thine is the kingdom,**
**the power, and the glory,**
**for ever and ever. Amen.**

*Silence*

# The Breaking of the Bread

*Then the celebrant breaks the consecrated bread. Then may be said,*

All    **We do not presume to come to this thy table, O merciful Lord, Trusting in our own righteousness, But in thy manifold and great mercies. We are not worthy So much as to gather up the crumbs under thy table. But thou art the same Lord, Whose property is always to have mercy: Grant us therefore, gracious Lord, So to eat the flesh of thy dear Son Jesus Christ, And to drink his blood, That we may evermore dwell in him, And he in us. Amen.**

# The Communion

*The celebrant and people receive the communion in both kinds. At the distribution the minister says to each communicant,*

The body of our Lord Jesus Christ, which was given for thee (preserve thy body and soul unto everlasting life: take and eat this in remembrance that Christ died for thee, and feed on him in thy heart by faith with thanksgiving).

The blood of our Lord Jesus Christ which was shed for thee (preserve thy body and soul unto everlasting life: drink this in remembrance that Christ's blood was shed for thee, and be thankful).

Or    The body of Christ, the bread of heaven.
The blood of Christ, the cup of salvation.

*The communicant responds each time,* **Amen.**

*During the breaking of the bread and the communion, psalms, hymns, and anthems such as the following may be sung or said.*

Celebrant    (Alleluia!) Christ our Passover is sacrificed for us;
People    **Therefore, let us keep the feast. (Alleluia!)**

O Lamb of God, that takest away the sin of the world: have mercy upon us.
O Lamb of God, that takest away the sin of the world: have mercy upon us.
O Lamb of God, that takest away the sin of the world: grant us thy peace.

*At the conclusion of the communion, silence may be kept.*

## Prayer after Communion

*Celebrant*  Let us pray.

*The celebrant may say the Prayer after Communion appointed for the day. At the conclusion of the prayer the congregation says,* **Amen.**

*Then the following doxology may be said.*

*Celebrant*  Glory to God,
*All*  **whose power, working in us,
can do infinitely more
than we can ask or imagine.
Glory to God from generation to generation,
in the Church and in Christ Jesus,
for ever and ever. Amen.**

*If Eucharistic Prayer A has been used, the following prayer may be said instead of the Prayer after Communion and the doxology.*

*All*  **Almighty and everliving God, We most heartily
thank thee That thou dost graciously feed us, in
these holy mysteries, With the spiritual food
of the most precious body and blood Of thy Son
our Saviour Jesus Christ; Assuring us thereby of
thy favour and goodness towards us; And that we
are living members of his mystical Body, Which is
the blessed company of all faithful people; And are
also heirs through hope of thy everlasting
kingdom.**

And here we offer and present unto thee, O Lord, Ourselves, our souls and bodies, To be a reasonable, holy, and living sacrifice unto thee. And although we are unworthy, Yet we beseech thee to accept this our bounden duty and service, Not weighing our merits, but pardoning our offences; Through Jesus Christ our Lord, To whom, with thee and the Holy Spirit, be all honour and glory, World without end. Amen.

*If Eucharistic Prayer B has been used, the following prayer may be said instead of the Prayer after Communion and the doxology.*

*All*      We most heartily thank thee, almighty and everliving God, That thou dost graciously feed us, in these holy mysteries, With the spiritual food of the most precious body and blood Of thy Son our Saviour Jesus Christ; Assuring us thereby of thy favour and goodness towards us; And that we are living members of his mystical Body, Which is the blessed company of all faithful people; And are also heirs through hope of thy everlasting kingdom.

And we humbly beseech thee, O heavenly Father, So to assist us with thy grace, That we may continue in that holy fellowship, And do all such good works as thou hast prepared for us to walk in; Through Jesus Christ our Lord, To whom, with thee and the Holy Spirit, be all honour and glory, World without end. Amen.

*The celebrant may bless the people.*

*Celebrant*      The peace of God, which passeth all understanding, keep your hearts and minds in the knowledge and love of God, and of his Son Jesus Christ our Lord: And the blessing of God almighty, the Father, the Son, and the Holy Spirit be amongst you and remain with you always. **Amen.**

# The Dismissal

*Then the deacon or the celebrant says,*

Go forth in the name of Christ.

*People*     **Thanks be to God.**

*Or the following:*

*Leader*     Go in peace to love and serve the Lord.

*People*     **Thanks be to God.**

*Or the following:*

*Leader*     Go forth into the world,
rejoicing in the power of the Spirit.

*People*     **Thanks be to God.**

*Or the following:*

*Leader*     Let us bless the Lord.

*People*     **Thanks be to God.**

*From Easter Day through the Day of Pentecost,* **Alleluia** *is added to the dismissal and the people's response.*

## The Decalogue

God spake these words and said: I am the Lord thy God who brought thee out of the land of Egypt, out of the house of bondage. Thou shalt have none other gods but me.
**Lord, have mercy upon us,**
**and incline our hearts to keep this law.**

Thou shalt not make to thyself any graven image, nor the likeness of any thing that is in heaven above, or in the earth beneath, or in the water under the earth; thou shalt not bow down to them, nor worship them.
**Lord, have mercy upon us,**
**and incline our hearts to keep this law.**

Thou shalt not take the name of the Lord thy God in vain.
**Lord, have mercy upon us,**
**and incline our hearts to keep this law.**

Remember that thou keep holy the Sabbath day.
**Lord, have mercy upon us,**
**and incline our hearts to keep this law.**

Honour thy father and thy mother.
**Lord, have mercy upon us,**
**and incline our hearts to keep this law.**

Thou shalt do no murder.
**Lord, have mercy upon us,**
**and incline our hearts to keep this law.**

Thou shalt not commit adultery.
**Lord, have mercy upon us,**
**and incline our hearts to keep this law.**

Thou shalt not steal.
**Lord, have mercy upon us,**
**and incline our hearts to keep this law.**

Thou shalt not bear false witness against thy neighbour.
**Lord, have mercy upon us,**
**and incline our hearts to keep this law.**

Thou shalt not covet.
**Lord, have mercy upon us,**
**and write all these thy laws in our hearts,**
**we beseech thee.**

## The Apostles' Creed

I believe in God the Father almighty,
maker of heaven and earth:

**And in Jesus Christ his only Son our Lord,**
**who was conceived by the Holy Ghost,**
**born of the Virgin Mary,**
**suffered under Pontius Pilate,**
**was crucified, dead, and buried;**
**he descended into hell;**
**the third day he rose again from the dead;**
**he ascended into heaven,**
**and sitteth on the right hand of God the Father almighty;**
**from thence he shall come to judge the quick and the dead.**

**I believe in the Holy Ghost;**
**the holy catholic Church;**
**the communion of saints;**
**the forgiveness of sins;**
**the resurrection of the body,**
**and the life everlasting. Amen.**

# Proper Prefaces

### Prefaces for the Lord's Day

*To be used on Sundays for which no other provision is made, but not on the succeeding weekdays.*

**1**

For thou art the fountain of light and life for all thy creation: thou hast made us in thine own image, and dost raise us to new life in Jesus Christ our Saviour. Therefore with angels . . . etc.

**2**

Through Jesus Christ our Lord; who on this first day of the week overcame death and the grave, and by his glorious resurrection opened to us the way of everlasting life. Therefore with angels . . . etc.

**3**

Who by water and the Holy Spirit hast made us a holy people in Jesus Christ our Lord; thou dost renew that mystery in bread and wine and nourish us, to show forth thy glory in all the world. Therefore with angels . . . etc.

*For weekdays when no other provision is made.*

Who hast gathered us together in this eucharistic feast that we may be renewed in love, joy, and peace. Therefore with angels . . . etc.

### Advent

Through Jesus Christ our Lord, who in the fullness of time came among us in our flesh and opened to us the way of salvation. Now we watch for the day when he will come again in power and great triumph to judge this world; that we, without shame or fear, may rejoice to behold his appearing. Therefore with angels . . . etc.

### Christmas

Because thou didst give Jesus Christ thine only Son to be born as at this time for us; who, by the operation of the Holy Spirit, was made very man of the substance of the Virgin Mary his mother; and that without spot of sin, to make us clean from all sin. Therefore with angels . . . etc.

### Incarnation

Because in the mystery of the Word made flesh, thou hast caused a new light to shine in our hearts, to give the knowledge of thy glory, in the face of thy Son Jesus Christ our Lord. Therefore with angels . . . etc.

### Epiphany

Through Jesus Christ our Lord, who, in substance of our mortal flesh, manifested forth his glory, that he might bring us out of darkness into his own marvellous light. Therefore with angels . . . etc.

### Lent

Who hast bidden us thy faithful people to cleanse our hearts and to prepare with joy for the paschal feast; that reborn through the waters of baptism, and renewed in the eucharistic mystery, we may be more fervent in prayer and more generous in works of love. Therefore with angels . . . etc.

### Holy Week

For the redemption of the world by the death and passion of our Saviour Christ, both God and Man; who did humble himself, even to the death upon the Cross for us sinners, who lay in darkness and the shadow of death; that he might make us the children of God, and exalt us to everlasting life. Therefore with angels . . . etc.

### Easter

But chiefly are we bound to praise thee for the glorious resurrection of thy Son Jesus Christ our Lord; for he is the very Paschal Lamb, which was offered for us, and hath taken away the sin of the world; who by his death hath destroyed death, and by his rising to life again hath restored to us everlasting life. Therefore with angels . . . etc.

### Ascension

Through thy most dearly beloved Son Jesus Christ our Lord; who after his most glorious resurrection manifestly appeared to all his apostles, and in their sight ascended up into heaven to prepare a place for us; that where he is, thither we might also ascend, and reign with him in glory. Therefore with angels . . . etc.

### Pentecost

Through Jesus Christ our Lord, according to whose most true promise thou dost pour forth thy Spirit upon us, filling us with gifts and leading us into all truth: who dost give us power to proclaim the gospel to all nations and to serve thee as a royal priesthood. Therefore with angels . . . etc.

### Trinity Sunday

For with thy co-eternal Son and Holy Spirit, thou art one God, one Lord, in trinity of persons and in unity of substance; and we celebrate the one and equal glory of thee, O Father, and of the Son, and of the Holy Spirit. Therefore with angels . . . etc.

### Last Sunday after Pentecost: The Reign of Christ

Through Jesus Christ our Lord; whom thou didst exalt as Lord of all creation, that he might present unto thee an eternal and universal kingdom: a kingdom of holiness and grace, a kingdom of justice, love and peace: that at the name of Jesus every knee should bow. Therefore with angels . . . etc.

### All Saints and other Saints Days

Who in the multitude of thy saints hast compassed us about with so great a cloud of witnesses, that we, rejoicing in their fellowship, may run with patience the race that is set before us, and together with them may receive the crown of glory that fadeth not away. Therefore with angels . . . etc.

### Marriage

Because thou dost unite husband and wife in a solemn covenant of love, as a witness of the bond and covenant between Christ and his Church. Therefore with angels . . . etc.

### Commemoration of the Dead

Through Jesus Christ our Lord; who rose victorious from the dead, and doth comfort us with the hope of resurrection and the promise of eternal life. Therefore with angels . . . etc.

# Communion under Special Circumstances

This rite is intended not only for use with the sick (cf. The Ministry to the Sick p. 553), but also for those who because of work schedules or physical or other types of limitations cannot be present at a public celebration of the eucharist.

Justin Martyr, in one of the earliest existing accounts of the Sunday eucharist, tells us that deacons left after the celebration to bring communion to the sick, to the imprisoned, and to those who for any reason were unable to be present at the community eucharist. Cyprian, a century later, tells us it was the custom for each member of the community to take home some of the consecrated bread so that each day could begin with communion. Regular reception of the eucharist was a primary sign of the communicant's desire to remain within the Body.

When a member of the community cannot be present at the community eucharist but wishes to receive communion, it is desirable that members of the community bring the consecrated elements to that person immediately upon completion of the Sunday celebration. The continuity between communion and community celebration is thus made clear. When this is not possible communion could either be brought from a weekday celebration or from the reserved sacrament.

If a person is unable to attend a public celebration of the eucharist for an extended period of time, it is appropriate that the eucharist be celebrated with them, members of their family, the parish community, and friends, if possible. The sign of the eucharist as an extension of the parish celebration, rather than as a private event, thus becomes clearer. In these cases it would be appropriate to involve others in the readings and prayers, using the proper of the day or other appropriate material.

# Communion under Special Circumstances

**For those not present at the celebration**

*This service may be conducted by a priest, or by a deacon or lay person authorized by the diocesan bishop.*

*This form is intended for use with those who for reasonable cause cannot be present at a public celebration of the eucharist.*

*When persons are unable to be present for extended periods, it is desirable that the priest arrange to celebrate the eucharist with them from time to time on a regular basis, using the Proper of the Day. At other times, or when desired, such persons may receive communion brought to them from a celebration of the eucharist, or from the reserved sacrament, using the following form. It is desirable that fellow parishioners, relatives, and friends be present, when possible, to communicate with them.*

*The minister conducting the service greets those present in these or similar words.*

**Brothers and sisters** in Christ,
God calls us to faithful service
by the proclamation of the word,
and sustains us with the sacrament
of the body and blood of Christ.
Hear now God's word,
and receive this holy food from the Lord's table.

*A passage of scripture appropriate to the day or occasion, or one of the following passages is read.*

God so loved the world that he gave his only Son, that whoever believes in him should not perish, but have eternal life.
*John 3.16*

Jesus said, "I am the bread of life; whoever comes to me shall not hunger, and whoever believes in me shall never thirst."
*John 6.35*

Jesus said, "I am the living bread which came down from heaven; if anyone eats of this bread, he will live for ever; and the bread which I shall give for the life of the world is my flesh. For my flesh is food indeed, and my blood is drink indeed. Whoever eats my flesh and drinks my blood abides in me, and I in him." *John 6.51, 55–56*

Jesus said, "Abide in me, as I in you. As the branch cannot bear fruit by itself, unless it abides in the vine, neither can you, unless you abide in me. I am the vine, you are the branches. By this my Father is glorified, that you bear much fruit, and so prove to be my disciples. As the Father has loved me, so have I loved you; abide in my love." *John 15.4–5a, 8–9*

*After the reading, the minister may comment on it briefly. Suitable prayers may be offered.*

*A confession of sin may follow. The following or some other form is used.*

| | |
|---|---|
| *Minister* | Most merciful God, |
| *All* | **we confess that we have sinned against you** |
| | **in thought, word, and deed,** |
| | **by what we have done,** |
| | **and by what we have left undone.** |
| | **We have not loved you with our whole heart;** |
| | **we have not loved our neighbours as ourselves.** |
| | **We are truly sorry and we humbly repent.** |
| | **For the sake of your Son Jesus Christ,** |
| | **have mercy on us and forgive us,** |
| | **that we may delight in your will,** |
| | **and walk in your ways,** |
| | **to the glory of your name. Amen.** |

*A priest says,*

> Almighty God have mercy upon you,
> pardon and deliver you from all your sins,
> confirm and strengthen you in all goodness,
> and keep you in eternal life;
> through Jesus Christ our Lord.

| | |
|---|---|
| *People* | **Amen.** |

*A deacon or lay person using the preceeding form substitutes* us *for* you *and* our *for* your.

*The Peace may then be exchanged. The Lord's Prayer is said.*

| | |
|---|---|
| *Minister* | As our Saviour taught us, let us pray, |
| *All* | **Our Father in heaven,** |
| | **hallowed be your name,** |
| | **your kingdom come,** |
| | **your will be done,** |
| | **on earth as in heaven.** |
| | **Give us today our daily bread.** |
| | **Forgive us our sins** |
| | **as we forgive those who sin against us.** |
| | **Save us from the time of trial,** |
| | **and deliver us from evil.** |
| | **For the kingdom, the power,** |
| | **and the glory are yours,** |
| | **now and for ever. Amen.** |

*Or*

| | |
|---|---|
| *Minister* | And now, as our Saviour Christ has taught us, |
| | we are bold to say, |
| *All* | **Our Father, who art in heaven,** |
| | **hallowed be thy name,** |
| | **thy kingdom come,** |
| | **thy will be done,** |
| | **on earth as it is in heaven.** |
| | **Give us this day our daily bread.** |
| | **And forgive us our trespasses,** |
| | **as we forgive those who trespass against us.** |
| | **And lead us not into temptation,** |
| | **but deliver us from evil.** |
| | **For thine is the kingdom,** |
| | **the power, and the glory,** |
| | **for ever and ever. Amen.** |

*The minister may say the following invitation.*

> The gifts of God for the People of God.

*People* **Thanks be to God.**

*The sacrament is given with the following words.*

> The body of Christ (given for you).
> The blood of Christ (shed for you).

*Or*   The body of Christ, the bread of heaven.
       The blood of Christ, the cup of salvation.

*The communicant responds each time,* **Amen.**

*The following doxology may be said.*

*Minister*   Glory to God,
*People*   **whose power, working in us,
           can do infinitely more
           than we can ask or imagine.
           Glory to God from generation to generation,
           in the Church and in Christ Jesus,
           for ever and ever. Amen.**

*A priest may bless those present. The service concludes with a dismissal.*

*Minister*   Let us bless the Lord.
*People*   **Thanks be to God.**

# The Proper of the
# Church Year

# The Proper of the Church Year

The systematic reading of Holy Scripture in accordance with a fixed calendar is very ancient. Some biblical scholars believe they can discern in the pattern of parts of the New Testament the structure of an older Jewish lectionary.

Different lectionaries, supplying readings for both eucharistic celebrations and the daily offices, evolved in the varied liturgical traditions of Christianity. Some churches had several readings at the eucharist, including one or more from the Old Testament; others chose to have two New Testament readings and to confine the Old Testament to the offices. Some lectionaries attempted to foster continuous reading of the Bible; others presented the biblical material thematically.

The churches of the Anglican communion inherited the Western (Roman) scheme of eucharistic readings: Epistle and Gospel lections for each Sunday and festival. While these lections show signs of having begun as a system of continuous reading, it is apparent that this was overlaid in the course of time by a more arbitrary approach to selection, based not only on the themes of the day or season, but even on the themes of nearby festivals of local import. There is, in addition, speculation that some of the Epistles and Gospels in the post-Trinity season were, at some ancient date, dislocated from their original order and consequently from any hope of thematic unity with each other or the Collect of the Day. It is difficult not to conclude that this scheme of readings, with its scanty use of the Old Testament and unrepresentative approach to the New Testament, provided a limited base for education in the Bible.

Fortunately for Anglicans, Archbishop Cranmer addressed himself vigorously to a reform of the lectionary used at the daily offices of Morning and Evening Prayer. He devised a scheme of continuous reading of the Bible with little interruption by festivals, consisting of four lessons a day, each of them usually a chapter in length, two from the Old Testament, and one each from the Gospels and the Epistles. Since the offices became the most frequently attended services on Sundays for a long period in Anglican history, the shortcomings of the eucharistic readings were mitigated. Cranmer's lectionary, with few revisions, remained in force in England until 1869. Since that date a large number of revisions has appeared in the various Anglican churches.

Lectionary revision took a new direction in the middle of the twentieth century with the realization that ecumenical agreement on common patterns would not only foster Christian unity but also would add to the richness of Christian experience, both through cooperation itself and through the use of common commentaries and other aids. The lectionary adopted by the Roman Catholic Church after the Second Vatican Council became the basis of this ecumenical cooperation. A process of experimentation, criticism, and revision has produced a situation in which a number of denominations now use lectionaries which are similar, but not identical. Agreement will eventually be reached only by continued commitment to ongoing use and revision, a process managed and facilitated by the ecumenical Consultation on Common Texts.

In 1980 the General Synod of the Anglican Church of Canada adopted the ecumenical lectionary at the point in the process of revision which had been reached at that time. Since then the Consultation on Common Texts has issued an amended edition for experimental use beginning in 1983, with a view to a final revision around the end of the decade (*Common Lectionary*, The Church Hymnal Corporation, New York). This experimental version constitutes the system of readings which follows.

The revision process which began in the mid-twentieth century was accompanied by a major shift in the conception of the role of lectionaries. The choice of lectionary was once dictated by the type of liturgical celebration: one lectionary was restricted to the eucharist, another to the offices. Now, in a number of denominations, a lectionary is intended to provide the readings for the principal acts of worship without reference to the particular form of worship involved. Thus in Anglican congregations where both Morning Prayer and the Holy Eucharist are celebrated as principal acts of worship on different Sundays each month, the alternation of two quite unrelated lectionaries is now to be replaced by a single coherent system of readings intended to engage the People of God with the deepest roots of their tradition.

Several other liturgical elements proper to the Sundays and holy days of the Church Year have been interpolated into the Lectionary:

Sentences, which may be recited at the beginning of Morning and Evening Prayer, or sung with Alleluia before the Gospel;

Collects, which are recited at the end of the Gathering of the Community in the eucharist, and may be recited at the end of the Intercessions in Morning and Evening Prayer;

Prayers over the Gifts, which may be recited at the conclusion of the Preparation of the Gifts in the eucharist;

a designation of the Preface proper to the day;

Prayers after Communion, which may be recited after the people have received communion in the eucharist.

This lectionary is intended to provide the primary structure for the proclamation of the word in the Anglican Church of Canada. General Synod, 1980, in approving an earlier edition of this lectionary, requested that "every diocese and parish, including those which in other respects substantially follow the Book of Common Prayer, give thoughtful consideration to the possibility of using this lectionary as a symbol and expression of unity in our Church and with many other Christians."

In addition to the Lectionary, three other guides to the liturgical reading of Holy Scripture are provided:

The Daily Office Lectionary, which may be used at Morning and Evening Prayer on weekdays (and on Sundays by those who have attended or will attend a celebration of the eucharist at which lections from the Lectionary are used), and at celebrations of the eucharist on weekdays for which no readings are provided in the Lectionary;

a weekday cycle of readings suitable for use at the offices or the eucharist on days for which no readings are provided in the Lectionary;

a short list of psalms and readings for use as required, e.g., at offices on days when the Daily Office Lectionary has been used at the eucharist, in time of haste, etc.

These resources must be used with a creative imagination sensitive to the needs of the congregation or individual involved. Clearly, lectionaries may fill several different functions, and sometimes more than one function for the same people. There remains a tension between thematic presentations of biblical material and continuous reading; modern lectionaries tend to hold this tension in balance.

Modern lectionaries intended for use at the daily offices provide shorter and fewer readings than their predecessors, chiefly because of a growing conviction among liturgists that the purpose of the readings is not only exposure to scripture but also opportunity for reflection, and three pericopes each day are all most active people are likely to be able to deal with. On the other hand, modern lectionaries intended for use at the eucharist provide more readings than Western Christians have been familiar with, restoring the Old Testament to its proper place in regular use and spreading a much larger body of biblical material over a three-year period.

# Concerning the Lectionary for Sundays and Holy Days

*The Lectionary for Sundays and holy days is arranged in a three-year cycle. Year A always begins on the First Sunday of Advent in those years evenly divisible by three (1986, 1989, etc.).*

*Readings are cited according to the versification of the Revised Standard Version translation. Versifications vary to some extent among translations and should be checked against the RSV.*

*Since all the readings are excerpted portions, the literal text may have to be adapted in order to preserve sense and maintain the continuity of the text. At the beginning of a reading, nouns should be substituted for pronouns ("Jesus said" for "he said"), phrases may be used instead of subordinate conjunctions ("At that time" for "then" or "when"), and co-ordinate conjunctions may be omitted ("for," "and," "but"). Some phrases in the text may have to be omitted, and others included, in order to begin or link certain passages sensibly. The proper sentence may also be adapted by the addition of an introduction as appropriate, eg., "Jesus said . . ."*

*Any reading may be lengthened at discretion, e.g., to set a passage in context or because a following passage will be displaced by a festival on the next Sunday. Some suggested lengthenings are shown in parentheses.*

*The Lectionary designates a psalm for every Sunday and holy day. A refrain is provided for responsorial recitation of the psalm, e.g., when the text of the psalm is said or sung by one voice or group of voices, and the congregation responds with the refrain at suitable intervals. Other suitable refrains may be chosen for good reason. In addition to the refrains suggested in connection with each psalm, eight common refrains and an alternative verse of the psalm are also indicated. The common refrains are*

CR 1  Give thanks to the Lord for he is good.
CR 2  We thank you, Lord, for your works are wonderful.
CR 3  Sing to the Lord a new song.
CR 4  The Lord is close to all who call him.
CR 5  Incline your ear, O Lord, and save us.
CR 6  The Lord is kind and merciful.
CR 7  Behold I come to do your will, O God.
CR 8  Remember, O Lord, your faithfulness and love.

*Those using refrains will have to select suitable stanza groupings.*

*Psalms may be shortened as appropriate to the liturgical context. When only a portion of a psalm is designated, more or all of the psalm may be recited. For traditional reasons, a longer psalm may be desired at Morning Prayer and Evening Prayer, and a shorter psalm at the eucharist.*

*The Lectionary suggests common readings for saints' days, from which appropriate selections may be made.*

*Years are designated by letter. When no letters appear, the material is intended for all three years.*

# Sundays and Holy Days

## First Sunday of Advent

### Sentence

Look up and raise your heads, because your redemption is
drawing near.   *Luke 21.28*

### Collect

Almighty God,
give us grace to cast away the works of darkness
and put on the armour of light,
now in the time of this mortal life
in which your Son Jesus Christ
came to us in great humility,
that on the last day,
when he shall come again in his glorious majesty
to judge both the living and the dead,
we may rise to the life immortal;
through him who lives and reigns
with you and the Holy Spirit,
one God, now and for ever.

### Readings

A     Isaiah 2.1–5     Psalm 122
      *Refrain*    I was glad when they said to me, "Let us go to the house of the
      Lord."    *Or v.7 or CR 1*
      Romans 13.11–14     Matthew 24.36–44

B     Isaiah 63.16—64.8     Psalm 80.1–7
      *Refrain*    Show the light of your countenance, and we shall be saved.
      *Or v.3 or CR 8*
      1 Corinthians 1.3–9     Mark 13.32–37

C     Jeremiah 33.14–16     Psalm 25.1–9
      *Refrain*    To you, O Lord, I lift up my soul.    *Or v.1 or CR 5*
      1 Thessalonians 3.9–13     Luke 21.25–36

**Prayer over the Gifts**

God of love and power,
your word stirs within us
the expectation of the coming of your Son.
Accept all we offer you this day,
and sustain us with your promise of eternal life.
We ask this in the name of Jesus Christ our Lord.

*Preface of Advent*

**Prayer after Communion**

God for whom we wait,
you have fed us with the bread of eternal life.
Keep us ever watchful,
that we may be ready to stand before the Son of man.
We ask this in the name of Christ the Lord.

# Second Sunday of Advent

**Sentence**

Prepare the way of the Lord, make his paths straight.
All flesh shall see the salvation of God.  *Luke 3.4, 6*

**Collect**

Almighty God,
who sent your servant John the Baptist
to prepare your people to welcome the Messiah,
inspire us, the ministers and stewards of your truth,
to turn our disobedient hearts to you,
that when the Christ shall come again to be our judge,
we may stand with confidence before his glory;
who is alive and reigns with you and the Holy Spirit,
one God, now and for ever.

**Readings**

A    Isaiah 11.1–10    Psalm 72.1–8
     *Refrain*  In his time shall peace and justice flourish.
     *Or v.7 or CR 3*
     Romans 15.4–13    Matthew 3.1–12

B     Isaiah 40.1–11     Psalm 85.8–13
*Refrain*   Show us your mercy, O Lord.   *Or v.7 or CR 4*
2 Peter 3.8–15a     Mark 1.1–8

C     Malachi 3.1–4 *or* Baruch 5.1–9     Psalm 126
*Refrain*   The Lord has done great things for us.   *Or v.4 or CR 1*
Philippians 1.3–11     Luke 3.1–6

**Prayer over the Gifts**

God our strength,
we are nothing without you.
Receive all we offer you this day
as you sustain us with your mercy;
in the name of Jesus Christ our Lord.

*Preface of Advent*

**Prayer after Communion**

Faithful God,
we thank you for feeding us with this heavenly banquet.
Help us always to hear the prophet's call
to turn our hearts to you;
in the name of Jesus Christ the Lord.

# Third Sunday of Advent

**Sentence**

The Spirit of the Lord God is upon me, because the Lord has
anointed me to bring good tidings to the afflicted.   *Isaiah 61.1*

**Collect**

God of power and mercy,
you call us once again
to celebrate the coming of your Son.
Remove those things which hinder love of you,
that when he comes,
he may find us waiting in awe and wonder
for him who lives and reigns with you and the Holy Spirit,
one God, now and for ever.

### Readings

A    Isaiah 35.1–10    Psalm 146.4–9
    *Refrain*    Come, O Lord, and save us.   *Or v.9 or* Alleluia!
    James 5.7–10    Matthew 11.2–11

B    Isaiah 61.1–4, 8–11    Canticle 18, The Song of Mary
    *Refrain*    My spirit rejoices in God my Saviour.   *Or v.1 or CR 1*
    1 Thessalonians 5.16–24    John 1.6–8, 19–28

C    Zephaniah 3.14–20    Canticle 3, Song of Thanksgiving
    *Refrain*    Ring out your joy, for the Holy One of Israel is in your midst.
    *Or v.7 or CR 1*
    Philippians 4.4–9    Luke 3.7–18

### Prayer over the Gifts

God of hope,
renew in us the joy of your salvation
and make us a living sacrifice to you,
for the sake of Jesus Christ our Lord.

*Preface of Advent*

### Prayer after Communion

Merciful God,
may this eucharist free us from our sins,
fill us with unending joy,
and prepare us for the birthday of our Saviour.
We ask this in the name of Jesus Christ,
who is Lord now and for ever.

# Fourth Sunday of Advent

### Sentence

A    A virgin shall conceive and bear a son, and his name shall
    be called Emmanuel: God with us.   *Matthew 1.23*

BC    I am the servant of the Lord; let it be to me according to
    his word.   *Luke 1.38*

## Collect

Heavenly Father,
who chose the Virgin Mary, full of grace,
to be the mother of our Lord and Saviour,
now fill us with your grace,
that we in all things may embrace your will
and with her rejoice in your salvation;
through Jesus Christ our Lord,
who lives and reigns with you and the Holy Spirit,
one God, now and for ever.

## Readings

A    Isaiah 7.10–16    Psalm 24
     *Refrain*  Let the King of glory enter.   *Or v.7 or CR 4*
     Romans 1.1–7    Matthew 1.18–25

B    2 Samuel 7.8–16    Psalm 89.1–4, 19–24
     *Refrain*  I will keep my love for him for ever.   *Or v.28 or CR 8*
     Romans 16.25–27    Luke 1.26–38

C    Micah 5.2–4    Psalm 80.1–7
     *Refrain*  Show the light of your countenance, and we shall be saved.
     *Or v.3 or CR 8*
     Hebrews 10.5–10    Luke 1.39–55

## Prayer over the Gifts

Gracious God,
by the power of the Spirit
who sanctified the mother of your Son,
make holy all we offer you this day.
We ask this in the name of Jesus Christ the Lord.

*Preface of Advent*

## Prayer after Communion

Faithful God,
in this sacrament we receive the promise of salvation.
May we, like the Virgin Mary,
be obedient to your will.
We ask this in the name of Jesus Christ the Lord.

# Christmas—at Midnight

I bring you good news of a great joy which will come to all the people; for to you is born this day a Saviour, Christ the Lord.
*Luke 2.10–11*

**Collect**

Eternal God,
this holy night is radiant
with the brilliance of your one true light.
As we have known
the revelation of that light on earth,
bring us to see the splendour of your heavenly glory;
through Jesus Christ our Lord,
who is alive and reigns with you and the Holy Spirit,
one God, now and for ever.

**Readings**

> Isaiah 9.2–7     Psalm 96
> *Refrain*   All the ends of the earth have seen the salvation of our God.
> *Or v.2 or CR 3*
> Titus 2.11–14     Luke 2.1–20

*Optional readings*

> Isaiah 62.6–7, 10–12     Psalm 97
> *Refrain*   As above   *Or v.11 or CR 3*
> Titus 3.4–7     Luke 2.8–20

*Or*   Isaiah 52.7–10     Psalm 98
> *Refrain*   As above   *Or v.5 or CR 3*
> Hebrews 1.1–12     John 1.1–14

**Prayer over the Gifts**

Source of light and gladness,
accept all we offer on this joyful feast.
May we grow up in him who unites our lives to yours;
for he is Lord now and for ever.

**Prayer after Communion**

Father of all,
tonight you have united earth and heaven
in sending your Son to take our human nature.
May we who have tasted heavenly things
share in the life of his eternal kingdom.
We ask this in the name of Jesus Christ our Lord.


# Christmas—in the Early Morning

**Sentence**

I bring you good news of a great joy which will come to all the
people; for to you is born this day a Saviour, Christ the Lord.
*Luke 2.10–11*

**Collect**

O God our Father,
whose Word has come among us
in the Holy Child of Bethlehem,
may the light of faith
illumine our hearts
and shine in our words and deeds;
through him who is Christ our Lord,
who lives and reigns with you and the Holy Spirit,
one God, now and for ever.

**Readings**

*As above*

**Prayer over the Gifts**

Generous Creator,
in faith and joy
we celebrate the birth of your Son.
Increase our understanding and our love
of the riches you have revealed in him,
who is Lord now and for ever.

**Prayer after Communion**

Source of truth and joy,
may we who have received the gift of divine life
always follow the way of your Son.
This we ask in the name of Jesus Christ the Lord.

# Christmas—during the Day

**Sentence**

I bring you good news of a great joy which will come to all the
people; for to you is born this day a Saviour, Christ the Lord.
*Luke 2.10–11*

**Collect**

Almighty God,
you wonderfully created
and yet more wonderfully restored our human nature.
May we share the divine life of your Son Jesus Christ,
who humbled himself to share our humanity,
and now lives and reigns with you and the Holy Spirit,
one God, now and for ever.

**Readings**

*As above*

**Prayer over the Gifts**

God of peace,
your Son Jesus Christ has reconciled us to you.
May all we offer you today
renew us as members of your household.
We ask this in his name.

*Preface of Christmas*

**Prayer after Communion**

Father of all,
the child born for us is the Saviour of the world.
May he who made us your children
welcome us into your kingdom,
where he is alive and reigns with you now and for ever.

# First Sunday after Christmas

*This Sunday takes precedence over any of the three holy days which follow
Christmas Day. When there is a conflict the holy day is transferred to 29
December or to the alternative day provided for its observance in the
Calendar. If there is only one Sunday between Christmas and the Epiphany,
the propers of the Epiphany may be used instead.*

### Sentence

Let the peace of Christ rule in your hearts; let the word of
Christ dwell in you richly.   *Colossians 3.15, 16*

### Collect

Almighty God,
you have shed upon us the new light
of your incarnate Word.
May this light, enkindled in our hearts,
shine forth in our lives;
through Jesus Christ our Lord,
who lives and reigns with you,
in the unity of the Holy Spirit,
one God, now and for ever.

### Readings

A    Isaiah 63.7–9    Psalm 111
       *Refrain*   God sent redemption to his people.   *Or v.9 or* Alleluia!
       Hebrews 2.10–18      Matthew 2.13–15, 19–23

B    Isaiah 61.10—62.3    Psalm 111
       *Refrain*   As Year A
       Galatians 4.4–7      Luke 2.22–40

C     1 Samuel 2.18–20, 26 *or* Sirach 3.3–7, 14–17     Psalm 111
       *Refrain*   As Year A
       Colossians 3.12–17     Luke 2.41–52

**Prayer over the Gifts**

God of light,
in the birth of your Son we see your glory.
May we who share in this mystery
grow daily in your love.
This we ask in the name of Jesus Christ the Lord.

*Preface of Christmas*

**Prayer after Communion**

Source of truth and joy,
may we who have received the gift of divine life
always follow the way of your Son.
This we ask in the name of Jesus Christ the Lord.

# The Naming of Jesus   *1 January*

*When 1 January is a Sunday these propers will be used instead of those for the
First Sunday after Christmas, or those of the Epiphany may be used.*

**Sentence**

God spoke of old by the prophets; but in these last days he has
spoken to us by a Son.     *Hebrews 1.1–2*

**Collect**

Eternal Father,
we give thanks for your incarnate Son,
whose name is our salvation.
Plant in every heart, we pray,
the love of him who is the Saviour of the world,
our Lord Jesus Christ;
who lives and reigns with you and the Holy Spirit,
one God, in glory everlasting.

### Readings

> Numbers 6.22–27　　Psalm 67
> *Refrain*　May God give us his blessing.　*Or v.1 or CR 4*
> Galatians 4.4–7 *or* Philippians 2.9–13　　Luke 2.15–21

### Prayer over the Gifts

Gracious God,
the name of Jesus brings salvation to the world.
In all we offer you this day,
may we honour him,
who is alive and reigns with you and the Holy Spirit,
one God, now and for ever.

*Preface of Christmas*

### Prayer after Communion

Father,
you have fed us heavenly food
in the sacrament of the body and blood of Christ.
Grant that we, sharing in this mystery,
may turn always to that name which is above all others,
Jesus Christ our Lord.

## Second Sunday of Christmas

*The readings and prayers for the Epiphany (6 January) may be read on the Sunday before the Epiphany instead of the readings and prayers assigned for that day.*

### Sentence

Glory to Christ who is preached among the nations, and
believed on in the world.　*See 1 Timothy 3.16*

### Collect

God of power and life,
the glory of all who believe in you,
fill the world with your splendour
and show the nations the light of your truth;

through Jesus Christ your Son our Lord,
who is alive and reigns with you and the Holy Spirit,
one God, now and for ever.

### Readings

> Jeremiah 31.7–14 *or* Sirach 24.1–4, 12–16    Psalm 147.13–21
> *Refrain*   Praise God, O Zion.   *Or v.13 or* Alleluia!
> Ephesians 1.3–6, 15–18    John 1.1–18

### Prayer over the Gifts

Source of love and life,
receive all we offer you this day,
and through the coming of your Son,
help us to see in others
him who is alive and reigns with you and the Holy Spirit,
one God, now and for ever.

*Preface of Christmas*

### Prayer after Communion

Light eternal,
you have nourished us in the mystery
of the body and blood of your Son.
By your grace keep us ever faithful to your word,
in the name of Jesus Christ our Lord.

# The Epiphany   *6 January*

*When 6 January is a Sunday these propers will be used instead of those for the Second Sunday after Christmas.*

### Sentence

We have seen his star in the East, and have come to worship him.    *Matthew 2.2*

## Collect

Eternal God,
who by a star
led wise men to the worship of your Son.
Guide by your light the nations of the earth,
that the whole world may know your glory;
through Jesus Christ our Lord,
who lives and reigns with you and the Holy Spirit,
one God, now and for ever.

## Readings

Isaiah 60.1–6      Psalm 72.1–14
*Refrain*   All nations shall serve him.   *Or v.11 or CR 1*
Ephesians 3.1–12      Matthew 2.1–12

## Prayer over the Gifts

Gracious God,
accept the offering of your Church,
the hearts of your people
joined in praise and thanksgiving,
in the name of Jesus Christ the Lord.

*Preface of the Epiphany*

## Prayer after Communion

God of all the nations of the earth,
guide us with your light.
Help us to recognize Christ as he comes to us
in this eucharist and in our neighbours.
May we welcome him with love,
for he is Lord now and for ever.

*Propers for the Sundays after the Epiphany may be found with other ferial
propers, in numerical order, beginning on p. 348.*

# Ash Wednesday

*On this day the liturgy begins as follows:*

| | |
|---|---|
| *Celebrant* | The Lord be with you. |
| *People* | **And also with you.** |

| | |
|---|---|
| *Celebrant* | Let us pray. |

*The community prays in silence; then follows the Collect of the Day.*

Almighty and everlasting God,
you despise nothing you have made
and forgive the sins of all who are penitent.
Create and make in us new and contrite hearts,
that we, worthily lamenting our sins
and acknowledging our brokenness,
may obtain of you, the God of all mercy,
perfect remission and forgiveness;
through Jesus Christ our Lord,
who lives and reigns with you and the Holy Spirit,
one God, for ever and ever.

### Readings

Joel 2.1–2, 12–17a        Psalm 103.8–18
*Refrain*    The Lord remembers that we are but dust.    *Or CR 8*
2 Corinthians 5.20b—6.2(3–10)        Matthew 6.1–6, 16–21

*A sermon may be preached. After the sermon all stand, and the celebrant or minister addresses the congregation, saying,*

Dear friends in Christ,
every year at the time of the Christian Passover
we celebrate our redemption
through the death and resurrection
of our Lord Jesus Christ.
Lent is a time to prepare for this celebration
and to renew our life in the paschal mystery.
We begin this holy season
by remembering our need for repentance,
and for the mercy and forgiveness
proclaimed in the Gospel of Jesus Christ.

*If ashes are used, the following may be said.*

We begin our journey to Easter with the sign of ashes,
an ancient sign,
speaking of the frailty and uncertainty of human life,
and marking the penitence of the community as a whole.

*The celebrant continues,*

I invite you therefore, in the name of the Lord,
to observe a holy Lent
by self-examination, penitence, prayer,
fasting, and almsgiving,
and by reading and meditating on the word of God.
Let us kneel before our Creator and Redeemer.

*Silence is then kept for reflection.*

*Psalm 51.1–18 is sung or said.*

*Refrain*   **Create in me a clean heart, O God.**

Have mercy on me, O God, according to your
                    loving kindness; *
  in your great compassion blot out my offences.
Wash me through and through from my wickedness *
  and cleanse me from my sin.

For I know my transgressions,*
  and my sin is ever before me.
Against you only have I sinned *
  and done what is evil in your sight.

And so you are justified when you speak *
  and upright in your judgement.
Indeed, I have been wicked from my birth,*
  a sinner from my mother's womb.

For behold, you look for truth deep within me,*
  and will make me understand wisdom secretly.
Purge me from my sin, and I shall be pure; *
  wash me, and I shall be clean indeed.

Make me hear of joy and gladness,*
   that the body you have broken may rejoice.
Hide your face from my sins *
   and blot out all my iniquities.

Create in me a clean heart, O God,*
   and renew a right spirit within me.
Cast me not away from your presence *
   and take not your Holy Spirit from me.

Give me the joy of your saving help again *
   and sustain me with your bountiful Spirit.
I shall teach your ways to the wicked,*
   and sinners shall return to you.

Deliver me from death, O God,*
   and my tongue shall sing of your righteousness,
   O God of my salvation.
Open my lips, O Lord,*
   and my mouth shall proclaim your praise.

Had you desired it, I would have offered sacrifice,*
   but you take no delight in burnt-offerings.
The sacrifice of God is a troubled spirit; *
   a broken and contrite heart, O God, you will not despise.

## Litany of Penitence

*The celebrant and people say together,*

**Most holy and merciful Father,
we confess to you, to one another,
and to the whole communion of saints
in heaven and on earth,
that we have sinned by our own fault
in thought, word, and deed;
by what we have done,
and by what we have left undone.**

We have not loved you with our whole heart, and mind, and strength. We have not loved our neighbours as ourselves. We have not forgiven others, as we have been forgiven.
**Have mercy on us, Lord.**

We have been deaf to your call to serve as Christ served us. We have not been true to the mind of Christ. We have grieved your Holy Spirit.
**Have mercy on us, Lord.**

We confess to you, Lord, all our past unfaithfulness: the pride, hypocrisy, and impatience of our lives,
**We confess to you, Lord.**

Our self-indulgent appetites and ways, and our exploitation of other people,
**We confess to you, Lord.**

Our anger at our own frustration, and our envy of those more fortunate than ourselves,
**We confess to you, Lord.**

Our intemperate love of worldly goods and comforts, and our dishonesty in daily life and work,
**We confess to you, Lord.**

Our negligence in prayer and worship, and our failure to commend the faith that is in us,
**We confess to you, Lord.**

Accept our repentance, Lord, for the wrongs we have done: for our blindness to human need and suffering, and our indifference to injustice and cruelty,
**Accept our repentance, Lord.**

For all false judgements, for uncharitable thoughts toward our neighbours  and for our prejudice and contempt toward those who differ trom us,
**Accept our repentance, Lord.**

For our waste and pollution of your creation, and our lack of
concern for those who come after us,
**Accept our repentance, Lord.**

Restore us, good Lord, and let your anger depart from us;
**Hear us, Lord, for your mercy is great.**

*If ashes are to be imposed, the celebrant may say the following prayer.*
Almighty God,
from the dust of the earth you have created us.
May these ashes be for us a sign
of our mortality and penitence,
and a reminder that only by your gracious gift
are we given eternal life;
through Jesus Christ our Saviour. **Amen.**

*Those who desire to receive ashes come forward, and the ashes are applied to
the forehead of each person with the following words.*
Remember you are dust, and to dust you shall return.

*After all who desire ashes have received them, the celebrant leads the
congregation in the conclusion of the confession, all kneeling.*

|           | Accomplish in us, O God, |
|-----------|---------------------------|

        Accomplish in us, O God,
        the work of your salvation,
*People*     **That we may show forth your glory**
        **in the world.**

*Celebrant*   By the cross and passion of your Son, our Lord,
*People*      **Bring us with all your saints**
        **to the joy of his resurrection.**

*The bishop, if present, or the priest stands and, facing the people, says,*
Almighty God have mercy on you,
forgive you all your sins
through our Lord Jesus Christ,
strengthen you in all goodness,
and by the power of the Holy Spirit
keep you in eternal life. **Amen.**

*In the absence of a bishop or priest, a deacon or lay person leading the service remains kneeling and substitutes* us *for* you *and* our *for* your.

*The Peace is exchanged. When the eucharist follows, the service continues with the offertory.*

## Prayer over the Gifts

Merciful God,
turn us from sin to faithfulness.
Accept our offering,
and prepare us to celebrate
the death and resurrection of Christ our Saviour,
who is alive and reigns with you now and for ever.

*Preface of Lent*

## Prayer after Communion

God of compassion,
through your Son Jesus Christ
you reconciled your people to yourself.
Following his example of prayer and fasting,
may we obey you with willing hearts
and serve one another in holy love;
through Jesus Christ our Lord.

*At services at which a Sentence is required, the following may be used.*

If today you hear his voice, harden not your hearts.
*Psalm 95.7–8*

# First Sunday in Lent

## Sentence

We shall not live by bread alone, but by every word that
proceeds from the mouth of God.    *Matthew 4.4*

## Collect

Almighty God,
whose Son fasted forty days in the wilderness,
and was tempted as we are but did not sin,

give us grace to discipline ourselves
in submission to your Spirit,
that as you know our weakness,
so we may know your power to save;
through Jesus Christ our Lord,
who lives and reigns with you and the Holy Spirit,
one God, now and for ever.

### Readings

A    Genesis 2.4b–9, 15–17, 25—3.7    Psalm 130
     *Refrain*   The Lord shall redeem us from all our sins.
     *Or v.7 or CR 5*
     Romans 5.12–19    Matthew 4.1–11

B    Genesis 9.8–17    Psalm 25.1–9
     *Refrain*   The paths of the Lord are love and faithfulness to those who
     keep his covenant.   *Or v.9 or CR 1*
     1 Peter 3.18–22    Mark 1.9–15

C    Deuteronomy 26.1–11    Psalm 91.9–16
     *Refrain*   He shall give his angels charge over you.
     *Or v.16 or CR 1*
     Romans 10.8b–13    Luke 4.1–13

### Prayer over the Gifts

God our refuge and our strength,
receive all we offer you this day,
and through the death and resurrection of your Son
transform us to his likeness.
We ask this in his name.

*Preface of Lent*

### Prayer after Communion

Faithful God,
in this holy bread
you increase our faith and hope and love.
Lead us in the path of Christ
who is your Word of life.
We ask this in his name.

# Second Sunday of Lent

## Sentence

A   The Son of man must be lifted up, that whoever believes in him may have eternal life.   *John 3.14–15*

B   I do not glory except in the cross of our Lord Jesus Christ, by which the world has been crucified to me, and I to the world.   *Galatians 6.14*

C   If you hear his voice, harden not your hearts.
*Psalm 95.7–8*

*When the alternative Gospels are read:*

This is my beloved Son, with whom I am well pleased; listen to him.   *Matthew 17.5*

## Collect

Almighty God,
whose Son was revealed in majesty
before he suffered death upon the cross,
give us faith to perceive his glory,
that being strengthened by his grace
we may be changed into his likeness, from glory to glory;
who lives and reigns with you and the Holy Spirit,
one God, now and for ever.

## Readings

A   Genesis 12.1–4a(4b–8)    Psalm 33.18–22
*Refrain*   Let your loving-kindness be upon us, O Lord.
*Or v.22 or CR 4*
Romans 4.1–5(6–12)13–17    John 3.1–17 *or* Matthew 17.1–9

B   Genesis 17.1–10, 15–19    Psalm 105.1–11
*Refrain*   The Lord has always been mindful of his covenant.
*Or v.8 or CR 6*
Romans 4.16–25    Mark 8.31–38 *or* Mark 9.1–9

C Genesis 15.1–12, 17–18    Psalm 127
   *Refrain*   Happy are they who fear the Lord.   *Or v.1 or CR 1*
   Philippians 3.17—4.1    Luke 13.31–35 *or* Luke 9.28–36

**Prayer over the Gifts**

God of wisdom,
may the light of the eternal Word,
our Lord and Saviour Jesus Christ,
guide us to your glory.
We ask this in his name.

*Preface of Lent*

**Prayer after Communion**

Creator of heaven and earth,
we thank you for these holy mysteries,
which bring us now a share in the life to come,
through Jesus Christ our Lord.

# Third Sunday of Lent—Year A

**Sentence**

Lord, you are indeed the Saviour of the world. Give us living
water, that we may not thirst.

**Collect**

Almighty God,
whose Son Jesus Christ gives the water of eternal life,
may we always thirst for you,
the spring of life and source of goodness;
through him who lives and reigns with you
and the Holy Spirit,
one God, now and for ever.

**Readings**

   Exodus 17.3–7    Psalm 95
   *Refrain*   Oh, that today you would hearken to his voice: harden not
   your hearts.   *Or v.8 or CR 8*
   Romans 5.1–11    John 4.5–26(27–42)

**Prayer over the Gifts**

Spring of life and Source of goodness,
receive all we offer you this day,
and bring us to the living water,
Jesus Christ, your Son our Lord.

*Preface of Lent*

**Prayer after Communion**

God of our pilgrimage,
we have found the living water.
Refresh and sustain us
as we go forth on our journey,
in the name of Jesus Christ the Lord.

# Third Sunday of Lent—Years B and C

**Sentence**

B    God so loved the world that he gave his only Son,
that whoever believes in him should not perish but have
eternal life.   *John 3.16*

C    Repent, says the Lord, for the kingdom of heaven is at
hand.   *Matthew 4.17*

**Collect**

Father of mercy,
alone we have no power in ourselves to help ourselves.
When we are discouraged by our weakness,
strengthen us to follow Christ,
our pattern and our hope;
who lives and reigns with you and the Holy Spirit,
one God, now and for ever.

**Readings**

B    Exodus 20.1–17     Psalm 19.7–14
     *Refrain*  The words of the Lord are spirit and life.
     *Or v.8 or CR 1*
     1 Corinthians 1.22–25    John 2.13–22

C     Exodus 3.1–15     Psalm 103.1–13

*Refrain*   The Lord is full of compassion and mercy.
*Or v.7 or CR 6*
1 Corinthians 10.1–13     Luke 13.1–9

**Prayer over the Gifts**

Gracious God,
we know your power to triumph over weakness.
May we who ask forgiveness
be ready to forgive one another,
in the name of Jesus the Lord.

*Preface of Lent*

**Prayer after Communion**

God of mercy and forgiveness,
may we who share this sacrament
live together in unity and peace,
in the name of Jesus Christ the Lord.

# Fourth Sunday of Lent—Year A

**Sentence**

I am the light of the world, says the Lord; those who follow me
will have the light of life.   *John 8.12*

**Collect**

Almighty God,
through the waters of baptism
your Son has made us children of light.
May we ever walk in his light
and show forth your glory in the world;
through Jesus Christ our Lord,
who is alive and reigns with you and the Holy Spirit,
one God, now and for ever.

### Readings

1 Samuel 16.1–13      Psalm 23

*Refrain*    The Lord has anointed his servant with oil.    *Or v.5 or CR 1*

Ephesians 5.8–14      John 9.1–41

### Prayer over the Gifts

God of light,
your Word brings to us a new vision of your glory.
Accept our offering of praise and thanksgiving,
through Jesus Christ our Lord.

*Preface of Lent*

### Prayer after Communion

Father,
through your goodness
we receive your Son in word and sacrament.
May we always have faith in him,
Jesus Christ the Lord.

# Fourth Sunday of Lent—Years B and C

### Sentence

B    God so loved the world that he gave his only Son, that
whoever believes in him should not perish but have
eternal life.   *John 3.16*

C    I will arise and go to my father, and I will say to him:
Father I have sinned against heaven and before you.
*Luke 15.18*

### Collect

Gracious Father,
whose blessed Son Jesus Christ came from heaven
to be the true bread which gives life to the world,
evermore give us this bread,
that he may live in us, and we in him,
who lives and reigns with you and the Holy Spirit,
one God, now and for ever.

### Readings

B   2 Chronicles 36.14–23      Psalm 137.1–6
    *Refrain*   May I never speak again if I forget you.   *Or v.6 or CR 5*
    Ephesians 2.4–10      John 3.14–21

C   Joshua 5.9–12      Psalm 34.1–8
    *Refrain*   Taste and see that the Lord is good.   *Or v.8 or CR 6*
    2 Corinthians 5.16–21      Luke 15.1–3, 11–32

### Prayer over the Gifts

God of mercy and compassion,
your Word calls us home to faith and love.
Accept all we offer you this day,
in the name of Jesus Christ the Lord.

*Preface of Lent*

### Prayer after Communion

Giver of life,
you enlighten all who come into the world.
Fill our hearts with the splendour of your grace,
that we may perfectly love you
and worthily praise your holy name,
through Jesus Christ the Lord.

# Fifth Sunday of Lent—Year A

### Sentence

I am the resurrection and the life, says the Lord; whoever lives
and believes in me shall never die.   *John 11.25, 26*

### Collect

Almighty God,
your Son came into the world
to free us all from sin and death.
Breathe upon us with the power of your Spirit,
that we may be raised to new life in Christ,
and serve you in holiness and righteousness all our days;
through the same Jesus Christ, our Lord.

### Readings

Ezekiel 37.1–14    Psalm 116.1–8
*Refrain*  You have rescued my soul from death.  *Or v.8 or CR 1*
Romans 8.6–11    John 11.(1–16)17–45

### Prayer over the Gifts

Giver of life,
your Son has destroyed the power of death
for all those who believe in him.
Accept all we offer you this day
and strengthen us in faith and hope;
through Jesus Christ, the Lord of all the living.

*Preface of Lent*

### Prayer after Communion

God of hope,
in this eucharist we have tasted the promise
of your heavenly banquet
and the richness of eternal life.
May we who bear witness to the death of your Son,
also proclaim the glory of his resurrection,
for he is Lord for ever and ever.

# Fifth Sunday of Lent—Years B and C

### Sentence

B    Anyone who serves me must follow me, says the Lord,
and where I am, there shall my servant be also.  *John 12.26*

C    All I care for is to know Christ and the power of his
resurrection.  *See Philippians 3.10*

## Collect

Most merciful God,
by the death and resurrection
of your Son Jesus Christ,
you created humanity anew.
May the power of his victorious cross
transform those who turn in faith
to him who lives and reigns with you
and the Holy Spirit,
one God, now and for ever.

## Readings

B    Jeremiah 31.31–34    Psalm 51.11–18
     *Refrain*  Create in me a clean heart, O God.   *Or v.11 or CR 5*
     Hebrews 5.7–10    John 12.20–33

C    Isaiah 43.16–21    Psalm 126
     *Refrain*  The Lord has done great things for us.   *Or v.4 or CR 1*
     Philippians 3.8–14    John 12.1–8

## Prayer over the Gifts

Eternal God,
your only Son suffered death upon the cross
to bring the world salvation.
Accept the praise and thanksgiving
we offer you this day,
in the name of Jesus Christ the Lord.

*Preface of Lent*

## Prayer after Communion

Merciful God,
you have called us to your table
and fed us with the bread of life.
Draw us and all people to your Son,
our Saviour Jesus Christ.

# Holy Week

The glory of Easter is the heart of the Christian gospel. It is the centre of the Church's faith and worship. In the earliest days of the Church it was the only Christian festival: an annual celebration, in one act, of Christ's life, death, resurrection, ascension, and his sending of the Holy Spirit. The celebration lasted fifty days in one continuous festival of adoration, joy, and thanksgiving, ending on the Feast of Pentecost. By the fourth century, the Church was adding to its celebration of Easter a week-long commemoration of the events which preceded our Lord's resurrection, beginning on Sunday with his triumphal entry into Jerusalem. Christians would recall the final meal Jesus had with his disciples and his institution of the sacrament of the eucharist. On the Friday they would commemorate Christ's agony and death on the cross. On Saturday night they would gather for the reading of the scripture, for prayers, for the baptism of their new converts, and then, as the day of the resurrection dawned, for the joyful celebration of Easter. The week before Easter became known as Holy Week. The focal points of this week would be

The Sunday of the Passion with the Liturgy of the Palms,

Maundy Thursday, with foot washing and a thanksgiving for the institution of the eucharist,

Good Friday, with a veneration of the cross,

Easter Eve, with the Great Vigil, paschal fire, initiation, and the Easter eucharist.

The services which follow contain suggestions for the observance of Holy Week and the celebration of Easter today. They represent an adaptation of a variety of services used through the centuries of the Church's life. Because they will be new to many people, they should be carefully explained and rehearsed before they are used. Members of congregations should be involved in the planning of the services and should be encouraged to participate in them.

# The Sunday of the Passion

With the Liturgy of the Palms

## The Liturgy of the Palms

*When circumstances are suitable, the people may assemble at a place apart from the church, so that all may enter the church in procession.*

*The branches of palm, or of other trees or shrubs to be carried in procession, may be distributed to the people before the service, or immediately before the procession. The following or some other suitable anthem is said or sung.*

Blessed is he who comes in the name of the Lord.
**Hosanna in the highest.**

*The priest then greets the people and gives a brief introduction, inviting them to participate in the celebration in these or similar words.*

Dear friends in Christ,
during Lent we have been preparing
for the celebration of our Lord's paschal mystery.
On this day our Lord Jesus Christ
entered the holy city of Jerusalem in triumph.
The people welcomed him with palms and shouts of praise,
but the path before him led to self-giving, suffering, and death.
Today we greet him as our King,
although we know his crown is thorns and his throne a cross.
We follow him this week from the glory of the palms
to the glory of the resurrection
by way of the dark road of suffering and death.
United with him in his suffering on the cross,
may we share his resurrection and new life.

Let us pray.

Assist us mercifully with your help,
Lord God of our salvation,
that we may enter with joy
into the celebration of those mighty acts
whereby you give us life and immortality;
through Jesus Christ our Lord. **Amen.**

*All remain standing for the Gospel.*

*Reader*   The Lord be with you.
*People*   **And also with you.**

*Reader*   The Holy Gospel of our Lord Jesus Christ
           according to . . .
*People*   **Glory to you, Lord Jesus Christ.**

*Then a deacon, a priest, or some other appointed person shall read one of the following:*

> A—*Matthew 21.1–11*
> B—*Mark 11.1–11 or John 12.12–16*
> C—*Luke 19.28–40*

*At the conclusion of the Gospel, the reader says,*

           The Gospel of Christ.
*People*   **Praise to you, Lord Jesus Christ.**

*The celebrant then says the following blessing.*

           The Lord be with you.
*People*   **And also with you.**

*Celebrant*   Let us give thanks to the Lord our God.
*People*   **It is right to give our thanks and praise.**

*The celebrant continues,*

It is right to praise you, almighty God,
for the acts of love by which you have redeemed us
through your Son Jesus Christ our Lord.
The Hebrews acclaimed Jesus as Messiah and King,
with palm branches in their hands, crying,
Hosanna in the highest.
May we also, carrying these emblems, go forth to meet Christ
and follow him in the way that leads to eternal life;
who lives and reigns in glory with you and the Holy Spirit,
now and for ever. **Amen.**

# The Procession

*Then may be said or sung,*

Let us go forth in peace.
*People*   **In the name of Christ. Amen.**

*During the procession, all hold branches in their hands, and suitable hymns, psalms (such as 118.19–29), or anthems are sung. At a suitable place, the procession may halt while the following or some other appropriate collect is said.*

Almighty God,
whose Son was crucified yet entered into glory,
may we, walking in the way of the cross,
find it is for us the way of life;
through Jesus Christ our Lord,
who is alive and reigns with you and the Holy Spirit,
one God, now and for ever.

*In the absence of a bishop or priest, the preceding service may be led by a deacon or lay person.*

# At the Eucharist

*When the Liturgy of the Palms precedes the eucharist, the celebration begins with the Collect of the Day.*

Let us pray.

Almighty and everliving God,
in tender love for all our human race
you sent your Son our Saviour Jesus Christ
to take our flesh
and suffer death upon a cruel cross.
May we follow the example of his great humility,
and share in the glory of his resurrection;
through Jesus Christ our Lord,
who is alive and reigns with you and the Holy Spirit,
one God, now and for ever.

### Readings

A   Isaiah 50.4–9a   Psalm 31.9–16
    *Refrain*   Into your hands, O Lord, I commend my spirit.
    *Or v.16 or CR 8*
    Philippians 2.5–11   Matthew 26.14—27.66 *or* Matthew 27.11–54

B   Isaiah 50.4–9a   Psalm 31.9–16
    *Refrain*   As Year A
    Philippians 2.5–11   Mark 14.1—15.47 *or* Mark 15.1–39

C   Isaiah 50.4–9a   Psalm 31.9–16
    *Refrain*   As Year A
    Philippians 2.5–11   Luke 22.14—23.56 *or* Luke 23.1–49

*Lay persons may read or chant the Passion. Specific roles may be assigned to individuals and to the congregation. After the Liturgy of the Palms, the creed and the confession of sin may be omitted at the eucharist.*

### Prayer over the Gifts

Gracious God,
the suffering and death of Jesus, your only Son,
makes us pleasing in your sight.
Alone we can do nothing,
but through his sacrifice,
may we receive your love and mercy.

*Preface of Holy Week*

### Prayer after Communion

God our help and strength,
you have satisfied our hunger with this eucharistic food.
Strengthen our faith,
that through the death and resurrection of your Son,
we may be led to salvation,
for he is Lord now and for ever.

*At services at which a Sentence is required, the following may be used.*
Christ became obedient unto death, even death on a cross.
Therefore God has highly exalted him and bestowed on him
the name which is above every name.   *Philippians 2.8–9*

# Monday in Holy Week

### Sentence

God sent his Son to be the expiation for our sins.   *1 John 4.10*

### Collect

Almighty God,
whose Son was crucified yet entered into glory,
may we, walking in the way of the cross,
find it is for us the way of life;
through Jesus Christ our Lord,
who is alive and reigns with you and the Holy Spirit,
one God, now and for ever.

### Readings

Isaiah 42.1–9      Psalm 36.5–10
*Refrain*   In your light, O God, we see light.   *Or v.5 or CR 7*
Hebrews 9.11–15      John 12.1–11

### Prayer over the Gifts

Ruler of all creation,
your Son was anointed with costly oil
in preparation for death and the grave.
Receive all we offer you this day
for the sake of him who died that we might live,
Jesus Christ the Lord.

*Preface of Holy Week*

### Prayer after Communion

God of our salvation,
in this eucharist
you have renewed us in your covenant.
Help us to follow in the path of him
who came to open the eyes of the blind
and bring prisoners out of darkness,
Jesus Christ our Lord.

# Tuesday in Holy Week

## Sentence

Anyone who serves me must follow me, says the Lord, and
where I am, there shall my servant be also.    *John 12.26*

## Collect

O God,
by the passion of your blessed Son,
you made an instrument of shameful death
to be for us the means of life.
May our lives be so transformed by his passion
that we may witness to his grace;
who lives and reigns with you and the Holy Spirit,
one God, now and for ever.

## Readings

> Isaiah 49.1–7        Psalm 71.1–12
> *Refrain*    From my mother's womb you have been my strength.
> *Or v.6 or CR 5*
> 1 Corinthians 1.18–31        John 12.20–36

## Prayer over the Gifts

Source of life,
accept all we offer you this day,
and turn us from sin and death,
that we may share in the tree of life,
through Jesus Christ our Lord.

*Preface of Holy Week*

## Prayer after Communion

Faithful God,
may we who share this banquet
glory in the cross of our Lord Jesus Christ,
our salvation, life, and hope,
who reigns as Lord now and for ever.

# Wednesday in Holy Week

### Sentence

By this will all know that you are my disciples, if you have love
for one another.   *John 13.35*

### Collect

Lord God,
your Son our Saviour gave his body to be whipped
and turned his face for men to spit upon.
Give your servants grace to accept suffering for his sake,
confident of the glory that will be revealed,
through Jesus Christ our Lord
who is alive and reigns with you and the Holy Spirit,
one God, now and for ever.

### Readings

Isaiah 50.4–9a     Psalm 70
*Refrain*   O Lord, make haste to help me.   *Or v.6 or CR 5*
Hebrews 12.1–3     John 13.21–30

### Prayer over the Gifts

God of glory,
may our worship this day
fix the eyes of our faith on Jesus,
the pioneer and perfecter of our new humanity,
who is seated at the right hand of your throne,
now and for ever.

*Preface of Holy Week*

### Prayer after Communion

God our help,
your Son was betrayed by one who called himself a friend.
May we who call him Lord
ever remain his faithful people,
for he lives and reigns with you now and for ever.

# Maundy Thursday

*This liturgy is celebrated once in the day and normally in the evening. The celebrant may address the congregation in these words.*

This is the day
that Christ the Lamb of God
gave himself into the hands of those who would slay him.

This is the day
that Christ gathered with his disciples in the upper room.

This is the day
that Christ took a towel
and washed the disciples' feet,
giving us an example that we should do to others
as he has done to us.

This is the day
that Christ our God gave us this holy feast,
that we who eat this bread
and drink this cup
may here proclaim his Holy Sacrifice
and be partakers of his resurrection,
and at the last day may reign with him in heaven.

*The eucharist follows in the usual manner, using the following collect, readings, and psalm.*

**Collect**

O God,
your Son Jesus Christ
has left to us this meal of bread and wine
in which we share his body and his blood.
May we who celebrate this sign of his great love
show in our lives the fruits of his redemption;
through Jesus Christ our Lord,
who lives and reigns with you and the Holy Spirit,
one God, now and for ever.

**Readings**

*The readings for Year A are used when the ceremony of the washing of feet is performed.*

A     Exodus 12.1–14     Psalm 116.10–17
       *Refrain*   I will lift up the cup of salvation.   *Or v.11 or CR 7*
       1 Corinthians 11.23–26     John 13.1–15

B     Exodus 24.3–8     Psalm 116.10–17
       *Refrain*   As Year A
       1 Corinthians 10.16–17     Mark 14.12–26

C     Jeremiah 31.31–34     Psalm 116.10–17
       *Refrain*   As Year A
       Hebrews 10.16–25     Luke 22.7–20

*When observed, the ceremony of the washing of feet follows the Gospel and sermon. The celebrant may introduce the ceremony using these or similar words.*

Fellow servants of our Lord Jesus Christ,
on the night before his death,
Jesus set an example for his disciples
by washing their feet, an act of humble service.
He taught that strength and growth
in the life of the kingdom of God
come not by power, authority, or even miracle,
but by such lowly service.

Therefore, I invite you
(who have been appointed as representatives
of the congregation and)
who share in the royal priesthood of Christ,
to come forward,
that I may recall whose servant I am
by following the example of my Master.
But come remembering his admonition
that what will be done for you
is also to be done by you to others,
for "a servant is not greater than his master,
nor is one who is sent greater than the one who sent him.
If you know these things, blessed are you if you do them."

*A basin of water is placed at the chancel step. Members of the congregation,*
*or their representatives, are seated on chairs near the front of the assembly.*
*The celebrant, carrying a towel, proceeds to wash the feet of those seated*
*before him.*

*During the ceremony suitable anthems or songs may be sung.*

*The service continues with the Prayers of the People. At the offertory the*
*following Prayer over the Gifts may be used.*

**Prayer over the Gifts**

Father,
we spread this table
to remember the loving sacrifice of Jesus Christ, your Son.
Accept all we offer you this day.
Bind us together in his love
and in the love he has commanded us to bring one another;
through Jesus Christ our Lord.

*Preface of Holy Week*

*In Eucharistic Prayer 3 the opening words of the institution narrative may be*
*changed to,*

On this very night,
when he was handed over to suffering and death . . .

*Eucharistic Prayers 1 and 6 are also appropriate on Maundy Thursday. In*
*Prayer 1 the opening words of the institution narrative may be changed to,*

On this very night,
when he freely gave himself to death . . .

*And in Prayer 6 they may be changed to,*

At supper with them on this night, he took bread . . .

*When it is desired to administer Holy Communion from the reserved*
*sacrament on Good Friday, the sacrament for that purpose is consecrated at*
*this service.*

### Prayer after Communion

Holy God,
source of all love,
on the night of his betrayal
Jesus gave his disciples a new commandment,
to love one another as he loved them.
Write this commandment in our hearts;
give us the will to serve others
as he was the servant of all,
who gave his life and died for us,
yet is alive and reigns with you and the Holy Spirit,
one God, now and for ever.

*At services at which a Sentence is required, the following may be used.*

A new commandment I give to you, that you love one another
as I have loved you.    *John 13.34*

*The Prayer after Communion may conclude the spoken part of the eucharistic liturgy.*

*At the end of the service, the ornaments and cloths on the altar and in other places in the church building may be removed. During their removal, Matthew 26.30–46 and Psalm 22 may be read.*

*The blessing or dismissal may be omitted. The congregation should leave in silence.*

# Good Friday

The Celebration of the Lord's Passion

## The Ministry of the Word

*When the congregation has assembled and the ministers, having entered in silence, are in their places, all shall stand.*

Celebrant   All we like sheep have gone astray;
            we have turned every one to his own way,

People      **And the Lord has laid on him
            the iniquity of us all.**

Celebrant   Christ the Lord became obedient unto death,
People      **Even death on a cross.**

*Silence may be kept.*

Celebrant   Almighty God,
All         **our heavenly Father,
            we have sinned
            in thought and word and deed;
            we have not loved you with our whole heart;
            we have not loved our neighbours as ourselves.
            We pray you of your mercy,
            forgive us all that is past,
            and grant that we may serve you
            in newness of life
            to the glory of your name. Amen.**

## The Collect of the Day

Celebrant   The Lord be with you.
People      **And also with you.**

Celebrant   Let us pray.

            Almighty God,
            look graciously, we pray, on this your family,

for whom our Lord Jesus Christ
was willing to be betrayed
and given into the hands of sinners,
and to suffer death upon the cross;
who now lives and reigns with you
and the Holy Spirit,
one God, for ever and ever.

### Readings

Isaiah 52.13—53.12      Psalm 22.1–17
*Refrain*   My God, my God, why have you forsaken me?   *Or v.1*
Hebrews 4.14–16; 5.7–9      John 18.1—19.42 *or* John 19.17–30

*The customary Gospel responses are omitted at the readings of the Passion.*
*The Passion may be read or chanted by lay persons. Roles may be assigned to*
*different people and the congregation.*

*The term "the Jews" in St John's Gospel applies to particular individuals and*
*not to the whole Jewish people. Insofar as we ourselves turn against Christ,*
*we are responsible for his death.*

*The congregation may be seated until the verse which mentions the arrival at*
*Golgotha (John 19.17) at which time all stand. The Passion Gospel is*
*announced in the following manner.*

*Reader*      **The Passion of our Lord Jesus Christ**
**according to John.**

*Then may follow a sermon. A hymn may be sung.*

## The Solemn Intercession

*All standing, the deacon or other person appointed says to the people,*
Dear people of God,
our heavenly Father sent his Son into the world,
not to condemn the world,
but that the world through him might be saved,
that all who believe in him
might be delivered from the power of sin and death
and become heirs with him of eternal life.

Let us pray for the one holy catholic
and apostolic Church of Christ throughout the world:

for its unity in witness and service,
for all bishops and other ministers
and the people whom they serve,
for N our bishop,
and all the people of this diocese,
for all Christians in this community,
for those about to be baptized
(particularly . . .),

that the Lord will confirm his Church in faith,
increase it in love,
and preserve it in peace.

*Silence*

Almighty and everlasting God,
by your Spirit the whole body of your faithful people
is governed and sanctified.
Receive our supplications and prayers
which we offer before you
for all members of your holy Church,
that in our vocation and ministry
we may truly and devoutly serve you;
through our Lord and Saviour Jesus Christ. **Amen.**


Let us pray for all nations and peoples of the earth,
and for those in authority among them:

for Elizabeth our Queen and all the Royal Family,
for N the Prime Minister
and for the government of this country,
for N the premier of this province
and the members of the legislature,
for N the mayor of this municipality

and those who serve with *him/her*
on the (city, town, village, district) council, †
for all who serve the common good,

that by God's help
they may seek justice and truth,
and live in peace and concord.

*Silence*

Almighty God,
kindle, we pray, in every heart
the true love of peace,
and guide with your wisdom
those who take counsel for the nations of the earth,
that justice and peace may increase,
until the earth is filled
with the knowledge of your love;
through Jesus Christ our Lord. **Amen.**

Let us pray for all who suffer
and are afflicted in body or in mind:

for the hungry and homeless,
the destitute and the oppressed,
and all who suffer persecution or prejudice,
for the sick, the wounded, and the handicapped,
for those in loneliness, fear, and anguish,
for those who face temptation, doubt, and despair,
for the sorrowful and bereaved,
for prisoners and captives
and those in mortal danger,

that God in his mercy will comfort and relieve them,
and grant them the knowledge of his love,
and stir up in us the will and patience
to minister to their needs.

† The name and title of the officers and the names of the governing bodies
  should be adapted in accordance with practice.

*Silence*

Gracious God,
the comfort of all who sorrow,
the strength of all who suffer,
hear the cry of those in misery and need.
In their afflictions show them your mercy,
and give us, we pray, the strength to serve them,
for the sake of him who suffered for us,
your Son Jesus Christ our Lord. **Amen.**


Let us pray for all
who have not received the gospel of Christ:

for all who have not heard the words of salvation,
for all who have lost their faith,
for all whose sin has made them indifferent to Christ,
for all who actively oppose Christ by word or deed,
for all who are enemies of the cross of Christ,
and persecutors of his disciples,
for all who in the name of Christ
have persecuted others,

that God will open their hearts to the truth,
and lead them to faith and obedience.

*Silence*

Merciful God,
creator of the peoples of the earth and lover of souls,
have compassion on all who do not know you
as you are revealed in your Son Jesus Christ.
Let your gospel be preached with grace and power
to those who have not heard it,
turn the hearts of those who resist it,
and bring home to your fold those who have gone astray;
that there may be one flock under one shepherd,
Jesus Christ our Lord. **Amen.**

Let us commit ourselves to God,
and pray for the grace of a holy life,
that with all who have departed this life
and have died in the peace of Christ,
and those whose faith is known to God alone,
we may be accounted worthy
to enter into the fullness of the joy of our Lord,
and receive the crown of life in the day of resurrection.

*Silence*

O God of unchangeable power and eternal light,
look favourably on your whole Church,
that wonderful and sacred mystery.
By the effectual working of your providence,
carry out in tranquillity the plan of salvation.
Let the whole world see and know
that things which were cast down are being raised up,
and things which had grown old are being made new,
and that all things are being brought to their perfection
by him through whom all things were made,
your Son Jesus Christ our Lord;
who lives and reigns with you,
in the unity of the Holy Spirit,
one God, for ever and ever. **Amen.**

*The service may be concluded here with a hymn, the Lord's Prayer (p. 318),
and the final prayer (p. 320).*

## Meditation on the Cross of Jesus

*If desired, a wooden cross may be brought into the church and placed in the
sight of the people. Then may be sung or said one of the following:*

| *Celebrant* | This is the wood of the cross, |
| | on which hung the Saviour of the world. |
| *People* | **Come let us worship.** |

*Or*

| *Celebrant* | Christ our Lord became obedient unto death. |
| *People* | **Come let us worship.** |

*Appropriate devotions may follow which may include any or all of the*
*following or other suitable anthems. If the texts are recited rather than sung,*
*the congregation reads the parts in heavy type.*

**Anthem 1** †

Is it nothing to you, all you who pass by?
Look and see if there is any sorrow like my sorrow
which was brought upon me,
which the Lord inflicted on the day of his fierce anger.
   **Holy God, holy and mighty,**
   **holy and immortal one, have mercy upon us.**

O my people, O my Church,
What have I done to you,
or in what have I offended you?
Testify against me.
I led you forth from the land of Egypt,
and delivered you by the waters of baptism,
but you have prepared a cross for your Saviour.
   **Holy God, holy and mighty,**
   **holy and immortal one, have mercy upon us.**

I led you through the desert forty years,
and fed you with manna.
I brought you through tribulation and penitence,
and gave you my body, the bread of heaven,
but you have prepared a cross for your Saviour.
   **Holy God, holy and mighty,**
   **holy and immortal one, have mercy upon us.**

What more could I have done for you
that I have not done?
I planted you, my chosen and fairest vineyard,
I made you the branches of my vine;
but when I was thirsty, you gave me vinegar to drink,
and pierced with a spear the side of your Saviour.

† Excerpted from *From Ashes to Fire*, Supplemental Worship Resource 8.
  Copyright © 1979 by Abingdon. Reprinted by permission.

**Holy God, holy and mighty,**
**holy and immortal one, have mercy upon us.**

I went before you in a pillar of cloud,
and you have led me to the judgement hall of Pilate.
I scourged your enemies and brought you
to a land of freedom,
but you have scourged, mocked, and beaten me.
I gave you the water of salvation from the rock,
but you have given me gall and left me to thirst.
  **Holy God, holy and mighty,**
  **holy and immortal one, have mercy upon us.**

I gave you a royal sceptre,
and bestowed the keys to the kingdom,
but you have given me a crown of thorns.
I raised you on high with great power,
but you have hanged me on the cross.
  **Holy God, holy and mighty,**
  **holy and immortal one, have mercy upon us.**

My peace I gave, which the world cannot give,
and washed your feet as a sign of my love,
but you draw the sword to strike in my name,
and seek high places in my kingdom.
I offered you my body and blood,
but you scatter and deny and abandon me.
  **Holy God, holy and mighty,**
  **holy and immortal one, have mercy upon us.**

I sent the Spirit of truth to guide you,
and you close your hearts to the Counsellor.
I pray that all may be as one in the Father and me,
but you continue to quarrel and divide.
I call you to go and bring forth fruit,
but you cast lots for my clothing.
  **Holy God, holy and mighty,**
  **holy and immortal one, have mercy upon us.**

I grafted you into the tree of my chosen Israel,
and you turned on them with persecution
and mass murder.
I made you joint heirs with them of my covenants,
but you made them scapegoats for your own guilt.
**Holy God, holy and mighty,**
**holy and immortal one, have mercy upon us.**

I came to you as the least of your brothers and sisters;
I was hungry and you gave me no food,
I was thirsty and you gave me no drink,
I was a stranger and you did not welcome me,
naked and you did not clothe me,
sick and in prison and you did not visit me.
**Holy God, holy and mighty,**
**holy and immortal one, have mercy upon us.**

### Anthem 2

We glory in your cross, O Lord,
**And praise and glorify your holy resurrection;**
**for by virtue of your cross**
**joy has come to the whole world.**

May God be merciful to us and bless us,
show us the light of his countenance, and come to us.
**Let your ways be known upon the earth,**
**your saving health among all nations.**

Let the peoples praise you, O God;
let all the peoples praise you.
**We glory in your cross, O Lord,**
**and praise and glorify your holy resurrection;**
**for by virtue of your cross**
**joy has come to the whole world.**

### Anthem 3

**We adore you, O Christ, and we bless you,**
**Because by your holy cross you have redeemed the world.**

If we have died with him, we shall also live with him;
if we endure, we shall also reign with him.
**We adore you, O Christ, and we bless you,
because of your holy cross you have redeemed the world.**

### Anthem 4

O Saviour of the world,
by your cross and precious blood you have redeemed us.
**Save us and help us, we humbly beseech you, O Lord.**

*The hymn "Sing, my tongue, the glorious battle," or some other hymn
extolling the glory of the cross, is then sung. The service may be concluded
with the Lord's Prayer (p. 318), and the final prayer (p. 320).*

## The Holy Communion

*In places where the eucharist is to be celebrated, the service continues with the
preparation of the gifts.*

### Prayer over the Gifts

Holy God,
your Son Jesus Christ carried our sins
in his own body on the tree,
so that we might have life.
May we and all who remember this day
find new life in him,
now and in the world to come,
where he lives with you and the Holy Spirit,
for ever and ever.

*Preface of Holy Week*

*In places where Holy Communion is to be administered from the reserved
sacrament, the following order is observed.*

*The table having been covered with a fair linen, and the sacrament having
been brought and placed on the altar, the celebrant shall say,*

As our Saviour taught us, let us pray,

*All*
**Our Father in heaven,
hallowed be your name,
your kingdom come,
your will be done,
on earth as in heaven.
Give us today our daily bread.
Forgive us our sins
as we forgive those who sin against us.
Save us from the time of trial,
and deliver us from evil.
For the kingdom, the power,
and the glory are yours,
now and forever. Amen.**

*Or*

*Celebrant*
And now, as our Saviour Christ has taught us,
we are bold to say,

*All*
**Our Father, who art in heaven,
hallowed be thy name,
thy kingdom come,
thy will be done,
on earth as it is in heaven.
Give us this day our daily bread.
And forgive us our trespasses,
as we forgive those who trespass against us.
And lead us not into temptation,
but deliver us from evil.
For thine is the kingdom,
the power, and the glory,
for ever and ever. Amen.**

*The celebrant invites the people to share in communion.*

*Celebrant*  The gifts of God for the People of God.
*People*  **Thanks be to God.**

*The sacrament is given with the following words.*

> The body of Christ (given for you).
> The blood of Christ (shed for you).

*Or*  The body of Christ, the bread of heaven.
> The blood of Christ, the cup of salvation.

*The communicant responds each time,* **Amen.**

**Prayer after Communion**

*Celebrant*  Let us pray.

*One of the following prayers is said.*

*Celebrant*  Almighty and eternal God,
*All*  **you have restored us to life**
> **by the triumphant death**
> **and resurrection of Christ.**
> **Continue this healing work within us.**
> **May we who partake of this mystery**
> **never cease to give you dedicated service.**
> **We ask this through Jesus Christ our Lord. Amen.**

*Or*

*Celebrant*  Lord Jesus Christ, Son of the living God,
*All*  **we pray you to set your passion, cross, and death**
> **between your judgement and our souls,**
> **now and in the hour of our death.**
> **Give mercy and grace to the living,**
> **pardon and rest to the dead,**
> **to your holy Church peace and concord,**
> **and to us sinners everlasting life and glory;**
> **for with the Father and the Holy Spirit,**
> **you live and reign,**
> **one God, now and for ever. Amen.**

*The service ends with the following prayer. No blessing or dismissal is added.*

Send down your abundant blessing, Lord,
upon your people
who have devoutly recalled the death of your Son
in the sure and certain hope of the resurrection.
Grant them pardon; bring them comfort.
May their faith grow stronger
and their eternal salvation be assured.
We ask this through Christ our Lord.

*At services at which a Sentence is required, the following may be used.*

Christ became obedient unto death, even death on a cross.
Therefore God has highly exalted him and bestowed on him
the name which is above every name.　　*Philippians 2.8–9*

# Holy Saturday

**Sentence**

Christ became obedient unto death, even death on a cross.
Therefore God has highly exalted him and bestowed on him
the name which is above every name.　　*Philippians 2.8–9*

**Collect**

O God,
creator of heaven and earth,
as the crucified body of your dear Son
was laid in the tomb and rested on this holy Sabbath,
so may we await with him the coming of the third day,
and rise with him to newness of life;
who now lives and reigns with you and the Holy Spirit,
one God, now and for ever.

**Readings**

> Job 14.1–14　　Psalm 31.1–4, 15–16
> *Refrain*　　Into your hands, O Lord, I commend my spirit.
> 1 Peter 4.1–8　　Matthew 27.57–66 *or* John 19.38–42

*The eucharist is not normally celebrated on Holy Saturday.*

# Concerning the Great Vigil of Easter

*The Great Vigil, when observed, is the first service of Easter. It is celebrated at a convenient time between sunset on Holy Saturday and sunrise on Easter morning.*

*The service normally consists of four parts:*

1 *The Service of Light,*
2 *The Liturgy of the Word,*
3 *Christian Initiation, or the Renewal of Baptismal Vows,*
4 *The Holy Eucharist with the administration of Easter Communion.*

*It is desirable for all the ordained ministers present, together with lay readers, singers, and other persons, to take active parts in the service.*

*The bishop, when present, is the chief celebrant. He presides at baptism and administers confirmation, and normally preaches the sermon.*

*The priests who are present share among them the reading of the collects which follow each lesson, and assist at baptism and the eucharist. In the absence of a bishop, a priest presides at the service.*

*It is the prerogative of a deacon to carry the paschal candle to its place, and to chant the Exsultet. Deacons likewise assist at baptism and the eucharist according to their order.*

*Lay persons read the lessons and the epistle, and assist in other ways. A lay person may be assigned to chant the Exsultet. It is desirable that each lesson be read by a different reader.*

*In the absence of a bishop or priest, a deacon or lay reader may lead the first two parts of the service, the Renewal of Baptismal Vows, and the Ministry of the Word of the Vigil Eucharist, concluding with the Prayers of the People, the Lord's Prayer, and the Dismissal.*

# The Great Vigil of Easter

## The Service of Light

*In the darkness, fire is kindled. The celebrant may then greet the people and address them in these or similar words.*

Dear friends in Christ,
on this most holy night,
when our Lord Jesus Christ passed from death to life,
the Church invites her children throughout the world
to come together in vigil and prayer.
This is the Passover of the Lord.
We remember his death and resurrection
by hearing his word and celebrating his mysteries;
we are confident
that we shall share his victory over death
and live with him for ever in God.

*The celebrant may say the following prayer.*

Let us pray.

Father,
we share in the light of your glory
through your Son, the light of the world.
Sanctify this new fire, and inflame us with new hope.
Purify our minds by this Easter celebration
and bring us one day to the feast of eternal light.
We ask this through Christ our Lord. **Amen.**

*In some places it may seem appropriate to stress the dignity and significance of the paschal candle with other symbolic rites. See p. 333.*

*The paschal candle is lighted from the new fire. The deacon (a priest if there is no deacon) takes the paschal candle, lifts it high, and sings,*

> The light of Christ.
> *People*      **Thanks be to God.**

*The procession enters the church, led by the deacon with the paschal candle. At a suitable place the deacon lifts the candle high, and sings a second time,*

The light of Christ.

*People*     **Thanks be to God.**

*If candles have been distributed to the congregation, they may be lighted now or when the procession ends. The procession continues until the deacon arrives before the altar. Turning to face the people, the deacon sings a third time,*

The light of Christ.

*People*     **Thanks be to God.**

*Other candles and lamps in the church may now be lighted. The paschal candle is placed in its stand in the middle of the sanctuary or near the lectern. The deacon, or other person appointed, standing near the candle, sings or says the Exsultet.*

Rejoice, heavenly powers! Sing, choirs of angels! Exult, all creation around God's throne! Jesus Christ, our King, is risen! Sound the trumpet of salvation!

Rejoice, O earth, in shining splendour, radiant in the brightness of your King! Christ has conquered! Glory fills you! Darkness vanishes for ever!

Rejoice, O Mother Church! Exult in glory! The risen Saviour shines upon you! Let this place resound with joy, echoing the mighty song of all God's people!

The Lord be with you.

*People*     **And also with you.**

*Deacon*     Let us give thanks to the Lord our God.

*People*     **It is right to give our thanks and praise.**

*Deacon*     It is truly right that with full hearts and minds and voices we should praise the unseen God, the all-powerful Father, and his only Son, our Lord Jesus Christ. For Christ has ransomed us with his blood, and paid for us the price of Adam's sin to our eternal Father!

This is our passover feast, when Christ, the true Lamb, is slain, whose blood consecrates the homes of all believers.

This is the night when first you saved our forebears: you freed the people of Israel from their slavery and led them dry-shod through the sea.

This is the night when Christians everywhere, washed clean of sin and freed from all defilement, are restored to grace and grow together in holiness.

This is the night when Jesus Christ broke the chains of death and rose triumphant from the grave.

Father, how wonderful your care for us! How boundless your merciful love! To ransom a slave you gave away your Son.

The power of this holy night dispels all evil, washes guilt away, restores lost innocence, brings mourners joy.

Night truly blessed when heaven is wedded to earth and we are reconciled with God!

Therefore, heavenly Father, in the joy of this night, receive our evening sacrifice of praise, your Church's solemn offering. Accept this Easter candle. May it always dispel the darkness of this night!

May the Morning Star which never sets find this flame still burning: Christ, that Morning Star, who came back from the dead, and shed his peaceful light on all creation, your Son who lives and reigns for ever and ever. **Amen.**

*After the Exsultet, if candles are being held, they may be extinguished. The paschal candle may burn at all services from Easter Day through the Day of Pentecost.*

# The Liturgy of the Word

*Before the readings begin, the celebrant may speak to the people in these or similar words.*

Dear friends in Christ,
let us now listen attentively to the word of God,
recalling how he saved his people throughout history
and in the fullness of time,
sent his own Son to be our Redeemer.

## Readings

*Ten readings from the Old Testament are provided. At least three are to be read. The passage from Exodus 14 is never to be omitted. Each Old Testament reading is followed by one or more of the following:*

1 *a suitable psalm, canticle, anthem, or hymn,*
2 *a period of silence,*
3 *a prayer.*

*Two readings from the New Testament are provided. Both are to be read.*

1    Genesis 1.1—2.2    Psalm 33
     *Refrain*   By the word of the Lord were the heavens made.

## Prayer

Almighty and eternal God,
you created all things in wonderful beauty and order.
Help us now to perceive
how still more wonderful is the new creation,
by which in the fullness of time
you redeemed your people
through the sacrifice of our Passover, Jesus Christ,
who lives and reigns for ever and ever.

2    Genesis 7.1–5, 11–18; 8.6–18; 9.8–13    Psalm 46
     *Refrain*   The Lord of hosts is with us; the God of Jacob is our
     stronghold.

**Prayer**

Faithful God,
you have placed the rainbow in the skies
as the sign of your covenant with all living things.
May we who are saved through water and the Spirit,
worthily offer to you our sacrifice of thanksgiving.
We ask this in the name of Jesus Christ our Lord.


3     Genesis 22.1–18     Psalm 16
      *Refrain*     Protect me, O God, for I take refuge in you.

**Prayer**

God and Father of all who believe in you,
you promised Abraham
that he would become the father of all nations,
and through the death and resurrection of Christ
you fulfil that promise;
everywhere throughout the world
you increase your chosen people.
May we respond to your call by joyfully accepting
your invitation to the new life of grace.
Grant this through Christ our Lord.


4     Exodus 14.10—15.1     Canticle: The Song of Moses (No. 1)
      *Refrain*     I will sing to the Lord for his glorious triumph.

**Prayer**

God of steadfast love,
your wonderful deeds of old shine forth even to our own day.
By the power of your mighty arm
you once delivered your chosen people
from slavery under Pharaoh,
to be a sign for us of the salvation of all nations
by the water of baptism.
Grant that all the peoples of the earth
may be numbered among the offspring of Abraham,
and rejoice in the inheritance of Israel.
We ask this through Jesus Christ our Lord.

**5**     Isaiah 54.5–14     Psalm 30
        *Refrain*   You have brought me up, O Lord, from the dead.

**Prayer**

O God,
you led your ancient people
in a pillar of cloud by day and a pillar of fire by night.
Grant that we who serve you now on earth,
may come to the joy of that heavenly Jerusalem,
where you wipe away all tears,
and where your saints for ever sing your praise.
Grant this through Christ our Lord.


**6**     Isaiah 55.1–11     Canticle: Song of Thanksgiving (No. 3)
        *Refrain*   You shall draw water with rejoicing.

**Prayer**

O God,
by the power of your Word
you have created all things,
and by your Spirit you renew the earth.
Give now the water of life to those who thirst for you,
that they may bring forth abundant fruit
in your glorious kingdom.
We ask this through Jesus Christ our Lord.


**7**     Baruch 3.9–15, 32—4.4     Psalm 19
        *Refrain*   The statutes of the Lord rejoice the heart.

**Prayer**

Creator of the universe, Source of all light,
teach us to hold fast to the ways of wisdom,
that we may live for ever in the radiance of your glory.
This we ask in the name of Jesus Christ our Saviour.

**8**      Ezekiel 36.24–28     Psalm 42

*Refrain*   As the deer longs for water-brooks, so longs my soul for you, O God.

**Prayer**

Almighty and everlasting God,
in the paschal mystery you established
the new covenant of reconciliation.
Grant that all who are born again in baptism
may show forth in their lives
what they profess by their faith.
Grant this in the name of Jesus Christ our Lord.


**9**      Ezekiel 37.1–14     Psalm 143

*Refrain*   Revive me, O Lord, for your name's sake.

**Prayer**

Living God,
by the Passover of your Son
you have brought us out of sin into righteousness,
and out of death into life.
Grant to those who are sealed by your Holy Spirit
the will and power to proclaim you to all the world;
through Jesus Christ our Lord.


**10**     Zephaniah 3.14–20     Psalm 98

*Refrain*   Lift up your voice, rejoice, and sing.

**Prayer**

O God of unchangeable power and eternal light,
look favourably on your whole Church,
that wonderful and sacred mystery.
By the effectual working of your providence,
carry out in tranquillity the plan of salvation.
Let the whole world see and know
that things which were cast down are being raised up,
and things which had grown old are being made new,
and that all things are being brought to their perfection

by him through whom all things were made,
your Son Jesus Christ our Lord.

*Glory to God, You are God, or some other suitable song of praise is sung.*
*Bells may be rung, according to local custom.*

## The Collect of the Day

*Celebrant*      Let us pray.

Eternal Giver of life and light,
this holy night shines with the radiance of the risen Christ.
Renew your Church with the Spirit given to us in baptism,
that we may worship you in sincerity and truth,
and shine as a light in the world;
through Jesus Christ our Lord,
who is alive and reigns with you and the Holy Spirit,
one God, now and for ever.

### Readings

|   | | |
|---|---|---|
|   | Romans 6.3–11 | Psalm 114 |
|   | *Refrain* Alleluia! | |
| A | Matthew 28.1–10 | |
| B | Mark 16.1–8 | |
| C | Luke 23.55—24.9 | |

## Sermon

*A silence for reflection may follow.*

## Holy Baptism

*Holy Baptism may follow, beginning with the Presentation and Examination*
*of the Candidates on p. 153.*

*During the procession to the font, which may take place here or immediately*
*before the Thanksgiving over the Water, a litany, psalm, anthem, or hymn*
*may be sung. The Presentation and Examination of the Candidates should*
*take place in a location which the congregation can see.*

# The Renewal of Baptismal Vows

*For use when there are no candidates for baptism or confirmation. The*
*following thanksgiving for water may be sung or said.*

Celebrant    Let us give thanks to the Lord our God.
People       **It is right to give our thanks and praise.**

Celebrant    We thank you, Almighty God, for the gift of water.
Over water the Holy Spirit moved in the beginning
of creation. Through water you led the children of
Israel out of their bondage in Egypt into the land of
promise. In water your Son Jesus received the
baptism of John and was anointed by the Holy
Spirit as the Messiah, the Christ, to lead us,
through his death and resurrection, from the
bondage of sin into everlasting life.

We thank you, Father, for the water of baptism. In
it we are buried with Christ in his death. By it we
share in his resurrection. Through it we are reborn
by the Holy Spirit. Therefore in joyful obedience to
your Son, we celebrate our fellowship in him in faith.

We pray that all who have passed through the water
of baptism may continue for ever in the risen life of
Jesus Christ our Saviour.

To him, to you, and to the Holy Spirit, be all honour
and glory, now and for ever. **Amen.**

*The celebrant may address the people in these or similar words.*

Dear friends,
through the paschal mystery
we have been buried with Christ in baptism,
so that we may rise with him to a new life.
Now that our Lenten observance is ended,
let us renew the promises we made in baptism,
when we rejected Satan and all his works,
and promised to serve God faithfully
in his holy catholic Church.

| | |
|---|---|
| *Celebrant* | Do you reaffirm your renunciation of evil and renew your commitment to Jesus Christ? |
| *People* | **I do.** |

| | |
|---|---|
| *Celebrant* | Do you believe in God the Father? |
| *People* | **I believe in God,**<br>**the Father almighty,**<br>**creator of heaven and earth.** |

| | |
|---|---|
| *Celebrant* | Do you believe in Jesus Christ, the Son of God? |
| *People* | **I believe in Jesus Christ,**<br>**his only Son, our Lord.**<br>**He was conceived by the power of the Holy Spirit**<br>**and born of the Virgin Mary.**<br>**He suffered under Pontius Pilate,**<br>**was crucified, died, and was buried.**<br>**He descended to the dead.**<br>**On the third day he rose again.**<br>**He ascended into heaven,**<br>**and is seated at the right hand of the Father.**<br>**He will come again**<br>**to judge the living and the dead.** |

| | |
|---|---|
| *Celebrant* | Do you believe in God the Holy Spirit? |
| *People* | **I believe in the Holy Spirit,**<br>**the holy catholic Church,**<br>**the communion of saints,**<br>**the forgiveness of sins,**<br>**the resurrection of the body,**<br>**and the life everlasting.** |

| | |
|---|---|
| *Celebrant* | Will you continue in the apostles' teaching and fellowship, in the breaking of bread, and in the prayers? |
| *People* | **I will, with God's help.** |

| | |
|---|---|
| *Celebrant* | Will you persevere in resisting evil and, whenever you fall into sin, repent and return to the Lord? |
| *People* | **I will, with God's help.** |

| | |
|---|---|
| *Celebrant* | Will you proclaim by word and example the good news of God in Christ? |
| *People* | **I will, with God's help.** |
| *Celebrant* | Will you seek and serve Christ in all persons, loving your neighbour as yourself? |
| *People* | **I will, with God's help.** |
| *Celebrant* | Will you strive for justice and peace among all people, and respect the dignity of every human being? |
| *People* | **I will, with God's help.** |

*The celebrant concludes the Renewal of Baptismal Vows with the following:*

God the creator, the rock of our salvation,
has given us new birth by water and the Holy Spirit,
and bestowed upon us the forgiveness of sins,
through our Lord Jesus Christ.
May he keep us faithful to our calling,
now and for ever. **Amen.**

*The Nicene Creed is not used at this service. The service continues with the Peace and the Preparation of the Gifts for the eucharist on p. 192.*

**Prayer over the Gifts**

God of life and health,
accept the offering of your holy people,
and grant that we who are baptized into Christ
may be perfected in your salvation,
in the name of Jesus Christ the risen Lord.

**Prayer after Communion**

Giver of all,
we are nourished with your Easter sacraments.
Fill us with the Spirit of love, and unite us in faith,
that we may be witnesses to the resurrection
and show your glory to all the world,
in the name of Jesus Christ the risen Lord.

# The Preparation of the Candle

*Any or all of the following rites may be used, depending on local circumstances.*

*A   After the blessing of the new fire, a lay person or one of the ministers brings the paschal candle to the celebrant, who cuts a cross in the wax and traces the Greek letter* alpha *above the cross, the letter* omega *below, and the numerals of the current year between the arms of the cross. Meanwhile he/she may say,*

1   Christ yesterday and today *(as he/she traces the vertical arm of the cross)*
2   the beginning and the end *(the horizontal arm)*
3   Alpha *(alpha, above the cross)*
4   and Omega *(omega, below the cross)*
5   all time belongs to him *(the first numeral, in the upper left corner of the cross)*
6   and all the ages *(the second numeral in the upper right corner)*
7   to him be glory and power *(the third numeral in the lower left corner)*
8   through every age for ever. Amen. *(the last numeral in the lower right corner)*

*B   When the cross and other marks have been made, the celebrant may insert five grains of incense into the candle. He/she does this in the form of a cross, saying,*

1   By his holy                     1
2   and glorious wounds
3   may Christ our Lord        4   2   5
4   guard us
5   and keep us. Amen.              3

*C   The celebrant lights the candle from the new fire, saying,*

May the light of Christ, rising in glory,
dispel the darkness of our hearts and minds.

# Additional Directions

When possible a large fire is prepared in a suitable place outside the church. The people assemble for the lighting of the new fire and of the paschal candle. All proceed to the darkened church, thus representing Christ and his antetype, the pillar of light leading the Israelites to their liberation.

Where it is difficult to have a large fire, the lighting of the new fire may be adapted to the circumstances. It may be lighted at the entrance to the church. The paschal candle, representing the risen Christ, is carried into the darkened church, the congregation waiting in silence.

In the absence of a deacon, the Exsultet may be sung by a priest or by a lay person. A different translation or musical setting may be substituted. Where it seems more fitting, an appropriate hymn or anthem may be sung in its place, for example, "Jesus Christ is risen today," "Come, ye faithful, raise the strain," "The strife is o'er."

The Service of Light may follow the Liturgy of the Word.

At the dismissal, "Alleluia" is added to the versicle and its response.

# Easter—during the Day

## Sentence

Christ our Passover has been sacrificed for us; therefore let us
keep the feast.   *1 Corinthians 5.7–8*

## Collect

Lord of life and power,
through the mighty resurrection of your Son,
you have overcome the old order of sin and death
and have made all things new in him.
May we, being dead to sin
and alive to you in Jesus Christ,
reign with him in glory,
who with you and the Holy Spirit is alive,
one God, now and for ever.

## Readings

*If the first reading is read from the Old Testament, the lection from Acts
should be the second reading.*

A    Acts 10.34–43 *or* Jeremiah 31.1–6    Psalm 118.14–24
     *Refrain*   On this day the Lord has acted; we will rejoice and be glad
     in it.   *Or* Alleluia!
     Colossians 3.1–4 *or* Acts 10.34–43     John 20.1–18 *or* Matthew 28.1–10

B    Acts 10.34–43 *or* Isaiah 25.6–9    Psalm 118.14–24
     *Refrain*   As in Year A
     1 Corinthians 15.1–11 *or* Acts 10.34–43    John 20.1–18 *or* Mark 16.1–8

C    Acts 10.34–43 *or* Isaiah 65.17–25    Psalm 118.14–24
     *Refrain*   As in Year A
     1 Corinthians 15.19–26 *or* Acts 10.34–43    John 20.1–18 *or* Luke 24.1–9

*Readings for Easter Evening*

     Daniel 12.1–3 *or* Acts 5.29–32     Psalm 150
     *Refrain*   Alleluia!
     1 Corinthians 5.6–8 *or* Acts 5.29–32     Luke 24.13–49

**Prayer over the Gifts**

God our strength and salvation,
receive all we offer you this day,
and grant that we who have confessed your name,
and received new life in baptism,
may live in the joy of the resurrection,
through Jesus Christ the Lord.

*Preface of Easter*

**Prayer after Communion**

God of life,
bring us to the glory of the resurrection
promised in this Easter sacrament.
We ask this in the name of Jesus Christ the risen Lord.

# Second Sunday of Easter

**Sentence**

Have you believed, Thomas, because you have seen me?
Blessed are those who have not seen and yet believe.
*John 20.29*

**Collect**

Almighty and eternal God,
the strength of those who believe
and the hope of those who doubt,
may we, who have not seen, have faith
and receive the fullness of Christ's blessing,
who is alive and reigns with you and the Holy Spirit,
one God, now and for ever.

**Readings**

A    Acts 2.14a, 22–32    Psalm 16.5–11
      *Refrain*   God will not abandon me to the grave.
      *Or v.10 or* Alleluia!
      1 Peter 1.3–9    John 20.19–31

B       Acts 4.32–35       Psalm 133
        *Refrain*   How good it is for all to live together in unity.
        *Or v.1 or* Alleluia!
        1 John 1.1—2.2       John 20.19–31

C       Acts 5.27–32       Psalm 2
        *Refrain*   God has exalted his anointed.   *Or v.6 or* Alleluia!
        Revelation 1.4–8       John 20.19–31

**Prayer over the Gifts**

God of grace,
you have freed us from our sins
and made us a kingdom in your Son
Jesus Christ our Lord.
Accept all we offer you this day,
and strengthen us in the new life you have given us,
through Jesus Christ our Lord.

*Preface of Easter*

**Prayer after Communion**

Father,
we have seen with our eyes
and touched with our hands
the bread of life.
Strengthen our faith
that we may grow in love for you and for each other;
through Jesus Christ the risen Lord.

# Third Sunday of Easter

**Sentence**

Lord Jesus, open to us the scriptures; make our hearts burn
within us while you speak.   *See Luke 24.32*

## Collect

O God,
your Son made himself known to his disciples
in the breaking of bread.
Open the eyes of our faith,
that we may see him in his redeeming work,
who is alive and reigns with you and the Holy Spirit,
one God, now and for ever.

## Readings

A    Acts 2.14a, 36–41      Psalm 116.10–17
     *Refrain*   I will call upon the name of the Lord.
     *Or v.11 or* Alleluia!
     1 Peter 1.17–23      Luke 24.13–35

B    Acts 3.12–19      Psalm 4
     *Refrain*   The Lord does wonders for the faithful.
     *Or v.3 or* Alleluia!
     1 John 3.1–7      Luke 24.35–48

C    Acts 9.1–20      Psalm 30.4–12
     *Refrain*   Remember God's holiness and praise him.
     *Or v.4 or* Alleluia!
     Revelation 5.11–14      John 21.1–19 *or* John 21.15–19

## Prayer over the Gifts

Creator of all,
you wash away our sins in water,
you give us new birth by the Spirit,
and redeem us in the blood of Christ.
As we celebrate the resurrection,
renew your gift of life within us.
We ask this in the name of Jesus Christ the risen Lord.

*Preface of Easter*

## Prayer after Communion

Author of life divine,
in the breaking of bread we know the risen Lord.
Feed us always in these mysteries,

that we may show your glory to all the world.
We ask this in the name of Jesus Christ our Lord.

## Fourth Sunday of Easter

### Sentence

I am the good shepherd, says the Lord: I know my own and my
own know me.   *John 10.14*

### Collect

O God of peace,
who brought again from the dead our Lord Jesus Christ,
that great shepherd of the sheep,
by the blood of the eternal covenant,
make us perfect in every good work to do your will,
and work in us that which is well-pleasing in your sight;
through Jesus Christ our Lord.

### Readings

A   Acts 2.42–47      Psalm 23
    *Refrain*   The Lord is my shepherd; I shall not be in want.
    *Or v.6 or* Alleluia!
    1 Peter 2.19–25       John 10.1–10

B   Acts 4.8–12      Psalm 23
    *Refrain*   As Year A
    1 John 3.18–24      John 10.11–18

C   Acts 13.15–16, 26–33      Psalm 23
    *Refrain*   As Year A
    Revelation 7.9–17       John 10.22–30

### Prayer over the Gifts

God of loving care,
you spread before us the table of life,
and give us the cup of salvation to drink.
Keep us always in the fold of your Son Jesus Christ,
our Saviour and our shepherd.

*Preface of Easter*

**Prayer after Communion**

God of steadfast love,
watch over the Church redeemed by the blood of your Son.
May we who share in these holy mysteries
come safely to your eternal kingdom,
where there is one flock and one shepherd.
We ask this in the name of Jesus Christ the risen Lord.

# Fifth Sunday of Easter

**Sentence**

A   I am the way, the truth, and the life, says the Lord; no one
comes to the Father, but by me.   *John 14.6*

B   I am the vine, you are the branches, says the Lord. Those
who abide in me, and I in them, bear much fruit.
*John 15.5*

C   A new commandment I give to you, that you love one
another as I have loved you.   *John 13.34*

**Collect**

Almighty God,
your Son Jesus Christ is the way, the truth, and the life.
Give us grace to love one another
and walk in the way of his commandments,
who lives and reigns with you and the Holy Spirit,
one God, now and for ever.

**Readings**

A   Acts 7.55–60      Psalm 31.1–8
*Refrain*   Into your hands, O Lord, I commend my spirit.
*Or v.5 or* Alleluia!
1 Peter 2.2–10      John 14.1–14

B   Acts 8.26–40      Psalm 22.24–30
*Refrain*   All the ends of the earth shall turn to the Lord.
*Or v.26 or* Alleluia!
1 John 4.7–12      John 15.1–8

C     Acts 14.8–18     Psalm 145.14–22
      *Refrain*  The Lord is close to all who call him.
      *Or v.19 or* Alleluia!
      Revelation 21.1–6     John 13.31–35

**Prayer over the Gifts**

Gracious God,
you show us your way
and give us your divine life.
May everything we do
be directed by the knowledge of your truth.
We ask this in the name of Jesus Christ the risen Lord.

*Preface of Easter*

**Prayer after Communion**

God of love,
in this eucharist we have heard your truth
and shared in your life.
May we always walk in your way,
in the name of Jesus Christ the Lord.

# Sixth Sunday of Easter

**Sentence**

If you love me, you will keep my word, and my Father will love
you, and we will come to you.     *See John 14.23*

**Collect**

Merciful God,
you have prepared for those who love you
riches beyond imagination.
Pour into our hearts such love toward you,
that we, loving you above all things,
may obtain your promises,
which exceed all that we can desire;
through Jesus Christ our Lord,
who is alive and reigns with you and the Holy Spirit,
one God, now and for ever.

**Readings**

A    Acts 17.22–31    Psalm 66.7–18
     *Refrain*    Be joyful in the Lord, all you lands.
     *Or v.7 or* Alleluia!
     1 Peter 3.13–22    John 14.15–21

B    Acts 10.44–48    Psalm 98
     *Refrain*    The Lord has made known his salvation.
     *Or v.3 or* Alleluia!
     1 John 5.1–6    John 15.9–17

C    Acts 15.1–2, 22–29    Psalm 67
     *Refrain*    Let all the peoples praise you, O God.
     *Or v.3 or* Alleluia!
     Revelation 21.10, 22–27    John 14.23–29

**Prayer over the Gifts**

God of glory,
accept all we offer you this day,
and bring us to that eternal city of love and light,
where Christ is King.
We ask this in his name.

*Preface of Easter*

**Prayer after Communion**

Father,
you restored us to life
by raising your Son from death.
May we who receive this sacrament
always be strengthened to do your will,
in the name of Jesus Christ the risen Lord.

# Ascension of the Lord

**Sentence**

Go and make disciples of all nations, says the Lord; I am with
you always, to the close of the age.    *Matthew 28.19, 20*

**Collect**

Almighty God,
your Son Jesus Christ ascended to the throne of heaven
that he might rule over all things as Lord.
Keep the Church in the unity of the Spirit
and in the bond of his peace,
and bring the whole of creation
to worship at his feet,
who is alive and reigns with you and the Holy Spirit,
one God, now and for ever.

**Readings**

> Acts 1.1–11      Psalm 47
> *Refrain*   God has gone up with a shout.   *Or v.5 or CR 3*
> Ephesians 1.15–23      Luke 24.46–53 *or* Mark 16.9–16, 19–20

**Prayer over the Gifts**

Eternal God,
our Saviour Jesus Christ
has promised to be with us until the end of time.
Accept all we offer you this day,
and renew us in his transfigured life;
for the sake of Jesus Christ our Lord.

*Preface of the Ascension*

**Prayer after Communion**

Eternal Giver of love and power,
your Son Jesus Christ has sent us into all the world
to preach the gospel of his kingdom.
Confirm us in this mission,
and help us to live the good news we proclaim;
through Jesus Christ our Lord.

# Seventh Sunday of Easter

## Sentence

I will not leave you desolate, says the Lord; I will come to
you.   *John 14.18*

## Collect

Almighty God,
you have exalted your only Son Jesus Christ
with great triumph to your kingdom in heaven.
Mercifully give us faith to know
that, as he promised,
he abides with us on earth to the end of time;
who is alive and reigns with you and the Holy Spirit,
one God, now and for ever.

## Readings

A     Acts 1.6–14      Psalm 68.1–10
      *Refrain*   Exalt him who rides upon the heavens.
      *Or v.4 or* Alleluia!
      1 Peter 4.12–14; 5.6–11      John 17.1–11

B     Acts 1.15–17, 21–26      Psalm 1
      *Refrain*   Happy are they who trust in the Lord.   *Or* Alleluia!
      1 John 5.9–13      John 17.11b–19

C     Acts 16.16–34      Psalm 97
      *Refrain*   Rejoice in the Lord, you righteous.
      *Or v.12 or* Alleluia!
      Revelation 22.12–14, 16–17, 20      John 17.20–26

## Prayer over the Gifts

Source of all joy,
receive our sacrifice of praise and thanksgiving.
Keep us in the love of Christ
and bring us to the vision of his glory;
through the same Jesus Christ our Lord.

*Preface of the Ascension*

**Prayer after Communion**

Eternal God,
may we who share Christ's banquet
be one with him as he is one with you.
We ask this in the name of Jesus Christ,
the risen and ascended Lord.

# The Day of Pentecost

**Sentence**

Come, Holy Spirit, fill the hearts of your faithful; and kindle in
us the fire of your love.

**Collect**

Almighty and everliving God,
who fulfilled the promises of Easter
by sending us your Holy Spirit
and opening to every race and nation
the way of life eternal,
keep us in the unity of your Spirit,
that every tongue may tell of your glory;
through Jesus Christ our Lord,
who lives and reigns with you and the Holy Spirit,
one God, now and for ever.

**Readings**

A    Acts 2.1–21 *or* Isaiah 44.1–8    Psalm 104.25–35
    *Refrain*   Send forth your Spirit, O Lord, and renew the face of the earth.
    *Or v.31 or* Alleluia!
    1 Corinthians 12.3b–13 *or* Acts 2.1–21    John 20.19–23 *or* John 7.37–39

B    Acts 2.1–21 *or* Ezekiel 37.1–14    Psalm 104.25–35
    *Refrain*   As Year A
    Romans 8.22–27 *or* Acts 2.1–21    John 15.26–27; 16.4b–15

C    Acts 2.1–21 *or* Genesis 11.1–9    Psalm 104.25–35
    *Refrain*   As Year A
    Romans 8.14–17 *or* Acts 2.1–21    John 14.8–17, 25–27

**Prayer over the Gifts**

Giver of life,
receive all we offer you this day.
Let the Spirit you bestow on your Church
continue to work in the world
through the hearts of all who believe.
We ask this in the name of Jesus Christ the Lord.

*Preface of Pentecost*

**Prayer after Communion**

Father,
may we who have received this eucharist
live in the unity of your Holy Spirit,
that we may show forth his gifts to all the world.
We ask this in the name of Jesus Christ our Lord.

# Trinity Sunday

**Sentence**

Holy, holy, holy is the Lord of hosts; the whole earth is full of
his glory.    *Isaiah 6.3*

**Collect**

Father, we praise you:
through your Word and Holy Spirit you created all things.
You reveal your salvation in all the world
by sending to us Jesus Christ, the Word made flesh.
Through your Holy Spirit
you give us a share in your life and love.
Fill us with the vision of your glory,
that we may always serve and praise you,
Father, Son, and Holy Spirit,
one God, for ever and ever.

## Readings

A    Deuteronomy 4.32–40      Psalm 33.1–12
     *Refrain*    Happy the people chosen by the Lord.    *Or v.12 or CR 1*
     2 Corinthians 13.5–14      Matthew 28.16–20

B    Isaiah 6.1–8      Psalm 29
     *Refrain*    Ascribe to the Lord glory and strength.    *Or v.1 or CR 3*
     Romans 8.12–17      John 3.1–17

C    Proverbs 8.22–31      Psalm 8
     *Refrain*    O Lord our governor, how exalted is your name in all the
     world!    *Or v.2 or CR 2*
     Romans 5.1–5      John 16.12–15

## Prayer over the Gifts

Living God,
receive all we offer you this day.
Grant that hearing your word and responding to your Spirit,
we may share in your divine life.
We ask this in the name of Jesus Christ the Lord.

*Preface of the Trinity*

## Prayer after Communion

Almighty and eternal God,
may we who have received this eucharist
worship you in all we do,
and proclaim the glory of your majesty.
We ask this in the name of Jesus Christ the Lord.

*Propers for the Sundays after Pentecost may be found with other ferial
propers, in numerical order, beginning on p. 354. The dates for their use are
identified.*

# The Baptism of the Lord   *Proper 1*

**Sentence**

A voice came from heaven, saying, "This is my beloved Son
with whom I am well pleased."   *Matthew 3.17*

**Collect**

Eternal Father,
who at the baptism of Jesus
revealed him to be your Son,
anointing him with the Holy Spirit,
keep your children, born of water and the Spirit,
faithful to their calling;
through Jesus Christ our Lord,
who lives and reigns with you and the Holy Spirit,
one God, now and for ever.

**Readings**

A    Isaiah 42.1–9    Psalm 29
     *Refrain*   The Lord shall give his people the blessing of peace.
     *Or v.11 or CR 1*
     Acts 10.34–43    Matthew 3.13–17

B    Genesis 1.1–5    Psalm 29
     *Refrain*   As Year A
     Acts 19.1–7    Mark 1.4–11

C    Isaiah 61.1–4    Psalm 29
     *Refrain*   As Year A
     Acts 8.14–17    Luke 3.15–17, 21–22

**Prayer over the Gifts**

God of life and freedom,
we celebrate the revelation of Jesus
as the Christ who makes all creation new.
Accept all we offer you this day
and make us new in him,
who is Lord for ever and ever.

*Third Preface of the Lord's Day*

**Prayer after Communion**

Gracious God, lover of all,
by this sacrament
you make us one family in Christ your Son,
one in the sharing of his body and blood,
one in the communion of his Spirit.
Help us to grow in love for one another
and come to the full maturity of the Body of Christ.
We ask this in his name.


## Second Sunday after Epiphany   *Proper 2*

**Sentence**

A   The Word of God became flesh and dwelt among us. To
all who receive him, he gave power to become children of
God.   *See John 1*

B   We have found the Messiah: Jesus Christ, who brings us
truth and grace.   *See John 1*

C   Jesus manifested his glory, and his disciples believed in
him.   *John 2.11*

**Collect**

Almighty God,
your Son our Saviour Jesus Christ
is the light of the world.
May your people,
illumined by your word and sacraments,
shine with the radiance of his glory,
that he may be known, worshipped, and obeyed
to the ends of the earth;
who lives and reigns with you and the Holy Spirit,
one God, now and for ever.

**Readings**

A   Isaiah 49.1–7      Psalm 40.1–11
*Refrain*   Behold, I come to do your will, O God.   *Or v.8*
1 Corinthians 1.1–9      John 1.29–34

B    1 Samuel 3.1–10(11–20)    Psalm 63.1–8
     *Refrain*  My soul thirsts for you, O God, my God.   *Or v.8 or CR 6*
     1 Corinthians 6.12–20    John 1.35–42

C    Isaiah 62.1–5    Psalm 36.5–10
     *Refrain*  We feast on the riches of your house, O Lord.
     *Or v.8 or CR 1*
     1 Corinthians 12.1–11    John 2.1–11

**Prayer over the Gifts**

Living God,
you have revealed your Son as the Messiah.
May we hear his word and follow it,
and live as children of light.
We ask this in the name of Jesus Christ the Lord.

*Preface of the Lord's Day*

**Prayer after Communion**

God of glory,
you nourish us with bread from heaven.
Fill us with your Holy Spirit,
that through us your light may shine in all the world.
We ask this in the name of Jesus Christ.

# Third Sunday after Epiphany   *Proper 3*

**Sentence**

A    Jesus preached the gospel of the kingdom and healed
     every infirmity among the people.   *See Matthew 4.23*

B    The time is fulfilled, and the kingdom of God is at hand;
     repent, and believe in the gospel.   *Mark 1.15*

C    The Lord has anointed me to preach good news to the
     poor and release to the captives.   *Luke 4.18*

**Collect**

Almighty God,
by grace alone you call us
and accept us in your service.
Strengthen us by your Spirit,
and make us worthy of your call;
through Jesus Christ our Lord,
who lives and reigns with you and the Holy Spirit,
one God, now and for ever.

**Readings**

A    Isaiah 9.1–4      Psalm 27.1–6
     *Refrain*   The Lord is my light and salvation.   *Or v.1 or CR 1*
     1 Corinthians 1.10–17      Matthew 4.12–23

B    Jonah 3.1–5, 10      Psalm 62.6–14
     *Refrain*   Take refuge in God, all you people.   *Or v.9 or CR 1*
     1 Corinthians 7.29–31(32–35)      Mark 1.14–20

C    Nehemiah 8.1–4a, 5–6, 8–10      Psalm 19.7–14
     *Refrain*   The words of the Lord are spirit and life.
     *Or v.8 or CR 1*
     1 Corinthians 12.12–30      Luke 4.14–21

**Prayer over the Gifts**

Loving God,
before the world began you called us.
Make holy all we offer you this day,
and strengthen us in that calling.
We ask this in the name of Jesus Christ the Lord.

*Preface of the Lord's Day*

**Prayer after Communion**

Gracious God,
our hands have taken holy things;
our lives have been nourished by the body of your Son.
May we who have eaten at this holy table
be strengthened for service in your world.
We ask this in the name of Jesus Christ the Lord.

# Fourth Sunday after Epiphany   *Proper 4*

## Sentence

A   Rejoice and be glad, for your reward is great in heaven.
*Matthew 5.12*

B   Jesus went about Galilee, teaching, preaching, and
healing every disease.   *See Matthew 4.23*

C   The Lord has anointed me to preach good news to the
poor and release to the captives.   *Luke 4.18*

## Collect

Living God,
in Christ you make all things new.
Transform the poverty of our nature
by the riches of your grace,
and in the renewal of our lives
make known your glory;
through Jesus Christ our Lord,
who is alive and reigns with you and the Holy Spirit,
one God, now and for ever.

## Readings

A   Micah 6.1–8      Psalm 37.1–12
*Refrain*   Put your trust in the Lord and do good.   *Or v.3 or CR 4*
1 Corinthians 1.18–31      Matthew 5.1–12

B   Deuteronomy 18.15–20      Psalm 111
*Refrain*   The fear of the Lord is the beginning of wisdom.
*Or v.10 or* Alleluia!
1 Corinthians 8.1–13      Mark 1.21–28

C   Jeremiah 1.4–10      Psalm 71.1–6
*Refrain*   From my mother's womb you have been my strength.
*Or v.6 or CR 5*
1 Corinthians 13.1–13      Luke 4.21–30

**Prayer over the Gifts**

God of steadfast love,
may our offering this day,
by the power of your Holy Spirit,
renew us for your service.
We ask this in the name of Jesus Christ the Lord.

*Preface of the Lord's Day*

**Prayer after Communion**

Source of all goodness,
in this eucharist
we are nourished by the bread of heaven
and invigorated with new wine.
May these gifts renew our lives,
that we may show your glory to all the world,
in the name of Jesus Christ the Lord.

# Fifth Sunday after Epiphany   *Proper 5*

**Sentence**

*AC*   I am the light of the world, says the Lord. Those who
follow me will not walk in darkness, but will have the
light of life.   *John 8.12*

*B*   He took our infirmities and bore our diseases.
*Matthew 8.17*

**Collect**

Merciful Lord,
grant to your faithful people pardon and peace,
that we may be cleansed from all our sins
and serve you with a quiet mind;
through Jesus Christ our Lord,
who is alive and reigns with you and the Holy Spirit,
one God, now and for ever.

### Readings

A    Isaiah 58.3–9a    Psalm 112.4–9
*Refrain*    The righteous are merciful and full of compassion.
*Or v.4 or* Alleluia!
1 Corinthians 2.1–11    Matthew 5.13–16

B    Job 7.1–7    Psalm 147.1–11
*Refrain*    Praise the Lord who heals the broken-hearted.
*Or v.3 or* Alleluia!
1 Corinthians 9.16–23    Mark 1.29–39

C    Isaiah 6.1–8(9–13)    Psalm 138
*Refrain*    The Lord will make good his purpose for me.
*Or v.4 or* Alleluia!
1 Corinthians 15.1–11    Luke 5.1–11

### Prayer over the Gifts

God of compassion and forgiveness,
receive our offering this day,
and make us one with him who is our peace,
Jesus Christ our Saviour.

*Preface of the Lord's Day*

### Prayer after Communion

Eternal God,
in you we find peace beyond all telling.
May we who share in this heavenly banquet
be instruments of your peace on earth,
in the name of Jesus Christ the Lord.

# Sixth Sunday after Epiphany
# or between 8 and 14 May   *Proper 6*

### Sentence

A    Blessed is our Father, Lord of heaven and earth, who has
revealed these things to the simple.

B A great prophet has arisen among us! God has visited his people! *Luke 7.16*

C Rejoice and leap for joy, for behold, your reward is great in heaven. *Luke 6.23*

**Collect**

Almighty and everliving God,
whose Son Jesus Christ healed the sick
and restored them to wholeness of life,
look with compassion on the anguish of the world,
and by your power make whole all peoples and nations;
through Jesus Christ our Lord,
who lives and reigns with you and the Holy Spirit,
one God, now and for ever.

**Readings**

A Deuteronomy 30.15–20 *or* Sirach 15.15–20  Psalm 119.1–8
 *Refrain* Happy are they who walk in the law of the Lord.
 *Or v.1 or CR 1*
 1 Corinthians 3.1–9  Matthew 5.17–26

B 2 Kings 5.1–14  Psalm 32
 *Refrain* You surround me with shouts of deliverance, O Lord.
 *Or v.8 or CR 1*
 1 Corinthians 9.24–27  Mark 1.40–45

C Jeremiah 17.5–10  Psalm 1
 *Refrain* Happy are they who trust in the Lord. *Or CR 4*
 1 Corinthians 15.12–20  Luke 6.17–26

**Prayer over the Gifts**

Eternal God,
you are the strength of the weak
and the comfort of sufferers,
receive all we offer you this day;
turn our sickness into health
and our sorrow into joy.
We ask this in the name of Jesus Christ the Lord.

**Prayer after Communion**

God of tender care,
in this eucharist we celebrate your love
for us and for all people.
May we show your love in our lives
and know its fulfilment in your presence.
We ask this in the name of Jesus Christ the Lord.

# Seventh Sunday after Epiphany
# or between 15 and 21 May   *Proper 7*

**Sentence**

A   Whoever keeps the word of Christ grows perfect in love
for God.   *See 1 John 2.5*

B   The Lord has anointed me to preach good news to the
poor and release to the captives.   *Luke 4.18*

C   A new commandment I give to you, that you love one
another as I have loved you.   *John 13.34*

**Collect**

Almighty God,
your Son revealed in signs and miracles
the wonder of your saving love.
Renew your people with your heavenly grace,
and in all our weakness
sustain us by your mighty power;
through Jesus Christ our Lord,
who is alive and reigns with you and the Holy Spirit,
one God, now and for ever.

**Readings**

A   Isaiah 49.8–13       Psalm 62.6–14
    *Refrain*   Take refuge in God, all you people.   *Or v.9 or CR 1*
    1 Corinthians 3.10–11, 16–23       Matthew 5.27–37

B     Isaiah 43.18–25     Psalm 41
      *Refrain*   Heal me, for I have sinned against you.   *Or v.4 or CR 4*
      2 Corinthians 1.18–22     Mark 2.1–12

C     Genesis 45.3–11, 15     Psalm 37.1–12
      *Refrain*   Put your trust in the Lord and do good.   *Or v.3 or CR 5*
      1 Corinthians 15.35–38, 42–50     Luke 6.27–38

### Prayer over the Gifts

Merciful God,
accept all we offer you this day.
Lead us to love you with all our heart,
and to love all people with your perfect love.
We ask this in the name of Jesus Christ.

*Preface of the Lord's Day*

### Prayer after Communion

Gracious God,
in the eucharist we celebrate your love
for us and for all people.
Grant that strengthened by these holy gifts,
we may show your love in our lives,
and know its fulfilment in your presence.
We ask this in the name of Jesus Christ our Lord.

# Eighth Sunday after Epiphany
# or between 22 and 28 May   *Proper 8*

### Sentence

A     The word of God is living and active. It sifts the thoughts
      and intentions of the heart.   *Hebrews 4.12*

B     The Father brought us forth by the word of truth that we
      should be a kind of first fruits of his creatures.   *James 1.18*

C     Shine as lights in the world, holding fast the word of
      life.   *See Philippians 2.15, 16*

**Collect**

Almighty God,
grant us the Spirit to think and do always
those things that are right,
that we who can do nothing good without you,
may live according to your holy will;
through Jesus Christ our Lord,
who lives and reigns with you and the Holy Spirit,
one God, now and for ever.

**Readings**

A   Leviticus 19.1–2, 9–18      Psalm 119.33–40
    *Refrain*   Instruct me in your statutes, O Lord.   *Or v.33 or CR 1*
    1 Corinthians 4.1–5       Matthew 5.38–48

B   Hosea 2.14–20      Psalm 103.1–13
    *Refrain*   The Lord is full of compassion and mercy.   *Or v.8 or CR 6*
    2 Corinthians 3.1–6       Mark 2.18–22

C   Sirach 27.4–7 *or* Isaiah 55.10–13      Psalm 92.1–4, 12–15
    *Refrain*   The righteous shall flourish like a palm tree.   *Or v.11 or CR 1*
    1 Corinthians 15.51–58       Luke 6.39–49

**Prayer over the Gifts**

Merciful God,
your word inspires us to bring an offering of our love.
May we always be ready to work according to your will.
We ask this in the name of Jesus Christ, the Lord.

*Preface of the Lord's Day*

**Prayer after Communion**

Faithful God,
as we are nourished by heavenly food,
may we live according to your will
and show the fruits of your love.
We ask this in the name of Jesus Christ the Lord.

# Ninth Sunday after Epiphany
## or between 29 May and 4 June *Proper 9*

### Sentence

A    I am the vine, and you are the branches, says the Lord.
Those who abide in me, and I in them, bear much fruit.
*John 15.5*

B    Your word, O Lord, is truth; sanctify us in the truth.
*John 17.17*

C    God so loved the world that he gave his only Son, that
whoever believes in him should not perish but have
eternal life.   *John 3.16*

### Collect

Lord God of the nations,
you have revealed your will to all people
and promised us your saving help.
May we hear and do what you command,
that the darkness may be overcome
by the power of your light;
through your Son Jesus Christ our Lord,
who lives and reigns with you and the Holy Spirit,
now and for ever.

### Readings

A    Genesis 12.1–9    Psalm 33.12–22
*Refrain*  Let your loving-kindness be upon us, O Lord.
*Or v.22 or CR 4*
Romans 3.21–28    Matthew 7.21–29

B    1 Samuel 16.1–13    Psalm 20
*Refrain*  The Lord gives victory to his anointed.   *Or v.6 or CR 7*
2 Corinthians 4.5–12    Mark 2.23—3.6

C    1 Kings 8.22–23, 41–43    Psalm 100
*Refrain*  The Lord is good; his mercy is everlasting.   *Or v.4 or CR 1*
Galatians 1.1–10    Luke 7.1–10

**Prayer over the Gifts**

Eternal God,
receive all we offer you this day.
Give us the wisdom of obedience
and help us to do your holy and life-giving will;
through Jesus Christ our Lord.

*Preface of the Lord's Day*

**Prayer after Communion**

Eternal God,
you have fed us at the table of your grace.
Deliver us from all spiritual pride,
and give us a quiet confidence in your mercy.
We ask this in the name of Jesus Christ our Lord.


# Sunday between 5 and 11 June  *Proper 10*

**Sentence**

A    The Lord has anointed me to preach good news to the
     poor and release to the captives.   *Luke 4.18*

B    The ruler of this world shall now be cast out; and when I
     am lifted up from the earth, I will draw all people to
     myself.   *John 12.31, 32*

C    A great prophet has arisen among us! God has visited his
     people!   *Luke 7.16*

**Collect**

O God,
you have assured the human family of eternal life
through Jesus Christ our Saviour.
Deliver us from the death of sin
and raise us to new life in him,
who lives and reigns with you and the Holy Spirit,
one God, now and for ever.

**Readings**

A     Genesis 22.1–18     Psalm 13
      *Refrain*  I will sing to the Lord, for he has dealt with me richly.
      *Or v.6 or CR 6*
      Romans 4.13–18     Matthew 9.9–13

B     1 Samuel 16.14–23     Psalm 57
      *Refrain*  In the shadow of your wings will I take refuge.
      *Or v.1 or CR 8*
      2 Corinthians 4.13—5.1     Mark 3.20–35

C     1 Kings 17.17–24     Psalm 113
      *Refrain*  Praise the name of the Lord.   *Or v.8 or CR 2*
      Galatians 1.11–24     Luke 7.11–17

**Prayer over the Gifts**

Merciful God and Father,
in Adam's fall we were born to death;
in the new Adam we are reborn to life.
In all we offer you this day
may we share a taste of your eternal kingdom.
We ask this in the name of Jesus Christ the Lord.

*Preface of the Lord's Day*

**Prayer after Communion**

O God,
we have shared in the mysteries
of the body and blood of Christ.
Nourish us by this feast,
that we may live the risen life
and serve you faithfully in the world.
We ask this in the name of Jesus Christ the Lord.

# Sunday between 12 and 18 June   *Proper 11*

**Sentence**

A     The kingdom of God is at hand; repent, and believe in the
     gospel.   *Mark 1.15*

B    Quietly accept the message planted in your hearts; it can
     bring you salvation.   *James 1.21*

C    In this is love, that God loved us and sent his Son to be the
     expiation for our sins.   *1 John 4.10*

**Collect**

Almighty God,
without you we are not able to please you.
Mercifully grant that your Holy Spirit
may in all things direct and rule our hearts;
through Jesus Christ our Lord,
who is alive and reigns with you and the Holy Spirit,
one God, now and for ever.

**Readings**

A    Genesis 25.19–34      Psalm 46
     *Refrain*  The God of Jacob is our stronghold.   *Or v.4 or CR 1*
     Romans 5.6–11        Matthew 9.35—10.8

B    2 Samuel 1.1, 17–27      Psalm 46
     *Refrain*  The God of Jacob is our stronghold.   *Or v.4 or CR 1*
     2 Corinthians 5.6–10, 14–17      Mark 4.26–34

C    1 Kings 19.1–8      Psalm 42
     *Refrain*  When shall I come to appear before the presence of God?
     *Or v.6 or CR 4*
     Galatians 2.15–21      Luke 7.36—8.3

**Prayer over the Gifts**

God of reconciliation and forgiveness,
the saving work of Christ has made our peace with you.
May that work grow toward its perfection
in all we offer you this day.
We ask this in his name.

*Preface of the Lord's Day*

**Prayer after Communion**

Holy and blessed God,
as you give us the body and blood of your Son,
guide us with your Holy Spirit,
that we may honour you not only with our lips
but also in our lives.
This we ask in the name of Jesus Christ our Lord.

## Sunday between 19 and 25 June   *Proper 12*

**Sentence**

A     The Spirit of truth will bear witness to me, says the Lord;
      and you also are witnesses.   *John 15.26, 27*

B     A great prophet has arisen among us! God has visited his
      people!   *Luke 7.16*

C     My sheep hear my voice, says the Lord; I know them and
      they follow me.   *John 10.27*

**Collect**

O God our defender,
storms rage about us and cause us to be afraid.
Rescue your people from despair,
deliver your sons and daughters from fear,
and preserve us all from unbelief;
through your Son, Jesus Christ our Lord,
who lives and reigns with you and the Holy Spirit,
one God, now and ever.

**Readings**

A     Genesis 28.10–17     Psalm 91.1–10
      *Refrain*   My God in whom I put my trust.   *Or v.2 or CR 4*
      Romans 5.12–19     Matthew 10.24–33

B     2 Samuel 5.1–12     Psalm 48
      *Refrain*   God shall be our guide for evermore.   *Or v.1 or CR 1*
      2 Corinthians 5.18—6.2     Mark 4.35–41

C    1 Kings 19.9–14     Psalm 43

    *Refrain*   Bring me to your holy hill and to your dwelling.

    *Or v.3 or CR 4*

    Galatians 3.23–29     Luke 9.18–24

**Prayer over the Gifts**

Eternal God,
you have made our Saviour Jesus Christ
the head of all creation.
Receive all we offer you this day
and renew us in his risen life,
in the name of Jesus Christ the Lord.

*Preface of the Lord's Day*

**Prayer after Communion**

Almighty God,
guide and protect your people
who share in this sacred mystery,
and keep us always in your love;
through Jesus Christ our Lord.

# Sunday between 26 June and 2 July   *Proper 13*

**Sentence**

A    You are a chosen race, a royal priesthood, a holy nation,
    that you may declare the wonderful deeds of him who
    called you out of darkness into his marvellous light.
    *1 Peter 2.9*

B    Our Saviour Jesus Christ has abolished death, and
    brought life and immortality to light through the gospel.
    *2 Timothy 1.10*

C    Speak Lord, for your servant is listening: you have the
    words of eternal life.   *See 1 Samuel 3.9; John 6.68*

## Collect

Almighty God,
you have taught us through your Son
that love fulfils the law.
May we love you with all our heart,
all our soul, all our mind, and all our strength,
and may we love our neighbour as ourselves;
through Jesus Christ our Lord,
who lives and reigns with you and the Holy Spirit,
one God, now and for ever.

## Readings

A    Genesis 32.22–32    Psalm 17.1–7, 16
     *Refrain*   Show me your marvellous loving-kindness, O Saviour of those
     who take refuge at your right hand.   *Or v.16 or CR 4*
     Romans 6.3–11    Matthew 10.34–42

B    2 Samuel 6.1–15    Psalm 24
     *Refrain*   Lift up your heads, O gates; and the King of glory shall come in.
     *Or v.7 or CR 2*
     2 Corinthians 8.7–15    Mark 5.21–43

C    1 Kings 19.15–21    Psalm 44.1–8
     *Refrain*   You drove the nations out and made your people flourish.
     *Or v.8 or CR 2*
     Galatians 5.1, 13–25    Luke 9.51–62

## Prayer over the Gifts

God of wisdom,
receive all we offer you this day.
Enrich our lives with the gifts of your Spirit,
that we may follow the way of our Lord Jesus Christ,
and serve one another in freedom.
We ask this in his name.

*Preface of the Lord's Day*

**Prayer after Communion**

God of power,
we are nourished by the riches of your grace.
Raise us to new life in your Son Jesus Christ
and fit us for his eternal kingdom,
that all the world may call him Lord.
We ask this in his name.

# Sunday between 3 and 9 July   *Proper 14*

**Sentence**

A    Blessed is our Father, Lord of heaven and earth, who has
     revealed these things to the simple.

B    The Lord has anointed me to preach good news to the
     poor and release to the captives.   *Luke 4.18*

C    Let the peace of Christ rule in your hearts; let the word of
     Christ dwell in you richly.   *Colossians 3.15, 16*

**Collect**

Almighty God,
your Son Jesus Christ has taught us
that what we do for the least of your children
we do also for him.
Give us the will to serve others
as he was the servant of all,
who gave up his life and died for us,
but lives and reigns with you and the Holy Spirit,
one God, now and for ever.

**Readings**

A    Exodus 1.6–14, 22—2.10      Psalm 124
     *Refrain*   Our help is in the name of the Lord.   *Or v.8 or CR 5*
     Romans 7.14–25a      Matthew 11.25–30

B    2 Samuel 7.1–17      Psalm 89.20–37
     *Refrain*   I will keep my love for him for ever.   *Or v.28 or CR 6*
     2 Corinthians 12.1–10      Mark 6.1–6

C     1 Kings 21.1–3, 17–21     Psalm 5.1–8

*Refrain*  Evil cannot dwell with you, my God.   *Or v.4 or CR 5*

Galatians 6.7–18     Luke 10.1–12, 17–20

**Prayer over the Gifts**

God of heaven and earth,
receive our sacrifice of praise,
and strengthen us
for the perfect freedom of your service,
through our Saviour Jesus Christ.

*Preface of the Lord's Day*

**Prayer after Communion**

O God,
may we who have shared in holy things
never fail to serve you in your world,
and so come to the fullness of joy,
in the name of Jesus Christ our Lord.

# Sunday between 10 and 16 July   *Proper 15*

**Sentence**

AB    The word is very near you; it is in your mouth and in your
heart, so that you can do it.   *Deuteronomy 30.14*

C     The words you have spoken are spirit and life, O Lord;
you have the words of eternal life.   *See John 6.63, 68*

**Collect**

Almighty God,
you have made us for yourself,
and our hearts are restless
until they find their rest in you.
May we find peace in your service,
and in the world to come, see you face to face;
through Jesus Christ our Lord,
who lives and reigns with you and the Holy Spirit,
one God, now and for ever.

**Readings**

A    Exodus 2.11–22    Psalm 69.6–15
     *Refrain*    Answer me, O Lord, for your love is kind.    *Or v.18 or CR 5*
     Romans 8.9–17    Matthew 13.1–9, 18–23

B    2 Samuel 7.18–29    Psalm 132.11–19
     *Refrain*    The Lord will dwell in Zion for ever.    *Or v.14 or CR 8*
     Ephesians 1.1–10    Mark 6.7–13

C    2 Kings 2.1, 6–14    Psalm 139.1–11
     *Refrain*    Lord, your hand will hold me fast.    *Or v.8, 9 or CR 2*
     Colossians 1.1–14    Luke 10.25–37

**Prayer over the Gifts**

Father,
your word creates in us a yearning for your kingdom.
Receive all we offer you this day, and keep us in your peace;
for the sake of Jesus Christ the Lord.

*Preface of the Lord's Day*

**Prayer after Communion**

Living God,
in this sacrament we have shared in your eternal kingdom.
May we who taste this mystery
forever serve you in faith, hope, and love.
We ask this in the name of Jesus Christ the Lord.

# Sunday between 17 and 23 July    *Proper 16*

**Sentence**

A    My word shall accomplish that which I purpose, and
     prosper in the thing for which I sent it.    *Isaiah 55.11*

B    My sheep hear my voice, says the Lord; I know them and
     they follow me.    *John 10.27*

C    Blessed are they who hold the word fast in an honest and
     good heart, and bring forth fruit with patience.
     *See Luke 8.15*

**Collect**

Almighty God,
your Son has opened for us
a new and living way into your presence.
Give us pure hearts and constant wills
to worship you in spirit and in truth;
through Jesus Christ our Lord,
who lives and reigns with you and the Holy Spirit,
one God, now and for ever.

**Readings**

A     Exodus 3.1–12     Psalm 103.1–13
      *Refrain*   The Lord is full of compassion and mercy.
      *Or v.7 or CR 6*
      Romans 8.18–25     Matthew 13.24–30, 36–43

B     2 Samuel 11.1–15     Psalm 53
      *Refrain*   God looks down from heaven upon us all.   *Or v.2 or CR 5*
      Ephesians 2.11–22     Mark 6.30–34

C     2 Kings 4.8–17     Psalm 139.12–17
      *Refrain*   Your works are wonderful, O Lord.   *Or v.13 or CR 2*
      Colossians 1.21–29     Luke 10.38–42

**Prayer over the Gifts**

O God,
accept our praise and thanksgiving.
Help us in all we do
to offer ourselves as a true and living sacrifice;
through Jesus Christ the Lord.

*Preface of the Lord's Day*

**Prayer after Communion**

O God,
as we are strengthened in these holy mysteries,
may our lives be a continual offering,
holy and acceptable in your sight;
through Jesus Christ our Lord.

# Sunday between 24 and 30 July  *Proper 17*

## Sentence

A    Lord, to whom shall we go? You have the words of eternal
     life.  *John 6.68*

B    A great prophet has arisen among us! God has visited his
     people!  *Luke 7.16*

C    When we cry, "Abba, Father!" it is the Spirit of God
     bearing witness with our spirit that we are children of
     God.  *Romans 8.15, 16*

## Collect

O God,
the protector of all who trust in you,
without whom nothing is strong, nothing is holy,
increase and multiply upon us your mercy,
that with you as our ruler and guide,
we may so pass through things temporal,
that we lose not the things eternal;
through Jesus Christ our Lord,
who lives and reigns with you and the Holy Spirit,
one God, for ever and ever.

## Readings

A    Exodus 3.13–20      Psalm 105.1–11
     *Refrain*  The Lord has always been mindful of his covenant.
     *Or v.8 or* Alleluia!
     Romans 8.26–30      Matthew 13.44–52

B    2 Samuel 12.1–14      Psalm 32
     *Refrain*  O Lord, you forgave me the guilt of my sin.
     *Or v.6 or* CR 6
     Ephesians 3.14–21      John 6.1–15

C    2 Kings 5.1–15ab (". . . in Israel.")      Psalm 21.1–7
     *Refrain*  He asked you for life, and you gave it to him.
     *Or v.4 or* CR 2
     Colossians 2.6–15      Luke 11.1–13

**Prayer over the Gifts**

God of grace,
accept all we offer you this day,
as we look toward the glory you have promised.
This we ask in the name of Jesus Christ our Lord.

*Preface of the Lord's Day*

**Prayer after Communion**

God of grace,
we have received the memorial
of the death and resurrection of your Son.
May your love, poured into us,
bring us to your promises.
We ask this in the name of our Redeemer Jesus Christ.

# Sunday between 31 July and 6 August  *Proper 18*

**Sentence**

*AB*   We do not live by bread alone, but by every word that
comes from the mouth of God.  *Matthew 4.4*

*C*   Blessed are the poor in spirit, for theirs is the kingdom of
heaven.  *Matthew 5.3*

**Collect**

Almighty God,
your Son Jesus Christ fed the hungry
with the bread of his life
and the word of his kingdom.
Renew your people with your heavenly grace,
and in all our weakness
sustain us by your true and living bread,
who lives and reigns with you and the Holy Spirit,
one God, now and for ever.

### Readings

A  Exodus 12.1–14   Psalm 143.1–10
   *Refrain*  Deliver us from our enemy, O Lord.   *Or v.9 or CR 5*
   Romans 8.31–39   Matthew 14.13–21

B  2 Samuel 12.15b–24   Psalm 34.11–22
   *Refrain*  Turn from evil and do good.   *Or v.14 or CR 5*
   Ephesians 4.1–6   John 6.24–35

C  2 Kings 13.14–20a   Psalm 28
   *Refrain*  The Lord is the strength of his people.   *Or v.10 or CR 8*
   Colossians 3.1–11   Luke 12.13–21

### Prayer over the Gifts

God our sustainer,
accept all we offer you this day,
and feed us continually with that bread
which satisfies all hunger,
your Son our Saviour Jesus Christ.

*Preface of the Lord's Day*

### Prayer after Communion

God of grace,
we have shared in the mystery
of the body and blood of Christ.
May we who have tasted the bread of life
live with you for ever.
We ask this in the name of Jesus Christ our Lord.

## Sunday between 7 and 13 August   *Proper 19*

### Sentence

A  I wait for the Lord; in his word is my hope.   *Psalm 130.4*

B  I am the living bread which came down from heaven, says
   the Lord; anyone who eats this bread will live for ever.
   *John 6.51*

C    Watch and be ready, for you do not know on what day
     your Lord is coming.    *Matthew 24.42, 44*

**Collect**

Almighty God,
you sent your Holy Spirit
to be the life and light of your Church.
Open our hearts to the riches of your grace,
that we may bring forth the fruit of the Spirit
in love, joy, and peace;
through Jesus Christ our Lord,
who is alive and reigns with you and the Holy Spirit,
one God, now and for ever.

**Readings**

A    Exodus 14.19–31    Psalm 106.4–12 *or* Canticle: Song of Moses (No.1)
     *Refrain*  I will sing to the Lord for his glorious triumph.
     *Or v.8 or CR 3*
     Romans 9.1–5    Matthew 14.22–33

B    2 Samuel 18.1, 5, 9–15    Psalm 143.1–8
     *Refrain*  Do not hide your face from me.    *Or v.1 or CR 5*
     Ephesians 4.25—5.2    John 6.35, 41–51

C    Jeremiah 18.1–11    Psalm 14
     *Refrain*  The Lord looks down from heaven upon us all.
     *Or v.2 or CR 5*
     Hebrews 11.1–3, 8–19    Luke 12.32–40

**Prayer over the Gifts**

Father,
receive all we offer you this day,
and grant that in this eucharist
we may be enriched by the gifts of the Spirit.
We ask this in the name of Jesus Christ our Lord.

*Preface of the Lord's Day*

**Prayer after Communion**

Eternal God,
grant to your Church the unity and peace
that we have tasted in this eucharist,
the fruit of your life-giving Spirit.
We ask this in the name of Jesus Christ the Lord.

# Sunday between 14 and 20 August   *Proper 20*

**Sentence**

A   Jesus preached the gospel of the kingdom and healed
    every infirmity among the people.   *See Matthew 4.23*

B   Those who eat my flesh and drink my blood abide in me
    and I in them, says the Lord.   *John 6.56*

C   My sheep hear my voice, says the Lord; I know them and
    they follow me.   *John 10.27*

**Collect**

Almighty God,
you have broken the tyranny of sin
and sent into our hearts the Spirit of your Son.
Give us grace to dedicate our freedom to your service,
that all people may know the glorious liberty
of the children of God;
through Jesus Christ our Lord,
who lives and reigns with you and the Holy Spirit,
one God, now and for ever.

**Readings**

A   Exodus 16.2–15      Psalm 78.1–3, 10–20
    *Refrain*   The Lord gave them bread from heaven.   *Or v.24 or CR 1*
    Romans 11.13–16, 29–32      Matthew 15.21–28

B       2 Samuel 18.24–33       Psalm 102.1–12
        *Refrain*   Hide not your face from me in the day of my trouble.
        *Or v.1 or CR 5*
        Ephesians 5.15–20       John 6.51–58

C       Jeremiah 20.7–13        Psalm 10.12–19
        *Refrain*   Rise up, O Lord; do not forget the afflicted.
        *Or v.12 or CR 8*
        Hebrews 12.1–2, 12–17       Luke 12.49–56

**Prayer over the Gifts**

Loving God and Father,
you have adopted us to be your heirs.
Accept all we offer you this day
and give us grace to live as faithful children.
We ask this in the name of Jesus Christ our Lord.

*Preface of the Lord's Day*

**Prayer after Communion**

Eternal God,
we have received a token of your promise.
May we who have been nourished by holy things
live as faithful heirs of your promised kingdom,
in the name of Jesus Christ our Lord.

# Sunday between 21 and 27 August   *Proper 21*

**Sentence**

A       Jesus is the Christ, the Son of the living God.
        *Matthew 16.16*

B       Lord, to whom shall we go? You have the words of eternal
        life.   *John 6.68*

C       I am the way, the truth, and the life, says the Lord; no one
        comes to the Father, but by me.   *John 14.6*

## Collect

Almighty God,
we are taught by your word
that all our doings without love are worth nothing.
Send your Holy Spirit and pour into our hearts
that most excellent gift of love,
the true bond of peace and of all virtue;
through Jesus Christ our Lord,
who lives and reigns with you and the Holy Spirit,
one God, now and for ever.

## Readings

A    Exodus 17.1–7      Psalm 95
     *Refrain*   Oh, that today you would hearken to his voice!
     *Or v.8 or CR 8*
     Romans 11.33–36       Matthew 16.13–20

B    2 Samuel 23.1–7      Psalm 67
     *Refrain*   Let the peoples praise you, O God.   *Or v.3 or CR 1*
     Ephesians 5.21–33      John 6.55–69

C    Jeremiah 28.1–9      Psalm 84
     *Refrain*   Happy are the people whose strength is in you!
     *Or v.4 or CR 8*
     Hebrews 12.18–29       Luke 13.22–30

## Prayer over the Gifts

God of glory,
receive all we offer this day as a symbol of our love,
and increase in us that true and perfect gift.
We ask this in the name of Jesus Christ our Lord.

*Preface of the Lord's Day*

## Prayer after Communion

Living God,
increase in us the healing power of your love.
Guide and direct us
that we may please you in all things,
for the sake of Jesus Christ our Lord.

# Sunday between 28 August and 3 September  *Proper 22*

**Sentence**

*A*  May the Father of our Lord Jesus Christ enlighten the eyes
of our hearts, that we may know what is the hope to
which he has called us.  *See Ephesians 1.17, 18*

*B*  The Father brought us forth by the word of truth that we
should be a kind of first fruits of his creatures.  *James 1.18*

*C*  Take my yoke upon you, and learn from me; for I am
gentle and lowly in heart.  *Matthew 11.29*

**Collect**

Author and Giver of all good things,
graft in our hearts the love of your name,
increase in us true religion,
nourish us in all goodness,
and of your great mercy keep us in the same;
through Jesus Christ our Lord,
who lives and reigns with you and the Holy Spirit,
one God, now and for ever.

**Readings**

*A*  Exodus 19.1–9     Psalm 114
*Refrain*  Alleluia!  *Or v.2*
Romans 12.1–13     Matthew 16.21–28

*B*  1 Kings 2.1–4, 10–12     Psalm 121
*Refrain*  The Lord himself watches over you.  *Or v.7 or CR 8*
Ephesians 6.10–20     Mark 7.1–8, 14–15, 21–23

*C*  Ezekiel 18.1–9, 25–29     Psalm 15
*Refrain*  Those who lead a blameless life will dwell in the presence of
the Lord.  *Or v.1 or CR 6*
Hebrews 13.1–8     Luke 14.1, 7–14

**Prayer over the Gifts**

Merciful God,
receive all we offer you this day.
Give us grace to love one another
that your love may be made perfect in us.
We ask this in the name of Jesus Christ our Lord.

*Preface of the Lord's Day*

**Prayer after Communion**

Almighty God,
you renew us at your table with the bread of life.
May your holy food strengthen us in love
and help us to serve you in each other.
We ask this in the name of Jesus Christ our Lord.

# Sunday between 4 and 10 September   *Proper 23*

**Sentence**

A   God was in Christ reconciling the world to himself, and he
has entrusted us with the message of reconciliation.
*2 Corinthians 5.19*

B   Jesus preached the gospel of the kingdom and healed
every infirmity among the people.   *Matthew 4.23*

C   Let your countenance shine upon your servant and teach
me your statutes.   *Psalm 119.135*

**Collect**

Stir up, O Lord,
the wills of your faithful people,
that richly bearing the fruit of good works,
we may by you be richly rewarded;
through Jesus Christ our Lord,
who is alive and reigns with you and the Holy Spirit,
one God, now and for ever.

### Readings

A     Exodus 19.16–24     Psalm 115.1–11
        *Refrain*    Not to us, O Lord, but to your name give glory.
        *Or v.1 or* Alleluia!
        Romans 13.1–10     Matthew 18.15–20

B     Sirach 5.8–15 *or* Proverbs 2.1–8     Psalm 119.129–136
        *Refrain*    Teach me your statutes, O Lord.    *Or v.135 or CR 8*
        James 1.17–27     Mark 7.31–37

C     Ezekiel 33.1–11     Psalm 94.12–22
        *Refrain*    Happy are they whom you instruct, O Lord.
        *Or v.12 or CR 8*
        Philemon 1–20     Luke 14.25–33

### Prayer over the Gifts

Great and holy God,
accept our offering of labour and love.
May we bring you true and spiritual worship
and be one with you.
We ask this in the name of Jesus Christ the Lord.

*Preface of the Lord's Day*

### Prayer after Communion

Father,
your word and sacrament give us food and life.
May we who have shared in holy things
bear fruit to your honour and glory,
in the name of Jesus Christ the Lord.

## Sunday between 11 and 17 September    *Proper 24*

### Sentence

A     A new commandment I give to you, that you love one
        another as I have loved you.    *John 13.34*

B     I do not glory except in the cross of our Lord Jesus Christ,
      by which the world has been crucified to me, and I to the
      world.    *Galatians 6.14*

C     There is joy before the angels of God over one sinner who
      repents.    *Luke 15.10*

**Collect**

Almighty God,
you call your Church to witness
that in Christ we are reconciled to you.
Help us so to proclaim the good news of your love,
that all who hear it may turn to you;
through Jesus Christ our Lord,
who lives and reigns with you and the Holy Spirit,
one God, now and for ever.

**Readings**

A     Exodus 20.1–20      Psalm 19.7–14
      *Refrain*   The words of the Lord are spirit and life.
      *Or v.8 or CR 1*
      Romans 14.5–12         Matthew 18.21–35

B     Proverbs 22.1–2, 8–9      Psalm 125
      *Refrain*   Those who trust in the Lord stand fast for ever.
      *Or v.1 or CR 8*
      James 2.1–5, 8–10, 14–17      Mark 8.27–38

C     Hosea 4.1–3; 5.15—6.6      Psalm 77.11–20
      *Refrain*   I will remember the works of the Lord.    *Or v.11 or CR 8*
      1 Timothy 1.12–17      Luke 15.1–10

**Prayer over the Gifts**

Holy God,
accept all we offer you this day.
May we who are reconciled at this table
bring wholeness to our broken world.
We ask this in the name of Jesus Christ the Lord.

*Preface of the Lord's Day*

**Prayer after Communion**

God of peace,
in this eucharist we have been reconciled
to you and to our neighbours.
May we who have been nourished by holy things
always have the courage to forgive.
We ask this in the name of Jesus Christ the Lord.

# Sunday between 18 and 24 September   *Proper 25*

**Sentence**

A   Open our hearts, O Lord, to give heed to what is said by
your Son.

B   God has called us through the gospel, so that we may
obtain the glory of our Lord Jesus Christ.
*See 2 Thessalonians 2.14*

C   You know the grace of our Lord Jesus Christ, that though
he was rich, yet for your sake he became poor, so that by
his poverty you might become rich.   *2 Corinthians 8.9*

**Collect**

Almighty God,
you have created the heavens and the earth,
and ourselves in your image.
Teach us to discern your hand in all your works
and to serve you with reverence and thanksgiving;
through Jesus Christ our Lord,
who is alive and reigns with you and the Holy Spirit,
one God, now and for ever.

**Readings**

A   Exodus 32.1–14     Psalm 106.7–8, 19–23
*Refrain*   Remember me, O Lord, with the love you have for your
people.   *Or v.4 or CR 8*
Philippians 1.21–27     Matthew 20.1–16

B      Job 28.20–28     Psalm 27.1–9
       *Refrain*   The Lord is my light and my salvation.   *Or v.1 or CR 8*
       James 3.13–18    Mark 9.30–37

C      Hosea 11.1–11    Psalm 107.1–9
       *Refrain*   Give thanks to the Lord, for he is good.   *Or v.1*
       1 Timothy 2.1–7    Luke 16.1–13

**Prayer over the Gifts**

God of power,
the glory of your works fills us with wonder and awe.
Accept our offering this day,
and help us to live in peace and harmony
with all your creation,
for the sake of Jesus Christ our Lord.

*Preface of the Lord's Day*

**Prayer after Communion**

Ruler of the universe,
all creation yearns for its fulfilment in your Son.
May we who have shared in holy things
grow into maturity in him.
This we ask in the name of the same Jesus Christ our Lord.

# Sunday between 25 September and 1 October   *Proper 26*

**Sentence**

A      My sheep hear my voice, says the Lord; I know them and
      they follow me.   *John 10.27*

B      Your word, O Lord, is truth; sanctify us in the truth.
      *John 17.17*

C      You know the grace of our Lord Jesus Christ, that though
      he was rich, yet for your sake he became poor, so that by
      his poverty you might become rich.   *2 Corinthians 8.9*

**Collect**

Grant, O merciful God,
that your Church,
being gathered by your Holy Spirit into one,
may show forth your power among all peoples,
to the glory of your name;
through Jesus Christ our Lord,
who lives and reigns with you and the Holy Spirit,
one God, now and for ever.

**Readings**

A    Exodus 33.12–23    Psalm 99
     *Refrain*   The Lord our God is the Holy One.   *Or v.1 or CR 4*
     Philippians 2.1–13    Matthew 21.28–32

B    Job 42.1–6    Psalm 27.10–18
     *Refrain*   Hide not your face from me, O Lord.   *Or v.12 or CR 5*
     James 4.13–17; 5.7–11    Mark 9.38–50

C    Joel 2.23–30    Psalm 107.1, 33–43
     *Refrain*   Give thanks to the Lord for he is good.
     1 Timothy 6.6–19    Luke 16.19–31

**Prayer over the Gifts**

Eternal God,
in Jesus Christ we behold your glory.
Receive the offering of your people gathered before you,
and open our hearts and mouths
to praise your great salvation,
the same Jesus Christ our Lord.

*Preface of the Lord's Day*

**Prayer after Communion**

Father in heaven,
strengthen the unity of your Church,
so that we who have been fed with holy things
may fulfil your will in the world.
We ask this in the name of Jesus Christ our Lord.

# Sunday between 2 and 8 October   *Proper 27*

## Sentence

A    I chose you and appointed you, says the Lord, that you
should go and bear fruit, fruit that will last.   *John 15.16*

B    If we love one another, God abides in us and his love is
perfected in us.   *1 John 4.12*

C    The word of the Lord abides for ever. That word is the
good news which was preached to you.   *1 Peter 1.25*

## Collect

Almighty God,
you have built your Church
on the foundation of the apostles and prophets,
Jesus Christ himself being the chief cornerstone.
Join us together in unity of spirit by their teaching,
that we may become a holy temple, acceptable to you;
through Jesus Christ our Lord,
who lives and reigns with you and the Holy Spirit,
one God, now and for ever.

## Readings

A    Numbers 27.12–23      Psalm 81.1–10
     *Refrain*   Sing with joy to God our strength.   *Or v.1 or CR 3*
     Philippians 3.12–21      Matthew 21.33–43

B    Genesis 2.18–24      Psalm 128
     *Refrain*   May the Lord bless you all the days of your life.
     *Or v.5 or CR 2*
     Hebrews 1.1–4; 2.9–11      Mark 10.2–16

C    Amos 5.6–7, 10–15      Psalm 101
     *Refrain*   I will sing of mercy and justice.   *Or v.1 or CR 3*
     2 Timothy 1.1–14      Luke 17.5–10

## Prayer over the Gifts

God of truth,
receive all we offer you this day.

Make us worthy servants,
strong to follow in the pattern
of our Lord and Saviour Jesus Christ.

*Preface of the Lord's Day*

**Prayer after Communion**

Almighty God,
may we who have been strengthened by this eucharist
remain in your steadfast love,
and show in our lives
the saving mystery that we celebrate.
This we ask in the name of Jesus Christ the Lord.

# Sunday between 9 and 15 October   *Proper 28*

**Sentence**

A    May the Father of our Lord Jesus Christ enlighten the eyes
of our hearts, that we may know what is the hope to
which he has called us.   *See Ephesians 1.17, 18*

B    Blessed are the poor in spirit, for theirs is the kingdom of
heaven.   *Matthew 5.3*

C    Give thanks in all circumstances, for this is the will of God
in Christ Jesus for you.   *1 Thessalonians 5.18*

**Collect**

Almighty God,
in our baptism you adopted us for your own.
Quicken, we pray, your Spirit within us,
that we, being renewed both in body and mind,
may worship you in sincerity and truth;
through Jesus Christ our Lord,
who lives and reigns with you and the Holy Spirit,
one God, now and for ever.

### Readings

A    Deuteronomy 34.1–12     Psalm 135.1–14
     *Refrain*   Give thanks to the Lord for he is good.
     *Or v.3 or Alleluia!*
     Philippians 4.1–9    Matthew 22.1–14

B    Genesis 3.8–19    Psalm 90.1–12
     *Refrain*   Teach us to number our days.  *Or v.12 or CR 5*
     Hebrews 4.1–3, 9–13    Mark 10.17–30

C    Micah 1.2; 2.1–10    Psalm 26
     *Refrain*   Do not sweep me away with sinners.  *Or v.9 or CR 8*
     2 Timothy 2.8–15    Luke 17.11–19

### Prayer over the Gifts

God of constant love,
in this eucharist you renew the covenant
made once with us in baptism.
As you are faithful in all things
may we, in our offering,
be faithful to our calling.
We ask this in the name of Jesus Christ our Lord.

*Preface of the Lord's Day*

### Prayer after Communion

Faithful God,
in baptism and eucharist we are made one with you.
May we who have shared in holy things
always bear witness to your covenant,
in the name of Jesus Christ the Lord.

# Sunday between 16 and 22 October  *Proper 29*

### Sentence

A    Shine as lights in the world, holding fast the word of
    life.  *See Philippians 2.15, 16*

B    The Son of man came also not to be served but to serve,
    and to give his life as a ransom for many.  *Mark 10.45*

C     The word of God is living and active; it sifts the thoughts and intentions of the heart.    *Hebrews 4.12*

**Collect**

Almighty and everliving God,
increase in us your gift of faith,
that forsaking what lies behind
and reaching out to what is before,
we may run the way of your commandments
and win the crown of everlasting joy;
through Jesus Christ our Lord,
who lives and reigns with you and the Holy Spirit,
one God, now and for ever.

**Readings**

A     Ruth 1.1–19a     Psalm 146
      *Refrain*   Happy are they who have the God of Jacob for their help.
      *Or v.4 or* Alleluia!
      1 Thessalonians 1.1–10     Matthew 22.15–22

B     Isaiah 53.7–12     Psalm 35.17–28
      *Refrain*   O Lord, be not far from me.    *Or v.23 or CR 5*
      Hebrews 4.14–16     Mark 10.35–45

C     Habakkuk 1.1–3; 2.1–4     Psalm 119.137–144
      *Refrain*   Grant me understanding, that I may live.
      *Or v.144 or CR 8*
      2 Timothy 3.14—4.5     Luke 18.1–8

**Prayer over the Gifts**

Eternal God,
your word inspires our faith.
May we who offer you our praise
trust you in all things.
We ask this in the name of Jesus Christ the Lord.

*Preface of the Lord's Day*

**Prayer after Communion**

God of peace,
you have nourished us in this sacrament
with the body and blood of Christ.
May we who have taken holy things
keep faith in our hearts and lives,
in the name of Jesus Christ the Lord.

# Sunday between 23 and 29 October  *Proper 30*

**Sentence**

A   If you love me, you will keep my word, and my Father
will love you, and we will come to you.   *John 14.23*

B   Our Saviour Jesus Christ has abolished death, and
brought life and immortality to light through the gospel.
*2 Timothy 1.10*

C   God was in Christ reconciling the world to himself, and he
has entrusted us with the message of reconciliation.
*2 Corinthians 5.19*

**Collect**

Lord God our redeemer,
who heard the cry of your people
and sent your servant Moses
to lead them out of slavery,
free us from the tyranny of sin and death,
and by the leading of your Spirit
bring us to our promised land;
through Jesus Christ our Lord,
who lives and reigns with you and the Holy Spirit,
one God, now and for ever.

**Readings**

A   Ruth 2.1–13      Psalm 128
*Refrain*   Happy are they who fear the Lord.   *Or v.1 or CR 1*
1 Thessalonians 2.1–8      Matthew 22.34–46

B     Jeremiah 31.7–9     Psalm 126
    *Refrain*   The Lord has done great things for us.   *Or v.4 or CR 1*
    Hebrews 5.1–6     Mark 10.46–52

C     Zephaniah 3.1–9     Psalm 3
    *Refrain*   Deliverance belongs to the Lord.   *Or v.8 or CR 8*
    2 Timothy 4.6–8, 16–18     Luke 18.9–14

**Prayer over the Gifts**

God of constant love,
you have guided your people
in all times and ages.
May we who offer you our praise today
always be ready to follow where you lead;
we ask this in the name of Jesus Christ our Lord.

*Preface of the Lord's Day*

**Prayer after Communion**

God our guide,
you have fed us with bread from heaven
as you fed the people of Israel.
May we who have been inwardly nourished
be ready to follow you all our days;
we ask this in the name of Jesus Christ our Lord.

# Sunday between 30 October and 5 November   *Proper 31*

**Sentence**

A     You have one Father, who is in heaven. You have one
    teacher, the Christ.   *Matthew 23.9, 10*

B     If you love me, you will keep my word, and my Father
    will love you, and we will come to you.   *John 14.23*

C     God so loved the world that he gave his only Son, that
    whoever believes in him should not perish but have
    eternal life.   *John 3.16*

## Collect

Almighty God,
whose chosen servant Abraham obeyed your call,
rejoicing in your promise
that in him the family of the earth is blessed,
give us faith like his,
that in us your promises may be fulfilled;
through Jesus Christ our Lord,
who lives and reigns with you and the Holy Spirit,
one God, now and for ever.

## Readings

A     Ruth 4.7–17     Psalm 127
      *Refrain*   Happy are they who fear the Lord.   *Or v.4 or CR 1*
      1 Thessalonians 2.9–13, 17–20     Matthew 23.1–12

B     Deuteronomy 6.1–9     Psalm 119.33–48
      *Refrain*   Teach me, O Lord, the way of your statutes.
      *Or v.1 or CR 5*
      Hebrews 7.23–28     Mark 12.28–34

C     Haggai 2.1–9     Psalm 65.1–8
      *Refrain*   To you shall vows be performed in Jerusalem.   *Or v.5 or CR 2*
      2 Thessalonians 1.5–12     Luke 19.1–10

## Prayer over the Gifts

God of freedom,
accept all we offer you this day.
May we embrace the law of your service
and know the glorious liberty of the children of God.
We ask this in the name of Jesus Christ the Lord.

*Preface of the Lord's Day*

## Prayer after Communion

Heavenly Father,
bring to perfection within us
the communion we share in this sacrament.

May the unity we know this day
live in our community and family.
This we pray in the name of Jesus Christ the Lord.

## Sunday between 6 and 12 November   *Proper 32*

### Sentence

A   Watch and be ready, for you do not know on what day
your Lord is coming.   *Matthew 24.42, 44*

B   Blessed are the poor in spirit, for theirs is the kingdom of
heaven.   *Matthew 5.3*

C   Jesus Christ is the first-born of the dead; to him be glory
and dominion for ever and ever. Amen.
*See Revelation 1.5, 6*

### Collect

Eternal God,
who caused all holy scriptures
to be written for our learning,
grant us so to hear them,
read, mark, learn, and inwardly digest them,
that we may embrace and ever hold fast
the blessed hope of everlasting life,
which you have given us in our Saviour Jesus Christ,
who lives and reigns with you and the Holy Spirit,
one God, for ever and ever.

### Readings

A   Amos 5.18–24      Psalm 50.7–15
*Refrain*   I will show my salvation to those who keep in my way.
*Or v.24 or CR 8*
1 Thessalonians 4.13–18      Matthew 25.1–13

B   1 Kings 17.8–16      Psalm 146
*Refrain*   Praise the Lord, O my soul!   *Or v.4 or CR 1*
Hebrews 9.24–28      Mark 12.38–44

C     Zechariah 7.1–10     Psalm 9.11–20

      *Refrain*  The Lord will not forget the cry of the afflicted.

      *Or v.18 or CR 4*

     2 Thessalonians 2.13—3.5     Luke 20.27–38

**Prayer over the Gifts**

Gracious God,
your word to us is food indeed.
Receive all we offer you this day,
and let your loving-kindness be our comfort,
for the sake of Jesus Christ, your living Word.

*Preface of the Lord's Day*

**Prayer after Communion**

Living God,
in the eucharist you fill us with new hope.
May the power of your love,
which we have known in word and sacrament,
continue your saving work among us,
and bring us to the joy you promise.
We ask this in the name of Jesus Christ our Lord.

# Sunday between 13 and 19 November   *Proper 33*

**Sentence**

A     I am the vine, you are the branches, says the Lord. Those
who abide in me, and I in them, bear much fruit.
*John 15.5*

B     Watch at all times, praying that you may stand before the
Son of man.  *Luke 21.36*

C     Look up and raise your heads, because your redemption is
drawing near.  *Luke 21.28*

**Collect**

Almighty God,
you sent your Son Jesus Christ

to be the light of the world.
Free us from all that darkens and ensnares us,
and bring us to eternal light and joy;
through the power of him
who is alive and reigns with you and the Holy Spirit,
one God, now and for ever.

### Readings

A    Zephaniah 1.7, 12–18    Psalm 76
     *Refrain*   The earth was still when God rose up to judgement.   *Or CR 8*
     1 Thessalonians 5.1–11    Matthew 25.14–30

B    Daniel 7.9–14    Psalm 145.8–14
     *Refrain*   Your kingdom is an everlasting kingdom.   *Or v.13 or CR 3*
     Hebrews 10.11–18    Mark 13.24–32

C    Malachi 4.1–6    Psalm 82
     *Refrain*   Arise, O God, and rule the earth.   *Or v.8 or CR 5*
     2 Thessalonians 3.6–13    Luke 21.5–19

### Prayer over the Gifts

Holy God,
in this eucharist we renew our baptismal covenant.
Help us, through our offering this day,
to renounce all things that draw us from your love.
This we ask in the name of Jesus Christ our Lord.

*Preface of The Lord's Day*

### Prayer after Communion

Gracious God,
in this sacrament
we have shared the body and blood of Christ.
May we who have been nourished by holy things
bear witness to his light,
and share in his eternal priesthood;
for he is Lord for ever and ever.

# The Last Sunday after Pentecost:
# the Reign of Christ  *Proper 34*

### Sentence

Blessed is he who comes in the name of the Lord! Blessed is the
kingdom of our father David that is coming!  *Mark 11.9, 10*

### Collect

Almighty and everlasting God,
whose will it is to restore all things
in your well-beloved Son, our Lord and King,
grant that the peoples of the earth,
now divided and enslaved by sin,
may be freed and brought together
under his gentle and loving rule;
who lives and reigns with you and the Holy Spirit,
one God, now and for ever.

### Readings

A    Ezekiel 34.11–16, 20–24      Psalm 23
      *Refrain*   The Lord is my shepherd; I shall not be in want.
      *Or v.6 or CR 4*
      1 Corinthians 15.20–28      Matthew 25.31–46

B    Jeremiah 23.1–6      Psalm 93
      *Refrain*   The Lord shall reign for ever and ever.   *Or v.1 or CR 3*
      Revelation 1.4b–8      John 18.33–37

C    2 Samuel 5.1–5      Psalm 95
      *Refrain*   The Lord is king; let the earth rejoice.   *Or v.3 or CR 3*
      Colossians 1.11–20      John 12.9–19

### Prayer over the Gifts

Eternal God,
by your grace you have raised us up
and enthroned us with Christ in the heavenly realms.

Receive all we offer you this day,
and lead us in those good works
for which you have created us.
We ask this in the name of Jesus Christ the Lord.

*Preface of the Last Sunday after Pentecost: the Reign of Christ*

**Prayer after Communion**

Almighty God,
you have made us a royal priesthood
in the kingdom of your Son our Saviour Jesus Christ.
Make known his victory through us, we pray,
that all the world may see his light.
We ask this in the name of Jesus Christ the Lord.

# Ember Days

*To be used at times of prayer for the whole ministry of the Church.*

**Sentence**

Grace was given to each of us according to the measure of
Christ's gift.    *Ephesians 4.7*

**Collect**

Almighty God,
by your grace alone
we are accepted and called to your service.
Strengthen us by your Holy Spirit
and make us worthy of our calling;
through Jesus Christ our Lord,
who is alive and reigns with you and the Holy Spirit,
one God, now and for ever.

**Readings**

  Isaiah 44.1–8  Psalm 87
  *Refrain* Glorious things are spoken of you, O city of our God. *Or CR 3*
  1 Peter 2.4–10  John 17.6–19

**Prayer over the Gifts**

God of faithfulness,
in every age you call men and women
to make known your love.
May we who celebrate this eucharist today
be so strengthened in the ministries to which we are called,
that we may always witness to your holy name.
This we pray in the name of Jesus Christ the Lord.

**Prayer after Communion**

God of our salvation,
your Spirit has given us new life,
and you have nourished us with holy things.
May we be living members of your Son Jesus Christ,
and exercise the ministry to which we are called.
This we pray in the name of Jesus Christ the Lord.

# Rogation Days and Harvest Thanksgiving

*To be used at the appropriate seasons of the year.*

**Sentence**

Those who sowed with tears will reap with songs of joy.
*Psalm 126.6*

**Collect**

Creator of the fruitful earth,
you made us stewards of all things.
Give us grateful hearts for all your goodness,
and steadfast wills to use your bounty well,
that the whole human family,
today and in generations to come,
may with us give thanks for the riches of your creation.
We ask this in the name of Jesus Christ the Lord.

## Readings

Deuteronomy 8.7–18     Psalm 65
*Refrain*   You crown the year with your goodness, O Lord.
*Or v.13 or CR 2*
2 Corinthians 9.6–15     Luke 17.11–19

*Or*   Joel 2.21–27     Psalm 126
*Refrain*   The Lord has done great things for us.   *Or v.4 or CR 1*
1 Timothy 2.1–7     Matthew 6.25–33

*Or*   Deuteronomy 26.1–11     Psalm 100
*Refrain*   The mercy of the Lord is everlasting.   *Or v.4 or CR 1*
Philippians 4.4–9     John 6.25–35

## Prayer over the Gifts

Source of all life,
the heaven and earth are yours,
yet you have given us dominion over all things.
Receive the symbols of our labour and love
which we offer you this day,
in the name of Jesus Christ our Lord.

## Prayer after Communion

God of our hope,
in this eucharist we find the source of all your blessings.
Nourished in these holy mysteries
may we, with our lives,
give you continual thanks and praise.
This we ask in the name of Jesus Christ our Lord.

# Saints' Days and Other Holy Days

## The Holy Innocents    *11 January (or 28 December)*

### Sentence

Blessed are those who are persecuted for righteousness' sake,
for theirs is the kingdom of heaven.    *Matthew 5.10*

### Collect

Almighty God, our heavenly Father,
whose children suffered at the hands of Herod,
receive, we pray, all innocent victims
into the arms of your mercy.
By your great might frustrate all evil designs
and establish your reign of justice, love, and peace;
through Jesus Christ our Lord,
who lives and reigns with you and the Holy Spirit,
one God, now and for ever.

### Readings

Jeremiah 31.15–17 *or* Revelation 21.1–7        Psalm 124
*Refrain*    We have escaped like a bird from the snare of the fowler.
*Or v.7 or CR 5*
Matthew 2.13–18

### Prayer over the Gifts

Merciful God,
accept all we offer you this day.
Preserve your people from cruelty
and indifference to violence,
that the weak may always be defended
from the tyranny of the strong.
We ask this in the name of Jesus Christ our Lord.

*Preface of a Martyr*

### Prayer after Communion

Eternal God,
comfort of the afflicted and healer of the broken,
you have fed us this day at the table of life and hope.
Teach us the ways of gentleness and peace,
that all the world may acknowledge
the kingdom of your Son Jesus Christ our Lord.

# The Confession of Saint Peter   *18 January*

### Sentence

Jesus is the Christ, the Son of the living God.   *Matthew 16.16*

### Collect

Almighty God,
you inspired Simon Peter, first among the apostles,
to confess Jesus as Messiah and Son of the living God.
Keep your Church steadfast upon the rock of this faith,
so that in unity and peace
we may proclaim the one truth
and follow the one Lord,
who lives and reigns with you and the Holy Spirit,
one God, now and for ever.

### Readings

Acts 4.8–13 *or* 1 Peter 5.1–4      Psalm 23
*Refrain*   The Lord is my shepherd; I shall not be in want.   *Or CR 4*
Matthew 16.13–19

### Prayer over the Gifts

Living God,
accept the offering of your holy Church.
As Peter confessed Jesus, the Messiah and your Son,
give us courage to follow him,
the Lord who reigns with you for ever.

*Preface of Apostles*

**Prayer after Communion**

Keep us, Father, in this fellowship of faith,
the Church of your Son Jesus Christ,
and help us to confess him as Messiah and Lord
in all we say and do.
We ask this in his name.

# The Conversion of Saint Paul  *25 January*

**Sentence**

This Jesus God raised up, and of that we all are witnesses.
*Acts 2.32*

**Collect**

Almighty God,
by the preaching of your servant Paul
you caused the light of the gospel
to shine throughout the world.
May we who celebrate his wonderful conversion
follow him in bearing witness to your truth;
through Jesus Christ our Lord,
who lives and reigns with you and the Holy Spirit,
one God, now and for ever.

**Readings**

> Acts 26.9–23 *or* Galatians 1.11–24  Psalm 67
> *Refrain*  Let all the peoples praise you, O God.  *Or v.3 or CR 1*
> Matthew 10.16–22

**Prayer over the Gifts**

Almighty God,
as we celebrate this holy eucharist,
may your Spirit fill us with the light of faith.
This we ask in the name of Jesus Christ the Lord.

*Preface of Apostles*

**Prayer after Communion**

Gracious God,
you filled your apostle Paul
with love for all the churches.
May the sacrament we have received
foster love and unity among your people.
This we ask in the name of Jesus Christ the Lord.

# The Presentation of our Lord Jesus Christ
# in the Temple   *2 February*

**Sentence**

This is a light to reveal God to the nations and the glory of his
people Israel.   *Luke 2.32*

**Collect**

Blessed are you, O Lord our God,
for you have sent us your salvation.
Inspire us by your Holy Spirit
to recognize him who is the glory of Israel
and the light for all nations,
your Son Jesus Christ our Lord.

**Readings**

Malachi 3.1–4      Psalm 84.1–7 *or* Psalm 24.7–10
*Refrain*   How dear to me is your dwelling, O Lord of hosts!   *Or CR 4*
Hebrews 2.14–18      Luke 2.22–40

**Prayer over the Gifts**

Almighty God,
accept the joyful offering of your Church,
and grant that your Son may shine in us
as the light that lightens every nation.
We ask this in the name of the same Jesus Christ our Lord.

*Preface of the Incarnation*

**Prayer after Communion**

God for whom we wait,
you fulfilled the hope of Simeon,
who did not die till he had welcomed the Messiah.
Complete in us your perfect will,
that we in Christ may share in your eternal kingdom;
for he is Lord for ever and ever.

# Saint Joseph of Nazareth   *19 March*

**Sentence**

Happy are they who dwell in your house! They will always be
praising you.   *Psalm 84.3*

**Collect**

O God,
from the family of your servant David
you raised up Joseph
to be the guardian of your incarnate Son.
Give us grace to follow him
in faithful obedience to your commands;
through Jesus Christ our Lord,
who lives and reigns with you and the Holy Spirit,
one God, now and for ever.

**Readings**

    2 Samuel 7.4, 8–16 *or* Romans 4.13–18    Psalm 89.1–4, 26–29
    *Refrain*   I will establish his line for ever.   *Or v.29 or CR 1*
    Luke 2.41–52

**Prayer over the Gifts**

Almighty God,
accept all we offer you this day,
and give us generous hearts
to serve you in all who claim our help.
We ask this in the name of Jesus Christ our Lord.

*Preface of the Incarnation*

**Prayer after Communion**

Heavenly Father,
your Son Jesus Christ, grew in wisdom and stature
in his home at Nazareth.
May we, nourished by this sacrament,
grow into the fullness of his new humanity,
who is Lord, now and for ever.

# The Annunciation of our Lord Jesus Christ to the Blessed Virgin Mary   *25 March*

**Sentence**

The Word became flesh and dwelt among us, full of grace and
truth; we have beheld his glory.   *John 1.14*

**Collect**

Pour your grace into our hearts, O Lord,
that we who have known the incarnation
of your Son Jesus Christ,
announced by an angel to the Virgin Mary,
may by his cross and passion
be brought to the glory of his resurrection;
who lives and reigns with you,
in the unity of the Holy Spirit,
one God, now and for ever.

**Readings**

> Isaiah 7.10–14      Psalm 40.5–10 *or* Psalm 45
> *Refrain*   I love to do your will, O my God.
> Hebrews 10.4–10      Luke 1.26–38

**Prayer over the Gifts**

Almighty God,
so fill us with your grace,
that we in all things may accept your holy will
and with the Virgin Mary, full of grace,
rejoice in your salvation;
through Jesus Christ our Lord.

**Prayer after Communion**

Almighty God,
your word proclaims our salvation;
your table gives us life.
Grant us the humble obedience we see in Mary,
that we too may respond as willing servants.
We ask this in the name of Jesus Christ the Lord.

# Saint Mark   *25 April*

**Sentence**

We preach Christ crucified, Christ the power of God and the
wisdom of God.   *1 Corinthians 1.23, 24*

**Collect**

Almighty God,
by the hand of Mark the evangelist
you gave to your Church
the gospel of Jesus Christ, the Son of God.
We thank you for his witness,
and pray that we may be grounded firmly in its truth;
through Jesus Christ our Lord,
who is alive and reigns with you and the Holy Spirit,
one God, now and for ever.

**Readings**

> Isaiah 52.7–10 *or* Ephesians 4.7–8, 11–16       Psalm 2.7–13
> *Refrain*   You are my Son; this day have I begotten you.
> *Or v.7 or* Alleluia!
> Mark 1.1–15 *or* Mark 16.15–20

**Prayer over the Gifts**

God of our salvation,
accept all we offer you this day.
May we learn to bear witness to the gospel of your Son
both in word and deed.
This we ask in the name of Jesus Christ our Lord.

Preface of a Saint

*Preface of a Saint*

**Prayer after Communion**

Gracious God,
may the gifts we have received at your table
strengthen us in the faith of the gospel preached by Mark.
This we ask in the name of Jesus Christ our Lord.

# Saint Philip and Saint James   *1 May*

**Sentence**

Whatever you ask in my name, I will do it, says the Lord; that
the Father may be glorified in the Son.   *John 14.13*

**Collect**

Almighty God,
you gave to your apostles Philip and James
grace and strength to bear witness to the truth.
Grant that we, mindful of their victory of faith,
may glorify in life and death the name of Jesus Christ,
who lives and reigns with you and the Holy Spirit,
one God, now and for ever.

**Readings**

> Isaiah 30.18–21 *or* 2 Corinthians 4.1–6      Psalm 119.33–40
> *Refrain*   Teach me, O Lord, the way of your statutes.
> *Or v.33 or CR 4*
> John 14.6–14

**Prayer over the Gifts**

Almighty God,
to know you is to have eternal life.
Grant us to know your Son
as the way, the truth, and the life;
and guide our footsteps
along the way of Jesus Christ our Lord,
who lives and reigns with you and the Holy Spirit,
one God, now and for ever.

**Prayer after Communion**

Holy God,
in Jesus Christ we find the way to you.
May we who have met him in this banquet
be kept in your unending love,
and see you working through your Son,
for he is Lord for ever and ever.

# Saint John the Evangelist  *6 May (or 27 December)*

**Sentence**

The word of the cross is the power of God to us who are being
saved.  *See 1 Corinthians 1.18*

**Collect**

Shed upon your Church, O Lord,
the brightness of your light,
that we being illumined by the teaching
of your apostle and evangelist John,
may walk in the light of your truth,
and come at last to the fullness of eternal life;
through Jesus Christ our Lord,
who lives and reigns with you and the Holy Spirit,
one God, now and for ever.

**Readings**

> Genesis 1.1–5, 12–19; *or* 1   1 John 1.1–9   Psalm 92.1–2, 11–14
> *Refrain*   The righteous shall flourish like a palm tree.
> *Or v.11 or CR 1*
> John 20.1–8

**Prayer over the Gifts**

Eternal Light,
receive all we offer you this day,
that we may share in the wisdom of your eternal Word

revealed at this eucharistic table.
We ask this in the name of Jesus Christ, the incarnate Word.

*Preface of Apostles*

**Prayer after Communion**

Eternal God,
your apostle and evangelist John proclaimed the Christ,
your Word made flesh among us.
May we who have shared the bread of life
remain for ever your children,
born according to your will;
through Jesus Christ our Lord.

# Saint Matthias  *14 May*

**Sentence**

I chose you and appointed you, says the Lord; that you should
go and bear fruit, fruit that will last.    *John 15.16*

**Collect**

Almighty God,
who in the place of Judas
chose Matthias to be numbered in the twelve,
preserve your Church from false apostles,
and by the ministry of faithful pastors and teachers
keep us steadfast in your truth;
through Jesus Christ our Lord,
who lives and reigns with you and the Holy Spirit,
one God, now and for ever.

**Readings**

>    Acts 1.15–26 *or* Philippians 3.13b–22      Psalm 15
>    *Refrain*   The just shall dwell on your holy mountain.
>    *Or v.1 or CR 3*
>    John 15.1, 6–16

**Prayer over the Gifts**

Father,
receive our offering of praise this day,
and when our faith is weak,
show us the light of your truth,
that we may continue in the way of righteousness,
revealed to us in Jesus Christ our Lord.

*Preface of Apostles*

**Prayer after Communion**

Gracious God,
you constantly give life to your people.
May we who receive these holy things
remain faithful to your call.
This we ask in the name of Jesus Christ our Lord.

# The Visit of the Blessed Virgin Mary to Elizabeth

*31 May*

**Sentence**

Blessed is she who believed that the Lord's promise would be
fulfilled.   *Luke 1.45*

**Collect**

Almighty God,
who looked with favour on your servant Mary,
and called her to be the mother of your Son,
nurture in us the humility and gentleness
that found favour in your sight,
that with her we may proclaim the greatness of your name
and find the mercy you show to those who fear you;
through Jesus Christ our Lord,
who lives and reigns with you and the Holy Spirit,
one God, for ever and ever.

### Readings

> 1 Samuel 2.1–10    Psalm 113
> *Refrain*   Let the name of the Lord be blessed for evermore.
> *Or v.2 or* Alleluia!
> Romans 12.9–16b    Luke 1.39–57

### Prayer over the Gifts

God of mercy,
accept all we offer you this day
as you accepted the love of Mary,
the mother of your Son Jesus Christ,
who is Lord, now and for ever.

*Preface of the Incarnation*

### Prayer after Communion

God of steadfast love,
may we who have been nourished
by your gifts in this sacrament,
always give you praise
for the great things you have done for us.
We ask this in the name of Jesus Christ the Lord.


## Saint Barnabas   *11 June*

### Sentence

This Jesus God raised up, and of that we all are witnesses.
*Acts 2.32*

### Collect

Merciful God,
help us to follow the example of your faithful servant Barnabas,
who, seeking not his own renown
but the well-being of your Church,
gave generously of his life and substance
for the relief of the poor and the spread of the gospel;
through Jesus Christ our Lord,
who lives and reigns with you and the Holy Spirit,
one God, for ever and ever.

### Readings

Isaiah 42.5–12 *or* Acts 11.19–30; 13.1–3     Psalm 112
*Refrain*   Happy are they who have given to the poor.
*Or v.9 or* Alleluia!
Matthew 10.7–16

### Prayer over the Gifts

Faithful God,
accept all we offer you this day.
Kindle in us the flame of love
by which your apostle Barnabas
bore witness to the gospel.
This we ask in the name of Jesus Christ our Lord.

*Preface of Apostles*

### Prayer after Communion

God of justice,
may we who have heard your word
and received new life at your table,
bear witness to your truth in the world,
so that all may come to share in your kingdom.
We ask this in the name of Jesus Christ the Lord.

# The Birth of Saint John the Baptist   24 *June*

### Sentence

You, my child, shall be called the prophet of the Most High, for
you will go before the Lord to prepare his way.   *Luke 1.76*

### Collect

Almighty God,
you called John the Baptist
to give witness to the coming of your Son
and to prepare his way.

Give your people the wisdom to see your purpose,
and the openness to hear your will,
that we too may witness to Christ's coming
and so prepare his way;
through your Son Jesus Christ our Lord,
who lives and reigns with you and the Holy Spirit,
one God, now and for ever.

### Readings

Isaiah 40.1–11     Psalm 85.7–13
*Refrain*   Show us your mercy.   *Or v.7 or CR 1*
Acts 13.14b–26     Luke 1.57–80

### Prayer over the Gifts

God of our salvation,
accept all we offer you this day,
and free us to worship you without fear,
in holiness and righteousness of life;
through Jesus Christ our Lord.

*Preface of Advent*

### Prayer after Communion

We thank you, Lord,
for your word and your table
which give us the knowledge of salvation.
Your compassion has broken on us like the dawn;
guide now our feet into the way of peace.
We ask this in the name of Jesus Christ the Lord.

# Saint Peter and Saint Paul   *29 June*

### Sentence

Lord, you know everything; you know that I love you.
*John 21.17*

## Collect

Almighty God,
your blessed apostles Peter and Paul
glorified you in their death as in their life.
Grant that your Church,
inspired by their teaching and example,
and made one by your Spirit,
may ever stand firm upon the one foundation,
Jesus Christ our Lord;
who lives and reigns with you and the Holy Spirit,
one God, now and for ever.

## Readings

Ezekiel 34.11–16      Psalm 87

*Refrain*   Glorious things are spoken of you, O city of our God.   *Or CR 1*

2 Timothy 4.1–8      John 21.15–19

## Prayer over the Gifts

Almighty God,
receive all we offer you on this feast of the apostles.
Help us to know our own weakness
and to rejoice in your saving power,
in the name of Jesus Christ our Lord.

*Preface of Apostles*

## Prayer after Communion

Heavenly Father,
renew the life of your Church
by the power of this sacrament.
May the breaking of bread
and the teaching of the apostles
keep us united in your love,
in the name of Jesus Christ the Lord.


# Canada Day   *1 July*

## Sentence

If any serve me, the Father will honour them.   *John 12.26*

### Collect

Almighty God,
whose wisdom and whose love are over all,
accept the prayers we offer for our nation.
Give integrity to its citizens
and wisdom to those in authority,
that harmony and justice may be secured
in obedience to your will;
through Jesus Christ our Lord,
who lives and reigns with you and the Holy Spirit,
one God, now and for ever.

### Readings

Isaiah 32.1–5, 16–18     Psalm 85.7–13
*Refrain*   Peace shall be a pathway for his feet.   *Or CR 8*
Colossians 3.12–17     John 15.12–17

### Prayer over the Gifts

Judge eternal,
accept all we offer you this day,
and grant to our nation unity and peace.
This we ask in the name of Jesus Christ the Lord.

*Preface of Trinity Sunday*

### Prayer after Communion

God of love,
may we who have taken holy things
grow in unity and peace.
We ask this in the name of Jesus Christ the Lord.

# Saint Thomas   *3 July*

### Sentence

Have you believed, Thomas, because you have seen me?
Blessed are those who have not seen and yet believe.
*John 20.29*

**Collect**

Almighty and everliving God,
who strengthened your apostle Thomas
with faith in the resurrection of your Son.
Strengthen us when we doubt,
and make us faithful disciples
of Jesus Christ our risen Lord;
who with you, O Father, and the Holy Spirit
lives and reigns eternally.

**Readings**

> Habakkuk 2.1–4 *or* Hebrews 10.35—11.1     Psalm 126
> *Refrain*   Those who sowed with tears will reap with songs of joy.
> *Or v.4 or CR 4*
> John 20.24–29

**Prayer over the Gifts**

Living God,
accept all we offer you this day,
and grant that we may find the presence of your Son
in the Church,
in each other,
and in the poor and wounded victims of the world,
for whom he gave his life,
Jesus Christ your Son our Lord.

*Preface of Apostles*

**Prayer after Communion**

God of truth,
we have seen with our eyes
and touched with our hands
the bread of life.
Strengthen our faith
that we may grow in love for you
and for each other;
through Jesus Christ the risen Lord.

# Saint Mary Magdalene  *22 July*

## Sentence

If any serve me, the Father will honour them.  *John 12.26*

## Collect

Almighty God,
whose Son restored Mary Magdalene
to health of mind and body,
and called her to be a witness of his resurrection,
forgive us and heal us by your grace,
that we may serve you in the power of his risen life;
who lives and reigns with you and the Holy Spirit,
one God, now and for ever.

## Readings

Judith 9.1, 11–14 *or* 2 Corinthians 5.14–18      Psalm 42.1–7
*Refrain*   My soul thirsts for you, O God, my God.   *Or v.1 or CR 4*
John 20.1–3, 11–18

## Prayer over the Gifts

God of life and health,
in your Son Jesus Christ
we find the forgiveness of all that is past.
Grant that in this eucharist today
we may find the healing of all our sins.
This we ask in the name of Jesus Christ our Lord.

*Preface of a Saint*

## Prayer after Communion

Compassionate God,
in this eucharist you have set aside our sins
and given us your healing.
Grant that all who have shared in holy things
may bring your healing to this broken world,
in the name of Jesus Christ our Lord.

# Saint James the Apostle   25 July

## Sentence

I chose you and appointed you, says the Lord; that you should
go and bear fruit, fruit that will last.   *John 15.16*

## Collect

Almighty God,
we remember today your servant James,
the first apostle to give his life
for faith in Jesus Christ.
Pour out on all your people
that spirit of self-denying service
which is the mark of true leadership.
We ask this in the name of Jesus Christ the Lord,
who lives and reigns with you and the Holy Spirit,
one God, now and for ever.

## Readings

> Jeremiah 45.1–5 *or* Acts 11.27—12.3      Psalm 7.1–10
> *Refrain*   God is the saviour of the true in heart.   *Or v.11 or CR 5*
> Matthew 20.20–28

## Prayer over the Gifts

Lord God,
today we honour your servant James,
the first apostle to share the cup of suffering and death.
Receive our offering of praise and thanksgiving,
and renew us in the service of your Son Jesus Christ,
who came not to be served but to serve,
and to give his life as a ransom for many.
We ask this in his name.

*Preface of Apostles*

## Prayer after Communion

Father,
we have eaten the bread of your table
and drunk from the cup of your kingdom.

Teach us, we pray, the way of service
that in compassion and humility
we may reflect the glory of Jesus Christ,
the Son of man and Son of God,
our Lord.

## Saint Stephen  *3 August (or 26 December)*

### Sentence

Blessed are those who are persecuted for righteousness' sake,
for theirs is the kingdom of heaven.   *Matthew 5.10*

### Collect

Grant us grace, O Lord,
that like Stephen we may learn to love even our enemies
and seek forgiveness for those who desire our hurt;
through your Son Jesus Christ our Lord,
who lives and reigns with you and the Holy Spirit,
one God now and for ever.

### Readings

(Jeremiah 26.1–9, 12–15) Acts 6.8—7.2a, 51c–60      Psalm 31.1–7, 16
*Refrain*   Into your hands, O Lord, I commend my spirit.
*Or v.5 or CR 4*
Matthew 23.34–39

### Prayer over the Gifts

Refuge of those who trust in you,
we give thanks for the witness of Stephen.
Accept our offering this day,
and grant your peace and consolation
to those who suffer for your truth.
We ask this in the name of Jesus Christ our Lord.

*Preface of a Martyr*

**Prayer after Communion**

Merciful God,
we have been gathered at the table of your Son.
Hear our prayer for all our sisters and brothers in faith
who suffer for truth, justice, and freedom.
Strengthen their witness
and keep them, with us,
under the protection of your wings.
We ask this in the name of Jesus Christ the Lord.

# The Transfiguration of the Lord   *6 August*

**Sentence**

This is my beloved Son, with whom I am well pleased; listen to
him.   *Matthew 17.5*

**Collect**

Almighty God,
on the holy mount you revealed to chosen witnesses
your well-beloved Son, wonderfully transfigured:
mercifully deliver us from the darkness of this world,
and change us into his likeness from glory to glory;
through Jesus Christ our Lord
who lives and reigns with you and the Holy Spirit,
one God, now and for ever.

**Readings**

> Daniel 7.9–10, 13–14       Psalm 99
> *Refrain*   The Lord our God is the Holy One.   *Or v.1 or CR 2*
> 2 Peter 1.16–19       Luke 9.28–36

**Prayer over the Gifts**

Holy God,
receive all we offer you this day,
and bring us to that radiant glory
which we see in the transfigured face
of Jesus Christ our Lord.

*Preface of the Incarnation*

### Prayer after Communion

Holy God,
we see your glory in the face of Jesus Christ.
May we who are partakers of his table
reflect his life in word and deed,
that all the world may know
his power to change and save.
We ask this in his name.

## Saint Mary the Virgin   *15 August*

### Sentence

Hail, O favoured one, the Lord is with you! The Holy Spirit will
come upon you.   *Luke 1.28, 35*

### Collect

O God,
you have taken to yourself the blessed Virgin Mary,
mother of your incarnate Son.
May we who have been redeemed by his blood,
share with her the glory of your eternal kingdom;
through Jesus Christ our Lord,
who lives and reigns with you and the Holy Spirit,
one God, now and for ever.

### Readings

Isaiah 7.10–15      Psalm 132.6–10, 13–14
*Refrain*   Arise, O Lord, into your resting place.   *Or v.8 or CR 2*
Galatians 4.4–7      Luke 1.46–55 *or* Luke 2.1–7

### Prayer over the Gifts

God of mercy,
receive all we offer you this day.
May we share with the Virgin Mary
the joys of your eternal kingdom,
and live with you in unending love.
We ask this in the name of Jesus Christ our Lord.

*Preface of Christmas*

**Prayer after Communion**

God of grace,
today we raise our voices
to magnify your holy name,
and, in our own generation, to call her blessed
who became the mother of our Saviour Jesus Christ.
May we who have shared this holy food
continue, with her, in your glorious kingdom,
founded and established in Jesus Christ our Lord.
We ask this in his name.

# Saint Bartholomew   *24 August*

**Sentence**

You are those who continued with me in my trials. You shall
eat and drink at my table in my kingdom.   *Luke 22.28, 30*

**Collect**

Almighty and everlasting God,
who gave to your apostle Bartholomew
grace to believe and preach your word,
may your Church truly love what he believed
and faithfully preach what he taught;
through Jesus Christ our Lord,
who lives and reigns with you and the Holy Spirit,
one God, now and for ever.

**Readings**

> Deuteronomy 18.15–18 *or* 1 Corinthians 4.9–15     Psalm 91
> *Refrain*   He shall give his angels charge over you.
> *Or v.11 or CR 4*
> Luke 22.24–30

**Prayer over the Gifts**

Faithful God,
receive all we offer you this day.
May we, like all your apostles,
so live the life of Christ

that your Church may be the sign of salvation
to all nations of the world.
We ask this in the name of Jesus Christ the Lord.

*Preface of Apostles*

**Prayer after Communion**

God of our salvation,
you have fed us at the table of your Son
Jesus Christ our Lord.
Lead us in his way of service,
that your kingdom may be known on earth.
We ask this in his name.

# The Beheading of Saint John the Baptist  *29 August*

**Sentence**

Blessed are those who are persecuted for righteousness' sake,
for theirs is the kingdom of heaven.   *Matthew 5.10*

**Collect**

Almighty God,
who called John the Baptist
to give witness to the coming of your Son
and to prepare his way,
strengthen us by your grace,
that as he suffered for the truth,
so we may boldly resist corruption and sin,
and receive with him the unfading crown of glory;
through Jesus Christ our Lord,
who lives and reigns with you and the Holy Spirit,
one God, now and for ever.

**Readings**

> 2 Chronicles 24.17–21 *or* Hebrews 11.32–40     Psalm 71.1–6, 15–17
> *Refrain*   My tongue will proclaim your righteousness.
> *Or v.15 or CR 5*
> Mark 6.17–29

**Prayer over the Gifts**

God of the prophets,
receive all we offer you this day,
and strengthen us to proclaim
your holy and righteous word.
We ask this in the name of Jesus Christ the Lord.

*Preface of a Saint*

**Prayer after Communion**

God of righteousness,
may we who honour John the Baptist,
the greatest of the prophets,
always turn to him who takes away the sin of the world,
our Saviour Jesus Christ.


# Holy Cross Day   *14 September*

**Sentence**

Far be it from me to glory except in the cross of our Lord Jesus
Christ.   *Galatians 6.14*

**Collect**

Almighty God,
whose Son our Saviour Jesus Christ
was lifted high upon the cross
that he might draw the whole world to himself,
may we who rejoice in the mystery of our redemption,
have grace to take up our cross and follow him,
who lives and reigns with you and the Holy Spirit,
one God, now and for ever.

**Readings**

>      Numbers 21.4b–9      Psalm 98.1–5
>      *Refrain*   The Lord has made known his victory.   *Or v.1 or CR 3*
>      1 Corinthians 1.18–24      John 3.13–17

**Prayer over the Gifts**

Merciful God,
through the death of your beloved Son
you transformed an instrument of shame
into a sign of hope and glory.
Receive all we offer you this day,
and renew in us the mystery of his love;
through the same Jesus Christ, the Lord of glory.

*Preface of Holy Week*

**Prayer after Communion**

Almighty God,
we give thanks that you have made us partakers
of the body and blood of your Son Jesus Christ our Lord,
who took our nature upon him
and suffered death upon the cross for our redemption;
who lives and reigns with you and the Holy Spirit,
one God, now and for ever.

# Saint Matthew   *21 September*

**Sentence**

You shall be my witnesses in Jerusalem and in all Judea and
Samaria and to the end of the earth.   *Acts 1.8*

**Collect**

Almighty God,
who through your Son
called Matthew to be your apostle and evangelist,
free us from all greed and selfish love,
that we may follow in the steps of Jesus Christ our Lord,
who lives and reigns with you and the Holy Spirit,
one God, now and for ever.

**Readings**

> Proverbs 3.1–6 *or* 2 Timothy 3.14–17      Psalm 119.33–40
> *Refrain*   Instruct me in your statutes, O Lord.   *Or v.33 or CR 4*
> Matthew 9.9–13

**Prayer over the Gifts**

Father,
accept all we offer you this day.
Guide us with your love
as you nourish the faith of the Church
by the preaching of your apostles.
We ask this in the name of Jesus Christ our Lord.

*Preface of Apostles*

**Prayer after Communion**

God of mercy and compassion,
we have shared the joy of salvation
that Matthew knew when Jesus called him.
May this food renew our life in him
who came not to call the righteous
but sinners to salvation in his kingdom,
your Son Jesus Christ our Lord.

# Saint Michael and All Angels   29 September

**Sentence**

Bless the Lord, all you his hosts, you ministers of his who do
his will.   *Psalm 103.21*

**Collect**

Eternal God,
you have ordained and constituted in a wonderful order
the ministries of angels and mortals.
Grant that as your holy angels stand before you in heaven,
so at your command
they may help and defend us here on earth;
through Jesus Christ our Lord,
who lives and reigns with you and the Holy Spirit,
one God, now and for ever.

### Readings

Genesis 28.10–17     Psalm 103.19–22
*Refrain*   Bless the Lord, O my soul.   *Or v.1 or CR 1*
Revelation 12.7–12     John 1.47–51

### Prayer over the Gifts

God of glory,
as you have appointed angels to minister in your presence,
so may all our worship bring you worthy praise.
We ask this in the name of Jesus Christ our Lord.

*Preface of Trinity Sunday*

### Prayer after Communion

Eternal God,
you have fed us with the bread of angels.
May we who come under their protection,
like them give you continual service and praise;
through Jesus Christ our Lord.

## Saint Luke   *18 October*

### Sentence

How beautiful upon the mountains are the feet of those who
bring good tidings, who publish salvation.   *Isaiah 52.7*

### Collect

Almighty God,
who inspired Luke the physician
to proclaim the love and healing power of your Son,
give your Church, by the grace of the Spirit
and the medicine of the gospel,
the same love and power to heal;
through Jesus Christ our Lord,
who lives and reigns with you and the Holy Spirit,
one God, now and for ever.

### Readings

Sirach 38.1–4, 6–10, 12–14 *or* 2 Timothy 4.5–13    Psalm 147.1–7

*Refrain*    Praise the Lord who heals the brokenhearted.

*Or v.3 or* Alleluia!

Luke 4.14–21

### Prayer over the Gifts

God of compassion,
you are a strong tower for all who trust in you.
Be now and evermore our defence,
that we may proclaim the only name under heaven
given for health and salvation,
the name of Jesus Christ our Lord.

*Preface of All Saints*

### Prayer after Communion

Living God,
may we who have shared in these holy mysteries
enjoy health of body and mind,
and witness faithfully to your gospel,
in the name of Jesus Christ our Lord.

# Saint Simon and Saint Jude    28 October

### Sentence

You shall be my witnesses in Jerusalem and in all Judea and
Samaria and to the end of the earth.    *Acts 1.8*

### Collect

Almighty God,
we thank you for the glorious company of the apostles,
and especially on this day for Simon and Jude.
As they were faithful and zealous in their mission,

so may we with ardent devotion
make known the love and mercy
of our Lord and Saviour Jesus Christ,
who lives and reigns with you and the Holy Spirit,
one God, now and for ever.

### Readings

Deuteronomy 32.1–4 *or* Ephesians 2.13–22        Psalm 119.89–96
*Refrain*   O Lord, your word is everlasting.   *Or v.89 or CR 4*
John 15.17–27

### Prayer over the Gifts

God of faithfulness,
accept our offering this day,
and give us grace to witness to your truth
and to follow in the path of those
who acknowledge Jesus as Lord for ever and ever.

*Preface of Apostles*

### Prayer after Communion

Eternal God,
we are nourished by the bread of life.
Strengthen us to witness to the gospel,
and bring us to reign with Jesus Christ your Son,
for he is Lord now and for ever.

# All Saints   *1 November*

*This festival may be observed on the Sunday following 1 November, in addition to its observance on the fixed date.*

### Sentence

They are before the throne of God, and he who sits upon the throne will shelter them with his presence.   *Revelation 7.15*

## Collect

Almighty God,
whose people are knit together in one holy Church,
the mystical Body of your Son,
grant us grace to follow your blessed saints
in lives of faith and commitment,
and to know the inexpressible joys you have prepared
for those who love you;
through your Son Jesus Christ our Lord,
who lives and reigns with you and the Holy Spirit,
one God, now and for ever.

## Readings

A    Revelation 7.9–17    Psalm 34.1–10
     *Refrain*  Taste and see that the Lord is good; happy are they who trust
     in him.  *Or v.9 or* Alleluia!
     1 John 3.1–3    Matthew 5.1–12

B    Revelation 21.1–6a    Psalm 24.1–6
     *Refrain*  The Lord of hosts, he is the King of glory.
     Colossians 1.9–14    John 11.32–44

C    Daniel 7.1–3, 15–18    Psalm 149
     *Refrain*  Sing to the Lord a new song.   *Or v.1 or* Alleluia!
     Ephesians 1.11–23    Luke 6.20–36

## Prayer over the Gifts

Holy and mighty God,
we give you thanks for the triumph of Christ
in the lives of all his saints.
Receive all we offer you this day,
and help us, like them, to run our course with faith,
that we may come to your eternal kingdom.
We ask this in the name of Jesus Christ our Lord.

*Preface of All Saints*

## Prayer after Communion

Lord of hosts,
we praise your glory reflected in your saints.

May we who share at this table
be filled with the joy of your eternal kingdom,
where Jesus is Lord, now and for ever.

## All Souls   *2 November*

*Or a convenient day in the week after All Saints.*

### Sentence

I am the resurrection and the life, says the Lord; whoever lives
and believes in me shall never die.   *John 11.25, 26*

### Collect

Father of all,
we pray to you for those we love, but see no longer.
Grant them your peace,
let light perpetual shine upon them,
and in your loving wisdom and almighty power,
work in them the good purpose of your perfect will;
through Jesus Christ our Lord,
who lives and reigns with you and the Holy Spirit,
one God, now and for ever.

### Readings

> Wisdom 3.1–9      Psalm 116.1–8
> *Refrain*   Precious in the sight of the Lord is the death of his servants.
> 1 Peter 1.3–9      John 6.37–40 *or* John 11.21–27

### Prayer over the Gifts

Gracious and righteous Lord,
we are united in the love of Jesus Christ.
Accept all we offer you this day,
and bring us, with all your faithful people
who have gone before us,
into his eternal glory;
who is Lord, now and for ever.

*Preface for the Commemoration of the Dead*

## Prayer after Communion

God of love,
may the death and resurrection of Christ,
which we celebrate in this eucharist,
bring us, with the faithful departed,
into the peace of your eternal home.
We ask this in the name of Jesus Christ,
our hope and our salvation.

# Saint Andrew  *30 November*

### Sentence

You shall be my witnesses in Jerusalem and in all Judea and
Samaria and to the end of the earth.   *Acts 1.8*

### Collect

Almighty God,
who gave your apostle Andrew
grace to believe in his heart
and to confess with his lips that Jesus is Lord,
touch our lips and our hearts
that faith may burn within us,
and we may share in the witness of your Church
to the whole human family;
through Jesus Christ our Lord,
who lives and reigns with you and the Holy Spirit,
one God, now and for ever.

### Readings

Deuteronomy 30.11–14 *or* Romans 10.8b–18       Psalm 19.1–6
*Refrain*   Their message has gone out to the ends of the world.
*Or v.4 or CR 2*
Matthew 4.18–22

**Prayer over the Gifts**

Eternal God, ruler of the universe,
may we who have heard your word
always be ready to answer your call
and to follow without fear.
We ask this in the name of Jesus Christ our Lord.

*Preface of Apostles*

**Prayer after Communion**

Father,
may the gifts we have received at your table
give us courage to follow the example of Andrew the apostle
and share in the ministry of your Son
Jesus Christ our Lord.

# Common Propers for Saints' Days

*The following sentences and prayers may be used on saints' days, either in conjunction with readings assigned for the day in the ongoing cycle of a lectionary, or in conjunction with readings appropriate to the day. Suggested readings follow the proper prayers.*

## Common of a Martyr 1

### Sentence

Blessed are those who are persecuted for righteousness' sake, for theirs is the kingdom of heaven.    *Matthew 5.10*

*Or*

Blessed are those who endure trial for Jesus' sake, for when they have stood the test, he will give them the crown of life.
*See James 1.12*

### Collect

Almighty God,
who gave your servant *N* courage
to confess Jesus Christ
and to die for this faith,
may we always be ready
to give a reason for the hope that is in us,
and to suffer gladly for his sake;
through Jesus Christ our Lord,
who lives and reigns with you and the Holy Spirit,
one God, now and for ever.

### Prayer over the Gifts

God of faithfulness,
your servant *N* praised you in *his/her* death.
Receive all we offer you this day,
and give us the strength of will
to proclaim your righteousness and love.
We ask this in the name of Jesus Christ the Lord.

*Preface of a Martyr*

### Prayer after Communion

God of courage,
we give thanks for this holy food,
and we praise you for your martyr *N*,
who ran with perseverance
the race that was set before *him/her*,
and won the victor's wreath that does not fade;
through Jesus Christ our Lord.

# Common of a Martyr 2

### Sentence

God is not ashamed to be called their God, for he has prepared
for them a city.   *Hebrews 11.16b*

*Or*

You are those who have continued with me in my trials; and I
assign to you, as my Father assigned to me a kingdom, that you
may eat and drink at my table in my kingdom.   *Luke 22.28–30a*

### Collect

Almighty and everlasting God,
who kindled the flame of your love
in the heart of your holy martyr *N*,
give us, your servants, the same faith and power of love,
that we who rejoice in *his/her* triumph
may profit by *his/her* example;
through Jesus Christ our Lord,
who lives and reigns with you and the Holy Spirit,
one God, now and for ever.

### Prayer over the Gifts

Father,
we give you thanks for the witness of your martyr *N*.
Accept our offering this day
and give your peace and consolation
to those who suffer for the proclamation of your name.
We ask this in the name of Jesus Christ our Lord.

**Prayer after Communion**

Father,
as we are nourished by the bread of life,
inspire us with the memory of your servant *N*,
and give us courage to witness with our lives
to your Son's victory over sin and death;
through Jesus Christ, the King of martyrs.

# Common of a Missionary

### Sentence

To all to whom I sent you you shall go, and whatever I
command you you shall speak.   *Jeremiah 1.7b*

### Collect

Almighty and everlasting God,
we thank you for your servant *N*,
whom you called to preach the gospel
to the people of . . .
(*or* to the . . . people).
Raise up in this and every land,
heralds and evangelists of your kingdom,
that your Church may make known the immeasurable riches
of our Saviour Jesus Christ,
who lives and reigns with you and the Holy Spirit,
one God, now and for ever.

### Prayer over the Gifts

God of our salvation,
your love for all the world is endless.
May all we offer you this day
renew our dedication to your mission;
in the name of Jesus Christ the Lord.

*Preface of a Saint*

**Prayer after Communion**

Father,
may we who share in these holy mysteries
receive health of body and mind,
and a continual will to witness to your gospel.
We ask this in the name of Jesus Christ our Lord.

# Common of a Pastor

**Sentence**

I have called you friends, says the Lord; for all that I have heard
from the Father I have made known to you.    *John 15.15*

*Or*

How beautiful on the mountains are the feet of those who bring
good tidings, who publish salvation.    *Isaiah 52.7*

**Collect**

God of love,
shepherd of your people,
we thank you for your servant *N*,
who was faithful in the care and nurture of your flock.
Taught by the example of *his/her* holy life,
may we by grace grow into the full stature
of our Lord and Saviour Jesus Christ,
who lives and reigns with you and the Holy Spirit,
one God, now and for ever.

**Prayer over the Gifts**

Shepherd of Israel,
your flock is never without care.
Accept our grateful offering
and grant that your Church
may always rejoice in faithful pastors
who are servants of Christ and stewards of your mysteries.
We ask this through Jesus Christ our Lord.

*Preface of a Saint or Martyr*

### Prayer after Communion

Father,
we thank you for your servant *N*,
in whom we see the loving service of Christ.
May we who receive these holy mysteries
be faithful in the ministry to which you call us,
through your Son Jesus Christ our Lord.

# Common of Doctors and Teachers of the Faith

### Sentence

If you continue in my word, you are truly my disciples, and
you will know the truth, and the truth will make you free.
*John 8.31–32*

*Or*

The word of the cross is the power of God to us who are being
saved.   *See 1 Corinthians 1.18*

### Collect

Almighty God,
who through the teaching of your servant *N*
enlightened and enabled all your Church
to understand the truth in Jesus Christ,
raise up among us teachers of your word,
that we, set free by truth from unbelief,
may come to know our great salvation;
through Jesus Christ our Lord,
who lives and reigns with you and the Holy Spirit,
one God, now and for ever.

### Prayer over the Gifts

God of truth,
receive all we offer you this day.
May we share in the wisdom of your eternal Word,
made known at this eucharistic table.
We ask this in the name of Jesus Christ the incarnate Word.

*Preface of a Saint*

**Prayer after Communion**

O God,
your Word is the light of our pilgrimage,
the end and fulfilment of our knowledge.
May we who have known him in the breaking of bread
await in love the dawning of his radiance,
the same Jesus Christ our Lord.

## Common of Virgins

**Sentence**

If any serve me, the Father will honour them.     *John 12.26*

**Collect**

God our Saviour,
today we celebrate with joy the memory of your servant *N*,
and we give thanks for her faithfulness and love.
May we, like her, serve you with generous hearts.
We ask this in the name of Jesus Christ the Lord.

**Prayer over the Gifts**

Lord,
we see the wonder of your faithful love
in the life of *N*.
Receive all we offer you this day,
and guide us too in the paths of your service.
We ask this in the name of Jesus Christ the Lord.

*Preface of a Saint*

**Prayer after Communion**

God of mercy,
we give thanks that on this feast of *N*
you give us the bread of heaven.
Grant us your grace in this life,
and glory in the world which is to come.
We ask this in the name of Jesus Christ the Lord.

# Common of a Saint 1

## Sentence

If any serve me, the Father will honour them. *John 12.26*

*Or*

Blessed are those who hunger and thirst for what is right, for they shall be satisfied. *Matthew 5.6*

*Or*

Come to me, all who labour and are heavy laden, and I will give you rest. *Matthew 11.28*

## Collect

Almighty and everlasting God,
who in the heart of your servant *N*
kindled the flame of your love,
give us, your humble servants,
such faith and power of love,
that as we rejoice in *his/her* triumph,
we may profit by *his/her* example;
through Jesus Christ our Lord,
who lives and reigns with you and the Holy Spirit,
one God, now and for ever.

## Prayer over the Gifts

God of love and justice,
you make known your ways in the lives of your saints.
Receive all we offer you this day,
and help us to know your holy will and do it;
through Jesus Christ the Lord.

*Preface of a Saint*

## Prayer after Communion

God of glory,
this table is a foretaste of the kingdom of your Son.
May we be faithful to him in this life
and rejoice with your servant *N* for ever;
through the same Jesus Christ our Lord.

# Common of a Saint 2

Walk in love, as Christ loved us and gave himself up for us.
*Ephesians 5.2a*

**Collect**

Almighty God,
who by your grace surrounds us
with so great a cloud of witnesses,
may we, encouraged by the example of your servant *N*,
persevere and run the race you set before us,
until at last, through your mercy,
we with *him/her* attain to your eternal joy;
through Jesus Christ our Lord,
the author and perfecter of our faith,
who lives and reigns with you and the Holy Spirit,
one God, now and for ever.

**Prayer over the Gifts**

Eternal God,
we give you thanks for the triumph of Christ
in the life of your servant *N*.
Accept our offering this day,
and give us grace to run our course with faith,
that we may come to your eternal kingdom.
We ask this in the name of Jesus Christ our Lord.

*Preface of a Saint*

**Prayer after Communion**

God of glory,
we give thanks for your likeness in your servant *N*.
May we who share at this table be transformed by your love
and display the joy of your kingdom,
where Jesus is Lord, now and for ever.

# Common Readings for Saints' Days

## Common of Martyrs

### Reading 1—outside Easter Season

2 Chronicles 24.17–22a   (They stoned him with stones in the court of the house of the Lord)

Sirach 51.1–12   (My soul drew near to death)

Wisdom 3.1–9   (The souls of the righteous are in the hand of God)

2 Maccabees 6.18, 21, 24–31   (I am glad to suffer these things because I fear him)

2 Maccabees 7.1–2, 9–14   (We are ready to die rather than transgress the laws of our fathers)

2 Maccabees 7.1, 20–23, 27b–29   (The mother was especially admirable . . . she encouraged each of them)

### Reading 1—during Easter Season

Acts 7.55—8.1a   (Lord Jesus, receive my spirit)

Revelation 7.9–17   (These are they who have come out of the great tribulation)

Revelation 12.10–12a   (They loved not their lives even unto death)

Revelation 21.5–7   (He who conquers shall have this heritage)

### Psalms and Suitable Refrains

31.1–5   (Into your hands I commend my spirit)

34.1–8   (The angel of the Lord encompasses those who fear him)

124   (Our help is in the name of the Lord)

126   (Those who sowed with tears will reap with songs of joy)

### Reading 2

Romans 5.1–5   (We rejoice in our sufferings)

Romans 8.31b–39   (Neither death nor life will be able to separate us from the love of God)

2 Corinthians 4.7–15   (Carrying in the body the death of Jesus)

2 Corinthians 6.3–10   (As dying, and behold we live)

2 Timothy 2.8–13; 3.10–12   (The Gospel for which I am suffering)

Hebrews 10.32–36   (You endured a hard struggle with sufferings)
James 1.2–4, 12   (Count it all joy . . . when you meet various trials)
1 Peter 3.13–17   (It is better to suffer for doing right)
1 Peter 4.12–19   (Do not be surprised by the fiery ordeal)
1 John 5.1–5   (This is the victory that overcomes the world, our faith)

## Gospel

Matthew 10.16–22   (I send you out as sheep in the midst of wolves)
Matthew 10.28–33   (Do not fear those who kill the body)
Matthew 10.34–39   (He who loses his life for my sake will find it)
Luke 9.23–26   (Whoever loses his life for my sake, he will save it)
John 12.24–26   (Unless a grain of wheat falls into the earth and dies, it remains alone)
John 15.18–21   (If they persecuted me, they will persecute you)
John 17.11b–19   (The world has hated them)

# Common of Pastors

### Reading 1—outside Easter Season

Exodus 32.7–14   (Moses besought the Lord his God)
Deuteronomy 10.8–9   (The Lord set apart the tribe of Levi)
1 Samuel 16.1, 6–13a   (The Spirit of the Lord came mightily upon David)
Isaiah 6.1–8   (Whom shall I send, and who will go for us?)
Isaiah 52.7–10   (All the ends of the earth shall see the salvation of our God)—for Missionaries
Isaiah 61.1–3   (The Lord has anointed me to bring good tidings)
Jeremiah 1.4–9   (I have put my words in your mouth)
Ezekiel 3.16–21   (I have made you a watchman for the house of Israel)
Ezekiel 34.11–16   (I seek out my sheep and I will rescue them)

### Reading 1—during Easter Season

Acts 13.46–49   (We turn to the gentiles)—for Missionaries
Acts 20.17–18a, 28–32, 36   (The Holy Spirit has made you overseers, to care for the Church of God)
Acts 26.19–23   (I was not disobedient to the heavenly vision)—for Missionaries

## Psalms and Suitable Refrains

16.5–11 (O Lord, you are my portion and my cup)
23 (The Lord is my shepherd; I shall not be in want)
96 (Ascribe to the Lord the honour due his name)
117 (Hallelujah!)

## Reading 2

Romans 12.3–13 (We, though many, are one body in Christ)
1 Corinthians 1.18–25 (Has not God made foolish the wisdom of the world?)
1 Corinthians 4.1–5 (Servants of Christ and stewards of the mysteries of God)
1 Corinthians 9.16–19, 22–23 (Woe to me if I do not preach the gospel!)
2 Corinthians 3.1–6a (Our competence is from God)
2 Corinthians 4.1–2, 5–7 (Ourselves as your servants for Jesus' sake)
2 Corinthians 5.14–20 (The love of Christ controls us)
Ephesians 4.1–7, 11–13 (To equip the saints for the work of ministry)
Colossians 1.24–29 (I became a minister according to the divine office which was given to me for you)
1 Thessalonians 2.1–8 (We had courage in our God to declare to you the gospel of God)
2 Timothy 1.13–14; 2.1–3 (Guard the truth that has been entrusted to you)
2 Timothy 4.1–5 (Do the work of an evangelist, fulfil your ministry)
1 Peter 5.1–4 (Tend the flock of God that is your charge)

## Gospel

Matthew 16.13–19 (You are Peter, and on this rock I will build my church)
Matthew 23.8–12 (He who is greatest among you shall be your servant)
Matthew 28.16–20 (Go therefore and make disciples of all nations)—for Missionaries
Mark 1.14–20 (I will make you become fishers of men)
Mark 16.15–20 (Go into all the world and preach the gospel to the whole creation)—for Missionaries
Luke 5.1–11 (They left everything and followed him)—for Missionaries
Luke 10.1–9 (The harvest is plentiful, but the labourers are few)
Luke 22.24–30 (I am among you as one who serves)
John 10.11–16 (I am the good shepherd)
John 15.9–17 (This is my commandment, that you love one another)
John 21.15–17 (Feed my sheep)

# Common of Doctors and Teachers of the Faith

### Reading 1—outside Easter Season

1 Kings 3.6–14  (I give you a wise and discerning mind)
Wisdom 7.7–10, 15–16  (The spirit of wisdom came to me)
Sirach 15.1–6  (Wisdom will feed him with the bread of understanding)
Sirach 39.6–14  (He will be filled with the spirit of understanding)

### Reading 1—during Easter Season

Acts 2.14a, 22–24, 32–36  (God has made him both Lord and Christ)
Acts 13.26–33  (God raised him from the dead)

### Psalms and Suitable Refrains

19.7–10  (The testimony of the Lord is sure and gives wisdom to the
  innocent)
37.32–42  (The mouth of the righteous utters wisdom)
119.9–16  (I will meditate on your commandments and give attention to your
  ways)
119.89–96  (I will never forget your commandments, because by them you
  give me life)

### Reading 2

1 Corinthians 1.18–25  (Has not God made foolish the wisdom of the world?)
1 Corinthians 2.1–10a  (I decided to know nothing among you except Jesus
  Christ and him crucified)
1 Corinthians 2.10b–16  (But we have the mind of Christ)
Ephesians 3.8–12  (That through the church the manifold wisdom of God
  might now be made known)
Ephesians 4.1–7, 11–13  (There is one body and one spirit)
2 Timothy 1.13–14; 2.1–3  (Guard the truth that has been entrusted to you)
2 Timothy 4.1–5  (Preach the word, be urgent in season and out of season)

### Gospel

Matthew 5.13–16  (You are the light of the world)
Matthew 23.8–12  (You are not to be called rabbi)
Mark 4.1–10, 13–20  (A sower went out to sow)

# Common of Virgins

## Reading 1—outside Easter Season

Song of Solomon 8.6–7   (Love is strong as death)

## Reading 1—during Easter Season

Revelation 19.1, 5–9a   (For the marriage of the Lamb has come)
Revelation 21.1–5a   (I saw the holy city . . . prepared as a bride)

## Psalms and Suitable Refrains

1   (The Lord knows the way of the righteous)
16.5–11   (O Lord, you are my portion and my cup)
34.1–8   (I will glory in the Lord; let the humble hear and rejoice)
45.1–16   (Hear, O daughter; consider and listen closely)
103   (Bless the Lord, O my soul, and all that is within me, bless his holy name)
112.1–9   (Happy are they who fear the Lord)
128   (Happy are they all who fear the Lord)
131   (O Israel, wait upon the Lord)
148   (Hallelujah!)

## Reading 2

1 Corinthians 7.25–35   (The form of this world is passing away)
2 Corinthians 10.17—11.2   (I betrothed you to Christ to present you as a pure bride to her one husband)

## Gospel

Matthew 19.3–12   (There are . . . eunuchs for the sake of the kingdom of heaven)
Matthew 25.1–13   (Behold the bridegroom! Come out to meet him)
Luke 10.38–42   (Mary has chosen the good portion)

# Common of Saints

## Reading 1—outside Easter Season

Genesis 12.1–4a   (Go from your country and your kindred)
Leviticus 19.1–2, 17–18   (Love your neighbour as yourself)
Deuteronomy 6.1–9   (Love the Lord your God with all your heart)

Deuteronomy 10.8–9   (The Lord set apart the tribe of Levi to carry the ark)

1 Kings 19.4–18   (Go forth and stand upon the mount before the Lord)

Proverbs 31.10–20, 30–31   (A woman who fears the Lord is to be praised)

Isaiah 58.6–11   (Share your bread with the hungry)—for Social Reformers

Jeremiah 20.7–9   (There is in my heart as it were a burning fire)

Micah 6.6–8   (To do justice, and to love kindness, and to walk humbly with your God)—for Social Reformers

Zephaniah 2.3; 3.11–13   (Seek the Lord, all you humble of the land)

Tobit 12.6–13   (Prayer is good when accompanied by fasting, almsgiving, and righteousness)

Judith 8.1a, 2–8   (She feared God with great devotion)

Esther 13.8–14, 17   (That I might not set the glory of man above the glory of God)

Sirach 2.7–13   (You who fear the Lord, wait for his mercy)

Sirach 3.18–26   (The greater you are the more you must humble yourself)

Sirach 26.1–4, 16–18   (The beauty of a good wife in her well-ordered home)

## Reading 1—during Easter Season

Acts 4.32–35   (The company of those who believed were of one heart and soul)

Revelation 3.14b, 20–22   (He who conquers, I will grant him to sit with me on my throne)

Revelation 19.1, 5–9a   (For the marriage of the Lamb has come)

Revelation 21.5–7   (He who conquers shall have this heritage, and I will be his God and he shall be my son)

## Psalms and Suitable Refrains

1   (The Lord knows the way of the righteous)

15   (Whoever leads a blameless life shall never be overthrown)

34.1–8   (Taste and see that the Lord is good)

34.9–22   (The eyes of the Lord are upon the righteous)

103   (Bless the Lord, O my soul, and all that is within me, bless his holy name)

112.1–9   (Happy are they who fear the Lord)

128   (Happy are they all who fear the Lord)

131   (O Israel, wait upon the Lord)

**Reading 2**

Romans 8.26–30 (Those whom he justified he also glorified)

1 Corinthians 1.26–31 (God chose what is foolish in the world to shame the wise)

1 Corinthians 12.31—13.13 (Love never ends)

2 Corinthians 10.17—11.2 (I betrothed you to Christ to present you as a pure bride to her one husband)

Galatians 2.19–20 (It is no longer I who live, but Christ who lives in me)

Galatians 6.14–16 (Far be it from me to glory except in the cross)

Ephesians 3.14–19 (To know the love of Christ which surpasses knowledge)

Ephesians 6.10–13, 18 (Put on the whole armour of God)

Philippians 3.8–14 (I press on toward the goal for the prize of the upward call of God in Christ Jesus)

Philippians 4.4–9 (Rejoice in the Lord always)

1 Timothy 5.3–10 (Honour widows who are real widows)—for Widows

James 2.14–17 (Faith by itself, if it has no works, is dead)

1 Peter 4.7–11 (As good stewards of God's varied grace)

1 John 3.14–18 (Let us not love in word or speech but in deed and in truth)—for Social Reformers

1 John 4.7–16 (If we love one another, God abides in us)

1 John 5.1–5 (This is the victory that overcomes the world, our faith)

**Gospel**

Matthew 5.1–12a (He went up on the mountain . . . and he opened his mouth and taught them)

Matthew 5.13–16 (You are the light of the world)

Matthew 11.25–30 (My yoke is easy, and my burden is light)

Matthew 13.44–46 (He goes and sells all that he has and buys that field)

Matthew 16.24–27 (Whoever loses his life for my sake will find it)

Matthew 18.1–4 (Unless you turn and become like children, you will never enter the kingdom of heaven)

Matthew 19.3–12 (There are . . . eunuchs for the sake of the kingdom of heaven)

Matthew 25.1–13 (Behold the bridegroom! Come out to meet him)

Matthew 25.14–30 (You have been faithful over a little, I will set you over much)

Matthew 25.31–46 (As you did it to one of the least of these my brethren, you did it to me)—for Social Reformers

Mark 3.31–35  (Whoever does the will of God is my brother, and sister, and mother)

Mark 9.33–37  (Whoever receives one such child in my name receives me)

Mark 10.13–16  (Let the children come to me, do not hinder them)

Mark 10.17–30  (Sell what you have, and give to the poor . . . and come, follow me)

Luke 9.57–62  (The Son of man has nowhere to lay his head)

Luke 10.38–42  (Mary has chosen the good portion)

Luke 12.32–34  (It is your Father's good pleasure to give you the kingdom)

Luke 12.35–40  (Blessed are those servants whom the master finds awake when he comes)

Luke 14.25–33  (Whoever of you does not renounce all that he has cannot be my disciple)

John 15.1–8  (I am the vine, you are the branches)

John 15.9–17  (This is my commandment, that you love one another)

John 17.20–26  (The glory which thou hast given me I have given to them)

# Alphabetical List of Abbreviations

## The Books of the Bible in the Revised Standard Version

| | | | |
|---|---|---|---|
| The Acts | Acts | Jude | Jude |
| Amos | Am | 1 Kings | 1 Kgs |
| 1 Chronicles | 1 Chr | 2 Kings | 2 Kgs |
| 2 Chronicles | 2 Chr | Lamentations | Lam |
| Colossians | Col | Leviticus | Lev |
| 1 Corinthians | 1 Cor | Luke | Lk |
| 2 Corinthians | 2 Cor | Malachi | Mal |
| Daniel | Dan | Micah | Mic |
| Deuteronomy | Dt | Mark | Mk |
| Ecclesiastes | Ec | Matthew | Mt |
| Ephesians | Eph | Nahum | Nah |
| Esther | Est | Nehemiah | Neh |
| Exodus | Ex | Numbers | Num |
| Ezekiel | Ezek | Obadiah | Ob |
| Ezra | Ezra | 1 Peter | 1 Pet |
| Galatians | Gal | 2 Peter | 2 Pet |
| Genesis | Gen | Philippians | Phil |
| Habakkuk | Hab | Philemon | Philem |
| Haggai | Hag | Proverbs | Pr |
| Hebrews | Heb | Psalms | Ps |
| Hosea | Hos | Revelation | Rev |
| Isaiah | Is | Romans | Rom |
| James | Jas | Ruth | Ru |
| Jeremiah | Jer | 1 Samuel | 1 Sam |
| Judges | Jg | 2 Samuel | 2 Sam |
| Joel | Jl | Song of Solomon | S of S |
| John | Jn | 1 Thessalonians | 1 Th |
| 1 John | 1 Jn | 2 Thessalonians | 2 Th |
| 2 John | 2 Jn | 1 Timothy | 1 Tim |
| 3 John | 3 Jn | 2 Timothy | 2 Tim |
| Job | Job | Titus | Tit |
| Jonah | Jon | Zechariah | Zech |
| Joshua | Jos | Zephaniah | Zeph |

## The Books of the Apocrypha

| | |
|---|---|
| The Additions to Esther | Ad Est |
| Baruch | Bar |
| The First Book of Esdras | 1 Esd |
| The Second Book of Esdras | 2 Esd |
| Judith | Jdt |
| The First Book of the Maccabees | 1 Macc |
| The Second Book of the Maccabees | 2 Macc |
| Ecclesiasticus, or the Wisdom of Jesus the Son of Sirach | Sir |
| The Prayer of Azariah and the Song of the Three Young Men | S of 3 Y |
| Susanna | Sus |
| Tobit | Tob |
| The Wisdom of Solomon | Wis |

# Concerning the Daily Office Lectionary

The Daily Office Lectionary is arranged in a two-year cycle. Year 1 always begins on the First Sunday of Advent in years divisible by two (1986, 1988, etc.).

Three readings are provided for every day. Two of the readings may be used in the morning and one in the evening. If two readings are desired at both morning and evening offices, the Old Testament reading for the alternative year may be used as a first reading. If the office occurs only once in the day, all three readings may be used.

The readings of the Daily Office Lectionary may be used at weekday celebrations of the eucharist for which no readings are provided in the Lectionary, or at Morning Prayer when it is attached to the eucharist as the liturgy of the word; in either case, the Gospel reading, preceded by at least one of the other readings, should be used.

When more than one reading is used at an office, the first is always from the Old Testament or the Apocrypha.

When a holy day interrupts the sequence of readings, they may be re-ordered by lengthening, combining, or omitting some of them, to secure continuity or avoid repetition.

In the Daily Office Lectionary the psalms are arranged in a seven-week pattern which recurs throughout the year, except for variations in the seasons of Christmas, Epiphany, Lent, and Easter.

In the citation of the psalms, those for the morning are given first, and then those for the evening. However, any of the psalms appointed for a given day may be used in the morning or in the evening, and any of the psalms appointed for any day may be used on any other day in the same week, except on major holy days.

Parentheses are used to indicate psalms and verses of psalms which may be omitted. In some instances, the entire portion of the psalter assigned to a given office is in parentheses and alternative psalmody is suggested. Those who wish to recite the psalter in its entirety should, in each instance, use the bracketed psalms rather than the alternatives.

Antiphons drawn from the psalms themselves, or from the opening sentences in the Propers, or from other passages of scripture, may be used with the psalms and the biblical canticles. The antiphons may be sung or said at the *beginning and end of each psalm or canticle, or may be used as refrains after each verse or group of verses.*

*On special occasions, suitable psalms and readings may be selected.*

**Signs**

1—*Year 1*
2—*Year 2*
M—*Morning*
E—*Evening*

# Daily Office Lectionary

## Week of 1 Advent

*Sun*    146, 147    \*    111, 112, 113
1        Is 1.1–9    2 Pet 3.1–10    Mt 25.1–13
2        Am 1.1–5, 13—2.8    1 Th 5.1–11    Lk 21.5–9

*Mon*    1, 2, 3    \*    4, 7
1        Is 1.10–20    1 Th 1.1–10    Lk 20.1–8
2        Am 2.6–16    2 Pet 1.1–11    Mt 21.1–11

*Tue*    5, 6    \*    10, 11
1        Is 1.21–31    1 Th 2.1–12    Lk 20.9–18
2        Am 3.1–11    2 Pet 1.12–21    Mt 21.12–22

*Wed*    119.1–24    \*    12, 13, 14
1        Is 2.1–11    1 Th 2.13–20    Lk 20.19–26
2        Am 3.12—4.5    2 Pet 3.1–10    Mt 21.23–32

*Thu*    18.1–20    \*    18.21–50
1        Is 2.12–22    1 Th 3.1–13    Lk 20.27–40
2        Am 4.6–13    2 Pet 3.11–18    Mt 21.33–46

*Fri*    16, 17    \*    22
1        Is 3.8–15    1 Th 4.1–12    Lk 20.41—21.4
2        Am 5.1–17    Jude 1–16    Mt 22.1–14

*Sat*    20, 21.1–7(8–14)    \*    110.1–5(6–7), 116, 117
1        Is 4.2–6    1 Th 4.13–18    Lk 21.5–19
2        Am 5.18–27    Jude 17–25    Mt 22.15–22

## Week of 2 Advent

*Sun*    148, 149, 150    \*    114, 115
1        Is 5.1–7    2 Pet 3.11–18    Lk 7.28–35
2        Am 6.1–14    2 Th 1.5–12    Lk 1.57–68

*Mon*    25    \*    9, 15
1        Is 5.8–12, 18–23    1 Th 5.1–11    Lk 21.20–28
2        Am 7.1–9    Rev 1.1–8    Mt 22.23–33

| *Tue* | 26, 28 | * | 36, 39 | |
|---|---|---|---|---|
| 1 | Is 5.13–17, 24–25 | 1 Th 5.12–28 | Lk 21.29–38 | |
| 2 | Am 7.10–17 | Rev 1.9–16 | Mt 22.34–46 | |

| *Wed* | 38 | * | 119.25–48 | |
|---|---|---|---|---|
| 1 | Is 6.1–13 | 2 Th 1.1–12 | Jn 7.53—8.11 | |
| 2 | Am 8.1–14 | Rev 1.17—2.7 | Mt 23.1–12 | |

| *Thu* | 37.1–18 | * | 37.19–42 | |
|---|---|---|---|---|
| 1 | Is 7.1–9 | 2 Th 2.1–12 | Lk 22.1–13 | |
| 2 | Am 9.1–10 | Rev 2.8–17 | Mt 23.13–26 | |

| *Fri* | 31 | * | 35 | |
|---|---|---|---|---|
| 1 | Is 7.10–25 | 2 Th 2.13—3.5 | Lk 22.14–30 | |
| 2 | Hag 1.1–15 | Rev 2.18–29 | Mt 23.27–39 | |

| *Sat* | 30, 32 | * | 42, 43 | |
|---|---|---|---|---|
| 1 | Is 8.1–15 | 2 Th 3.6–18 | Lk 22.31–38 | |
| 2 | Hag 2.1–9 | Rev 3.1–6 | Mt 24.1–14 | |

## Week of 3 Advent

| *Sun* | 63.1–8(9–11), 98 | * | 103 | |
|---|---|---|---|---|
| 1 | Is 13.6–13 | Heb 12.18–29 | Jn 3.22–30 | |
| 2 | Am 9.11–15 | 2 Th 2.1–3, 13–17 | Jn 5.30–47 | |

*The readings below are interrupted after 17 December in favour of the
readings identified by date in the week of 4 Advent.*

| *Mon* | 41, 52 | * | 44 | |
|---|---|---|---|---|
| 1 | Is 8.16—9.1 | 2 Pet 1.1–11 | Lk 22.39–53 | |
| 2 | Zech 1.7–17 | Rev 3.7–13 | Mt 24.15–31 | |

| *Tue* | 45 | * | 47, 48 | |
|---|---|---|---|---|
| 1 | Is 9.1–7 | 2 Pet 1.12–21 | Lk 22.54–69 | |
| 2 | Zech 2.1–13 | Rev 3.14–22 | Mt 24.32–44 | |

| *Wed* | 119.49–72 | * | 49, [53] | |
|---|---|---|---|---|
| 1 | Is 9.8–17 | 2 Pet 2.1–10a | Mk 1.1–8 | |
| 2 | Zech 3.1–10 | Rev 4.1–8 | Mt 24.45–51 | |

| *Thu* | 50 | * | [59, 60] *or* 33 | |
|---|---|---|---|---|
| 1 | Is 9.18—10.4 | | 2 Pet 2.10b–16 | Mt 3.1–12 |
| 2 | Zech 4.1–14 | | Rev 4.9—5.5 | Mt 25.1–13 |

| *Fri* | 40, 54 | * | 51 | |
|---|---|---|---|---|
| 1 | Is 10.5–19 | | 2 Pet 2.17–22 | Mt 11.2–15 |
| 2 | Zech 7.8—8.8 | | Rev 5.6–14 | Mt 25.14–30 |

| *Sat* | 55 | * | 138, 139.1–17(18–23) | |
|---|---|---|---|---|
| 1 | Is 10.20–27 | | Jude 17–25 | Lk 3.1–9 |
| 2 | Zech 8.9–17 | | Rev 6.1–17 | Mt 25.31–46 |

## Week of 4 Advent

*The readings provided for the dates below serve as Sunday readings if the date happens to be a Sunday.*

| *18 Dec* | 24, 29 | * | 8, 84 | |
|---|---|---|---|---|
| 1 | Is 42.1–12 | | Eph 6.10–20 | Jn 3.16–21 |
| 2 | Gen 3.8–15 | | Rev 12.1–10 | Jn 3.16–21 |

| *19 Dec* | 61, 62 | * | 112, 115 | |
|---|---|---|---|---|
| 1 | Is 11.1–9 | | Rev 20.1–10 | Jn 5.30–47 |
| 2 | Zeph 3.14–20 | | Tit 1.1–16 | Lk 1.1–25 |

| *20 Dec* | 66, 67 | * | 116, 117 | |
|---|---|---|---|---|
| 1 | Is 11.10–16 | | Rev 20.11—21.8 | Lk 1.5–25 |
| 2 | 1 Sam 2.1b–10 | | Tit 2.1–10 | Lk 1.26–38 |

| *21 Dec* | 72 | * | 111, 113 | |
|---|---|---|---|---|
| 1 | Is 28.9–22 | | Rev 21.9–21 | Lk 1.26–38 |
| 2 | 2 Sam 7.1–17 | | Tit 2.11—3.8a | Lk 1.39–48a(48b–56) |

| *22 Dec* | 80 | * | 146, 147 | |
|---|---|---|---|---|
| 1 | Is 29.13–24 | | Rev 21.22—22.5 | Lk 1.39–48a(48b–56) |
| 2 | 2 Sam 7.18–29 | | Gal 3.1–14 | Lk 1.57–66 |

| *23 Dec* | 93, 96 | * | 148, 150 | |
|---|---|---|---|---|
| 1 | Is 33.17–22 | | Rev 22.6–11, 18–20 | Lk 1.57–66 |
| 2 | Bar 4.21–29 | | Gal 3.15–22 | Lk 1.67–80 *or* Mt 1.1–17 |

| *24 Dec* | 45, 46 | * | | |
|---|---|---|---|---|
| 1M | Is 35.1–10 | | Rev 22.12–17, 21 | Lk 1.67–80 |
| 2M | Bar 4.36—5.9 | | Gal 3.23—4.7 | Mt 1.18–25 |

## Christmas and Following

*Christmas Eve*      *      89.1–29
         Is 59.15b–21      Phil 2.5–11

*Christmas Day*      2, 85      *      110.1–5(6–7), 132
1       Zech 2.10–13      1 Jn 4.7–16      Jn 3.31–36
2       Mic 4.1–5; 5.2–4      1 Jn 4.7–16      Jn 3.31–36

*First Sunday after Christmas*      93, 96      *      34
1       Is 62.6–7, 10–12      Heb 2.10–18      Mt 1.18–25
2       1 Sam 1.1–2, 7b–28      Col 1.9–20      Lk 2.22–40

*If St Stephen, St John, Apostle and Evangelist, and the Holy Innocents are observed on the days after Christmas, the following readings will be used on December 29, 30, and 31.*

*29 Dec*      18.1–20      *      18.21–50 †
1       Is 12.1–6      Rev 1.1–8      Jn 7.37–52
2       2 Sam 23.13–17b      2 Jn 1–13      Jn 2.1–11

*30 Dec*      20, 21.1–7(8–14)      *      23, 27
1       Is 25.1–9      Rev 1.9–20      Jn 7.53—8.11
2       1 Kg 17.17–24      3 Jn 1–15      Jn 4.46–54

*31 Dec*      46, 48      *
1       Is 26.1–9      2 Cor 5.16—6.2      Jn 8.12–19
2       1 Kg 3.5–14      Jas 4.13–17; 5.7–11      Jn 5.1–15

*If St Stephen, St John, Apostle and Evangelist, and the Holy Innocents are not observed on the days after Christmas, the following readings will be used until the Eve of the Naming of Jesus, except on the First Sunday after Christmas.*

*26 Dec*      145      *      146, 147
1       Is 12.1–6      Heb 1.1–12      Lk 2.22–40
2       Is 41.8–10      Heb 1.1–12      Lk 2.15–21

*27 Dec*      148, 149, 150      *      125, 126
1       Is 25.1–9      Col 1.11–19      Lk 2.41–52
2       Is 41.17–20      Heb 2.10–18      Mt 1.18–25

† If today is Saturday, use Psalms 23 and 27 at Evening Prayer.

| | | | |
|---|---|---|---|
| *28 Dec* | 26 | * | 2, 8 |
| 1 | Is 26.1–9 | Col 1.20–29 | Mt 2.13–18 |
| 2 | Jer 31.10–17 | Gal 4.1–7 | Jn 1.1–18 |

| | | | |
|---|---|---|---|
| *29 Dec* | 18.1–20 | * | 18.21–50 † |
| 1 | Is 60.1–5 | Rev 1.1–8 | Jn 7.37–52 |
| 2 | 2 Sam 23.13–17b | 2 Jn 1–13 | Jn 2.1–11 |

| | | | |
|---|---|---|---|
| *30 Dec* | 20, 21.1–7(8–14) | * | 23, 27 |
| 1 | Is 60.19–22 | Rev 1.9–20 | Jn 7.53—8.11 |
| 2 | 1 Kg 17.17–24 | 3 Jn 1–15 | Jn 4.46–54 |

| | | | |
|---|---|---|---|
| *31 Dec* | 46, 48 | * | |
| 1M | Is 62.10–12 | 2 Cor 5.16—6.2 | Jn 8.12–19 |
| 2M | 1 Kg 3.5–14 | Jas 4.13–17; 5.7–11 | Jn 5.1–15 |

*Eve of the Naming of Jesus*     *     90

        Is 65.15b–25      Rev 21.1–6

| | | | |
|---|---|---|---|
| *The Naming of Jesus* | 103 | * | 148 |
| 1 | Gen 17.1–12a, 15–16 | Col 2.6–12 | Jn 16.23b–30 |
| 2 | Is 62.1–5, 10–12 | Rev 19.11–16 | Mt 1.18–25 |

| | | | |
|---|---|---|---|
| *Second Sunday after Christmas* | 66, 67 | * | 145 |
| 1 | Ec 3.3–9, 14–17 | 1 Jn 2.12–17 | Jn 6.41–47 |
| 2 | Wis 7.3–14 | Col 3.12–17 | Jn 6.41–47 |

| | | | |
|---|---|---|---|
| *2 Jan* | 34 | * | 33 |
| 1 | Gen 12.1–7 | Heb 11.1–12 | Jn 6.35–42, 48–51 |
| 2 | 1 Kg 19.1–8 | Eph 4.1–16 | Jn 6.1–14 |

| | | | |
|---|---|---|---|
| *3 Jan* | 68 | * | 72 †† |
| 1 | Gen 28.10–22 | Heb 11.13–22 | Jn 10.7–17 |
| 2 | 1 Kg 19.9–18 | Eph 4.17–32 | Jn 6.15–27 |

| | | | |
|---|---|---|---|
| *4 Jan* | 85, 87 | * | 89.1–29 †† |
| 1 | Ex 3.1–12 | Heb 11.23–31 | Jn 14.6–14 |
| 2 | Jos 3.14—4.7 | Eph 5.1–20 | Jn 9.1–12, 35–38 |

†   If today is Saturday, use Psalms 23 and 27 at Evening Prayer.
††   If today is Saturday, use Psalm 136 at Evening Prayer.

*5 Jan*    2, 110.1–5(6–7)    *
1          Jos 1.1–9    Heb 11.32—12.2    Jn 15.1–16
2          Jon 2.2–9    Eph 6.10–20    Jn 11.17–27, 38–44

## The Epiphany and Following

*Eve of Epiphany*    *    29, 98
          Is 66.18–23    Rom 15.7–13

*Epiphany*    46, 97    *    96, 100
1          Is 52.7–10    Rev 21.22–27    Mt 12.14–21
2          Is 49.1–7    Rev 21.22–27    Mt 12.14–21

*7 Jan* †    103    *    114, 115
1          Is 52.3–6    Rev 2.1–7    Jn 2.1–11
2          Dt 8.1–3    Col 1.1–14    Jn 6.30–33, 48–51

*8 Jan*    117, 118    *    112, 113
1          Is 59.15–21    Rev 2.8–17    Jn 4.46–54
2          Ex 17.1–7    Col 1.15–23    Jn 7.37–52

*9 Jan*    121, 122, 123    *    131, 132
1          Is 63.1–5    Rev 2.18–29    Jn 5.1–15
2          Is 45.14–19    Col 1.24—2.7    Jn 8.12–19

*10 Jan*    138, 139.1–17(18–23)    *    147
1          Is 65.1–9    Rev 3.1–6    Jn 6.1–14
2          Jer 23.1–8    Col 2.8–23    Jn 10.7–17

*11 Jan*    148, 150    *    91, 92
1          Is 65.13–16    Rev 3.7–13    Jn 6.15–27
2          Is 55.3–9    Col 3.1–17    Jn 14.6–14

*12 Jan*    98, 99 [100]    *
1          Is 66.1–2, 22–23    Rev 3.14–22    Jn 9.1–12, 35–38
2          Gen 49.1–2, 8–12    Col 3.18—4.6    Jn 15.1–16

*Eve of the Baptism of the Lord*    *    104
          Is 61.1–9    Gal 3.23–29; 4.4–7

†    The psalms and readings for the dated days after the Epiphany are used
     only until the following Saturday evening.

*Psalms and readings between the Eve of the Baptism of the Lord and the week of the beginning of Lent may be found on p. 468.*

## Week of the Beginning of Lent

| *Sun* | 148, 149, 150 | * | 114, 115 |
|---|---|---|---|
| 1 | Dt 6.1–9 | Heb 12.18–29 | Jn 12.24–32 |
| 2 | Sir 48.1–11 | 2 Cor 3.7–18 | Lk 9.18–27 |

| *Mon* | 25 | * | 9, 15 |
|---|---|---|---|
| 1 | Dt 6.10–15 | Heb 1.1–14 | Jn 1.1–18 |
| 2 | Pr 27.1–6, 10–12 | Phil 2.1–13 | Jn 18.15–18, 25–27 |

| *Tue* | 26, 28 | * | 36, 39 |
|---|---|---|---|
| 1 | Dt 6.16–25 | Heb 2.1–10 | Jn 1.19–28 |
| 2 | Pr 30.1–4, 24–33 | Phil 3.1–11 | Jn 18.28–38 |

| *Ash Wednesday* | 95 (Invitatory), 32, 143 | * | 102, 130 |
|---|---|---|---|
| 1 | Jon 3.1—4.11 | Heb 12.1–14 | Lk 18.9–14 |
| 2 | Am 5.6–15 | Heb 12.1–14 | Lk 18.9–14 |

| *Thu* | 37.1–18 | * | 37.19–42 |
|---|---|---|---|
| 1 | Dt 7.6–11 | Tit 1.1–16 | Jn 1.29–34 |
| 2 | Hab 3.1–10(11–15)16–18 | Phil 3.12–21 | Jn 17.1–8 |

| *Fri* | 95 (Invitatory), 31 | * | 35 |
|---|---|---|---|
| 1 | Dt 7.12–16 | Tit 2.1–15 | Jn 1.35–42 |
| 2 | Ezek 18.1–4, 25–32 | Phil 4.1–9 | Jn 17.9–19 |

| *Sat* | 30, 32 | * | 42, 43 |
|---|---|---|---|
| 1 | Dt 7.17–26 | Tit 3.1–15 | Jn 1.43–51 |
| 2 | Ezek 39.21–29 | Phil 4.10–20 | Jn 17.20–26 |

## Week of 1 Lent

| *Sun* | 63.1–8(9–11), 98 | * | 103 |
|---|---|---|---|
| 1 | Dt 8.1–10 | 1 Cor 1.17–31 | Mk 2.18–22 |
| 2 | Dan 9.3–10 | Heb 2.10–18 | Jn 12.44–50 |

| *Mon* | 41, 52 | * | 44 |
|---|---|---|---|
| 1 | Dt 8.11–20 | Heb 2.11–18 | Jn 2.1–12 |
| 2 | Gen 37.1–11 | 1 Cor 1.1–19 | Mk 1.1–13 |

| *Tue* | 45 | * | 47, 48 | |
|---|---|---|---|---|
| 1 | Dt 9.4–12 | Heb 3.1–11 | Jn 2.13–22 | |
| 2 | Gen 37.12–24 | 1 Cor 1.20–31 | Mk 1.14–28 | |

| *Wed* | 119.49–72 | * | 49, [53] | |
|---|---|---|---|---|
| 1 | Dt 9.13–21 | Heb 3.12–19 | Jn 2.23—3.15 | |
| 2 | Gen 37.25–36 | 1 Cor 2.1–13 | Mk 1.29–45 | |

| *Thu* | 50 | * | [59, 60] *or* 19, 46 | |
|---|---|---|---|---|
| 1 | Dt 9.23—10.5 | Heb 4.1–10 | Jn 3.16–21 | |
| 2 | Gen 39.1–23 | 1 Cor 2.14—3.15 | Mk 2.1–12 | |

| *Fri* | 95 (Invitatory), 40, 54 | * | 51 | |
|---|---|---|---|---|
| 1 | Dt 10.12–22 | Heb 4.11–16 | Jn 3.22–36 | |
| 2 | Gen 40.1–23 | 1 Cor 3.16–23 | Mk 2.13–22 | |

| *Sat* | 55 | * | 138, 139.1–17(18–23) | |
|---|---|---|---|---|
| 1 | Dt 11.18–28 | Heb 5.1–10 | Jn 4.1–26 | |
| 2 | Gen 41.1–13 | 1 Cor 4.1–7 | Mk 2.23—3.6 | |

## Week of 2 Lent

| *Sun* | 24, 29 | * | 8, 84 | |
|---|---|---|---|---|
| 1 | Jer 1.1–10 | 1 Cor 3.11–23 | Mk 3.31—4.9 | |
| 2 | Gen 41.14–45 | Rom 6.3–14 | Jn 5.19–24 | |

| *Mon* | 56, 57, [58] | * | 64, 65 | |
|---|---|---|---|---|
| 1 | Jer 1.11–19 | Rom 1.1–15 | Jn 4.27–42 | |
| 2 | Gen 41.46–57 | 1 Cor 4.8–20(21) | Mk 3.7–19a | |

| *Tue* | 61, 62 | * | 68.1–20(21–23)24–36 | |
|---|---|---|---|---|
| 1 | Jer 2.1–13 | Rom 1.16–25 | Jn 4.43–54 | |
| 2 | Gen 42.1–17 | 1 Cor 5.1–8 | Mk 3.19b–35 | |

| *Wed* | 72 | * | 119.73–96 | |
|---|---|---|---|---|
| 1 | Jer 3.6–18 | Rom 1.28—2.11 | Jn 5.1–18 | |
| 2 | Gen 42.18–28 | 1 Cor 5.9—6.8 | Mk 4.1–20 | |

| *Thu* | [70], 71 | * | 74 | |
|---|---|---|---|---|
| 1 | Jer 4.9–10, 19–28 | Rom 2.12–24 | Jn 5.19–29 | |
| 2 | Gen 42.29–38 | 1 Cor 6.12–20 | Mk 4.21–34 | |

| Fri | 95 (Invitatory), 69.1–23(24–30)31–38 | * | 73 |

| *Fri* | 95 (Invitatory), 69.1–23(24–30)31–38 | * | 73 |
|---|---|---|---|
| 1 | Jer 5.1–9 | Rom 2.25—3.18 | Jn 5.30–47 |
| 2 | Gen 43.1–15 | 1 Cor 7.1–9 | Mk 4.35–41 |

| *Sat* | 75, 76 | * | 23, 27 |
|---|---|---|---|
| 1 | Jer 5.20–31 | Rom 3.19–31 | Jn 7.1–13 |
| 2 | Gen 43.16–34 | 1 Cor 7.10–24 | Mk 5.1–20 |

## Week of 3 Lent

| *Sun* | 93, 96 | * | 34 |
|---|---|---|---|
| 1 | Jer 6.9–15 | 1 Cor 6.12–20 | Mk 5.1–20 |
| 2 | Gen 44.1–17 | Rom 8.1–10 | Jn 5.25–29 |

| *Mon* | 80 | * | 77, [79] |
|---|---|---|---|
| 1 | Jer 7.1–15 | Rom 4.1–12 | Jn 7.14–36 |
| 2 | Gen 44.18–34 | 1 Cor 7.25–31 | Mk 5.21–43 |

| *Tue* | 78.1–39 | * | 78.40–72 |
|---|---|---|---|
| 1 | Jer 7.21–34 | Rom 4.13–25 | Jn 7.37–52 |
| 2 | Gen 45.1–15 | 1 Cor 7.32–40 | Mk 6.1–13 |

| *Wed* | 119.97–120 | * | 81, 82 |
|---|---|---|---|
| 1 | Jer 8.18—9.6 | Rom 5.1–11 | Jn 8.12–20 |
| 2 | Gen 45.16–28 | 1 Cor 8.1–13 | Mk 6.13–29 |

| *Thu* | [83] *or* 42, 43 | * | 85, 86 |
|---|---|---|---|
| 1 | Jer 10.11–24 | Rom 5.12–21 | Jn 8.21–32 |
| 2 | Gen 46.1–7, 28–34 | 1 Cor 9.1–15 | Mk 6.30–46 |

| *Fri* | 95 (Invitatory), 88 | * | 91, 92 |
|---|---|---|---|
| 1 | Jer 11.1–8, 14–20 | Rom 6.1–11 | Jn 8.33–47 |
| 2 | Gen 47.1–26 | 1 Cor 9.16–27 | Mk 6.47–56 |

| *Sat* | 87, 90 | * | 136 |
|---|---|---|---|
| 1 | Jer 13.1–11 | Rom 6.12–23 | Jn 8.47–59 |
| 2 | Gen 47.27—48.7 | 1 Cor 10.1–13 | Mk 7.1–23 |

## Week of 4 Lent

| *Sun* | 66, 67 | * | 19, 46 |
|---|---|---|---|
| 1 | Jer 14.1–9, 17–22 | Gal 4.21—5.1 | Mk 8.11–21 |
| 2 | Gen 48.8–22 | Rom 8.11–25 | Jn 6.27–40 |

| *Mon* | 89.1–18 | * | 89.19–52 | | |
|---|---|---|---|---|---|
| 1 | Jer 16.10–21 | Rom 7.1–12 | Jn 6.1–15 | | |
| 2 | Gen 49.1–28 | 1 Cor 10.14—11.1 | Mk 7.24–37 | | |

| *Tue* | 97, 99, [100] | * | 94, [95] | | |
|---|---|---|---|---|---|
| 1 | Jer 17.19–27 | Rom 7.13–25 | Jn 6.16–27 | | |
| 2 | Gen 49.29—50.14 | 1 Cor 11.17–34 | Mk 8.1–10 | | |

| *Wed* | 101, 109.1–4(5–19)20–30 | * | 119.121–144 | | |
|---|---|---|---|---|---|
| 1 | Jer 18.1–11 | Rom 8.1–11 | Jn 6.27–40 | | |
| 2 | Gen 50.15–26 | 1 Cor 12.1–11 | Mk 8.11–26 | | |

| *Thu* | 69.1–23(24–30)31–38 | * | 73 | | |
|---|---|---|---|---|---|
| 1 | Jer 22.13–23 | Rom 8.12–27 | Jn 6.41–51 | | |
| 2 | Ex 1.6–22 | 1 Cor 12.12–26 | Mk 8.27—9.1 | | |

| *Fri* | 95 (Invitatory), 102 | * | 107.1–32 | | |
|---|---|---|---|---|---|
| 1 | Jer 23.1–8 | Rom 8.28–39 | Jn 6.52–59 | | |
| 2 | Ex 2.1–22 | 1 Cor 12.27—13.3 | Mk 9.2–13 | | |

| *Sat* | 107.33–43, 108.1–6(7–13) | * | 33 | | |
|---|---|---|---|---|---|
| 1 | Jer 23.9–15 | Rom 9.1–18 | Jn 6.60–71 | | |
| 2 | Ex 2.23—3.15 | 1 Cor 13.1–13 | Mk 9.14–29 | | |

## Week of 5 Lent

| *Sun* | 118 | * | 145 | | |
|---|---|---|---|---|---|
| 1 | Jer 23.16–32 | 1 Cor 9.19–27 | Mk 8.31—9.1 | | |
| 2 | Ex 3.16—4.12 | Rom 12.1–21 | Jn 8.46–59 | | |

| *Mon* | 31 | * | 35 | | |
|---|---|---|---|---|---|
| 1 | Jer 24.1–10 | Rom 9.19–33 | Jn 9.1–17 | | |
| 2 | Ex 4.10–20(21–26)27–31 | 1 Cor 14.1–19 | Mk 9.30–41 | | |

| *Tue* | [120], 121, 122, 123 | * | 124, 125, 126, [127] | | |
|---|---|---|---|---|---|
| 1 | Jer 25.8–17 | Rom 10.1–13 | Jn 9.18–41 | | |
| 2 | Ex 5.1—6.1 | 1 Cor 14.20–33a, 39–40 | Mk 9.42–50 | | |

| *Wed* | 119.145–176 | * | 128, 129, 130 | | |
|---|---|---|---|---|---|
| 1 | Jer 25.30–38 | Rom 10.14–21 | Jn 10.1–18 | | |
| 2 | Ex 7.8–24 | 2 Cor 2.14—3.6 | Mk 10.1–16 | | |

| *Thu* | 131, 132, [133] | * | 140, 142 | |
| 1 | Jer 26.1–16 | Rom 11.1–12 | Jn 10.19–42 |
| 2 | Ex 7.25—8.19 | 2 Cor 3.7–18 | Mk 10.17–31 |

| *Fri* | 95 (Invitatory), 22 | * | 141, 143.1–11(12) | |
| 1 | Jer 29.1, 4–13 | Rom 11.13–24 | Jn 11.1–27 *or* 12.1–10 |
| 2 | Ex 9.13–35 | 2 Cor 4.1–12 | Mk 10.32–45 |

| *Sat* | 137.1–6(7–9), 144 | * | 42, 43 | |
| 1 | Jer 31.27–34 | Rom 11.25–36 | Jn 11.28–44 *or* 12.37–50 |
| 2 | Ex 10.21—11.8 | 2 Cor 4.13–18 | Mk 10.46–52 |

## Holy Week

| *Sunday of the Passion* | 24, 29 | * | 103 | |
| M | Zech 9.9–12 | 1 Tim 6.12–16 | |
| 1E | Zech 12.9–11; 13.1, 7–9 | Mt 21.12–17 | |
| 2E | Zech 12.9–11; 13.1, 7–9 | Lk 19.41–48 | |

| *Mon* | 51.1–18(19–20) | * | 69.1–23 | |
| 1 | Jer 12.1–16 | Phil 3.1–14 | Jn 12.9–19 |
| 2 | Lam 1.1–2, 6–12 | 2 Cor 1.1–7 | Mk 11.12–25 |

| *Tue* | 6, 12 | * | 94 | |
| 1 | Jer 15.10–21 | Phil 3.15–21 | Jn 12.20–26 |
| 2 | Lam 1.17–22 | 2 Cor 1.8–22 | Mk 11.27–33 |

| *Wed* | 55 | * | 74 | |
| 1 | Jer 17.5–10, 14–17 | Phil 4.1–13 | Jn 12.27–36 |
| 2 | Lam 2.1–9 | 2 Cor 1.23—2.11 | Mk 12.1–11 |

| *Maundy Thursday* | 102 | * | 142, 143 | |
| 1 | Jer 20.7–11 | 1 Cor 10.14–17; 11.27–32 | Jn 17.1–11(12–26) |
| 2 | Lam 2.10–18 | 1 Cor 10.14–17; 11.27–32 | Mk 14.12–25 |

| *Good Friday* | 95 (Invitatory), 22 | * | 40.1–14(15–19), 54 | |
| 1 | Wis 1.16—2.1, 12–22 *or* Gen 22.1–14 | | 1 Pet 1.10–20 |
| | Jn 13.36–38 *M, or* Jn 19.38–42 *E* | | |
| 2 | Lam 3.1–9, 19–33 | 1 Pet 1.10–20 | Jn 13.36–38 *M or* Jn 19.38–42 *E* |

| *Holy Saturday* | 95 (Invitatory), 88 | * | 27 | |
| 1 | Job 19.21–27a | Heb 4.1–16 *M* | Rom 8.1–11 *E* |
| 2 | Lam 3.37–58 | Heb 4.1–16 *M* | Rom 8.1–11 *E* |

**Easter Week**

*Easter Day*    148, 149, 150   *   113, 114, *or* 118
M     Ex 12.1–14    Jn 1.1–18
E     Is 51.9–11    Lk 24.13–35 *or* Jn 20.19–23

*Mon*    93, 98   *   66
1     Jon 2.1–9    Acts 2.14, 22–32 †    Jn 14.1–14
2     Ex 12.14–27    1 Cor 15.1–11    Mk 16.1–8

*Tue*    103   *   111, 114
1     Is 30.18–21    Acts 2.36–41(42–47) †    Jn 14.15–31
2     Ex 12.28–39    1 Cor 15.12–28    Mk 16.9–20

*Wed*    97, 99   *   115
1     Mic 7.7–15    Acts 3.1–10 †    Jn 15.1–11
2     Ex 12.40–51    1 Cor 15.(29)30–41    Mt 28.1–16

*Thu*    146, 147   *   148, 149
1     Ezek 37.1–14    Acts 3.11–26 †    Jn 15.12–27
2     Ex 13.3–10    1 Cor 15.41–50    Mt 28.16–20

*Fri*    136   *   118
1     Dan 12.1–4, 13    Acts 4.1–12 †    Jn 16.1–15
2     Ex 13.1–2, 11–16    1 Cor 15.51–58    Lk 24.1–12

*Sat*    145   *   104
1     Is 25.1–9    Acts 4.13–21(22–31) †    Jn 16.16–33
2     Ex 13.17—14.4    2 Cor 4.16—5.10    Mk 12.18–27

**Week of 2 Easter**

*Sun*    146, 147   *   111, 112, 113
1     Is 43.8–13    1 Pet 2.2–10    Jn 14.1–7
2     Ex 14.5–22    1 Jn 1.1–7    Jn 14.1–7

*Mon*    1, 2, 3   *   4, 7
1     Dan 1.1–21    1 Jn 1.1–10    Jn 17.1–11
2     Ex 14.21–31    1 Pet 1.1–12    Jn 14.(1–7)8–17

†   Duplicates the first lesson at the eucharist. Readings from Year 2 may be substituted.

| *Tue* | 5, 6 | * | 10, 11 | |
|---|---|---|---|---|
| 1 | Dan 2.1–16 | 1 Jn 2.1–11 | Jn 17.12–19 | |
| 2 | Ex 15.1–21 | 1 Pet 1.13–25 | Jn 14.18–31 | |

| *Wed* | 119.1–24 | * | 12, 13, 14 | |
|---|---|---|---|---|
| 1 | Dan 2.17–30 | 1 Jn 2.12–17 | Jn 17.20–26 | |
| 2 | Ex 15.22—16.10 | 1 Pet 2.1–10 | Jn 15.1–11 | |

| *Thu* | 18.1–20 | * | 18.21–50 | |
|---|---|---|---|---|
| 1 | Dan 2.31–49 | 1 Jn 2.18–29 | Lk 3.1–14 | |
| 2 | Ex 16.10–22 | 1 Pet 2.11–25 | Jn 15.12–27 | |

| *Fri* | 16, 17 | * | 134, 135 | |
|---|---|---|---|---|
| 1 | Dan 3.1–18 | 1 Jn 3.1–10 | Lk 3.15–22 | |
| 2 | Ex 16.23–36 | 1 Pet 3.13—4.6 | Jn 16.1–15 | |

| *Sat* | 20, 21.1–7(8–14) | * | 110.1–5(6–7), 116, 117 | |
|---|---|---|---|---|
| 1 | Dan 3.19–30 | 1 Jn 3.11–18 | Lk 4.1–13 | |
| 2 | Ex 17.1–16 | 1 Pet 4.7–19 | Jn 16.16–33 | |

## Week of 3 Easter

| *Sun* | 148, 149, 150 | * | 114, 115 | |
|---|---|---|---|---|
| 1 | Dan 4.1–18 | 1 Pet 4.7–11 | Jn 21.15–25 | |
| 2 | Ex 18.1–12 | 1 Jn 2.7–17 | Mk 16.9–20 | |

| *Mon* | 25 | * | 9, 15 | |
|---|---|---|---|---|
| 1 | Dan 4.19–27 | 1 Jn 3.19—4.6 | Lk 4.14–30 | |
| 2 | Ex 18.13–27 | 1 Pet 5.1–14 | Mt (1.1–17) 3.1–6 | |

| *Tue* | 26, 28 | * | 36, 39 | |
|---|---|---|---|---|
| 1 | Dan 4.28–37 | 1 Jn 4.7–21 | Lk 4.31–37 | |
| 2 | Ex 19.1–16 | Col 1.1–14 | Mt 3.7–12 | |

| *Wed* | 38 | * | 119.25–48 | |
|---|---|---|---|---|
| 1 | Dan 5.1–12 | 1 Jn 5.1–12 | Lk 4.38–44 | |
| 2 | Ex 19.16–25 | Col 1.15–23 | Mt 3.13–17 | |

| *Thu* | 37.1–18 | * | 37.19–42 | |
|---|---|---|---|---|
| 1 | Dan 5.13–30 | 1 Jn 5.13–20(21) | Lk 5.1–11 | |
| 2 | Ex 20.1–21 | Col 1.24—2.7 | Mt 4.1–11 | |

| *Fri* | 105.1–22 | * | 105.23–45 |
| 1 | Dan 6.1–15 | 2 Jn 1.1–13 | Lk 5.12–26 |
| 2 | Ex 24.1–18 | Col 2.8–23 | Mt 4.12–17 |

| *Sat* | 30, 32 | * | 42, 43 |
| 1 | Dan 6.16–28 | 3 Jn 1.1–15 | Lk 5.27–39 |
| 2 | Ex 25.1–22 | Col 3.1–17 | Mt 4.18–25 |

## Week of 4 Easter

| *Sun* | 63.1–8(9–11), 98 | * | 103 |
| 1 | Wis 1.1–15 | 1 Pet 5.1–11 | Mt 7.15–29 |
| 2 | Ex 28.1–4, 30–38 | 1 Jn 2.18–29 | Mk 6.30–44 |

| *Mon* | 41, 52 | * | 44 |
| 1 | Wis 1.16—2.11, 21–24 | Col 1.1–14 | Lk 6.1–11 |
| 2 | Ex 32.1–20 | Col 3.18—4.6(7–18) | Mt 5.1–10 |

| *Tue* | 45 | * | 47, 48 |
| 1 | Wis 3.1–9 | Col 1.15–23 | Lk 6.12–26 |
| 2 | Ex 32.21–34 | 1 Th 1.1–10 | Mt 5.11–16 |

| *Wed* | 119.49–72 | * | 49, [53] |
| 1 | Wis 4.16—5.8 | Col 1.24—2.7 | Lk 6.27–38 |
| 2 | Ex 33.1–23 | 1 Th 2.1–12 | Mt 5.17–20 |

| *Thu* | 50 | * | [59, 60] *or* 114, 115 |
| 1 | Wis 5.9–23 | Col 2.8–23 | Lk 6.39–49 |
| 2 | Ex 34.1–17 | 1 Th 2.13–20 | Mt 5.21–26 |

| *Fri* | 40, 54 | * | 51 |
| 1 | Wis 6.12–23 | Col 3.1–11 | Lk 7.1–17 |
| 2 | Ex 34.18–35 | 1 Th 3.1–13 | Mt 5.27–37 |

| *Sat* | 55 | * | 138, 139.1–17(18–23) |
| 1 | Wis 7.1–14 | Col 3.12–17 | Lk 7.18–28(29–30)31–35 |
| 2 | Ex 40.18–38 | 1 Th 4.1–12 | Mt 5.38–48 |

## Week of 5 Easter

| *Sun* | 24, 29 | * | 8, 84 |
| 1 | Wis 7.22—8.1 | 2 Th 2.13–17 | Mt 7.7–14 |
| 2 | Lev 8.1–13, 30–36 | Heb 12.1–14 | Lk 4.16–30 |

| *Mon* | 56, 57, [58] | * | 64, 65 |
| 1 | Wis 9.1, 7–18 | Col (3.18—4.1)4.2–18 | Lk 7.36–50 |
| 2 | Lev 16.1–19 | 1 Th 4.13–18 | Mt 6.1–6, 16–18 |

| *Tue* | 61, 62 | * | 68.1–20(21–23)24–36 |
| 1 | Wis 10.1–4(5–12)13–21 | Rom 12.1–21 | Lk 8.1–15 |
| 2 | Lev 16.20–34 | 1 Th 5.1–11 | Mt 6.7–15 |

| *Wed* | 72 | * | 119.73–96 |
| 1 | Wis 13.1–9 | Rom 13.1–14 | Lk 8.16–25 |
| 2 | Lev 19.1–18 | 1 Th 5.12–28 | Mt 6.19–24 |

| *Thu* | [70], 71 | * | 74 |
| 1 | Wis 14.27—15.3 | Rom 14.1–12 | Lk 8.26–39 |
| 2 | Lev 19.26–37 | 2 Th 1.1–12 | Mt 6.25–34 |

| *Fri* | 106.1–18 | * | 106.19–48 |
| 1 | Wis 16.15—17.1 | Rom 14.13–23 | Lk 8.40–56 |
| 2 | Lev 23.1–22 | 2 Th 2.1–17 | Mt 7.1–12 |

| *Sat* | 75, 76 | * | 23, 27 |
| 1 | Wis 19.1–8, 18–22 | Rom 15.1–13 | Lk 9.1–17 |
| 2 | Lev 23.23–44 | 2 Th 3.1–18 | Mt 7.13–21 |

## Week of 6 Easter

| *Sun* | 93, 96 | * | 34 |
| 1 | Ec 43.1–12, 27–32 | 1 Tim 3.14—4.5 | Mt 13.24–34a |
| 2 | Lev 25.1–17 | Jas 1.2–8, 16–18 | Lk 12.13–21 |

| *Mon* | 80 | * | 77, [79] |
| 1 | Dt 8.1–10 | Jas 1.1–15 | Lk 9.18–27 |
| 2 | Lev 25.35–55 | Col 1.9–14 | Mt 13.1–16 |

| *Tue* | 78.1–39 | * | 78.40–72 |
| 1 | Dt 8.11–20 | Jas 1.16–27 | Lk 11.1–13 |
| 2 | Lev 26.1–20 | 1 Tim 2.1–6 | Mt 13.18–23 |

| *Wed* | 119.97–120 | * | |
| 1M | Bar 3.24–37 | Jas 5.13–18 | Lk 12.22–31 |
| 2M | Lev 26.27–42 | Eph 1.1–10 | Mt 22.41–46 |

*Eve of Ascension*     *     68.1–20
         2 Kg 2.1–15     Rev 5.1–14

*Ascension Day*    8, 47    *    24, 96
1        Ezek 1.1–14, 24–28b    Heb 2.5–18    Mt 28.16–20
2        Dan 7.9–14    Heb 2.5–18    Mt 28.16–20

*Fri*     85, 86    *    91, 92
1        Ezek 1.28—3.3    Heb 4.14—5.6    Lk 9.28–36
2        1 Sam 2.1–10    Eph 2.1–10    Mt 7.22–27

*Sat*     87, 90    *    136
1        Ezek 3.4–17    Heb 5.7–14    Lk 9.37–50
2        Num 11.16–17, 24–29    Eph 2.11–22    Mt 7.28—8.4

## Week of 7 Easter

*Sun*     66, 67    *    19, 46
1        Ezek 3.16–27    Eph 2.1–10    Mt 10.24–33, 40–42
2        Ex 3.1–12    Heb 12.18–29    Lk 10.17–24

*Mon*    89.1–18    *    89.19–52
1        Ezek 4.1–17    Heb 6.1–12    Lk 9.51–62
2        Jos 1.1–9    Eph 3.1–13    Mt 8.5–17

*Tue*     97, 99, [100]    *    94, [95]
1        Ezek 7.10–15, 23b–27    Heb 6.13–20    Lk 10.1–17
2        1 Sam 16.1–13a    Eph 3.14–21    Mt 8.18–27

*Wed*    101, 109.1–4(5–19)20–30    *    119.121–144
1        Ezek 11.14–25    Heb 7.1–17    Lk 10.17–24
2        Is 4.2–6    Eph 4.1–16    Mt 8.28–34

*Thu*     105.1–22    *    105.23–45
1        Ezek 18.1–4, 19–32    Heb 7.18–28    Lk 10.25–37
2        Zech 4.1–14    Eph 4.17–32    Mt 9.1–8

*Fri*     102    *    107.1–32
1        Ezek 34.17–31    Heb 8.1–13    Lk 10.38–42
2        Jer 31.27–34    Eph 5.1–20    Mt 9.9–17

*Sat*     107.33–43, 108.1–6(7–13)    *
1M       Ezek 43.1–12    Heb 9.1–14    Lk 11.14–23
2M       Ezek 36.22–27    Eph 6.10–24    Mt 9.18–26

*Eve of Pentecost*     \*     33
        Ex 19.3–8a, 16–20     1 Pet 2.4–10

*Day of Pentecost*     118     \*     145
1       Is 11.1–9     1 Cor 2.1–13     Jn 14.21–29
2       Dt 16.9–12     Acts 4.18–21, 23–33     Jn 4.19–26

*On the weekdays which follow the Day of Pentecost, the readings are taken
from the numbered proper (six through eleven) which corresponds most
closely to the date of the day of Pentecost.*

*Eve of Trinity Sunday*     \*     104
        Sir 42.15–25     Eph 3.14–21

*Trinity Sunday*     146, 147     \*     111, 112, 113
1       Sir 43.1–12(27–33)     Eph 4.1–16     Jn 1.1–18
2       Job 38.1–11; 42.1–5     Rev 19.4–16     Jn 1.29–34

*On the weekdays which follow Trinity Sunday, the readings are taken from
the numbered proper (seven through twelve) which corresponds most closely
to the date of Trinity Sunday.*

## Week of the Baptism of the Lord    *Proper 1*

*Sun*     146, 147     \*     111, 112, 113
1       Is 40.1–11     Heb 1.1–12     Jn 1.1–7, 19–20, 29–34
2       Gen 1.1—2.3     Eph 1.3–14     Jn 1.29–34

*Mon*     1, 2, 3     \*     4, 7
1       Is 40.12–23     Eph 1.1–14     Mk 1.1–13
2       Gen 2.4–9(10–15)16–25     Heb 1.1–14     Jn 1.1–18

*Tue*     5, 6     \*     10, 11
1       Is 40.25–31     Eph 1.15–23     Mk 1.14–28
2       Gen 3.1–24     Heb 2.1–10     Jn 1.19–28

*Wed*     119.1–24     \*     12, 13, 14
1       Is 41.1–16     Eph 2.1–10     Mk 1.29–45
2       Gen 4.1–16     Heb 2.11–18     Jn 1.(29–34)35–42

*Thu*     18.1–20     \*     18.21–50
1       Is 41.17–29     Eph 2.11–22     Mk 2.1–12
2       Gen 4.17–26     Heb 3.1–11     Jn 1.43–51

| *Fri* | 16, 17 | * | 22 | |
|---|---|---|---|---|
| *1* | Is 42.(1–9)10–17 | | Eph 3.1–13 | Mk 2.13–22 |
| *2* | Gen 6.1–8 | | Heb 3.12–19 | Jn 2.1–12 |

| *Sat* | 20, 21.1–7(8–14) | * | 110.1–5(6–7), 116, 117 | |
|---|---|---|---|---|
| *1* | Is 43.1–13 | | Eph 3.14–21 | Mk 2.23—3.6 |
| *2* | Gen 6.9–22 | | Heb 4.1–13 | Jn 2.13–22 |

## Week of 2 Epiphany   *Proper 2*

| *Sun* | 148, 149, 150 | * | 114, 115 | |
|---|---|---|---|---|
| *1* | Is 43.14—44.5 | | Heb 6.17—7.10 | Jn 4.27–42 |
| *2* | Gen 7.1–10, 17–23 | | Eph 4.1–16 | Mk 3.7–19 |

| *Mon* | 25 | * | 9, 15 | |
|---|---|---|---|---|
| *1* | Is 44.6–8, 21–23 | | Eph 4.1–16 | Mk 3.7–19a |
| *2* | Gen 8.6–22 | | Heb 4.14—5.6 | Jn 2.23—3.15 |

| *Tue* | 26, 28 | * | 36, 39 | |
|---|---|---|---|---|
| *1* | Is 44.9–20 | | Eph 4.17–32 | Mk 3.19b–35 |
| *2* | Gen 9.1–17 | | Heb 5.7–14 | Jn 3.16–21 |

| *Wed* | 38 | * | 119.25–48 | |
|---|---|---|---|---|
| *1* | Is 44.24—45.7 | | Eph 5.1–14 | Mk 4.1–20 |
| *2* | Gen 9.18–29 | | Heb 6.1–12 | Jn 3.22–36 |

| *Thu* | 37.1–18 | * | 37.19–42 | |
|---|---|---|---|---|
| *1* | Is 45.5–17 | | Eph 5.15–33 | Mk 4.21–34 |
| *2* | Gen 11.1–9 | | Heb 6.13–20 | Jn 4.1–15 |

| *Fri* | 31 | * | 35 | |
|---|---|---|---|---|
| *1* | Is 45.18–25 | | Eph 6.1–9 | Mk 4.35–41 |
| *2* | Gen 11.27—12.8 | | Heb 7.1–17 | Jn 4.16–26 |

| *Sat* | 30, 32 | * | 42, 43 | |
|---|---|---|---|---|
| *1* | Is 46.1–13 | | Eph 6.10–24 | Mk 5.1–20 |
| *2* | Gen 12.9—13.1 | | Heb 7.18–28 | Jn 4.27–42 |

## Week of 3 Epiphany   *Proper 3*

| *Sun* | 63.1–8(9–11), 98 | * | 103 | |
|---|---|---|---|---|
| *1* | Is 47.1–15 | | Heb 10.19–31 | Jn 5.2–18 |
| *2* | Gen 13.2–18 | | Gal 2.1–10 | Mk 7.31–37 |

| Mon | 41, 52 | * | 44 |
| --- | --- | --- | --- |
| 1 | Is 48.1–11 | Gal 1.1–17 | Mk 5.21–43 |
| 2 | Gen 14.(1–7)8–24 | Heb 8.1–13 | Jn 4.43–54 |

| Tue | 45 | * | 47, 48 |
| --- | --- | --- | --- |
| 1 | Is 48.12–21 | Gal 1.18—2.10 | Mk 6.1–13 |
| 2 | Gen 15.1–11, 17–21 | Heb 9.1–14 | Jn 5.1–18 |

| Wed | 119.49–72 | * | 49, [53] |
| --- | --- | --- | --- |
| 1 | Is 49.1–12 | Gal 2.11–21 | Mk 6.13–29 |
| 2 | Gen 16.1–14 | Heb 9.15–28 | Jn 5.19–29 |

| Thu | 50 | * | [59, 60] or 118 |
| --- | --- | --- | --- |
| 1 | Is 49.13–23 | Gal 3.1–14 | Mk 6.30–46 |
| 2 | Gen 16.15—17.14 | Heb 10.1–10 | Jn 5.30–47 |

| Fri | 40, 54 | * | 51 |
| --- | --- | --- | --- |
| 1 | Is 50.1–11 | Gal 3.15–22 | Mk 6.47–56 |
| 2 | Gen 17.15–27 | Heb 10.11–25 | Jn 6.1–15 |

| Sat | 55 | * | 138, 139.1–17(18–23) |
| --- | --- | --- | --- |
| 1 | Is 51.1–8 | Gal 3.23–29 | Mk 7.1–23 |
| 2 | Gen 18.1–16 | Heb 10.26–39 | Jn 6.16–27 |

**Week of 4 Epiphany**   *Proper 4*

| Sun | 24, 29 | * | 8, 84 |
| --- | --- | --- | --- |
| 1 | Is 51.9–16 | Heb 11.8–16 | Jn 7.14–31 |
| 2 | Gen 18.16–33 | Gal 5.13–25 | Mk 8.22–30 |

| Mon | 56, 57, [58] | * | 64, 65 |
| --- | --- | --- | --- |
| 1 | Is 51.17–23 | Gal 4.1–11 | Mk 7.24–37 |
| 2 | Gen 19.1–17(18–23)24–29 | Heb 11.1–12 | Jn 6.27–40 |

| Tue | 61, 62 | * | 68.1–20(21–23)24–36 |
| --- | --- | --- | --- |
| 1 | Is 52.1–12 | Gal 4.12–20 | Mk 8.1–10 |
| 2 | Gen 21.1–21 | Heb 11.13–22 | Jn 6.41–51 |

| Wed | 72 | * | 119.73–96 |
| --- | --- | --- | --- |
| 1 | Is 54.1–10(11–17) | Gal 4.21–31 | Mk 8.11–26 |
| 2 | Gen 22.1–18 | Heb 11.23–31 | Jn 6.52–59 |

| | | | | |
|---|---|---|---|---|
| *Thu* | [70], 71 | * | 74 | |
| 1 | Is 55.1–13 | Gal 5.1–15 | Mk 8.27—9.1 | |
| 2 | Gen 23.1–20 | Heb 11.32—12.2 | Jn 6.60–71 | |
| | | | | |
| *Fri* | 69.1–23(24–30)31–38 | * | 73 | |
| 1 | Is 56.1–8 | Gal 5.16–24 | Mk 9.2–13 | |
| 2 | Gen 24.1–27 | Heb 12.3–11 | Jn 7.1–13 | |
| | | | | |
| *Sat* | 75, 76 | * | 23, 27 | |
| 1 | Is 57.3–13 | Gal 5.25—6.10 | Mk 9.14–29 | |
| 2 | Gen 24.28–38, 49–51 | Heb 12.12–29 | Jn 7.14–36 | |

**Week of 5 Epiphany**   *Proper 5*

| | | | | |
|---|---|---|---|---|
| *Sun* | 93, 96 | * | 34 | |
| 1 | Is 57.14–21 | Heb 12.1–6 | Jn 7.37–46 | |
| 2 | Gen 24.50–67 | 2 Tim 2.14–21 | Mk 10.13–22 | |
| | | | | |
| *Mon* | 80 | * | 77, [79] | |
| 1 | Is 58.1–12 | Gal 6.11–18 | Mk 9.30–41 | |
| 2 | Gen 25.19–34 | Heb 13.1–16 | Jn 7.37–52 | |
| | | | | |
| *Tue* | 78.1–39 | * | 78.40–72 | |
| 1 | Is 59.1–15a | 2 Tim 1.1–14 | Mk 9.42–50 | |
| 2 | Gen 26.1–6, 12–33 | Heb 13.17–25 | Jn 7.53—8.11 | |
| | | | | |
| *Wed* | 119.97–120 | * | 81, 82 | |
| 1 | Is 59.15b–21 | 2 Tim 1.15—2.13 | Mk 10.1–16 | |
| 2 | Gen 27.1–29 | Rom 12.1–8 | Jn 8.12–20 | |
| | | | | |
| *Thu* | [83] *or* 146, 147 | * | 85, 86 | |
| 1 | Is 60.1–17 | 2 Tim 2.14–26 | Mk 10.17–31 | |
| 2 | Gen 27.30–45 | Rom 12.9–21 | Jn 8.21–32 | |
| | | | | |
| *Fri* | 88 | * | 91, 92 | |
| 1 | Is 61.1–9 | 2 Tim 3.1–17 | Mk 10.32–45 | |
| 2 | Gen 27.46—28.4, 10–22 | Rom 13.1–14 | Jn 8.33–47 | |
| | | | | |
| *Sat* | 87, 90 | * | 136 | |
| 1 | Is 61.10—62.5 | 2 Tim 4.1–8 | Mk 10.46–52 | |
| 2 | Gen 29.1–20 | Rom 14.1–23 | Jn 8.47–59 | |

**Week of 6 Epiphany**
**or Sunday between 8 and 14 May**   *Proper 6*

| | | | | |
|---|---|---|---|---|
| *Sun* | 66, 67 | * | 19, 46 | |
| 1 | Is 62.6–12 | 1 Jn 2.3–11 | Jn 8.12–19 | |
| 2 | Gen 29.20–35 | 1 Tim 3.14—4.10 | Mk 10.23–31 | |

*When Proper 6 is used after Epiphany and before Lent, the following are the weekday readings.*

| | | | | |
|---|---|---|---|---|
| *Mon* | 89.1–18 | * | 89.19–52 | |
| 1 | Is 63.1–6 | 1 Tim 1.1–17 | Mk 11.1–11 | |
| 2 | Gen 30.1–24 | 1 Jn 1.1–10 | Jn 9.1–17 | |
| | | | | |
| *Tue* | 97, 99, [100] | * | 94, [95] | |
| 1 | Is 63.7–14 | 1 Tim 1.18—2.8 | Mk 11.12–25 | |
| 2 | Gen 31.1–24 | 1 Jn 2.1–11 | Jn 9.18–41 | |
| | | | | |
| *Wed* | 101, 109.1–4(5–19)20–30 | * | 119.121–144 | |
| 1 | Is 63.15—64.9 | 1 Tim 3.1–16 | Mk 11.27—12.12 | |
| 2 | Gen 31.25–50 | 1 Jn 2.12–17 | Jn 10.1–18 | |
| | | | | |
| *Thu* | 105.1–22 | * | 105.23–45 | |
| 1 | Is 65.1–12 | 1 Tim 4.1–16 | Mk 12.13–27 | |
| 2 | Gen 32.3–21 | 1 Jn 2.18–29 | Jn 10.19–30 | |
| | | | | |
| *Fri* | 102 | * | 107.1–32 | |
| 1 | Is 65.17–25 | 1 Tim 5.17–22(23–25) | Mk 12.28–34 | |
| 2 | Gen 32.22—33.17 | 1 Jn 3.1–10 | Jn 10.31–42 | |
| | | | | |
| *Sat* | 107.33–43, 108.1–6(7–13) | * | 33 | |
| 1 | Is 66.1–6 | 1 Tim 6.6–21 | Mk 12.35–44 | |
| 2 | Gen 35.1–20 | 1 Jn 3.11–18 | Jn 11.1–16 | |

*When Proper 6 is used after Pentecost, the following are the weekday readings.*

| | | | | |
|---|---|---|---|---|
| *Mon* | 106.1–18 | * | 106.19–48 | |
| 1 | Is 63.7–14 | 2 Tim 1.1–14 | Lk 11.24–36 | |
| 2 | Ezek 33.1–11 | 1 Jn 1.1–10 | Mt 9.27–34 | |
| | | | | |
| *Tue* | [120], 121, 122, 123 | * | 124, 125, 126, [127] | |
| 1 | Is 63.15—64.9 | 2 Tim 1.15—2.13 | Lk 11.37–52 | |
| 2 | Ezek 33.21–33 | 1 Jn 2.1–11 | Mt 9.35—10.4 | |

| _Wed_ | 119.145–176 | * | 128, 129, 130 | |
| 1 | Is 65.1–12 | 2 Tim 2.14–26 | Lk 11.53—12.12 |
| 2 | Ezek 34.1–16 | 1 Jn 2.12–17 | Mt 10.5–15 |

| _Thu_ | 131, 132, [133] | * | 134, 135 | |
| 1 | Is 65.17–25 | 2 Tim 3.1–17 | Lk 12.13–31 |
| 2 | Ezek 37.21b–28 | 1 Jn 2.18–29 | Mt 10.16–23 |

| _Fri_ | 140, 142 | * | 141, 143.1–11(12) | |
| 1 | Is 66.1–6 | 2 Tim 4.1–8 | Lk 12.32–48 |
| 2 | Ezek 39.21–29 | 1 Jn 3.1–10 | Mt 10.24–33 |

| _Sat_ | 137.1–6(7–9), 144 | * | 104 | |
| 1 | Is 66.7–14 | 2 Tim 4.9–22 | Lk 12.49–59 |
| 2 | Ezek 47.1–12 | 1 Jn 3.11–18 | Mt 10.34–42 |

## Week of 7 Epiphany
## or Sunday between 15 and 21 May   _Proper 7_

| _Sun_ | 118 | * | 145 | |
| 1 | Is 66.7–14 | 1 Jn 3.4–10 | Jn 10.7–16 |
| 2 | Pr 1.20–33 | 2 Cor 5.11–21 | Mk 10.35–45 |

_When Proper 7 is used after Epiphany and before Lent, the following are the weekday readings._

| _Mon_ | 106.1–18 | * | 106.19–48 | |
| 1 | Ru 1.1–14 | 2 Cor 1.1–11 | Mt 5.1–12 |
| 2 | Pr 3.11–20 | 1 Jn 3.18—4.6 | Jn 11.17–29 |

| _Tue_ | [120], 121, 122, 123 | * | 124, 125, 126, [127] | |
| 1 | Ru 1.15–22 | 2 Cor 1.12–22 | Mt 5.13–20 |
| 2 | Pr 4.1–27 | 1 Jn 4.7–21 | Jn 11.30–44 |

| _Wed_ | 119.145–176 | * | 128, 129, 130 | |
| 1 | Ru 2.1–13 | 2 Cor 1.23—2.17 | Mt 5.21–26 |
| 2 | Pr 6.1–19 | 1 Jn 5.1–12 | Jn 11.45–54 |

| _Thu_ | 131, 132, [133] | * | 134, 135 | |
| 1 | Ru 2.14–23 | 2 Cor 3.1–18 | Mt 5.27–37 |
| 2 | Pr 7.1–27 | 1 Jn 5.13–21 | Jn 11.55—12.8 |

| Fri | 140, 142 | * | 141, 143.1–11(12) | |
| 1 | Ru 3.1–18 | 2 Cor 4.1–12 | Mt 5.38–48 |
| 2 | Pr 8.1–21 | Philem 1–25 | Jn 12.9–19 |

| Sat | 137.1–6(7–9), 144 | * | 104 | |
| 1 | Ru 4.1–17 | 2 Cor 4.13—5.10 | Mt 6.1–6 |
| 2 | Pr 8.22–36 | 2 Tim 1.1–14 | Jn 12.20–26 |

*When Proper 7 is used after Pentecost, the following are the weekday readings.*

| Mon | 1, 2, 3 | * | 4, 7 | |
| 1 | Ru 1.1–18 | 1 Tim 1.1–17 | Lk 13.1–9 |
| 2 | Pr 3.11–20 | 1 Jn 3.18—4.6 | Mt 11.1–6 |

| Tue | 5, 6 | * | 10, 11 | |
| 1 | Ru 1.19—2.13 | 1 Tim 1.18—2.8 | Lk 13.10–17 |
| 2 | Pr 4.1–27 | 1 Jn 4.7–21 | Mt 11.7–15 |

| Wed | 119.1–24 | * | 12, 13, 14 | |
| 1 | Ru 2.14–23 | 1 Tim 3.1–16 | Lk 13.18–30 |
| 2 | Pr 6.1–19 | 1 Jn 5.1–12 | Mt 11.16–24 |

| Thu | 18.1–20 | * | 18.21–50 | |
| 1 | Ru 3.1–18 | 1 Tim 4.1–16 | Lk 13.31–35 |
| 2 | Pr 7.1–27 | 1 Jn 5.13–21 | Mt 11.25–30 |

| Fri | 16, 17 | * | 22 | |
| 1 | Ru 4.1–17 | 1 Tim 5.17–22(23–25) | Lk 14.1–11 |
| 2 | Pr 8.1–21 | 2 Jn 1–13 | Mt 12.1–14 |

| Sat | 20, 21.1–7(8–14) | * | 110.1–5(6–7), 116, 117 | |
| 1 | Dt 1.1–8 | 1 Tim 6.6–21 | Lk 14.12–24 |
| 2 | Pr 8.22–36 | 3 Jn 1–15 | Mt 12.15–21 |

## Week of 8 Epiphany
## or Sunday between 22 and 28 May   *Proper 8*

*When Proper 8 is used after Epiphany and before Lent, the following are the readings.*

| Sun | 146, 147 | * | 111, 112, 113 | |
| 1 | Dt 4.1–9 | 2 Tim 4.1–8 | Jn 12.1–8 |
| 2 | Pr 9.1–12 | 2 Cor 9.6b–15 | Mk 10.46–52 |

| *Mon* | 1, 2, 3 | * | 4, 7 | |
|---|---|---|---|---|
| 1 | Dt 4.9–14 | 2 Cor 10.1–18 | Mt 6.7–15 | |
| 2 | Pr 10.1–12 | 2 Tim 1.15—2.13 | Jn 12.27–36a | |

| *Tue* | 5, 6 | * | 10, 11 | |
|---|---|---|---|---|
| 1 | Dt 4.15–24 | 2 Cor 11.1–21a | Mt 6 16–23 | |
| 2 | Pr 15.16–33 | 2 Tim 2.14–26 | Jn 12.36b–50 | |

| *Wed* | 119.1–24 | * | 12, 13, 14 | |
|---|---|---|---|---|
| 1 | Dt 4.25–31 | 2 Cor 11.21b–33 | Mt 6.24–34 | |
| 2 | Pr 17.1–20 | 2 Tim 3.1–17 | Jn 13.1–20 | |

| *Thu* | 18.1–20 | * | 18.21–50 | |
|---|---|---|---|---|
| 1 | Dt 4.32–40 | 2 Cor 12.1–10 | Mt 7.1–12 | |
| 2 | Pr 21.30—22.6 | 2 Tim 4.1–8 | Jn 13.21–30 | |

| *Fri* | 16, 17 | * | 22 | |
|---|---|---|---|---|
| 1 | Dt 5.1–22 | 2 Cor 12.11–21 | Mt 7.13–21 | |
| 2 | Pr 23.19–21, 29—24.2 | 2 Tim 4.9–22 | Jn 13.31–38 | |

| *Sat* | 20, 21.1–7(8–14) | * | 110.1–5(6–7), 116, 117 | |
|---|---|---|---|---|
| 1 | Dt 5.22–33 | 2 Cor 13.1–14 | Mt 7.22–29 | |
| 2 | Pr 25.15–28 | Phil 1.1–11 | Jn 18.1–14 | |

*When Proper 8 is used after Pentecost, the following are the readings.*

| *Sun* | 148, 149, 150 | * | 114, 115 | |
|---|---|---|---|---|
| 1 | Dt 4.1–9 | Rev 7.1–4, 9–17 | Mt 12.33–45 | |
| 2 | Pr 9.1–12 | Acts 8.14–25 | Lk 10.25–28, 38–42 | |

| *Mon* | 25 | * | 9, 15 | |
|---|---|---|---|---|
| 1 | Dt 4.9–14 | 2 Cor 1.1–11 | Lk 14.25–35 | |
| 2 | Pr 10.1–12 | 1 Tim 1.1–17 | Mt 12.22–32 | |

| *Tue* | 26, 28 | * | 36, 39 | |
|---|---|---|---|---|
| 1 | Dt 4.15–24 | 2 Cor 1.12–22 | Lk 15.1–10 | |
| 2 | Pr 15.16–33 | 1 Tim 1.18—2.8 | Mt 12.33–42 | |

| *Wed* | 38 | * | 119.25–48 | |
|---|---|---|---|---|
| 1 | Dt 4.25–31 | 2 Cor 1.23—2.17 | Lk 15.1–2, 11–32 | |
| 2 | Pr 17.1–20 | 1 Tim 3.1–16 | Mt 12.43–50 | |

| Thu | 37.1–18 | * | 37.19–42 | |
|---|---|---|---|---|
| 1 | Dt 4.32–40 | 2 Cor 3.1–18 | Lk 16.1–9 | |
| 2 | Pr 21.30—22.6 | 1 Tim 4.1–16 | Mt 13.24–30 | |

| Fri | 31 | * | 35 | |
|---|---|---|---|---|
| 1 | Dt 5.1–22 | 2 Cor 4.1–12 | Lk 16.10–17(18) | |
| 2 | Pr 23.19–21, 29—24.2 | 1 Tim 5.17–22(23–25) | Mt 13.31–35 | |

| Sat | 30, 32 | * | 42, 43 | |
|---|---|---|---|---|
| 1 | Dt 5.22–33 | 2 Cor 4.13—5.10 | Lk 16.19–31 | |
| 2 | Pr 25.15–28 | 1 Tim 6.6–21 | Mt 13.36–43 | |

## Week of Sunday between 29 May and 4 June   *Proper 9*

| Sun | 63.1–8(9–11), 98 | * | 103 | |
|---|---|---|---|---|
| 1 | Dt 11.1–12 | Rev 10.1–11 | Mt 13.44–58 | |
| 2 | Ec 1.1–11 | Acts 8.26–40 | Lk 11.1–13 | |

| Mon | 41, 52 | * | 44 | |
|---|---|---|---|---|
| 1 | Dt 11.13–19 | 2 Cor 5.11—6.2 | Lk 17.1–10 | |
| 2 | Ec 2.1–15 | Gal 1.1–17 | Mt 13.44–52 | |

| Tue | 45 | * | 47, 48 | |
|---|---|---|---|---|
| 1 | Dt 12.1–12 | 2 Cor 6.3–13(14—7.1) | Lk 17.11–19 | |
| 2 | Ec 2.16–26 | Gal 1.18—2.10 | Mt 13.53–58 | |

| Wed | 119.49–72 | * | 49, [53] | |
|---|---|---|---|---|
| 1 | Dt 13.1–11 | 2 Cor 7.2–16 | Lk 17.20–37 | |
| 2 | Ec 3.1–15 | Gal 2.11–21 | Mt 14.1–12 | |

| Thu | 50 | * | [59, 60] *or* 8, 84 | |
|---|---|---|---|---|
| 1 | Dt 16.18–20; 17.14–20 | 2 Cor 8.1–16 | Lk 18.1–8 | |
| 2 | Ec 3.16—4.3 | Gal 3.1–14 | Mt 14.13–21 | |

| Fri | 40, 54 | * | 51 | |
|---|---|---|---|---|
| 1 | Dt 26.1–11 | 2 Cor 8.16–24 | Lk 18.9–14 | |
| 2 | Ec 5.1–7 | Gal 3.15–22 | Mt 14.22–36 | |

| Sat | 55 | * | 138, 139.1–17(18–23) | |
|---|---|---|---|---|
| 1 | Dt 29.2–15 | 2 Cor 9.1–15 | Lk 18.15–30 | |
| 2 | Ec 5.8–20 | Gal 3.23—4.11 | Mt 15.1–20 | |

## Week of Sunday between 5 and 11 June    *Proper 10*

| Sun | 24, 29 | * | 8, 84 | |
|---|---|---|---|---|
| 1 | Dt 29.16–29 | Rev 12.1–12 | Mt 15.29–39 | |
| 2 | Ec 6.1–12 | Acts 10.9–23 | Lk 12.32–40 | |

| Mon | 56, 57, [58] | * | 64, 65 | |
|---|---|---|---|---|
| 1 | Dt 30.1–10 | 2 Cor 10.1–18 | Lk 18.31–43 | |
| 2 | Ec 7.1–14 | Gal 4.12–20 | Mt 15.21–28 | |

| Tue | 61, 62 | * | 68.1–20(21–23)24–36 | |
|---|---|---|---|---|
| 1 | Dt 30.11–20 | 2 Cor 11.1–21a | Lk 19.1–10 | |
| 2 | Ec 8.14—9.10 | Gal 4.21–31 | Mt 15.29–39 | |

| Wed | 72 | * | 119.73–96 | |
|---|---|---|---|---|
| 1 | Dt 31.30—32.14 | 2 Cor 11.21b–33 | Lk 19.11–27 | |
| 2 | Ec 9.11–18 | Gal 5.1–15 | Mt 16.1–12 | |

| Thu | [70], 71 | * | 74 | |
|---|---|---|---|---|
| 1 | Sir 44.19—45.5 | 2 Cor 12.1–10 | Lk 19.28–40 | |
| 2 | Ec 11.1–8 | Gal 5.16–24 | Mt 16.13–20 | |

| Fri | 69.1–23(24–30)31–38 | * | 73 | |
|---|---|---|---|---|
| 1 | Sir 45.6–16 | 2 Cor 12.11–21 | Lk 19.41–48 | |
| 2 | Ec 11.9—12.14 | Gal 5.25—6.10 | Mt 16.21–28 | |

| Sat | 75, 76 | * | 23, 27 | |
|---|---|---|---|---|
| 1 | Sir 46.1–10 | 2 Cor 13.1–14 | Lk 20.1–8 | |
| 2 | Num 3.1–13 | Gal 6.11–18 | Mt 17.1–13 | |

## Week of Sunday between 12 and 18 June    *Proper 11*

| Sun | 93, 96 | * | 34 | |
|---|---|---|---|---|
| 1 | Sir 46.11–20 | Rev 15.1–8 | Mt 18.1–14 | |
| 2 | Num 6.22–27 | Acts 13.1–12 | Lk 12.41–48 | |

| Mon | 80 | * | 77, [79] | |
|---|---|---|---|---|
| 1 | 1 Sam 1.1–20 | Acts 1.1–14 | Lk 20.9–19 | |
| 2 | Num 9.15–23; 10.29–36 | Rom 1.1–15 | Mt 17.14–21 | |

| Tue | 78.1–39 | * | 78.40–72 | |
|---|---|---|---|---|
| 1 | 1 Sam 1.21—2.11 | Acts 1.15–26 | Lk 20.19–26 | |
| 2 | Num 11.1–23 | Rom 1.16–25 | Mt 17.22–27 | |

| Wed | 119.97–120 | * | 81, 82 | |
|---|---|---|---|---|
| 1 | 1 Sam 2.12–26 | Acts 2.1–21 | Lk 20.27–40 | |
| 2 | Num 11.24–33(34–35) | Rom 1.28—2.11 | Mt 18.1–9 | |

| Thu | [83] or 34 | * | 85, 86 | |
|---|---|---|---|---|
| 1 | 1 Sam 2.27–36 | Acts 2.22–36 | Lk 20.41—21.4 | |
| 2 | Num 12.1–16 | Rom 2.12–24 | Mt 18.10–20 | |

| Fri | 88 | * | 91, 92 | |
|---|---|---|---|---|
| 1 | 1 Sam 3.1–21 | Acts 2.37–47 | Lk 21.5–19 | |
| 2 | Num 13.1–3, 21–30 | Rom 2.25—3.8 | Mt 18.21–35 | |

| Sat | 87, 90 | * | 136 | |
|---|---|---|---|---|
| 1 | 1 Sam 4.1b–11 | Acts 4.32—5.11 | Lk 21.20–28 | |
| 2 | Num 13.31—14.25 | Rom 3.9–20 | Mt 19.1–12 | |

## Week of Sunday between 19 and 25 June   *Proper 12*

| Sun | 66, 67 | * | 19, 46 | |
|---|---|---|---|---|
| 1 | 1 Sam 4.12–22 | Jas 1.1–18 | Mt 19.23–30 | |
| 2 | Num 14.26–45 | Acts 15.1–12 | Lk 12.49–56 | |

| Mon | 89.1–18 | * | 89.19–52 | |
|---|---|---|---|---|
| 1 | 1 Sam 5.1–12 | Acts 5.12–26 | Lk 21.29–36 | |
| 2 | Num 16.1–19 | Rom 3.21–31 | Mt 19.13–22 | |

| Tue | 97, 99, [100] | * | 94, [95] | |
|---|---|---|---|---|
| 1 | 1 Sam 6.1–16 | Acts 5.27–42 | Lk 21.37—22.13 | |
| 2 | Num 16.20–35 | Rom 4.1–12 | Mt 19.23–30 | |

| Wed | 101, 109.1–4(5–19)20–30 | * | 119.121–144 | |
|---|---|---|---|---|
| 1 | 1 Sam 7.2–17 | Acts 6.1–15 | Lk 22.14–23 | |
| 2 | Num 16.36–50 | Rom 4.13–25 | Mt 20.1–16 | |

| Thu | 105.1–22 | * | 105.23–45 | |
|---|---|---|---|---|
| 1 | 1 Sam 8.1–22 | Acts 6.15—7.16 | Lk 22.24–30 | |
| 2 | Num 17.1–11 | Rom 5.1–11 | Mt 20.17–28 | |

| Fri | 102 | * | 107.1–32 | |
|---|---|---|---|---|
| 1 | 1 Sam 9.1–14 | Acts 7.17–29 | Lk 22.31–38 | |
| 2 | Num 20.1–13 | Rom 5.12–21 | Mt 20.29–34 | |

| Sat | 107.33–43, 108.1–6(7–13) | * | 33 | |
|-----|---------|---|----|---|
| 1 | 1 Sam 9.15—10.1 | Acts 7.30–43 | Lk 22.39–51 | |
| 2 | Num 20.14–29 | Rom 6.1–11 | Mt 21.1–11 | |

## Week of Sunday between 26 June and 2 July  *Proper 13*

| Sun | 118 | * | 145 | |
|-----|-----|---|-----|---|
| 1 | 1 Sam 10.1–16 | Rom 4.13–25 | Mt 21.23–32 | |
| 2 | Num 21.4–9, 21–35 | Acts 17.(12–21)22–34 | Lk 13.10–17 | |

| Mon | 106.1–18 | * | 106.19–48 | |
|-----|-----|---|-----|---|
| 1 | 1 Sam 10.17–27 | Acts 7.44—8.1a | Lk 22.52–62 | |
| 2 | Num 22.1–21 | Rom 6.12–23 | Mt 21.12–22 | |

| Tue | [120], 121, 122, 123 | * | 124, 125, 126, [127] | |
|-----|-----|---|-----|---|
| 1 | 1 Sam 11.1–15 | Acts 8.1–13 | Lk 22.63–71 | |
| 2 | Num 22.21–38 | Rom 7.1–12 | Mt 21.23–32 | |

| Wed | 119.145–176 | * | 128, 129, 130 | |
|-----|-----|---|-----|---|
| 1 | 1 Sam 12.1–6, 16–25 | Acts 8.14–25 | Lk 23.1–12 | |
| 2 | Num 22.41—23.12 | Rom 7.13–25 | Mt 21.33–46 | |

| Thu | 131, 132, [133] | * | 134, 135 | |
|-----|-----|---|-----|---|
| 1 | 1 Sam 13.5–18 | Acts 8.26–40 | Lk 23.13–25 | |
| 2 | Num 23.11–26 | Rom 8.1–11 | Mt 22.1–14 | |

| Fri | 140, 142 | * | 141, 143.1–11(12) | |
|-----|-----|---|-----|---|
| 1 | 1 Sam 13.19—14.15 | Acts 9.1–9 | Lk 23.26–31 | |
| 2 | Num 24.1–13 | Rom 8.12–17 | Mt 22.15–22 | |

| Sat | 137.1–6(7–9), 144 | * | 104 | |
|-----|-----|---|-----|---|
| 1 | 1 Sam 14.16–30 | Acts 9.10–19a | Lk 23.32–43 | |
| 2 | Num 24.12–25 | Rom 8.18–25 | Mt 22.23–40 | |

## Week of Sunday between 3 and 9 July  *Proper 14*

| Sun | 146, 147 | * | 111, 112, 113 | |
|-----|-----|---|-----|---|
| 1 | 1 Sam 14.36–45 | Rom 5.1–11 | Mt 22.1–14 | |
| 2 | Num 27.12–23 | Acts 19.11–20 | Mk 1.14–20 | |

| Mon | 1, 2, 3 | * | 4, 7 | |
|-----|-----|---|-----|---|
| 1 | 1 Sam 15.1–3, 7–23 | Acts 9.19b–31 | Lk 23.44–56a | |
| 2 | Num 32.1–6, 16–27 | Rom 8.26–30 | Mt 23.1–12 | |

| Tue | 5, 6 | * | 10, 11 |
| 1 | 1 Sam 15.24–35 | Acts 9.32–43 | Lk 23.56b—24.11 |
| 2 | Num 35.1–3, 9–15, 30–34 | Rom 8.31–39 | Mt 23.13–26 |

| Wed | 119.1–24 | * | 12, 13, 14 |
| 1 | 1 Sam 16.1–13 | Acts 10.1–16 | Lk 24.13–35 |
| 2 | Dt 1.1–18 | Rom 9.1–18 | Mt 23.27–39 |

| Thu | 18.1–20 | * | 18.21–50 |
| 1 | 1 Sam 16.14—17.11 | Acts 10.17–33 | Lk 24.36–53 |
| 2 | Dt 3.18–28 | Rom 9.19–33 | Mt 24.1–14 |

| Fri | 16, 17 | * | 22 |
| 1 | 1 Sam 17.17–30 | Acts 10.34–48 | Mk 1.1–13 |
| 2 | Dt 31.7–13, 24—32.4 | Rom 10.1–13 | Mt 24.15–31 |

| Sat | 20, 21.1–7(8–14) | * | 110.1–5(6–7), 116, 117 |
| 1 | 1 Sam 17.31–49 | Acts 11.1–18 | Mk 1.14–28 |
| 2 | Dt 34.1–12 | Rom 10.14–21 | Mt 24.32–51 |

## Week of Sunday between 10 and 16 July    *Proper 15*

| Sun | 148, 149, 150 | * | 114, 115 |
| 1 | 1 Sam 17.50—18.4 | Rom 10.4–17 | Mt 23.29–39 |
| 2 | Jos 1.1–18 | Acts 21.3–15 | Mk 1.21–27 |

| Mon | 25 | * | 9, 15 |
| 1 | 1 Sam 18.5–16, 27b–30 | Acts 11.19–30 | Mk 1.29–45 |
| 2 | Jos 2.1–14 | Rom 11.1–12 | Mt 25.1–13 |

| Tue | 26, 28 | * | 36, 39 |
| 1 | 1 Sam 19.1–18 | Acts 12.1–17 | Mk 2.1–12 |
| 2 | Jos 2.15–24 | Rom 11.13–24 | Mt 25.14–30 |

| Wed | 38 | * | 119.25–48 |
| 1 | 1 Sam 20.1–23 | Acts 12.18–25 | Mk 2.13–22 |
| 2 | Jos 3.1–13 | Rom 11.25–36 | Mt 25.31–46 |

| Thu | 37.1–18 | * | 37.19–42 |
| 1 | 1 Sam 20.24–42 | Acts 13.1–12 | Mk 2.23—3.6 |
| 2 | Jos 3.14—4.7 | Rom 12.1–8 | Mt 26.1–16 |

| Fri | 31 | * | 35 |
|---|---|---|---|
| 1 | 1 Sam 21.1–15 | Acts 13.13–25 | Mk 3.7–19a |
| 2 | Jos 4.19—5.1, 10–15 | Rom 12.9–21 | Mt 26.17–25 |

| Sat | 30, 32 | * | 42, 43 |
|---|---|---|---|
| 1 | 1 Sam 22.1–23 | Acts 13.26–43 | Mk 3.19b–35 |
| 2 | Jos 6.1–14 | Rom 13.1–7 | Mt 26.26–35 |

## Week of Sunday between 17 and 23 July   *Proper 16*

| Sun | 63.1–8(9–11), 98 | * | 103 |
|---|---|---|---|
| 1 | 1 Sam 23.7–18 | Rom 11.33—12.2 | Mt 25.14–30 |
| 2 | Jos 6.15–27 | Acts 22.30—23.11 | Mk 2.1–12 |

| Mon | 41, 52 | * | 44 |
|---|---|---|---|
| 1 | 1 Sam 24.1–22 | Acts 13.44–52 | Mk 4.1–20 |
| 2 | Jos 7.1–13 | Rom 13.8–14 | Mt 26.36–46 |

| Tue | 45 | * | 47, 48 |
|---|---|---|---|
| 1 | 1 Sam 25.1–22 | Acts 14.1–18 | Mk 4.21–34 |
| 2 | Jos 8.1–22 | Rom 14.1–12 | Mt 26.47–56 |

| Wed | 119.49–72 | * | 49, [53] |
|---|---|---|---|
| 1 | 1 Sam 25.23–44 | Acts 14.19–28 | Mk 4.35–41 |
| 2 | Jos 8.30–35 | Rom 14.13–23 | Mt 26.57–68 |

| Thu | 50 | * | [59, 60] *or* 66, 67 |
|---|---|---|---|
| 1 | 1 Sam 28.3–20 | Acts 15.1–11 | Mk 5.1–20 |
| 2 | Jos 9.3–21 | Rom 15.1–13 | Mt 26.69–75 |

| Fri | 40, 54 | * | 51 |
|---|---|---|---|
| 1 | 1 Sam 31.1–13 | Acts 15.12–21 | Mk 5.21–43 |
| 2 | Jos 9.22—10.15 | Rom 15.14–24 | Mt 27.1–10 |

| Sat | 55 | * | 138, 139.1–17(18–23) |
|---|---|---|---|
| 1 | 2 Sam 1.1–16 | Acts 15.22–35 | Mk 6.1–13 |
| 2 | Jos 23.1–16 | Rom 15.25–33 | Mt 27.11–23 |

## Week of Sunday between 24 and 30 July   *Proper 17*

| Sun | 24, 29 | * | 8, 84 |
|---|---|---|---|
| 1 | 2 Sam 1.17–27 | Rom 12.9–21 | Mt 25.31–46 |
| 2 | Jos 24.1–15 | Acts 28.23–31 | Mk 2.23–28 |

| Mon | 56, 57, [58] | * | 64, 65 | |
|---|---|---|---|---|
| 1 | 2 Sam 2.1–11 | Acts 15.36—16.5 | Mk 6.14–29 |
| 2 | Jos 24.16–33 | Rom 16.1–16 | Mt 27.24–31 |

| Tue | 61, 62 | * | 68.1–20(21–23)24–36 | |
|---|---|---|---|---|
| 1 | 2 Sam 3.6–21 | Acts 16.6–15 | Mk 6.30–46 |
| 2 | Jg 2.1–5, 11–23 | Rom 16.17–27 | Mt 27.32–44 |

| Wed | 72 | * | 119.73–96 | |
|---|---|---|---|---|
| 1 | 2 Sam 3.22–39 | Acts 16.16–24 | Mk 6.47–56 |
| 2 | Jg 3.12–30 | Acts 1.1–14 | Mt 27.45–54 |

| Thu | [70], 71 | * | 74 | |
|---|---|---|---|---|
| 1 | 2 Sam 4.1–12 | Acts 16.25–40 | Mk 7.1–23 |
| 2 | Jg 4.4–23 | Acts 1.15–26 | Mt 27.55–66 |

| Fri | 69.1–23(24–30)31–38 | * | 73 | |
|---|---|---|---|---|
| 1 | 2 Sam 5.1–12 | Acts 17.1–15 | Mk 7.24–37 |
| 2 | Jg 5.1–18 | Acts 2.1–21 | Mt 28.1–10 |

| Sat | 75, 76 | * | 23, 27 | |
|---|---|---|---|---|
| 1 | 2 Sam 5.22—6.11 | Acts 17.16–34 | Mk 8.1–10 |
| 2 | Jg 5.19–31 | Acts 2.22–36 | Mt 28.11–20 |

## Week of Sunday between 31 July and 6 August   Proper 18

| Sun | 93, 96 | * | 34 | |
|---|---|---|---|---|
| 1 | 2 Sam 6.12–23 | Rom 14.7–12 | Jn 1.43–51 |
| 2 | Jg 6.1–24 | 2 Cor 9.6–15 | Mk 3.20–30 |

| Mon | 80 | * | 77, [79] | |
|---|---|---|---|---|
| 1 | 2 Sam 7.1–17 | Acts 18.1–11 | Mk 8.11–21 |
| 2 | Jg 6.25–40 | Acts 2.37–47 | Jn 1.1–18 |

| Tue | 78.1–39 | * | 78.40–72 | |
|---|---|---|---|---|
| 1 | 2 Sam 7.18–29 | Acts 18.12–28 | Mk 8.22–33 |
| 2 | Jg 7.1–18 | Acts 3.1–11 | Jn 1.19–28 |

| Wed | 119.97–120 | * | 81, 82 | |
|---|---|---|---|---|
| 1 | 2 Sam 9.1–13 | Acts 19.1–10 | Mk 8.34—9.1 |
| 2 | Jg 7.19—8.12 | Acts 3.12–26 | Jn 1.29–42 |

| Thu | [83] *or* 145 | * | 85, 86 | |
|------|------|------|------|------|
| 1 | 2 Sam 11.1–27 | Acts 19.11–20 | Mk 9.2–13 | |
| 2 | Jg 8.22–35 | Acts 4.1–12 | Jn 1.43–51 | |

| Fri | 88 | * | 91, 92 | |
|------|------|------|------|------|
| 1 | 2 Sam 12.1–14 | Acts 19.21–41 | Mk 9.14–29 | |
| 2 | Jg 9.1–16, 19–21 | Acts 4.13–31 | Jn 2.1–12 | |

| Sat | 87, 90 | * | 136 | |
|------|------|------|------|------|
| 1 | 2 Sam 12.15–31 | Acts 20.1–16 | Mk 9.30–41 | |
| 2 | Jg 9.22–25, 50–57 | Acts 4.32—5.11 | Jn 2.13–25 | |

## Week of Sunday between 7 and 13 August   *Proper 19*

| Sun | 66, 67 | * | 19, 46 | |
|------|------|------|------|------|
| 1 | 2 Sam 13.1–22 | Rom 15.1–13 | Jn 3.22–36 | |
| 2 | Jg 11.1–11, 29–40 | 2 Cor 11.21b–31 | Mk 4.35–41 | |

| Mon | 89.1–18 | * | 89.19–52 | |
|------|------|------|------|------|
| 1 | 2 Sam 13.23–39 | Acts 20.17–38 | Mk 9.42–50 | |
| 2 | Jg 12.1–7 | Acts 5.12–26 | Jn 3.1–21 | |

| Tue | 97, 99, [100] | * | 94, [95] | |
|------|------|------|------|------|
| 1 | 2 Sam 14.1–20 | Acts 21.1–14 | Mk 10.1–16 | |
| 2 | Jg 13.1–15 | Acts 5.27–42 | Jn 3.22–36 | |

| Wed | 101, 109.1–4(5–19)20–30 | * | 119.121–144 | |
|------|------|------|------|------|
| 1 | 2 Sam 14.21–33 | Acts 21.15–26 | Mk 10.17–31 | |
| 2 | Jg 13.15–24 | Acts 6.1–15 | Jn 4.1–26 | |

| Thu | 105.1–22 | * | 105.23–45 | |
|------|------|------|------|------|
| 1 | 2 Sam 15.1–18 | Acts 21.27–36 | Mk 10.32–45 | |
| 2 | Jg 14.1–19 | Acts 6.15—7.16 | Jn 4.27–42 | |

| Fri | 102 | * | 107.1–32 | |
|------|------|------|------|------|
| 1 | 2 Sam 15.19–37 | Acts 21.37—22.16 | Mk 10.46–52 | |
| 2 | Jg 14.20—15.20 | Acts 7.17–29 | Jn 4.43–54 | |

| Sat | 107.33–43, 108.1–6(7–13) | * | 33 | |
|------|------|------|------|------|
| 1 | 2 Sam 16.1–23 | Acts 22.17–29 | Mk 11.1–11 | |
| 2 | Jg 16.1–14 | Acts 7.30–43 | Jn 5.1–18 | |

## Week of Sunday between 14 and 20 August    *Proper 20*

| | | | |
|---|---|---|---|
| *Sun* | 118 | * | 145 |
| 1 | 2 Sam 17.1–23 | Gal 3.6–14 | Jn 5.30–47 |
| 2 | Jg 16.15–31 | 2 Cor 13.1–11 | Mk 5.25–34 |

| | | | |
|---|---|---|---|
| *Mon* | 106.1–18 | * | 106.19–48 |
| 1 | 2 Sam 17.24—18.8 | Acts 22.30—23.11 | Mk 11.12–26 |
| 2 | Jg 17.1–13 | Acts 7.44—8.1a | Jn 5.19–29 |

| | | | |
|---|---|---|---|
| *Tue* | [120], 121, 122, 123 | * | 124, 125, 126, [127] |
| 1 | 2 Sam 18.9–18 | Acts 23.12–24 | Mk 11.27—12.12 |
| 2 | Jg 18.1–15 | Acts 8.1–13 | Jn 5.30–47 |

| | | | |
|---|---|---|---|
| *Wed* | 119.145–176 | * | 128, 129, 130 |
| 1 | 2 Sam 18.19–33 | Acts 23.23–35 | Mk 12.13–27 |
| 2 | Jg 18.16–31 | Acts 8.14–25 | Jn 6.1–15 |

| | | | |
|---|---|---|---|
| *Thu* | 131, 132, [133] | * | 134, 135 |
| 1 | 2 Sam 19.1–23 | Acts 24.1–23 | Mk 12.28–34 |
| 2 | Job 1.1–22 | Acts 8.26–40 | Jn 6.16–27 |

| | | | |
|---|---|---|---|
| *Fri* | 140, 142 | * | 141, 143.1–11(12) |
| 1 | 2 Sam 19.24–43 | Acts 24.24—25.12 | Mk 12.35–44 |
| 2 | Job 2.1–13 | Acts 9.1–9 | Jn 6.27–40 |

| | | | |
|---|---|---|---|
| *Sat* | 137.1–6(7–9), 144 | * | 104 |
| 1 | 2 Sam 23.1–7, 13–17 | Acts 25.13–27 | Mk 13.1–13 |
| 2 | Job 3.1–26 | Acts 9.10–19a | Jn 6.41–51 |

## Week of Sunday between 21 and 27 August    *Proper 21*

| | | | |
|---|---|---|---|
| *Sun* | 146, 147 | * | 111, 112, 113 |
| 1 | 2 Sam 24.1–2, 10–25 | Gal 3.23—4.7 | Jn 8.12–20 |
| 2 | Job 4.1–6, 12–21 | Rev 4.1–11 | Mk 6.1–6a |

| | | | |
|---|---|---|---|
| *Mon* | 1, 2, 3 | * | 4, 7 |
| 1 | 1 Kg 1.5–31 | Acts 26.1–23 | Mk 13.14–27 |
| 2 | Job 4.1; 5.1–11, 17–21, 26–27 | Acts 9.19b–31 | Jn 6.52–59 |

| | | | |
|---|---|---|---|
| *Tue* | 5, 6 | * | 10, 11 |
| 1 | 1 Kg 1.38—2.4 | Acts 26.24—27.8 | Mk 13.28–37 |
| 2 | Job 6.1–4, 8–15, 21 | Acts 9.32–43 | Jn 6.60–71 |

| Wed | 119.1–24 | * | 12, 13, 14 | |
| 1 | 1 Kg 3.1–15 | Acts 27.9–26 | Mk 14.1–11 |
| 2 | Job 6.1; 7.1–21 | Acts 10.1–16 | Jn 7.1–13 |

| Thu | 18.1–20 | * | 18.21–50 | |
| 1 | 1 Kg 3.16–28 | Acts 27.27–44 | Mk 14.12–26 |
| 2 | Job 8.1–10, 20–22 | Acts 10.17–33 | Jn 7.14–36 |

| Fri | 16, 17 | * | 22 | |
| 1 | 1 Kg 5.1—6.1, 7 | Acts 28.1–16 | Mk 14.27–42 |
| 2 | Job 9.1–15, 32–35 | Acts 10.34–48 | Jn 7.37–52 |

| Sat | 20, 21.1–7(8–14) | * | 110.1–5(6–7), 116, 117 | |
| 1 | 1 Kg 7.51—8.21 | Acts 28.17–31 | Mk 14.43–52 |
| 2 | Job 9.1; 10.1–9, 16–22 | Acts 11.1–18 | Jn 8.12–20 |

## Week of Sunday between 28 August and 3 September  *Proper 22*

| Sun | 148, 149, 150 | * | 114, 115 | |
| 1 | 1 Kg 8.22–30(31–40) | 1 Tim 4.7b–16 | Jn 8.47–59 |
| 2 | Job 11.1–9, 13–20 | Rev 5.1–14 | Mt 5.1–12 |

| Mon | 25 | * | 9, 15 | |
| 1 | 2 Chr 6.32—7.7 | Jas 2.1–13 | Mk 14.53–65 |
| 2 | Job 12.1–6, 13–25 | Acts 11.19–30 | Jn 8.21–30 |

| Tue | 26, 28 | * | 36, 39 | |
| 1 | 1 Kg 8.65—9.9 | Jas 2.14–26 | Mk 14.66–72 |
| 2 | Job 12.1; 13.3–17, 21–27 | Acts 12.1–17 | Jn 8.31–47 |

| Wed | 38 | * | 119.25–48 | |
| 1 | 1 Kg 9.24—10.13 | Jas 3.1–12 | Mk 15.1–11 |
| 2 | Job 12.1; 14.1–22 | Acts 12.18–25 | Jn 8.47–59 |

| Thu | 37.1–18 | * | 37.19–42 | |
| 1 | 1 Kg 11.1–13 | Jas 3.13—4.12 | Mk 15.12–21 |
| 2 | Job 16.16–22; 17.1, 13–16 | Acts 13.1–12 | Jn 9.1–17 |

| Fri | 31 | * | 35 | |
| 1 | 1 Kg 11.26–43 | Jas 4.13—5.6 | Mk 15.22–32 |
| 2 | Job 19.1–7, 14–27 | Acts 13.13–25 | Jn 9.18–41 |

| Sat | 30, 32 | * | 42, 43 | | |
|---|---|---|---|---|---|
| 1 | 1 Kg 12.1–20 | Jas 5.7–12, 19–20 | Mk 15.33–39 | | |
| 2 | Job 22.1–4, 21—23.7 | Acts 13.26–43 | Jn 10.1–18 | | |

## Week of Sunday between 4 and 10 September *Proper 23*

| Sun | 63.1–8(9–11), 98 | * | 103 | | |
|---|---|---|---|---|---|
| 1 | 1 Kg 12.21–33 | Acts 4.18–31 | Jn 10.31–42 | | |
| 2 | Job 25.1–6; 27.1–6 | Rev 14.1–7, 13 | Mt 5.13–20 | | |

| Mon | 41, 52 | * | 44 | | |
|---|---|---|---|---|---|
| 1 | 1 Kg 13.1–10 | Phil 1.1–11 | Mk 15.40–47 | | |
| 2 | Job 32.1–10, 19—33.1, 19–28 | Acts 13.44–52 | Jn 10.19–30 | |

| Tue | 45 | * | 47, 48 | | |
|---|---|---|---|---|---|
| 1 | 1 Kg 16.23–34 | Phil 1.12–30 | Mk 16.1–8(9–20) | | |
| 2 | Job 29.1–20 | Acts 14.1–18 | Jn 10.31–42 | | |

| Wed | 119.49–72 | * | 49, [53] | | |
|---|---|---|---|---|---|
| 1 | 1 Kg 17.1–24 | Phil 2.1–11 | Mt 2.1–12 | | |
| 2 | Job 29.1; 30.1–2, 16–31 | Acts 14.19–28 | Jn 11.1–16 | |

| Thu | 50 | * | [59, 60] *or* 93, 96 | | |
|---|---|---|---|---|---|
| 1 | 1 Kg 18.1–19 | Phil 2.12–30 | Mt 2.13–23 | | |
| 2 | Job 29.1; 31.1–23 | Acts 15.1–11 | Jn 11.17–29 | |

| Fri | 40, 54 | * | 51 | | |
|---|---|---|---|---|---|
| 1 | 1 Kg 18.20–40 | Phil 3.1–16 | Mt 3.1–12 | | |
| 2 | Job 29.1; 31.24–40 | Acts 15.12–21 | Jn 11.30–44 | |

| Sat | 55 | * | 138, 139.1–17(18–23) | | |
|---|---|---|---|---|---|
| 1 | 1 Kg 18.41—19.8 | Phil 3.17—4.7 | Mt 3.13–17 | | |
| 2 | Job 38.1–17 | Acts 15.22–35 | Jn 11.45–54 | | |

## Week of Sunday between 11 and 17 September *Proper 24*

| Sun | 24, 29 | * | 8, 84 | | |
|---|---|---|---|---|---|
| 1 | 1 Kg 19.8–21 | Acts 5.34–42 | Jn 11.45–57 | | |
| 2 | Job 38.1, 18–41 | Rev 18.1–8 | Mt 5.21–26 | | |

| Mon | 56, 57, [58] | * | 64, 65 | | |
|---|---|---|---|---|---|
| 1 | 1 Kg 21.1–16 | 1 Cor 1.1–19 | Mt 4.1–11 | | |
| 2 | Job 40.1–24 | Acts 15.36—16.5 | Jn 11.55—12.8 | |

| Tue | 61, 62 | * | 68.1–20(21–23)24–36 | |
|---|---|---|---|---|
| 1 | 1 Kg 21.17–29 | 1 Cor 1.20–31 | Mt 4.12–17 | |
| 2 | Job 40.1; 41.1–11 | Acts 16.6–15 | Jn 12.9–19 | |

| Wed | 72 | * | 119.73–96 | |
|---|---|---|---|---|
| 1 | 1 Kg 22.1–28 | 1 Cor 2.1–13 | Mt 4.18–25 | |
| 2 | Job 42.1–17 | Acts 16.16–24 | Jn 12.20–26 | |

| Thu | [70], 71 | * | 74 | |
|---|---|---|---|---|
| 1 | 1 Kg 22.29–45 | 1 Cor 2.14—3.15 | Mt 5.1–10 | |
| 2 | Job 28.1–28 | Acts 16.25–40 | Jn 12.27–36a | |

| Fri | 69.1–23(24–30)31–38 | * | 73 | |
|---|---|---|---|---|
| 1 | 2 Kg 1.2–17 | 1 Cor 3.16–23 | Mt 5.11–16 | |
| 2 | Est 1.1–4, 10–19 † | Acts 17.1–15 | Jn 12.36b–43 | |

| Sat | 75, 76 | * | 23, 27 | |
|---|---|---|---|---|
| 1 | 2 Kg 2.1–18 | 1 Cor 4.1–7 | Mt 5.17–20 | |
| 2 | Est 2.5–8, 15–23 † | Acts 17.16–34 | Jn 12.44–50 | |

## Week of Sunday between 18 and 24 September   *Proper 25*

| Sun | 93, 96 | * | 34 | |
|---|---|---|---|---|
| 1 | 2 Kg 4.8–37 | Acts 9.10–31 | Lk 3.7–18 | |
| 2 | Est 3.1—4.3 † | Jas 1.19–27 | Mt 6.1–6, 16–18 | |

| Mon | 80 | * | 77, [79] | |
|---|---|---|---|---|
| 1 | 2 Kg 5.1–19 | 1 Cor 4.8–21 | Mt 5.21–26 | |
| 2 | Est 4.4–17 † | Acts 18.1–11 | Lk (1.1–4); 3.1–14 | |

| Tue | 78.1–39 | * | 78.40–72 | |
|---|---|---|---|---|
| 1 | 2 Kg 5.19–27 | 1 Cor 5.1–8 | Mt 5.27–37 | |
| 2 | Est 5.1–14 † | Acts 18.12–28 | Lk 3.15–22 | |

| Wed | 119.97–120 | * | 81, 82 | |
|---|---|---|---|---|
| 1 | 2 Kg 6.1–23 | 1 Cor 5.9—6.8 | Mt 5.38–48 | |
| 2 | Est 6.1–14 † | Acts 19.1–10 | Lk 4.1–13 | |

† Judith may be read from this Friday until the next Friday instead of Esther.

| | | |
|---|---|---|
| *Fri* 4.1–15 | *Sun* 5.22–6.4, 10–21 | *Tue* 8.9–17; 9.1, 7–10 |
| *Sat* 5.1–21 | *Mon* 7.1–7, 19–32 | *Wed* 10.1–23 |

| Thu | [83] *or* 116, 117 | * | 85, 86 | |
|---|---|---|---|---|
| 1 | 2 Kg 9.1–16 | 1 Cor 6.12–20 | Mt 6.1–6, 16–18 | |
| 2 | Est 7.1–10 † | Acts 19.11–20 | Lk 4.14–30 | |

| Fri | 88 | * | 91, 92 | |
|---|---|---|---|---|
| 1 | 2 Kg 9.17–37 | 1 Cor 7.1–9 | Mt 6.7–15 | |
| 2 | Est 8.1–8, 15–17 † | Acts 19.21–41 | Lk 4.31–37 | |

| Sat | 87, 90 | * | 136 | |
|---|---|---|---|---|
| 1 | 2 Kg 11.1–20a | 1 Cor 7.10–24 | Mt 6.19–24 | |
| 2 | Hos 1.1—2.1 | Acts 20.1–16 | Lk 4.38–44 | |

## Week of Sunday between 25 September and 1 October    *Proper 26*

| Sun | 66, 67 | * | 19, 46 | |
|---|---|---|---|---|
| 1 | 2 Kg 17.1–18 | Acts 9.36–43 | Lk 5.1–11 | |
| 2 | Hos 2.2–14 | Jas 3.1–13 | Mt 13.44–52 | |

| Mon | 89.1–18 | * | 89.19–52 | |
|---|---|---|---|---|
| 1 | 2 Kg 17.24–41 | 1 Cor 7.25–31 | Mt 6.25–34 | |
| 2 | Hos 2.14–23 | Acts 20.17–38 | Lk 5.1–11 | |

| Tue | 97, 99, [100] | * | 94, [95] | |
|---|---|---|---|---|
| 1 | 2 Chr 29.1–3; 30.1(2–9)10–27 | 1 Cor 7.32–40 | Mt 7.1–12 | |
| 2 | Hos 4.1–10 | Acts 21.1–14 | Lk 5.12–26 | |

| Wed | 101, 109.1–4(5–19)20–30 | * | 119.121–144 | |
|---|---|---|---|---|
| 1 | 2 Kg 18.9–25 | 1 Cor 8.1–13 | Mt 7.13–21 | |
| 2 | Hos 4.11–19 | Acts 21.15–26 | Lk 5.27–39 | |

| Thu | 105.1–22 | * | 105.23–45 | |
|---|---|---|---|---|
| 1 | 2 Kg 18.28–37 | 1 Cor 9.1–15 | Mt 7.22–29 | |
| 2 | Hos 5.8—6.6 | Acts 21.27–36 | Lk 6.1–11 | |

| Fri | 102 | * | 107.1–32 | |
|---|---|---|---|---|
| 1 | 2 Kg 19.1–20 | 1 Cor 9.16–27 | Mt 8.1–17 | |
| 2 | Hos 10.1–15 | Acts 21.37—22.16 | Lk 6.12–26 | |

† Judith may be read from the previous Friday to this Friday instead of Esther.

    *Thu* 12.1–20      *Fri* 13.1–20

| Sat | 107.33–43, 108.1–6(7–13) | * | 33 | |
| 1 | 2 Kg 19.21–36 | 1 Cor 10.1–13 | Mt 8.18–27 |
| 2 | Hos 11.1–9 | Acts 22.17–29 | Lk 6.27–38 |

## Week of Sunday between 2 and 8 October  *Proper 27*

| Sun | 118 | * | 145 | |
| 1 | 2 Kg 20.1–21 | Acts 12.1–17 | Lk 7.11–17 |
| 2 | Hos 13.4–14 | 1 Cor 2.6–16 | Mt 14.1–12 |

| Mon | 106.1–18 | * | 106.19–48 | |
| 1 | 2 Kg 21.1–18 | 1 Cor 10.14—11.1 | Mt 8.28–34 |
| 2 | Hos 14.1–9 | Acts 22.30—23.11 | Lk 6.39–49 |

| Tue | [120], 121, 122, 123 | * | 124, 125, 126, [127] | |
| 1 | 2 Kg 22.1–13 | 1 Cor 11.2, 17–22 | Mt 9.1–8 |
| 2 | Mic 1.1–9 | Acts 23.12–24 | Lk 7.1–17 |

| Wed | 119.145–176 | * | 128, 129, 130 | |
| 1 | 2 Kg 22.14—23.3 | 1 Cor 11.23–34 | Mt 9.9–17 |
| 2 | Mic 2.1–13 | Acts 23.23–35 | Lk 7.18–35 |

| Thu | 131, 132, [133] | * | 134, 135 | |
| 1 | 2 Kg 23.4–25 | 1 Cor 12.1–11 | Mt 9.18–26 |
| 2 | Mic 3.1–8 | Acts 24.1–23 | Lk 7.36–50 |

| Fri | 140, 142 | * | 141, 143.1–11(12) | |
| 1 | 2 Kg 23.36—24.17 | 1 Cor 12.12–26 | Mt 9.27–34 |
| 2 | Mic 3.9—4.5 | Acts 24.24—25.12 | Lk 8.1–15 |

| Sat | 137.1–6(7–9), 144 | * | 104 | |
| 1 | Jer 35.1–19 | 1 Cor 12.27—13.3 | Mt 9.35—10.4 |
| 2 | Mic 5.1–4, 10–15 | Acts 25.13–27 | Lk 8.16–25 |

## Week of Sunday between 9 and 15 October  *Proper 28*

| Sun | 146, 147 | * | 111, 112, 113 | |
| 1 | Jer 36.1–10 | Acts 14.8–18 | Lk 7.36–50 |
| 2 | Mic 6.1–8 | 1 Cor 4.9–16 | Mt 15.21–28 |

| Mon | 1, 2, 3 | * | 4, 7 | |
| 1 | Jer 36.11–26 | 1 Cor 13.(1–3), 4–13 | Mt 10.5–15 |
| 2 | Mic 7.1–7 | Acts 26.1–23 | Lk 8.26–39 |

| Tue | 5, 6 | * | 10, 11 | |
|---|---|---|---|---|
| 1 | Jer 36.27—37.2 | 1 Cor 14.1–12 | Mt 10.16–23 | |
| 2 | Jon 1.1–17a | Acts 26.24—27.8 | Lk 8.40–56 | |

| Wed | 119.1–24 | * | 12, 13, 14 | |
|---|---|---|---|---|
| 1 | Jer 37.3–21 | 1 Cor 14.13–25 | Mt 10.24–33 | |
| 2 | Jon 1.17—2.10 | Acts 27.9–26 | Lk 9.1–17 | |

| Thu | 18.1–20 | * | 18.21–50 | |
|---|---|---|---|---|
| 1 | Jer 38.1–13 | 1 Cor 14.26–33a, 37–40 | Mt 10.34–42 | |
| 2 | Jon 3.1—4.11 | Acts 27.27–44 | Lk 9.18–27 | |

| Fri | 16, 17 | * | 22 | |
|---|---|---|---|---|
| 1 | Jer 38.14–28 | 1 Cor 15.1–11 | Mt 11.1–6 | |
| 2 | Sir 1.1–10, 18–27 | Acts 28.1–6 | Lk 9.28–36 | |

| Sat | 20, 21.1–7(8–14) | * | 110.1–5(6–7), 116, 117 | |
|---|---|---|---|---|
| 1 | 2 Kg 25.8–12, 22–26 | 1 Cor 15.12–29 | Mt 11.7–15 | |
| 2 | Sir 3.17–31 | Acts 28.17–31 | Lk 9.37–50 | |

## Week of Sunday between 16 and 22 October   *Proper 29*

| Sun | 148, 149, 150 | * | 114, 115 | |
|---|---|---|---|---|
| 1 | Jer 29.1, 4–14 | Acts 16.6–15 | Lk 10.1–12, 17–20 | |
| 2 | Sir 4.1–10 | 1 Cor 10.1–13 | Mt 16.13–20 | |

| Mon | 25 | * | 9, 15 | |
|---|---|---|---|---|
| 1 | Jer 44.1–14 | 1 Cor 15.30–41 | Mt 11.16–24 | |
| 2 | Sir 4.20—5.7 | Rev 7.1–8 | Lk 9.51–62 | |

| Tue | 26, 28 | * | 36, 39 | |
|---|---|---|---|---|
| 1 | Lam 1.1–5(6–9)10–12 | 1 Cor 15.41–50 | Mt 11.25–30 | |
| 2 | Sir 6.5–17 | Rev 7.9–17 | Lk 10.1–16 | |

| Wed | 38 | * | 119.25–48 | |
|---|---|---|---|---|
| 1 | Lam 2.8–15 | 1 Cor 15.51–58 | Mt 12.1–14 | |
| 2 | Sir 7.4–14 | Rev 8.1–13 | Lk 10.17–24 | |

| Thu | 37.1–18 | * | 37.19–42 | |
|---|---|---|---|---|
| 1 | Ezra 1.1–11 | 1 Cor 16.1–9 | Mt 12.15–21 | |
| 2 | Sir 10.1–18 | Rev 9.1–12 | Lk 10.25–37 | |

| Fri | 31 | * | 35 |
| 1 | Ezra 3.1–13 | 1 Cor 16.10–24 | Mt 12.22–32 |
| 2 | Sir 11.2–20 | Rev 9.13–21 | Lk 10.38–42 |

| Sat | 30, 32 | * | 42, 43 |
| 1 | Ezra 4.7, 11–24 | Philem 1–25 | Mt 12.33–42 |
| 2 | Sir 15.9–20 | Rev 10.1–11 | Lk 11.1–13 |

## Week of Sunday between 23 and 29 October   *Proper 30*

| Sun | 63.1–8(9–11), 98 | * | 103 |
| 1 | Hag 1.1—2.9 | Acts 18.24—19.7 | Lk 10.25–37 |
| 2 | Sir 18.19–33 | 1 Cor 10.15–24 | Mt 18.15–20 |

| Mon | 41, 52 | * | 44 |
| 1 | Zech 1.7–17 | Rev 1.4–20 | Mt 12.43–50 |
| 2 | Sir 19.4–17 | Rev 11.1–14 | Lk 11.14–26 |

| Tue | 45 | * | 47, 48 |
| 1 | Ezra 5.1–17 | Rev 4.1–11 | Mt 13.1–9 |
| 2 | Sir 24.1–12 | Rev 11.14–19 | Lk 11.27–36 |

| Wed | 119.49–72 | * | 49, [53] |
| 1 | Ezra 6.1–22 | Rev 5.1–10 | Mt 13.10–17 |
| 2 | Sir 28.14–26 | Rev 12.1–6 | Lk 11.37–52 |

| Thu | 50 | * | [59, 60] *or* 103 |
| 1 | Neh 1.1–11 | Rev 5.11—6.11 | Mt 13.18–23 |
| 2 | Sir 31.12–18, 25—32.2 | Rev 12.7–17 | Lk 11.53—12.12 |

| Fri | 40, 54 | * | 51 |
| 1 | Neh 2.1–20 | Rev 6.12—7.4 | Mt 13.24–30 |
| 2 | Sir 34.1–8, 18–22 | Rev 13.1–10 | Lk 12.13–31 |

| Sat | 55 | * | 138, 139.1–17(18–23) |
| 1 | Neh 4.1–23 | Rev 7.(4–8)9–17 | Mt 13.31–35 |
| 2 | Sir 35.1–17 | Rev 13.11–18 | Lk 12.32–48 |

## Week of Sunday between 30 October and 5 November   *Proper 31*

| Sun | 24, 29 | * | 8, 84 |
| 1 | Neh 5.1–19 | Acts 20.7–12 | Lk 12.22–31 |
| 2 | Sir 36.1–17 | 1 Cor 12.27—13.13 | Mt 18.21–35 |

| Mon | 56, 57, [58] | * | 64, 65 | |
|---|---|---|---|---|
| 1 | Neh 6.1–19 | Rev 10.1–11 | Mt 13.36–43 | |
| 2 | Sir 38.24–34 | Rev 14.1–13 | Lk 12.49–59 | |

| Tue | 61, 62 | * | 68.1–20(21–23)24–36 | |
|---|---|---|---|---|
| 1 | Neh 12.27–31a, 42b–47 | Rev 11.1–19 | Mt 13.44–52 | |
| 2 | Sir 43.1–22 | Rev 14.14—15.8 | Lk 13.1–9 | |

| Wed | 72 | * | 119.73–96 | |
|---|---|---|---|---|
| 1 | Neh 13.4–22 | Rev 12.1–12 | Mt 13.53–58 | |
| 2 | Sir 43.23–33 | Rev 16.1–11 | Lk 13.10–17 | |

| Thu | [70], 71 | * | 74 | |
|---|---|---|---|---|
| 1 | Ezra 7.(1–10)11–26 | Rev 14.1–13 | Mt 14.1–12 | |
| 2 | Sir 44.1–15 | Rev 16.12–21 | Lk 13.18–30 | |

| Fri | 69.1–23(24–30)31–38 | * | 73 | |
|---|---|---|---|---|
| 1 | Ezra 7.27–28; 8.21–36 | Rev 15.1–8 | Mt 14.13–21 | |
| 2 | Sir 50.1, 11–24 | Rev 17.1–18 | Lk 13.31–35 | |

| Sat | 75, 76 | * | 23, 27 | |
|---|---|---|---|---|
| 1 | Ezra 9.1–15 | Rev 17.1–14 | Mt 14.22–36 | |
| 2 | Sir 51.1–12 | Rev 18.1–14 | Lk 14.1–11 | |

## Week of Sunday between 6 and 12 November   *Proper 32*

| Sun | 93, 96 | * | 34 | |
|---|---|---|---|---|
| 1 | Ezra 10.1–17 | Acts 24.10–21 | Lk 14.12–24 | |
| 2 | Sir 51.13–22 | 1 Cor 14.1–12 | Mt 20.1–16 | |

| Mon | 80 | * | 77, [79] | |
|---|---|---|---|---|
| 1 | Neh 9.1–15(16–25) | Rev 18.1–8 | Mt 15.1–20 | |
| 2 | Jl 1.1–13 | Rev 18.15–24 | Lk 14.12–24 | |

| Tue | 78.1–39 | * | 78.40–72 | |
|---|---|---|---|---|
| 1 | Neh 9.26–38 | Rev 18.9–20 | Mt 15.21–28 | |
| 2 | Jl 1.15—2.2(3–11) | Rev 19.1–10 | Lk 14.25–35 | |

| Wed | 119.97–120 | * | 81, 82 | |
|---|---|---|---|---|
| 1 | Neh 7.73b—8.3, 5–18 | Rev 18.21–24 | Mt 15.29–39 | |
| 2 | Jl 2.12–19 | Rev 19.11–21 | Lk 15.1–10 | |

| Thu | [83] *or* 23, 27 | * | 85, 86 | |
|---|---|---|---|---|
| 1 | 1 Macc 1.1–28 | Rev 19.1–10 | Mt 16.1–12 | |
| 2 | Jl 2.21–27 | Jas 1.1–15 | Lk 15.1–2, 11–32 | |

| Fri | 88 | * | 91, 92 | |
|---|---|---|---|---|
| 1 | 1 Macc 1.41–63 | Rev 19.11–16 | Mt 16.13–20 | |
| 2 | Jl 2.28—3.8 | Jas 1.16–27 | Lk 16.1–9 | |

| Sat | 87, 90 | * | 136 | |
|---|---|---|---|---|
| 1 | 1 Macc 2.1–28 | Rev 20.1–6 | Mt 16.21–28 | |
| 2 | Jl 3.9–17 | Jas 2.1–13 | Lk 16.10–17(18) | |

## Week of Sunday between 13 and 19 November   *Proper 33*

| Sun | 66, 67 | * | 19, 46 | |
|---|---|---|---|---|
| 1 | 1 Macc 2.29–43, 49–50 | Acts 28.14b–23 | Lk 16.1–13 | |
| 2 | Hab 1.1–4(5–11)12—2.1 | Phil 3.13—4.1 | Mt 23.13–24 | |

| Mon | 89.1–18 | * | 89.19–52 | |
|---|---|---|---|---|
| 1 | 1 Macc 3.1–24 | Rev 20.7–15 | Mt 17.1–13 | |
| 2 | Hab 2.1–4, 9–20 | Jas 2.14–26 | Lk 16.19–31 | |

| Tue | 97, 99, [100] | * | 94, [95] | |
|---|---|---|---|---|
| 1 | 1 Macc 3.25–41 | Rev 21.1–8 | Mt 17.14–21 | |
| 2 | Hab 3.1–10(11–15)16–18 | Jas 3.1–12 | Lk 17.1–10 | |

| Wed | 101, 109.1–4(5–19)20–30 | * | 119.121–144 | |
|---|---|---|---|---|
| 1 | 1 Macc 3.42–60 | Rev 21.9–21 | Mt 17.22–27 | |
| 2 | Mal 1.1, 6–14 | Jas 3.13—4.12 | Lk 17.11–19 | |

| Thu | 105.1–22 | * | 105.23–45 | |
|---|---|---|---|---|
| 1 | 1 Macc 4.1–25 | Rev 21.22—22.5 | Mt 18.1–9 | |
| 2 | Mal 2.1–16 | Jas 4.13—5.6 | Lk 17.20–37 | |

| Fri | 102 | * | 107.1–32 | |
|---|---|---|---|---|
| 1 | 1 Macc 4.36–59 | Rev 22.6–13 | Mt 18.10–20 | |
| 2 | Mal 3.1–12 | Jas 5.7–12 | Lk 18.1–8 | |

| Sat | 107.33–43, 108.1–6(7–13) | * | 33 | |
|---|---|---|---|---|
| 1 | Is 65.17–25 | Rev 22.14–21 | Mt 18.21–35 | |
| 2 | Mal 3.13—4.6 | Jas 5.13–20 | Lk 18.9–14 | |

**Week of the Reign of Christ between 20 and 26 November**  *Proper 34*

| | | | |
|---|---|---|---|
| *Sun* | 118 | * 145 | |
| 1 | Is 19.19–25 | Rom 15.5–13 | Lk 19.11–27 |
| 2 | Zech 9.9–16 | 1 Pet 3.13–22 | Mt 21.1–13 |

| | | | |
|---|---|---|---|
| *Mon* | 106.1–18 | * 106.19–48 | |
| 1 | Jl 3.1–2, 9–17 | 1 Pet 1.1–12 | Mt 19.1–12 |
| 2 | Zech 10.1–12 | Gal 6.1–10 | Lk 18.15–30 |

| | | | |
|---|---|---|---|
| *Tue* | [120], 121, 122, 123 | * 124, 125, 126, [127] | |
| 1 | Nah 1.1–13 | 1 Pet 1.13–25 | Mt 19.13–22 |
| 2 | Zech 11.4–17 | 1 Cor 3.10–23 | Lk 18.31–43 |

| | | | |
|---|---|---|---|
| *Wed* | 119.145–176 | * 128, 129, 130 | |
| 1 | Ob 15–21 | 1 Pet 2.1–10 | Mt 19.23–30 |
| 2 | Zech 12.1–10 | Eph 1.3–14 | Lk 19.1–10 |

| | | | |
|---|---|---|---|
| *Thu* | 131, 132, [133] | * 134, 135 | |
| 1 | Zeph 3.1–13 | 1 Pet 2.11–25 | Mt 20.1–16 |
| 2 | Zech 13.1–9 | Eph 1.15–23 | Lk 19.11–27 |

| | | | |
|---|---|---|---|
| *Fri* | 140, 142 | * 141, 143.1–11(12) | |
| 1 | Is 24.14–23 | 1 Pet 3.13—4.6 | Mt 20.17–28 |
| 2 | Zech 14.1–11 | Rom 15.7–13 | Lk 19.28–40 |

| | | | |
|---|---|---|---|
| *Sat* | 137.1–6(7–9), 144 | * 104 | |
| 1 | Mic 7.11–20 | 1 Pet 4.7–19 | Mt 20.29–34 |
| 2 | Zech 14.12–21 | Phil 2.1–11 | Lk 19.41–48 |

## Holy Days

| | | | | |
|---|---|---|---|---|
| 11 Jan | *Holy Innocents* | 2, 26 | * 19, 126 | |
| or 28 Dec | M | Is 49.13–23 | Mt 18.1–14 | |
| | E | Is 54.1–13 | Mk 10.13–16 | |

| | | | | |
|---|---|---|---|---|
| 18 Jan | *Confession of St Peter the Apostle* | 66, 67 | * 118 | |
| | M | Ezek 3.4–11 | Acts 10.34–44 | |
| | E | Ezek 34.11–16 | Jn 21.15–22 | |

| | | | | |
|---|---|---|---|---|
| 25 Jan | *Conversion of St Paul the Apostle* | 19 | * 119.89–112 | |
| | M | Is 45.18–25 | Phil 3.4b–11 | |
| | E | Sir 39.1–10 | Acts 9.1–22 | |

*Eve of the Presentation*          *          113, 122
          1 Sam 1.20–28a          Rom 8.14–21

2 Feb      *Presentation of the Lord*          42, 43          *          48, 87
          M          1 Sam 2.1–10          Jn 8.31–36
          E          Hag 2.1–9          1 Jn 3.1–8

19 Mar     *St Joseph*          132          *          34
          M          Is 63.7–16          Mt 1.18–25
          E          2 Chr 6.12–17          Eph 3.14–21

*Eve of the Annunciation*          *          8, 138
          Gen 3.1–15          Rom 5.12–21 *or* Gal 4.1–7

25 Mar     *Annunciation*          85, 87          *          110.1–5(6–7), 132
          M          Is 52.7–12          Heb 2.5–10
          E          Wis 9.1–12          Jn 1.9–14

25 Apr     *St Mark*          145          *          67, 96
          M          Sir 2.1–11          Acts 12.25—13.3
          E          Is 62.6–12          2 Tim 4.1–11

1 May      *St Philip and St James*          119.137–160          *          139
          M          Job 23.1–12          Jn 1.43–51
          E          Pr 4.7–18          Jn 12.20–26

6 May      *St John the Evangelist*          97, 98          *          145
or 27 Dec  M          Pr 8.22–30          Jn 13.20–35
          E          Is 44.1–8          1 Jn 5.1–12

14 May     *St Matthias*          80          *          33
          M          1 Sam 16.1–13          1 Jn 2.18–25
          E          1 Sam 12.1–5          Acts 20.17–35

*Eve of the Visitation*          *          132
          Is 11.1–10          Heb 2.11–18

31 May     *The Visit of Mary to Elizabeth*          72          *          146, 147
          M          1 Sam 1.1–20          Heb 3.1–6
          E          Zech 2.10–13          Jn 3.25–30

11 Jun    *St Barnabas*    15, 67    *    19, 146
       M     Sir 31.3–11     Acts 4.32–37
       E     Job 29.1–16     Acts 9.26–31

*Eve of St John*    *    103
       Sir 48.1–11     Lk 1.5–23

24 Jun    *Birth of St John the Baptist*    82, 98    *    80
       M     Mal 3.1–5     Jn 3.22–30
       E     Mal 4.1–6     Mt 11.2–19

29 Jun    *St Peter and St Paul*    66    *    97, 138
       M     Ezek 2.1–7     Acts 11.1–18
       E     Is 49.1–6     Gal 2.1–9

3 Jul    *St Thomas*    23, 121    *    27
       M     Job 42.1–6     1 Pet 1.3–9
       E     Is 43.8–13     Jn 14.1–7

22 Jul    *St Mary Magdalene*    116    *    30, 149
       M     Zeph 3.14–20     Mk 15.37—16.7
       E     Ex 15.19–21     2 Cor 1.3–7

25 Jul    *St James the Apostle*    34    *    33
       M     Jer 16.14–21     Mk 1.14–20
       E     Jer 26.1–15     Mt 10.16–32

3 Aug    *St Stephen*    28, 30    *    118
or 26 Dec M     2 Chr 24.17–22     Acts 6.1–7
       E     Wis 4.7–15     Acts 7.59—8.8

*Eve of the Transfiguration*    *    84
       1 Kg 19.1–12     2 Cor 3.1–9, 18

6 Aug    *Transfiguration of the Lord*    2, 24    *    72
       M     Ex 24.12–18     2 Cor 4.1–6
       E     Dan 7.9–10, 13–14     Jn 12.27–36a

15 Aug    *St Mary the Virgin*    113, 115    *    45 *or* 138, 149
       M     1 Sam 2.1–10     Jn 2.1–12
       E     Jer 31.1–14 *or* Zech 2.10–13     Jn 19.23–27 *or* Acts 1.6–14

24 Aug  *St Bartholomew*     86        *      15, 67
        M     Gen 28.10–17       Jn 1.43–51
        E     Is 66.1–2, 18–23      1 Pet 5.1–11

29 Aug  *Beheading of St John the Baptist*     102      *      86
        M     Jer 38.1–6      Rev 7.13–17
        E     Jg 16.28–30      1 Pet 3.13–18

*Eve of Holy Cross*      *      46, 87
        1 Kg 8.22–30      Eph 2.11–22

14 Sep  *Holy Cross Day*     66      *      118
        M     Num 21.4–9      Jn 3.11–17
        E     Gen 3.1–15      1 Pet 3.17–22

21 Sep  *St Matthew*      119.41–64      *      19, 112
        M     Is 8.11–20      Rom 10.1–15
        E     Job 28.12–28      Mt 13.44–52

29 Sep  *St Michael and All Angels*      8, 148      *      34, 150 or 104
        M     Job 38.1–7      Heb 1.1–14
        E     Dan 12.1–3 or 2 Kg 6.8–17      Mk 13.21–27 or Rev 5.1–14

18 Oct  *St Luke*     103      *      67, 96
        M     Ezek 47.1–12      Lk 1.1–4
        E     Is 52.7–10      Acts 1.1–8

28 Oct  *St Simon and St Jude*     66      *      116, 117
        M     Is 28.9–16      Eph 4.1–16
        E     Is 4.2–6      Jn 14.15–31

*Eve of All Saints*      *      34
        Wis 3.1–9      Rev 19.1, 4–10

1 Nov   *All Saints' Day*     111, 112      *      148, 150
        M     2 Esd 2.42–47      Heb 11.32—12.2
        E     Wis 5.1–5, 14–16      Rev 21.1–4, 22—22.5

30 Nov  *St Andrew*     34      *      96, 100
        M     Is 49.1–6      1 Cor 4.1–16
        E     Is 55.1–5      Jn 1.35–42

# Concerning the Weekday Eucharistic Lectionary

*The Weekday Lectionary is intended primarily for use at celebrations of the eucharist on days for which the Lectionary does not provide readings.*

*The Weekday Lectionary is arranged in a two-year cycle. Year 1 always begins on the First Sunday of Advent in years divisible by two (1986, 1988, etc.).*

*Two daily readings are provided. All references to readings are based on the Revised Standard Version of the Bible. Versification varies among translations; if another translation is being used, the RSV should be checked. Suggestions on p. 266 for the adaptation of excerpted texts for public reading should be consulted.*

*All references to psalms are based on the psalter appended to this book; if another translation is used, that psalter should be checked. Verse selections are suggested for many psalms, but selections may be lengthened or shortened as appropriate.*

*The Collect, the Prayer over the Gifts, and the Prayer after Communion of the previous Sunday may be used on ordinary weekdays, except that one of the sets of Christmas prayers may be used on ordinary weekdays between Christmas Day and the First Sunday after Christmas, and the prayers of Ash Wednesday may be used between Ash Wednesday and the First Sunday of Lent.*

## Signs

1—*Year 1*

2—*Year 2*

C—*Canticle*

# Weekday Eucharistic Lectionary

## Advent

### Week of 1 Advent

| | | | |
|---|---|---|---|
| *Mon* | Is 2.1–5 (Year 1 Is 4.2–6) | Ps 122 | Mt 8.5–13 |
| *Tue* | Is 11.1–10 | Ps 72.1–8 | Lk 10.21–24 |
| *Wed* | Is 25.6–9 | Ps 23 | Mt 15.29–39 |
| *Thu* | Is 26.1–6 | Ps 118.19–24 | Mt 7.21–27 |
| *Fri* | Is 29.17–24 | Ps 27.1–6, 17–18 | Mt 9.27–31 |
| *Sat* | Is 30.19–21, 23–26 | Ps 147.1–12 | Mt 9.35—10.1, 5–8 |

### Week of 2 Advent

| | | | |
|---|---|---|---|
| *Mon* | Is 35.1–10 | Ps 85.8–13 | Lk 5.17–26 |
| *Tue* | Is 40.1–11 | Ps 96 | Mt 18.12–14 |
| *Wed* | Is 40.25–31 | Ps 103.1–10 | Mt 11.28–30 |
| *Thu* | Is 41.13–20 | Ps 145.1–4, 8–13 | Mt 11.7–15 |
| *Fri* | Is 48.17–19 | Ps 1 | Mt 11.16–19 |
| *Sat* | Sir 48.1–11 | Ps 80.1–3, 14–18 | Mt 17.9–13 |

### Week of 3 Advent

| | | | |
|---|---|---|---|
| *Mon* | Num 24.2–7, 15–17a | Ps 25.3–8 | Mt 21.23–27 |
| *Tue* | Zeph 3.1–2, 9–13 | Ps 34.1–8, 15–22 | Mt 21.28–32 |
| *Wed* | Is 45.5–8(9–17), 18–25 | Ps 85.8–13 | Lk 7.19–23 |
| *Thu* | Is 54.1–10 | Ps 30 | Lk 7.24–30 |
| *Fri* | Is 56.1–8 | Ps 67 | Jn 5.33–36 |

### 17 to 24 December

| | | | |
|---|---|---|---|
| 17 | Gen 49.2, 8–10 | Ps 72.1–8 | Mt 1.1–7, 17 |
| 18 | Jer 23.5–8 | Ps 72.11–19 | Mt 1.18–25 |
| 19 | Jg 13.2–7, 24–25 | Ps 71.1–8 | Lk 1.5–25 |
| 20 | Is 7.10–14 | Ps 24 | Lk 1.26–38 |
| 21 | S of S 2.8–14 *or* Zeph 3.14–18a | Ps 33.1–5, 20–22 | Lk 1.39–45 |
| 22 | 1 Sam 1.19–28 | C 3 *or* Ps 113 *or* Ps 122 | Lk 1.46–56 |
| 23 | Mal 3.1–5 | Ps 25.1–14 | Lk 1.57–66 |
| 24 | 2 Sam 7.1–16 | Ps 89.1–4, 19–29 | Lk 1.67–79 |

# Christmas and Epiphany

## 26 to 31 December

| | | | |
|----|----|----|----|
| 26 | 1 Jn 1.1–4 | Ps 136.1–9, 23–26 | Jn 1.1–5 |
| 27 | 1 Jn 1.5–10 | Ps 27.5–13 | Jn 1.6–14 |
| 28 | 1 Jn 2.1–6 | Ps 16 | Mt 2.13–18 |
| 29 | 1 Jn 2.7–11 | Ps 96.1–9 | Lk 2.22–35 |
| 30 | 1 Jn 2.12–17 | Ps 96.7–10 | Lk 2.36–40 |
| 31 | 1 Jn 2.18–21 | Ps 96.1–2, 11–13 | Jn 1.1–18 |

## 2 to 12 January

| | | | |
|----|----|----|----|
| 2 | 1 Jn 2.22–29 | Ps 98.1–5 | Jn 1.19–28 |
| 3 | 1 Jn 3.1–6 | Ps 98.1–2, 4–7 | Jn 1.29–34 |
| 4 | 1 Jn 3.7–10 | Ps 98.1–2, 8–10 | Jn 1.35–42 |
| 5 | 1 Jn 3.11–18 | Ps 100 | Jn 1.43–51 |
| 7 | 1 Jn 3.18—4.6 | Ps 2 | Mt 4.12–17, 23–25 |
| 8 | 1 Jn 4.7–12 | Ps 72.1–8 | Mk 6.30–44 |
| 9 | 1 Jn 4.11–19 | Ps 72.1–2, 10–13 | Mk 6.45–52 |
| 10 | 1 Jn 4.19—5.4 | Ps 72.1–2, 14–19 | Lk 4.14–22 |
| 11 | 1 Jn 5.5–12 | Ps 147.13–21 | Lk 5.12–16 |
| 12 | 1 Jn 5.13–21 | Ps 149.1–4 | Jn 3.22–30 |

*The Monday after the Baptism of the Lord begins the Ferial Cycle.*

# Lent

| | | | |
|-----|----|----|----|
| Thu | Dt 30.15–20 | Ps 1 | Lk 9.18–25 |
| Fri | Is 58.1–9a | Ps 51.1–4, 17–18 | Mt 9.14–17 |
| Sat | Is 58.9b–14 | Ps 86.1–6 | Lk 5.27–32 |

## Week of 1 Lent

| | | | |
|-----|----|----|----|
| Mon | Lev 19.1–2, 11–18 | Ps 19.7–14 | Mt 25.31–46 |
| Tue | Is 55.10–11 | Ps 34.1–8(15–22) | Mt 6.7–15 |
| Wed | Jon 3.1–10 | Ps 51.1–2, 11–13 | Lk 11.29–32 |
| Thu | Ad Est 14.1, 3–5, 12–14 | Ps 138 | Mt 7.7–12 |
| Fri | Ezek 18.21–28 | Ps 130 | Mt 5.20–26 |
| Sat | Dt 26.16–19 | Ps 119.1–8 | Mt 5.43–48 |

## Week of 2 Lent

| | | | |
|---|---|---|---|
| *Mon* | Dan 9.3–10 | Ps 79 | Lk 6.36–38 |
| *Tue* | Is 1.10–20 | Ps 50.7–15 | Mt 23.1–12 |
| *Wed* | Jer 18.18–20 | Ps 31.1–5, 13–16 | Mt 20.17–28 |
| *Thu* | Jer 17.5–10 | Ps 1 | Lk 16.19–31 |
| *Fri* | Gen 37.3–4, 12–28 | Ps 17.1–8 | Mt 21.33–46 |
| *Sat* | Mic 7.14–20 | Ps 103.1–12 | Lk 15.1–3, 11–32 |

## Week of 3 Lent

| | | | |
|---|---|---|---|
| *Mon* | 2 Kg 5.1–15a | Ps 42.1–2, 11–15 | Lk 4.24–30 |
| *Tue* | S of 3 Y 1.2, 11–20 | Ps 25.3–8 | Mt 18.21–35 |
| *Wed* | Dt 4.1, 5–10 | Ps 147.13–21 | Mt 5.17–20 |
| *Thu* | Jer 7.21–28 | Ps 95.1–9 | Lk 11.14–23 |
| *Fri* | Hos 14.1–9 | Ps 81 | Mk 12.28–34 |
| *Sat* | Hos 5.13—6.6 | Ps 51.1–2, 17–20 | Lk 18.9–14 |

## Week of 4 Lent

| | | | |
|---|---|---|---|
| *Mon* | Is 65.17–21 | Ps 30 | Jn 4.43–54 |
| *Tue* | Ezek 47.1–9, 12 | Ps 46 | Jn 5.1–18 |
| *Wed* | Is 49.8–15 | Ps 145.8–15 | Jn 5.19–30 |
| *Thu* | Ex 32.7–14 | Ps 103.1–12 | Jn 5.31–47 |
| *Fri* | Wis 2.1a, 12–22 | Ps 34.15–22 | Jn 7.1–2, 10, 25–30 |
| *Sat* | Jer 11.18–20 | Ps 7.1–2, 9–12 | Jn 7.40–53 |

## Week of 5 Lent

| | | | | |
|---|---|---|---|---|
| *Mon* | Sus 1.1–9, 15–17, 19–30, 33–62 *or* Sus 1.41c–62 | Ps 23 | Jn 8.1–11 | |
| *Tue* | Num 21.4–9 | Ps 102.1–2, 15–22 | Jn 8.21–30 | |
| *Wed* | Dan 3.13–28 | C 13 *or* Ps 24.1–6 | Jn 8.31–47 | |
| *Thu* | Gen 17.3–9 | Ps 105.1–9 | Jn 8.51–59 | |
| *Fri* | Jer 20.7–13 | Ps 18.1–7 | Jn 10.31–42 | |
| *Sat* | Ezek 37.21b–28 | C 8 *or* Ps 121 | Jn 11.45–57 | |

# Easter Season

## Easter Week

| | | | |
|---|---|---|---|
| *Mon* | Acts 2.14, 22–32 | Ps 16.1, 5–11 | Mt 28.8–15 |
| *Tue* | Acts 2.14, 36–41 | Ps 33.1–5, 18–22 | Jn 20.11–18 |
| *Wed* | Acts 3.1–10 | Ps 105.1–9 | Lk 24.13–35 |
| *Thu* | Acts 3.11–26 | Ps 8 *or* 114 | Lk 24.36b–48 |
| *Fri* | Acts 4.1–12 | Ps 116.1–8 | Jn 21.1–14 |
| *Sat* | Acts 4.13–21 | Ps 118.1–4, 22–29 | Mk 16.9–15 |

## Week of 2 Easter

| | | | |
|---|---|---|---|
| *Mon* | Acts 4.23–31 | Ps 2 | Jn 3.1–8 |
| *Tue* | Acts 4.32–37 | Ps 93 | Jn 3.7–15 |
| *Wed* | Acts 5.17–26 | Ps 34.1–8 | Jn 3.16–21 |
| *Thu* | Acts 5.27–33 | Ps 34.15–22 | Jn 3.31–36 |
| *Fri* | Acts 5.34–42 | Ps 27.1–8, 17–18 | Jn 6.1–15 |
| *Sat* | Acts 6.1–7 | Ps 33.1–5, 18–22 | Jn 6.16–21 |

## Week of 3 Easter

| | | | |
|---|---|---|---|
| *Mon* | Acts 6.8–15 | Ps 119.161–168 | Jn 6.22–29 |
| *Tue* | Acts 7.51—8.1a | Ps 31.1–5 | Jn 6.30–35 |
| *Wed* | Acts 8.1b–8 | Ps 66.1–6 | Jn 6.35–40 |
| *Thu* | Acts 8.26–40 | Ps 66.7–8, 14–18 | Jn 6.44–51 |
| *Fri* | Acts 9.1–20 | Ps 117 | Jn 6.52–59 |
| *Sat* | Acts 9.31–42 | Ps 116.10–17 | Jn 6.60–69 |

## Week of 4 Easter

| | | | |
|---|---|---|---|
| *Mon* | Acts 11.1–18 | Ps 43 | Jn 10.1–10 |
| *Tue* | Acts 11.19–26 | Ps 87 | Jn 10.22–30 |
| *Wed* | Acts 12.24—13.5a | Ps 67 | Jn 12.44–50 |
| *Thu* | Acts 13.13–25 | Ps 89.1–2, 19–26 | Jn 13.16–20 |
| *Fri* | Acts 13.26–33 | Ps 2 | Jn 14.1–7 |
| *Sat* | Acts 13.44–52 | Ps 98 | Jn 14.7–14 |

## Week of 5 Easter

| | | | |
|---|---|---|---|
| *Mon* | Acts 14.5–18 | Ps 115.1–12 | Jn 14.21–26 |
| *Tue* | Acts 14.19–27 | Ps 145.10–13, 22 | Jn 14.27–31a |
| *Wed* | Acts 15.1–6 | Ps 122 | Jn 15.1–8 |
| *Thu* | Acts 15.7–21 | Ps 96.1–3, 10–13 | Jn 15.9–11 |
| *Fri* | Acts 15.22–31 | Ps 57.6–11 | Jn 15.12–17 |
| *Sat* | Acts 16.1–10 | Ps 100 | Jn 15.18–21 |

## Week of 6 Easter

| | | | |
|---|---|---|---|
| *Mon* | Acts 16.11–15 | Ps 149 | Jn 15.26—16.4a |
| *Tue* | Acts 16.19b–34 | Ps 138 | Jn 16.4b–11 |
| *Wed* | Acts 17.15, 22—18.8 | Ps 148 | Jn 16.12–20 |
| *Thu* | *Ascension Day* | | |
| *Fri* | Acts 18.9–18 | Ps 47.1–6 | Jn 16.20–24 |
| *Sat* | Acts 18.23–28 | Ps 47.1–2, 7–10 | Jn 16.23b–28 |

## Week of 7 Easter

| | | | |
|---|---|---|---|
| *Mon* | Acts 19.1–10 | Ps 68.1–6 | Jn 16.29–33 |
| *Tue* | Acts 20.17–27 | Ps 68.7–20 | Jn 17.1–11a |
| *Wed* | Acts 20.28–38 | Ps 68.28–36 | Jn 17.11b–19 |
| *Thu* | Acts 22.30; 23.6–11 | Ps 16 | Jn 17.20–26 |
| *Fri* | Acts 25.13–21 | Ps 103.1–2, 19–22 | Jn 21.15–19 |
| *Sat* | Acts 28.16–20, 30–31 | Ps 11 | Jn 21.20–25 |

## Week of the Baptism of the Lord—Proper 1

| *Mon* | | | |
|---|---|---|---|
| 1 | Heb 1.1–6 | Ps 97 | Mk 1.14–20 |
| 2 | 1 Sam 1.1–8 | Ps 116.10–17 | Mk 1.14–20 |

| *Tue* | | | |
|---|---|---|---|
| 1 | Heb 2.5–12 | Ps 8 | Mk 1.21–28 |
| 2 | 1 Sam 1.9–20 | C 18 *or* Ps 123 | Mk 1.21–28 |

| *Wed* | | | |
|---|---|---|---|
| 1 | Heb 2.14–18 | Ps 105.1–15 | Mk 1.29–39 |
| 2 | 1 Sam 3.1–20 | Ps 40.1–10 | Mk 1.29–39 |

| *Thu* | | | |
|---|---|---|---|
| 1 | Heb 3.1–14 | Ps 95.6–11 | Mk 1.40–45 |
| 2 | 1 Sam 4.1c–11 | Ps 44.7–14, 23–26 | Mk 1.40–45 |

*Fri*

1      Heb 4.1–5, 11     Ps 78.3–8     Mk 2.1–12

2      1 Sam 8.4–7, 10–22a     Ps 89.15–18     Mk 2.1–12

*Sat*

1      Heb 4.12–16     Ps 19.7–14     Mk 2.13–17

2      1 Sam 9.1–4,15–19; 10.1ab (not c)     Ps 21.1–7     Mk 2.13–17

## Week of Proper 2

*Mon*

1      Heb 5.1–10     Ps 110     Mk 2.18–22

2      1 Sam 15.16–23     Ps 50.7–15, 24     Mk 2.18–22

*Tue*

1      Heb 6.10–20     Ps 111     Mk 2.23–28

2      1 Sam 16.1–13     Ps 89.19–27     Mk 2.23–28

*Wed*

1      Heb 7.1–3, 15–17     Ps 110     Mk 3.1–6

2      1 Sam 17.32–51     Ps 144.1–10     Mk 3.1–6

*Thu*

1      Heb 7.23—8.7     Ps 40.8–12, 17–19     Mk 3.7–12

2      1 Sam 18.6–9; 19.1–8     Ps 56     Mk 3.7–12

*Fri*

1      Heb 8.6–13     Ps 85.7–13     Mk 3.13–19

2      1 Sam 24.2–20     Ps 57     Mk 3.13–19

*Sat*

1      Heb 9.2–3, 11–14     Ps 47     Jn 8.51–59

2      2 Sam 1.1–4, 11–12, 19–27     Ps 80.1–7     Jn 8.51–59

## Week of Proper 3

*Mon*

1      Heb 9.15, 24–28     Ps 98     Mk 3.19b–30

2      2 Sam 5.1–7, 10     Ps 89.19–28     Mk 3.19b–30

*Tue*

1      Heb 10.1–10     Ps 40.1–11     Mk 3.31–35

2      2 Sam 6.12b–19     Ps 24.7–10     Mk 3.31–35

*Wed*

| 1 | Heb 10.11–18 | Ps 110.1–4 | Mk 4.1–20 |
| 2 | 2 Sam 7.4–17 | Ps 89.1–4 | Mk 4.1–20 |

*Thu*

| 1 | Heb 10.19–25 | Ps 24.1–6 | Mk 4.21–25 |
| 2 | 2 Sam 7.18–19, 24–29 | Ps 132.1–5, 11–15 | Mk 4.21–25 |

*Fri*

| 1 | Heb 10.32–39 | Ps 37.1–7, 24–25, 41–42 | Mk 4.26–34 |
| 2 | 2 Sam 11.1–17 | Ps 51.1–10 | Mk 4.26–34 |

*Sat*

| 1 | Heb 11.1–2, 8–19 | C 19 *or* Ps 89.19–29 | Mk 4.35–41 |
| 2 | 2 Sam 12.1–25 | Ps 51.11–18 | Mk 4.35–41 |

## Week of Proper 4

*Mon*

| 1 | Heb 11.32–40 | Ps 31.19–24 | Mk 5.1–20 |
| 2 | 2 Sam 15.13–14, 30; 16.5–14 | Ps 3 | Mk 5.1–20 |

*Tue*

| 1 | Heb 12.1–4 | Ps 22.22–30 | Mk 5.21–43 |
| 2 | 2 Sam 18.9–14, 24—19.3 | Ps 86.1–6 | Mk 5.21–43 |

*Wed*

| 1 | Heb 12.4–7, 11–15 | Ps 103.1–2, 13–18 | Mk 6.1–6 |
| 2 | 2 Sam 24.2, 9–17 | Ps 32.1–8 | Mk 6.1–6 |

*Thu*

| 1 | Heb 12.18–24 | Ps 48.1–3, 7–9 | Mk 6.7–13 |
| 2 | 1 Kg 2.1–4, 10–12 | Ps 132.10–19 | Mk 6.7–13 |

*Fri*

| 1 | Heb 13.1–8 | Ps 27.1–13 | Mk 6.14–29 |
| 2 | Sir 47.2–11 | Ps 18.31–33, 46–50 | Mk 6.14–29 |

*Sat*

| 1 | Heb 13.9–17, 20–21 | Ps 23 | Mk 6.30–34 |
| 2 | 1 Kg 3.3–14 | Ps 119.9–16 | Mk 6.30–34 |

## Week of Proper 5

*Readings for days between Ash Wednesday and 1 Lent are found on page 500.*

*Mon*

1    Gen 1.1–19       Ps 104.1–12, 25      Mk 6.53–56
2    1 Kg 8.1–7, 9–13      Ps 132.6–10      Mk 6.53–56

*Tue*

1    Gen 1.20—2.4a      Ps 8      Mk 7.1–13
2    1 Kg 8.22–23, 27–30      Ps 84      Mk 7.1–13

*Wed*

1    Gen 2.4b–9, 15–17      Ps 104.25, 28–31      Mk 7.14–23
2    1 Kg 10.1–10      Ps 37.1–7, 32–33, 41–42      Mk 7.14–23

*Thu*

1    Gen 2.18–25      Ps 128      Mk 7.24–30
2    1 Kg 11.4–13      Ps 132.11–19      Mk 7.24–30

*Fri*

1    Gen 3.1–8      Ps 32.1–8      Mk 7.31–37
2    1 Kg 11.29–32; 12.19      Ps 81.8–16      Mk 7.31–37

*Sat*

1    Gen 3.9–24      Ps 90.1–12      Mk 8.1–10
2    1 Kg 12.26–33; 13.33–34      Ps 106.19–22      Mk 8.1–10

## Week of Proper 6

*Mon*

1    Gen 4.1–15, 25      Ps 50.7–24      Mk 8.11–13
2    Jas 1.1–11      Ps 119.65–72      Mk 8.11–13

*Tue*

1    Gen 6.5–8; 7.1–5, 10      Ps 29      Mk 8.14–21
2    Jas 1.12–18      Ps 94.12–19      Mk 8.14–21

*Wed*

1    Gen 8.6–13, 20–22      Ps 116.10–17      Mk 8.22–26
2    Jas 1.19–27      Ps 15      Mk 8.22–26

*Thu*

1    Gen 9.1–13      Ps 102.15–22      Mk 8.27–33
2    Jas 2.1–9      Ps 72.1–4, 13–14      Mk 8.27–33

*Fri*

| 1 | Gen 11.1–9 | Ps 33.6–18 | Mk 8.34—9.1 |
| 2 | Jas 2.14–26 | Ps 112 | Mk 8.34—9.1 |

*Sat*

| 1 | Heb 11.1–7 | Ps 145.1–4, 10–13 | Mk 9.2–13 |
| 2 | Jas 3.1–10 | Ps 12.1–7 | Mk 8.2–13 |

## Week of Proper 7

*Mon*

| 1 | Sir 1.1–10 | Ps 93 | Mk 9.14–29 |
| 2 | Jas 3.13–18 | Ps 19.7–14 | Mk 9.14–29 |

*Tue*

| 1 | Sir 2.1–11 | Ps 37.3–6, 27–28 | Mk 9.30–37 |
| 2 | Jas 4.1–10 | Ps 51.11–18 | Mk 9.30–37 |

*Wed*

| 1 | Sir 4.11–19 | Ps 119.161–168 | Mk 9.38–41 |
| 2 | Jas 4.13–17 | Ps 49.1–9, 16–20 | Mk 9.38–41 |

*Thu*

| 1 | Sir 5.1–8 | Ps 1 | Mk 9.42–50 |
| 2 | Jas 5.1–6 | Ps 49.12–19 | Mk 9.42–50 |

*Fri*

| 1 | Sir 6.5–17 | Ps 119.17–24 | Mk 10.1–12 |
| 2 | Jas 5.9–12 | Ps 103.1–4, 8–13 | Mk 10.1–12 |

*Sat*

| 1 | Sir 17.1–15 | Ps 103.1–4, 13–18 | Mk 10.13–16 |
| 2 | Jas 5.13–20 | Ps 141 | Mk 10.13–16 |

## Week of Proper 8

*Mon*

| 1 | Sir 17.24–29 | Ps 32.1–8 | Mk 10.17–27 |
| 2 | 1 Pet 1.3–9 | Ps 111 | Mk 10.17–27 |

*Tue*

| 1 | Sir 35.1–12 | Ps 50.7–15 | Mk 10.28–31 |
| 2 | 1 Pet 1.10–16 | Ps 98 | Mk 10.28–31 |

*Wed*

| 1 | Sir 36.1–2, 5–6, 13–17 | Ps 79.8–13 | Mk 10.32–45 |
| 2 | 1 Pet 1.18—2.1 | Ps 147.13–21 | Mk 10.32–45 |

*Thu*

| 1 | Sir 42.15–25 | Ps 33.1–9 | Mk 10.46–52 |
| 2 | 1 Pet 2.2–5, 9–12 | Ps 100 | Mk 10.46–52 |

*Fri*

| 1 | Sir 44.1–13 | Ps 149.1–5 | Mk 11.11–26 |
| 2 | 1 Pet 4.7–13 | Ps 96.7–13 | Mk 11.11–26 |

*Sat*

| 1 | Sir 51.11b–22 | Ps 19.7–14 | Mk 11.27–33 |
| 2 | Jude 1.17–25 | Ps 63.1–8 | Mk 11.27–33 |

## Week of Proper 9

*Mon*

| 1 | Tob 1.1–2; 2.1–8 | Ps 112.1–6 | Mk 12.1–12 |
| 2 | 2 Pet 1.2–7 | Ps 91 | Mk 12.1–12 |

*Tue*

| 1 | Tob 2.9–14 | Ps 112.1–2, 7–9 | Mk 12.13–17 |
| 2 | 2 Pet 3.11–18 | Ps 90.1–6, 13–17 | Mk 12.13–17 |

*Wed*

| 1 | Tob 3.1–11, 16–17 | Ps 25.1–8 | Mk 12.18–27 |
| 2 | 2 Tim 1.1–12 | Ps 123 | Mk 12.18–27 |

*Thu*

| 1 | Tob 6.9–11; 7.1–15; 8.4–8 | Ps 128 | Mk 12.28–34 |
| 2 | 2 Tim 2.8–15 | Ps 25.1–12 | Mk 12.28–34 |

*Fri*

| 1 | Tob 11.5–15 | Ps 146 | Mk 12.35–37 |
| 2 | 2 Tim 3.10–17 | Ps 119.161–168 | Mk 12.35–37 |

*Sat*

| 1 | Tob 12.1, 5–15, 20 | Ps 65.1–4 | Mk 12.38–44 |
| 2 | 2 Tim 4.1–8 | Ps 71.8–17 | Mk 12.38–44 |

**Week of Proper 10**

*Mon*

| | | | |
|---|---|---|---|
| 1 | 2 Cor 1.1–7 | Ps 34.1–8 | Mt 5.1–12 |
| 2 | 1 Kg 17.1–6 | Ps 121 | Mt 5.1–12 |

*Tue*

| | | | |
|---|---|---|---|
| 1 | 2 Cor 1.18–22 | Ps 119.129–136 | Mt 5.13–16 |
| 2 | 1 Kg 17.7–16 | Ps 4 | Mt 5.13–16 |

*Wed*

| | | | |
|---|---|---|---|
| 1 | 2 Cor 3.4–11 | Ps 99 | Mt 5.17–19 |
| 2 | 1 Kg 18.20–39 | Ps 16.1, 6–11 | Mt 5.17–19 |

*Thu*

| | | | |
|---|---|---|---|
| 1 | 2 Cor 3.12—4.6 | Ps 85.7–13 | Mt 5.20–26 |
| 2 | 1 Kg 18.41–46 | Ps 65.1, 8–14 | Mt 5.20–26 |

*Fri*

| | | | |
|---|---|---|---|
| 1 | 2 Cor 4.7–15 | Ps 116.9–17 | Mt 5.27–32 |
| 2 | 1 Kg 19.9–16 | Ps 27.10–18 | Mt 5.27–32 |

*Sat*

| | | | |
|---|---|---|---|
| 1 | 2 Cor 5.14–21 | Ps 103.1–12 | Mt 5.33–37 |
| 2 | 1 Kg 19.19–21 | Ps 16.1–7 | Mt 5.33–37 |

**Week of Proper 11**

*Mon*

| | | | |
|---|---|---|---|
| 1 | 2 Cor 6.1–10 | Ps 98 | Mt 5.38–42 |
| 2 | 1 Kg 21.1–16 | Ps 5.1–6 | Mt 5.38–42 |

*Tue*

| | | | |
|---|---|---|---|
| 1 | 2 Cor 8.1–9 | Ps 146 | Mt 5.43–48 |
| 2 | 1 Kg 21.17–29 | Ps 51.1–11 | Mt 5.43–48 |

*Wed*

| | | | |
|---|---|---|---|
| 1 | 2 Cor 9.6–11 | Ps 112.1–9 | Mt 6.1–6, 16–18 |
| 2 | 2 Kg 2.1, 6–14 | Ps 31.19–24 | Mt 6.1–6, 16–18 |

*Thu*

| | | | |
|---|---|---|---|
| 1 | 2 Cor 11.1–11 | Ps 111 | Mt 6.7–15 |
| 2 | Sir 48.1–14 | Ps 97 | Mt 6.7–15 |

*Fri*

1       2 Cor 11.18, 21b–30       Ps 34.1–6       Mt 6.19–23
2       2 Kg 11.1–4, 9–20       Ps 132.11–19       Mt 6.19–23

*Sat*

1       2 Cor 12.1–10       Ps 34.7–14       Mt 6.24–34
2       2 Chr 24.17–25       Ps 89.19–33       Mt 6.24–34

## Week of Proper 12

*Mon*

1       Gen 12.1–9       Ps 33.12–22       Mt 7.1–5
2       2 Kg 17.5–8, 13–18       Ps 60       Mt 7.1–5

*Tue*

1       Gen 13.2, 5–18       Ps 15       Mt 7.6, 12–14
2       2 Kg 19.9–21, 31–36       Ps 48       Mt 7.6, 12–14

*Wed*

1       Gen 15.1–12, 17–18       Ps 105.1–9       Mt 7.15–20
2       2 Kg 22.8–13; 23.1–3       Ps 119.33–40       Mt 7.15–20

*Thu*

1       Gen 16.1–12, 15–16       Ps 106.1–5       Mt 7.21–29
2       2 Kg 24.8–17       Ps 79       Mt 7.21–29

*Fri*

1       Gen 17.1, 9–10, 15–22       Ps 128       Mt 8.1–4
2       2 Kg 25.1–12       Ps 137.1–6       Mt 8.1–4

*Sat*

1       Gen 18.1–15       C 18 *or* Ps 123       Mt 8.5–17
2       Lam 2.2, 10–14, 18–19       Ps 74.1–8, 17–20       Mt 8.5–17

## Week of Proper 13

*Mon*

1       Gen 18.16–33       Ps 103.1–10       Mt 8.18–22
2       Am 2.6–10, 13–16       Ps 50.14–24       Mt 8.18–22

*Tue*

1       Gen 19.15–29       Ps 26       Mt 8.23–27
2       Am 3.1–8; 4.11–12       Ps 5       Mt 8.23–27

*Wed*

1       Gen 21.5, 8–20      Ps 34.1–8      Mt 8.28–34

2       Am 5.14–15, 21–24      Ps 50.7–15      Mt 8.28–34

*Thu*

1       Gen 22.1–14      Ps 116.1–8      Mt 9.1–8

2       Am 7.10–17      Ps 19.7–10      Mt 9.1–8

*Fri*

1       Gen 23.1–4, 19; 24.1–8, 62–67      Ps 106.1–5      Mt 9.9–13

2       Am 8.4–6, 9–12      Ps 119.1–8      Mt 9.9–13

*Sat*

1       Gen 27.1–9, 15–29      Ps 135.1–6      Mt 9.14–17

2       Am 9.11–15      Ps 85.7–13      Mt 9.14–17

## Week of Proper 14

*Mon*

1       Gen 28.10–22      Ps 91.1–6, 14–16      Mt 9.18–26

2       Hos 2.16–23      Ps 145.1–9      Mt 9.18–26

*Tue*

1       Gen 32.22–32      Ps 17.1–8      Mt 9.32–38

2       Hos 8.4–7, 11–13      Ps 115.1–10      Mt 9.32–38

*Wed*

1       Gen 41.55–57; 42.5–7a, 17–24a      Ps 33.1–4, 18–22      Mt 10.1–7

2       Hos 10.1–3, 7–8, 12      Ps 105.1–7      Mt 10.1–7

*Thu*

1       Gen 44.18—45.5      Ps 105.7–21      Mt 10.7–15

2       Hos 11.1–9      Ps 80.1–7      Mt 10.7–15

*Fri*

1       Gen 46.1–7, 28–30      Ps 37.3–4, 19–20, 28–29, 41–42
        Mt 10.16–23

2       Hos 14.1–9      Ps 51.1–12      Mt 10.16–23

*Sat*

1       Gen 49.29–33      Ps 105.1–7      Mt 10.24–33

2       Is 6.1–8      Ps 93      Mt 10.24–33

## Week of Proper 15

*Mon*
1     Ex 1.8–14, 22     Ps 124     Mt 10.34—11.1
2     Is 1.10–17     Ps 50.7–15     Mt 10.34—11.1

*Tue*
1     Ex 2.1–15     Ps 69.1–2, 31–38     Mt 11.20–24
2     Is 7.1–9     Ps 48     Mt 11.20–24

*Wed*
1     Ex 3.1–12     Ps 103.1–7     Mt 11.25–27
2     Is 10.5–7, 13–16     Ps 94.5–15     Mt 11.25–27

*Thu*
1     Ex 3.13–20     Ps 105.1–15     Mt 11.28–30
2     Is 26.7–9, 12, 16–19     Ps 102.12–22     Mt 11.28–30

*Fri*
1     Ex 11.10—12.14     Ps 116.10–17     Mt 12.1–8
2     Is 38.1–6, 21     Ps 6     Mt 12.1–8

*Sat*
1     Ex 12.37–42     Ps 136.1–3, 10–15     Mt 12.14–21
2     Mic 2.1–5     Ps 10.1–9, 18–19     Mt 12.14–21

## Week of Proper 16

*Mon*
1     Ex 14.5–18     C 1 *or* Ps 114     Mt 12.38–42
2     Mic 6.1–8     Ps 50.5–15     Mt 12.38–42

*Tue*
1     Ex 14.21—15.1     C 1 *or* Ps 114     Mt 12.46–50
2     Mic 7.14–15, 18–20     Ps 85.1–7     Mt 12.46–50

*Wed*
1     Ex 16.1–5, 9–15     Ps 78.18–29     Mt 13.1–9
2     Jer 1.1, 4–10     Ps 71.1–6, 15–17     Mt 13.1–9

*Thu*
1     Ex 19.1–20     C 13 *or* Ps 24.1–6     Mt 13.10–17
2     Jer 2.1–3, 7–13     Ps 36.5–10     Mt 13.10–17

*Fri*

| | | | |
|---|---|---|---|
| 1 | Ex 20.1–17 | Ps 19.7–10 | Mt 13.18–23 |
| 2 | Jer 3.14–18 | C 8 *or* Ps 121 | Mt 13.18–23 |

*Sat*

| | | | |
|---|---|---|---|
| 1 | Ex 24.3–8 | Ps 50.1–15 | Mt 13.24–30 |
| 2 | Jer 7.1–11 | Ps 84 | Mt 13.24–30 |

## Week of Proper 17

*Mon*

| | | | |
|---|---|---|---|
| 1 | Ex 32.15–24, 30–34 | Ps 106.19–23 | Mt 13.31–35 |
| 2 | Jer 13.1–11 | Ps 95 | Mt 13.31–35 |

*Tue*

| | | | |
|---|---|---|---|
| 1 | Ex 33.7–11; 34.5–10, 27–28 | Ps 103.5–13 | Mt 13.36–43 |
| 2 | Jer 14.17–22 | Ps 79.9–13 | Mt 13.36–43 |

*Wed*

| | | | |
|---|---|---|---|
| 1 | Ex 34.29–35 | Ps 99 | Mt 13.44–46 |
| 2 | Jer 15.10, 15–21 | Ps 59.1–4, 18–20 | Mt 13.44–46 |

*Thu*

| | | | |
|---|---|---|---|
| 1 | Ex 40.16–21, 34–38 | Ps 84 | Mt 13.47–53 |
| 2 | Jer 18.1–6 | Ps 146.1–5 | Mt 13.47–53 |

*Fri*

| | | | |
|---|---|---|---|
| 1 | Lev 23.1–11, 26–38 | Ps 81.1–10 | Mt 13.54–58 |
| 2 | Jer 26.1–9 | Ps 69.1–9, 14–15 | Mt 13.54–58 |

*Sat*

| | | | |
|---|---|---|---|
| 1 | Lev 25.1, 8–17 | Ps 67 | Mt 14.1–12 |
| 2 | Jer 26.11–16, 24 | Ps 69.16–17, 31–35 | Mt 14.1–12 |

## Week of Proper 18

*Mon*

| | | | |
|---|---|---|---|
| 1 | Num 11.4–15 | Ps 81.10–16 | Mt 14.22–36 |
| 2 | Jer 28.1–17 | Ps 119.89–96 | Mt 14.13–21 |

*Tue*

| | | | |
|---|---|---|---|
| 1 | Num 12.1–17 | Ps 51.1–12 | Mt 15.1–2, 10–14 |
| 2 | Jer 30.1–2, 12–22 | Ps 102.16–22 | Mt 14.22–36 |

*Wed*

1    Num 13.1–2, 25—14.1, 26–35   Ps 106.6–14, 21–23
      Mt 15.21–28

2    Jer 31.1–7  C 8 *or* Ps 121   Mt 15.21–28

*Thu*

1    Num 20.1–13  Ps 95.1–9  Mt 16.13–23

2    Jer 31.31–34  Ps 51.11–18  Mt 16.13–23

*Fri*

1    Dt 4.32–40  Ps 77.11–20  Mt 16.24–28

2    Nah 1.15; 2.2; 3.1–3, 6–7  Ps 124  Mt 16.24–28

*Sat*

1    Dt 6.4–13  Ps 18.1–2, 48–50  Mt 17.14–20

2    Hab 1.12—2.4  Ps 9.7–12  Mt 17.14–20

## Week of Proper 19

*Mon*

1    Dt 10.12–22  Ps 148  Mt 17.22–27

2    Ezek 1.1–5, 24–28  Ps 148.1–4, 13–14  Mt 17.22–27

*Tue*

1    Dt 31.1–8  Ps 111  Mt 18.1–5, 10, 12–14

2    Ezek 2.8—3.4  Ps 119.65–72  Mt 18.1–5, 10, 12–14

*Wed*

1    Dt 34.1–12  Ps 66.1–8  Mt 18.15–20

2    Ezek 9.1–7; 10.18–22  Ps 113  Mt 18.15–20

*Thu*

1    Jos 3.7–17  Ps 114  Mt 18.21—19.1

2    Ezek 12.1–16  Ps 39.11–15  Mt 18.21—19.1

*Fri*

1    Jos 24.1–13  Ps 136.1–3, 16–22  Mt 19.3–12

2    Ezek 16.1–15, 59–63  C 6 *or* Ps 11  Mt 19.3–12

*Sat*

1    Jos 24.14–29  Ps 16.1, 5–11  Mt 19.13–15

2    Ezek 18.1–13, 30–32  Ps 51.11–18  Mt 19.13–15

## Week of Proper 20

*Mon*

| 1 | Jg 2.11–19 | Ps 51.1–10 | Mt 19.16–22 |
| 2 | Ezek 24.15–24 | Ps 79.1–8 | Mt 19.16–22 |

*Tue*

| 1 | Jg 5.11–24a | Ps 85.8–13 | Mt 19.23–30 |
| 2 | Ezek 28.1–10 | Ps 60.1–5 | Mt 19.23–30 |

*Wed*

| 1 | Jg 9.6–15 | Ps 21.1–6 | Mt 20.1–16a |
| 2 | Ezek 34.1–11 | Ps 23 | Mt 20.1–16a |

*Thu*

| 1 | Jg 11.29–40 | Ps 130 | Mt 22.1–14 |
| 2 | Ezek 36.22–28 | Ps 51.8–13 | Mt 22.1–14 |

*Fri*

| 1 | Ru 1.1–22 | Ps 146 | Mt 22.34–40 |
| 2 | Ezek 37.1–14 | Ps 107.1–8 | Mt 22.34–40 |

*Sat*

| 1 | Ru 2.1–11; 4.13–17 | Ps 128 | Mt 23.1–12 |
| 2 | Ezek 43.1–7 | Ps 85.8–13 | Mt 23.1–12 |

## Week of Proper 21

*Mon*

| 1 | 1 Th 1.1–10 | Ps 149.1–5 | Mt 23.13–22 |
| 2 | 2 Th 1.1–5, 11–12 | Ps 96.1–5 | Mt 23.13–22 |

*Tue*

| 1 | 1 Th 2.1–8 | Ps 139.1–9 | Mt 23.23–26 |
| 2 | 2 Th 2.1–17 | Ps 96.7–13 | Mt 23.23–26 |

*Wed*

| 1 | 1 Th 2.9–13 | Ps 126 | Mt 23.27–32 |
| 2 | 2 Th 3.6–10, 16–18 | Ps 128 | Mt 23.27–32 |

*Thu*

| 1 | 1 Th 3.6–13 | Ps 90.13–17 | Mt 24.42–51 |
| 2 | 1 Cor 1.1–9 | Ps 145.1–7 | Mt 24.42–51 |

*Fri*

1     1 Th 4.1–8     Ps 97     Mt 25.1–13
2     1 Cor 1.17–25     Ps 33.1–11     Mt 25.1–13

*Sat*

1     1 Th 4.9–12     Ps 98     Mt 25.14–30
2     1 Cor 1.26–31     Ps 33.12–22     Mt 25.14–30

## Week of Proper 22

*Mon*

1     1 Th 4.13–18     Ps 96     Lk 4.16–30
2     1 Cor 2.1–5     Ps 119.97–103     Lk 4.16–30

*Tue*

1     1 Th 5.1–11     Ps 27.1–6, 17–18     Lk 4.31–37
2     1 Cor 2.10–16     Ps 145.8–15     Lk 4.31–37

*Wed*

1     Col 1.1–8     Ps 34.9–22     Lk 4.38–44
2     1 Cor 3.1–9     Ps 62     Lk 4.38–44

*Thu*

1     Col 1.9–14     Ps 98     Lk 5.1–11
2     1 Cor 3.18–23     Ps 24.1–6     Lk 5.1–11

*Fri*

1     Col 1.15–20     Ps 100     Lk 5.33–39
2     1 Cor 4.1–5     Ps 37.1–12     Lk 5.33–39

*Sat*

1     Col 1.21–23     Ps 54     Lk 6.1–5
2     1 Cor 4.6–15     Ps 145.14–22     Lk 6.1–5

## Week of Proper 23

*Mon*

1     Col 1.24—2.3     Ps 62.1–7     Lk 6.6–11
2     1 Cor 5.1–8     Ps 5     Lk 6.6–11

*Tue*

1     Col 2.6–15     Ps 145.1–9     Lk 6.12–19
2     1 Cor 6.1–11     Ps 149.1–5     Lk 6.12–19

*Wed*

| 1 | Col 3.1–11 | Ps 145.10–13 | Lk 6.20–26 |
| 2 | 1 Cor 7.25–31 | Ps 45.11–18 | Lk 6.20–26 |

*Thu*

| 1 | Col 3.12–17 | Ps 150 | Lk 6.27–38 |
| 2 | 1 Cor 8.1–13 | Ps 139.1–9, 22–23 | Lk 6.27–38 |

*Fri*

| 1 | 1 Tim 1.1–2, 12–14 | Ps 16 | Lk 6.39–42 |
| 2 | 1 Cor 9.16–27 | Ps 84 | Lk 6.39–42 |

*Sat*

| 1 | 1 Tim 1.15–17 | Ps 113 | Lk 6.43–49 |
| 2 | 1 Cor 10.14–22 | Ps 116.10–17 | Lk 6.43–49 |

## Week of Proper 24

*Mon*

| 1 | 1 Tim 2.1–8 | Ps 28 | Lk 7.1–10 |
| 2 | 1 Cor 11.17–28, 33 | Ps 40.8–12 | Lk 7.1–10 |

*Tue*

| 1 | 1 Tim 3.1–13 | Ps 101 | Lk 7.11–17 |
| 2 | 1 Cor 12.12–14, 27–31 | Ps 100 | Lk 7.11–17 |

*Wed*

| 1 | 1 Tim 3.14–16 | Ps 111.1–6 | Lk 7.31–35 |
| 2 | 1 Cor 12.31—13.13 | Ps 33.1–12, 22 | Lk 7.31–35 |

*Thu*

| 1 | 1 Tim 4.12–16 | Ps 111.7–10 | Lk 7.36–50 |
| 2 | 1 Cor 15.1–11 | Ps 118.14–29 | Lk 7.36–50 |

*Fri*

| 1 | 1 Tim 6.1–12 | Ps 49.1–9 | Lk 8.1–3 |
| 2 | 1 Cor 15.12–20 | Ps 17.1–7 | Lk 8.1–3 |

*Sat*

| 1 | 1 Tim 6.13–16 | Ps 100 | Lk 8.4–15 |
| 2 | 1 Cor 15.35–49 | Ps 30.1–5 | Lk 8.4–15 |

## Week of Proper 25

*Mon*

1    Ezra 1.1–6      Ps 126     Lk 8.16–18
2    Pr 3.27–35      Ps 15      Lk 8.16–18

*Tue*

1    Ezra 6.1–8, 12–19     Ps 124     Lk 8.19–21
2    Pr 21.1–6, 10–13     Ps 119.1–8     Lk 8.19–21

*Wed*

1    Ezra 9.5–9      C 7 *or* Ps 48     Lk 9.1–6
2    Pr 30.5–9       Ps 119.105–112     Lk 9.1–6

*Thu*

1    Hag 1.1–8       Ps 149.1–5     Lk 9.7–9
2    Ec 1.1–11       Ps 90.1–6      Lk 9.7–9

*Fri*

1    Hag 1.15b—2.9      Ps 43     Lk 9.18–22
2    Ec 3.1–11       Ps 144.1–4     Lk 9.18–22

*Sat*

1    Zech 2.1–11     C 8 *or* Ps 121     Lk 9.43b–45
2    Ec 11.9—12.8     Ps 90.1–2, 12–17     Lk 9.43b–45

## Week of Proper 26

*Mon*

1    Zech 8.1–8      Ps 102.11–22     Lk 9.46–50
2    Job 1.6–22      Ps 17.1–7      Lk 9.46–50

*Tue*

1    Zech 8.20–23     Ps 87     Lk 9.51–56
2    Job 3.1–3, 11–23     Ps 88.1–8     Lk 9.51–56

*Wed*

1    Neh 2.1–8       Ps 137.1–6     Lk 9.57–62
2    Job 9.1–16      Ps 88.10–15     Lk 9.57–62

*Thu*

1    Neh 8.1–12      Ps 19.7–10     Lk 10.1–12
2    Job 19.21–27     Ps 27.10–18     Lk 10.1–12

*Fri*

| | | | |
|---|---|---|---|
| 1 | Bar 1.15–21 | Ps 79.1–9 | Lk 10.13–16 |
| 2 | Job 38.1, 12–21; 40.1–5 | Ps 139.1–17 | Lk 10.13–16 |

*Sat*

| | | | |
|---|---|---|---|
| 1 | Bar 4.5–12, 27–29 | Ps 69.34–38 | Lk 10.17–24 |
| 2 | Job 42.1–6, 12–17 | Ps 119.169–176 | Lk 10.17–24 |

## Week of Proper 27

*Mon*

| | | | |
|---|---|---|---|
| 1 | Jon 1.1–17; 2.10 | Ps 130 | Lk 10.25–37 |
| 2 | Gal 1.6–12 | Ps 111.1–6 | Lk 10.25–37 |

*Tue*

| | | | |
|---|---|---|---|
| 1 | Jon 3.1–10 | Ps 6 | Lk 10.38–42 |
| 2 | Gal 1.13–24 | Ps 139.1–14 | Lk 10.38–42 |

*Wed*

| | | | |
|---|---|---|---|
| 1 | Jon 4.1–11 | Ps 86.1–10 | Lk 11.1–4 |
| 2 | Gal 2.1–2, 7–14 | Ps 117 | Lk 11.1–4 |

*Thu*

| | | | |
|---|---|---|---|
| 1 | Mal 3.13—4.2a | Ps 1 | Lk 11.5–13 |
| 2 | Gal 3.1–5 | C 19 *or* Ps 89.19–29 | Lk 11.5–13 |

*Fri*

| | | | |
|---|---|---|---|
| 1 | Jl 1.13–15; 2.1–2 | Ps 9.1–8 | Lk 11.14–26 |
| 2 | Gal 3.7–14 | Ps 111.4–10 | Lk 11.14–26 |

*Sat*

| | | | |
|---|---|---|---|
| 1 | Jl 3.12–21 | Ps 97 | Lk 11.27–28 |
| 2 | Gal 3.21–29 | Ps 105.1–7 | Lk 11.27–28 |

## Week of Proper 28

*Mon*

| | | | |
|---|---|---|---|
| 1 | Rom 1.1–7 | Ps 98 | Lk 11.29–32 |
| 2 | Gal 4.21—5.1 | Ps 113 | Lk 11.29–32 |

*Tue*

| | | | |
|---|---|---|---|
| 1 | Rom 1.16–25 | Ps 19.1–4 | Lk 11.37–41 |
| 2 | Gal 5.1–6 | Ps 119.41–48 | Lk 11.37–41 |

*Wed*

| 1 | Rom 2.1–11 | Ps 62.1–9 | Lk 11.42–46 |
| 2 | Gal 5.16–25 | Ps 1 | Lk 11.42–46 |

*Thu*

| 1 | Rom 3.21–31 | Ps 130 | Lk 11.47–54 |
| 2 | Eph 1.1–10 | Ps 98 | Lk 11.47–54 |

*Fri*

| 1 | Rom 4.1–8 | Ps 32 | Lk 12.1–7 |
| 2 | Eph 1.11–14 | Ps 33.1–12 | Lk 12.1–7 |

*Sat*

| 1 | Rom 4.13–18 | Ps 105.5–10, 42–45 | Lk 12.8–12 |
| 2 | Gal 1.15–23 | Ps 8 | Lk 12.8–12 |

## Week of Proper 29

*Mon*

| 1 | Rom 4.13, 19–25 | C 19 *or* Ps 89.19–29 | Lk 12.13–21 |
| 2 | Eph 2.1–10 | Ps 100 | Lk 12.13–21 |

*Tue*

| 1 | Rom 5.6–21 | Ps 40.8–11 | Lk 12.35–38 |
| 2 | Eph 2.11–22 | Ps 85.8–13 | Lk 12.35–38 |

*Wed*

| 1 | Rom 6.12–18 | Ps 124 | Lk 12.39–48 |
| 2 | Eph 3.4–12 | C 3 *or* Ps 113 *or* 122 | Lk 12.39–48 |

*Thu*

| 1 | Rom 6.19–23 | Ps 1 | Lk 12.49–53 |
| 2 | Eph 3.14–21 | Ps 33.1–11 | Lk 12.49–53 |

*Fri*

| 1 | Rom 7.18–25a | Ps 119.33–40 | Lk 12.54–59 |
| 2 | Eph 4.1–6 | Ps 24.1–6 | Lk 12.54–59 |

*Sat*

| 1 | Rom 8.1–11 | Ps 24.1–6 | Lk 13.1–9 |
| 2 | Eph 4.7–16 | Ps 122 | Lk 13.1–9 |

## Week of Proper 30

*Mon*

| | | | |
|---|---|---|---|
| 1 | Rom 8.12–17 | Ps 68.1–6, 19–20 | Lk 13.10–17 |
| 2 | Eph 5.1–8 | Ps 1 | Lk 13.10–17 |

*Tue*

| | | | |
|---|---|---|---|
| 1 | Rom 8.18–25 | Ps 126 | Lk 13.18–21 |
| 2 | Eph 5.21–33 | Ps 128 | Lk 13.18–21 |

*Wed*

| | | | |
|---|---|---|---|
| 1 | Rom 8.26–30 | Ps 13 | Lk 13.22–30 |
| 2 | Eph 6.1–9 | Ps 145.10–19 | Lk 13.22–30 |

*Thu*

| | | | |
|---|---|---|---|
| 1 | Rom 8.31–39 | Ps 30 | Lk 13.31–35 |
| 2 | Eph 6.10–20 | Ps 144.1–10 | Lk 13.31–35 |

*Fri*

| | | | |
|---|---|---|---|
| 1 | Rom 9.1–5 | Ps 147.13–21 | Lk 14.1–6 |
| 2 | Phil 1.1–11 | Ps 111 | Lk 14.1–6 |

*Sat*

| | | | |
|---|---|---|---|
| 1 | Rom 11.1–6, 11–12, 25–29 | Ps 94.14–19 | Lk 14.1, 7–11 |
| 2 | Phil 1.12–26 | Ps 42.1–7 | Lk 14.1, 7–11 |

## Week of Proper 31

*Mon*

| | | | |
|---|---|---|---|
| 1 | Rom 11.29–36 | Ps 69.31–38 | Lk 14.12–14 |
| 2 | Phil 2.1–4 | Ps 131 | Lk 14.12–14 |

*Tue*

| | | | |
|---|---|---|---|
| 1 | Rom 12.1–16 | Ps 131 | Lk 14.15–24 |
| 2 | Phil 2.5–11 | Ps 22.22–28 | Lk 14.15–24 |

*Wed*

| | | | |
|---|---|---|---|
| 1 | Rom 13.8–10 | Ps 112 | Lk 14.25–33 |
| 2 | Phil 2.12–18 | Ps 27.1–6, 17–18 | Lk 14.25–33 |

*Thu*

| | | | |
|---|---|---|---|
| 1 | Rom 14.7–12 | Ps 27.1–6, 17–18 | Lk 15.1–10 |
| 2 | Phil 3.3–8a | Ps 105.1–7 | Lk 15.1–10 |

*Fri*

| 1 | Rom 15.14–21 | Ps 98 | Lk 16.1–8 | |
| 2 | Phil 3.17—4.1 | Ps 122 | Lk 16.1–8 | |

*Sat*

| 1 | Rom 16.3–9, 16, 22–27 | Ps 145.1–7 | Lk 16.9–15 |
| 2 | Phil 4.10–19 | Ps 112 | Lk 16.9–15 | |

## Week of Proper 32

*Mon*

| 1 | Wis 1.1–7 | Ps 139.1–9 | Lk 17.1–6 |
| 2 | Tit 1.1–9 | Ps 24.1–6 | Lk 17.1–6 |

*Tue*

| 1 | Wis 2.23—3.9 | Ps 34.15–22 | Lk 17.7–10 |
| 2 | Tit 2.1–14 | Ps 37.1–6, 28–29 | Lk 17.7–10 |

*Wed*

| 1 | Wis 6.1–11 | Ps 82 | Lk 17.11–19 |
| 2 | Tit 3.1–7 | Ps 23 | Lk 17.11–19 |

*Thu*

| 1 | Wis 7.21—8.1 | Ps 119.89–96 | Lk 17.20–25 |
| 2 | Philem 1.4–20 | Ps 146 | Lk 17.20–25 |

*Fri*

| 1 | Wis 13.1–9 | Ps 19.1–4 | Lk 17.26–37 |
| 2 | 2 Jn 4–9 | Ps 119.1–8 | Lk 17.26–37 |

*Sat*

| 1 | Wis 18.14–16; 19.6–9 | Ps 105.1–6, 37–45 | Lk 18.1–8 |
| 2 | 3 Jn 5–8 | Ps 112 | Lk 18.1–8 |

## Week of Proper 33

*Mon*

| 1 | 1 Macc 1.1–15, 54–57, 62–64 | Ps 79 | Lk 18.35–43 |
| 2 | Rev 1.1–4; 2.1–5 | Ps 1 | Lk 18.35–43 |

*Tue*

| 1 | 2 Macc 6.18–31 | Ps 3 | Lk 19.1–10 |
| 2 | Rev 3.1–6, 14–22 | Ps 15 | Lk 19.1–10 |

*Wed*

1     2 Macc 7.1, 20–31, 39–42    Ps 17.1–8    Lk 19.11–28

2     Rev 4.1–11    Ps 150    Lk 19.11–28

*Thu*

1     1 Macc 2.15–29    Ps 129    Lk 19.41–44

2     Rev 5.1–10    Ps 149.1–5    Lk 19.41–44

*Fri*

1     1 Macc 4.36–37, 52–59    C 3 *or* Ps 113 *or* 122    Lk 19.45–48

2     Rev 10.8–11    Ps 119.65–72    Lk 19.45–48

*Sat*

1     1 Macc 6.1–13    Ps 124    Lk 20.27–40

2     Rev 11.1–12    Ps 144.1–10    Lk 20.27–40

## Week of the Reign of Christ—Proper 34

*Mon*

1     Dan 1.1–20    C 13 *or* Ps 24.1–6    Lk 21.1–4

2     Rev 14.1–5    Ps 24.1–6    Lk 21.1–4

*Tue*

1     Dan 2.31–45    C 14 *or* Ps 96    Lk 21.5–9

2     Rev 14.14–20    Ps 96    Lk 21.5–9

*Wed*

1     Dan 5.1–6, 13–28    C 14 *or* Ps 98    Lk 21.10–19

2     Rev 15.1–4    Ps 98    Lk 21.10–19

*Thu*

1     Dan 6.6–27    C 14 *or* Ps 99    Lk 21.20–28

2     Rev 18.1–2, 21—19.3, 9    Ps 100    Lk 21.20–28

*Fri*

1     Dan 7.1–14    C 15 *or* Ps 93    Lk 21.29–33

2     Rev 20.1–4, 11—21.4    Ps 84    Lk 21.29–33

*Sat*

1     Dan 7.15–27    C 16 *or* Ps 95.1–7    Lk 21.34–36

2     Rev 22.1–7    Ps 95.1–7    Lk 21.34–36

# A Short Table of Psalms and Readings

### In the Morning

Psalms 51, 63.1–8, 95.1–7, 100, 148, 149, 150.

Deuteronomy 4.39–40, Deuteronomy 6.4–9, Isaiah 55.1–3, Matthew 5.1–12, John 14.15–17, Romans 12.9–13, Romans 12.14–21, I John 2.7–10.

### At Mid–Day

Psalms 19.1–6, 91, a portion of 119, 122, 124, 126, 127, 128, 130.

Isaiah 60.19–21, Malachi 1.11, John 15.12–17, 2 Corinthians 5.17–18, Galatians 5.22–25.

### In the Early Evening

Psalms 23, 117, 121, 140, 141.

Isaiah 62.6–7, 10–12, Hosea 6.1–3, Matthew 15.32–38, Mark 4.35–41, Mark 8.1–10, Mark 8.34–38, Luke 12.32–40, Romans 5.6–11, Ephesians 6.10–18, Philippians 4.4–9, Colossians 3.12–17.

### In the Late Evening

Psalms 4, 31.1–5, 91.

Isaiah 45.18–19, Hosea 14.4–7, 9, Luke 24.13–17, 28–35, Luke 24.36–43, John 3.1–8, John 21.4–8, John 21.9–14, John 21.15–17, Ephesians 1.3–14, 1 Timothy 6.12–16, Titus 2.11–14, Hebrews 12.1–2, I Peter 5.6–11, Revelation 22.1–5.

# Pastoral Offices

# Concerning Marriage in the Church

*The Canon Law concerning Marriage in the Church is contained in Canon XXI of General Synod. The rubrics that follow are intended to apply the directions of the Canon to the services, and the full text of the Canon should be consulted where necessary.*

*Marriage is a public service of the Church. It should therefore be solemnized in the body of the church (except for sufficient cause to the contrary) in the presence of the friends and neighbours of those who come to be married and of the congregation of the Church.*

*The requirements of the civil laws of the province or territory must be met.*

*It shall be the duty of those who intend to marry to give notice to the minister at least thirty days before the day proposed for the wedding. The minister may at his/her discretion waive this requirement for sufficient cause, in which case the bishop of the diocese shall be notified in writing, with a statement of the cause for the decision.*

*It shall be the duty of the minister, when application is made for a marriage to be solemnized, to enquire whether there is any impediment to the marriage and its solemnization. It shall also be the duty of the minister to provide or secure appropriate means of education, so that all who seek marriage in the Church may attain a Christian understanding of its purpose and may be encouraged to give effect, with God's help, to the vows which they are preparing to make.*

*No minister shall solemnize the marriage of two persons neither of whom has been baptized. If two persons, one of whom has not been baptized, desire to be married, the matter shall be referred to the bishop of the diocese; the bishop's order and direction shall be followed.*

*When banns are to be published, they shall be published in the church where the marriage is to be celebrated and in any other church as required by civil law. In addition they may be published in any other church at the request of a party to the marriage. The following form of banns appears in Canon XXI:*

   *The minister shall say together with such addition as the civil law may require:*

I publish the Banns of Marriage between N
of . . . and N of . . . If any of you know cause or just
impediment why these two persons should not be joined
together in Holy Matrimony, you are to declare it. This is the
first (or second or third) time of asking.

*Any person knowing of a lawful reason why a marriage may not be
solemnized should inform the officiating minister before the service.*

## Concerning the Service

*Every marriage shall be solemnized in the presence of at least two witnesses in
addition to the officiating minister.*

*The incumbent shall be responsible for the conduct of the marriage service.
Hymns, anthems, and readings at the service shall be those only which may
be found in Holy Scripture, in the* Book of Common Prayer, *the Hymn
Book, or in texts approved by ecclesiastical authority. Relatives or members of
the wedding party may be invited to read the scripture lessons and lead the
intercessions.*

*Where both bride and bridegroom are entitled to receive communion, it is
desirable that the form of service in which the marriage rite is incorporated in
the celebration of the eucharist be used (p. 528).*

*A proper preface for Marriage has been provided for Eucharistic Prayer 3.
One of the other eucharistic prayers may be used, if desired.*

*Variations in the text may be made by the couple with the consent of the
minister, according to diocesan policy, but no alterations may be made in the
declarations to be made by the parties or in the marriage vows themselves.*

*Suitable points in the service for hymns or anthems are at the opening, before
or after the sermon, after the couple have been declared to be husband and
wife, during or after the communion, or at the close of the service. It may be
necessary to provide seating for the bridal party if there is to be a sermon.*

*When the form of service on page 541 is celebrated by a deacon, the nuptial
blessing and the blessing of the ring(s) shall be appropriately changed.*

*It is desirable that the register be signed publicly in the body of the church.*

# The Celebration and Blessing of a Marriage

with the Holy Eucharist

## The Gathering of the Community

*The people stand. The bride and bridegroom stand before the celebrant.*

Celebrant The grace of our Lord Jesus Christ,
   and the love of God,
   and the fellowship of the Holy Spirit,
   be with you all.

People  **And also with you.**

Celebrant Dear friends, we have come together in the presence of God to witness the marriage of N and N, and to rejoice with them.

   Marriage is a gift of God and a means of his grace, in which man and woman become one flesh. It is God's purpose that, as husband and wife give themselves to each other in love, they shall grow together and be united in that love, as Christ is united with his Church.

   The union of man and woman in heart, body, and mind is intended for their mutual comfort and help, that they may know each other with delight and tenderness in acts of love [and that they may be blessed in the procreation, care, and upbringing of children].

   In marriage, husband and wife give themselves to each other, to care for each other in good times and in bad. They are linked to each other's families, and they begin a new life together in the community.

It is a way of life that all should reverence, and none should lightly undertake.

If anyone present knows a reason why N and N may not lawfully marry, they must declare it now.

N and N, if either of you knows a reason why you may not lawfully marry, you must declare it now.

N and N have come to enter this holy state. They have complied with Civil and Canon Law and have been duly prepared to enter into marriage. They will each give their consent to the other; they will exchange solemn vows, and in token of this, they will (each) give and receive a ring.

We pray with them that by God's help they may fulfil his purpose for the whole of their earthly life together.

Let us pray.

God our Father,
you have taught us through your Son
that love is the fulfilling of the law.
Grant to these your servants
that loving one another
they may continue in your love
until their lives' end;
through Jesus Christ our Lord.

*People*    **Amen.**

# The Proclamation of the Word

*Two or three readings, including a Gospel reading, shall normally be read.*
*Members of the family and friends of the bride and groom may read lessons.*
*A psalm, canticle, hymn, anthem, or period of silence may follow the lessons.*
*Suggested readings may be found on p. 549. The readings and the response*
*shall be selected in consultation with the bride and groom.*

*At the conclusion of readings from the Old Testament and the New Testament writings other than the Gospels, the reader says,*

The word of the Lord.
*People*       **Thanks be to God.**

*Silence may be kept. A psalm, canticle, hymn, or anthem may follow.*

*All stand for the Gospel.*

*Reader*       The Lord be with you.
*People*       **And also with you.**

*Reader*       The Holy Gospel of our Lord Jesus Christ
               according to . . .
*People*       **Glory to you, Lord Jesus Christ.**

*At the conclusion of the Gospel, the reader says,*

The Gospel of Christ.
*People*       **Praise to you, Lord Jesus Christ.**

*A sermon may follow.*


# The Wedding

*The people stand. The celebrant says to the bridegroom,*

               *N* will you give yourself to *N* to be her husband:
               to love her, comfort her, honour and protect her;
               and forsaking all others, to be faithful to her
               so long as you both shall live?
*Bridegroom*   **I will.**

*The celebrant says to the bride,*

               *N* will you give yourself to *N* to be his wife:
               to love him, comfort him, honour and protect him;
               and forsaking all others, to be faithful to him
               so long as you both shall live?
*Bride*        **I will.**

*The celebrant may address the following question to the families of the bride and bridegroom.*

Do you, members of the families of N and N, give your blessing to this marriage?

*Answer*     **We do.**

*The celebrant addresses the following to all present.*

You are the witnesses to these vows now being made. Will you do all in your power to support and uphold this marriage?

*Answer*     **We will.**

*The bride and bridegroom face each other and join hands.*

*Bridegroom*    I N take you N to be my wife,
to have and to hold
from this day forward;
for better, for worse,
for richer, for poorer,
in sickness and in health,
to love and to cherish
for the rest of our lives,
according to God's holy law.
This is my solemn vow.

*Bride*    I N take you N to be my husband,
to have and to hold
from this day forward;
for better, for worse,
for richer, for poorer,
in sickness and in health,
to love and to cherish
for the rest of our lives,
according to God's holy law.
This is my solemn vow.

*They loose hands. The celebrant receives the ring(s) and addresses the congregation in these or similar words.*

> Dear friends in Christ,
> let us ask God to bless *this ring*,
> that *it* may be a symbol of the vow and covenant
> N and N have made this day.

*The community may pray silently. The celebrant then says,*

> Blessed are you,
> God of steadfast love,
> source of our joy and end of our hope.
> Bless *this ring* given and received
> that *it* may be a symbol of the vow and covenant
> N and N have made this day,
> through Jesus Christ our Lord.

People      **Amen.**

*The bridegroom (and the bride in her turn) places the ring on the ring-finger of the other's hand and says,*

> N, I give you this ring
> as a symbol of my vow.
> With all that I am and all that I have,
> I honour you in the name of God.

*The bride and bridegroom join right hands.*

Celebrant    N and N have joined themselves to each other by solemn vows, signified by the joining of hands and the giving and receiving of *a ring*. I declare that they are husband and wife, in the name of the Father, and of the Son, and of the Holy Spirit.

           Those whom God has joined together let no one put asunder.

People      **Amen.**

## The Prayers of the People

*The Prayers of the People may be led by a friend or member of a family of the bride or groom, or by the celebrant or another minister.*

| Leader | Let us pray. |
|---|---|
|  | Almighty God, in whom we live and move and have our being, look graciously upon the world which you have made and for which your Son gave his life, and especially on all whom you make to be one flesh in holy marriage. May their lives together be a sacrament of your love to this broken world, so that unity may overcome estrangement, forgiveness heal guilt, and joy overcome despair. |
|  | Lord, in your mercy, |
| People | **Hear our prayer.** |
| Leader | May N and N so live together that the strength of their love may enrich our common life and become a sign of your faithfulness. |
|  | Lord, in your mercy, |
| People | **Hear our prayer.** |
| [Leader | May they receive the gift and heritage of children and the grace to bring them up to know and love you. |
|  | Lord, in your mercy, |
| People | **Hear our prayer.**] |
| Leader | May their home be a place of truth, security, and love; and their lives an example of concern for others. |
|  | Lord, in your mercy; |
| People | **Hear our prayer.** |
| Leader | May those who have witnessed these vows find their lives strengthened and their loyalties confirmed. |
|  | Lord, in your mercy, |
| People | **Hear our prayer.** |

*Other suitable prayers may be used.*

# The Blessing of the Marriage

*The people remain standing. The husband and wife kneel, and the celebrant says one of the following prayers.*

Most gracious God, we give you thanks for your tender love in sending Jesus Christ to come among us, to be born of a human mother, and to make the way of the cross to be the way of life. We thank you, also, for consecrating the union of man and woman in his name. By the power of your Holy Spirit, pour out the abundance of your blessing upon this man and this woman. Defend them from every enemy. Lead them into all peace. Let their love for each other be a seal upon their hearts, a mantle about their shoulders, and a crown upon their foreheads. Bless them in their work and in their companionship; in their sleeping and in their waking; in their joys and in their sorrows; in their life and in their death. Finally, in your mercy, bring them to that table where your saints feast for ever in your heavenly home; through Jesus Christ our Lord, who with you and the Holy Spirit lives and reigns, one God, for ever and ever.

*People*   **Amen.**

*Or*

*Celebrant*   O God, you have so consecrated the covenant of marriage that in it is represented the spiritual unity between Christ and his Church. Send therefore your blessing upon these your servants, that they may so love, honour, and cherish each other in faithfulness and patience, in wisdom and true godliness, that their home may be a haven of blessing and peace; through Jesus Christ our Lord, who lives and reigns with you and the Holy Spirit, one God, now and for ever.

*People*   **Amen.**

*The husband and wife still kneeling, the celebrant adds this blessing.*

God the Father, God the Son, God the Holy Spirit,
bless, preserve, and keep you; the Lord mercifully
with his favour look upon you, and fill you with all
spiritual benediction and grace; that you may
faithfully live together in this life, and in the age to
come have life everlasting.

*People*    **Amen.**

## The Peace

*Celebrant*    The peace of the Lord be always with you.
*People*    **And also with you.**

*The newly married couple may greet each other. The register may be signed at
this time or before the dismissal.*

# The Liturgy of the Eucharist

## The Preparation of the Gifts

*The bread and wine may be presented to the celebrant by the husband and
wife. When the gifts have been prepared, the celebrant may say the Prayer
over the Gifts, as follows:*

God of the covenant, hear our prayer,
and accept all we offer you this day.
You have made N and N one
in the sacrament of marriage.
May the mystery of Christ's unselfish love,
which we celebrate in this eucharist,
increase their love for you and for each other;
through Christ our Lord.

*People*    **Amen.**

# The Great Thanksgiving

*Celebrant*   The Lord be with you.
*People*      **And also with you.**

*Celebrant*   Lift up your hearts.
*People*      **We lift them to the Lord.**

*Celebrant*   Let us give thanks to the Lord our God.
*People*      **It is right to give our thanks and praise.**

*Celebrant*   Blessed are you, gracious God,
creator of heaven and earth;
we give you thanks and praise
in the assembly of your people.
You made us in your image:
male and female you created us.
You give us the gift of marriage
and call us to reflect your faithfulness
as we serve one another
in the bond of covenant love.
Therefore we raise our voices,
with all who have served you in every age,
to proclaim the glory of your name.

*All*   **Holy, holy, holy Lord,
God of power and might,
heaven and earth are full of your glory.
Hosanna in the highest.**

**Blessed is he who comes in the name of the Lord.
Hosanna in the highest.**

*Celebrant*   We give thanks to you, Lord our God,
for the goodness and love
you have made known to us in creation;
in calling Israel to be your people;
in your Word spoken through the prophets;
and above all in the Word made flesh,
Jesus your Son.

For in these last days you sent him
to be incarnate from the Virgin Mary,
to be the Saviour and Redeemer of the world.
In him, you have delivered us from evil,
and made us worthy to stand before you.
In him, you have brought us
out of error into truth,
out of sin into righteousness,
out of death into life.

On the night he was handed over
to suffering and death,
a death he freely accepted,
our Lord Jesus Christ took bread;
and when he had given thanks to you,
he broke it, and gave it to his disciples,
and said, "Take, eat:
this is my body, which is given for you.
Do this for the remembrance of me."

After supper he took the cup of wine;
and when he had given thanks,
he gave it to them,
and said, "Drink this, all of you:
this is my blood of the new covenant,
which is shed for you and for many
for the forgiveness of sins.
Whenever you drink it,
do this for the remembrance of me."

*All*    Therefore, Father, according to his command,
**we remember his death,**
**we proclaim his resurrection,**
**we await his coming in glory;**

*Celebrant*    and we offer our sacrifice
of praise and thanksgiving
to you, Lord of all;
presenting to you, from your creation,
this bread and this wine.

We pray you, gracious God,
to send your Holy Spirit upon these gifts,
that they may be the sacrament
of the body of Christ
and his blood of the new covenant.
Unite us to your Son in his sacrifice,
that we, made acceptable in him,
may be sanctified by the Holy Spirit.

In the fullness of time,
reconcile all things in Christ,
and make them new,
and bring us to that city of light
where you dwell with all your sons and daughters;
through Jesus Christ our Lord,
the firstborn of all creation,
the head of the Church,
and the author of our salvation;

by whom, and with whom, and in whom,
in the unity of the Holy Spirit,
all honour and glory are yours, almighty Father,
now and for ever.

*People*　　　**Amen.**

## The Lord's Prayer

*Celebrant*　　As our Saviour taught us, let us pray,
*All*　　　　　**Our Father in heaven,**
　　　　　　　**hallowed be your name,**
　　　　　　　**your kingdom come,**
　　　　　　　**your will be done,**
　　　　　　　**on earth as in heaven.**
　　　　　　　**Give us today our daily bread.**
　　　　　　　**Forgive us our sins**
　　　　　　　**as we forgive those who sin against us.**
　　　　　　　**Save us from the time of trial,**
　　　　　　　**and deliver us from evil.**
　　　　　　　**For the kingdom, the power,**
　　　　　　　**and the glory are yours,**
　　　　　　　**now and for ever. Amen.**

| | |
|---|---|
| *Celebrant* | And now, as our Saviour Christ has taught us, we are bold to say, |
| *All* | **Our Father, who art in heaven, hallowed be thy name, thy kingdom come, thy will be done, on earth as it is in heaven. Give us this day our daily bread. And forgive us our trespasses, as we forgive those who trespass against us. And lead us not into temptation, but deliver us from evil. For thine is the kingdom, the power, and the glory, for ever and ever. Amen.** |

*Silence*

*The celebrant breaks the consecrated bread for distribution, and may say,*

We break the bread of life,
and that life is the light of the world.

*All*    **God here among us,
light in the midst of us,
bring us to light and life.**

## The Communion

*The celebrant invites the people to share in communion and may say,*

| | |
|---|---|
| *Celebrant* | The gifts of God for the People of God. |
| *People* | **Thanks be to God.** |

*The celebrant receives the sacrament first and then delivers it to the husband and wife, and to such of the congregation as wish to receive communion.*

*The sacrament is given with the following words.*

The body of Christ (given for you).
The blood of Christ (shed for you).

*Or*                The body of Christ, the bread of heaven.
                    The blood of Christ, the cup of salvation.

*The communicant responds each time,* **Amen.**

*During the communion, hymns or anthems may be sung.*

## Prayer after Communion

*Celebrant*         Let us pray.

*Standing, the community prays in silence. The celebrant then says,*

                    Gracious God,
                    may *N* and *N*, who have been bound together
                    in these holy mysteries,
                    become one in heart and soul.
                    May they live in fidelity and peace
                    and obtain those eternal joys
                    prepared for all who love you;
                    through your Son, Jesus Christ the Lord.
*People*            **Amen.**

*Then the following doxology may be said.*

*Celebrant*         Glory to God,
*People*            **whose power, working in us,**
                    **can do infinitely more**
                    **than we can ask or imagine.**
                    **Glory to God from generation to generation,**
                    **in the Church and in Christ Jesus,**
                    **for ever and ever. Amen.**

## The Dismissal

*The celebrant may bless the people. The deacon, or other leader, dismisses the people saying,*

*Leader*            Go in peace to love and serve the Lord.
*People*            **Thanks be to God.**

*From Easter Day through the Day of Pentecost,* **Alleluia** *may be added to the dismissal and the people's response.*

# The Celebration and Blessing of a Marriage

*This service will be used when there is to be no celebration of the eucharist.*

## The Gathering of the Community

*The people stand. The bride and bridegroom stand before the celebrant.*

Celebrant  The grace of our Lord Jesus Christ,
and the love of God,
and the fellowship of the Holy Spirit,
be with you all.

People  **And also with you.**

Celebrant  Dear friends, we have come together in the presence of God to witness the marriage of N and N, and to rejoice with them.

Marriage is a gift of God and a means of his grace, in which man and woman become one flesh. It is God's purpose that, as husband and wife give themselves to each other in love, they shall grow together and be united in that love, as Christ is united with his Church.

The union of man and woman in heart, body, and mind is intended for their mutual comfort and help, that they may know each other with delight and tenderness in acts of love [and that they may be blessed in the procreation, care, and upbringing of children].

In marriage, husband and wife give themselves to each other, to care for each other in good times and in bad. They are linked to each other's families, and they begin a new life together in the community.

It is a way of life that all should reverence, and none should lightly undertake.

If anyone present knows a reason why N and N may not lawfully marry, they must declare it now.

N and N, if either of you knows a reason why you may not lawfully marry, you must declare it now.

N and N have come to enter this holy state. They have complied with Civil and Canon Law and have been duly prepared to enter into marriage. They will each give their consent to the other; they will exchange solemn vows, and in token of this, they will (each) give and receive a ring.

We pray with them that by God's help they may fulfil his purpose for the whole of their earthly life together.

Let us pray.

God our Father,
you have taught us through your Son
that love is the fulfilling of the law.
Grant to these your servants
that loving one another
they may continue in your love
until their lives' end;
through Jesus Christ our Lord.

*People*      **Amen.**


# The Proclamation of the Word

*One or more readings, including a Gospel reading, shall normally be read.*
*Members of the family and friends of the bride and groom may read lessons.*
*A psalm, canticle, hymn, anthem, or period of silence may follow the lessons.*
*Suggested readings may be found on p. 549. The readings and the response*
*shall be selected in consultation with the bride and groom.*

*At the conclusion of readings from the Old Testament and the New
Testament writings other than the Gospels, the reader says,*

> The word of the Lord.

*People* **Thanks be to God.**

*Silence may be kept. A psalm, canticle, hymn, or anthem may follow.*

*All stand for the Gospel.*

*Reader* The Lord be with you.

*People* **And also with you.**

*Reader* The Holy Gospel of our Lord Jesus Christ
according to . . .

*People* **Glory to you, Lord Jesus Christ.**

*At the conclusion of the Gospel, the reader says,*

> The Gospel of Christ.

*People* **Praise to you, Lord Jesus Christ.**

*A sermon may follow.*


# The Wedding

*The people stand. The celebrant says to the bridegroom,*

> N will you give yourself to N to be her husband:
> to love her, comfort her, honour and protect her;
> and forsaking all others, to be faithful to her
> so long as you both shall live?

*Bridegroom* **I will.**

*The celebrant says to the bride,*

> N will you give yourself to N to be his wife:
> to love him, comfort him, honour and protect him;
> and forsaking all others, to be faithful to him
> so long as you both shall live?

*Bride* **I will.**

*The celebrant may address the following question to the families of the bride and bridegroom.*

Do you, members of the families of N and N, give your blessing to this marriage?

*Answer* **We do.**

*The celebrant addresses the following to all present.*

You are the witnesses to these vows now being made. Will you do all in your power to support and uphold this marriage?

*Answer* **We will.**

*The bride and bridegroom face each other and join hands.*

*Bridegroom* I N take you N to be my wife,
to have and to hold
from this day forward;
for better, for worse,
for richer, for poorer,
in sickness and in health,
to love and to cherish
for the rest of our lives,
according to God's holy law.
This is my solemn vow.

*Bride* I N take you N to be my husband,
to have and to hold
from this day forward;
for better, for worse,
for richer, for poorer,
in sickness and in health,
to love and to cherish
for the rest of our lives,
according to God's holy law.
This is my solemn vow.

*They loose hands. The celebrant receives the ring(s) and addresses the*
*congregation in these or similar words.*

> Dear friends in Christ,
> let us ask God to bless *this ring*,
> that *it* may be a symbol of the vow and covenant
> N and N have made this day.

*The community may pray silently. The celebrant then says,*

> Blessed are you,
> God of steadfast love,
> source of our joy and end of our hope.
> Bless *this ring* given and received
> that *it* may be a symbol of the vow and covenant
> N and N have made this day,
> through Jesus Christ our Lord.

People   **Amen.**

*The bridegroom (and the bride in her turn) places the ring on the ring-finger*
*of the other's hand and says,*

> N, I give you this ring
> as a symbol of my vow.
> With all that I am and all that I have,
> I honour you in the name of God.

*The bride and bridegroom join right hands.*

Celebrant   N and N have joined themselves to each other by
solemn vows, signified by the joining of hands and
the giving and receiving of *a ring*. I declare that they
are husband and wife, in the name of the Father,
and of the Son, and of the Holy Spirit.

Those whom God has joined together let no one put
asunder.

People   **Amen.**

*The register may be signed at this time or at the end of the service.*

# The Prayers of the People

*The Prayers of the People may be led by a friend or member of a family of the bride or groom, or by the celebrant or another minister.*

Leader      Let us pray.

Almighty God, in whom we live and move and have our being, look graciously upon the world which you have made and for which your Son gave his life, and especially on all whom you make to be one flesh in holy marriage. May their lives together be a sacrament of your love to this broken world, so that unity may overcome estrangement, forgiveness heal guilt, and joy overcome despair.

Lord, in your mercy,

People      **Hear our prayer.**

Leader      May N and N so live together that the strength of their love may enrich our common life and become a sign of your faithfulness.

Lord, in your mercy,

People      **Hear our prayer.**

[Leader      May they receive the gift and heritage of children and the grace to bring them up to know and love you.

Lord, in your mercy,

People      **Hear our prayer.**]

Leader      May their home be a place of truth, security, and love; and their lives an example of concern for others.

Lord, in your mercy,

People      **Hear our prayer.**

Leader      May those who have witnessed these vows find their lives strengthened and their loyalties confirmed.

Lord, in your mercy,
*People*    **Hear our prayer.**

*Other suitable prayers may be used.*

## The Lord's Prayer

*Celebrant*    Gathering our prayers and praises into one,
let us pray as our Saviour taught us,
*All*    **Our Father in heaven,
hallowed be your name,
your kingdom come,
your will be done,
on earth as in heaven.
Give us today our daily bread.
Forgive us our sins
as we forgive those who sin against us.
Save us from the time of trial,
and deliver us from evil.
For the kingdom, the power,
and the glory are yours,
now and for ever. Amen.**

*Or*

*Celebrant*    And now, as our Saviour Christ has taught us,
we are bold to say,
*All*    **Our Father, who art in heaven,
hallowed be thy name,
thy kingdom come,
thy will be done,
on earth as it is in heaven.
Give us this day our daily bread.
And forgive us our trespasses,
as we forgive those who trespass against us.
And lead us not into temptation,
but deliver us from evil.
For thine is the kingdom,
the power, and the glory,
for ever and ever. Amen.**

# The Blessing of the Marriage

*The people remain standing. The husband and wife kneel, and the celebrant says one of the following prayers.*

Most gracious God, we give you thanks for your tender love in sending Jesus Christ to come among us, to be born of a human mother, and to make the way of the cross to be the way of life. We thank you, also, for consecrating the union of man and woman in his name. By the power of your Holy Spirit, pour out the abundance of your blessing upon this man and this woman. Defend them from every enemy. Lead them into all peace. Let their love for each other be a seal upon their hearts, a mantle about their shoulders, and a crown upon their foreheads. Bless them in their work and in their companionship; in their sleeping and in their waking; in their joys and in their sorrows; in their life and in their death. Finally, in your mercy, bring them to that table where your saints feast for ever in your heavenly home; through Jesus Christ our Lord, who with you and the Holy Spirit lives and reigns, one God, for ever and ever.

*People*    **Amen.**

*Or*

*Celebrant*    O God, you have so consecrated the covenant of marriage that in it is represented the spiritual unity between Christ and his Church. Send therefore your blessing upon these your servants, that they may so love, honour, and cherish each other in faithfulness and patience, in wisdom and true godliness, that their home may be a haven of blessing and peace; through Jesus Christ our Lord, who lives and reigns with you and the Holy Spirit, one God, now and for ever.

*People*    **Amen.**

*The husband and wife still kneeling, the celebrant adds this blessing.*

God the Father, God the Son, God the Holy Spirit, bless, preserve, and keep you; the Lord mercifully with his favour look upon you, and fill you with all spiritual benediction and grace; that you may faithfully live together in this life, and in the age to come have life everlasting.

*People* **Amen.**

## The Peace

*Celebrant* The peace of the Lord be always with you.
*People* **And also with you.**

*The newly married couple may greet each other.*

## Readings and Psalms Suitable for Marriage Liturgies

### Old Testament and New Testament Readings

Genesis 1.27–28,31a  (God created man in his own image; in the image of God he created him; male and female he created them)

Tobit 8.5b–8  (Not . . . because of lust, but with sincerity)

Romans 12.1–2,9–13  (Let love be genuine; hate what is evil, hold fast to what is good)

1 Corinthians 13  (So faith, hope, love abide, these three; but the greatest of these is love)

Ephesians 3.14–19  (To comprehend with all the saints what is the breadth and length and height and depth, and to know the love of Christ)

Colossians 3.12–17  (Put on love, which binds everything together in perfect harmony)

1 John 4.7–12  (If we love one another, God abides in us)

### Psalms and Suitable Refrains

67  (May God be merciful to us and bless us)
112.1–6  (Happy are they who fear the Lord *or* Hallelujah!)
148.1–6  (Hallelujah!)
150  (Hallelujah!)

## Gospel Readings

Matthew 5.1–10   (Blessed are those who hunger and thirst for righteousness, for they shall be satisfied)

Matthew 22.35–40   (You shall love the Lord your God . . . You shall love your neighbour as yourself)

Mark 10.6–9   (The two shall become one flesh)

John 2.1–11   (On the third day there was a marriage at Cana in Galilee)

John 15.9–12 (This is my commandment, that you love one another)

# Ministry to the Sick

The Church's ministry to the sick is based on Jesus' constant concern and care for the sick. It is reinforced by the Epistle of James' admonition to the sick to call for the elders of the Church to pray over them and anoint them with oil in the name of the Lord. James expects this rite to have three effects: the prayer of faith will save the sick, the Lord will raise them up, and their sins will be forgiven.

James' suggestion that the sick should call for the leaders and rulers of the Christian assembly ties the Church's ministry to the sick to its Sunday worship from a very early date. If the sick could not get to church, then the Church, through the leaders of its worship, would come to them. Justin Martyr spoke of the early Christian practice of taking communion to those absent from the Christian community.[1]

We may draw two conclusions from our knowledge of early Christian ministry to the sick: Christians were not to rely on the multitude of faith-healers and wonder-workers who abounded in their society but were to send for senior members of their own community. Second, the ministry those leaders offered was an extension of the Church's basic act of worship, i.e., the gathering around the word and the bread and wine each Sunday.

This office of the Ministry to the Sick has been prepared in an attempt to be faithful to these two principles. The minister represents not only the congregation but also its holy activity to the sick person. The minister brings the Church, the community of wholeness, to the sick person. It is not essential that the minister be ordained (unless the eucharist is to be celebrated instead of offering communion reserved at the congregational assembly); it is sufficient that the minister be authorized (by the diocesan bishop) to undertake this ministry. The rite itself is based in shape and pattern on the Church's Sunday liturgy and consists of reading and proclaiming of the word; intercessory prayer, culminating in prayer for the sick person with actions of touching and anointing; and the sharing of holy communion.

The service normally consists of four parts:

1   *The Ministry of the Word*—Following the opening acclamations and prayer, portions of scripture are read. A brief reflection on the reading(s) is also appropriate.

The intercession may take any of the following forms: biddings followed by silence, free prayer, or formal prayers such as those provided on pp. 110–132.

2 *Confession and Absolution*—Anglican Prayer Books have traditionally provided for the sick to have opportunity to confess their sins if their "conscience feel troubled with any weighty matter." A number of forms of confession are available, including those found in the forms of prayer for morning and evening (p. 45), in the Penitential Order (p. 217), and in the office for the Reconciliation of a Penitent (p. 168).

3 *The Laying on of Hands and Anointing*—The laying on of hands and anointing provide the moment when the prayer of the Church for the healing power of God is made specific and particular in relation to this sick person. It is also a sign of forgiveness and consequently of reconciliation in and with the Christian community.

In accordance with ancient practice the oil used by the minister (whether ordained or lay) will have been blessed by the bishop.

4 *Holy Communion*—The service may conclude with holy communion. The relationship between the sick person and the Sunday assembly is best demonstrated when bread and wine set aside at the Sunday eucharist are brought for communion. Others present may receive holy communion.

Provision is also made in this rite for the celebration of the eucharist with the sick and their family. This would be appropriate during an extended illness when the sick person has been unable to join with the eucharistic assembly for a long time.

1   Justin, "First Apology," 66.

# Concerning the Service

*In case of illness, the minister of the congregation is to be notified.*

*One or more parts of the following service may be used, as appropriate; however, when two or more parts of the service are used together, they are used in the order indicated. The Lord's Prayer is always included.*

*When the Laying on of Hands or Anointing takes place at a public celebration of the eucharist, it should precede the exchange of the Peace and the Preparation of the Gifts.*

# Ministry to the Sick

## The Ministry of the Word

*The minister begins with the following or other appropriate greeting.*

> The grace of our Lord Jesus Christ,
> and the love of God,
> and the fellowship of the Holy Spirit,
> be with you (all).

*Response*  **And also with you.**

*Then the minister may say the following or another appropriate prayer.*

O God of peace,
who taught us that in returning and rest we shall be saved,
in quietness and confidence shall be our strength;
by the might of your Spirit lift us, we pray, to your presence,
where we may be still and know that you are God;
through Jesus Christ our Lord. **Amen.**

*One or more of the Sunday lessons, or of the passages of scripture on p. 558, or of other appropriate passages of scripture, is read. The readings may be followed by silence, by a psalm, or by a brief reflection on their content.*

*Prayers may be offered according to the occasion. The minister concludes with the following or other suitable collect.*

Gracious God,
you have heard the prayers of your faithful people;
you know our needs before we ask,
and our ignorance in asking.
Grant our requests as may be best for us.
This we ask in the name of your Son
Jesus Christ our Lord. **Amen.**

## Confession and Absolution

*If confession is desired, the form found on p. 168 or in the Penitential Order on p. 217 may be used.*

# The Laying on of Hands and Anointing

*The oil for the anointing of the sick is to be used only by clergy and those lay persons who have received authorization by the diocesan bishop.*

*The minister begins with the following declaration.*

Holy scripture teaches us
that in acts of healing and restoration
our Lord Jesus and his disciples
laid hands upon the sick (and anointed them).
By so doing they made known
the healing power and presence of God.
Pray that as we follow our Lord's example,
you may know his unfailing love.

*Then the minister lays hands upon the sick person, saying the following:*

N, may the Lord in his love and mercy uphold you
by the grace and power of the Holy Spirit. **Amen.**

*Or, if the person is to be anointed, the minister anoints the person's forehead with oil, making the sign of the cross and saying,*

N, through this holy anointing
may the Lord in his love and mercy uphold you
by the grace and power of the Holy Spirit. **Amen.**

*When the anointing is completed, the minister may add,*

As you are outwardly anointed with this holy oil,
so may our heavenly Father grant you
the inward anointing of the Holy Spirit.
Of his great mercy,
may he forgive you your sins,
release you from suffering,
and restore you to wholeness and strength.
May he deliver you from all evil,
preserve you in all goodness,
and bring you to everlasting life;
through Jesus Christ our Lord. **Amen.**

# Holy Communion

*Minister*    The peace of the Lord be always with you.
*Response*    **And also with you.**

*If the Holy Eucharist is celebrated, the service will continue with the Great
Thanksgiving, the Lord's Prayer, and the Communion on pp. 192–215.*

*If the sacrament has been brought from the church, the service continues as
follows:*

*Minister*    The Church of Christ,
              of which we are members,
              has taken this bread and wine
              and given thanks according to the Lord's command.
              We now share together
              in the communion of his body and blood.

              As our Saviour taught us, let us pray,
*All*         **Our Father in heaven,
              hallowed be your name,
              your kingdom come,
              your will be done,
              on earth as in heaven.
              Give us today our daily bread.
              Forgive us our sins
              as we forgive those who sin against us.
              Save us from the time of trial,
              and deliver us from evil.
              For the kingdom, the power,
              and the glory are yours,
              now and for ever. Amen.**

*Or*

*Minister*    And now, as our Saviour Christ has taught us,
              we are bold to say,
*All*         **Our Father, who art in heaven,
              hallowed be thy name,
              thy kingdom come,
              thy will be done,
              on earth as it is in heaven.**

Give us this day our daily bread.
And forgive us our trespasses,
as we forgive those who trespass against us.
And lead us not into temptation,
but deliver us from evil.
For thine is the kingdom,
the power, and the glory,
for ever and ever. Amen.

*The minister may say the following invitation.*

The gifts of God for the People of God.

*People*  **Thanks be to God.**

*The sacrament is then given with the following words.*

The body of Christ (given for you).
The blood of Christ (shed for you).

*Or*  The body of Christ, the bread of heaven.
The blood of Christ, the cup of salvation.

*The communicant responds each time,* **Amen.**

*The following doxology may be said.*

*Minister*  Glory to God,
*People*  **whose power, working in us,**
**can do infinitely more**
**than we can ask or imagine.**
**Glory to God from generation to generation,**
**in the Church and in Christ Jesus,**
**for ever and ever. Amen.**

*A priest may bless those present. The service concludes with a dismissal.*

*Minister*  Let us bless the Lord.
*People*  **Thanks be to God.**

# Readings and Psalms Suitable for the Ministry to the Sick

### Old Testament Readings

Isaiah 35.1–10   (The eyes of the blind shall be opened)

Isaiah 53.1–12   (Surely he has borne our griefs)

Isaiah 61.1–3   (Good tidings to the afflicted)

Wisdom 9.1, 9–18   (Who has traced out what is in the heavens?)

### Psalms and Suitable Refrains

Psalm 23   (The Lord is my shepherd, I shall not be in want)

Psalm 91   (You are my refuge and my stronghold)

Psalm 103   (Bless the Lord, O my soul)

Psalm 145.14–22   (The Lord is near to those who call upon him)

### New Testament Readings

Romans 8.18–27   (The creation waits with eager longing for the revealing of the sons of God)

Romans 8.31b–35, 37–39   (If God is for us, who is against us?)

Romans 12.1–12   (Be transformed by the renewal of your mind)

1 Corinthians 1.18–25   (Christ the power of God and the wisdom of God)

Colossians 1.22–29   (Christ in you, the hope of glory)

Hebrews 4.14–16   (Let us then with confidence draw near to the throne of grace)

James 5.13–16   (Is any among you sick? Let him call for the elders of the church)

1 John 4.16   (God is love)

### Gospel Readings

Matthew 9.2–8   (Your sins are forgiven)

Matthew 11.25–30   (You will find rest for your souls)

Mark 6.7, 12–13   (They anointed with oil many that were sick)

John 6.47–51   (I am the bread of life)

John 10.14–15, 27–28   (I am the good shepherd)

# Concerning Ministry at the Time of Death

*Ministry at the time of death may be offered to a number of people: first, to the dying person, especially if still conscious; second, to family and friends who may have been gathered by this event. Different words are required for different people on such an occasion, and at different moments.*

*The prayers which follow have been divided into several groups: prayers for and with the dying person, prayers with family and friends, prayers when the person has died.*

*It is appropriate that these prayers be led by someone who has already ministered to those involved, whether minister of the congregation, lay visitor, hospital chaplain, or other person exercising the ministry of the Church. However, a family member, or friend, or anyone else, may lead in the offering of these prayers.*

### A Prayer for a Person Near Death

*This prayer may be offered in the presence of a person who is dying.*

Almighty God, look on this your servant, lying in great weakness, and comfort *him/her* with the promise of life everlasting, given in the resurrection of your Son Jesus Christ our Lord. **Amen.**

# Ministry at the Time of Death

## Prayers with a Person Who Is Dying

*One or more of these prayers may be said slowly, phrase by phrase, with a
dying person, or in his/her name.*

Our Father in heaven,
hallowed be your name,
your kingdom come,
your will be done,
on earth as in heaven.
Give us today our daily bread.
Forgive us our sins
as we forgive those who sin against us.
Save us from the time of trial,
and deliver us from evil.
For the kingdom, the power,
and the glory are yours,
now and for ever. Amen.

*Or*

Our Father, who art in heaven,
hallowed be thy name,
thy kingdom come,
thy will be done,
on earth as it is in heaven.
Give us this day our daily bread.
And forgive us our trespasses,
as we forgive those who trespass against us.
And lead us not into temptation,
but deliver us from evil.
For thine is the kingdom,
the power, and the glory,
for ever and ever. Amen.

Glory to the Father, and to the Son,
and to the Holy Spirit:
as it was in the beginning, is now,
and will be for ever. Amen.

*Or*  Glory be to the Father, and to the Son,
and to the Holy Spirit:
as it was in the beginning, is now,
and ever shall be, world without end. Amen.

Father, Son, and Holy Spirit, help me.

Father, I place myself in your hands.

Holy God, I believe in you.
I trust you.
I love you.

*Family members and friends may lay their hands on the dying person in a
moment of silent prayer.*

*The minister leading the prayers may say,*

God of mercy,
look with love on *N*,
and receive *him/her* into your heavenly kingdom.
Bless *him/her*
and let *him/her* live with you for ever.
We ask this grace through Christ the Lord.

*People*  **Amen.**

# Prayers with Family and Friends

*One or more of the following may be read.*

Psalm 23          Psalm 121          John 14.1–6, 23, 27
Psalm 91          John 6.37–40

## A Litany

God the Father,
**Have mercy on your servant.**

God the Son,
**Have mercy on your servant.**

God the Holy Spirit,
**Have mercy on your servant.**

Holy Trinity, one God,
**Have mercy on your servant.**

From all evil, from all sin, from all tribulation,
**Have mercy on your servant.**

By your holy incarnation, by your cross and passion, by your
precious death and burial,
**Have mercy on your servant.**

By your glorious resurrection and ascension, and by the
coming of the Holy Spirit,
**Have mercy on your servant.**

We sinners beseech you to hear us, Lord Christ, that it may
please you to deliver the soul of your servant from the power of
evil, and from eternal death,
**Have mercy on your servant.**

That it may please you mercifully to pardon all *his/her* sins,
**Have mercy on your servant.**

That it may please you to grant *him/her* a place of refreshment
and everlasting blessedness,
**Have mercy on your servant.**

That it may please you to give *him/her* joy and gladness in your
kingdom, with your saints in light,
**Have mercy on your servant.**

Lamb of God, you take away the sin of the world,
**Have mercy on your servant.**

Lamb of God, you take away the sin of the world,
**Have mercy on your servant.**

Lamb of God, you take away the sin of the world,
**Have mercy on your servant.**

Let us pray.

God of mercy,
into whose hands your Son Jesus Christ
commended his spirit at his last hour,
into those same hands
we now commend your servant N,
that death may be for *him/her* the gate to life
and to eternal fellowship with you;
through Jesus Christ our Lord. **Amen.**

## Prayers at Death

*One of the following commendations may be said.*

Give rest, O Christ, to your servant with your saints,
where sorrow and pain are no more,
neither sighing, but life everlasting.

You only are immortal, the creator and maker of all;
and we are mortal, formed of the earth,
and to earth shall we return.
For so did you ordain when you created me, saying,
"You are dust, and to dust you shall return."
All of us go down to the dust;
yet even at the grave we make our song:
Alleluia, alleluia, alleluia.

Give rest, O Christ, to your servant with your saints,
where sorrow and pain are no more,
neither sighing, but life everlasting.

*Or*

Depart, O Christian soul, out of this world;
in the name of God the Father almighty who created you;
in the name of Jesus Christ who redeemed you;
in the name of the Holy Spirit who sanctifies you.
May your rest be this day in peace,
and your dwelling place in the paradise of God.

*Or*

Loving and merciful God,
we entrust our *brother/sister* to your mercy.
You loved *him/her* greatly in this life;
now that *he/she* is freed from all its cares,
give *him/her* happiness and peace for ever.
The old order has passed away;
welcome *him/her* now into paradise
where there will be no more sorrow,
no more weeping or pain,
but only peace and joy
with Jesus, your Son,
and the Holy Spirit,
for ever and ever. **Amen.**

*The minister may conclude these prayers with a simple blessing, in these or similar words.*

God grant us to share
in the inheritance of his saints in glory;
and the blessing of God almighty,
the Father, the Son, and the Holy Spirit,
be with us, now and always. **Amen.**

# The Funeral Liturgy

The origins of funeral practices, whether burial or other forms of
reverent disposal of the bodies of those who have died, are lost in the
furthest mists of human history. Many of the oldest remains of our
most ancient ancestors are their burial sites and it is not impossible
that the appearance of rites associated with mourning and the final
disposal of the bodies of the dead mark the emergence of humanity as
we understand that term. Funerals are universal in the human
species, both historically and geographically.

Funeral practices are unlike some of the other rites and ceremonies of
the Church precisely because of their universal nature. People do
them first of all because they are human. Many people who do not
belong to the Christian Church (or any other worshipping body or
faith community) and who do not describe themselves as "religious,"
are among the most assiduous in the exercise of funeral rites.

It is important for Christians to be aware of the universal dimensions
of funeral practices, partly out of sensitivity to the basic needs,
conscious and unconscious, which mourners bring to these rituals,
and partly so they can identify clearly the particular insights and
interpretations which Christian faith brings to bear on the reality of
death and the experience of bereavement.

The Bible reflects many attitudes to death, ranging from belief that
death is a judgement for sin (and its prolonged deferral a reward for
righteousness), through resigned acceptance of the inevitable and
inexplicable, to the belief in the goodness of both the Creator and the
creation which eventually found expression in a theology of
resurrection.

A Christian attitude to death is inseparable from the biblical accounts
of the resurrection of Jesus Christ and his followers' experience of the
saving power of his renewed presence. Yet even on this central issue
the biblical account is varied. The fourth Gospel sees the whole of
Jesus' ministry as an expression of glory in which death itself is an act
of triumph and resurrection an inevitable conclusion. The cry of
abandonment in Matthew and Mark and of resignation in Luke reflect
another perception of Jesus' experience of death. Early Christians who
expected the imminent return of the Lord were particularly
threatened by the death of fellow-believers who might, it was

assumed, be deprived of full participation in the realization of the new age. The author of the Epistle to the Hebrews developed a theology of the death of Jesus as a "school of suffering." And so on. There is no single biblical attitude to death, not even to the death of Jesus. The biblical narratives and letters reflect a mixture of grief and hope, suffering and glory. This mixture is found in Jesus' attitude to his own death and in his followers' attitude to his death and the death of other members of their company.[1]

It is entirely fitting that Christian funerals reflect these various dimensions of the experience of death. Faith is not only belief: faith embraces even its own shadow, which is doubt. Liturgical expressions of faith and hope in the face of death should consequently leave room for the radical sense of anxiety and loss which the mourners experience. They should also enable, rather than deny, the grief process about which so much has been learned in recent years. On the other hand, Christian funerals should not become unrelieved expressions of anguish and despair: there is a time for thanksgiving even in the midst of mourning.

This note of thanksgiving even in a time of tears explains, in part, the ancient association of Christian funerals with celebrations of the eucharist. Thanksgiving for the death and victory of the Christ vibrates with different and more basic tones at the time of the death of a fellow disciple. Further, the bread and wine of holy communion, that foretaste of the messianic banquet, convey an experience of the solidarity of the Christian community which is particularly appropriate to the moment. All our experience of the kingdom of God takes place between the poles of "already" and "not yet," a tension which is only temporarily resolved for us when we remember with thanks the basic Christian story, and in the case of a funeral, the story of this particular Christian as well.

Christian funerals have been shaped over the centuries by a variety of notions of what happens to those who have died. In earlier centuries the idea of solidarity was paramount: the Church was a single body moving towards an ultimate destiny which neither living nor dead had yet experienced. This view of things gradually gave way to a more individualistic preoccupation with immediate personal destiny. Pagan influences also entered the scheme and it is sometimes unclear if prayers for the rest and peace of the deceased were intended to secure their welfare or the protection of their survivors. Certainly much Christian piety became an expression of identification with the individual soul in its ongoing purgation and development rather than with the whole redeemed humanity of which that individual is a significant but not distinguishable member.[2]

These nuances of piety can be helpful if they are held in some kind of balance and with a strong sense of their symbolic structure. They are less helpful, and even destructive, when they are held with conviction in their exact and literal correspondence to an unseen reality. For the truth is that we do not know the condition of the dead, and while faith may consign their well-being to the creative and redemptive remembrance of God, everything we say about them remains, as thing said, at the level of symbol. This is precisely the level at which Paul worked when he wrote the great fifteenth chapter of his first letter to the Corinthians, drawing on images of seeds and stars and bodies to communicate his belief in the ultimate transformation of mortal human nature. It is important that funeral liturgies enable people to act at this poetic and symbolic level of their being.

The original ministers of funeral liturgies were the family or tribe of the dead person, and this is still true in many parts of the world today. Comparatively little is known about the development of Christian funerals, but it is clear that Christian families, from an early date, chose to celebrate their funeral liturgies within the larger family of the Christian community. Christian cemeteries became places of great importance for the Christian community, especially in times of persecution. The cleric in charge of the burying-place was an important leader of the Church.

An effect of this consignment of the rites of the family to the care of the larger Christian community was the gradual withdrawal of responsibility from the immediate family and friends of the dead person. The Church gradually took on roles which once had been the inalienable responsibility of the family or tribe and the secularization of this process in more recent times has led to the development of a profession which relieves bereaved families of many burdens but also sometimes functions as a barrier between families and their funeral rites.

It is important to note that funerals are the property of neither undertakers nor clergy. They belong to the circle of family and friends of the person who has died and, when that circle is Christian, they find an appropriate setting in the larger Christian fellowship. Both undertakers and clergy may provide valued support and resources, and clergy have a particular responsibility to make sure that the rituals observed (at least those which take place in church) are appropriate expressions of Christian faith and hope. The family and friends who come to bury their dead should be encouraged to take an active role in the liturgy.

Funeral rites, unlike most other liturgical observances, normally consist of a number of distinct liturgical events spread over a period of time, usually several days. They may include such elements as prayers in the home, prayers in the presence of the body (whether in the home or in church or in an undertaker's premises), the reception of the body at the church, a liturgy of the word in an undertaker's chapel, a liturgy of the word (and possibly of the sacrament) in church, the committal of the body to the grave, the flames, or the sea, and the disposal of ashes at a later date.

Obviously not all of these elements will be observed in each case. The resources which follow are, however, intended to provide for these various events and aspects of a funeral, with such adaptation as may be necessary. The family and friends of the dead person are encouraged to consult as early as possible with the priest or other person responsible in their parish, as well as with the undertaker who may be involved, to plan the various events which will constitute the funeral. Particular sensitivity is required in planning the funerals of suicides, whose deaths are often to be regarded as more tragic than sinful.

This material provides for three forms of funeral:

a  A funeral composed of three events separated by two processions. Prayers are provided for use in the home or in an undertaker's premises; a liturgy is provided for use in church; a committal is provided for use at the grave or other appropriate place.

b  A funeral composed of two events: a liturgy in a chapel and a committal at the grave;

c  A funeral which takes place entirely in a home or other suitable place. (This form would usually be observed in special circumstances, e.g., when a committal must be deferred because of inclement weather or the distance of the grave.)

These various forms of services are provided as broad outlines for different kinds of circumstances and not as rigid alternatives. For instance, although Form I is intended for use in a church ceremony (whether the eucharist is celebrated or not), sometimes Form II may be better suited to a funeral in church. Similarly, prayers and readings with the family and friends some time before the principal funeral service are not forbidden when Form II is used, although it may be decided not to read all the opening sentences on each occasion and to substitute one of the additional prayers for the opening prayer at one of the services.

1  Cf. Schuyler Brown, "Bereavement in New Testament Perspective," *Worship*, Vol. 48, No. 2, 1974, pp. 93–98.

2  Cf. John P. Meier, "Catholic Funerals in the Light of Scripture," *Worship*, Vol. 48, No. 4, 1974, pp. 206–216.

# Concerning the Services

*The family or friends of a person who has died should consult the responsible minister as soon as possible. Together they should make appropriate arrangements for the funeral.*

*The conduct of the funeral should allow for the expression of the grief of the mourners within the context of the Easter hope.*

*The coffin may be draped with a pall during the service. In ritual matters, liturgical practice should be considerate of the cultural traditions of the mourners.*

*These services may be adapted for use apart from the funeral rite, e.g., as memorial services, as a commemoration of the anniversary of a death, on All Souls' Day, or at the time of a funeral by family and friends whose presence is made impossible for such reasons as distance.*

*If the body is to be cremated, any of the following procedures is appropriate, subject to the regulations of the Ordinary:*

   *the Funeral Liturgy, followed by committal of the body to the fire;*

   *the Funeral Liturgy, followed by private cremation, after which the final committal of the ashes takes place;*

   *the committal of the body to the fire, followed by the Funeral Liturgy;*

   *cremation, followed by the Funeral Liturgy and the committal of the ashes to their final resting place;*

   *the committal of the body to the fire and another committal of the ashes to their final resting place.*

# The Funeral Liturgy

**Form I**

*This form of the Funeral Liturgy consists of three parts: prayers for use in the home of the deceased or in another appropriate place (these prayers may, in abbreviated form, be used to greet the body at the door of the church); a form of service for use in church, which may or may not include a celebration of the eucharist; and a form of committal.*

*When the eucharist is celebrated in Part 2 of this form of the Funeral Liturgy, the celebrant shall be a bishop or priest. At other times the celebrant may be a deacon or lay person.*

**Part 1**

# Prayers in the Home or Elsewhere

*The following form of service may be used in the home of the deceased (or elsewhere) or in the church at some suitable interval of time before the Funeral Liturgy.*

*If this form of service is used to greet the body at the door of the church, it should be limited to one or more of the opening sentences and a prayer.*

*The celebrant shall greet those present with words of Holy Scripture such as the following:*

I am Resurrection and I am Life, says the Lord.
Whoever has faith in me shall have life,
even though he die.
And everyone who has life,
and is committed to me in faith,
shall not die for ever.    *John 11.25–26*

Let not your hearts be troubled;
believe in God, believe also in me.
In my Father's house are many rooms;
if it were not so, would I have told you
that I go to prepare a place for you?
And when I go and prepare a place for you,
I will come again and will take you to myself,
that where I am you may be also.   *John 14.1–3*

I am sure that neither death, nor life,
nor angels, nor principalities,
nor things present, nor things to come,
nor powers, nor height, nor depth,
nor anything else in all creation,
will be able to separate us from the love of God
in Christ Jesus our Lord.   *Romans 8.38–39*

*Then all may say one of the following psalms.*

## Psalm 23

The Lord is my shepherd; *
  I shall not be in want.
He makes me lie down in green pastures *
  and leads me beside still waters.
He revives my soul *
  and guides me along right pathways for his name's sake.

Though I walk through the valley of the shadow of death,
I shall fear no evil; *
  for you are with me;
  your rod and your staff, they comfort me.
You spread a table before me in the presence of those
               who trouble me; *
  you have anointed my head with oil,
  and my cup is running over.

Surely your goodness and mercy shall follow me all the
             days of my life,*
  and I will dwell in the house of the Lord for ever.

# Psalm 130

Out of the depths have I called to you, O Lord;
Lord, hear my voice *
  let your ears consider well the voice of my supplication.
If you, Lord, were to note what is done amiss,*
  O Lord, who could stand?
For there is forgiveness with you; *
  therefore you shall be feared.

I wait for the Lord; my soul waits for him; *
  in his word is my hope.
My soul waits for the Lord,
more than watchmen for the morning,*
  more than watchmen for the morning.

O Israel, wait for the Lord,*
  for with the Lord there is mercy;
With him there is plenteous redemption,*
  and he shall redeem Israel from all their sins.

*Other suitable psalms are 90, 121, 122, 126, 132, 134. Silence may be kept after the psalm and an appropriate Psalm Prayer may be said; or the following may be said:*

Glory to the Father, and to the Son, and to the Holy Spirit: *
  as it was in the beginning, is now, and will be for ever.
            Amen.

*One of the readings suggested on p. 604 may be read.*

*Then the celebrant shall say,*

        The Lord be with you.
*People*     **And also with you.**

*Celebrant*    Let us pray.

        God of all consolation,
        in your unending love and mercy
        you turn the darkness of death
        into the dawn of new life.

Show compassion to your people in their sorrow.
Be our refuge and our strength
to lift us from the darkness of grief
to the peace and light of your presence.

Your Son, our Lord Jesus Christ,
by dying for us, conquered death
and by rising again, restored life.

May we then go forward eagerly to meet him,
and after our life on earth
be reunited with our brothers and sisters
where every tear will be wiped away.
We ask this through Jesus Christ, the Lord.

*People*     **Amen.**

*Other suitable prayers may be used and silence may be kept for a time.*
*Additional prayers may be found on pp. 601–603.*

*Then the celebrant shall say,*

Gathering all our cares into one,
let us pray as our Saviour taught us,

*All*     **Our Father in heaven,**
**hallowed be your name,**
**your kingdom come,**
**your will be done,**
**on earth as in heaven.**
**Give us today our daily bread.**
**Forgive us our sins**
**as we forgive those who sin against us.**
**Save us from the time of trial,**
**and deliver us from evil.**
**For the kingdom, the power,**
**and the glory are yours,**
**now and for ever. Amen**

*Or*

Celebrant    And now, as our Saviour Christ has taught us,
             we are bold to say,
             **Our Father, who art in heaven,**
             **hallowed be thy name,**
             **Thy kingdom come,**
             **thy will be done,**
             **on earth as it is in heaven.**
             **Give us this day our daily bread.**
             **And forgive us our trespasses,**
             **as we forgive those who trespass against us.**
             **And lead us not into temptation,**
             **but deliver us from evil.**
             **For thine is the kingdom,**
             **the power, and the glory,**
             **for ever and ever. Amen.**


*Then the celebrant shall dismiss the congregation with these or other words.*

             The eternal God is your dwelling place,
             and underneath are the everlasting arms.
People       **Blessed is the Lord,**
             **our strength and our salvation.**

# Funeral Liturgy for Use in Church

*The celebrant welcomes the congregation and may at this time, or after the*
*readings, express thanksgiving for the gifts of the deceased person, especially*
*the marks of a Christian life. Such remarks, without denying the legitimate*
*grief of the mourners, should relate the life and death of the Christian to the*
*victory of Christ.*

| | |
|---|---|
| *Celebrant* | **The grace of our Lord Jesus Christ,**<br>**and the love of God,**<br>**and the fellowship of the Holy Spirit,**<br>**be with you all.** |
| *People* | **And also with you.** |

*Then may follow a hymn, anthem, or canticle, or the following. The refrain*
*alone may be said or sung.*

> In the midst of life we are in death;
> from whom can we seek help?
> From you alone, O Lord,
> who by our sins are justly angered.

> **Holy God,**
> **holy and mighty,**
> **holy immortal one,**
> **have mercy upon us.**

> Lord you know the secrets of our hearts;
> shut not your ears to our prayers,
> but spare us, O Lord.

> **Holy God,**
> **holy and mighty,**
> **holy immortal one,**
> **have mercy upon us.**

> O worthy and eternal Judge,
> do not let the pains of death
> turn us away from you at our last hour.

**Holy God,**
**holy and mighty,**
**holy immortal one,**
**have mercy upon us.**

## The Collect

*Celebrant*    Let us pray.

*All may pray silently. The celebrant then sings or says the collect.*

O God, the maker and redeemer of all,
grant us, with your servant *N*
and all the faithful departed,
the sure benefits of your Son's saving passion
and glorious resurrection;
that in the last day,
when you gather up all things in Christ,
we may with them enjoy the fullness of your promises;
through Jesus Christ our Lord,
who lives and reigns with you in the unity of the Holy Spirit,
God for ever and ever. **Amen.**

## The Proclamation of the Word

*Two or three readings shall normally be read. A Gospel reading is read when
the eucharist is celebrated. Members of the family and friends of the deceased
person may read readings. A psalm, canticle, hymn, anthem, or period of
silence may follow. Suggested readings may be found on p. 604.*

*At the conclusion of readings from the Old Testament and the Epistles, the
reader shall say,* The word of the Lord, *and the congregation shall reply,*
**Thanks be to God.**

*Before the Gospel the reader shall say,*

           The Lord be with you.
*People*        **And also with you.**

The Holy Gospel of our Lord Jesus Christ
according to . . .
**Glory to you, Lord Jesus Christ.**

*At the conclusion of the Gospel, the reader says,*

The Gospel of Christ.
*People* **Praise to you, Lord Jesus Christ.**

## The Apostles' Creed

*The celebrant may invite the people, in these or similar words, to join in the recitation of the creed.*

*Celebrant* Let us confess the faith of our baptism, as we say,
*All* **I believe in God,**
**the Father almighty,**
**creator of heaven and earth.**

**I believe in Jesus Christ,**
**his only Son, our Lord.**
**He was conceived by the power of the Holy Spirit**
**and born of the Virgin Mary.**
**He suffered under Pontius Pilate,**
**was crucified, died, and was buried.**
**He descended to the dead.**
**On the third day he rose again.**
**He ascended into heaven,**
**and is seated at the right hand of the Father.**
**He will come again**
**to judge the living and the dead.**

**I believe in the Holy Spirit,**
**the holy catholic Church,**
**the communion of saints,**
**the forgiveness of sins,**
**the resurrection of the body,**
**and the life everlasting. Amen.**

# The Prayers of the People

*A deacon or lay member of the community (appropriately a member of the family or a friend of the deceased person) leads the Prayers of the People. A time for silent remembrance and thanksgiving may be kept. All or part of the following form, or a similar form, may be used.*

Leader     Let us pray.

Almighty God, you have knit your chosen people together in one communion, in the mystical body of your Son, Jesus Christ our Lord. Give to your whole Church in heaven and on earth your light and your peace.

People     **Hear us, Lord.**

Leader     May all who have been baptized into Christ's death and resurrection die to sin and rise to newness of life, and may we with him pass through the grave and gate of death to our joyful resurrection.

People     **Hear us, Lord.**

Leader     Grant to us who are still in our pilgrimage, and who walk as yet by faith, that your Holy Spirit may lead us in holiness and righteousness all our days.

People     **Hear us, Lord.**

Leader     Grant to your faithful people pardon and peace, that we may be cleansed from all our sins and serve you with a quiet mind.

People     **Hear us, Lord.**

Leader     Grant to all who mourn a sure confidence in your loving care that casting all their sorrow on you, they may know the consolation of your love.

People     **Hear us, Lord.**

Leader     Give courage and faith to those who are bereaved, that they may have strength to meet the days ahead in the comfort of a holy and certain hope, and in the joyful expectation of eternal life with those they love.

People     **Hear us, Lord.**

| Leader | Grant us grace to entrust *N* to your never-failing love which sustained *him/her* in this life. Receive *him/her* into the arms of your mercy, and remember *him/her* according to the favour you bear for your people. |
| People | **Hear us, Lord.** |

*If the eucharist is not to be celebrated, the service continues with the Lord's Prayer on p. 583 or 584, followed by the Commendation on p. 586.*


## The Peace

*All stand, and the presiding celebrant addresses the people.*

| | The peace of the Lord be always with you. |
| People | **And also with you.** |


# The Celebration of the Eucharist

## The Preparation of the Gifts

*A hymn may be sung. Members of the family or friends of the deceased person may present the gifts of bread and wine for the eucharist to the deacon or celebrant.*

*When the gifts have been prepared, the celebrant may say the Prayer over the Gifts.*

| Celebrant | God of mercy, accept the worship we offer you this day. Increase, we pray, our faith, deepen our hope, and confirm us in your eternal love. We ask this in the name of Jesus Christ the Lord. |
| People | **Amen.** |

# The Great Thanksgiving

*Other eucharistic prayers may be found on pp. 193–210.*

| | |
|---|---|
| *Celebrant* | The Lord be with you. |
| *People* | **And also with you.** |

| | |
|---|---|
| *Celebrant* | Lift up your hearts. |
| *People* | **We lift them to the Lord.** |

| | |
|---|---|
| *Celebrant* | Let us give thanks to the Lord our God. |
| *People* | **It is right to give our thanks and praise.** |

*Celebrant*    Blessed are you, gracious God,
creator of heaven and earth;
we give you thanks and praise
through Jesus Christ our Lord,
whose victorious rising from the dead
has given to us the hope of resurrection
and the promise of eternal life.
Therefore with angels and archangels
and all who have served you in every age,
we raise our voices
to proclaim the glory of your name.

*All*    **Holy, holy, holy Lord,
God of power and might,
heaven and earth are full of your glory.
Hosanna in the highest.**

**Blessed is he who comes in the name of the Lord.
Hosanna in the highest.**

*Celebrant*    We give thanks to you, Lord our God,
for the goodness and love
you have made known to us in creation;
in calling Israel to be your people;
in your Word spoken through the prophets;
and above all in the Word made flesh,
Jesus your Son.

For in these last days you sent him
to be incarnate from the Virgin Mary,
to be the Saviour and Redeemer of the world.
In him, you have delivered us from evil,
and made us worthy to stand before you.
In him, you have brought us
out of error into truth,
out of sin into righteousness,
out of death into life.

On the night he was handed over
to suffering and death,
a death he freely accepted,
our Lord Jesus Christ took bread;
and when he had given thanks to you,
he broke it, and gave it to his disciples,
and said, "Take, eat:
this is my body, which is given for you.
Do this for the remembrance of me."

After supper he took the cup of wine;
and when he had given thanks,
he gave it to them,
and said, "Drink this, all of you:
this is my blood of the new covenant,
which is shed for you and for many
for the forgiveness of sins.
Whenever you drink it,
do this for the remembrance of me."

Therefore, Father, according to his command,

*All*     **we remember his death,**
**we proclaim his resurrection,**
**we await his coming in glory;**

*Celebrant*     and we offer our sacrifice
of praise and thanksgiving
to you, Lord of all;
presenting to you, from your creation,
this bread and this wine.

We pray you, gracious God,
to send your Holy Spirit upon these gifts,
that they may be the sacrament
of the body of Christ
and his blood of the new covenant.
Unite us to your Son in his sacrifice,
that we, made acceptable in him,
may be sanctified by the Holy Spirit.

In the fullness of time,
reconcile all things in Christ,
and make them new,
and bring us to that city of light
where you dwell with all your sons and daughters;
through Jesus Christ our Lord,
the firstborn of all creation,
the head of the Church,
and the author of our salvation;

by whom, and with whom, and in whom,
in the unity of the Holy Spirit,
all honour and glory are yours, almighty Father,
now and for ever.

*People*     **Amen.**

## The Lord's Prayer

*Celebrant*     As our Saviour taught us, let us pray,
*All*     **Our Father in heaven,
hallowed be your name,
your kingdom come,
your will be done,
on earth as in heaven.
Give us today our daily bread.
Forgive us our sins
as we forgive those who sin against us.
Save us from the time of trial,
and deliver us from evil.
For the kingdom, the power,
and the glory are yours,
now and for ever. Amen.**

*Or*

| | |
|---|---|
| *Celebrant* | And now, as our Saviour Christ has taught us, we are bold to say, |
| *All* | **Our Father, who art in heaven,**<br>**hallowed be thy name,**<br>**thy kingdom come,**<br>**thy will be done,**<br>**on earth as it is in heaven.**<br>**Give us this day our daily bread.**<br>**And forgive us our trespasses,**<br>**as we forgive those who trespass against us.**<br>**And lead us not into temptation,**<br>**but deliver us from evil.**<br>**For thine is the kingdom,**<br>**the power, and the glory,**<br>**for ever and ever. Amen.** |

*If the eucharist is not celebrated the service continues with the Commendation on p. 586.*

*Silence*

*The celebrant breaks the consecrated bread for distribution, and may say the following:*

This is the bread which has come down from heaven.

*All* **Those who eat this bread will live for ever.**

*The celebrant invites the people to share in communion and may say,*

The gifts of God for the People of God.

*People* **Thanks be to God.**

*The sacrament is given with the following words.*

The body of Christ (given for you).
The blood of Christ (shed for you).

*Or* The body of Christ, the bread of heaven.
The blood of Christ, the cup of salvation.

*The communicant responds each time,* **Amen.**

*During the breaking of the bread and the communion, psalms, hymns, and anthems such as the following may be sung.*

**(Alleluia!) Christ our passover is sacrificed for us; therefore let us keep the feast (Alleluia!).**

**Lamb of God, you take away the sin of the world: have mercy on us (*or* grant them rest).**
**Lamb of God, you take away the sin of the world: have mercy on us (*or* grant them rest).**
**Lamb of God, you take away the sin of the world: grant us peace (*or* grant them rest eternal).**

## Prayer after Communion

*Celebrant*    Let us pray.

*Standing, the community prays in silence. Then the celebrant says one of the following:*

God of love,
you have fed us at the table of your kingdom.
Teach us to trust, without fear,
in your eternal goodness and mercy.
We ask this in the name of Jesus Christ the Lord. **Amen.**

*Or*

Almighty God, we thank you
that in your great love you have fed us
with the spiritual food and drink
of the body and blood of your Son Jesus Christ,
and have given us a foretaste
of your heavenly banquet.
Grant that this sacrament may be to us
a comfort in affliction,
and a pledge of our inheritance
in that kingdom where there is no death,
neither sorrow nor crying,
but fullness of joy with all your saints;
through Jesus Christ our Saviour. **Amen.**

# The Commendation

*The celebrant and other ministers stand by the body, where they may be joined by members of the family and friends of the deceased person.*

*This anthem, or some other suitable anthem, or a hymn, may be sung or said.*

**Give rest, O Christ, to your servants with your saints,
where sorrow and pain are no more,
neither sighing, but life everlasting.**

**You only are immortal, the creator and maker of all;
and we are mortal, formed of the earth,
and to earth shall we return.
For so did you ordain when you created me, saying,
"You are dust, and to dust you shall return."
All of us go down to the dust;
yet even at the grave we make our song:
Alleluia, alleluia, alleluia.**

**Give rest, O Christ, to your servants with your saints,
where sorrow and pain are no more,
neither sighing, but life everlasting.**

*The celebrant, facing the body, says,*

Into your hands, O merciful Saviour,
we commend your servant *N*.
Acknowledge, we pray, a sheep of your own fold,
a lamb of your own flock,
a sinner of your own redeeming.
Receive *him/her* into the arms of your mercy,
into the blessed rest of everlasting peace,
and into the glorious company of the saints in light. **Amen.**

*The celebrant, or the bishop if present, may then bless the people, and a deacon or other minister may dismiss them, saying,*

Let us go forth in the name of Christ.

*People*    **Thanks be to God.**

*As the body is borne from the church, a psalm (or part thereof), a hymn, an anthem, or a canticle may be sung or said. The following are appropriate: The Song of Zechariah, The Song of Simeon, Christ our Passover.*

# The Committal

*The following anthem, or a similar anthem, is sung or said.*

Everyone the Father gives to me will come to me; I will never
turn away anyone who believes in me.    *John 6.37*

He who raised Jesus Christ from the dead will also give new life
to our mortal bodies through his indwelling Spirit.    *Romans 8.11*

My heart, therefore, is glad, and my spirit rejoices; my body
also shall rest in hope.    *Psalm 16.9*

You will show me the path of life; in your presence there is
fullness of joy, and in your right hand are pleasures for
evermore.    *Psalm 16.11*

*Then (while earth is cast upon the coffin if appropriate), the celebrant says,*

In sure and certain hope of the resurrection to eternal life
through our Lord Jesus Christ,
we commend to almighty God our *brother/sister N*,
and we commit *his/her* body to the ground; †
earth to earth, ashes to ashes, dust to dust.
The Lord bless *him/her* and keep *him/her*,
the Lord make his face to shine upon *him/her*
and be gracious to *him/her*,
the Lord lift up his countenance upon *him/her*
and give *him/her* peace. **Amen.**

† *Or* to be consumed by fire, *or* to its resting place, *or* to the deep.

*The celebrant says,*

|  | The Lord be with you. |
|---|---|
| *People* | **And also with you.** |
| *Celebrant* | Let us pray. |

*The celebrant may offer any of the prayers on pp. 601–603, or other suitable prayers. If the committal does not take place immediately following the Funeral Liturgy in church, the Lord's Prayer may be said.*

*Then may be said,*

| | |
|---|---|
| Celebrant | Rest eternal grant to *him/her*, O Lord. |
| People | **And let light perpetual shine upon *him/her*.** |

| | |
|---|---|
| Celebrant | May *his/her* soul, |
| | and the souls of all the departed, |
| | through the mercy of God, rest in peace. |
| People | **Amen.** |

*The celebrant dismisses the people with these or similar words.*

May the God of peace
who brought again from the dead our Lord Jesus,
the great shepherd of the sheep,
by the blood of the eternal covenant,
equip you with everything good
that you may do his will,
working in you that which is pleasing in his sight,
through Jesus Christ,
to whom be glory for ever and ever.

People     **Amen.**

Go forth in the name of Christ.
People     **Thanks be to God.**

# The Funeral Liturgy
**Form II**

*This form of the Funeral Liturgy is for use in a church or a chapel or other suitable place.*

*The celebrant welcomes the congregation and may at this time, or after the readings, express thanksgiving for the gifts of the deceased person, especially the marks of a Christian life. Such remarks, without denying the legitimate grief of the mourners, should relate the life and death of the Christian to the victory of Christ. The celebrant then says,*

I am Resurrection and I am Life, says the Lord.
Whoever has faith in me shall have life,
even though he die.
And everyone who has life,
and is committed to me in faith,
shall not die for ever.    *John 11.25–26*

Let not your hearts be troubled;
believe in God, believe also in me.
In my Father's house are many rooms;
if it were not so, would I have told you
that I go to prepare a place for you?
And when I go and prepare a place for you,
I will come again and will take you to myself,
that where I am you may be also.    *John 14.1–3*

I am sure that neither death, nor life,
nor angels, nor principalities,
nor things present, nor things to come,
nor powers, nor height, nor depth,
nor anything else in all creation,
will be able to separate us from the love of God
in Christ Jesus our Lord.    *Romans 8.38–39*

*Then a hymn may be sung, or a psalm or canticle said or sung. The following are suitable psalms.*

# Psalm 121

I lift up my eyes to the hills; *
    from where is my help to come?
My help comes from the Lord,*
    the maker of heaven and earth.

He will not let your foot be moved *
    and he who watches over you will not fall asleep.
Behold, he who keeps watch over Israel *
    shall neither slumber nor sleep;

The Lord himself watches over you; *
    the Lord is your shade at your right hand,
So that the sun shall not strike you by day,*
    nor the moon by night.

The Lord shall preserve you from all evil; *
    it is he who shall keep you safe.
The Lord shall watch over your going out and
                        your coming in,*
    from this time forth for evermore.

# Psalm 139

Lord, you have searched me out and known me; *
    you know my sitting down and my rising up;
    you discern my thoughts from afar.
You trace my journeys and my resting-places *
    and are acquainted with all my ways.
Indeed, there is not a word on my lips,*
    but you, O Lord, know it altogether.

You press upon me behind and before *
    and lay your hand upon me.
Such knowledge is too wonderful for me; *
    it is so high that I cannot attain to it.

Where can I go then from your Spirit? *
    where can I flee from your presence?

If I climb up to heaven, you are there; *
  if I make the grave my bed, you are there also.

If I take the wings of the morning *
  and dwell in the uttermost parts of the sea,
Even there your hand will lead me *
  and your right hand hold me fast.

If I say, "Surely the darkness will cover me,*
  and the light around me turn to night,"
Darkness is not dark to you;
the night is as bright as the day; *
  darkness and light to you are both alike.

*Other suitable psalms are 23, 122, 126, 130, 132, 134. After a psalm or canticle the following may be said or sung.*
Glory to the Father, and to the Son, and to the Holy Spirit: *
  as it was in the beginning, is now, and will be for ever.
            Amen.

*Then the celebrant shall say,*

            The Lord be with you.
*People*     **And also with you.**

*Celebrant*  Let us pray.

            God of all consolation,
            in your unending love and mercy
            you turn the darkness of death
            into the dawn of new life.

            Show compassion to your people in their sorrow.
            Be our refuge and our strength
            to lift us from the darkness of grief
            to the peace and light of your presence.

            Your Son, our Lord Jesus Christ,
            by dying for us, conquered death
            and by rising again, restored life.

| Leader | Grant us grace to entrust N to your never-failing love which sustained *him/her* in this life. Receive *him/her* into the arms of your mercy, and remember *him/her* according to the favour you bear for your people. |
| People | **Hear us, Lord.** |

## The Lord's Prayer

| Celebrant | Gathering all our cares into one, let us pray as our Saviour taught us, |
| All | **Our Father in heaven, hallowed be your name, your kingdom come, your will be done, on earth as in heaven. Give us today our daily bread. Forgive us our sins as we forgive those who sin against us. Save us from the time of trial, and deliver us from evil. For the kingdom, the power, and the glory are yours, now and for ever. Amen.** |

*Or*

| Celebrant | And now, as our Saviour Christ has taught us, we are bold to say, |
| All | **Our Father, who art in heaven, hallowed be thy name, thy kingdom come, thy will be done, on earth as it is in heaven. Give us this day our daily bread. And forgive us our trespasses, as we forgive those who trespass against us. And lead us not into temptation, but deliver us from evil. For thine is the kingdom, the power, and the glory, for ever and ever. Amen.** |

# The Commendation

*A hymn may be sung, or this anthem or some other suitable anthem may be sung or said.*

**Give rest, O Christ, to your servants with your saints,**
**where sorrow and pain are no more,**
**neither sighing, but life everlasting.**

**You only are immortal, the creator and maker of all;**
**and we are mortal, formed of the earth,**
**and to earth shall we return.**
**For so did you ordain when you created me, saying,**
**"You are dust, and to dust you shall return."**
**All of us go down to the dust;**
**yet even at the grave we make our song:**
**Alleluia, alleluia, alleluia.**

**Give rest, O Christ, to your servants with your saints,**
**where sorrow and pain are no more,**
**neither sighing, but life everlasting.**

*The celebrant, facing the body, says,*

Into your hands, O merciful Saviour,
we commend your servant N.
Acknowledge, we pray, a sheep of your own fold,
a lamb of your own flock,
a sinner of your own redeeming.
Receive *him/her* into the arms of your mercy,
into the blessed rest of everlasting peace,
and into the glorious company of the saints in light. **Amen.**

*The celebrant may then bless the people and dismiss them with these or similar words.*

|  | The eternal God is your dwelling place, |
|  | and underneath are the everlasting arms. |
| *People* | **Blessed is the Lord,** |
|  | **our strength and our salvation.** |

*Or*

| | |
|---|---|
| *Celebrant* | Go forth in the name of Christ. |
| *People* | **Thanks be to God.** |

*As the body is removed, a psalm (or part thereof), a hymn, an anthem, or a canticle may be sung or said. The following are appropriate: The Song of Zechariah, The Song of Simeon, Christ our Passover.*

## The Committal

*The following anthem, or a similar anthem, is sung or said.*

Everyone the Father gives to me will come to me; I will never turn away anyone who believes in me.   *John 6.37*

He who raised Jesus Christ from the dead will also give new life to our mortal bodies through his indwelling Spirit.   *Romans 8.11*

My heart, therefore, is glad, and my spirit rejoices; my body also shall rest in hope.   *Psalm 16.9*

You will show me the path of life; in your presence there is fullness of joy, and in your right hand are pleasures for evermore.   *Psalm 16.11*

*Then (while earth is cast upon the coffin if appropriate), the celebrant says,*

In sure and certain hope of the resurrection to eternal life
through our Lord Jesus Christ,
we commend to almighty God our *brother/sister N*,
and we commit *his/her* body to the ground; †
earth to earth, ashes to ashes, dust to dust.
The Lord bless *him/her* and keep *him/her*,
the Lord make his face to shine upon *him/her*
and be gracious to *him/her*,
the Lord lift up his countenance upon *him/her*
and give *him/her* peace. **Amen.**

† *Or* to be consumed by fire, *or* to its resting place, *or* to the deep.

The Lord be with you.

*People* **And also with you.**

*Celebrant* Let us pray.

*The celebrant may offer any of the prayers on pp. 601–603, or other suitable prayers. If the committal does not take place immediately following the Funeral Liturgy in church, the Lord's Prayer may be said.*

*Then may be said,*

*Celebrant* Rest eternal grant to *him/her*, O Lord.

*People* **And let light perpetual shine upon *him/her*.**

*Celebrant* May *his/her* soul,
and the souls of all the departed,
through the mercy of God, rest in peace.

*People* **Amen.**

*The celebrant dismisses the people with these or similar words.*

May the God of peace
who brought again from the dead our Lord Jesus,
the great shepherd of the sheep,
by the blood of the eternal covenant,
equip you with everything good
that you may do his will,
working in you that which is pleasing in his sight,
through Jesus Christ,
to whom be glory for ever and ever.

*People* **Amen.**

*Celebrant* Go forth in the name of Christ.

*People* **Thanks be to God.**

# The Funeral Liturgy

## Form III

*This form of the Funeral Liturgy is for use in those circumstances in which it is necessary for the entire public act of worship to take place as a single event and in one place. It is suitable for use in a home or hall when a church building is too far away or unusable because of bad weather, and when the committal must be deferred because of weather or the distance of the grave.*

*The celebrant may be a bishop, priest, deacon, or lay person.*

*A number of options are open to those planning the service.*

*Prayers in the Home or Elsewhere beginning on p. 571, may be used as the basic Funeral Liturgy. More than one lesson may be read, and comment on the scriptures may include an expression of thanksgiving for the gifts of the deceased person, especially the marks of a Christian life.*

*A Funeral Liturgy for Use in Church, beginning on p. 576, may be used, with such amendments as are appropriate to the time and place. If a bishop or priest presides, the eucharist may be celebrated.*

*The blessing and dismissal provided at the end of these services are omitted and appear at the end of the Commendation (p. 586) which immediately follows.*

*When the body is to be interred privately or at a later date, or when the body is for some reason unrecoverable, the Committal may be recited, in which case the blessing and dismissal are deferred until after the Committal.*

*The Lord's Prayer may be recited at any of the suggested points in any of these rites, but should not be recited more than once in the course of the liturgy.*

# The Interment of Ashes

*The celebrant may greet those present with words of Holy Scripture such as the following:*

I know that my Redeemer lives, and at last he will stand upon the earth; and after my skin has been thus destroyed, then from my flesh I shall see God, whom I shall see on my side, and my eyes shall behold, and not another.   *Job 19.25–27*

I heard a voice from heaven saying, "Write this: Blessed are the dead who die in the Lord henceforth." "Blessed indeed," says the Spirit, "that they may rest from their labours, for their deeds follow them!"   *Revelation 14.13*

*One or more of the psalms and one or more of the readings suggested on p. 604 may be read.*

*While the ashes are put in their final resting place, the celebrant says these words.*

In sure and certain hope of the resurrection to eternal life
through our Lord Jesus Christ,
we commend to almighty God our *brother/sister N,*
and we commit *his/her* ashes to the ground; †
earth to earth, ashes to ashes, dust to dust.
The Lord bless *him/her* and keep *him/her,*
the Lord make his face to shine upon *him/her*
and be gracious to *him/her,*
the Lord lift up his countenance upon *him/her*
and give *him/her* peace. **Amen.**

† *Or* the deep, *or* their resting place.

*The celebrant says,*

|          | The Lord be with you.       |
|----------|------------------------------|
| *People* | **And also with you.**       |

*Celebrant*    Let us pray.

*The celebrant may offer any of the prayers on pp. 601–603, or other suitable prayers. The Lord's Prayer may be said.*

| | |
|---|---|
| *Celebrant* | Rest eternal grant to *him/her*, O Lord. |
| *People* | **And let light perpetual shine upon *him/her*.** |

| | |
|---|---|
| *Celebrant* | May *his/her* soul,<br>and the souls of all the departed,<br>through the mercy of God, rest in peace. |
| *People* | **Amen.** |

*The celebrant dismisses the people with these or similar words.*

> May the God of peace
> who brought again from the dead our Lord Jesus,
> the great shepherd of the sheep,
> by the blood of the eternal covenant,
> equip you with everything good
> that you may do his will,
> working in you that which is pleasing in his sight,
> through Jesus Christ,
> to whom be glory for ever and ever.

| | |
|---|---|
| *People* | **Amen.** |

| | |
|---|---|
| *Celebrant* | Go forth in the name of Christ. |
| *People* | **Thanks be to God.** |

## The Consecration of a Grave

*If the grave is in a place that has not previously been set apart for Christian burial, the celebrant (if a bishop or priest) may use the following prayer, either before the service of committal or at some other convenient time.*

O God, whose blessed Son was laid in a sepulchre in the garden: bless, we pray, this grave, and grant that *he/she* whose body is to be buried here may dwell with Christ in paradise, and may come to your heavenly kingdom; through your Son Jesus Christ our Lord. **Amen.**

## Additional Prayers

Almighty and everlasting God, with whom still live the spirits of those who die in the Lord, and with whom the souls of the faithful are in joy and felicity: we give you heartfelt thanks for the good examples of all your servants, who having finished their course in faith, now find rest and refreshment. May we, with all who have died in the true faith of your holy name, have perfect fulfilment and bliss in your eternal and everlasting glory, through Jesus Christ our Lord. **Amen.**

O God, whose days are without end and whose mercies cannot be numbered: make us, we pray, deeply aware of the shortness and uncertainty of human life, and let your Holy Spirit lead us in holiness and righteousness all our days; that when we shall have served you in our generation, we may be gathered to our ancestors, having the testimony of a good conscience, in the communion of the catholic Church, in the confidence of a certain faith, in the comfort of a religious and holy hope, in favour with you, our God, and in perfect charity with all. We ask this through Jesus Christ our Lord. **Amen.**

O God, the king of saints, we praise and glorify your holy name for all your servants who have finished their course in your faith and fear: for the blessed Virgin Mary; for the holy patriarchs, prophets, apostles, and martyrs; and for all your other righteous servants, known to us and unknown; and we pray that, encouraged by their examples, aided by their prayers, and strengthened by their fellowship, we also may be partakers of the inheritance of the saints in light; through the merits of your Son Jesus Christ our Lord. **Amen.**

Merciful God, Father of our Lord Jesus Christ who is the Resurrection and the Life: raise us, we humbly pray, from the death of sin to the life of righteousness; that when we depart this life we may rest in him, and at the resurrection receive that blessing which your well-beloved Son shall then pronounce: "Come, you blessed of my Father, receive the kingdom prepared for you from the beginning of the world." Grant this, O merciful Father, through Jesus Christ, our Mediator and Redeemer. **Amen.**

Lord Jesus Christ, by your death you took away the sting of death. Grant to us your servants so to follow in faith where you have led the way, that we may at length fall asleep peacefully in you and wake up in your likeness, for your tender mercies' sake. **Amen.**

Father of all, we pray to you for those we love but see no longer. Grant them your peace; let light perpetual shine upon them; and in your loving wisdom and almighty power, work in them the good purpose of your perfect will, through Jesus Christ our Lord. **Amen.**

Grant, O Lord, to all who are bereaved the spirit of faith and courage, that they may have strength to meet the days to come with steadfastness and patience; not sorrowing as those without hope, but in thankful remembrance of your great goodness, and in the joyful expectation of eternal life with those they love. And this we ask in the name of Jesus Christ our Saviour. **Amen.**

Almighty God, Father of mercies and giver of comfort, deal graciously, we pray, with all who mourn; that casting all their care on you, they may know the consolation of your love, through Jesus Christ our Lord. **Amen.**

*The following prayer may be adapted to reflect the age, sex, and other aspects of the deceased person. It may be used as the Prayers of the People.*

God of grace and glory, we thank you for N, who was so near and dear to us, and who has now been taken from us.

We thank you for the friendship *he/she* gave and for the strength and peace *he/she* brought.

We thank you for the love *he/she* offered and received while *he/she* was with us on earth.

We pray that nothing good in this *man's/woman's* life will be lost, but will be of benefit to the world; that all that was important to *him/her* will be respected by those who follow; and that everything in which *he/she* was great will continue to mean much to us now that *he/she* is dead.

We ask you that *he/she* may go on living in *his/her children*, *his/her* family and *his/her* friends; in their hearts and minds, in their courage and their consciences.

We ask you that we who were close to *him/her* may now, because of *his/her* death, be even closer to each other, and that we may, in peace and friendship here on earth, always be deeply conscious of your promise to be faithful to us in death.

We pray for ourselves, who are severely tested by this death, that we do not try to minimize this loss, or seek refuge from it in words alone, and also that we do not brood over it so that it overwhelms us and isolates us from others.

May God grant us courage and confidence in the new life of Christ.

We ask this in the name of the risen Lord. **Amen.** †

## Prayers for the Funeral of a Child

O God, whose beloved Son took children into his arms and blessed them, give us grace to entrust *N* to your never-failing care and love, and bring us all to your heavenly kingdom; through Jesus Christ our Lord, who lives and reigns with you and the Holy Spirit, one God, now and for ever. **Amen.**

Most merciful God, whose wisdom is beyond our understanding, deal graciously with *NN* in *their* grief. Surround *them* with your love, that *they* may not be overwhelmed by *their* loss, but have confidence in your goodness and strength to meet the days to come; through Jesus Christ our Lord. **Amen.**

Lord, listen to the prayers of this family that put their trust in you. In their sorrow at the death of this child, may they find hope in your infinite mercy. We ask this through Christ our Lord. **Amen.**

†   Adapted from "For a Dead Person" from *Your Word is Near* by Huub
    Oosterhuis. © 1968 by the Missionary Society of St. Paul the Apostle in the
    State of New York. Used by permission of the Paulist Press.

# Readings and Psalms Suitable for Funeral Liturgies

## Old Testament Readings

Job 19.1, 21–27a   (I know that my Redeemer lives)

Isaiah 25.6–9   (He will swallow up death for ever)

Isaiah 61.1–3   (To comfort all who mourn)

Lamentations 3.17–26, 31–33   (The steadfast love of the Lord never ceases)

Daniel 12.1–3   (Every one whose name shall be found written in the book)

Wisdom 3.1–6(7–9)   (The souls of the righteous are in the hand of God)

## Psalms and Suitable Refrains

23   (I will dwell in the house of the Lord for ever)

25   (Remember me according to your love, O Lord)

42   (I will give thanks to him who is my help and my God)

51   (Have mercy on me, O God, according to your loving-kindness)

90   (From age to age you are God)

121   (My help comes from the Lord, the maker of heaven and earth)

122   (May they prosper who love Jerusalem)

126   (Those who sowed with tears will reap with songs of joy)

130   (My soul waits for the Lord, for with the Lord there is mercy)

134   (Bless the Lord who made heaven and earth)

139   (Lead me in the way that is everlasting)

## New Testament Readings

Romans 6.3–9   (All of us who have been baptized into Christ Jesus were baptized into his death)

Romans 8.14–19(34–35, 37–39)   (The glory that is to be revealed)

Romans 14.7–9   (Whether we live or whether we die, we are the Lord's)

1 Corinthians 15.20–28(35–44a)   (In Christ shall all be made alive)

1 Corinthians 15.51–57   (Death is swallowed up in victory)

2 Corinthians 4.7–18   (The things that are unseen are eternal)

2 Corinthians 5.1–9   (What is mortal may be swallowed up by life)

Philippians 3.20–21   (To be like his glorious body)

1 Thessalonians 4.13–18   (So we shall always be with the Lord)

2 Timothy 2.8–12a   (If we have died with him, we shall also live with him)

1 Peter 1.3–9   (We have been born anew to a living hope)

1 John 3.1–2   (We shall be like him)

1 John 4.7–18a   (We may have confidence for the day of judgement)

Revelation 21.1–7   (Behold I make all things new)

## Gospel Readings

Matthew 5.1–12a   (Rejoice and be glad, for your reward is great in heaven)
Matthew 11.25–30   (Come to me . . . and I will give you rest)
Mark 15.33–39; 16.1–7   (He has risen, he is not here)
Luke 24.13–16(17–27)28–35   (He was known to them in the breaking of the
    bread)
John 5.24–27   (Who hears my word and believes him who sent me, has
    eternal life)
John 6.37–40   (All that the Father gives me will come to me)
John 10.11–16   (I am the good shepherd)
John 11.17–27   (I am the resurrection and the life)
John 14.1–6   (In my Father's house are many rooms)
John 20.1–9   (The stone had been taken away from the tomb)

## Non-Biblical Readings

A short, appropriate reading from a non-biblical source may be read instead of
one of the readings before the Gospel, or at the time of the sermon, or at
another suitable point in the service.

# Thanksgiving for the Gift of a Child

This service provides an alternative to the Prayer Book rite of the Churching of Women, expanding the focus of thanksgiving to include the child and the whole family.

It may be helpful to explore some biblical and human history in order to appreciate this change in emphasis. There is an ancient and basic impulse in human society to treat as special or sacred those whom circumstances have brought into contact with the forces of life and death. Often this sacred status is both holy and polluting. In Numbers 19.14 everyone who enters the tent of a dead person is unclean, and in Leviticus 12 a woman who bears a child is unclean; both require ritual purification in order to be restored to ordinary membership in the community.

The New Testament recognizes this impulse and at the same time resists the theological and moral vision of reality on which it is based. On one hand we have Luke's beautiful account of the ritual purification of Mary after the birth of Jesus (2.22–39); on the other hand we have Jesus' statement that it is unethical behaviour and not technical impurity which defiles a person (Matthew 15.16–20), and Paul's warning against an obsessive preoccupation with the traditional ritual calendar (Galatians 4.10f). The freedom of the Gospel includes freedom from technical, ritual status.

In spite of Christian emancipation from the notion that certain life experiences make people more or less holy without regard to their ethical implications, it has remained true for generations of Christians that close contact with the springs of life and the gates of death produces a particular kind of consciousness, in both the individual and his or her society, which may demand expression and resolution in a particular kind of prayer. Thus forms of prayer for and by women who have recently given birth have been common among Christians at least since the fourth century.

Sometimes these forms of prayer have reflected a vision of technical impurity which is hard to reconcile with the spirit of the New Testament. In some societies women who have not performed certain rituals have been isolated and ostracized. In other cases these forms of prayer have reflected the simple fact that pregnancy and the special care it requires creates in some cases a distance between a woman and her community, as well as the fact that the delivery of a child is not without risk even in a technologically developed society.

The development of these forms of prayer may be traced in the names which have been given to them in the various Books of Common Prayer. In 1549 it was "The Order of the Purification of Women"; in 1552 it became, "The Thanksgiving of Women after Childbirth, commonly called the Churching of Women"; it now becomes, "A Thanksgiving for the Gift of a Child." The rubrics directing the place of the woman during the ceremony also provide a clue to the changing mind of the Church: the Sarum rite directed the woman to stand "before the church door"; the 1549 Prayer Book said, "nigh unto the quire door"; in 1552 it was "nigh unto the place where the table standeth"; in 1662 it was "in some convenient place as hath been accustomed, or as the ordinary shall direct."[1] Our new rite instructs the celebrant to "invite the parents and other members of the family (or families) to present themselves before the congregation."

Clearly the mind of the Church has been moving and the focus of these forms of prayer has shifted, not only away from notions of pollution and purification but also away from exclusive concentration on the mother towards inclusion of the child and the father, and even other members of the family. This shift is entirely consistent with the New Testament's emphasis on thanksgiving as well as its suspicion of ritual status. However, those who use this rite should be conscious of two areas in which it could be open to misunderstanding.

First, moments of deep involvement in the process of life and death are turning points in our lives; the need for rituals at such moments varies in intensity from one person to another and no one can decide for another whether a ritual action is important or even necessary. Such rituals are legitimate, even healthy, when they are not allowed to degenerate into mere ritualism and when neither their form nor their absence is used to dehumanize the persons involved.

Second, the concentration of attention on the child as the cause of thanksgiving should not lead to confusion of this rite with Christian initiation. The normative form of initiation remains the baptism of adults on their profession of faith; initiation may also be extended to the children of faithful parents. Thanksgiving for the birth or adoption of a child is not baptism, even though it may be an appropriate action on the part of parents who have decided (for whatever reason is good to them) to defer the baptism of a child. Confusion of a service of thanksgiving with Christian initiation will only result in the denigration of both.

This liturgy has been prepared to meet a number of human situations: a mother's delivery of a child, the thanksgiving of a family for the birth of a child, the thanksgiving of a family for the adoption of a child. Not all these elements will be present on any given occasion. This material must therefore be used with discrimination and sensitivity relevant to the immediate context.

1   *The Oxford Dictionary of the Christian Church*, Oxford University Press, London, 1958, p. 290.

# Concerning the Service

*This service provides an opportunity for parents to give thanks for the birth or adoption of a child and to offer prayer for the life of their family. This service must not be confused with Holy Baptism, which is the sacrament of initiation into the People of God. The Service of Thanksgiving for the Gift of a Child may precede or follow Holy Baptism, on the same occasion or at some other time, or it may be used by those parents who do not, for some reason, wish to present a child for baptism at that time. Holy Baptism is administered with water in the name of the Father, the Son, and the Holy Spirit; the Service of Thanksgiving for the Gift of a Child does not replace Holy Baptism and should not be conducted at the font.*

*As soon as may be convenient after the birth of a child, or after receiving a child for adoption, the parents, with other members of the family, may come to the Church to give thanks to God and to be greeted by the congregation. It is desirable that this take place at a public service on a Sunday. If the child is not to be baptized on that occasion, this service may follow or take the place of the Prayers of the People in the eucharist or the Intercessions and Thanksgivings in Morning or Evening Prayer.*

*A reading, such as Luke 2.41–51 or Luke 18.15–17, may follow the psalm.*

*At the appointed time the celebrant shall invite the parents and other members of the family (or families) to present themselves before the congregation.*

# Thanksgiving for the Gift of a Child

*The celebrant greets the people, saying,*

> The Lord be with you.

*People*   **And also with you.**

*The celebrant addresses the congregation in these or similar words.*

Dear friends in Christ, we have come to thank God our creator for the gift of *this child N*; therefore let us join with *his/her family* in this song of praise.

## Psalm 103   *1–4, 13, 17, 18, 22*

Bless the Lord, O my soul,*
   and all that is within me, bless his holy name.
Bless the Lord, O my soul,*
   and forget not all his benefits.

He forgives all your sins *
   and heals all your infirmities;
He redeems your life from the grave *
   and crowns you with mercy and loving kindness;

As a father cares for his children,*
   so does the Lord care for those who fear him.
The merciful goodness of the Lord endures for ever
                  on those who fear him,*
   and his righteousness on children's children;
On those who keep his covenant *
   and remember his commandments and do them.

Bless the Lord, all you works of his,
in all places of his dominion; *
   bless the Lord, O my soul.

Glory to the Father, and to the Son, and to the Holy Spirit: *
    as it was in the beginning, is now, and will be for ever. Amen.

*Or*

# Psalm 23

The Lord is my shepherd; *
    I shall not be in want.
He makes me lie down in green pastures *
    and leads me beside still waters.
He revives my soul *
    and guides me along right pathways for his name's sake.

Though I walk through the valley of the shadow of death,
I shall fear no evil; *
    for you are with me;
    your rod and your staff, they comfort me.
You spread a table before me in the presence of those
                who trouble me; *
    you have anointed my head with oil,
    and my cup is running over.

Surely your goodness and mercy shall follow me all
                the days of my life,*
    and I will dwell in the house of the Lord forever.

Glory to the Father, and to the Son, and to the Holy Spirit: *
    as it was in the beginning, is now and will be for ever. Amen.

*The celebrant then says,*

Let us pray.

God, giver of life,
we thank you for the gift of *this child.*
Confirm our joy by your presence;
give us quiet strength and patient wisdom
as we seek to nurture *him/her*
in all that is good, true, just, and pure,
through Jesus Christ our Lord. **Amen.**

*The parents of the child may say together,*

God our creator and redeemer,
thank you for the gift of *this child*,
entrusted to our care for a time.
May we be patient and understanding,
ready to guide and forgive,
that in our love *this child* may know your love,
and learn to love your world
and the whole family of your children;
through Jesus Christ our Lord. Amen.

*If only one parent of a child is present the above form may be used or the parent may say,*

God our creator and redeemer,
thank you for the gift of *this child*,
entrusted to my care for a time.
May I be patient and understanding,
ready to guide and forgive,
that in my love *this child* may know your love,
and learn to love your world
and the whole family of your children;
through Jesus Christ our Lord. Amen.

*The celebrant may add one or more of the following prayers.*

### Thanksgiving after Delivery

Gracious God, creator and sustainer of human life, we praise you that you have called *N* to share in your creative acts in the great mystery of childbirth. We give you thanks that she has been brought safely through the time of pregnancy and labour. Grant that she may know your joy in bringing new life into this world which you love, in the name of him who was born of a woman, Jesus Christ our Redeemer. **Amen.**

### For the Family

Lord and Saviour Jesus Christ, who shared in Nazareth the life of an earthly home, dwell in the *home* of these your servants, give them grace to serve others as you have served, and grant that by deed and word they may be witnesses of your saving love to those among whom they live, for the sake of your holy name. **Amen.**

### For a Child Born Handicapped

O God, creator of us all, we give you thanks for the life of this child. Grant us understanding, compassionate, and accepting hearts, and the gifts of courage and patience to face the challenge of caring for *him/her*; let your love for us show forth in our lives, that we may create an atmosphere in which *he/she* will live a life full of dignity and worth. We ask this in the name of Jesus Christ the Lord. **Amen.**

*The celebrant and people together may say,*

> **God, giver of all life,**
> **we thank you for calling us**
> **to share in your work of creation,**
> **and especially for giving us this child N.**
> **Help us to show *him/her* such faith and love**
> **that *he/she* may daily grow in grace**
> **and live to serve you and your people,**
> **through Jesus Christ our Lord. Amen.**

*Unless the Lord's Prayer is said elsewhere in the service, the celebrant shall say,*

> Gathering our prayers and praises into one,
> let us pray as our Saviour taught us,

*All*
> **Our Father in heaven,**
> **hallowed be your name,**
> **your kingdom come,**
> **your will be done,**
> **on earth as in heaven.**
> **Give us today our daily bread.**
> **Forgive us our sins**
> **as we forgive those who sin against us.**

Save us from the time of trial,
and deliver us from evil.
For the kingdom, the power,
and the glory are yours,
now and for ever. Amen.

*Or*

*Celebrant*    And now as our Saviour Christ has taught us,
we are bold to say,

*All*    **Our Father, who art in heaven,
hallowed be thy name,
thy kingdom come,
thy will be done,
on earth as it is in heaven.
Give us this day our daily bread.
And forgive us our trespasses,
as we forgive those who trespass against us.
And lead us not into temptation,
but deliver us from evil.
For thine is the kingdom,
the power, and the glory,
for ever and ever. Amen.**

*The celebrant may then bless the family.*

The Lord bless you and keep you. **Amen.**
The Lord make his face shine on you
and be gracious to you. **Amen.**
The Lord look upon you with favour
and grant you peace. **Amen.**

*A deacon or lay person says,*

The Lord bless us and keep us. **Amen.**
The Lord make his face shine on us
and be gracious to us. **Amen.**
The Lord look upon us with favour
and grant us peace. **Amen.**

# Episcopal Offices

# The Blessing of Oil

The use of oil for religious purposes was common in Mediterranean culture. It was Jewish practice to anoint kings, as well as converts to the faith, and the sick. These practices were carried over into the life of the Church. In James (5.13–16) we find the Church ministering to the sick in a rite that included anointing with oil. In baptism anointing with oil early became a vivid sign of the belief that the new Christian was sealed with the Holy Spirit.

It is in the *Apostolic Tradition* of Hippolytus (c. 215) that we have the earliest existing witness to the manner in which oil was blessed for the use of the Church. The form was quite simple. Oil to be blessed was placed on the altar along with the bread and wine at the preparation of the gifts. The presiding celebrant included a prayer in the Great Thanksgiving asking that God would grant the desired effect (in this case healing) to those who were anointed.

In time the rite for the blessing of oil grew increasingly elaborate. In the West the blessing of oil came to take place on Maundy Thursday, as this was the last celebration of the eucharist before the Great Vigil of Easter when most baptisms occurred. In some Churches in the East the blessing of oil only takes place every seven years, when all the bishops of the church assemble for the occasion.

This rite takes the simplicity of the Hippolytan text as its model. Oil to be blessed is placed on the holy table in suitable vessels when the bread and wine are prepared. One vessel should be used for oil for anointing the sick and another vessel for oil for baptism (chrism). Appropriate forms of blessing are inserted into the Great Thanksgiving.

The day on which the blessing takes place is not specified. In some urban dioceses clergy and laity gather at mid–day on Maundy Thursday for this event. In other dioceses distance would make this impossible. It is important to find an occasion on which as many clergy and lay people of the diocese as possible may be present, e.g., one of the services at a synod, so that the blessing of oil will be seen as an action of the whole diocesan Church.

# Concerning the Service

## Preparation

*The oil to be consecrated is normally olive oil or, according to circumstances, other plant oil.*

*Traditionally, a small amount of oil of balsam or other fragrant oil is added to the oil to be set aside for use as chrism.*

*The oil should be prepared beforehand in the sacristy or other suitable place. Vessels large enough to be seen clearly by the congregation should be used—one vessel for the oil for anointing the sick and one vessel for the oil for baptism.*

## The Service

*Oil is blessed during a celebration of the eucharist. The diocesan bishop is the minister of this service. It is appropriately celebrated when there is a gathering of clergy and lay people from the whole diocese. Priests from various parts of the diocese may preside with the bishop.*

*The oil to be blessed is placed on the altar during the Preparation of the Gifts. It may be presented along with bread and wine in an offertory procession.*

*If there is a procession at the end of the service, the oil that has been blessed is carried out to the sacristy during that procession.*

*After the service, the oil for anointing the sick and the oil of baptism are poured into separate small bottles for distribution to parishes. Sufficient quantity should remain at the cathedral or some other central place to supply further need during the year.*

*Blessed oil should be kept reverently and in a safe place.*

*The oil should be renewed each time the bishop blesses oil. Old oil should either be poured onto the earth or into some absorbent material and then burned.*

*The oil for anointing the sick is to be used only by clergy and those lay persons who have received due authorization by the Ordinary.*

# The Blessing of Oil

*The following proper prayers and readings, and Great Thanksgiving shall be used.*

**Collect**

Heavenly Father,
you anointed your Son Jesus Christ
with the Holy Spirit and with power
to bring the good news of your kingdom.
Anoint your Church with the same Holy Spirit,
that we who share in his suffering and his victory
may bear witness to the gospel of salvation;
through Jesus Christ our Lord,
who lives and reigns with you and the Holy Spirit,
one God, now and forever.

**Readings**

> Isaiah 61.1–9     Psalm 89.19–29
> *Refrain*   The Lord is the rock of our salvation.   *Or v. 20*
> James 5.13–16a *or* Revelation 1.4b–8     Luke 4.16–21

**Prayer over the Gifts**

Loving God,
your Son was anointed by the Holy Spirit
not to be served but to serve.
Receive all we offer you this day,
that we who are called to serve you in the world
may be effective ministers of your healing love.
This we ask in the name of Jesus, the Christ, our Lord.

# The Eucharistic Prayer

| | |
|---|---|
| *Bishop* | The Lord be with you. |
| *People* | **And also with you.** |

| | |
|---|---|
| *Bishop* | Lift up your hearts. |
| *People* | **We lift them to the Lord.** |

| | |
|---|---|
| *Bishop* | Let us give thanks to the Lord our God. |
| *People* | **It is right to give our thanks and praise.** |

*Bishop*

Blessed are you, gracious God,
creator of heaven and earth;
for you anointed your Son Jesus Christ
with the Holy Spirit and with power;
and you anoint us
with the same Spirit in baptism,
making us a holy people
in the royal priesthood of the new covenant.
Your apostles anointed the sick
and healed them,
and by your grace
the ministry of healing continues in your Church;
for you sustain us with your presence
and drive away sickness of body and spirit,
giving us new life and health
that we may serve you both now and ever more.
Therefore we praise you
with angels and archangels,
and with all the company of heaven,
who for ever sing this hymn
to proclaim the glory of your name.

*All*

**Holy, holy, holy Lord,
God of power and might,
heaven and earth are full of your glory.
Hosanna in the highest.**

**Blessed is he who comes in the name of the Lord.
Hosanna in the highest.**

Bishop   We give thanks to you, Lord our God,
for the goodness and love
you have made known to us in creation;
in calling Israel to be your people;
in your Word spoken through the prophets;
and above all in the Word made flesh,
Jesus your Son.
For in these last days you sent him
to be incarnate from the Virgin Mary,
to be the Saviour and Redeemer of the world.
In him, you have delivered us from evil,
and made us worthy to stand before you.
In him, you have brought us
out of error into truth,
out of sin into righteousness,
out of death into life.

On the night he was handed over
to suffering and death,
a death he freely accepted,
our Lord Jesus Christ took bread;
and when he had given thanks to you,
he broke it, and gave it to his disciples,
and said, "Take, eat:
this is my body, which is given for you.
Do this for the remembrance of me."

After supper he took the cup of wine;
and when he had given thanks,
he gave it to them,
and said, "Drink this, all of you:
this is my blood of the new covenant,
which is shed for you and for many
for the forgiveness of sins.
Whenever you drink it,
do this for the remembrance of me."

Therefore, Father, according to his command,
All   **we remember his death,**
**we proclaim his resurrection,**
**we await his coming in glory;**

Celebrant  and we offer our sacrifice
of praise and thanksgiving
to you, Lord of all;
presenting to you, from your creation,
this bread and this wine.

We pray you, gracious God,
to send your Holy Spirit upon these gifts
that they may be the sacrament
of the body of Christ
and his blood of the new covenant.
Unite us to your Son in his sacrifice,
that we, made acceptable in him,
may be sanctified by the Holy Spirit.

Send your Holy Spirit on this oil,
that those who in faith and repentance
receive this holy unction may be made whole,
[and that those who are sealed with this chrism
may share in the royal priesthood
of Jesus Christ].

In the fullness of time,
reconcile all things in Christ,
and make them new,
and bring us to that city of light
where you dwell with all your sons and daughters;
through Jesus Christ our Lord,
the firstborn of all creation,
the head of the Church,
and the author of our salvation;

by whom, and with whom, and in whom,
in the unity of the Holy Spirit,
all honour and glory are yours, almighty Father,
now and for ever.

People  **Amen.**

*If chrism is not being consecrated, the words in brackets are omitted.*

*The service continues with the Lord's Prayer on p. 211.*

**Prayer after Communion**

Lord God,
in baptism you anoint us with your Holy Spirit,
and in this eucharist you feed us with the bread of life.
Strengthen us in our ministry of service
that we may preach good news to the poor,
proclaim release to the captives
and recovery of sight to the blind,
set at liberty those who are oppressed,
and proclaim the acceptable year of the Lord.
This we ask in the name of Jesus, the Christ, our Lord.

# Confirmation

*When the rites of Confirmation, Reception, and the Reaffirmation of Baptismal Vows are administered apart from the administration of baptism, the following form is used.*

*The Nicene Creed is not used at this service.*

*All stand. The bishop greets the community.*

Bishop    The grace of our Lord Jesus Christ,
and the love of God,
and the fellowship of the Holy Spirit,
be with you all.
People    **And also with you.**

*Or from Easter Day through the Day of Pentecost,*

Bishop    Alleluia! Christ is risen.
People    **The Lord is risen indeed. Alleluia!**

Bishop    May his grace and peace be with you.
People    **May he fill our hearts with joy.**

*The bishop then continues,*

    There is one body and one Spirit,
People    **There is one hope in God's call to us;**

Bishop    One Lord, one faith, one baptism,
People    **One God and Father of all.**

*Then may follow a canticle or a hymn.*

## The Collect

*At the principal service on a Sunday or other feast, the proper is of the day.*

Bishop    Let us pray.

*The community may pray silently for a while. The bishop sings or says the collect, at the conclusion of which all respond,* **Amen.**

*At the discretion of the bishop, however, the following collect and readings appropriate to the occasion may be used instead.*

Almighty God,
grant that we who have been buried with Christ in baptism
may be raised with him to newness of life.
Renew us by the power of your Holy Spirit
that we may live in righteousness and true holiness,
through Jesus Christ our Lord,
who lives and reigns with you and the Holy Spirit,
one God, now and for ever. **Amen.**

## The Proclamation of the Word

*The readings are those of the Sunday or feast day if the confirmation takes place at the principal service. At the discretion of the bishop one or more of the readings on p. 630 may be used instead. Lay persons may act as readers.*

*The people sit for the first reading.*

*Reader*     A reading from . . .

*At the conclusion of the passage, the reader says,*

The word of the Lord.
*People*     **Thanks be to God.**

*Then shall follow a psalm as appointed.*

*The second reading as appointed.*

*Reader*     A reading from . . .

*At the conclusion of the passage, the reader says,*

The word of the Lord.
*People*     **Thanks be to God.**

*A psalm, canticle, hymn, or anthem may follow the reading.*

*All stand for the Gospel.*

*Reader*     The Lord be with you.
*People*     **And also with you.**

| Reader | The Holy Gospel of our Lord Jesus Christ according to . . . |
|---|---|
| People | **Glory to you, Lord Jesus Christ.** |

*At the conclusion of the Gospel, the reader says,*

| | The Gospel of Christ. |
|---|---|
| People | **Praise to you, Lord Jesus Christ.** |

## The Sermon

*A silence for reflection may follow.*

## Presentation and Examination

*The presenters say to the bishop,*

> I present *these persons* for confirmation.

Or
> I present *these persons* to be received into this Communion.

Or
> I present *these persons* who *desire* to reaffirm *their* baptismal vows.

*The bishop asks those who have been presented to renew their baptismal commitment,*

| | Do you reaffirm your renunciation of evil? |
|---|---|
| Response | I do. |

| Bishop | Do you renew your commitment to Jesus Christ? |
|---|---|
| Response | I do. |

| Bishop | Do you put your whole trust in his grace and love? |
|---|---|
| Response | I do, and with God's grace I will follow him as my Saviour and Lord. |

*After all have been presented, the bishop addresses the congregation, saying,*

| | Will you who witness these vows do all in your power to support *these persons* in *their* life in Christ? |
|---|---|
| People | **We will.** |

*The bishop then says in these or similar words,*

Let us join with those who commit themselves again to Christ and renew our own baptismal covenant.

## The Baptismal Covenant

*Bishop*  Do you believe in God the Father?
*People*  **I believe in God,**
**the Father almighty,**
**creator of heaven and earth.**

*Bishop*  Do you believe in Jesus Christ, the Son of God?
*People*  **I believe in Jesus Christ,**
**his only Son, our Lord.**
**He was conceived by the power of the Holy Spirit**
**and born of the Virgin Mary.**
**He suffered under Pontius Pilate,**
**was crucified, died, and was buried.**
**He descended to the dead.**
**On the third day he rose again.**
**He ascended into heaven,**
**and is seated at the right hand of the Father.**
**He will come again**
**to judge the living and the dead.**

*Bishop*  Do you believe in God the Holy Spirit?
*People*  **I believe in God the Holy Spirit,**
**the holy catholic Church,**
**the communion of saints,**
**the forgiveness of sins,**
**the resurrection of the body,**
**and the life everlasting.**

*Bishop*  Will you continue in the apostles' teaching and fellowship, in the breaking of bread, and in the prayers?
*People*  **I will, with God's help.**

| | |
|---|---|
| Bishop | Will you persevere in resisting evil and, whenever you fall into sin, repent and return to the Lord? |
| People | **I will, with God's help.** |
| Bishop | Will you proclaim by word and example the good news of God in Christ? |
| People | **I will, with God's help.** |
| Bishop | Will you seek and serve Christ in all persons, loving your neighbour as yourself? |
| People | **I will, with God's help.** |
| Bishop | Will you strive for justice and peace among all people, and respect the dignity of every human being? |
| People | **I will, with God's help.** |

## Prayers

*The bishop says to the congregation,*

Let us pray for those who are affirming their baptism, and for all the baptized everywhere, saying, "Lord, hear our prayer."

*A person appointed leads the following litany.*

| | |
|---|---|
| Leader | That they may be redeemed from all evil and rescued from the way of sin and death; in your mercy, |
| People | **Lord, hear our prayer.** |
| Leader | That the Holy Spirit may open their hearts to your grace and truth; in your mercy, |
| People | **Lord, hear our prayer.** |
| Leader | That they may be kept in the faith and communion of your holy Church; in your mercy, |
| People | **Lord, hear our prayer.** |

| Leader | That they may be sent into the world |
|---|---|
| | in witness to your love; |
| | in your mercy, |
| People | **Lord, hear our prayer.** |

| Leader | That they may be brought |
|---|---|
| | to the fullness of your peace and glory; |
| | in your mercy, |
| People | **Lord, hear our prayer.** |

*Other prayers may be added.*

| Bishop | Into your hands, O Lord, we commend all for whom we pray, trusting in your mercy, through your Son, Jesus Christ our Lord. |
|---|---|
| People | **Amen.** |

*Silence may be kept. Then the bishop says,*

Almighty God, we thank you that by the death and resurrection of your Son Jesus Christ you have overcome sin and brought us to yourself, and that by the sealing of your Holy Spirit you have bound us to your service. Renew in *these* your *servants* the covenant you made with *them* at *their* baptism. Send *them* forth in the power of that Spirit to perform the service you set before *them;* through Jesus Christ your Son our Lord, who lives and reigns with you and the Holy Spirit, one God, now and for ever. **Amen.**

*The bishop lays his hand upon each one and says,*

**For Confirmation**

Strengthen, O Lord, your servant N with your Holy Spirit; empower *him/her* for your service; and sustain *him/her* all the days of *his/her* life. **Amen.**

*Or this:*

Defend, O Lord, your servant N with your heavenly grace, that *he/she* may continue yours for ever, and daily increase in your Holy Spirit more and more, until *he/she* comes to your everlasting kingdom. **Amen.**

### For Reception

N, we recognize you as a member of the one holy catholic and apostolic Church, and we receive you into the fellowship of this Communion. God, the Father, Son, and Holy Spirit, bless, preserve, and keep you. **Amen.**

### For Reaffirmation

N, may the Holy Spirit, who has begun a good work in you, direct and uphold you in the service of Christ and his kingdom. **Amen.**

*The bishop may say,*

Almighty and everliving God, let your fatherly hand ever be over *these* your *servants*; let your Holy Spirit ever be with *them*; and so lead *them* in the knowledge and obedience of your word, that *they* may serve you in this life, and dwell with you in the life to come; through Jesus Christ our Lord. **Amen.**

## The Peace

*All stand, and the bishop addresses the people.*

The peace of the Lord be always with you.
*People*    **And also with you.**

*The members of the community, ministers and people, may greet one another in the name of the Lord.*

*The service continues with the preparation of the gifts for the eucharist, at which the bishop should be the principal celebrant.*

*It is appropriate that the oblations of bread and wine be presented by persons newly confirmed.*

*The preface is normally that of the day. The third Preface of the Lord's Day may be used.*

*If there is no celebration of the eucharist, the service continues with the Lord's Prayer and other concluding prayers.*

# Readings and Psalms Suitable for Confirmation

## Old Testament Readings

Jeremiah 31.31–34   (I will make a new covenant with the house of Israel)
Isaiah 61.1–9   (The Spirit of the Lord God is upon me)

## Psalm and Suitable Refrain

Psalm 139.1–9   (Your hand will lead me and your right hand hold me fast)

## New Testament Readings

Ephesians 4.7,11–16   (To equip the saints for the work of ministry)
Romans 12.1–8   (To present your bodies as a living sacrifice)

## Gospel Readings

Matthew 5.1–12   (Blessed are the poor in spirit)
Luke 4.16–21   (The Spirit of the Lord is upon me)

# Preface to the Ordination Rites

The Holy Scriptures and ancient Christian writers make it clear that from the apostles' time there have been different ministries within the Church. In particular, since the time of the New Testament, three distinct orders of ordained ministers have been characteristic of Christ's holy catholic Church. First, there is the order of bishops who carry on the apostolic work of leading, supervising, and uniting the Church. Secondly, associated with them are the presbyters, or ordained elders, in subsequent times generally known as priests. Together with the bishops, they take part in the governance of the Church, in the carrying out of its missionary and pastoral work, and in the preaching of the word of God and the administration of his holy sacraments. Thirdly, there are deacons who, in addition to assisting bishops and priests in all this work, have a special responsibility to minister in Christ's name to the poor, the sick, the suffering, and the helpless.

The persons who are chosen and recognized by the Church as being called by God to the ordained ministry are admitted to these sacred orders by solemn prayer and the laying on of episcopal hands. It has been, and is, the intention and purpose of this Church to maintain and continue these three orders; and for this purpose these services of ordination and consecration are appointed. No persons are allowed to exercise the offices of bishop, priest, or deacon in this Church unless they are so ordained, or have already received such ordination with the laying on of hands by bishops who are themselves duly qualified to confer holy orders.

It is also recognized and affirmed that the threefold ministry is not the exclusive property of this portion of Christ's catholic Church, but is a gift from God for the nurture of his people and the proclamation of his gospel everywhere. Accordingly, the manner of ordaining in this Church is to be such as has been, and is, most generally recognized by Christian people as suitable for the conferring of the sacred orders of bishop, priest, and deacon.

# Concerning the Ordination of a Bishop

*In accordance with ancient custom, it is desirable, if possible, that bishops be ordained on Sundays or other feasts of our Lord, or on the feasts of apostles or evangelists.*

*When a bishop is to be ordained, the archbishop, or a bishop appointed by him, presides and serves as chief consecrator. At least two other bishops serve as co-consecrators. Representatives of the presbyterate, diaconate, and laity of the diocese for which the new bishop is to be consecrated, are assigned appropriate duties in the service.*

*From the beginning of the service until the offertory the chief consecrator presides from a chair placed close to the people, so that all may see and hear what is done. The other bishops, or a convenient number of them, sit to the right and left of the chief consecrator.*

*When the bishop-elect is presented, his full name (designated by the sign NN) is used. Thereafter, it is appropriate to refer to him only by the Christian name by which he wishes to be known.*

# The Ordination of a Bishop

*A hymn may be sung at the entry of the bishops and others. All stand. The presiding archbishop greets the community.*

> The grace of our Lord Jesus Christ,
> and the love of God,
> and the fellowship of the Holy Spirit,
> be with you all.

*People* **And also with you.**

*Or from Easter Day through the Day of Pentecost,*

*Archbishop* Alleluia! Christ is risen.
*People* **The Lord is risen indeed. Alleluia!**

*Archbishop* May his grace and peace be with us.
*People* **May he fill our hearts with joy.**

*The following prayer may be said.*

*Archbishop* Almighty God,
*All* **to you all hearts are open,**
**all desires known,**
**and from you no secrets are hidden.**
**Cleanse the thoughts of our hearts**
**by the inspiration of your Holy Spirit,**
**that we may perfectly love you,**
**and worthily magnify your holy name;**
**through Christ our Lord. Amen.**

*Glory to God (or other customary hymn) is not sung.*

*The prayers, readings, and preface are normally those of the day. If the propers are inappropriate, the following prayer may be used, a selection may be made from the list of readings on pp. 659–660, the Prayer over the Gifts for Ember Days on p. 396 or for the Common of a Pastor on p. 435, and the Preface of Ordination may be used.*

*The archbishop says,* **Let us pray.** *The community may pray silently.*

*The archbishop sings or says either the Collect of the Day or the following:*

O God of unchangeable power and eternal light,
look favourably on your whole Church,
that wonderful and sacred mystery.
By the effectual working of your providence,
carry out in tranquillity the plan of salvation.
Let the whole world see and know
that things which were cast down are being raised up,
and things which had grown old are being made new,
and that all things are being brought to their perfection
by him through whom all things were made,
your Son Jesus Christ our Lord;
who lives and reigns with you,
in the unity of the Holy Spirit,
one God, for ever and ever. **Amen.**

# The Readings

*Three lessons are read. Lay persons should normally be assigned the readings which precede the Gospel. A psalm, canticle, hymn, anthem, or period of silence may follow the lessons.*

# The Sermon

*A silence for reflection may follow.*

# The Presentation

*After the sermon, while the bishops and others sit, representatives of the diocese and province (priests, deacons, and lay persons), standing before the archbishop, present the bishop-elect, saying,*

N, bishop in the Church of God,
the clergy and people of the Diocese (or province) of N,
trusting in the guidance of the Holy Spirit,
have chosen NN to be a bishop and chief pastor.

We therefore ask you to lay your hands upon him
and in the power of the Holy Spirit
to consecrate him a bishop
in the one, holy, catholic, and apostolic Church.

*The archbishop then directs that testimonials of the election be read. When the
reading of the testimonials is ended, the archbishop requires the following
promise from the bishop-elect.*

In the name of the Father, and of the Son, and of the Holy
Spirit, I, *NN*, chosen bishop of the Church and see of *N*,
solemnly declare that I do believe the holy scriptures of the Old
and New Testaments to be the word of God, and to contain all
things necessary to salvation; I do solemnly promise to conform
to the doctrine, discipline, and worship of the Anglican Church
of Canada; and I do pledge myself to render due obedience to
the Metropolitan of *N* and to his successors. So help me God,
through Jesus Christ.

*The bishop-elect then signs the above declaration in the sight of all present.
The witnesses add their signatures.*

*All stand. The archbishop then asks the response of the people in these or
similar words.*

Brothers and sisters in Christ Jesus, you have heard testimony
given that *NN* has been duly and lawfully elected to be a bishop
of the Church of God to serve in the Diocese of *N*. You have
been assured of his suitability and that the Church has
approved him for this sacred responsibility. Nevertheless, if
any of you know any reason why we should not proceed, let it
now be made known.

*If no objection is made, the archbishop continues,*

Is it your will that we ordain *N* a bishop?
*People*      **It is.**

*Archbishop*  Will you uphold *N* as bishop?
*People*      **We will.**

# The Examination

*All now sit except the bishop-elect, who stands facing the bishops. The archbishop addresses the bishop-elect.*

N, the people have chosen you and have affirmed their trust in you by acclaiming your election. A bishop in God's holy Church is called to be one with the apostles in proclaiming Christ's resurrection and interpreting the Gospel, and to testify to Christ's sovereignty as Lord of lords and King of kings.

You are called to guard the faith, unity, and discipline of the Church; to celebrate and to provide for the administration of the sacraments of the new covenant; to ordain priests and deacons, and to join in ordaining bishops; and to be in all things a faithful pastor and wholesome example for the entire flock of Christ.

With your fellow bishops you will share in the leadership of the Church throughout the world. Your heritage is the faith of patriarchs, prophets, apostles, and martyrs, and those of every generation who have looked to God in hope. Your joy will be to follow him who came not to be served but to serve, and to give his life a ransom for many.

Are you persuaded that God has called you to the office of bishop?

*Answer*     I am so persuaded.

*The following questions are then addressed to the bishop-elect by one or more of the other bishops.*

*Bishop*     Will you accept this call and fulfil this trust in obedience to Christ?

*Answer*     I will obey Christ, and will serve in his name.

*Bishop*     Will you be faithful in prayer, and in the study of holy scripture, that you may have the mind of Christ?

*Answer*     I will, for he is my help.

| | |
|---|---|
| *Bishop* | Will you boldly proclaim and interpret the gospel of Christ, enlightening the minds and stirring up the conscience of your people? |
| *Answer* | I will, in the power of the Spirit. |
| *Bishop* | As a chief priest and pastor, will you encourage and support all baptized people in their gifts and ministries, nourish them from the riches of God's grace, pray for them without ceasing, and celebrate with them the sacraments of our redemption? |
| *Answer* | I will, in the name of Christ, the shepherd and bishop of our souls. |
| *Bishop* | Will you guard the faith, unity, and discipline of the Church? |
| *Answer* | I will, for the love of God. |
| *Bishop* | Will you share with your fellow bishops in the government of the whole Church; will you sustain your fellow presbyters and take counsel with them; will you guide and strengthen the deacons and all others who minister in the Church? |
| *Answer* | I will, by the grace given me. |
| *Bishop* | Will you be merciful to all, show compassion to the poor and strangers, and defend those who have no helper? |
| *Answer* | I will, for the sake of Jesus Christ. |

*All stand. The archbishop then says,*

N, through these promises you have committed yourself to God, to serve his Church in the office of bishop. We therefore call upon you, chosen to be a guardian of the Church's faith, to lead us in confessing that faith.

*All say the Nicene Creed (p. 188) together, the bishop-elect beginning,*

We believe in one God, . . .

# The Consecration of the Bishop

*All remain standing, except the bishop-elect, who kneels before the*
*archbishop. The other bishops stand to the right and left of the archbishop.*
*The archbishop says,*

The scriptures tell us that our Saviour Christ spent the whole
night in prayer before he chose and sent forth his twelve
apostles. Likewise, the apostles prayed before they appointed
Matthias to be one of their number. Let us, therefore, follow
their examples, and offer our prayers to Almighty God before
we ordain N for the work to which we trust the Holy Spirit has
called him.

*The people remain standing or kneel, as directed by the archbishop.*

*The Litany for Ordinations is sung or said, according to one of the two forms*
*provided on pp. 661–664.*

*The hymn Veni Creator Spiritus or the hymn Veni Sancte Spiritus is sung.*
*(Some suitable translations are listed on p. 665.)*

*A period of silent prayer follows.*

*The archbishop stands with the bishops who assist him, the bishop-elect*
*kneeling before him; he stretches out his hands toward him, and begins this*
*Prayer of Consecration.*

We praise and glorify you, almighty Father, because you have
formed throughout the world a holy people for your own
possession, a royal priesthood, a universal Church.

We praise and glorify you because you have given us your only
Son Jesus Christ to be the Apostle and High Priest of our faith,
and the Shepherd of our souls.

We praise and glorify you that by his death he has overcome
death; and that, having ascended into heaven, he has given his
gifts abundantly to your people, making some, apostles; some,
prophets; some, evangelists; some, pastors and teachers; to
equip them for the work of ministry and to build up his Body.

And now we give you thanks that you have called this your servant to share this ministry entrusted to your Church.

*Here the archbishop and other bishops lay their hands on the head of the bishop-elect, and the archbishop says,*

Send down your Holy Spirit upon your servant N, whom we consecrate in your name to the office and work of a bishop in the Church.

*The archbishop then continues, with hands extended,*

Almighty Father, fill this your servant with the grace and power which you gave to your apostles, that he may lead those committed to his charge in proclaiming the gospel of salvation. Through him increase your Church, renew its ministry, and unite its members in a holy fellowship of truth and love. Enable him as a true shepherd to feed and govern your flock; make him wise as a teacher, and steadfast as a guardian of its faith and sacraments. Guide and direct him in presiding at the worship of your people. Give him humility, that he may use his authority to heal, not to hurt; to build up, not to destroy. Defend him from all evil, that, as a ruler over your household and an ambassador for Christ, he may stand before you blameless, and finally, with all your servants, enter your eternal joy.

Accept our prayers, most merciful Father, through your Son Jesus Christ our Lord, to whom, with you and your Holy Spirit, belong glory and honour, worship and praise, now and for ever.

*People*     **Amen.**

*The new bishop is now vested according to the order of bishops. Symbols of office, such as a ring and pectoral cross, may be presented to him. The archbishop presents him with a Bible, saying,*

Receive the holy scriptures. Feed the flock of Christ committed to your charge, guard and defend them in his truth, and be a faithful steward of his holy word and sacraments.

*The archbishop presents him with a pastoral staff, saying,*

Receive this staff as a sign of your pastoral office; keep watch over the whole flock in which the Holy Spirit has appointed you to shepherd the Church of God. Encourage the faithful, restore the lost, build up the Body of Christ; that when the Chief Shepherd shall appear, you may receive the unfading crown of glory.

## The Peace

*The archbishop presents to the people the new bishop, saying,*

I present N, bishop in the Church of God.

*The new bishop then says,*

The peace of the Lord be always with you.

People     **And also with you.**

## Offertory, Thanksgiving, and Communion

*The liturgy continues with the offertory. The archbishop or senior bishop, joined by the new bishop, other bishops, and presbyters, presides at the eucharist as chief celebrant.*

## After Communion

*One of the bishops leads the people in the following:*

**Almighty Father,
we thank you for feeding us with the holy food
of the body and blood of your Son,
and for uniting us through him
in the fellowship of your Holy Spirit.
We thank you for raising up among us
faithful servants for the ministry
of your word and sacraments.
We pray that N may be to us
a godly example in word and action,
in love and patience,
and in holiness of life.**

Grant that we, with him, may serve you now,
and always rejoice in your glory;
through Jesus Christ your Son our Lord,
who lives and reigns with you and the Holy Spirit,
one God, now and for ever. Amen.

*The new bishop blesses the people, first saying,*

Our help is in the name of the Lord,
*People* **The maker of heaven and earth.**

*Bishop* Blessed be the name of the Lord,
*People* **From this time forth for evermore.**

*Bishop* The blessing, mercy, and grace of God almighty,
the Father, the Son, and the Holy Spirit,
be upon you and remain with you for ever.
*People* **Amen.**

*Or the bishop may bless the people with one of the forms of blessing on p. 683.*

*A deacon dismisses the people with these words.*

Go forth into the world,
rejoicing in the power of the Spirit.
*People* **Thanks be to God.**

*From Easter Day through the Day of Pentecost,* **Alleluia** *is added to the
dismissal and the people's response. A hymn may be sung as the bishops and
others leave the church.*

*Further directions for this and the other rites of ordination may be found on
p. 666.*

# Concerning the Ordination of a Priest

*It is desirable, if possible, that priests be ordained on Sundays or other feasts. Whenever a bishop is to confer holy orders, at least two presbyters should be present.*

*From the beginning of the service until the offertory, the bishop presides from a chair placed close to the people, so that all may see and hear what is done.*

*When each ordinand is presented, his/her full name (designated by the sign NN) is used. Thereafter, it is appropriate to refer to him/her only by the Christian name by which he/she wishes to be known.*

# The Ordination of a Priest

*A hymn may be sung at the entry of the bishop and others. All stand. The bishop greets the community.*

Bishop      The grace of our Lord Jesus Christ,
                 and the love of God,
                 and the fellowship of the Holy Spirit,
                 be with you all.

People      **And also with you.**

*Or from Easter Day through the Day of Pentecost,*

Bishop      Alleluia! Christ is risen.

People      **The Lord is risen indeed. Alleluia!**

Bishop      May his grace and peace be with us.

People      **May he fill our hearts with joy.**

*The following prayer may be said.*

Bishop      Almighty God,

All      **to you all hearts are open,
all desires known,
and from you no secrets are hidden.
Cleanse the thoughts of our hearts
by the inspiration of your Holy Spirit,
that we may perfectly love you,
and worthily magnify your holy name;
through Christ our Lord. Amen.**

*Glory to God (or other customary hymn) is not sung.*

*The prayers, readings, and preface are normally those of the day. If the propers are inappropriate, the following prayer may be used, a selection may be made from the list of readings on pp. 659–660, the Prayer over the Gifts for Ember Days on p. 396 or for the Common of a Pastor on p. 435, and the Preface of Ordination may be used.*

*The bishop says,* **Let us pray.** *The community may pray silently.*

*The bishop sings or says either the Collect of the Day or the following:*

O God of unchangeable power and eternal light,
look favourably on your whole Church,
that wonderful and sacred mystery.
By the effectual working of your providence,
carry out in tranquillity the plan of salvation.
Let the whole world see and know
that things which were cast down are being raised up,
and things which had grown old are being made new,
and that all things are being brought to their perfection
by him through whom all things were made,
your Son Jesus Christ our Lord;
who lives and reigns with you,
in the unity of the Holy Spirit,
one God, for ever and ever. **Amen.**

## The Readings

*Three lessons are read. Lay persons should normally be assigned the readings which precede the Gospel. A psalm, canticle, hymn, anthem, or period of silence may follow the lessons.*

## The Sermon

*A silence for reflection may follow*

## The Presentation

*After the sermon and the Nicene Creed (p. 188), the bishop and people sit. A priest and a lay person, and additional presenters if desired, standing before the bishop, present the* ordinand, *saying,*

N, bishop in the Church of God,
on behalf of the clergy and people of the Diocese of N,
we present you NN to be ordained *a priest*
in Christ's holy catholic Church.

Bishop      Has *he/she* been selected in accordance with the
            canons and customs of this Church? And do you
            believe *his/her* manner of life to be suitable to the
            exercise of this ministry?

Presenters  We certify to you that *he/she has* been duly selected,
            and we believe *him/her* to be qualified for this order.

*The bishop says to the* ordinand,

Will you be loyal to the doctrine, discipline, and worship of
Christ as this Church has received them? And will you, in
accordance with the canons of this Church, obey your bishop
and other ministers who may have authority over you and your
work?

*The* ordinand answers,

I am willing and ready to do so; and I solemnly declare that I do
believe the holy scriptures of the Old and New Testaments to
be the word of God, and to contain all things necessary to
salvation; and I do solemnly promise to conform to the
doctrine, discipline, and worship of the Anglican Church of
Canada.

*The* ordinand *then* signs *the above declaration in the sight of all present.*

*All stand. The bishop says to the people,*

Dear friends in Christ, you know the importance of this
ministry, and the weight of your responsibility in presenting
NN for ordination to the sacred priesthood. Therefore, if any of
you know any impediment or crime for which we should not
proceed, come forward now, and make it known.

*If no objection is made, the bishop continues,*

            Is it your will that N be ordained *a priest?*
People      **It is.**

Bishop      Will you uphold *him/her* in this ministry?
People      **We will.**

# The Examination

*All now sit except the* ordinand, *who* stands *before the bishop. The bishop addresses the* ordinand *as follows:*

N, the Church is the family of God, the body of Christ, and the temple of the Holy Spirit. All baptized people are called to make Christ known as Saviour and Lord, and to share in the renewing of his world. Now you are called to work as *a pastor, priest, and teacher,* together with your bishop and fellow presbyters, and to take your share in the councils of the Church.

As *a priest,* it will be your task to proclaim by word and deed the gospel of Jesus Christ, and to fashion your *life* in accordance with its precepts. You are to love and serve the people among whom you work, caring alike for young and old, strong and weak, rich and poor. You are to preach, to declare God's forgiveness to penitent sinners, to pronounce God's blessing, to preside at the administration of holy baptism and at the celebration of the mysteries of Christ's body and blood, and to perform the other ministrations entrusted to you.

In all that you do, you are to nourish Christ's people from the riches of his grace, and strengthen them to glorify God in this life and in the life to come.

Do you believe that you are truly called by God and his Church to this priesthood?

| | |
|---|---|
| *Answer* | I believe I am so called. |
| *Bishop* | Do you now in the presence of the Church commit *yourself* to this trust and responsibility? |
| *Answer* | I do. |
| *Bishop* | Will you respect and be guided by the pastoral direction and leadership of your bishop? |
| *Answer* | I will. |

| Bishop | Will you be diligent in the reading and study of the holy scriptures, and in seeking the knowledge of such things as may make you *a* stronger and more able *minister* of Christ? |
|---|---|
| Answer | I will. |

| Bishop | Will you endeavour so to minister the word of God and the sacraments of the new covenant, that the reconciling love of Christ may be known and received? |
|---|---|
| Answer | I will. |

| Bishop | Will you undertake to be *a* faithful *pastor* to all whom you are called to serve, labouring together with them and with your fellow ministers to build up the family of God? |
|---|---|
| Answer | I will. |

| Bishop | Will you do your best to pattern your *life* (and *that* of your *family*) in accordance with the teachings of Christ, so that you may be *a* wholesome *example* to your people? |
|---|---|
| Answer | I will. |

| Bishop | Will you persevere in prayer, both in public and in private, asking God's grace, both for *yourself* and for others, and offering all your labours to God, through the mediation of Jesus Christ, and in the sanctification of the Holy Spirit? |
|---|---|
| Answer | I will. |

| Bishop | May the Lord who has given you the will to do these things give you the grace and power to perform them. |
|---|---|
| Answer | Amen. |

# The Consecration of the Priest

*Now all stand except the* ordinand, *who kneels facing the bishop and the presbyters, who stand to the right and left of the bishop. The bishop calls the people to prayer with these or similar words.*

In peace let us pray to the Lord.

*The people remain standing or kneel, as directed by the bishop.*

*The Litany for Ordinations is sung or said, according to one of the two forms provided on pp. 661–664.*

*The hymn Veni Creator Spiritus or the hymn Veni Sancte Spiritus is sung. (Some suitable translations are listed on p. 665.)*

*A period of silent prayer follows.*

*The bishop stands with the priests who assist him, the* ordinand *kneeling before him; he stretches out his hands toward* him/her, *and begins this Prayer of Consecration.*

We praise and glorify you, almighty Father, because you have formed throughout the world a holy people for your own possession, a royal priesthood, a universal Church.

We praise and glorify you because you have given us your only Son Jesus Christ to be the Apostle and High Priest of our faith, and the Shepherd of our souls.

We praise and glorify you that by his death he has overcome death; and that, having ascended into heaven, he has given his gifts abundantly to your people, making some, apostles; some, prophets; some, evangelists; some, pastors and teachers; to equip them for the work of ministry and to build up his Body.

And now we give you thanks that you have called *this* your *servant* to share this ministry entrusted to your Church.

*Here the bishop and priests lay their hands on the head of each ordinand, and the bishop says,*

Send down your Holy Spirit upon your *servant N*, whom we consecrate in your name to the office and work of a priest in the Church.

Almighty Father, give to *this* your *servant* grace and power to fulfil *his/her* ministry among the people committed to *his/her* charge; to watch over them and care for them; to absolve and bless them in your name; and to proclaim the gospel of your salvation. Set *him/her* among your people to offer spiritual sacrifices acceptable in your sight, and as you have called *him/her* to your service, make *him/her* by the gift of your Holy Spirit worthy of *his/her* calling. Give *him/her* wisdom and discipline to work faithfully with all *his/her* fellow servants in Christ, that the world may come to know your glory and your love.

Accept our prayers, most merciful Father, through your Son Jesus Christ our Lord, to whom, with you and your Holy Spirit, belong glory and honour, worship and praise, now and for ever.

*People* **Amen.**

*The new priest is now vested according to the order of priests. The bishop hands a Bible and a chalice and paten to each new priest, saying,*

Receive this Bible and this chalice and paten as signs of the authority given you to preach the word of God and to administer his holy sacraments. Do not forget the trust committed to you as a priest of the Church of God.

## The Peace

*The bishop presents the new priest to the congregation. A new priest then says to the congregation,*

The peace of the Lord be always with you.
*People* **And also with you.**

## Offertory, Thanksgiving, and Communion

*The liturgy continues with the offertory. The newly ordained priest joins with the bishop and other presbyters in the celebration of the eucharist and in the breaking of the bread.*

# After Communion

*The bishop says the following prayer.*

Almighty Father, we thank you for feeding us with the holy food of the body and blood of your Son, and for uniting us through him in the fellowship of your Holy Spirit. We thank you for raising up among us faithful servants for the ministry of your word and sacraments. We pray that *N* may be to us *a* godly *example* in word and action, in love and patience, and in holiness of life. Grant that we, with *him/her*, may serve you now, and always rejoice in your glory; through Jesus Christ your Son our Lord, who lives and reigns with you and the Holy Spirit, one God, now and for ever. **Amen.**

*The bishop blesses the people, first saying,*

> Our help is in the name of the Lord,

People    **The maker of heaven and earth.**

Bishop    Blessed be the name of the Lord,
People    **From this time forth for evermore.**

Bishop    The blessing, mercy, and grace of God Almighty,
> the Father, the Son, and the Holy Spirit,
> be upon you and remain with you for ever.

People    **Amen.**

*Or the bishop may bless the people with one of the forms of blessing on p. 683.*

*A deacon dismisses the people with these words.*

> Go forth into the world,
> rejoicing in the power of the Spirit.

People    **Thanks be to God.**

*From Easter Day through the Day of Pentecost,* **Alleluia** *is added to the dismissal and the people's response. A hymn may be sung as the bishop and others leave the church.*

*Further directions for this and the other rites of ordination may be found on p. 666.*

# Concerning the Ordination of a Deacon

*It is desirable, if possible, that deacons be ordained on Sundays or other feasts. Whenever a bishop is to confer holy orders, at least two presbyters should be present.*

*From the beginning of the service until the offertory the bishop presides from a chair placed close to the people, so that all may see and hear what is done.*

*When each ordinand is presented, his/her full name (designated by the sign NN) is used. Thereafter, it is appropriate to refer to him/her only by the Christian name by which he/she wishes to be known.*

# The Ordination of a Deacon

*A hymn may be sung at the entry of the bishop and others.*
*All stand. The bishop greets the community.*

Bishop     **The grace of our Lord Jesus Christ,**
              **and the love of God,**
              **and the fellowship of the Holy Spirit,**
              **be with you all.**
People     **And also with you.**

*Or from Easter Day through the Day of Pentecost,*

Bishop     Alleluia! Christ is risen.
People     **The Lord is risen indeed. Alleluia!**

Bishop     May his grace and peace be with us.
People     **May he fill our hearts with joy.**

*The following prayer may be said.*

Bishop     **Almighty God,**
All         **to you all hearts are open,**
              **all desires known,**
              **and from you no secrets are hidden.**
              **Cleanse the thoughts of our hearts**
              **by the inspiration of your Holy Spirit,**
              **that we may perfectly love you,**
              **and worthily magnify your holy name;**
              **through Christ our Lord. Amen.**

*Glory to God (or other customary hymn) is not sung.*

*The prayers, readings, and preface are normally those of the day. If the propers are inappropriate, the following prayer may be used, a selection may be made from the list of readings on pp. 659–660, the Prayer over the Gifts for Ember Days on p. 396 or for the Common of a Pastor on p. 435, and the Preface of Ordination may be used.*

*The bishop says,* **Let us pray.** *The community may pray silently.*

*The bishop sings or says either the Collect of the Day or the following:*

O God of unchangeable power and eternal light,
look favourably on your whole Church,
that wonderful and sacred mystery.
By the effectual working of your providence,
carry out in tranquillity the plan of salvation.
Let the whole world see and know
that things which were cast down are being raised up,
and things which had grown old are being made new,
and that all things are being brought to their perfection
by him through whom all things were made,
your Son Jesus Christ our Lord;
who lives and reigns with you,
in the unity of the Holy Spirit,
one God, for ever and ever. **Amen.**

## The Readings

*Three lessons are read. Lay persons should normally be assigned the readings
which precede the Gospel. A psalm, canticle, hymn, anthem, or period of
silence may follow the lessons.*

## The Sermon

*A silence for reflection may follow.*

## The Presentation

*After the sermon and the Nicene Creed (p. 188), the bishop and people sit. A
priest and a lay person, and additional presenters if desired, standing before
the bishop, present the* ordinand, *saying,*

N, bishop in the Church of God,
on behalf of the clergy and people of the diocese of N,
we present you NN to be ordained *a deacon*
in Christ's holy catholic Church.

| Bishop | Has *he/she* been selected in accordance with the canons and customs of this Church? And do you believe *his/her* manner of life to be suitable to the exercise of this ministry? |
| --- | --- |
| Presenters | We certify to you that *he/she has* been duly selected, and we believe *him/her* to be qualified for this order. |

*The bishop says to the* ordinand,

Will you be loyal to the doctrine, discipline, and worship of Christ as this Church has received them? And will you, in accordance with the canons of this Church, obey your bishop and other ministers who may have authority over you and your work?

*The* ordinand answers,

I am willing and ready to do so; and I solemnly declare that I do believe the holy scriptures of the Old and New Testaments to be the word of God, and to contain all things necessary to salvation; and I do solemnly promise to conform to the doctrine, discipline, and worship of the Anglican Church of Canada.

*The* ordinand *then* signs *the above declaration in the sight of all present.*

*All stand. The bishop says to the people,*

Dear friends in Christ, you know the importance of this ministry, and the weight of your responsibility in presenting *NN* for ordination to the sacred order of deacons. Therefore, if any of you know any impediment or crime for which we should not proceed, come forward now and make it known.

*If no objection is made, the bishop continues,*

| | Is it your will that *N* be ordained *a deacon?* |
| --- | --- |
| People | **It is.** |

| Bishop | Will you uphold *him/her* in this ministry? |
| --- | --- |
| People | **We will.** |

# The Examination

*All now sit except the ordinand, who stands before the bishop. The bishop addresses the* ordinand *as follows.*

N, every Christian is called to follow Jesus Christ, serving God the Father, through the power of the Holy Spirit. God now calls you to a special ministry of servanthood, directly under the authority of your bishop. In the name of Jesus Christ, you are to serve all people, particularly the poor, the weak, the sick, and the lonely.

As *a deacon* in the Church, you are to study the holy scriptures, to seek nourishment from them, and to model your *life* upon them. You are to make Christ and his redemptive love known, by your word and example, to those among whom you live and work and worship. You are to interpret to the Church the needs, concerns, and hopes of the world. You are to assist the bishop and priests in public worship, and in the ministration of God's word and sacraments, and you are to carry out other duties assigned to you from time to time. At all times, your life and teaching are to show Christ's people that in serving the helpless they are serving Christ himself.

Do you believe that you are truly called by God and his Church to the life and work of a deacon?

| | |
|---|---|
| Answer | I believe I am so called. |
| Bishop | Do you now in the presence of the Church commit *yourself* to this trust and responsibility? |
| Answer | I do. |
| Bishop | Will you be guided by the pastoral direction and leadership of your bishop? |
| Answer | I will. |
| Bishop | Will you be faithful in prayer, and in the reading and study of the holy scriptures? |
| Answer | I will. |
| Bishop | Will you look for Christ in all others, being ready to help and serve those in need? |
| Answer | I will. |

| Bishop | Will you do your best to pattern your *life* (and *that* of your *family)* in accordance with the teachings of Christ, so that you may be *a* wholesome *example* to your people? |
| Answer | I will. |
| Bishop | Will you in all things seek not your glory but the glory of the Lord Christ? |
| Answer | I will. |
| Bishop | May the Lord by his grace uphold you in the service to which you are called. |
| Answer | Amen. |

# The Consecration of the Deacon

*Now all stand except the* ordinand, *who kneels facing the bishop. The bishop calls the people to prayer with these or similar words.*

**In peace let us pray to the Lord.**

*The people remain standing or kneel, as directed by the bishop.*

*The Litany for Ordinations is sung or said, according to one of the two forms provided on pp. 661–664.*

*The hymn Veni Creator Spiritus or the hymn Veni Sancte Spiritus is sung. (Some suitable translations are listed on p. 665).*

*A period of silent prayer follows.*

*The bishop stands with the priests who assist him; the* ordinand *kneels before him; he stretches out his hands toward* him/her *and begins this Prayer of Consecration.*

**We praise and glorify you, most merciful Father, because in your great love of our human race you sent your only Son Jesus Christ to take the form of a servant; he came to serve and not to be served; and to teach us that he who would be great among us must be the servant of all; he humbled himself for our sake, and in obedience accepted death, even death on a cross; therefore you highly exalted him and gave him the name which is above every name.**

And now we give you thanks that you have called *this* your *servant* to share this ministry entrusted to your Church.

*Here the bishop lays his hands on the head of each ordinand.*

Send down your Holy Spirit upon your servant N, whom we now consecrate in your name to the office and work of a deacon in the Church.

*The bishop continues.*

Almighty Father, give to *this* your *servant* grace and power to fulfil *his/her* ministry. Make *him/her* faithful to serve, ready to teach, and constant to advance your gospel; and grant that always having full assurance of faith, abounding in hope, and being rooted and grounded in love, *he/she* may continue strong and steadfast in your Son Jesus Christ our Lord, to whom, with you and your Holy Spirit, belong glory and honour, worship and praise, now and for ever.

*People*    **Amen.**

*The new deacon is now vested according to the order of deacons. The bishop gives a Bible to each of the newly ordained, saying,*

Receive this Bible as the sign of your authority to proclaim God's word and to assist in the ministration of his holy sacraments.

## The Peace

*The bishop presents the new* deacon *to the congregation. The bishop then says to the congregation,*

The peace of the Lord be always with you.

*People*    **And also with you.**

## Offertory, Thanksgiving, and Communion

*The liturgy continues with the offertory. The newly ordained* deacon *prepares the elements and places the vessels on the Lord's Table. The bishop, joined (if possible) by presbyters, presides at the celebration of the eucharist.*

# After Communion

*The bishop says the following prayer.*

Almighty Father, we thank you for feeding us with the holy food of the body and blood of your Son, and for uniting us through him in the fellowship of your Holy Spirit. We thank you for raising up among us faithful servants for the ministry of your word and sacraments. We pray that *N* may be to us *a* godly *example* in word and action, in love and patience, and in holiness of life. Grant that we, with *him/her*, may serve you now, and always rejoice in your glory; through Jesus Christ our Lord, who lives and reigns with you and the Holy Spirit, one God, now and for ever. **Amen.**

*The bishop blesses the people, first saying,*

|          | Our help is in the name of the Lord, |
|----------|--------------------------------------|
| *People* | **The maker of heaven and earth.**   |

| *Bishop* | Blessed be the name of the Lord,     |
|----------|--------------------------------------|
| *People* | **From this time forth for evermore.** |

| *Bishop* | The blessing, mercy, and grace of God almighty, the Father, the Son, and the Holy Spirit, be upon you and remain with you for ever. |
|----------|---|
| *People* | **Amen.** |

*Or the bishop may bless the people with one of the forms of blessing on p. 683.*

*A deacon dismisses the people with these words.*

|          | Go forth into the world, rejoicing in the power of the Spirit. |
|----------|---|
| *People* | **Thanks be to God.** |

*From Easter Day to the Day of Pentecost,* **Alleluia** *is added to the dismissal and the people's response. A hymn may be sung as the bishops and others leave the church.*

*Further directions for this and the other rites of ordination may be found on p. 666.*

# Readings and Psalms Suitable for Ordinations

## For a Bishop

### Old Testament Readings

Isaiah 42.1–9   (I am the Lord, I have called you in righteousness)
Ezekiel 34.11–16   (I myself will search for my sheep, and will seek them out)

### Psalms and Suitable Refrains

99   (Proclaim the greatness of the Lord our God; he is the Holy One)
40   (Behold, I come to do your will, O God)
100   (We are his people and the sheep of his pasture)

### New Testament Readings

2 Corinthians 4.1–10   (Having this ministry by the mercy of God, we do not lose heart)
Hebrews 5.1–10   (Christ did not exalt himself to be made a high priest, but was appointed by him who said to him, 'Thou art my Son . . .')

### Gospel Readings

John 20.19–23   (Receive the Holy Spirit)
John 21.15–17   (Feed my sheep)

## For a Priest

### Old Testament Readings

Isaiah 61.1–8   (The Spirit of the Lord God is upon me)
Ezekiel 33.1–9   (So you, son of man, I have made a watchman for the house of Israel)

### Psalms and Suitable Readings

43   (Send out your light and your truth, that they may lead me)
132   (Let your priests be clothed with righteousness; let your faithful people sing with joy)

### New Testament Readings

Ephesians 4.7–13   (And his gifts were that some should be apostles, some prophets, some evangelists, some pastors and teachers)

1 Peter 5.1–11   (Tend the flock of God that is your charge)

### Gospel Readings

Matthew 9.35–38   (The harvest is plentiful, but the labourers are few)

John 10.1–16   (I am the good shepherd)

# For a Deacon

### Old Testament Readings

Isaiah 6.1–8   (Whom shall I send, and who will go for us?)

Jeremiah 1.4–9   (Behold, I have put my words in your mouth)

### Psalms and Suitable Refrains

84   (O Lord of hosts, happy are they who put their trust in you)

119.33–40   (Teach me, O Lord, the way of your statutes)

### New Testament Readings

2 Corinthians 4.1–10   (Having this ministry by the mercy of God, we do not lose heart)

Philippians 4.4–9   (Rejoice in the Lord always)

### Gospel Readings

Mark 10.35–45   (Whoever would be great among you must be your servant)

Luke 12.35–38   (Blessed are those servants whom the master finds awake when he comes)

# Ordination Litany

**Form A**

God the Father,
**Have mercy on us.**

God the Son,
**Have mercy on us.**

God the Holy Spirit,
**Have mercy on us.**

Holy Trinity, one God,
**Have mercy on us.**

We pray to you, Lord Christ.
**Lord, hear our prayer.**

For the holy Church of God, that it may be filled with truth and
love, and be found without fault at the day of your coming, we
pray to you, O Lord.
**Lord, hear our prayer.**

For all members of your Church in their vocation and ministry,
that they may serve you in a true and godly life,
we pray to you, O Lord.
**Lord, hear our prayer.**

For *N*, our *archbishop/bishop,* and for all bishops, priests, and
deacons, that they may be filled with your love, may hunger
for truth, and may thirst after righteousness, we pray to you,
O Lord.
**Lord, hear our prayer.**

For *N*, chosen (*bishop/priest/deacon*) in your Church, we pray to
you, O Lord.
**Lord, hear our prayer.**

That *he/she* may faithfully fulfil the duties of this ministry,
build up your Church, and glorify your name, we pray to
you, O Lord.
**Lord, hear our prayer.**

That by the indwelling of the Holy Spirit *he/she* may be
sustained and encouraged to persevere to the end, we pray
to you, O Lord.
**Lord, hear our prayer.**

For all who fear God and believe in you, Lord Christ, that our
divisions may cease and that all may be one as you and the
Father are one, we pray to you, O Lord.
**Lord, hear our prayer.**

For the mission of the Church, that in faithful witness it may
preach the gospel to the ends of the earth, we pray to you,
O Lord.
**Lord hear our prayer.**

For those who do not yet believe, and for those who have lost
their faith, that they may receive the light of the gospel, we
pray to you, O Lord.
**Lord, hear our prayer.**

For ourselves: for the forgiveness of our sins, and for the grace
of the Holy Spirit to amend our lives, we pray to you, O Lord.
**Lord, hear our prayer.**

For all who have died in the communion of the Church, and
those whose faith is known to you alone, that, with all the
saints, they may have rest in that place where there is no pain
or grief, but life eternal, we pray to you, O Lord.
**Lord, hear our prayer.**

Rejoicing in the fellowship of [the ever-blessed Virgin Mary,
(blessed *N*) and] all the saints, let us commend ourselves, and
one another, and all our life to Christ our God.
**To you, O Lord.**

*The bishop prays,*

Almighty and eternal God, ruler of all things in heaven and
earth, mercifully accept the prayers of your people, and
strengthen us to do your will; through Jesus Christ our Lord.
**Amen.**

**Form B**

God the Father,
**Have mercy on us.**

God the Son,
**Have mercy on us.**

God the Holy Spirit,
**Have mercy on us.**

Holy, blessed, and glorious Trinity,
**Have mercy on us.**

From all evil and mischief; from pride, vanity, and hypocrisy;
from envy, hatred, and malice; and from all evil intent,
**Good Lord, deliver us.**

From sloth, worldliness, and love of money; from hardness of
heart and contempt for your word and your laws,
**Good Lord, deliver us.**

From sins of body and mind; from the deceits of the world, the
flesh, and the devil,
**Good Lord, deliver us.**

In all times of sorrow, in all times of joy; in the hour of death,
and at the day of judgement,
**Good Lord, deliver us.**

Govern and direct your holy Church; fill it with love and truth;
and grant it that unity which is your will.
**Hear us, good Lord.**

Give us boldness to preach the gospel in all the world, and to
make disciples of all the nations.
**Hear us, good Lord.**

Enlighten your ministers with knowledge and understanding,
that by their teaching and their lives they may proclaim your
word.
**Hear us, good Lord.**

Bless your *servant* now to be made *(bishop/priest/deacon)*, that *he/she* may serve your Church and reveal your glory in the world.
**Hear us, good Lord.**

Give your people grace to hear and receive your word, and to bring forth the fruit of the Spirit.
**Hear us, good Lord.**

Bring into the way of truth all who have erred and are deceived.
**Hear us, good Lord.**

Strengthen those who stand; comfort and help the fainthearted; raise up the fallen; and finally beat down Satan under our feet.
**Hear us, good Lord.**

Give us true repentance; forgive our sins of negligence and ignorance, and our deliberate sins; and grant us the grace of your Holy Spirit, to amend our lives according to your holy word.
**Holy God,**
**holy and mighty,**
**holy and immortal one,**
**have mercy upon us.**

*The bishop prays,*

Almighty God, you have promised to hear those who pray in the name of your Son. Grant that what we have asked in faith we may obtain according to your will; through Jesus Christ our Lord. **Amen.**

# Ordination Hymns

The following translations of *Veni Creator Spiritus* and *Veni Sancte Spiritus* are suitable.

## A  Veni Creator Spiritus

1 "O Holy Spirit, by whose breath." Tr. John Webster Grant
   *The Hymn Book of the Anglican Church of Canada and the United Church of Canada*, No. 246 (Modern-language version).

2 "Creator Spirit, Lord of grace." Tr. James Quinn. *New Hymns for all Seasons*, No. 75 (Modern-language version).

3 "Come Holy Ghost, Creator blest." Tr. Edward Caswall and others. *Catholic Book of Worship*, No. 277b (Modern-language version).

4 "Come Holy Ghost, Creator blest." Tr. Edward Caswall, Richard Mant, and Robert Campbell. *The Book of Common Praise*, No. 477 (Traditional original of the preceding version).

5 "Come, O Creator Spirit, come." Tr. Robert Bridges. *The English Hymnal*, No. 154 (Traditional version).

## B  Veni Sancte Spiritus

1 "Holy Spirit, font of light." Tr. John Webster Grant. *The Hymn Book of the Anglican Church of Canada and the United Church of Canada*, No. 248 (Modern-language version).

2 "Holy Spirit, God of light." Tr. A.G.P. *New Catholic Hymnal*, No. 93 (Modern-language version).

3 "Come, thou Holy Spirit, come." Tr. Edward Caswall. *The Book of Common Praise*, No. 481 (Traditional version).

4 "Come, thou holy Paraclete." Tr. John Mason Neale. *The English Hymnal*, No. 155 (Traditional version).

Other translations may be used at the discretion of the ordaining archbishop or bishop. Many hymns in a traditional idiom will continue to be used in these ordination rites, as well as in other modern-language services. The above list includes good (and readily accessible) traditional versions.

Either *Veni Creator Spiritus* or *Veni Sancte Spiritus* is to be sung at the appointed place in all ordinations. Other hymns to the Holy Spirit, while appropriate for use elsewhere in services of ordination, are not to be substituted for these historic expressions of Christian devotion.

## Further Directions

A candidate for ordination may be vested in an alb or surplice (or, in the case of a bishop-elect, a rochet), as the ordaining archbishop or bishop shall direct. If stoles are used, a stole is placed over the left shoulder of a newly ordained deacon, and over both shoulders of a newly ordained priest. If desired, the newly ordained may be vested in the full eucharistic vestments proper to their respective orders.

According to the rubrics, the ordination eucharist is to be concelebrated. In such celebrations of the eucharist, other bishops and presbyters stand at the Lord's Table with the presiding celebrant. It is fitting for them to express their participation by suitable gestures—for example, by extending their right hands over the elements being consecrated. They may also say appropriate portions of the Great Thanksgiving with the presiding celebrant.

Newly ordained deacons should take part in the administration of communion. They may administer either the bread or the wine. One of the new deacons should dismiss the congregation after the bishop's blessing.

If convenient, the family and friends of the newly ordained may fittingly bring the eucharistic elements to the altar at the offertory. It is appropriate for the family of the newly ordained to receive Holy Communion before the other members of the congregation.

The congregation must always be given an opportunity to communicate at an ordination eucharist. The adminstration may take place at several conveniently separated places in the Church.

If two or more priests or deacons are ordained together, they should have their own presenters. The ordinands may be presented together, or in succession, as the bishop shall direct. The ordinands are to be examined together.

At the imposition of hands in the ordination of a bishop or priest, care should be taken to avoid unseemly crowding around the ordinand. It is appropriate for those bishops or presbyters who cannot reach conveniently to extend their right hands toward the ordinand.

# Parish Thanksgiving and Prayers

# Thanksgiving on the Anniversary of a Parish

**or on the Feast of Dedication**

*This service may also be used as a thanksgiving on becoming free of debt.*

*All stand. The presiding celebrant greets the community.*

| | |
|---|---|
| *Celebrant* | The grace of our Lord Jesus Christ, and the love of God, and the fellowship of the Holy Spirit, be with you all. |
| *People* | **And also with you.** |

*Or from Easter Day through the Day of Pentecost,*

| | |
|---|---|
| *Celebrant* | Alleluia! Christ is risen. |
| *People* | **The Lord is risen indeed. Alleluia!** |

| | |
|---|---|
| *Celebrant* | May his grace and peace be with you. |
| *People* | **May he fill our hearts with joy.** |

*Then may follow an act of praise.*

*At the principal service on a Sunday or other feast, the prayers, readings, and preface are normally those of the day. If the propers are inappropriate, the following prayer may be used, a selection may be made from the list of readings on p. 674, and the Prayer over the Gifts, the Preface, and the Prayer after Communion on p. 673 may be used.*

*The celebrant says,* Let us pray. *The community may pray silently.*

*The celebrant sings or says either the Collect of the Day or the following:*

Almighty God,
watchful and caring,
our source and our end,
all that we are and all that we have are yours.

Accept us now,
as we give thanks to you for this place
where we have come to praise your name,
to ask your forgiveness,
to know your healing power,
to hear your word,
and to be nourished by the body and blood of your Son.
Be present always to guide and to judge,
to illumine and to bless your people.
This we pray in the name of Jesus Christ our Lord. **Amen.**

*The celebrant and attendants proceed to the font. Psalms 42 and 43, or a hymn, may be sung.*

### At the Font

*When the procession has arrived at the font, the celebrant says,*

Let us give thanks to the Lord our God.

*All* **It is right to give our thanks and praise.**

*The celebrant says,*

We thank you, Almighty God, for the gift of water. Over water the Holy Spirit moved in the beginning of creation. Through water you led the children of Israel out of their bondage in Egypt into the land of promise. In water your Son Jesus received the baptism of John and was anointed by the Holy Spirit as the Messiah, the Christ, to lead us, through his death and resurrection, from the bondage of sin into everlasting life.

We thank you, Father, for the water of baptism. In it we are buried with Christ in his death. By it we share in his resurrection. Through it we are reborn by the Holy Spirit. Therefore in joyful obedience to your Son, we celebrate our fellowship in him in faith.

We pray that all who here pass through the water of baptism may continue for ever in the risen life of Jesus Christ our Saviour.

To him, to you, and to the Holy Spirit, be all honour and glory, now and for ever. **Amen.**

*The celebrant and attendants proceed to the lectern. Portions of Psalm 119, 89–112, or a hymn, may be sung.*

**At the Lectern**

*The celebrant says,*

Almighty God, your eternal Word speaks to us through the words of holy scripture. Here we have read of your mighty acts and purposes in history, and here we have learned about those whom you have chosen to be agents of your will. Inspired by the revelation of your Son, we seek your present purposes. Give us ears to hear and hearts to obey. This we ask through Jesus Christ our Lord. **Amen.**


## The Readings

*A first reading as appointed.*

Reader      A reading from . . .

*At the conclusion of the passage, the reader says,*

         The word of the Lord.
People      **Thanks be to God.**

*Silence may be kept. Then shall follow a psalm as appointed.*

*On Sundays and major festivals a second reading as appointed is read.*

Reader      A reading from . . .

*At the conclusion of the passage, the reader says,*

         The word of the Lord.
People      **Thanks be to God.**

*Silence may be kept. A psalm, canticle, hymn, or anthem may follow.*

*All stand for the Gospel.*

Reader      The Lord be with you.
People      **And also with you.**

| Reader | The Holy Gospel of our Lord Jesus Christ according to . . . |
| People | **Glory to you, Lord Jesus Christ.** |

*At the conclusion of the Gospel, the reader says,*

|  | The Gospel of Christ. |
| People | **Praise to you, Lord Jesus Christ.** |

### At the Pulpit

*The following prayer is said at the pulpit before the sermon, while the congregation remains standing.*

Almighty God, we have heard your words to us in holy scripture, and know your call to each of us. In every age you have spoken through the voices of prophets, pastors, and teachers. We give you thanks that over the years we have heard you speak to us through the preaching of your word in this place. Grant that those who preach in this place may proclaim the crucified and risen Christ and interpret your word with sensitivity and insight, that we may hear that word inwardly and respond to it in all our life. This we ask in the name of Jesus Christ, your living Word. **Amen.**

## The Sermon

*A silence for reflection may follow.*

## The Prayers of the People

*A deacon or a lay person leads the following litany.*

For the Church universal, of which these buildings are a visible symbol,
    **We thank you, Lord.**

For your presence whenever two or three have gathered in your name,
    **We thank you, Lord.**

For this place where we may be still and know that you are God,
**We thank you, Lord.**

For the fulfilling of our desires and petitions as you see best for us,
**We thank you, Lord.**

For our past and a vision of the future that lies ahead,
**We thank you, Lord.**

For the gift of the Holy Spirit and new life in baptism,
**We thank you, Lord.**

For the pardon of our sins when we have fallen short of your glory,
**We thank you, Lord.**

For the holy eucharist in which we have a foretaste of your eternal kingdom,
**We thank you, Lord.**

For the blessing of our vows and the crowning of our years with your goodness,
**We thank you, Lord.**

For the faith of those who have gone before us and for our encouragement by their perseverance,
**We thank you, Lord.**

For all the benefactors of this place who have died in the peace of Christ and are at rest (especially *N*),
**We thank you, Lord.**

For the fellowship of all your saints, and especially for *N*, our patron,
**We thank you, Lord.**

*After a period of silence the litany is concluded with the following prayer.*

O God, from living and chosen stones you prepare an everlasting dwelling place for your majesty. Grant that in the power of the Holy Spirit those who serve you here may always be kept within your presence. This we pray through Jesus

Christ our Lord, who lives and reigns with you and the Holy
Spirit, one God, now and ever. **Amen.**

*The service continues with the Peace and the Preparation of the Gifts (p. 192).*

### Prayer over the Gifts

Father, hear the prayers of your faithful people.
Grant that all who celebrate this eucharist
may please you by the offering of themselves
and the fulfilling of your will.
This we ask in the name of Jesus Christ the Lord. **Amen.**

### Proper Preface

Blessed are you, gracious God,
creator of heaven and earth;
heaven itself cannot contain you
and your glory fills all the world.
You accept our setting apart of places for your worship
and in them pour out your gifts of grace
upon your faithful people.
This table is a sign to us of the heavenly altar,
where your saints and angels praise you.
Here we have recalled the sacrifice of your Son;
here we have been fed with the body and blood of your Son;
here our sins have been forgiven;
here we have tasted the joys of your eternal kingdom.
Grant that in these mysteries
we may be united with one another
and strengthened for service in your world.
Therefore with angels and archangels
and those who worship you in every age,
we raise our voices in joyful praise
to proclaim the glory of your name.

### Prayer after Communion

Father, you have given us this time of joy
and have nourished us in heavenly things.
Grant that we may show in our lives the love of Christ
who is our God and Saviour. **Amen.**

# Readings and Psalms Suitable for the Anniversary of a Parish

## Old Testament Readings

Genesis 28.10–17   (How awesome is this place! This is none other than the house of God)

1 Kings 8.22–30   (That thy eyes may be open night and day toward this house)

1 Chronicles 29.6–19   (All things come from thee, and of thy own have we given thee)

## Psalms and Suitable Refrains

84   (My soul has a desire and longing for the courts of the Lord)

122   (Peace be within your walls and quietness within your towers)

## New Testament Readings

1 Peter 2.1–5, 9–10   (Like living stones be yourselves built into a spiritual house)

Revelation 21.1–4, 22—22.5   (Its temple is the Lord God the Almighty and the Lamb)

## Gospel Readings

Matthew 21.12–16   (My house shall be called a house of prayer)

John 20.19–21   (Jesus came and stood among them)

# Occasional Prayers

### 1 For the Unity of Christians

Lord Jesus Christ, you said to your apostles, "Peace I give to you; my own peace I leave with you." Regard not our sins, but the faith of your Church, and give to us the peace and unity of that heavenly city, where with the Father and the Holy Spirit you live and reign, now and for ever.

### 2 For the Mission of the Church

Draw your Church together, O Lord, into one great company of disciples, together following our Lord Jesus Christ into every walk of life, together serving him in his mission to the world, and together witnessing to his love on every continent and island. We ask this in his name and for his sake.

### 3 At a Time of Election or Appointment in the Church

Almighty God, giver of all good gifts, look on your Church with grace, and guide the minds of those who shall choose a . . . for this . . ., that we may receive a faithful servant who will care for your people and support us in our ministries; through Jesus Christ our Lord.

### 4 For a Synod

Almighty and everliving God, source of all wisdom and understanding, be present with those who take counsel (in . . . ) for the renewal and mission of your Church. Teach us in all things to seek first your honour and glory. Guide us to perceive what is right, and grant us both the courage to pursue it and the grace to accomplish it; through Jesus Christ our Lord.

### 5 For the Ministry of the Church

*i For all Christians in their vocation*

Almighty and everlasting God, by whose Spirit the whole body of your faithful people is governed and sanctified, receive our supplications and prayers, which we offer before you for all members of your holy Church, that in their vocation and ministry they may truly and devoutly serve you; through our Lord and Saviour Jesus Christ, who lives and reigns with you, in the unity of the Holy Spirit, one God, now and for ever.

*ii   For the choice of suitable persons for the ordained ministry*

O God, you led your holy apostles to ordain ministers in every place. Grant that your Church, under the guidance of the Holy Spirit, may choose suitable persons for the ministry of word and sacrament, and may uphold them in their work for the extension of your kingdom; through him who is the shepherd and bishop of our souls, Jesus Christ our Lord, who lives and reigns with you and the Holy Spirit, one God, for ever and ever.

*iii   For those to be ordained*

Almighty God, the giver of all good gifts, in your divine providence you have appointed various orders in your Church. Give your grace, we humbly pray, to all who are (now) called to any office and ministry for your people; and so fill them with the truth of your doctrine and clothe them with holiness of life, that they may faithfully serve before you, to the glory of your great name and for the benefit of your holy Church; through Jesus Christ our Lord, who lives and reigns with you, in the unity of the Holy Spirit, one God, now and for ever.

### 6   For Peace

O God, it is your will to hold both heaven and earth in a single peace. Let the design of your great love shine on the waste of our wraths and sorrows, and give peace to your Church, peace among nations, peace in our homes, and peace in our hearts; through your Son Jesus Christ our Lord.

### 7   For the Commonwealth

God of all, by your providence we are bound with many peoples in the fellowship of a commonwealth of nations. Give us, we pray, such unity as may enable us to promote the peace of your creation and the glory of its creator; in the name of Jesus Christ, the Prince of Peace.

### 8   For the Queen

Almighty God, fountain of all goodness, bless our Sovereign Lady, Queen Elizabeth, and all who are in authority under her; that they may order all things in wisdom and equity, righteousness and peace, to the honour of your name, and the good of your Church and people; through Jesus Christ our Lord.

### 9 For the Royal Family

Almighty God, the fountain of all goodness, bless, we pray, our Sovereign Lady, Queen Elizabeth, († . . . ), and all the Royal Family. Endue them with your Holy Spirit; enrich them with your heavenly grace, prosper them with all happiness; and bring them to your everlasting kingdom; through Jesus Christ our Lord.

### 10 For the Nation

Almighty God, you have given us this good land as our heritage. May we prove ourselves a people mindful of your generosity and glad to do your will. Bless our land with honest industry, truthful education, and an honourable way of life. Save us from violence, discord, and confusion; from pride and arrogance; and from every evil course of action. Make us who came from many nations with many different languages a united people. Defend our liberties and give those whom we have entrusted with the authority of government the spirit of wisdom, that there may be justice and peace in our land. When times are prosperous, let our hearts be thankful; and, in troubled times, do not let our trust in you fail. We ask this through Jesus Christ our Lord.

### 11 For Responsible Citizenship or for an Election

Lord, keep this nation under your care. Bless the leaders of our land, that we may be a people at peace among ourselves and a blessing to other nations of the earth. Help us elect trustworthy leaders, contribute to wise decisions for the general welfare, and thus serve you faithfully in our generation to the honour of your holy name; through Jesus Christ our Lord.

† Here shall be named, as determined by authority from time to time, the several members of the Royal Family.

## 12 For Courts of Justice

Almighty God, creator, judge, and redeemer of all: we pray
you to bless the courts of justice and the magistrates in all this
land, and give them the spirit of wisdom and understanding,
that they may discern the truth, and impartially administer the
law in reverence of you alone; through him who shall come to
be our judge, your Son our Saviour Jesus Christ.

## 13 For the Armed Forces

Almighty God, we commend to your gracious care and keeping
all the men and women of our armed forces at home and
abroad. Defend them day by day with your heavenly grace;
strengthen them in their trials and temptations; give them
courage to face the perils which beset them; and grant them a
sense of your abiding presence wherever they may be; through
Jesus Christ our Lord.

## 14 For the Oppressed in this Land

Look with pity, O heavenly Father, upon those in this land
who live with injustice, terror, disease, and death as their
constant companions. Have mercy upon us and help us to
eliminate cruelty wherever it is found. Strengthen those who
seek equality for all. Grant that every one of us may enjoy a fair
portion of the abundance of this land; through your Son Jesus
Christ our Lord.

## 15 For Good Use of Leisure

O God, in the course of this busy life give us times of
refreshment and peace; and grant that we may so use our
leisure to rebuild our bodies and renew our minds, that our
spirits may be opened to the goodness of your creation;
through Jesus Christ our Lord.

## 16 For Educational Institutions

O Eternal God, bless all schools, colleges, and universities
(especially . . . ), that they may be lively centres for sound
learning, new discovery, and the pursuit of wisdom; and grant
that those who teach and those who learn may find you to be
the source of all truth; through Jesus Christ our Lord.

### 17 For Industry and Commerce

Almighty God, your Son Jesus Christ dignified our labour by sharing our toil. Be with your people where they work; make those who carry on the industries and commerce of this land responsive to your will; and to all of us, give pride in what we do and a just return for our labour; through your Son Jesus Christ our Lord.

### 18 For Fisheries

Holy God, creator of the universe, you have given the seas and the life they contain for the use and benefit of all. Protect our fishermen during this fishing season, and give them a bountiful catch. We ask your help through our Lord Jesus Christ, your Son, in the unity of the Holy Spirit, one God, for ever and ever.

### 19 For Agriculture

Almighty God, we thank you for making the fruitful earth produce what is needed for life. Bless those who work in the fields; give us favourable weather; and grant that all may share the fruits of the earth, rejoicing in your goodness; through your Son Jesus Christ our Lord.

*See also prayers for Rogation and Harvest Thanksgiving, pp. 396–397.*

### 20 For the Unemployed

Heavenly Father, we remember before you those who suffer want and anxiety from lack of work. Guide the people of this land so to use their wealth and resources that everyone may find suitable and fulfilling employment and receive just payment for their labour; through your Son Jesus Christ our Lord.

### 21 For the Neighbourhood

O Lord our creator, by your holy prophet you taught your ancient people to seek the welfare of the cities in which they lived. We commend our neighbourhood to your care, that it might be kept free from social strife and decay. Give us strength of purpose and concern for others, that we may create here a community of justice and peace where your will may be done; through your Son Jesus Christ our Lord.

## 22  For the Poor and Neglected

Almighty and most merciful God, we remember before you the homeless, the destitute, the sick, the aged, and all who have none to care for them. Heal those who are broken in body or spirit, and turn their sorrow into joy. Grant this for the love of your Son, who for our sake became poor, Jesus Christ our Lord.

## 23  For Our Enemies

O God, the Lord of all, your Son commanded us to love our enemies and to pray for them. Lead us from prejudice to truth; deliver us from hatred, cruelty, and revenge; and enable us to stand before you, reconciled through your Son Jesus Christ our Lord.

## 24  For Prisons and Correctional Institutions

Gracious God, help us to be obedient to your command to love and serve you in all people. Make us conscious of your loving presence everywhere, and especially with those in prison. Comfort the prisoners in their loneliness and uphold their families during separation. Remember those who work in our justice system, that they may perform their duties in a spirit of fairness and patience. Bring us to a closer relationship with our sisters and brothers who as prisoners and staff share with us the joy of your release from human bondage. We ask this in the name of Jesus Christ the Lord.

## 25  For Those Who Suffer for the Sake of Conscience

God of love and strength, your Son forgave his enemies even while he was suffering shame and death. Strengthen those who suffer for the sake of conscience. When they are accused, save them from speaking in hate; when they are rejected, save them from bitterness; when they are imprisoned, save them from despair. Give us grace to discern the truth, that our society may be cleansed and strengthened. This we ask for the sake of our merciful and righteous judge, Jesus Christ our Lord.

## 26  For Those in Affliction

Almighty and everlasting God, the comfort of the sad and the strength of those who suffer, hear the prayers of your people who are in any trouble. Grant to everyone in distress mercy, relief, and refreshment; through Jesus Christ our Lord.

## 27  For Those in Mental Distress

Heavenly Father, have mercy on all your children who live in mental distress. Restore them to strength of mind and cheerfulness of spirit, and give them health and peace; through Jesus Christ our Lord.

## 28  For Those Suffering from Addiction

O blessed Jesus, you ministered to all who came to you. Look with compassion upon all who through addiction have lost their health and freedom. Restore to them the assurance of your unfailing mercy; remove the fears that attack them; strengthen them in the work of their recovery; and to those who care for them, give patient understanding and persevering love; for your mercy's sake.

## 29  For the Aged

O Lord God, look with mercy on all whose increasing years bring them isolation, distress, or weakness. Provide for them homes of dignity and peace; give them understanding helpers and the willingness to accept help; and, as their strength diminishes, increase their faith and their assurance of your love. We pray in the name of Jesus Christ our Lord.

## 30  For Those Who Travel

God whose glory fills the whole creation, and whose presence we find wherever we go, preserve those who travel (in particular . . . ); surround them with your loving care; protect them from every danger; and bring them in safety to their journey's end; through Jesus Christ our Lord.

## 31  A Prayer of Christian Life

Lord, make us instruments of your peace. Where there is hatred, let us sow love; where there is injury, pardon; where there is discord, union; where there is doubt, faith; where there is despair, hope; where there is darkness, light; where there is sadness, joy. Grant that we may not so much seek to be consoled as to console; to be understood as to understand; to be loved as to love. For it is in giving that we receive; it is in pardoning that we are pardoned; and it is in dying that we are born to eternal life.

### 32   A General Intercession

Remember, Lord, your people bowed before you, and those who are absent through age, sickness, or any other cause. Care for the infants, guide the young, support the aged, inspire the faint-hearted, and bring the wandering to your fold. Journey with the travellers, encourage the oppressed, defend the widows, deliver the captives, heal the sick. Strengthen all who are in tribulation, necessity, or distress. Remember for good those who love us, and those who hate us, and those who have asked us, unworthy as we are, to pray for them. Remember especially, Lord, those whom we have forgotten. For you are the helper of the helpless, the saviour of the lost, the refuge of the wanderer, the healer of the sick. You know the need of all and have heard each prayer: save us in your merciful loving-kindness and eternal love; through Jesus Christ our Lord.

### 33   Blessings

*i*   The Lord bless you and keep you. The Lord make his face shine on you and be gracious to you. The Lord look upon you with favour and grant you peace.

*ii*   The peace of God which passes all understanding keep your hearts and minds in the knowledge and love of God, and of his Son Jesus Christ our Lord; and the blessing of God almighty, the Father, the Son, and the Holy Spirit, be among you and remain with you always.

*Advent*

Be steadfast in faith, joyful in hope, and untiring in love all the days of your life; and the blessing of God almighty, the Father, the Son, and the Holy Spirit, be among you and remain with you always.

## Incarnation

May the God of infinite goodness scatter the darkness of sin and brighten your hearts with holiness; and the blessing of God almighty, the Father, the Son, and the Holy Spirit, be among you and remain with you always.

## Lent

May the God of mercy transform you by his grace, and the blessing of God almighty, the Father, the Son, and the Holy Spirit, be among you and remain with you always.

## Easter

May the God of peace who brought again from the dead our Lord Jesus, the great shepherd of the sheep, by the blood of the eternal covenant, equip you with everything good that you may do his will, working in you that which is pleasing in his sight, through Jesus Christ; to whom be glory for ever and ever.

# Home Prayers

Christian households should consider a regular pattern of worship and celebration in the home. An individual who lives alone, a family group, friends or Christians in an institutional setting may develop their own particular style of prayer. It is impossible to offer one form of worship which will meet all needs. Indeed, it is not desirable to do so, for each community is shaped by God in a unique way. Home Prayers suggests a pattern which may be adapted quite freely:

preparation—a gathering of the community around a theme
praise—music, psalms, poetry
readings and study of scripture
intercession
the Lord's Prayer
conclusion.

The Divine Office also follows this pattern and may be adapted for use by families.

Each community will find an appropriate time for devotions. For some, this may only be on special occasions; for others, a regular daily or weekly event.

There are occasions in the lives of families and communities when special prayers are appropriate: meals, bedtime, family festivals such as birthdays, anniversaries and reunions, and times of mourning. Suitable prayers will be found in the Occasional Prayers section (p. 675).

The following form for Home Prayers, although designed for use in the context of the evening meal, may be used at any time. Alternate sentences and prayers are provided for morning and day-time use.

The service may be adapted as needed.

# Concerning the Service

*The Preparation may be used as a separate devotion, or the service may be used at other times of the day without the Preparation.*

*The service is most appropriately held in a place where it is usual for the whole group to gather, e.g. the dining area. Seasonal symbols may be put in an appropriate place.*

*Advent—the Advent wreath may be placed on the table. One candle is lit in the first week of Advent. An additional candle is lit each week until Christmas Day.*

*Christmas Season—a crèche may be arranged on the table. The Christmas candle is lit.*

*Epiphany—the wreath is removed but the Christmas candle remains. The wise men may be placed in the crèche.*

*Lent—there is no candle. A plain cross may be placed on the table. If mite boxes are being used, it is appropriate to place them on the table.*

*Holy Week—branches of palm trees or other trees may be placed around the cross.*

*Easter Season—on Easter Eve or Morning a new white candle may be placed on the table. It may be decorated, and may be surrounded by a small garden scene, flowers and/or eggs.*

*Pentecost—one or more candles are lit.*

*Saints' Days—the table may be decorated with symbols of the saints who are being commemorated.*

*A seasonal affirmation may be used during a special season in the church year (pp. 687–689).*

*In choosing psalms and scripture passages, the lectionary may be used. If the group has already heard the readings for the day, those from another cycle may be used. A book of the Bible may be read sequentially.*

*Music may be used before or during the service.*

*Individuals may lead different parts of the service.*

# Home Prayers

## A Form of Prayer for Groups or Families

### 1  The Preparation

*The candle or candles on the table or in the worship area may be lit. The one*
*who lights them says one of the following:*

Leader  God is our light and our salvation, and in his name
we light *these candles*. May *they* remind us of the
beauty of his truth and the radiance of his love. May
our hearts be open to the light of Christ now and at
all times.

All  **Lord, in your mercy, let there be light.**

*Or*

Leader  O God, you command a light to shine out of
darkness. Shine in our hearts that we may be as
lights in the world reflecting the glory of Jesus in
our lives.

All  **God is light and in him is no darkness.**

*Advent*

Leader  Jesus said, "I am the light of the world. Those
who follow me will not walk in darkness, but will
have the light of life."

All  **Come, Lord Jesus, come quickly.**

Leader  Source of all light, send your Son Jesus Christ to
shine in our dark world. Help us to prepare our
hearts to receive him who lives and reigns with you
and the Holy Spirit, now and for ever. **Amen.**

*Christmas Season*

Leader  Unto us a child is born.
All  **Unto us a Son is given.**

| Leader | O God, your love was so great for us that you gave us your Son to shine out in our darkness. Help us to make that love known to all the world, through Jesus Christ our Lord. **Amen.** |

*Epiphany*

| Leader | Arise, shine, for our light has come. |
| All | **And the glory of the Lord has dawned upon us.** |

| Leader | Eternal God, who by a star led wise men to the worship of your Son. Guide by your light the nations of the earth, that the whole world may know your glory; through Jesus Christ our Lord, who lives and reigns with you and the Holy Spirit, one God, now and for ever. **Amen.** |

*Lent*

| Leader | Jesus said, "And if I am lifted up, I will draw the whole world to myself." |
| All | **We will take up our cross and follow him.** |

| Leader | We adore you, O Christ, and we bless you, |
| All | **Because by your holy cross you have redeemed the world.** |

| Leader | Almighty God, by the suffering of your Son you have brought hope to the whole world. Help us in our trials and be the strength of our human weakness, through Jesus Christ our Lord. **Amen.** |

*Holy Week*

| Leader | Hosanna to the Son of David. |
| All | **Blessed is he who comes in the name of the Lord.** |

| Leader | Father, your Son Jesus humbled himself and accepted death on a cross for us. Help us to walk with him to Calvary and to bring your love to all who suffer, through Jesus Christ our Lord. **Amen.** |

*Easter Season*

Leader  May the light of Christ in glory rising scatter the darkness of heart and mind. Alleluia! Christ is risen.

All  **The Lord is risen indeed. Alleluia!**

Leader  O God, the source of light and life, by the resurrection of your only Son you have led us out of darkness into your marvellous light, from death into life, from slavery into freedom. Bring the light of your new creation to us and to our world, through Jesus Christ our Lord, who is alive and reigns with you and the Holy Spirit for ever. **Amen.**

*Pentecost*

Leader  Come, Holy Spirit, and renew the face of the earth.

All  **Come, Holy Spirit, and kindle in our hearts the fire of your love.**

Leader  God of love, of your goodness set us aflame with that fire of the Spirit which Christ brought upon the earth and longs to see blazing throughout the world, through him who lives and reigns with you and the Spirit now and for ever. **Amen.**

*Saints' Days*

Leader  The saints are your witnesses to the ends of the earth.

All  **And lights of the world in their generations.**

Leader  Almighty God, by your grace your servant *N*, was kindled with the fires of your love and became a shining light in your Church. Inflame us with the same spirit of discipline and love, that we may always walk before you as children of light, through Jesus Christ our Lord. **Amen.**

*This hymn may be sung.* *Tune: Tallis's Canon*

> O gracious Light, Lord Jesus Christ,
> in you the Father's glory shone.
> Immortal, holy, blest is he,
> and blest are you, his holy Son.
>
> Now sunset comes, but light shines forth,
> the lamps are lit to pierce the night.
> Praise Father, Son, and Spirit: God
> who dwells in the eternal light.
>
> Worthy are you of endless praise,
> O Son of God, Life-giving Lord;
> wherefore you are through all the earth
> and in the highest heaven adored.

*The Collect of the Day may be said.*

## 2  The Meal  *if desired*

*For forms of grace before and after meals, see pp. 694–695.*

## 3  Praise

*Here may follow a psalm, hymn, song, or instrumental music.*

## 4  Readings

*One or more passages of scripture may be read.*

## 5  Response

*Any of the following may follow the readings: silence, discussion of the scripture passage or theme of the day, reading of a related work of literature, telling of a related story, study of special material from the parish, diocese, or national Church, discussion of family concerns in the light of scripture or the theme of the day.*

## 6  Intercession

*Prayer may be offered for the Church, the Queen and all in authority, the world, the special needs of the group, those in need, and the departed. The following litany may be used, or a seasonal litany (pp. 119–123), or any prayers from the Occasional Prayers (p. 675); or individuals may offer their own prayers, silently or aloud.*

| Leader | Let us pray together to the Lord, saying, "Lord, hear our prayer." |
|---|---|
| All | **Lord, hear our prayer.** |

| Leader | Loving God, we thank you for your many gifts to us, for the love which brings us together, for the earth which provides for our needs, for the new life you have given us in Jesus Christ, (for . . . ). |
|---|---|
| All | **Lord, hear our prayer.** |

| Leader | We pray to you for our Christian family (especially for . . . ) and for grace to grow in your love. |
|---|---|
| All | **Lord, hear our prayer.** |

| Leader | We pray to you for our world, for all its cares and needs, and for all who lead us and care for us, (especially . . . ). |
|---|---|
| All | **Lord, hear our prayer.** |

| Leader | We pray to you for those in need, for the sick and the lonely, for the hurt and the frightened, and for those who live without hope (especially . . . ). |
|---|---|
| All | **Lord, hear our prayer.** |

| Leader | We pray for those we love who have died, that you will surround them with your care and love (especially . . . ). |
|---|---|
| All | **Lord, hear our prayer.** |

| Leader | We pray for one another, asking you to bless us, our friends, and relatives. Bless the places where we work, and bless our home and our life together. |
|---|---|
| All | **Lord, hear our prayer.** |

*Members of the home may wish to share in personal prayer. Then may be said,*

| Leader | Let us remember before God our selfish ways, the things we have done wrong, the sorrows we have caused, the love we have not shown. |
|---|---|

*Silence for reflection is kept.*

All     **Most merciful Father,**
              **forgive us our sins against you**
              **and against each other.**
              **Strengthen us to overcome our weaknesses,**
              **that we may live in love**
              **as you would have us live,**
              **for the sake of Jesus Christ our Saviour. Amen.**

*One of the following prayers may be said.*

Evening     The Lord almighty grant us a quiet night and peace at the last. **Amen.**

Or     Be our light in the darkness, O Lord, and in your great mercy defend us from all perils and dangers of this night; for the love of your only Son, our Saviour Jesus Christ. **Amen.**

Or     Remain with us, Lord, for the day is far spent and evening is at hand. Kindle our hearts on our way that we may recognize you in the scriptures and the breaking of bread. Grant this for the sake of your love. **Amen.**

Morning     Fill our hearts, O God, with your Holy Spirit that we may go forth this day in peace and joy, serving you eagerly in all we do, for Jesus' sake. **Amen.**

*Other prayers for morning and evening may be found on pp. 130 to 132.*

## 7   The Lord's Prayer

Leader     As our Saviour taught us, let us pray,

All     **Our Father in heaven,**
              **hallowed be your name,**
              **your kingdom come,**
              **your will be done,**
              **on earth as in heaven.**
              **Give us today our daily bread.**

Forgive us our sins
as we forgive those who sin against us.
Save us from the time of trial,
and deliver us from evil.
For the kingdom, the power,
and the glory are yours,
now and forever. Amen.

*Or*

*Leader*    And now, as our Saviour Christ has taught us,
we are bold to say,

*All*    **Our Father, who art in heaven,
hallowed be thy name,
thy kingdom come,
thy will be done,
on earth as it is in heaven.
Give us this day our daily bread.
And forgive us our trespasses,
as we forgive those who trespass against us.
And lead us not into temptation,
but deliver us from evil.
For thine is the kingdom,
the power, and the glory,
for ever and ever. Amen.**

## 8  Conclusion

*One of the following may be said.*

The grace of the Lord Jesus Christ, and the love of
God, and the fellowship of the Holy Spirit, be with
us all evermore. **Amen.**

*Or*    Grace to you and peace from God our Father and
the Lord Jesus Christ.

*Or*    Jesus said, "I am the light of the world; whoever
follows me will not walk in darkness, but will have
the light of life."

**Grace at Meals**

1   Blessed are you, Lord our God, ruler of the universe; you give us food from the earth. **Amen.**

2   Creator of the universe, you give us this gift of food to nourish us and give us life. Bless this food that you have made and human hands have prepared. May it satisfy our hunger, and in sharing it together may we come closer to one another. **Amen.**

3   For what we are about to receive, may the Lord make us truly thankful, through Jesus Christ our Lord. **Amen.**

4   The eyes of all wait upon you, O Lord,
    **And you give them their food in due season.**
You open wide your hand
    **And satisfy the needs of every living creature.**
Glory to the Father, and to the Son, and to the
Holy Spirit.
    **As it was in the beginning, is now, and will be**
    **for ever. Amen.**

Bless, O Lord, this food to our use and bless us to your service, and make us ever mindful of the needs of others; through Jesus Christ our Lord. **Amen.**

5   Come, Lord Jesus, be our guest,
and let these gifts to us be blessed. **Amen.**

6   God is great, God is good,
and we thank him for this food.
By his hand we all are fed;
give us, Lord, our daily bread.
Bless our home with peace and love,
and grant in Christ a home above. **Amen.**

7   For this our daily food, and for every gift which comes from you, O God, we bless your holy name (through Jesus Christ our Lord). **Amen.**

8  For these and all our blessings, God's holy name be praised
   (through Jesus Christ our Lord). **Amen.**

9  All good gifts around us
   are sent from heaven above,
   then thank the Lord, O thank the Lord,
   for all his love.

10  For health and strength and daily food,
   we praise your name, O Lord.

11  Lord, may our fellowship be the revelation of your
   presence and turn our daily bread into bread of life. **Amen.**

12  Blessed are you, Lord our God, ruler of the universe;
   we have shared of your bounty, and through your
   goodness we live. **Amen.**

*Or the Prayer over the Gifts from the propers of the day may be used when
suitable.*

### On the Anniversary of a Baptism

Blessed are you, Lord God, ruler of the universe; we praise you
for your love and mercy which you have shown to all your
people.

Today we give you thanks and glory as we celebrate the
anniversary of the day when you made N your *son/daughter* in
baptism.

Give *him/her* the grace to live in your love, and help this family
to come closer to you by faith, prayer, and example.

All glory is yours, Father, through Jesus your Son in the
communion of your Spirit, now and for ever. **Amen.**

# Additional Home Prayers

### 1 For a Birthday

God our Father, the birth of your Son Jesus Christ brought
great joy to Mary and Joseph. We give thanks to you for *N*,
whose birthday we celebrate today. May *he/she* ever grow in
your faith, hope, and love. We ask this in the name of our Lord
Jesus Christ.

### 2 For the Blessing of a New Home

Let us ask God to bless our home.

Jesus, King of love, you shared in the life of your earthly home
at Nazareth with Mary and Joseph. Bless, we pray, our new
home and our life here, that we may help each other and those
who visit us to grow more and more in your love. We ask this
in your name and for your sake.

### 3 For the Anniversary of a Marriage

Gracious God, on this our special day we remember with
thanksgiving our vows of love and commitment to you and to
each other in marriage. We pray for your continued blessing.
May we learn from both our joys and sorrows, and discover
new riches in our life together in you. We ask this in the name
of Jesus Christ our Lord.

### 4 For a Member Leaving Home

Let us ask God to bless us at this time of separation.

Gracious God, look on us in your love and give us your
blessing. Be with *N*, as *he/she* leaves us, and be with those of us
who remain here. You know our feelings at this time. Help us
to remember that we are always united to one another in your
love, made known to us in Jesus Christ our Lord.

### 5 For Reconciliation in a Home

Let us ask God for his healing peace.

God of peace, forgive us as we forgive each other for all the hurt we have brought into our lives. Let your healing love rest upon the wounds we have caused by our anger. Deepen our love in a new understanding for each other and for you. We ask this in the name of Jesus Christ who carried on his cross our discord and our grief.

### 6 A Thanksgiving

Our Lord God, we thank you for all your blessings,
for life and health,
for laughter and fun,
for all our powers of mind and body,
for our homes and the love of dear ones,
for everything that is beautiful, good and true.
But above all we thank you for giving your Son
to be our Saviour and Friend.
May we always find our true happiness
in pleasing you and helping others
to know and love you,
for Jesus Christ's sake.

*ther Thanksgivings may be found on p. 129.*

### 7 For Home and Family

O God whose desire is that all the peoples of the world should be one human family, living together in harmony, grant that our home, by its worship and its witness, may help to hasten the day when your will is done on earth as it is in heaven.

# The Psalter

# The Psalter

The Psalter is not only the oldest hymn book of the Church, it is also the hymn book of ancient Israel as well as the basis of much of the worship of Jews today. The Psalter is consequently a sign of the continuity of Christianity with its Jewish origins and of the solidarity of Christians with their Jewish brothers and sisters in the contemporary world. The piety of the Psalter transcends the divisions of the Jewish-Christian faith communities, and overarches their history.

The origins of the Psalter were liturgical. Even the psalms which speak in singular voice presuppose a corporate setting and presentation. They are the voice of a people in the various moments of its experience of life: moments of aspiration, degradation, ecstasy, and hope. Those who read the psalms, even in solitude, should be conscious of the host of voices that accompany them, stretched across two and a half millenia and more.

From an early date, Christians have attempted to make the Psalter their own. In Acts 13.30–39, for instance, two psalms (2 and 16) are used as the basis of a developing Christology. Later Christian piety attempted to treat all the psalms in this way, as descriptions of Christ, as prayers to Christ, or as the voice of Christ speaking to his people.

This "Christianizing" of the psalms is not inappropriate and it continues among Christians to the present day. Many of the psalms appointed for Fridays in the Daily Office Lectionary are laments and provide vivid images for reflection on the cross. On the other hand, the psalms continue to have a life and integrity of their own and their openness to a particular interpretation does not exclude other interpretations. Sometimes in the psalms of the exile the reader may hear primarily the anguish of those who suffered the pains of imprisonment and isolation from their homeland, and may add to their complaint the burdens of the present moment. All this may be subsumed into a theology of the cross without insistence that that theology function always as the first level of interpretation.

The psalms began as the cry of a people in moments of pain and joy. They are an intensely human cry. When Christians use the psalms they do not leave their Christianity behind, but they do not abandon their humanity either. Christians also experience doubt and anger as well as joy and hope and the psalms encourage them to give vent to that darker side of their humanity. To do so is not to fail in faith or love but to recognize that faith and love cannot be claimed as mere palliatives of present pain. Present pain must be owned if life is to be transformed.

When the *Book of Common Prayer* of 1962 was published it was an accepted practice in the Church to delete from the Psalter those sections which were judged to be too negative and violent. That practice has not been followed in the translation of the Psalter which follows. The psalms are all here, much as Jesus found them in Jewish liturgical tradition. Not every psalm or section of a psalm has been suggested for public recitation in the various lectionaries in this book, but they are all here for study, and reflection, and for use when appropriate.

An early method of appropriating the psalms to Christian worship was the offering of a "psalm prayer" after a period of reflective silence at the end of the recitation of the psalm. Psalm prayers have been attached to the psalms which follow, not as rigid and unvarying liturgical forms but as suggestions and models for Christian use. Another Christian device with which contemporary Anglicans are more familiar is the singing or saying of the short canticle *Glory to the Father* at the end of each psalm or collection of psalms. Psalm prayers and the canticle may be used separately or together.

Matthew and Mark report that the last supper Jesus ate with his disciples ended with a hymn. We may assume that the hymn was a psalm. Certainly by the time of Tertullian a psalm was sung between the readings at the eucharist and by the fifth century a psalm was sung during the procession at the beginning of the liturgy. The appearance of psalms as the central core and substance of both the monastic and cathedral offices in the fourth century suggests that they were already firmly established in Christian worship. It is true that Christians had made early attempts at the composition of their own psalms but the low survival rate of these compositions suggests that few of the imitations matched the model. (*Glory to God* and *Phos Hilaron* are among the few that survive in widespread liturgical use.)

The psalms, like other hymns, are poems, i.e., they are ceremonial forms of speech which observe recognized canons of structure and express themselves in powerful and evocative images through the use of metaphor, simile, and other literary constructs. The structural form of the psalms is based primarily on two devices: parallelism and stress. Parallelism is apparent even to a casual reader of the psalms, for they contain a recurring tendency to say things twice, usually in slightly different ways and often with some expansion of the subject in the second statement. Thus,

> Come, let us sing to the Lord; let us shout for joy to the rock of our salvation,

is paralleled by

> Let us come before his presence with thanksgiving and raise a loud shout to him with psalms.

The second device, stress, is less apparent, especially in traditional English translations, although it is not foreign to older forms of the English language and poetry and has attracted contemporary attention through the poems of the nineteenth century Jesuit, Gerard Manley Hopkins. Stress (unlike metre, which is rhythmic) consists simply in the emphasis of certain predetermined syllables, usually three or four in number, in each line. A modern English version of a stressed line written by the fourteenth-century poet Langland might read,

> In a *sum*mer *sea*son, when *soft* was the *sun*.

If the italicized syllables are emphasized or stressed when the line is read, the ceremonial structure of the poetic form becomes clear. The pattern of words informs the reader that the telling of the story which follows is no mere exercise in marketplace gossip but a manifestation of that artistry of language which, from ancient times, we have called poetry.

The Hebrew psalms rely heavily on the form of stress, but this dimension of their poetry has, until recently, been hidden from most English language readers. The family of Psalters which is found in various forms in the traditional Prayer Books of the Anglican Communion is based on Miles Coverdale's translation which was used with the first Prayer Book of 1549. This translation, a work of great beauty and a cornerstone of Anglican piety, did not contain the device of stress, and a significant element of Hebrew poetry, not unsusceptible of translation, did not enter Anglican vernacular tradition. Coverdale's omission is understandable: he did not translate from the Hebrew original but from the Latin Psalter (with unstressed lines) which was itself a translation from the Greek Septuagint.

The Psalter which appears in the *Book of Common Prayer* of the Episcopal Church (U.S.A.) has been selected as an appendix to the *Book of Alternative Services*. It was chosen because of the verbal accuracy of its translation, because the form is familiar and is highly suitable for use with both plainsong and Anglican chant, and because the translators made an earnest (although not always successful) attempt to use gender-inclusive language whenever possible. This is a good translation, recognizably Anglican in flavour.

It should, however, be noted that the world of the Psalter is, at the time of writing, in a very fluid state. Some years ago a translation of the psalms appeared in French with lines designed for stressed recitation. Joseph Gelineau adapted traditional modes to provide appropriate music for this translation of the psalms. This style of recitation has been made available to the English-speaking world by the Grail (*The Psalms*, Fontana Books, London and Glasgow, 1966, 1976). In the meantime, a new translation was prepared in England, along more traditional lines, at the request of the Liturgical Commission of the Church of England (*The Psalms: A New Translation for Worship*, Collins Liturgical Publications, London, 1977). This translation, which does not contain stress, was approved for inclusion in the *Alternative Service Book* of the Church of England in 1979.

More recently, the International Commission on English in the Liturgy has initiated a pilot project on a liturgical psalter. Twenty-two psalms have been translated in forms open to a wide variety of musical styles and an evaluation will determine if translation of the rest of the psalter is to be addressed.

A particular translation is attached to this book to provide a basis for regular use. It also happens to be the translation from which the psalms are usually quoted throughout the *Book of Alternative Services*. But those responsible for planning worship should be free to choose other translations appropriate to the liturgical needs and abilities of a congregation. The metric translations of the Reformed tradition should not be forgotten.

There are many ways to recite the psalms. The psalms may be recited in unison, or antiphonally between two sections of a choir, or antiphonally between a cantor or reader and a congregation, or by a cantor with congregational refrains. It is possible for a single reader, or a chorus of readers, to read the verses in spoken voice in alternation with refrains sung by a congregation. There is room for innovation here.

It should also be remembered that sung recitation of the psalms is normative (although not always possible). Traditional Anglican chant is a demanding legacy of great beauty, as is plainsong. Both are highly suited to the Office, but not exclusively. Some music, as already noted, is intended for use with stressed lines: the reciting tone is usually accompanied by a compatible refrain melody. Some settings of music for the psalms are "through composed," like anthems. There is a wealth of music available, and it is growing.

# The Psalter

## 1

1   Happy are they who have not walked in the counsel of
        the wicked,*
      nor lingered in the way of sinners,
      nor sat in the seats of the scornful!

2   Their delight is in the law of the Lord,*
      and they meditate on his law day and night.

3   They are like trees planted by streams of water,
      bearing fruit in due season, with leaves that do not wither; *
      everything they do shall prosper.

4   It is not so with the wicked; *
      they are like chaff which the wind blows away.

5   Therefore the wicked shall not stand upright when
        judgement comes,*
      nor the sinner in the council of the righteous.

6   For the Lord knows the way of the righteous,*
      but the way of the wicked is doomed.

Giver of life, save us from the desert of faithlessness and nourish
us with the living water of your word, that we may bring forth
fruit that will last, in the name of Jesus Christ our Saviour.

## 2

1   Why are the nations in an uproar? *
      Why do the peoples mutter empty threats?

2   Why do the kings of the earth rise up in revolt,
    and the princes plot together,*
      against the Lord and against his anointed?

3   "Let us break their yoke," they say; *
     "let us cast off their bonds from us."

4   He whose throne is in heaven is laughing; *
     the Lord has them in derision.

5   Then he speaks to them in his wrath,*
     and his rage fills them with terror.

6   "I myself have set my king *
     upon my holy hill of Zion."

7   Let me announce the decree of the Lord: *
     he said to me, "You are my Son;
     this day have I begotten you.

8   Ask of me, and I will give you the nations for
              your inheritance *
     and the ends of the earth for your possession.

9   You shall crush them with an iron rod *
     and shatter them like a piece of pottery."

10   And now, you kings, be wise; *
     be warned, you rulers of the earth.

11   Submit to the Lord with fear,*
     and with trembling bow before him;

12   Lest he be angry and you perish; *
     for his wrath is quickly kindled.

13   Happy are they all *
     who take refuge in him!

Ruler of heaven and earth, you sent your only Son into the
world to be our Redeemer, and by raising him from the dead
you gave him the victory over all his enemies. Show us the
power of your saving love and bring us to share in your eternal
kingdom; through Jesus Christ our Saviour.

# 3

1   Lord, how many adversaries I have! *
     how many there are who rise up against me!

2 How many there are who say of me,*
   "There is no help for him in his God."

3 But you, O Lord, are a shield about me; *
   you are my glory, the one who lifts up my head.

4 I call aloud upon the Lord,*
   and he answers me from his holy hill;

5 I lie down and go to sleep; *
   I wake again, because the Lord sustains me.

6 I do not fear the multitudes of people *
   who set themselves against me all around.

7 Rise up, O Lord; set me free, O my God; *
   surely, you will strike all my enemies across the face,
   you will break the teeth of the wicked.

8 Deliverance belongs to the Lord.*
   Your blessing be upon your people!

Shield and protector of all, hear the prayers of those who call
upon you, and set them free from violence, persecution, and
fear, that all may know that deliverance belongs to you. We ask
this in the name of Jesus Christ, our Saviour and Redeemer.

# 4

1 Answer me when I call, O God, defender of my cause; *
   you set me free when I am hard-pressed;
   have mercy on me and hear my prayer.

2 "You mortals, how long will you dishonour my glory; *
   how long will you worship dumb idols
   and run after false gods?"

3 Know that the Lord does wonders for the faithful; *
   when I call upon the Lord, he will hear me.

4 Tremble, then, and do not sin; *
   speak to your heart in silence upon your bed.

5 Offer the appointed sacrifices *
   and put your trust in the Lord.

6 Many are saying,
"Oh, that we might see better times!" *
Lift up the light of your countenance upon us, O Lord.

7 You have put gladness in my heart,*
more than when grain and wine and oil increase.

8 I lie down in peace; at once I fall asleep; *
for only you, Lord, make me dwell in safety.

Faithful defender, do not let our hearts be troubled, but fill us
with such confidence and joy that we may sleep in peace and
rise in your light; through Jesus Christ our Saviour.

# 5

1 Give ear to my words, O Lord; *
consider my meditation.

2 Hearken to my cry for help, my King and my God,*
for I make my prayer to you.

3 In the morning, Lord, you hear my voice; *
early in the morning I make my appeal and watch for you.

4 For you are not a God who takes pleasure in wickedness,*
and evil cannot dwell with you.

5 Braggarts cannot stand in your sight; *
you hate all those who work wickedness.

6 You destroy those who speak lies; *
the bloodthirsty and deceitful, O Lord, you abhor.

7 But as for me, through the greatness of your mercy I will
go into your house; *
I will bow down toward your holy temple in awe of you.

8 Lead me, O Lord, in your righteousness,
because of those who lie in wait for me; *
make your way straight before me.

9 For there is no truth in their mouth; *
there is destruction in their heart;

10    Their throat is an open grave; *
        they flatter with their tongue.

11    Declare them guilty, O God; *
        let them fall, because of their schemes.

12    Because of their many transgressions cast them out,*
        for they have rebelled against you.

13    But all who take refuge in you will be glad; *
        they will sing out their joy for ever.

14    You will shelter them,*
        so that those who love your name may exult in you.

15    For you, O Lord, will bless the righteous; *
        you will defend them with your favour as with a shield.

Source of all justice and goodness, you hate deception and evil.
Lead us in the paths of righteousness and keep us from falling
into sin, that we may sing out our joy in Jesus Christ our
Redeemer.

# 6

1    Lord, do not rebuke me in your anger; *
        do not punish me in your wrath.

2    Have pity on me, Lord, for I am weak; *
        heal me, Lord, for my bones are racked.

3    My spirit shakes with terror; *
        how long, O Lord, how long?

4    Turn, O Lord, and deliver me; *
        save me for your mercy's sake.

5    For in death no one remembers you; *
        and who will give you thanks in the grave?

6    I grow weary because of my groaning; *
        every night I drench my bed
        and flood my couch with tears.

7    My eyes are wasted with grief *
        and worn away because of all my enemies.

8    Depart from me, all evildoers,*
        for the Lord has heard the sound of my weeping.

9    The Lord has heard my supplication; *
        the Lord accepts my prayer.

10    All my enemies shall be confounded and quake with fear; *
        they shall turn back and suddenly be put to shame.

God of mercy and tenderness, giver of life and conqueror of
death, look upon our weakness and grief, and restore us to
health, that we may sing a new song to your praise; through
Jesus Christ our risen Lord.

# 7

1    O Lord my God, I take refuge in you; *
        save and deliver me from all who pursue me;

2    Lest like a lion they tear me in pieces *
        and snatch me away with none to deliver me.

3    O Lord my God, if I have done these things: *
        if there is any wickedness in my hands,

4    If I have repaid my friend with evil,*
        or plundered him who without cause is my enemy;

5    Then let my enemy pursue and overtake me,*
        trample my life into the ground,
        and lay my honour in the dust.

6    Stand up, O Lord, in your wrath; *
        rise up against the fury of my enemies.

7    Awake, O my God, decree justice; *
        let the assembly of the peoples gather round you.

8    Be seated on your lofty throne, O Most High; *
        O Lord, judge the nations.

9    Give judgement for me according to my
                    righteousness, O Lord,*
        and according to my innocence, O Most High.

10   Let the malice of the wicked come to an end,
     but establish the righteous; *
         for you test the mind and heart, O righteous God.

11   God is my shield and defence; *
         he is the saviour of the true in heart.

12   God is a righteous judge; *
         God sits in judgement every day.

13   If they will not repent, God will whet his sword; *
         he will bend his bow and make it ready.

14   He has prepared his weapons of death; *
         he makes his arrows shafts of fire.

15   Look at those who are in labour with wickedness,*
         who conceive evil, and give birth to a lie.

16   They dig a pit and make it deep *
         and fall into the hole that they have made.

17   Their malice turns back upon their own head; *
         their violence falls on their own scalp.

18   I will bear witness that the Lord is righteous; *
         I will praise the name of the Lord Most High.

Righteous judge of the nations, you know the secrets of our
hearts; our sins are not hidden from you. Rise to our defence
and strengthen us in the faith, that we may struggle against
evil and bear witness to your justice, in the name of Jesus
Christ our Redeemer.

# 8

1    O Lord our governor,*
         how exalted is your name in all the world!

2    Out of the mouths of infants and children *
         your majesty is praised above the heavens.

3    You have set up a stronghold against your adversaries,*
         to quell the enemy and the avenger.

4    When I consider your heavens, the work of your fingers,*
     the moon and the stars you have set in their courses,

5    What is man that you should be mindful of him? *
     the son of man that you should seek him out?

6    You have made him but little lower than the angels; *
     you adorn him with glory and honour;

7    You give him mastery over the works of your hands; *
     you put all things under his feet;

8    All sheep and oxen,*
     even the wild beasts of the field,

9    The birds of the air, the fish of the sea,*
     and whatsoever walks in the paths of the sea.

10    O Lord our governor,*
     how exalted is your name in all the world!

Blessed are you, creator of heaven and earth; amid the
immensity of the universe, you are mindful of us and seek us
out. Blessed are you for the gift of your Son, who humbled
himself to share our life that we might be raised with him to
glory and splendour. Blessed be your holy name, Father, Son,
and Holy Spirit, now and for ever.

# 9

1    I will give thanks to you, O Lord, with my whole heart; *
     I will tell of all your marvellous works.

2    I will be glad and rejoice in you; *
     I will sing to your name, O Most High.

3    When my enemies are driven back,*
     they will stumble and perish at your presence.

4    For you have maintained my right and my cause; *
     you sit upon your throne judging right.

5    You have rebuked the ungodly and destroyed the wicked; *
     you have blotted out their name for ever and ever.

6    As for the enemy, they are finished, in perpetual ruin,*
         their cities ploughed under, the memory of them perished;

7    But the Lord is enthroned for ever; *
         he has set up his throne for judgement.

8    It is he who rules the world with righteousness; *
         he judges the peoples with equity.

9    The Lord will be a refuge for the oppressed,*
         a refuge in time of trouble.

10   Those who know your name will put their trust in you,*
         for you never forsake those who seek you, O Lord.

11   Sing praise to the Lord who dwells in Zion; *
         proclaim to the peoples the things he has done.

12   The avenger of blood will remember them; *
         he will not forget the cry of the afflicted.

13   Have pity on me, O Lord; *
         see the misery I suffer from those who hate me,
         O you who lift me up from the gate of death;

14   So that I may tell of all your praises
     and rejoice in your salvation *
         in the gates of the city of Zion.

15   The ungodly have fallen into the pit they dug,*
         and in the snare they set is their own foot caught.

16   The Lord is known by his acts of justice; *
         the wicked are trapped in the works of their own hands.

17   The wicked shall be given over to the grave,*
         and also all the peoples that forget God.

18   For the needy shall not always be forgotten,*
         and the hope of the poor shall not perish for ever.

19   Rise up, O Lord, let not the ungodly have the upper hand; *
         let them be judged before you.

20   Put fear upon them, O Lord; *
         let the ungodly know they are but mortal.

Righteous Judge, hear the cries of your people. Rescue them from the hands of their oppressors, and save them from the gates of death, that we may always rejoice in your help; through Jesus Christ our Saviour and Defender.

# 10

1 Why do you stand so far off, O Lord,*
     and hide yourself in time of trouble?

2 The wicked arrogantly persecute the poor,*
     but they are trapped in the schemes they have devised.

3 The wicked boast of their heart's desire; *
     the covetous curse and revile the Lord.

4 The wicked are so proud that they care not for God; *
     their only thought is, "God does not matter."

5 Their ways are devious at all times;
   your judgements are far above out of their sight; *
     they defy all their enemies.

6 They say in their heart, "I shall not be shaken; *
     no harm shall happen to me ever."

7 Their mouth is full of cursing, deceit, and oppression; *
     under their tongue are mischief and wrong.

8 They lurk in ambush in public squares
   and in secret places they murder the innocent; *
     they spy out the helpless.

9 They lie in wait, like a lion in a covert;
   they lie in wait to seize upon the lowly; *
     they seize the lowly and drag them away in their net.

10 The innocent are broken and humbled before them; *
     the helpless fall before their power.

11 They say in their heart, "God has forgotten; *
     he hides his face; he will never notice."

12 Rise up, O Lord;
   lift up your hand, O God; *
     do not forget the afflicted.

13 Why should the wicked revile God? *
    why should they say in their heart, "You do not care"?

14 Surely, you behold trouble and misery; *
    you see it and take it into your own hand.

15 The helpless commit themselves to you,*
    for you are the helper of orphans.

16 Break the power of the wicked and evil; *
    search out their wickedness until you find none.

17 The Lord is king for ever and ever; *
    the ungodly shall perish from his land.

18 The Lord will hear the desire of the humble; *
    you will strengthen their heart and your ears shall hear;

19 To give justice to the orphan and oppressed,*
    so that mere mortals may strike terror no more.

Helper of the helpless, do not hide your face from the troubles
of your people. Give them strength and comfort in times of
affliction, that we may proclaim the joyous news of freedom
in Jesus Christ our Saviour.

# 11

1 In the Lord have I taken refuge; *
    how then can you say to me,
    "Fly away like a bird to the hilltop;

2 For see how the wicked bend the bow
and fit their arrows to the string,*
    to shoot from ambush at the true of heart.

3 When the foundations are being destroyed,*
    what can the righteous do?"

4 The Lord is in his holy temple; *
    the Lord's throne is in heaven.

5 His eyes behold the inhabited world; *
    his piercing eye weighs our worth.

6　The Lord weighs the righteous as well as the wicked,*
　　but those who delight in violence he abhors.

7　Upon the wicked he shall rain coals of fire and
　　　　　　　　burning sulphur; *
　　a scorching wind shall be their lot.

8　For the Lord is righteous;
　　he delights in righteous deeds; *
　　and the just shall see his face.


God our refuge, deliver us from violence and evil, and guide
us in the paths of righteousness, that on the day of judgement
we may rejoice to see you face to face; through Jesus Christ our
Redeemer.

# 12

1　Help me, Lord, for there is no godly one left; *
　　the faithful have vanished from among us.

2　Everyone speaks falsely with his neighbour; *
　　with a smooth tongue they speak from a double heart.

3　Oh, that the Lord would cut off all smooth tongues,*
　　and close the lips that utter proud boasts!

4　Those who say, "With our tongue will we prevail; *
　　our lips are our own; who is lord over us?"

5　"Because the needy are oppressed,
　　and the poor cry out in misery,*
　　　I will rise up," says the Lord,
　　"and give them the help they long for."

6　The words of the Lord are pure words,*
　　like silver refined from ore
　　and purified seven times in the fire.

7　O Lord, watch over us *
　　and save us from this generation for ever.

8　The wicked prowl on every side,*
　　and that which is worthless is highly prized by everyone.

God of truth, protector of your people, come to the aid of all who are poor and oppressed. By the power of your life-giving word lead us in the ways of peace and integrity, and give us the help we long for in Jesus Christ our Saviour.

# 13

1 How long, O Lord?
will you forget me for ever? *
  how long will you hide your face from me?

2 How long shall I have perplexity in my mind,
and grief in my heart, day after day? *
  how long shall my enemy triumph over me?

3 Look upon me and answer me, O Lord my God; *
  give light to my eyes, lest I sleep in death;

4 Lest my enemy say, "I have prevailed over him," *
  and my foes rejoice that I have fallen.

5 But I put my trust in your mercy; *
  my heart is joyful because of your saving help.

6 I will sing to the Lord, for he has dealt with me richly; *
  I will praise the name of the Lord Most High.

Loving and merciful God, hear the prayers of those who cry to you, and shine with the light of your presence on those who live in the shadow of death. May we rejoice in your saving help and sing you songs of praise in the name of our risen Saviour, Jesus Christ.

# 14

1 The fool has said in his heart, "There is no God." *
  All are corrupt and commit abominable acts;
  there is none who does any good.

2 The Lord looks down from heaven upon us all,*
  to see if there is any who is wise,
  if there is one who seeks after God.

3   Every one has proved faithless;
    all alike have turned bad; *
        there is none who does good; no, not one.

4   Have they no knowledge, all those evildoers *
        who eat up my people like bread
        and do not call upon the Lord?

5   See how they tremble with fear, *
        because God is in the company of the righteous.

6   Their aim is to confound the plans of the afflicted, *
        but the Lord is their refuge.

7   Oh, that Israel's deliverance would come out of Zion! *
        when the Lord restores the fortunes of his people,
        Jacob will rejoice and Israel be glad.

God of wisdom and love, without you neither truth nor holiness can survive. Show your mighty presence among us, and make us glad in proclaiming your deliverance in Jesus Christ our Lord.

# 15

1   Lord, who may dwell in your tabernacle? *
        who may abide upon your holy hill?

2   Whoever leads a blameless life and does what is right, *
        who speaks the truth from his heart.

3   There is no guile upon his tongue;
    he does no evil to his friend; *
        he does not heap contempt upon his neighbour.

4   In his sight the wicked is rejected, *
        but he honours those who fear the Lord.

5   He has sworn to do no wrong *
        and does not take back his word.

6   He does not give his money in hope of gain, *
        nor does he take a bribe against the innocent.

7   Whoever does these things *
        shall never be overthrown.

God of love, teach us to walk blamelessly in your ways, that
our whole life may be established in you, and that we may
come to the place prepared for us by your Son, Jesus Christ
our Redeemer.


# 16

1   Protect me, O God, for I take refuge in you; *
        I have said to the Lord, "You are my Lord,
        my good above all other."

2   All my delight is upon the godly that are in the land,*
        upon those who are noble among the people.

3   But those who run after other gods *
        shall have their troubles multiplied.

4   Their libations of blood I will not offer,*
        nor take the names of their gods upon my lips.

5   O Lord, you are my portion and my cup; *
        it is you who uphold my lot.

6   My boundaries enclose a pleasant land; *
        indeed, I have a goodly heritage.

7   I will bless the Lord who gives me counsel; *
        my heart teaches me, night after night.

8   I have set the Lord always before me; *
        because he is at my right hand I shall not fall.

9   My heart, therefore, is glad, and my spirit rejoices; *
        my body also shall rest in hope.

10  For you will not abandon me to the grave,*
        nor let your holy one see the Pit.

11  You will show me the path of life; *
        in your presence there is fullness of joy,
        and in your right hand are pleasures for evermore.

Gracious God, we bless your holy name for the heritage you
have given us. Show us the path of life, that we may follow it
in hope, and come to know the joy of the resurrection of your
Son, Jesus Christ.

# 17

1    Hear my plea of innocence, O Lord;
     give heed to my cry; *
          listen to my prayer, which does not come from lying lips.

2    Let my vindication come forth from your presence; *
          let your eyes be fixed on justice.

3    Weigh my heart, summon me by night,*
          melt me down; you will find no impurity in me.

4    I give no offence with my mouth as others do; *
          I have heeded the words of your lips.

5    My footsteps hold fast to the ways of your law; *
          in your paths my feet shall not stumble.

6    I call upon you, O God, for you will answer me; *
          incline your ear to me and hear my words.

7    Show me your marvellous loving-kindness,*
          O Saviour of those who take refuge at your right hand
          from those who rise up against them.

8    Keep me as the apple of your eye; *
          hide me under the shadow of your wings,

9    From the wicked who assault me,*
          from my deadly enemies who surround me.

10   They have closed their heart to pity,*
          and their mouth speaks proud things.

11   They press me hard,
     now they surround me,*
          watching how they may cast me to the ground,

12   Like a lion, greedy for its prey,*
          and like a young lion lurking in secret places.

13   Arise, O Lord; confront them and bring them down; *
        deliver me from the wicked by your sword.

14   Deliver me, O Lord, by your hand *
        from those whose portion in life is this world;

15   Whose bellies you fill with your treasure,*
        who are well supplied with children
        and leave their wealth to their little ones.

16   But at my vindication I shall see your face; *
        when I awake, I shall be satisfied, beholding
                your likeness.


God of truth and justice, watch over your people in adversity,
that we may know the wonders of your love and see the glory
of your presence; through Jesus Christ our Saviour.


# 18

**Part I**

1   I love you, O Lord my strength,*
        O Lord my stronghold, my crag, and my haven.

2   My God, my rock in whom I put my trust,*
        my shield, the horn of my salvation, and my refuge;
        you are worthy of praise.

3   I will call upon the Lord,*
        and so shall I be saved from my enemies.

4   The breakers of death rolled over me,*
        and the torrents of oblivion made me afraid.

5   The cords of hell entangled me,*
        and the snares of death were set for me.

6   I called upon the Lord in my distress *
        and cried out to my God for help.

7   He heard my voice from his heavenly dwelling; *
        my cry of anguish came to his ears.

8     The earth reeled and rocked; *
      the roots of the mountains shook;
      they reeled because of his anger.

9     Smoke rose from his nostrils
      and a consuming fire out of his mouth; *
      hot burning coals blazed forth from him.

10    He parted the heavens and came down *
      with a storm cloud under his feet.

11    He mounted on Cherubim and flew; *
      he swooped on the wings of the wind.

12    He wrapped darkness about him; *
      he made dark waters and thick clouds his pavilion.

13    From the brightness of his presence, through the clouds,*
      burst hailstones and coals of fire.

14    The Lord thundered out of heaven; *
      the Most High uttered his voice.

15    He loosed his arrows and scattered them; *
      he hurled thunderbolts and routed them.

16    The beds of the seas were uncovered,
      and the foundations of the world laid bare,*
        at your battle cry, O Lord,
        at the blast of the breath of your nostrils.

17    He reached down from on high and grasped me; *
      he drew me out of great waters.

18    He delivered me from my strong enemies
      and from those who hated me; *
      for they were too mighty for me.

19    They confronted me in the day of my disaster; *
      but the Lord was my support.

20    He brought me out into an open place; *
      he rescued me because he delighted in me.

# 18

Part II

21 The Lord rewarded me because of my righteous dealing; *
   because my hands were clean he rewarded me;

22 For I have kept the ways of the Lord *
   and have not offended against my God;

23 For all his judgements are before my eyes,*
   and his decrees I have not put away from me;

24 For I have been blameless with him *
   and have kept myself from iniquity;

25 Therefore the Lord rewarded me according to my
                              righteous dealing,*
   because of the cleanness of my hands in his sight.

26 With the faithful you show yourself faithful, O God; *
   with the forthright you show yourself forthright.

27 With the pure you show yourself pure,*
   but with the crooked you are wily.

28 You will save a lowly people,*
   but you will humble the haughty eyes.

29 You, O Lord, are my lamp; *
   my God, you make my darkness bright.

30 With you I will break down an enclosure; *
   with the help of my God I will scale any wall.

31 As for God, his ways are perfect;
   the words of the Lord are tried in the fire; *
   he is a shield to all who trust in him.

32 For who is God, but the Lord? *
   who is the rock, except our God?

33 It is God who girds me about with strength *
   and makes my way secure.

34 He makes me sure-footed like a deer *
   and lets me stand firm on the heights.

35 He trains my hands for battle *
  and my arms for bending even a bow of bronze.

36 You have given me your shield of victory; *
  your right hand also sustains me;
  your loving care makes me great.

37 You lengthen my stride beneath me,*
  and my ankles do not give way.

38 I pursue my enemies and overtake them; *
  I will not turn back till I have destroyed them.

39 I strike them down, and they cannot rise; *
  they fall defeated at my feet.

40 You have girded me with strength for the battle; *
  you have cast down my adversaries beneath me;
  you have put my enemies to flight.

41 I destroy those who hate me;
  they cry out, but there is none to help them; *
  they cry to the Lord, but he does not answer.

42 I beat them small like dust before the wind; *
  I trample them like mud in the streets.

43 You deliver me from the strife of the peoples; *
  you put me at the head of the nations.

44 A people I have not known shall serve me;
  no sooner shall they hear than they shall obey me; *
  strangers will cringe before me.

45 The foreign peoples will lose heart; *
  they shall come trembling out of their strongholds.

46 The Lord lives! Blessed is my rock! *
  Exalted is the God of my salvation!

47 He is the God who gave me victory *
  and cast down the peoples beneath me.

48 You rescued me from the fury of my enemies;
  you exalted me above those who rose against me; *
  you saved me from my deadly foe.

49  Therefore will I extol you among the nations, O Lord,*
        and sing praises to your name.

50  He multiplies the victories of his king; *
        he shows loving-kindness to his anointed,
        to David and his descendants for ever.

Praise to you, God of our salvation; you come to our help and
set us free. May your strength be our shield and your word be
our lamp, that we may serve you with pure hearts and find
victory through our Saviour Jesus Christ.

# 19

1  The heavens declare the glory of God,*
        and the firmament shows his handiwork.

2  One day tells its tale to another,*
        and one night imparts knowledge to another.

3  Although they have no words or language,*
        and their voices are not heard,

4  Their sound has gone out into all lands,*
        and their message to the ends of the world.

5  In the deep has he set a pavilion for the sun; *
        it comes forth like a bridegroom out of his chamber;
        it rejoices like a champion to run its course.

6  It goes forth from the uttermost edge of the heavens
    and runs about to the end of it again; *
        nothing is hidden from its burning heat.

7  The law of the Lord is perfect
                    and revives the soul; *
    the testimony of the Lord is sure
                    and gives wisdom to the innocent.

8  The statutes of the Lord are just
                    and rejoice the heart; *
    the commandment of the Lord is clear
                    and gives light to the eyes.

9     The fear of the Lord is clean
           and endures for ever; *
     the judgements of the Lord are true
           and righteous altogether.

10    More to be desired are they than gold,
           more than much fine gold,*
     sweeter far than honey,
           than honey in the comb.

11    By them also is your servant enlightened,*
     and in keeping them there is great reward.

12    Who can tell how often he offends? *
     cleanse me from my secret faults.

13    Above all, keep your servant from presumptuous sins;
     let them not get dominion over me; *
     then shall I be whole and sound,
     and innocent of a great offense.

14    Let the words of my mouth and the meditation of my
           heart be acceptable in your sight,*
     O Lord, my strength and my redeemer.

Gracious creator of heaven and earth, your Word has come
among us as the true Sun of righteousness, and the good news
of his birth has gone out to the ends of the world. Open our
eyes to the light of your law, that we may be purified from sin
and serve you without reproach for the sake of Jesus Christ,
our Light and our Life.

# 20

1     May the Lord answer you in the day of trouble,*
     the name of the God of Jacob defend you;

2     Send you help from his holy place *
     and strengthen you out of Zion;

3     Remember all your offerings *
     and accept your burnt sacrifice;

4	Grant you your heart's desire *
	and prosper all your plans.

5	We will shout for joy at your victory
	and triumph in the name of our God; *
		may the Lord grant all your requests.

6	Now I know that the Lord gives victory to his anointed; *
		he will answer him out of his holy heaven,
		with the victorious strength of his right hand.

7	Some put their trust in chariots and some in horses,*
		but we will call upon the name of the Lord our God.

8	They collapse and fall down,*
		but we will arise and stand upright.

9	O Lord, give victory to the king *
		and answer us when we call.

God, our hope and our defence, protect all those who call
upon your name, that they may stand upright in the day of
trouble, and share in the victory of your Son our Saviour Jesus
Christ.

# 21

1	The king rejoices in your strength, O Lord; *
		how greatly he exults in your victory!

2	You have given him his heart's desire; *
		you have not denied him the request of his lips.

3	For you meet him with blessings of prosperity,*
		and set a crown of fine gold upon his head.

4	He asked you for life, and you gave it to him; *
		length of days, for ever and ever.

5	His honour is great, because of your victory; *
		splendour and majesty have you bestowed upon him.

6	For you will give him everlasting felicity *
		and will make him glad with the joy of your presence.

7  For the king puts his trust in the Lord; *
   because of the loving-kindness of the Most High, he
      will not fall.

8  Your hand will lay hold upon all your enemies; *
   your right hand will seize all those who hate you.

9  You will make them like a fiery furnace *
   at the time of your appearing, O Lord;

10 You will swallow them up in your wrath,*
   and fire shall consume them.

11 You will destroy their offspring from the land *
   and their descendants from among the
      peoples of the earth.

12 Though they intend evil against you
   and devise wicked schemes,*
      yet they shall not prevail.

13 For you will put them to flight *
   and aim your arrows at them.

14 Be exalted, O Lord, in your might; *
   we will sing and praise your power.


Giver of life and source of all blessings, may the leaders of the
nations serve your people with justice and protect them from
violence, hardship, and exploitation. We ask this in the name
of Jesus Christ, our Lord and our King.

# 22

1  My God, my God, why have you forsaken me? *
   and are so far from my cry
   and from the words of my distress?

2  O my God, I cry in the daytime, but you do not answer; *
   by night as well, but I find no rest.

3  Yet you are the Holy One,*
   enthroned upon the praises of Israel.

4   Our forefathers put their trust in you; *
        they trusted, and you delivered them.

5   They cried out to you and were delivered; *
        they trusted in you and were not put to shame.

6   But as for me, I am a worm and no man,*
        scorned by all and despised by the people.

7   All who see me laugh me to scorn; *
        they curl their lips and wag their heads, saying,

8   "He trusted in the Lord; let him deliver him; *
        let him rescue him, if he delights in him."

9   Yet you are he who took me out of the womb,*
        and kept me safe upon my mother's breast.

10  I have been entrusted to you ever since I was born; *
        you were my God when I was still in my mother's womb.

11  Be not far from me, for trouble is near,*
        and there is none to help.

12  Many young bulls encircle me; *
        strong bulls of Bashan surround me.

13  They open wide their jaws at me,*
        like a ravening and a roaring lion.

14  I am poured out like water;
    all my bones are out of joint; *
        my heart within my breast is melting wax.

15  My mouth is dried out like a pot-sherd;
    my tongue sticks to the roof of my mouth; *
        and you have laid me in the dust of the grave.

16  Packs of dogs close me in,
    and gangs of evildoers circle around me; *
        they pierce my hands and my feet;
        I can count all my bones.

17  They stare and gloat over me; *
        they divide my garments among them;
        they cast lots for my clothing.

18 Be not far away, O Lord; *
    you are my strength; hasten to help me.

19 Save me from the sword,*
    my life from the power of the dog.

20 Save me from the lion's mouth,*
    my wretched body from the horns of wild bulls.

21 I will declare your name to my brethren; *
    in the midst of the congregation I will praise you.


22 Praise the Lord, you that fear him; *
    stand in awe of him, O offspring of Israel;
    all you of Jacob's line, give glory.

23 For he does not despise nor abhor the poor in their poverty;
  neither does he hide his face from them; *
    but when they cry to him he hears them.

24 My praise is of him in the great assembly; *
    I will perform my vows in the presence of those who
        worship him.

25 The poor shall eat and be satisfied,
  and those who seek the Lord shall praise him: *
    "May your heart live for ever!"

26 All the ends of the earth shall remember and turn to
        the Lord,*
    and all the families of the nations shall bow before him.

27 For kingship belongs to the Lord; *
    he rules over the nations.

28 To him alone all who sleep in the earth bow down
        in worship; *
    all who go down to the dust fall before him.

29 My soul shall live for him;
  my descendants shall serve him; *
    they shall be known as the Lord's for ever.

30 They shall come and make known to a people yet unborn *
    the saving deeds that he has done.

Father, your tortured Son felt abandoned, and cried out in anguish from the cross, yet you delivered him. He overcame the bonds of death and rose in triumph from the grave. Do not hide your face from those who cry out to you: feed the hungry, strengthen the weak, and break the chains of the oppressed, that your people may rejoice in your saving deeds. This we ask in the name of Jesus Christ our Saviour.

# 23

1   The Lord is my shepherd; *
        I shall not be in want.

2   He makes me lie down in green pastures *
        and leads me beside still waters.

3   He revives my soul *
        and guides me along right pathways for his name's sake.

4   Though I walk through the valley of the shadow of death,
    I shall fear no evil; *
        for you are with me;
        your rod and your staff, they comfort me.

5   You spread a table before me in the presence of those
                    who trouble me; *
        you have anointed my head with oil,
        and my cup is running over.

6   Surely your goodness and mercy shall follow me all the
                    days of my life,*
        and I will dwell in the house of the Lord for ever.


Glory to you, Jesus Christ, our good shepherd. In the waters of baptism you give us new birth, at your table you nourish us with heavenly food, and in your goodness and mercy, you guide us beyond the terrors of evil and death to your Father's home to dwell in eternal light. Glory to you for ever.

# 24

1  The earth is the Lord's and all that is in it,*
   the world and all who dwell therein.

2  For it is he who founded it upon the seas *
   and made it firm upon the rivers of the deep.

3  "Who can ascend the hill of the Lord? *
   and who can stand in his holy place?"

4  "Those who have clean hands and a pure heart,*
   who have not pledged themselves to falsehood,
   nor sworn by what is a fraud.

5  They shall receive a blessing from the Lord *
   and a just reward from the God of their salvation."

6  Such is the generation of those who seek him,*
   of those who seek your face, O God of Jacob.

7  Lift up your heads, O gates;
   lift them high, O everlasting doors; *
   and the King of glory shall come in.

8  "Who is this King of glory?" *
   "The Lord, strong and mighty,
   the Lord, mighty in battle."

9  Lift up your heads, O gates;
   lift them high, O everlasting doors; *
   and the King of glory shall come in.

10 "Who is he, this King of glory?" *
   "The Lord of hosts,
   he is the King of glory."

Creator and ruler of all, open our hearts that the King of glory
may enter, and bring us rejoicing to your holy mountain,
where you live and reign, now and for ever.

## 25

1   To you, O Lord, I lift up my soul;
    my God, I put my trust in you; *
        let me not be humiliated,
        nor let my enemies triumph over me.

2   Let none who look to you be put to shame; *
        let the treacherous be disappointed in their schemes.

3   Show me your ways, O Lord,*
        and teach me your paths.

4   Lead me in your truth and teach me,*
        for you are the God of my salvation;
        in you have I trusted all the day long.

5   Remember, O Lord, your compassion and love,*
        for they are from everlasting.

6   Remember not the sins of my youth and my transgressions; *
        remember me according to your love
        and for the sake of your goodness, O Lord.

7   Gracious and upright is the Lord; *
        therefore he teaches sinners in his way.

8   He guides the humble in doing right *
        and teaches his way to the lowly.

9   All the paths of the Lord are love and faithfulness *
        to those who keep his covenant and his testimonies.

10  For your name's sake, O Lord,*
        forgive my sin, for it is great.

11  Who are they who fear the Lord? *
        he will teach them the way that they should choose.

12  They shall dwell in prosperity,*
        and their offspring shall inherit the land.

13  The Lord is a friend to those who fear him *
        and will show them his covenant.

14  My eyes are ever looking to the Lord,*
        for he shall pluck my feet out of the net.

15  Turn to me and have pity on me,*
        for I am left alone and in misery.

16  The sorrows of my heart have increased; *
        bring me out of my troubles.

17  Look upon my adversity and misery *
        and forgive me all my sin.

18  Look upon my enemies, for they are many,*
        and they bear a violent hatred against me.

19  Protect my life and deliver me; *
        let me not be put to shame, for I have trusted in you.

20  Let integrity and uprightness preserve me,*
        for my hope has been in you.

21  Deliver Israel, O God,*
        out of all his troubles.

God of compassion and love, forgive our sins, relieve our
misery, satisfy our longing, and fulfil all our hopes for peace;
through your Son Jesus Christ our Redeemer.

# 26

1  Give judgement for me, O Lord,
    for I have lived with integrity; *
        I have trusted in the Lord and have not faltered.

2  Test me, O Lord, and try me; *
        examine my heart and my mind.

3  For your love is before my eyes; *
        I have walked faithfully with you.

4  I have not sat with the worthless,*
        nor do I consort with the deceitful.

5  I have hated the company of evildoers; *
        I will not sit down with the wicked.

6  I will wash my hands in innocence, O Lord,*
        that I may go in procession round your altar,

7  Singing aloud a song of thanksgiving *
      and recounting all your wonderful deeds.

8  Lord, I love the house in which you dwell *
      and the place where your glory abides.

9  Do not sweep me away with sinners,*
      nor my life with those who thirst for blood,

10  Whose hands are full of evil plots,*
      and their right hand full of bribes.

11  As for me, I will live with integrity; *
      redeem me, O Lord, and have pity on me.

12  My foot stands on level ground; *
      in the full assembly I will bless the Lord.

God of love and mercy, give us clean hands and pure hearts,
that we may walk in innocence and come to your eternal
dwelling, to praise you in the company of your saints for ever.

# 27

1  The Lord is my light and my salvation;
   whom then shall I fear? *
      the Lord is the strength of my life;
      of whom then shall I be afraid?

2  When evildoers came upon me to eat up my flesh,*
      it was they, my foes and my adversaries, who
                              stumbled and fell.

3  Though an army should encamp against me,*
      yet my heart shall not be afraid;

4  And though war should rise up against me,*
      yet will I put my trust in him.

5  One thing have I asked of the Lord;
   one thing I seek; *
      that I may dwell in the house of the Lord all the days
                              of my life;

6     To behold the fair beauty of the Lord *
       and to seek him in his temple.

7     For in the day of trouble he shall keep me safe
                  in his shelter; *
       he shall hide me in the secrecy of his dwelling
       and set me high upon a rock.

8     Even now he lifts up my head *
       above my enemies round about me.

9     Therefore I will offer in his dwelling an oblation
       with sounds of great gladness; *
       I will sing and make music to the Lord.

10    Hearken to my voice, O Lord, when I call; *
       have mercy on me and answer me.

11    You speak in my heart and say, "Seek my face." *
       Your face, Lord, will I seek.

12    Hide not your face from me,*
       nor turn away your servant in displeasure.

13    You have been my helper;
   cast me not away; *
       do not forsake me, O God of my salvation.

14    Though my father and my mother forsake me,*
       the Lord will sustain me.

15    Show me your way, O Lord; *
       lead me on a level path, because of my enemies.

16    Deliver me not into the hand of my adversaries,*
       for false witnesses have risen up against me,
       and also those who speak malice.

17    What if I had not believed
   that I should see the goodness of the Lord *
       in the land of the living!

18    O tarry and await the Lord's pleasure;
   be strong, and he shall comfort your heart; *
       wait patiently for the Lord.

Faithful God, the shelter of all who hope in you, may those who seek your face be set free from fear and distress, and come to see your goodness in the land of the living; through Jesus Christ, our Light and our Salvation.

# 28

1 O Lord, I call to you;
my rock, do not be deaf to my cry; *
    lest, if you do not hear me,
    I become like those who go down to the Pit.

2 Hear the voice of my prayer when I cry out to you,*
    when I lift up my hands to your holy of holies.

3 Do not snatch me away with the wicked or with the
                        evildoers,*
    who speak peaceably with their neighbours,
    while strife is in their hearts.

4 Repay them according to their deeds,*
    and according to the wickedness of their actions.

5 According to the work of their hands repay them,*
    and give them their just deserts.

6 They have no understanding of the Lord's doings,
    nor of the works of his hands; *
    therefore he will break them down and not
                        build them up.

7 Blessed is the Lord! *
    for he has heard the voice of my prayer.

8 The Lord is my strength and my shield; *
    my heart trusts in him, and I have been helped;

9 Therefore my heart dances for joy,*
    and in my song will I praise him.

10 The Lord is the strength of his people,*
    a safe refuge for his anointed.

11 Save your people and bless your inheritance; *
    shepherd them and carry them for ever.

Blessed are you, strong Shepherd of your people. You hear us
when we lift up our hands in prayer, and through your Son
Jesus Christ you give us the promise of an eternal inheritance.
Blessed are you for ever.

# 29

1   Ascribe to the Lord, you gods,*
      ascribe to the Lord glory and strength.

2   Ascribe to the Lord the glory due his name; *
      worship the Lord in the beauty of holiness.

3   The voice of the Lord is upon the waters;
    the God of glory thunders; *
      the Lord is upon the mighty waters.

4   The voice of the Lord is a powerful voice; *
      the voice of the Lord is a voice of splendour.

5   The voice of the Lord breaks the cedar trees; *
      the Lord breaks the cedars of Lebanon;

6   He makes Lebanon skip like a calf,*
      and Mount Hermon like a young wild ox.

7   The voice of the Lord splits the flames of fire;
    the voice of the Lord shakes the wilderness; *
      the Lord shakes the wilderness of Kadesh.

8   The voice of the Lord makes the oak trees writhe *
      and strips the forests bare.

9   And in the temple of the Lord *
      all are crying, "Glory!"

10  The Lord sits enthroned above the flood; *
      the Lord sits enthroned as king for evermore.

11  The Lord shall give strength to his people; *
      the Lord shall give his people the blessing of peace.

God of mystery and power, open our eyes to the flame of your
love, and open our ears to the thunder of your justice, that we
may receive your gifts of blessing and peace, to the glory of
your name; through Jesus Christ our Lord.

# 30

1   I will exalt you, O Lord,
    because you have lifted me up *
        and have not let my enemies triumph over me.

2   O Lord my God, I cried out to you,*
        and you restored me to health.

3   You brought me up, O Lord, from the dead; *
        you restored my life as I was going down to the grave.

4   Sing to the Lord, you servants of his; *
        give thanks for the remembrance of his holiness.

5   For his wrath endures but the twinkling of an eye,*
        his favour for a lifetime.

6   Weeping may spend the night,*
        but joy comes in the morning.

7   While I felt secure, I said,
    "I shall never be disturbed.*
        You, Lord, with your favour, made me as strong as
                the mountains."

8   Then you hid your face,*
        and I was filled with fear.

9   I cried to you, O Lord; *
        I pleaded with the Lord, saying,

10  "What profit is there in my blood, if I go down to the Pit? *
        will the dust praise you or declare your faithfulness?

11  Hear, O Lord, and have mercy upon me; *
        O Lord, be my helper."

12  You have turned my wailing into dancing; *
        you have put off my sack-cloth and clothed me with joy.

13  Therefore my heart sings to you without ceasing; *
        O Lord my God, I will give you thanks for ever.

God our Father, glorious in giving and restoring life, do not
hide your face from your people overcome with loneliness and
fear; turn our mourning into dancing and raise us up with your
Son, that we may rejoice in your presence for ever.

# 31

1 In you, O Lord, have I taken refuge;
   let me never be put to shame; *
      deliver me in your righteousness.

2 Incline your ear to me; *
      make haste to deliver me.

3 Be my strong rock, a castle to keep me safe,
   for you are my crag and my stronghold; *
      for the sake of your name, lead me and guide me.

4 Take me out of the net that they have secretly set for me,*
      for you are my tower of strength.

5 Into your hands I commend my spirit,*
      for you have redeemed me,
      O Lord, O God of truth.

6 I hate those who cling to worthless idols,*
      and I put my trust in the Lord.

7 I will rejoice and be glad because of your mercy; *
      for you have seen my affliction;
      you know my distress.

8 You have not shut me up in the power of the enemy; *
      you have set my feet in an open place.

9 Have mercy on me, O Lord, for I am in trouble; *
      my eye is consumed with sorrow,
      and also my throat and my belly.

10 For my life is wasted with grief,
    and my years with sighing; *
       my strength fails me because of affliction,
       and my bones are consumed.

11 I have become a reproach to all my enemies and
                        even to my neighbours,
    a dismay to those of my acquaintance; *
       when they see me in the street they avoid me.

12 I am forgotten like a dead man, out of mind; *
       I am as useless as a broken pot.

13  For I have heard the whispering of the crowd;
    fear is all around; *
        they put their heads together against me;
        they plot to take my life.

14  But as for me, I have trusted in you, O Lord.*
        I have said, "You are my God.

15  My times are in your hand; *
        rescue me from the hand of my enemies,
        and from those who persecute me.

16  Make your face to shine upon your servant,*
        and in your loving-kindness save me."

17  Lord, let me not be ashamed for having called upon you; *
        rather, let the wicked be put to shame;
        let them be silent in the grave.

18  Let the lying lips be silenced which speak against
                        the righteous,*
        haughtily, disdainfully, and with contempt.

19  How great is your goodness, O Lord!
    which you have laid up for those who fear you; *
        which you have done in the sight of all
        for those who put their trust in you.

20  You hide them in the covert of your presence from those
                        who slander them; *
        you keep them in your shelter from the strife of tongues.

21  Blessed be the Lord! *
        for he has shown me the wonders of his love in a
                        besieged city.

22  Yet I said in my alarm,
    "I have been cut off from the sight of your eyes." *
        Nevertheless, you heard the sound of my entreaty
        when I cried out to you.

23  Love the Lord, all you who worship him; *
        the Lord protects the faithful,
        but repays to the full those who act haughtily.

24  Be strong and let your heart take courage,*
        all you who wait for the Lord.

Helper of the helpless, comfort of the afflicted, may your servants who stand in the midst of evil find strength in the knowledge of your presence, and praise you for the wonders of your love; through Jesus Christ our Redeemer.

# 32

1 Happy are they whose transgressions are forgiven,*
   and whose sin is put away!

2 Happy are they to whom the Lord imputes no guilt,*
   and in whose spirit there is no guile!

3 While I held my tongue, my bones withered away,*
   because of my groaning all day long.

4 For your hand was heavy upon me day and night; *
   my moisture was dried up as in the heat of summer.

5 Then I acknowledged my sin to you,*
   and did not conceal my guilt.

6 I said, "I will confess my transgressions to the Lord." *
   Then you forgave me the guilt of my sin.

7 Therefore all the faithful will make their prayers to you in
                     time of trouble; *
   when the great waters overflow, they shall not reach them.

8 You are my hiding-place;
   you preserve me from trouble; *
   you surround me with shouts of deliverance.

9 "I will instruct you and teach you in the way that you
                     should go; *
   I will guide you with my eye.

10 Do not be like horse or mule, which have no understanding; *
   who must be fitted with bit and bridle,
   or else they will not stay near you."

11 Great are the tribulations of the wicked; *
   but mercy embraces those who trust in the Lord.

12 Be glad, you righteous, and rejoice in the Lord; *
   shout for joy, all who are true of heart.

Watch over us, loving God, and when we fall into sin teach us to acknowledge our guilt. May we forgive and be forgiven, for the sake of the one who was wounded for our transgressions, Jesus Christ your Son our Saviour.

# 33

1 Rejoice in the Lord, you righteous; *
   it is good for the just to sing praises.

2 Praise the Lord with the harp; *
   play to him upon the psaltery and lyre.

3 Sing for him a new song; *
   sound a fanfare with all your skill upon the trumpet.

4 For the word of the Lord is right,*
   and all his works are sure.

5 He loves righteousness and justice; *
   the loving-kindness of the Lord fills the whole earth.

6 By the word of the Lord were the heavens made,*
   by the breath of his mouth all the heavenly hosts.

7 He gathers up the waters of the ocean as in a water-skin *
   and stores up the depths of the sea.

8 Let all the earth fear the Lord; *
   let all who dwell in the world stand in awe of him.

9 For he spoke, and it came to pass; *
   he commanded, and it stood fast.

10 The Lord brings the will of the nations to naught; *
   he thwarts the designs of the peoples.

11 But the Lord's will stands fast for ever,*
   and the designs of his heart from age to age.

12 Happy is the nation whose God is the Lord! *
   happy the people he has chosen to be his own!

13 The Lord looks down from heaven,*
   and beholds all the people in the world.

14 From where he sits enthroned he turns his gaze *
   on all who dwell on the earth.

15    He fashions all the hearts of them*
      and understands all their works.

16    There is no king that can be saved by a mighty army; *
      a strong man is not delivered by his great strength.

17    The horse is a vain hope for deliverance; *
      for all its strength it cannot save.

18    Behold, the eye of the Lord is upon those who fear him,*
      on those who wait upon his love,

19    To pluck their lives from death,*
      and to feed them in time of famine.

20    Our soul waits for the Lord; *
      he is our help and our shield.

21    Indeed, our heart rejoices in him,*
      for in his holy name we put our trust.

22    Let your loving-kindness, O Lord, be upon us,*
      as we have put our trust in you.

Blessed are you, Creator of the universe. In your loving
kindness you watch over your chosen people. Make us
witnesses to your truth and instruments of your peace,
that all may know you as the God of justice, and praise
your holy name; through Jesus Christ our Saviour.

# 34

1    I will bless the Lord at all times; *
      his praise shall ever be in my mouth.

2    I will glory in the Lord; *
      let the humble hear and rejoice.

3    Proclaim with me the greatness of the Lord; *
      let us exalt his name together.

4    I sought the Lord, and he answered me *
      and delivered me out of all my terror.

5    Look upon him and be radiant,*
      and let not your faces be ashamed.

6   I called in my affliction and the Lord heard me *
        and saved me from all my troubles.

7   The angel of the Lord encompasses those who fear him,*
        and he will deliver them.

8   Taste and see that the Lord is good; *
        happy are they who trust in him!

9   Fear the Lord, you that are his saints,*
        for those who fear him lack nothing.

10  The young lions lack and suffer hunger,*
        but those who seek the Lord lack nothing that is good.

11  Come, children, and listen to me; *
        I will teach you the fear of the Lord.

12  Who among you loves life *
        and desires long life to enjoy prosperity?

13  Keep your tongue from evil-speaking *
        and your lips from lying words.

14  Turn from evil and do good; *
        seek peace and pursue it.

15  The eyes of the Lord are upon the righteous,*
        and his ears are open to their cry.

16  The face of the Lord is against those who do evil,*
        to root out the remembrance of them from the earth.

17  The righteous cry, and the Lord hears them *
        and delivers them from all their troubles.

18  The Lord is near to the brokenhearted *
        and will save those whose spirits are crushed.

19  Many are the troubles of the righteous,*
        but the Lord will deliver him out of them all.

20  He will keep safe all his bones; *
        not one of them shall be broken.

21  Evil shall slay the wicked,*
        and those who hate the righteous will be punished.

22     The Lord ransoms the life of his servants,\*
      and none will be punished who trust in him.

Hear us, Lord, when we cry to you. Calm our bodies and
minds with the peace which passes understanding, and make
us radiant with the knowledge of your goodness; through
Jesus Christ our Saviour.

# 35

1     Fight those who fight me, O Lord; \*
      attack those who are attacking me.

2     Take up shield and armour \*
      and rise up to help me.

3     Draw the sword and bar the way against those
                        who pursue me; \*
      say to my soul, "I am your salvation."

4     Let those who seek after my life be shamed and humbled; \*
      let those who plot my ruin fall back and be dismayed.

5     Let them be like chaff before the wind,\*
      and let the angel of the Lord drive them away.

6     Let their way be dark and slippery,\*
      and let the angel of the Lord pursue them.

7     For they have secretly spread a net for me without a cause; \*
      without a cause they have dug a pit to take me alive.

8     Let ruin come upon them unawares; \*
      let them be caught in the net they hid;
      let them fall into the pit they dug.

9     Then I will be joyful in the Lord; \*
      I will glory in his victory.

10    My very bones will say, "Lord, who is like you? \*
      You deliver the poor from those who are too
                   strong for them,
      the poor and needy from those who rob them."

11    Malicious witnesses rise up against me; \*
      they charge me with matters I know nothing about.

12 They pay me evil in exchange for good; *
    my soul is full of despair.

13 But when they were sick I dressed in sack-cloth *
    and humbled myself by fasting;

14 I prayed with my whole heart,
  as one would for a friend or a brother; *
    I behaved like one who mourns for his mother,
    bowed down and grieving.

15 But when I stumbled, they were glad and gathered together;
  they gathered against me; *
    strangers whom I did not know tore me to pieces and
            would not stop.

16 They put me to the test and mocked me; *
    they gnashed at me with their teeth.

17 O Lord, how long will you look on? *
    rescue me from the roaring beasts,
    and my life from the young lions.

18 I will give you thanks in the great congregation; *
    I will praise you in the mighty throng.

19 Do not let my treacherous foes rejoice over me,*
    nor let those who hate me without a cause
          wink at each other.

20 For they do not plan for peace,*
    but invent deceitful schemes against the
          quiet in the land.

21 They opened their mouths at me and said,*
  "Aha! we saw it with our own eyes."

22 You saw it, O Lord; do not be silent; *
    O Lord, be not far from me.

23 Awake, arise, to my cause! *
    to my defence, my God and my Lord!

24 Give me justice, O Lord my God,
  according to your righteousness; *
    do not let them triumph over me.

25     Do not let them say in their hearts,
      "Aha! just what we want!" *
        Do not let them say, "We have swallowed him up."

26     Let all who rejoice at my ruin be ashamed and disgraced; *
      let those who boast against me be clothed with
                       dismay and shame.

27     Let those who favour my cause sing out with
                    joy and be glad; *
      let them say always, "Great is the Lord,
        who desires the prosperity of his servant."

28     And my tongue shall be talking of your righteousness *
      and of your praise all the day long.

God of our salvation, come quickly to free the poor from their
oppressors, and establish your reign of justice on earth, that your
people may sing out with joy; through Jesus Christ our Lord.

# 36

1     There is a voice of rebellion deep in the heart of the wicked; *
      there is no fear of God before his eyes.

2     He flatters himself in his own eyes *
      that his hateful sin will not be found out.

3     The words of his mouth are wicked and deceitful; *
      he has left off acting wisely and doing good.

4     He thinks up wickedness upon his bed
      and has set himself in no good way; *
      he does not abhor that which is evil.

5     Your love, O Lord, reaches to the heavens,*
      and your faithfulness to the clouds.

6     Your righteousness is like the strong mountains,
      your justice like the great deep; *
      you save both man and beast, O Lord.

7     How priceless is your love, O God! *
      your people take refuge under the shadow of your wings.

8   They feast upon the abundance of your house; *
      you give them drink from the river of your delights.

9   For with you is the well of life,*
      and in your light we see light.

10   Continue your loving-kindness to those who know you,*
      and your favour to those who are true of heart.

11   Let not the foot of the proud come near me.*
      nor the hand of the wicked push me aside.

12   See how they are fallen, those who work wickedness! *
      they are cast down and shall not be able to rise.

God of justice and of mercy, open the eyes of sinners that they
may see the light of your truth, know the power of your love,
and share in the bounty of your heavenly table; through Jesus
Christ our Saviour.

# 37

**Part I**

1   Do not fret yourself because of evildoers; *
      do not be jealous of those who do wrong.

2   For they shall soon wither like the grass,*
      and like the green grass fade away.

3   Put your trust in the Lord and do good; *
      dwell in the land and feed on its riches.

4   Take delight in the Lord,*
      and he shall give you your heart's desire.

5   Commit your way to the Lord and put your trust in him,*
      and he will bring it to pass.

6   He will make your righteousness as clear as the light *
      and your just dealing as the noonday.

7   Be still before the Lord *
      and wait patiently for him.

8     Do not fret yourself over the one who prospers,*
      the one who succeeds in evil schemes.

9     Refrain from anger, leave rage alone; *
      do not fret yourself; it leads only to evil.

10    For evildoers shall be cut off,*
      but those who wait upon the Lord shall possess the land.

11    In a little while the wicked shall be no more; *
      you shall search out their place, but they will not be there.

12    But the lowly shall possess the land; *
      they will delight in abundance of peace.

13    The wicked plot against the righteous *
      and gnash at them with their teeth.

14    The Lord laughs at the wicked,*
      because he sees that their day will come.

15    The wicked draw their sword and bend their bow
      to strike down the poor and needy,*
      to slaughter those who are upright in their ways.

16    Their sword shall go through their own heart,*
      and their bow shall be broken.

17    The little that the righteous has *
      is better than great riches of the wicked.

18    For the power of the wicked shall be broken,*
      but the Lord upholds the righteous.

# 37

**Part II**

19    The Lord cares for the lives of the godly,*
      and their inheritance shall last for ever.

20    They shall not be ashamed in bad times,*
      and in days of famine they shall have enough.

21    As for the wicked, they shall perish,*
      and the enemies of the Lord, like the glory of
                the meadows, shall vanish;
      they shall vanish like smoke.

22 The wicked borrow and do not repay,*
    but the righteous are generous in giving.

23 Those who are blessed by God shall possess the land,*
    but those who are cursed by him shall be destroyed.

24 Our steps are directed by the Lord; *
    he strengthens those in whose way he delights.

25 If they stumble, they shall not fall headlong,*
    for the Lord holds them by the hand.

26 I have been young and now I am old,*
    but never have I seen the righteous forsaken,
    or their children begging bread.

27 The righteous are always generous in their lending,*
    and their children shall be a blessing.

28 Turn from evil, and do good,*
    and dwell in the land for ever.

29 For the Lord loves justice; *
    he does not forsake his faithful ones.

30 They shall be kept safe for ever,*
    but the offspring of the wicked shall be destroyed.

31 The righteous shall possess the land *
    and dwell in it for ever.

32 The mouth of the righteous utters wisdom,*
    and their tongue speaks what is right.

33 The law of their God is in their heart,*
    and their footsteps shall not falter.

34 The wicked spy on the righteous *
    and seek occasion to kill them.

35 The Lord will not abandon them to their hand,*
    nor let them be found guilty when brought to trial.

36 Wait upon the Lord and keep his way; *
    he will raise you up to possess the land,
    and when the wicked are cut off, you will see it.

37  I have seen the wicked in their arrogance,*
       flourishing like a tree in full leaf.

38  I went by, and behold, they were not there; *
       I searched for them, but they could not be found.

39  Mark those who are honest;
     observe the upright; *
       for there is a future for the peaceable.

40  Transgressors shall be destroyed, one and all; *
       the future of the wicked is cut off.

41  But the deliverance of the righteous comes from the Lord; *
       he is their stronghold in time of trouble.

42  The Lord will help them and rescue them; *
       he will rescue them from the wicked and deliver them,
       because they seek refuge in him.

God our strength, give us the humility to trust in your loving
care, and the patience to be faithful in seeking your kingdom,
that we may come to share in the inheritance of your saints;
through Jesus Christ our Saviour.

# 38

1  O Lord, do not rebuke me in your anger; *
     do not punish me in your wrath.

2  For your arrows have already pierced me,*
     and your hand presses hard upon me.

3  There is no health in my flesh,
   because of your indignation; *
       there is no soundness in my body, because of my sin.

4  For my iniquities overwhelm me; *
     like a heavy burden they are too much for me to bear.

5  My wounds stink and fester *
     by reason of my foolishness.

6  I am utterly bowed down and prostrate; *
     I go about in mourning all the day long.

7   My loins are filled with searing pain; *
        there is no health in my body.

8   I am utterly numb and crushed; *
        I wail, because of the groaning of my heart.

9   O Lord, you know all my desires,*
        and my sighing is not hidden from you.

10  My heart is pounding, my strength has failed me,*
        and the brightness of my eyes is gone from me.

11  My friends and companions draw back from my affliction; *
        my neighbours stand afar off.

12  Those who seek after my life lay snares for me; *
        those who strive to hurt me speak of my ruin
        and plot treachery all the day long.

13  But I am like the deaf who do not hear,*
        like those who are mute and do not open their mouth.

14  I have become like one who does not hear *
        and from whose mouth comes no defence.

15  For in you, O Lord, have I fixed my hope; *
        you will answer me, O Lord my God.

16  For I said, "Do not let them rejoice at my expense,*
        those who gloat over me when my foot slips."

17  Truly, I am on the verge of falling,*
        and my pain is always with me.

18  I will confess my iniquity *
        and be sorry for my sin.

19  Those who are my enemies without cause are mighty,*
        and many in number are those who wrongfully hate me.

20  Those who repay evil for good slander me,*
        because I follow the course that is right.

21  O Lord, do not forsake me; *
        be not far from me, O my God.

22  Make haste to help me,*
        O Lord of my salvation.

God of compassion, when we are weighed down by the
burden of our sins, help us to remember that you do not
forsake us, but show mercy through Jesus Christ our Saviour.

## 39

1   I said, "I will keep watch upon my ways,*
    so that I do not offend with my tongue.

2   I will put a muzzle on my mouth *
    while the wicked are in my presence."

3   So I held my tongue and said nothing; *
    I refrained from rash words;
    but my pain became unbearable.

4   My heart was hot within me;
    while I pondered, the fire burst into flame; *
    I spoke out with my tongue:

5   Lord, let me know my end and the number of my days,*
    so that I may know how short my life is.

6   You have given me a mere handful of days,
    and my lifetime is as nothing in your sight; *
    truly, even those who stand erect are but a puff of wind.

7   We walk about like a shadow,
    and in vain we are in turmoil; *
    we heap up riches and cannot tell who will gather them.

8   And now, what is my hope? *
    O Lord, my hope is in you.

9   Deliver me from all my transgressions *
    and do not make me the taunt of the fool.

10  I fell silent and did not open my mouth,*
    for surely it was you that did it.

11  Take your affliction from me; *
    I am worn down by the blows of your hand.

12  With rebukes for sin you punish us;
    like a moth you eat away all that is dear to us; *
    truly, everyone is but a puff of wind.

13     Hear my prayer, O Lord,
      and give ear to my cry; *
        hold not your peace at my tears.

14     For I am but a sojourner with you,*
        a wayfarer, as all my forbears were.

15     Turn your gaze from me, that I may be glad again,*
        before I go my way and am no more.

God our hope, when we are troubled by fear and uncertainty,
teach us to commit our lives to your care and to go forward on
our pilgrimage, trusting in the knowledge of your love and
forgiveness; through Jesus Christ our Redeemer.

# 40

1     I waited patiently upon the Lord; *
        he stooped to me and heard my cry.

2     He lifted me out of the desolate pit, out of the mire and clay; *
        he set my feet upon a high cliff and made my footing sure.

3     He put a new song in my mouth,
      a song of praise to our God; *
        many shall see, and stand in awe,
        and put their trust in the Lord.

4     Happy are they who trust in the Lord! *
        they do not resort to evil spirits or turn to false gods.

5     Great things are they that you have done, O Lord my God!
    how great your wonders and your plans for us! *
        there is none who can be compared with you.

6     Oh, that I could make them known and tell them! *
        but they are more than I can count.

7     In sacrifice and offering you take no pleasure *
        (you have given me ears to hear you);

8     Burnt-offering and sin-offering you have not required,*
        and so I said, "Behold, I come.

9     In the roll of the book it is written concerning me: *
       'I love to do your will, O my God;
       your law is deep in my heart.'"

10    I proclaimed righteousness in the great congregation; *
       behold, I did not restrain my lips;
       and that, O Lord, you know.

11    Your righteousness have I not hidden in my heart;
       I have spoken of your faithfulness and
                  your deliverance; *
       I have not concealed your love and faithfulness from
                  the great congregation.

12    You are the Lord;
       do not withhold your compassion from me; *
       let your love and your faithfulness keep me safe for ever,

13    For innumerable troubles have crowded upon me;
       my sins have overtaken me, and I cannot see; *
       they are more in number than the hairs of my head,
       and my heart fails me.

14    Be pleased, O Lord, to deliver me; *
       O Lord, make haste to help me.

15    Let them be ashamed and altogether dismayed
       who seek after my life to destroy it; *
       let them draw back and be disgraced
       who take pleasure in my misfortune.

16    Let those who say "Aha!" and gloat over me be confounded,*
       because they are ashamed.

17    Let all who seek you rejoice in you and be glad; *
       let those who love your salvation continually say,
     "Great is the Lord!"

18    Though I am poor and afflicted,*
       the Lord will have regard for me.

19    You are my helper and my deliverer; *
       do not tarry, O my God.

God our saviour, hear our prayer for all who suffer at the hands of others, and especially for those who suffer for the sake of justice. Raise and comfort them, and lead us all in the paths of loving service. We ask this in the name of Jesus Christ the Lord.

# 41

1 Happy are they who consider the poor and needy! *
    the Lord will deliver them in the time of trouble.

2 The Lord preserves them and keeps them alive,
so that they may be happy in the land; *
    he does not hand them over to the will of their enemies.

3 The Lord sustains them on their sickbed *
    and ministers to them in their illness.

4 I said, "Lord, be merciful to me; *
    heal me, for I have sinned against you."

5 My enemies are saying wicked things about me: *
    "When will he die, and his name perish?"

6 Even if they come to see me, they speak empty words; *
their heart collects false rumours;
    they go outside and spread them.

7 All my enemies whisper together about me *
    and devise evil against me.

8 "A deadly thing," they say, "has fastened on him; *
    he has taken to his bed and will never get up again."

9 Even my best friend, whom I trusted,
who broke bread with me,*
    has lifted up his heel and turned against me.

10 But you, O Lord, be merciful to me and raise me up,*
    and I shall repay them.

11 By this I know you are pleased with me,*
    that my enemy does not triumph over me.

12 In my integrity you hold me fast,*
    and shall set me before your face for ever.

13 Blessed be the Lord God of Israel,*
      from age to age. Amen. Amen.

Remember us, gracious God, when we are lonely and
depressed, and support us in the dark night of grief and
despair, for your love is faithful and you do not forget your
broken ones. We ask this in the name of Jesus Christ the Lord.

## Book Two

# 42

1 As the deer longs for the water-brooks,*
      so longs my soul for you, O God.

2 My soul is athirst for God, athirst for the living God; *
      when shall I come to appear before the presence of God?

3 My tears have been my food day and night,*
      while all day long they say to me,
      "Where now is your God?"

4 I pour out my soul when I think on these things: *
      how I went with the multitude and led them into the
            house of God,

5 With the voice of praise and thanksgiving,*
      among those who keep holy-day.

6 Why are you so full of heaviness, O my soul? *
      and why are you so disquieted within me?

7 Put your trust in God; *
      for I will yet give thanks to him,
      who is the help of my countenance, and my God.

8 My soul is heavy within me; *
      therefore I will remember you from the land of Jordan,
      and from the peak of Mizar among the heights of Hermon.

9 One deep calls to another in the noise of your cataracts; *
      all your rapids and floods have gone over me.

10    The Lord grants his loving-kindness in the daytime; *
          in the night season his song is with me,
          a prayer to the God of my life.

11    I will say to the God of my strength,
          "Why have you forgotten me? *
          and why do I go so heavily while the enemy
                                    oppresses me?"

12    While my bones are being broken,*
          my enemies mock me to my face;

13    All day long they mock me *
          and say to me, "Where now is your God?"

14    Why are you so full of heaviness, O my soul? *
          and why are you so disquieted within me?

15    Put your trust in God; *
          for I will yet give thanks to him,
          who is the help of my countenance, and my God.

Gracious God, in the night of distress we forget the days of sun
and joy. Even when we do not know your presence, preserve
us from the dark torrent of despair. We ask this in the name of
Jesus Christ our Lord.

# 43

1    Give judgement for me, O God,
          and defend my cause against an ungodly people; *
          deliver me from the deceitful and the wicked.

2    For you are the God of my strength;
          why have you put me from you? *
          and why do I go so heavily while the enemy
                                    oppresses me?

3    Send out your light and your truth, that they may lead me,*
          and bring me to your holy hill
          and to your dwelling;

4   That I may go to the altar of God,
    to the God of my joy and gladness; *
        and on the harp I will give thanks to you, O God my God.

5   Why are you so full of heaviness, O my soul? *
        and why are you so disquieted within me?

6   Put your trust in God; *
        for I will yet give thanks to him,
        who is the help of my countenance, and my God.

God of mercy, deliver those who are weighed down by fear
and depression, and give them joy and gladness in your
presence. We ask this in the name of Jesus Christ the Lord.

# 44

1   We have heard with our ears, O God,
    our forefathers have told us,*
        the deeds you did in their days,
        in the days of old.

2   How with your hand you drove the peoples out
    and planted our forefathers in the land; *
        how you destroyed nations and made your people flourish.

3   For they did not take the land by their sword,
    nor did their arm win the victory for them; *
        but your right hand, your arm, and the
                            light of your countenance,
        because you favoured them.

4   You are my King and my God; *
        you command victories for Jacob.

5   Through you we pushed back our adversaries; *
        through your name we trampled on those who
        rose up against us.

6   For I do not rely on my bow,*
        and my sword does not give me the victory.

7   Surely, you gave us victory over our adversaries *
        and put those who hate us to shame.

8    Every day we gloried in God,*
       and we will praise your name for ever.

9    Nevertheless, you have rejected and humbled us *
       and do not go forth with our armies.

10    You have made us fall back before our adversary,*
       and our enemies have plundered us.

11    You have made us like sheep to be eaten *
       and have scattered us among the nations.

12    You are selling your people for a trifle *
       and are making no profit on the sale of them.

13    You have made us the scorn of our neighbours,*
       a mockery and derision to those around us.

14    You have made us a byword among the nations,*
       a laughing-stock among the peoples.

15    My humiliation is daily before me,*
       and shame has covered my face;

16    Because of the taunts of the mockers and blasphemers,*
       because of the enemy and avenger.

17    All this has come upon us; *
       yet we have not forgotten you,
       nor have we betrayed your covenant.

18    Our heart never turned back,*
       nor did our footsteps stray from your path;

19    Though you thrust us down into a place of misery,*
       and covered us over with deep darkness.

20    If we have forgotten the name of our God,*
       or stretched out our hands to some strange god,

21    Will not God find it out? *
       for he knows the secrets of the heart.

22    Indeed, for your sake we are killed all the day long; *
       we are accounted as sheep for the slaughter.

23    Awake, O Lord! why are you sleeping? *
       Arise! do not reject us for ever.

24     Why have you hidden your face *
        and forgotten our affliction and oppression?

25     We sink down into the dust; *
        our body cleaves to the ground.

26     Rise up, and help us,*
        and save us, for the sake of your steadfast love.

God of hosts, be present with those who suffer for no fault of
their own: the broken victims of war, oppression, indifference,
and neglect. May we see in their sufferings the wounds of
Christ, and share with them in his gift of new life. We ask this
in his name.

# 45

1     My heart is stirring with a noble song;
        let me recite what I have fashioned for the king; *
        my tongue shall be the pen of a skilled writer.

2     You are the fairest of men; *
        grace flows from your lips,
        because God has blessed you for ever.

3     Strap your sword upon your thigh, O mighty warrior,*
        in your pride and in your majesty.

4     Ride out and conquer in the cause of truth *
        and for the sake of justice.

5     Your right hand will show you marvellous things; *
        your arrows are very sharp, O mighty warrior.

6     The peoples are falling at your feet,*
        and the king's enemies are losing heart.

7     Your throne, O God, endures for ever and ever,*
        a sceptre of righteousness is the sceptre of your kingdom;
        you love righteousness and hate iniquity.

8     Therefore God, your God, has anointed you *
        with the oil of gladness above your fellows.

9  All your garments are fragrant with myrrh, aloes, and cassia,*
     and the music of strings from ivory palaces makes you glad.

10  Kings' daughters stand among the ladies of the court; *
     on your right hand is the queen,
     adorned with the gold of Ophir.

11  "Hear, O daughter; consider and listen closely; *
     forget your people and your father's house.

12  The king will have pleasure in your beauty; *
     he is your master; therefore do him honour.

13  The people of Tyre are here with a gift; *
     the rich among the people seek your favour."

14  All glorious is the princess as she enters; *
     her gown is cloth-of-gold.

15  In embroidered apparel she is brought to the king; *
     after her the bridesmaids follow in procession.

16  With joy and gladness they are brought,*
     and enter into the palace of the king.

17  "In place of fathers, O king, you shall have sons; *
     you shall make them princes over all the earth.

18  I will make your name to be remembered
     from one generation to another; *
        therefore nations will praise you for ever and ever."

Gracious God, your love unites heaven and earth in a new
festival of gladness. Lift our spirits to learn the way of joy that
leads us to your banquet hall, where all is golden with praise.
We ask this through Jesus Christ the Lord.

# 46

1  God is our refuge and strength,*
     a very present help in trouble.

2  Therefore we will not fear, though the earth be moved,*
     and though the mountains be toppled into the
                              depths of the sea;

3    Though its waters rage and foam,*
        and though the mountains tremble at its tumult.

4    The Lord of hosts is with us; *
        the God of Jacob is our stronghold.

5    There is a river whose streams make glad the city of God,*
        the holy habitation of the Most High.

6    God is in the midst of her;
        she shall not be overthrown; *
        God shall help her at the break of day.

7    The nations make much ado, and the kingdoms are shaken; *
        God has spoken, and the earth shall melt away.

8    The Lord of hosts is with us; *
        the God of Jacob is our stronghold.

9    Come now and look upon the works of the Lord,*
        what awesome things he has done on earth.

10   It is he who makes war to cease in all the world; *
        he breaks the bow, and shatters the spear,
        and burns the shields with fire.

11   "Be still, then, and know that I am God; *
        I will be exalted among the nations;
        I will be exalted in the earth."

12   The Lord of hosts is with us; *
        the God of Jacob is our stronghold.


God our strength, your power is for peace, and the pride of
your mighty acts secures the city of the humble. Teach us to
put our trust in your salvation, through Jesus Christ our Lord.

# 47

1    Clap your hands, all you peoples; *
        shout to God with a cry of joy.

2     For the Lord Most High is to be feared; *
       he is the great king over all the earth.

3     He subdues the peoples under us,*
       and the nations under our feet.

4     He chooses our inheritance for us,*
       the pride of Jacob whom he loves.

5     God has gone up with a shout,*
       the Lord with the sound of the ram's-horn.

6     Sing praises to God, sing praises; *
       sing praises to our king, sing praises.

7     For God is king of all the earth; *
       sing praises with all your skill.

8     God reigns over the nations; *
       God sits upon his holy throne.

9     The nobles of the peoples have gathered together *
       with the people of the God of Abraham.

10    The rulers of the earth belong to God,*
       and he is highly exalted.


Blessed are you, God of all the earth; you have called us out of
every people and nation to be a royal priesthood and citizens of
your holy city. May our words of praise call the world to turn to
the joy of fellowship with you, through Jesus Christ our Lord.


# 48

1     Great is the Lord, and highly to be praised; *
       in the city of our God is his holy hill.

2     Beautiful and lofty, the joy of all the earth, is the
                     hill of Zion,*
       the very centre of the world and the city of the great king.

3     God is in her citadels; *
       he is known to be her sure refuge.

4     Behold, the kings of the earth assembled *
       and marched forward together.

5   They looked and were astounded; *
        they retreated and fled in terror.

6   Trembling seized them there; *
        they writhed like a woman in childbirth,
        like ships of the sea when the east wind shatters them.

7   As we have heard, so have we seen,
    in the city of the Lord of hosts, in the city of our God; *
        God has established her for ever.

8   We have waited in silence on your loving-kindness, O God,*
        in the midst of your temple.

9   Your praise, like your name, O God, reaches to
                            the world's end; *
        your right hand is full of justice.

10  Let Mount Zion be glad
    and the cities of Judah rejoice,*
        because of your judgements.

11  Make the circuit of Zion;
    walk round about her; *
        count the number of her towers.

12  Consider well her bulwarks;
    examine her strongholds; *
        that you may tell those who come after.

13  This God is our God for ever and ever; *
        he shall be our guide for evermore.


Gracious God, you have made us fellow-citizens with the
saints in the city of your eternal light. In the time of storm,
when the foundations shake, teach us to wait in silence on
your steadfast and transforming love, made known to us in
Jesus Christ our Lord.

# 49

1   Hear this, all you peoples;
    hearken, all you who dwell in the world,*
        you of high degree and low, rich and poor together.

2 My mouth shall speak of wisdom,*
    and my heart shall meditate on understanding.

3 I will incline my ear to a proverb *
    and set forth my riddle upon the harp.

4 Why should I be afraid in evil days,*
    when the wickedness of those at my heels surrounds me,

5 The wickedness of those who put their trust in their goods,*
    and boast of their great riches?

6 We can never ransom ourselves,*
    or deliver to God the price of our life;

7 For the ransom of our life is so great,*
    that we should never have enough to pay it,

8 In order to live for ever and ever,*
    and never see the grave.

9 For we see that the wise die also;
  like the dull and stupid they perish *
    and leave their wealth to those who come after them.

10 Their graves shall be their homes for ever,
   their dwelling places from generation to generation,*
    though they call the lands after their own names.

11 Even though honoured, they cannot live for ever; *
    they are like the beasts that perish.

12 Such is the way of those who foolishly trust in themselves,*
    and the end of those who delight in their own words.

13 Like a flock of sheep they are destined to die;
   Death is their shepherd; *
    they go down straightway to the grave.

14 Their form shall waste away,*
    and the land of the dead shall be their home.

15 But God will ransom my life; *
    he will snatch me from the grasp of death.

16 Do not be envious when some become rich,*
    or when the grandeur of their house increases;

17  For they will carry nothing away at their death,*
        nor will their grandeur follow them.

18  Though they thought highly of themselves while they lived,*
        and were praised for their success,

19  They shall join the company of their forebears,*
        who will never see the light again.

20  Those who are honoured, but have no understanding,*
        are like the beasts that perish.


God of our salvation, save us from envy, and teach us to be
content with what is enough. We ask this in the name of Jesus
Christ the Lord.


# 50

1   The Lord, the God of gods, has spoken; *
        he has called the earth from the rising of the sun to
                its setting.

2   Out of Zion, perfect in its beauty,*
        God reveals himself in glory.

3   Our God will come and will not keep silence; *
        before him there is a consuming flame,
        and round about him a raging storm.

4   He calls the heavens and the earth from above *
        to witness the judgement of his people.

5   "Gather before me my loyal followers,*
        those who have made a covenant with me
        and sealed it with sacrifice."

6   Let the heavens declare the rightness of his cause; *
        for God himself is judge.


7   Hear, O my people, and I will speak:
        "O Israel, I will bear witness against you; *
        for I am God, your God.

8 I do not accuse you because of your sacrifices; *
　　your offerings are always before me.

9 I will take no bull-calf from your stalls,*
　　nor he-goats out of your pens;

10 For the beasts of the forest are mine,*
　　the herds in their thousands upon the hills.

11 I know every bird in the sky,*
　　and the creatures of the fields are in my sight.

12 If I were hungry, I would not tell you,*
　　for the whole world is mine and all that is in it.

13 Do you think I eat the flesh of bulls,*
　　or drink the blood of goats?

14 Offer to God a sacrifice of thanksgiving *
　　and make good your vows to the Most High.

15 Call upon me in the day of trouble; *
　　I will deliver you, and you shall honour me."


16 But to the wicked God says: *
　　"Why do you recite my statutes,
　　and take my covenant upon your lips;

17 Since you refuse discipline,*
　　and toss my words behind your back?

18 When you see a thief, you make him your friend,*
　　and you cast in your lot with adulterers.

19 You have loosed your lips for evil,*
　　and harnessed your tongue to a lie.

20 You are always speaking evil of your brother *
　　and slandering your own mother's son.

21 These things you have done, and I kept still,*
　　and you thought that I am like you."


22 "I have made my accusation; *
　　I have put my case in order before your eyes.

23   Consider this well, you who forget God,*
      lest I rend you and there be none to deliver you.

24   Whoever offers me the sacrifice of thanksgiving
                        honours me; *
      but to those who keep in my way will I show
                        the salvation of God.''

Blessed are you, God of glory; you call us to give up all our vain
attempts to reach you, and to come before you in thanksgiving
for your great salvation, shown to us in Jesus Christ our Lord.

# 51

1   Have mercy on me, O God, according to your
                        loving-kindness; *
      in your great compassion blot out my offenses.

2   Wash me through and through from my wickedness *
      and cleanse me from my sin.

3   For I know my transgressions,*
      and my sin is ever before me.

4   Against you only have I sinned *
      and done what is evil in your sight.

5   And so you are justified when you speak *
      and upright in your judgement.

6   Indeed, I have been wicked from my birth,*
      a sinner from my mother's womb.

7   For behold, you look for truth deep within me,*
      and will make me understand wisdom secretly.

8   Purge me from my sin, and I shall be pure; *
      wash me, and I shall be clean indeed.

9   Make me hear of joy and gladness,*
      that the body you have broken may rejoice.

10  Hide your face from my sins *
      and blot out all my iniquities.

11 Create in me a clean heart, O God,*
   and renew a right spirit within me.

12 Cast me not away from your presence *
   and take not your holy Spirit from me.

13 Give me the joy of your saving help again *
   and sustain me with your bountiful Spirit.

14 I shall teach your ways to the wicked,*
   and sinners shall return to you.

15 Deliver me from death, O God,*
   and my tongue shall sing of your righteousness,
   O God of my salvation.

16 Open my lips, O Lord,*
   and my mouth shall proclaim your praise.

17 Had you desired it, I would have offered sacrifice,*
   but you take no delight in burnt-offerings.

18 The sacrifice of God is a troubled spirit; *
   a broken and contrite heart, O God, you will not despise.

19 Be favourable and gracious to Zion,*
   and rebuild the walls of Jerusalem.

20 Then you will be pleased with the appointed sacrifices,
   with burnt-offerings and oblations; *
   then shall they offer young bullocks upon your altar.

Almighty God, to you all hearts are open, all desires known,
and from you no secrets are hidden. Cleanse the thoughts of
our hearts by the inspiration of your Holy Spirit, that we may
perfectly love you, and worthily magnify your holy name;
through Christ our Lord.

# 52

1 You tyrant, why do you boast of wickedness *
   against the godly all day long?

2 You plot ruin;
    your tongue is like a sharpened razor,*
        O worker of deception.

3 You love evil more than good *
        and lying more than speaking the truth.

4 You love all words that hurt,*
        O you deceitful tongue.

5 Oh, that God would demolish you utterly,*
        topple you, and snatch you from your dwelling,
        and root you out of the land of the living!

6 The righteous shall see and tremble,*
        and they shall laugh at him, saying,

7 "This is the one who did not take God for a refuge,*
        but trusted in great wealth
        and relied upon wickedness."

8 But I am like a green olive tree in the house of God; *
        I trust in the mercy of God for ever and ever.

9 I will give you thanks for what you have done *
        and declare the goodness of your name in the presence
                of the godly.

God of the oppressed, we pray for all those who suffer injustice
at the hands of cruel and indifferent rulers, especially for the
innocent victims of war. Give them strength and patience, and
hasten the day when the kingdoms of this world will own the
perfect law of love, made known to us in Jesus Christ our Lord.

# 53

1 The fool has said in his heart, "There is no God." *
        All are corrupt and commit abominable acts;
        there is none who does any good.

2 God looks down from heaven upon us all,*
        to see if there is any who is wise,
        if there is one who seeks after God.

3    Every one has proved faithless;
     all alike have turned bad; *
         there is none who does good; no, not one.

4    Have they no knowledge, those evildoers *
         who eat up my people like bread
         and do not call upon God?

5    See how greatly they tremble,
     such trembling as never was; *
         for God has scattered the bones of the enemy;
         they are put to shame, because God has rejected them.

6    Oh, that Israel's deliverance would come out of Zion! *
         when God restores the fortunes of his people
         Jacob will rejoice and Israel be glad.

God of hope, in times of trouble save us from blind despair and
help us to wait in confidence for the bloom of new life which,
in the darkness, we cannot imagine. We ask this in the name of
Jesus Christ the Lord.

# 54

1    Save me, O God, by your name; *
         in your might, defend my cause.

2    Hear my prayer, O God; *
         give ear to the words of my mouth.

3    For the arrogant have risen up against me,
     and the ruthless have sought my life,*
         those who have no regard for God.

4    Behold, God is my helper; *
         it is the Lord who sustains my life.

5    Render evil to those who spy on me; *
         in your faithfulness, destroy them.

6    I will offer you a freewill sacrifice *
         and praise your name, O Lord, for it is good.

7    For you have rescued me from every trouble,*
         and my eye has seen the ruin of my foes.

God of mercy, hear our prayer and come to our aid, that from
the rising of the sun to its setting we may offer you a pure
sacrifice of praise, through Jesus Christ our Lord.

# 55

1 Hear my prayer, O God; *
  do not hide yourself from my petition.

2 Listen to me and answer me; *
  I have no peace, because of my cares.

3 I am shaken by the noise of the enemy *
  and by the pressure of the wicked;

4 For they have cast an evil spell upon me *
  and are set against me in fury.

5 My heart quakes within me,*
  and the terrors of death have fallen upon me.

6 Fear and trembling have come over me,*
  and horror overwhelms me.

7 And I said, "Oh, that I had wings like a dove! *
  I would fly away and be at rest.

8 I would flee to a far-off place *
  and make my lodging in the wilderness.

9 I would hasten to escape *
  from the stormy wind and tempest."

10 Swallow them up, O Lord;
   confound their speech; *
   for I have seen violence and strife in the city.

11 Day and night the watchmen make their rounds
                        upon her walls,*
   but trouble and misery are in the midst of her.

12 There is corruption at her heart; *
   her streets are never free of oppression and deceit.

13  For had it been an adversary who taunted me,
    then I could have borne it; *
        or had it been an enemy who vaunted himself against me,
        then I could have hidden from him.

14  But it was you, a man after my own heart,*
        my companion, my own familiar friend.

15  We took sweet counsel together,*
        and walked with the throng in the house of God.

16  Let death come upon them suddenly;
    let them go down alive into the grave; *
        for wickedness is in their dwellings, in their very midst.

17  But I will call upon God,*
        and the Lord will deliver me.

18  In the evening, in the morning, and at noonday,
    I will complain and lament,*
        and he will hear my voice.

19  He will bring me safely back from the battle
                            waged against me; *
        for there are many who fight me.

20  God, who is enthroned of old, will hear me and
                            bring them down; *
        they never change; they do not fear God.

21  My companion stretched forth his hand against
                            his comrade; *
        he has broken his covenant.

22  His speech is softer than butter,*
        but war is in his heart.

23  His words are smoother than oil,*
        but they are drawn swords.

24  Cast your burden upon the Lord,
    and he will sustain you; *
        he will never let the righteous stumble.

25  For you will bring the bloodthirsty and deceitful *
        down to the pit of destruction, O God.

26    They shall not live out half their days,*
          but I will put my trust in you.

      God of grace, when we are frightened and alone, help us to trust
      you and cast our burdens upon you, that we may be upheld by
      your saving strength. We ask this in the name of Jesus Christ.

# 56

1     Have mercy on me, O God,
      for my enemies are hounding me; *
          all day long they assault and oppress me.

2     They hound me all the day long; *
          truly there are many who fight against me, O Most High.

3     Whenever I am afraid,*
          I will put my trust in you.

4     In God, whose word I praise,
      in God I trust and will not be afraid,*
          for what can flesh do to me?

5     All day long they damage my cause; *
          their only thought is to do me evil.

6     They band together; they lie in wait; *
          they spy upon my footsteps;
          because they seek my life.

7     Shall they escape despite their wickedness? *
          O God, in your anger, cast down the peoples.

8     You have noted my lamentation;
      put my tears into your bottle; *
          are they not recorded in your book?

9     Whenever I call upon you, my enemies will be put to flight; *
          this I know, for God is on my side.

10    In God the Lord, whose word I praise,
      in God I trust and will not be afraid,*
          for what can mortals do to me?

11    I am bound by the vow I made to you, O God; *
      I will present to you thank-offerings;

12    For you have rescued my soul from death and my feet
                      from stumbling,*
      that I may walk before God in the light of the living.

Giver of courage, when our path is hard and dangerous, give
us the grace of quiet confidence. We ask this in the name of
Jesus Christ, the way, the truth, and the life.

# 57

1    Be merciful to me, O God, be merciful,
   for I have taken refuge in you; *
      in the shadow of your wings will I take refuge
      until this time of trouble has gone by.

2    I will call upon the Most High God,*
      the God who maintains my cause.

3    He will send from heaven and save me;
   he will confound those who trample upon me; *
      God will send forth his love and his faithfulness.

4    I lie in the midst of lions that devour the people; *
      their teeth are spears and arrows,
      their tongue a sharp sword.

5    They have laid a net for my feet,
   and I am bowed low; *
      they have dug a pit before me,
      but have fallen into it themselves.

6    Exalt yourself above the heavens, O God,*
      and your glory over all the earth.

7    My heart is firmly fixed, O God, my heart is fixed; *
      I will sing and make melody.

8    Wake up, my spirit;
   awake, lute and harp; *
      I myself will waken the dawn.

9     I will confess you among the peoples, O Lord; *
      I will sing praise to you among the nations.

10    For your loving-kindness is greater than the heavens,*
      and your faithfulness reaches to the clouds.

11    Exalt yourself above the heavens, O God,*
      and your glory over all the earth.

God our help and strength, look with mercy on all who are
oppressed in mind, body, or human dignity. Shield and protect
them, and give them that wholeness which is your will for all
your children. We ask this in the name of Jesus Christ the Lord.

# 58

1     Do you indeed decree righteousness, you rulers? *
      do you judge the peoples with equity?

2     No; you devise evil in your hearts,*
      and your hands deal out violence in the land.

3     The wicked are perverse from the womb; *
      liars go astray from their birth.

4     They are as venomous as a serpent,*
      they are like the deaf adder which stops its ears.

5     Which does not heed the voice of the charmer,*
      no matter how skilful his charming.

6     O God, break their teeth in their mouths; *
      pull the fangs of the young lions, O Lord.

7     Let them vanish like water that runs off; *
      let them wither like trodden grass.

8     Let them be like the snail that melts away,*
      like a stillborn child that never sees the sun.

9     Before they bear fruit, let them be cut down like a brier; *
      like thorns and thistles let them be swept away.

10    The righteous will be glad when they see the vengeance; *
      they will bathe their feet in the blood of the wicked.

11 And they will say,
"Surely, there is a reward for the righteous; *
surely, there is a God who rules in the earth."

God of justice, sweep away all tyranny and violence that
righteousness and equity may prevail among your people.
We ask in the name of Jesus Christ.

# 59

1 Rescue me from my enemies, O God; *
protect me from those who rise up against me.

2 Rescue me from evildoers *
and save me from those who thirst for my blood.

3 See how they lie in wait for my life,
how the mighty gather together against me; *
not for any offence or fault of mine, O Lord.

4 Not because of any guilt of mine *
they run and prepare themselves for battle.

5 Rouse yourself, come to my side, and see; *
for you, Lord God of hosts, are Israel's God.

6 Awake, and punish all the ungodly; *
show no mercy to those who are faithless and evil.

7 They go to and fro in the evening; *
they snarl like dogs and run about the city.

8 Behold, they boast with their mouths,
and taunts are on their lips; *
"For who," they say, "will hear us?"

9 But you, O Lord, you laugh at them; *
you laugh all the ungodly to scorn.

10 My eyes are fixed on you, O my Strength; *
for you, O God, are my stronghold.

11 My merciful God comes to meet me; *
God will let me look in triumph on my enemies.

12  Slay them, O God, lest my people forget; *
        send them reeling by your might
        and put them down, O Lord our shield.

13  For the sins of their mouths, for the words of their lips,
        for the cursing and lies that they utter,*
        let them be caught in their pride.

14  Make an end of them in your wrath; *
        make an end of them, and they shall be no more.

15  Let everyone know that God rules in Jacob,*
        and to the ends of the earth.

16  They go to and fro in the evening; *
        they snarl like dogs and run about the city.

17  They forage for food,*
        and if they are not filled, they howl.

18  For my part, I will sing of your strength; *
        I will celebrate your love in the morning;

19  For you have become my stronghold,*
        a refuge in the day of my trouble.

20  To you, O my Strength, will I sing; *
        for you, O God, are my stronghold and my merciful God.

God of power, deliver us from evil and confirm our trust in you,
that with our rising we may sing of your justice and exult in
your mercy. We ask this in the name of Jesus Christ the Lord.

# 60

1  O God, you have cast us off and broken us; *
        you have been angry;
        oh, take us back to you again.

2  You have shaken the earth and split it open; *
        repair the cracks in it, for it totters.

3  You have made your people know hardship; *
        you have given us wine that makes us stagger.

4    You have set up a banner for those who fear you,*
        to be a refuge from the power of the bow.

5    Save us by your right hand and answer us,*
        that those who are dear to you may be delivered.


6    God spoke from his holy place and said: *
        "I will exult and parcel out Shechem;
        I will divide the valley of Succoth.

7    Gilead is mine and Manasseh is mine; *
        Ephraim is my helmet and Judah my sceptre.

8    Moab is my wash-basin,
        on Edom I throw down my sandal to claim it,*
        and over Philistia will I shout in triumph."

9    Who will lead me into the strong city? *
        who will bring me into Edom?

10   Have you not cast us off, O God? *
        you no longer go out, O God, with our armies.

11   Grant us your help against the enemy,*
        for vain is the help of man.

12   With God we will do valiant deeds,*
        and he shall tread our enemies under foot.


God of mercy, you have called us out of exile and darkness to
be citizens and priests in your kingdom of light. Make us
strong in your cause of steadfast love and justice. We ask this
in the name of our Lord Jesus Christ.


# 61

1    Hear my cry, O God,*
        and listen to my prayer.

2    I call upon you from the ends of the earth
        with heaviness in my heart; *
        set me upon the rock that is higher than I.

3 For you have been my refuge,*
   a strong tower against the enemy.

4 I will dwell in your house for ever; *
   I will take refuge under the cover of your wings.

5 For you, O God, have heard my vows; *
   you have granted me the heritage of those
                     who fear your name.

6 Add length of days to the king's life; *
   let his years extend over many generations.

7 Let him sit enthroned before God for ever; *
   bid love and faithfulness watch over him.

8 So will I always sing the praise of your name,*
   and day by day I will fulfil my vows.


God of our salvation, when we are depressed and fearful,
teach us the way of quiet confidence and hope. We ask this in
the name of Jesus Christ the Lord.


# 62

1 For God alone my soul in silence waits; *
   from him comes my salvation.

2 He alone is my rock and my salvation,*
   my stronghold, so that I shall not be greatly shaken.

3 How long will you assail me to crush me,
   all of you together,*
       as if you were a leaning fence, a toppling wall?

4 They seek only to bring me down from my place of honour; *
   lies are their chief delight.

5 They bless with their lips,*
   but in their hearts they curse.

6 For God alone my soul in silence waits; *
   truly, my hope is in him.

7 He alone is my rock and my salvation,*
   my stronghold, so that I shall not be shaken.

8     In God is my safety and my honour; *
       God is my strong rock and my refuge.

9     Put your trust in him always, O people,*
       pour out your hearts before him, for God is our refuge.

10     Those of high degree are but a fleeting breath,*
       even those of low estate cannot be trusted.

11     On the scales they are lighter than a breath,*
       all of them together.

12     Put no trust in extortion;
       in robbery take no empty pride; *
       though wealth increase, set not your heart upon it.

13     God has spoken once, twice have I heard it,*
       that power belongs to God.

14     Steadfast love is yours, O Lord,*
       for you repay everyone according to his deeds.

Lord God, in a threatening world we look to you as our rock of
hope. Hear us as we pour out our hearts to you, and give us your
grace and protection, through your Son Jesus Christ our Lord.

## 63

1     O God, you are my God; eagerly I seek you; *
       my soul thirsts for you, my flesh faints for you,
       as in a barren and dry land where there is no water.

2     Therefore I have gazed upon you in your holy place,*
       that I might behold your power and your glory.

3     For your loving-kindness is better than life itself; *
       my lips shall give you praise.

4     So will I bless you as long as I live *
       and lift up my hands in your name.

5     My soul is content, as with marrow and fatness,*
       and my mouth praises you with joyful lips,

6     When I remember you upon my bed,*
       and meditate on you in the night watches.

7    For you have been my helper,*
     and under the shadow of your wings I will rejoice.

8    My soul clings to you; *
     your right hand holds me fast.

9    May those who seek my life to destroy it *
     go down into the depths of the earth;

10    Let them fall upon the edge of the sword,*
     and let them be food for jackals.

11    But the king will rejoice in God;
     all those who swear by him will be glad,*
       for the mouth of those who speak lies shall be stopped.

Eternal Love, our hearts are restless until they rest in you. Let
your glory shine on us, that our lives may proclaim your
goodness, our work give you honour, and our voices praise
you forever; for the sake of Jesus Christ our Lord.

# 64

1    Hear my voice, O God, when I complain; *
     protect my life from fear of the enemy.

2    Hide me from the conspiracy of the wicked,*
     from the mob of evildoers.

3    They sharpen their tongue like a sword,*
     and aim their bitter words like arrows,

4    That they may shoot down the blameless from ambush; *
     they shoot without warning and are not afraid.

5    They hold fast to their evil course; *
     they plan how they may hide their snares.

6    They say, "Who will see us?
who will find out our crimes? *
     we have thought out a perfect plot."

7 The human mind and heart are a mystery; *
    but God will loose an arrow at them,
    and suddenly they will be wounded.

8 He will make them trip over their tongues,*
    and all who see them will shake their heads.

9 Everyone will stand in awe and declare God's deeds; *
    they will recognize his works.

10 The righteous will rejoice in the Lord and put their
                      trust in him,*
    and all who are true of heart will glory.

Heavenly Father, you gave your Son victory over those who
plotted evil against him and when he cried to you in his agony,
you delivered him from the fear of his enemies. May those
who suffer with him find refuge in you, for the sake of Jesus
Christ our Lord.

# 65

1 You are to be praised, O God, in Zion; *
    to you shall vows be performed in Jerusalem.

2 To you that hear prayer shall all flesh come,*
    because of their transgressions.

3 Our sins are stronger than we are,*
    but you will blot them out.

4 Happy are they whom you choose
and draw to your courts to dwell there! *
    they will be satisfied by the beauty of your house,
    by the holiness of your temple.

5 Awesome things will you show us in your righteousness,
O God of our salvation,*
    O Hope of all the ends of the earth
    and of the seas that are far away.

6 You make fast the mountains by your power; *
    they are girded about with might.

7  You still the roaring of the seas,*
   the roaring of their waves,
   and the clamour of the peoples.

8  Those who dwell at the ends of the earth will tremble at
                               your marvellous signs; *
   you make the dawn and the dusk to sing for joy.

9  You visit the earth and water it abundantly;
   you make it very plenteous; *
   the river of God is full of water.

10 You prepare the grain,*
   for so you provide for the earth.

11 You drench the furrows and smooth out the ridges; *
   with heavy rain you soften the ground and bless
                               its increase.

12 You crown the year with your goodness,*
   and your paths overflow with plenty.

13 May the fields of the wilderness be rich for grazing,*
   and the hills be clothed with joy.

14 May the meadows cover themselves with flocks,
   and the valleys cloak themselves with grain; *
   let them shout for joy and sing.

Lord God, joy marks your presence; beauty, abundance, and
peace are the tokens of your work in all creation. Work also in
our lives, that by these signs we may see the splendour of your
love and praise you through Jesus Christ our Lord.

# 66

1  Be joyful in God, all you lands; *
   sing the glory of his name;
   sing the glory of his praise.

2  Say to God, "How awesome are your deeds! *
   because of your great strength your enemies
                               cringe before you.

3    All the earth bows down before you,*
     sings to you, sings out your name.''

4    Come now and see the works of God,*
     how wonderful he is in his doing toward all people.

5    He turned the sea into dry land,
   so that they went through the water on foot,*
     and there we rejoiced in him.

6    In his might he rules for ever;
   his eyes keep watch over the nations; *
     let no rebel rise up against him.

7    Bless our God, you peoples; *
     make the voice of his praise to be heard;

8    Who holds our souls in life,*
     and will not allow our feet to slip.

9    For you, O God, have proved us; *
     you have tried us just as silver is tried.

10    You brought us into the snare; *
     you laid heavy burdens upon our backs.

11    You let enemies ride over our heads;
   we went through fire and water; *
     but you brought us out into a place of refreshment.


12    I will enter your house with burnt-offerings
   and will pay you my vows,*
     which I promised with my lips
     and spoke with my mouth when I was in trouble.

13    I will offer you sacrifices of fat beasts
   with the smoke of rams; *
     I will give you oxen and goats.

14    Come and listen, all you who fear God,*
     and I will tell you what he has done for me.

15    I called out to him with my mouth,*
     and his praise was on my tongue.

16    If I had found evil in my heart,*
     the Lord would not have heard me;

17 But in truth God has heard me; *
   he has attended to the voice of my prayer.

18 Blessed be God, who has not rejected my prayer,*
   nor withheld his love from me.

God of power and might, you bring your people out of
darkness and slavery into light and freedom through the
waters of salvation. Receive our sacrifice of praise and
thanksgiving, and keep us always in your steadfast love,
through Jesus Christ our Lord.

# 67

1 May God be merciful to us and bless us,*
   show us the light of his countenance and come to us.

2 Let your ways be known upon earth,*
   your saving health among all nations.

3 Let the peoples praise you, O God; *
   let all the peoples praise you.

4 Let the nations be glad and sing for joy,*
   for you judge the peoples with equity
   and guide all the nations upon earth.

5 Let the peoples praise you, O God; *
   let all the peoples praise you.

6 The earth has brought forth her increase; *
   may God, our own God, give us his blessing.

7 May God give us his blessing,*
   and may all the ends of the earth stand in awe of him.

Blessed are you, Lord our God, light of the earth and health of
the nations; you lead us in the way of justice and mercy,
through Jesus Christ our Lord.

# 68

1 Let God arise, and let his enemies be scattered; *
   let those who hate him flee before him.

2 Let them vanish like smoke when the wind drives it away; *
   as the wax melts at the fire, so let the wicked perish at
          the presence of God.

3 But let the righteous be glad and rejoice before God; *
   let them also be merry and joyful.

4 Sing to God, sing praises to his name;
   exalt him who rides upon the heavens; *
     Yahweh is his name, rejoice before him!

5 Father of orphans, defender of widows,*
   God in his holy habitation!

6 God gives the solitary a home and brings forth prisoners
          into freedom; *
   but the rebels shall live in dry places.

7 O God, when you went forth before your people,*
   when you marched through the wilderness,

8 The earth shook, and the skies poured down rain,
   at the presence of God, the God of Sinai,*
     at the presence of God, the God of Israel.

9 You sent a gracious rain, O God, upon your inheritance; *
   you refreshed the land when it was weary.

10 Your people found their home in it; *
   in your goodness, O God, you have made provision
          for the poor.

11 The Lord gave the word; *
   great was the company of women who bore the tidings:

12 "Kings with their armies are fleeing away; *
   the women at home are dividing the spoils."

13 Though you lingered among the sheepfolds,*
   you shall be like a dove whose wings are
          covered with silver,
   whose feathers are like green gold.

14 When the Almighty scattered kings,*
       it was like snow falling in Zalmon.

15 O mighty mountain, O hill of Bashan! *
       O rugged mountain, O hill of Bashan!

16 Why do you look with envy, O rugged mountain,
   at the hill which God chose for his resting place? *
       truly, the Lord will dwell there for ever.

17 The chariots of God are twenty thousand,
   even thousands of thousands; *
       the Lord comes in holiness from Sinai.

18 You have gone up on high and led captivity captive;
   you have received gifts even from your enemies,*
       that the Lord God might dwell among them.

19 Blessed be the Lord day by day,*
       the God of our salvation, who bears our burdens.

20 He is our God, the God of our salvation; *
       God is the Lord, by whom we escape death.


21 God shall crush the heads of his enemies,*
       and the hairy scalp of those who go on still in their
                                wickedness.

22 The Lord has said, "I will bring them back from Bashan; *
       I will bring them back from the depths of the sea;

23 That your foot may be dipped in blood,*
       the tongues of your dogs in the blood of your enemies."


24 They see your procession, O God,*
       your procession into the sanctuary, my God and my King.

25 The singers go before, musicians follow after,*
       in the midst of maidens playing upon the hand-drums.

26 Bless God in the congregation; *
       bless the Lord, you that are of the fountain of Israel.

27  There is Benjamin, least of the tribes, at the head;
    the princes of Judah in a company; *
        and the princes of Zebulon and Naphtali.

28  Send forth your strength, O God; *
        establish, O God, what you have wrought for us.

29  Kings shall bring gifts to you,*
        for your temple's sake at Jerusalem.

30  Rebuke the wild beast of the reeds,*
        and the peoples, a herd of wild bulls with its calves.

31  Trample down those who lust after silver; *
        scatter the peoples that delight in war.

32  Let tribute be brought out of Egypt; *
        let Ethiopia stretch out her hands to God.

33  Sing to God, O kingdoms of the earth; *
        sing praises to the Lord.

34  He rides in the heavens, the ancient heavens; *
        he sends forth his voice, his mighty voice.

35  Ascribe power to God; *
        his majesty is over Israel;
        his strength is in the skies.

36  How wonderful is God in his holy places! *
        the God of Israel giving strength and power to his people!
        Blessed be God!


Blessed are you, Lord God of truth and justice; you open our
hearts and our mouths to pray and to praise. Guide now our
feet in your holy way, through Jesus Christ our Lord.

# 69

1  Save me, O God,*
        for the waters have risen up to my neck.

2  I am sinking in deep mire,*
        and there is no firm ground for my feet.

3   I have come into deep waters,*
        and the torrent washes over me.

4   I have grown weary with my crying;
    my throat is inflamed; *
        my eyes have failed from looking for my God.

5   Those who hate me without a cause are more than the hairs
                of my head;
        my lying foes who would destroy me are mighty.*
        Must I then give back what I never stole?

6   O God, you know my foolishness,*
        and my faults are not hidden from you.

7   Let not those who hope in you be put to shame through me,
                Lord God of hosts; *
        let not those who seek you be disgraced because of me,
                O God of Israel.

8   Surely, for your sake have I suffered reproach,*
        and shame has covered my face.

9   I have become a stranger to my own kindred,*
        an alien to my mother's children.

10  Zeal for your house has eaten me up; *
        the scorn of those who scorn you has fallen upon me.

11  I humbled myself with fasting,*
        but that was turned to my reproach.

12  I put on sack-cloth also,*
        and became a byword among them.

13  Those who sit at the gate murmur against me,*
        and the drunkards make songs about me.

14  But as for me, this is my prayer to you,*
        at the time you have set, O Lord:

15  "In your great mercy, O God,*
        answer me with your unfailing help.

16  Save me from the mire; do not let me sink; *
        let me be rescued from those who hate me
        and out of the deep waters.

17    Let not the torrent of waters wash over me,
      neither let the deep swallow me up; *
         do not let the Pit shut its mouth upon me.

18    Answer me, O Lord, for your love is kind; *
         in your great compassion, turn to me."

19    "Hide not your face from your servant; *
         be swift and answer me, for I am in distress.

20    Draw near to me and redeem me; *
         because of my enemies deliver me.

21    You know my reproach, my shame, and my dishonour; *
         my adversaries are all in your sight."

22    Reproach has broken my heart, and it cannot be healed; *
         I looked for sympathy, but there was none,
         for comforters, but I could find no one.

23    They gave me gall to eat,*
         and when I was thirsty, they gave me vinegar to drink.

24    Let the table before them be a trap *
         and their sacred feasts a snare.

25    Let their eyes be darkened, that they may not see,*
         and give them continual trembling in their loins.

26    Pour out your indignation upon them,*
         and let the fierceness of your anger overtake them.

27    Let their camp be desolate,*
         and let there be none to dwell in their tents.

28    For they persecute him whom you have stricken *
         and add to the pain of those whom you have pierced.

29    Lay to their charge guilt upon guilt,*
         and let them not receive your vindication.

30    Let them be wiped out of the book of the living *
         and not be written among the righteous.

31 As for me, I am afflicted and in pain; *
   your help, O God, will lift me up on high.

32 I will praise the name of God in song; *
   I will proclaim his greatness with thanksgiving.

33 This will please the Lord more than an offering of oxen,*
   more than bullocks with horns and hoofs.

34 The afflicted shall see and be glad; *
   you who seek God, your heart shall live.

35 For the Lord listens to the needy,*
   and his prisoners he does not despise.

36 Let the heavens and the earth praise him,*
   the seas and all that moves in them;

37 For God will save Zion and rebuild the cities of Judah; *
   they shall live there and have it in possession.

38 The children of his servants will inherit it,*
   and those who love his name will dwell therein.


Blessed are you, God of our hope; you restore the fallen and
rebuild the broken walls. Teach us the song of thanksgiving,
for you are the strength of your people; through Jesus Christ
our Lord.

# 70

1 Be pleased, O God, to deliver me; *
   O Lord, make haste to help me.

2 Let those who seek my life be ashamed
and altogether dismayed; *
   let those who take pleasure in my misfortune
   draw back and be disgraced.

3 Let those who say to me "Aha!" and gloat over
                              me turn back,*
   because they are ashamed.

4   Let all who seek you rejoice and be glad in you; *
     let those who love your salvation say for ever,
    "Great is the Lord!"

5   But as for me, I am poor and needy; *
     come to me speedily, O God.

6   You are my helper and my deliverer; *
     O Lord, do not tarry.

Deliver us, Lord, from every evil, and grant us peace in our
day. In your mercy keep us free from sin and protect us from
all anxiety, as we wait in joyful hope for the coming of your
Son, Jesus Christ our Lord.

# 71

1   In you, O Lord, have I taken refuge; *
     let me never be ashamed.

2   In your righteousness, deliver me and set me free; *
     incline your ear to me and save me.

3   Be my strong rock, a castle to keep me safe; *
     you are my crag and my stronghold.

4   Deliver me, my God, from the hand of the wicked,*
     from the clutches of the evildoer and the oppressor.

5   For you are my hope, O Lord God,*
     my confidence since I was young.

6   I have been sustained by you ever since I was born;
   from my mother's womb you have been my strength; *
     my praise shall be always of you.

7   I have become a portent to many; *
     but you are my refuge and my strength.

8   Let my mouth be full of your praise *
     and your glory all the day long.

9   Do not cast me off in my old age; *
     forsake me not when my strength fails.

10     For my enemies are talking against me,*
      and those who lie in wait for my life take counsel together.

11     They say, "God has forsaken him;
      go after him and seize him; *
      because there is none who will save."

12     O God, be not far from me; *
      come quickly to help me, O my God.

13     Let those who set themselves against me be put to
           shame and be disgraced; *
      let those who seek to do me evil be covered with
           scorn and reproach.

14     But I shall always wait in patience,*
      and shall praise you more and more.

15     My mouth shall recount your mighty acts
      and saving deeds all day long; *
      though I cannot know the number of them.

16     I will begin with the mighty works of the Lord God; *
      I will recall your righteousness, yours alone.

17     O God, you have taught me since I was young,*
      and to this day I tell of your wonderful works.

18     And now that I am old and gray-headed, O God, do not
           forsake me,*
      till I make known your strength to this generation
      and your power to all who are to come.

19     Your righteousness, O God, reaches to the heavens; *
      you have done great things;
      who is like you, O God?

20     You have showed me great troubles and adversities,*
      but you will restore my life
      and bring me up again from the deep places of the earth.

21     You strengthen me more and more; *
      you enfold and comfort me,

22    Therefore I will praise you upon the lyre for your
                  faithfulness, O my God; *
      I will sing to you with the harp, O Holy One of Israel.

23    My lips will sing with joy when I play to you,*
      and so will my soul, which you have redeemed.

24    My tongue will proclaim your righteousness all day long,*
      for they are ashamed and disgraced who sought
                to do me harm.

Holy God, be our strength and our salvation, that we may
never be ashamed to praise you for your mighty acts. We ask
this through Jesus Christ.

# 72

1    Give the king your justice, O God,*
      and your righteousness to the king's son;

2    That he may rule your people righteously *
      and the poor with justice;

3    That the mountains may bring prosperity to the people,*
      and the little hills bring righteousness.

4    He shall defend the needy among the people; *
      he shall rescue the poor and crush the oppressor.

5    He shall live as long as the sun and moon endure,*
      from one generation to another.

6    He shall come down like rain upon the mown field,*
      like showers that water the earth.

7    In his time shall the righteous flourish; *
      there shall be abundance of peace till the moon shall
                be no more.

8    He shall rule from sea to sea,*
      and from the River to the ends of the earth.

9    His foes shall bow down before him,*
      and his enemies lick the dust.

10     The kings of Tarshish and of the isles shall pay tribute,*
       and the kings of Arabia and Saba offer gifts.

11     All kings shall bow down before him,*
       and all the nations do him service.

12     For he shall deliver the poor who cries out in distress,*
       and the oppressed who has no helper.

13     He shall have pity on the lowly and poor; *
       he shall preserve the lives of the needy.

14     He shall redeem their lives from oppression and violence,*
       and dear shall their blood be in his sight.

15     Long may he live!
       and may there be given to him gold from Arabia; *
       may prayer be made for him always,
       and may they bless him all the day long.

16     May there be abundance of grain on the earth,
       growing thick even on the hilltops; *
       may its fruit flourish like Lebanon,
       and its grain like grass upon the earth.

17     May his name remain for ever
       and be established as long as the sun endures; *
       may all the nations bless themselves in him and
                 call him blessed.


18     Blessed be the Lord God, the God of Israel,*
       who alone does wondrous deeds!

19     And blessed be his glorious name for ever! *
       and may all the earth be filled with his glory.
       Amen. Amen.


O God, bring our nation and all nations to a sense of justice
and equity, that poverty, oppression, and violence may vanish
and all may know peace and plenty. We ask this in the name of
Jesus Christ.

## Book Three

# 73

1 Truly, God is good to Israel,*
   to those who are pure in heart.

2 But as for me, my feet had nearly slipped; *
   I had almost tripped and fallen;

3 Because I envied the proud *
   and saw the prosperity of the wicked:

4 For they suffer no pain,*
   and their bodies are sleek and sound;

5 In the misfortunes of others they have no share; *
   they are not afflicted as others are;

6 Therefore they wear their pride like a necklace *
   and wrap their violence about them like a cloak.

7 Their iniquity comes from gross minds,*
   and their hearts overflow with wicked thoughts.

8 They scoff and speak maliciously; *
   out of their haughtiness they plan oppression.

9 They set their mouths against the heavens,*
   and their evil speech runs through the world.

10 And so the people turn to them *
   and find in them no fault.

11 They say, "How should God know? *
   is there knowledge in the Most High?"

12 So then, these are the wicked; *
   always at ease, they increase their wealth.

13 In vain have I kept my heart clean,*
   and washed my hands in innocence.

14 I have been afflicted all day long,*
   and punished every morning.

15 Had I gone on speaking this way,*
   I should have betrayed the generation of your children.

16     When I tried to understand these things,*
       it was too hard for me;

17     Until I entered the sanctuary of God *
       and discerned the end of the wicked.

18     Surely, you set them in slippery places; *
       you cast them down in ruin.

19     Oh, how suddenly do they come to destruction,*
       come to an end, and perish from terror!

20     Like a dream when one awakens, O Lord,*
       when you arise you will make their image vanish.

21     When my mind became embittered,*
       I was sorely wounded in my heart.

22     I was stupid and had no understanding; *
       I was like a brute beast in your presence.

23     Yet I am always with you; *
       you hold me by my right hand.

24     You will guide me by your counsel,*
       and afterwards receive me with glory.

25     Whom have I in heaven but you? *
       and having you I desire nothing upon earth.

26     Though my flesh and my heart should waste away,*
       God is the strength of my heart and my portion for ever.

27     Truly, those who forsake you will perish; *
       you destroy all who are unfaithful.

28     But it is good for me to be near God; *
       I have made the Lord God my refuge.

29     I will speak of all your works *
       in the gates of the city of Zion.


Most High, you know our faithlessness, and our blindness to
the rewards of goodness. Guide us with your counsel and be
the strength of our hearts, that we may not fall but rejoice in
the life of your eternal city; through Jesus Christ our Mediator.

# 74

1 O God, why have you utterly cast us off? *
   why is your wrath so hot against the sheep of your pasture?

2 Remember your congregation that you purchased long ago, *
   the tribe you redeemed to be your inheritance,
   and Mount Zion where you dwell.

3 Turn your steps toward the endless ruins; *
   the enemy has laid waste everything in your sanctuary.

4 Your adversaries roared in your holy place; *
   they set up their banners as tokens of victory.

5 They were like men coming up with axes to a grove of trees; *
   they broke down all your carved work with hatchets
      and hammers.

6 They set fire to your holy place; *
   they defiled the dwelling-place of your name
      and razed it to the ground.

7 They said to themselves, "Let us destroy them altogether." *
   They burned down all the meeting-places of God
      in the land.

8 There are no signs for us to see;
   there is no prophet left; *
      there is not one among us who knows how long.

9 How long, O God, will the adversary scoff? *
   will the enemy blaspheme your name for ever?

10 Why do you draw back your hand? *
   why is your right hand hidden in your bosom?

11 Yet God is my king from ancient times, *
   victorious in the midst of the earth.

12 You divided the sea by your might *
   and shattered the heads of the dragons upon the waters;

13 You crushed the heads of Leviathan *
   and gave him to the people of the desert for food.

14 You split open spring and torrent; *
   you dried up ever-flowing rivers.

15 Yours is the day, yours also the night; *
    you established the moon and the sun.

16 You fixed all the boundaries of the earth; *
    you made both summer and winter.

17 Remember, O Lord, how the enemy scoffed,*
    how a foolish people despised your name.

18 Do not hand over the life of your dove to wild beasts; *
    never forget the lives of your poor.

19 Look upon your covenant; *
    the dark places of the earth are haunts of violence.

20 Let not the oppressed turn away ashamed; *
    let the poor and needy praise your name.

21 Arise, O God, maintain your cause; *
    remember how fools revile you all day long.

22 Forget not the clamour of your adversaries,*
    the unending tumult of those who rise up against you.

O God, when violence threatens and destruction seems at
hand, help us to remember that you maintain your cause and
still rule your universe through Jesus Christ our Saviour.

# 75

1 We give you thanks, O God, we give you thanks,*
    calling upon your name and declaring all your
                wonderful deeds.

2 "I will appoint a time," says God; *
    "I will judge with equity.

3 Though the earth and all its inhabitants are quaking,*
    I will make its pillars fast.

4 I will say to the boasters, 'Boast no more,' *
    and to the wicked, 'Do not toss your horns;

5 Do not toss your horns so high,*
    nor speak with a proud neck.'"

12     He worked marvels in the sight of their forefathers,*
      in the land of Egypt, in the field of Zoan.

13     He split open the sea and let them pass through; *
      he made the waters stand up like walls.

14     He led them with a cloud by day,*
      and all the night through with a glow of fire.

15     He split the hard rocks in the wilderness *
      and gave them drink as from the great deep.

16     He brought streams out of the cliff,*
      and the waters gushed out like rivers.

17     But they went on sinning against him,*
      rebelling in the desert against the Most High.

18     They tested God in their hearts,*
      demanding food for their craving.

19     They railed against God and said,*
      "Can God set a table in the wilderness?

20     True, he struck the rock, the waters gushed out, and the
                   gullies overflowed; *
      but is he able to give bread
      or to provide meat for his people?"

21     When the Lord heard this, he was full of wrath; *
      a fire was kindled against Jacob,
      and his anger mounted against Israel;

22     For they had no faith in God,*
      nor did they put their trust in his saving power.

23     So he commanded the clouds above *
      and opened the doors of heaven.

24     He rained down manna upon them to eat *
      and gave them grain from heaven.

25     So mortals ate the bread of angels; *
      he provided for them food enough.

26     He caused the east wind to blow in the heavens *
      and led out the south wind by his might.

27 He rained down flesh upon them like dust *
    and winged birds like the sand of the sea.

28 He let it fall in the midst of their camp *
    and round about their dwellings.

29 So they ate and were well filled,*
    for he gave them what they craved.

30 But they did not stop their craving,*
    though the food was still in their mouths.

31 So God's anger mounted against them; *
    he slew their strongest men
    and laid low the youth of Israel.

32 In spite of all this, they went on sinning *
    and had no faith in his wonderful works.

33 So he brought their days to an end like a breath *
    and their years in sudden terror.

34 Whenever he slew them, they would seek him,*
    and repent, and diligently search for God.

35 They would remember that God was their rock,*
    and the Most High God their redeemer.

36 But they flattered him with their mouths *
    and lied to him with their tongues.

37 Their heart was not steadfast toward him,*
    and they were not faithful to his covenant.

38 But he was so merciful that he forgave their sins
and did not destroy them; *
    many times he held back his anger
    and did not permit his wrath to be roused.

39 For he remembered that they were but flesh,*
    a breath that goes forth and does not return.

# 78

40    How often the people disobeyed him in the wilderness *
     and offended him in the desert!

41    Again and again they tempted God *
     and provoked the Holy One of Israel.

42    They did not remember his power *
     in the day when he ransomed them from the enemy;

43    How he wrought his signs in Egypt *
     and his omens in the field of Zoan.

44    He turned their rivers into blood,*
     so that they could not drink of their streams.

45    He sent swarms of flies among them, which ate them up,*
     and frogs, which destroyed them.

46    He gave their crops to the caterpillar,*
     the fruit of their toil to the locust.

47    He killed their vines with hail *
     and their sycamores with frost.

48    He delivered their cattle to hailstones *
     and their livestock to hot thunderbolts.

49    He poured out upon them his blazing anger: *
     fury, indignation, and distress,
     a troop of destroying angels.

50    He gave full rein to his anger;
     he did not spare their souls from death; *
     but delivered their lives to the plague.

51    He struck down all the firstborn of Egypt,*
     the flower of manhood in the dwellings of Ham.

52    He led out his people like sheep *
     and guided them in the wilderness like a flock.

53    He led them to safety, and they were not afraid; *
     but the sea overwhelmed their enemies.

54 He brought them to his holy land,*
    the mountain his right hand had won.

55 He drove out the Canaanites before them
    and apportioned an inheritance to them by lot; *
      he made the tribes of Israel to dwell in their tents.

56 But they tested the Most High God, and defied him,*
      and did not keep his commandments.

57 They turned away and were disloyal like their fathers; *
      they were undependable like a warped bow.

58 They grieved him with their hill-altars *
      and provoked his displeasure with their idols.

59 When God heard this, he was angry *
      and utterly rejected Israel.

60 He forsook the shrine at Shiloh,*
      the tabernacle where he had lived among his people.

61 He delivered the ark into captivity,*
      his glory into the adversary's hand.

62 He gave his people to the sword *
      and was angered against his inheritance.

63 The fire consumed their young men; *
      there were no wedding songs for their maidens.

64 Their priests fell by the sword,*
      and their widows made no lamentation.

65 Then the Lord woke as though from sleep,*
      like a warrior refreshed with wine.

66 He struck his enemies on the backside *
      and put them to perpetual shame.

67 He rejected the tent of Joseph *
      and did not choose the tribe of Ephraim;

68 He chose instead the tribe of Judah *
      and Mount Zion, which he loved.

69   He built his sanctuary like the heights of heaven,*
      like the earth which he founded for ever.

70   He chose David his servant,*
      and took him away from the sheepfolds.

71   He brought him from following the ewes,*
      to be a shepherd over Jacob his people
      and over Israel his inheritance.

72   So he shepherded them with a faithful and true heart *
      and guided them with the skilfulness of his hands.

God of pilgrims, strengthen our faith, we pray. Guide us
through the uncertainties of our journey, and hold before us
the vision of your eternal kingdom, made known to us in Jesus
Christ our Lord.

# 79

1   O God, the heathen have come into your inheritance;
    they have profaned your holy temple; *
      they have made Jerusalem a heap of rubble.

2   They have given the bodies of your servants as food for
         the birds of the air,*
      and the flesh of your faithful ones to the beasts
         of the field.

3   They have shed their blood like water on every side
         of Jerusalem,*
      and there was no one to bury them.

4   We have become a reproach to our neighbours,*
      an object of scorn and derision to those around us.

5   How long will you be angry, O Lord? *
      will your fury blaze like fire for ever?

6   Pour out your wrath upon the heathen who have not
         known you *
      and upon the kingdoms that have not called upon
         your name.

7 For they have devoured Jacob *
    and made his dwelling a ruin.

8 Remember not our past sins;
    let your compassion be swift to meet us; *
      for we have been brought very low.

9 Help us, O God our Saviour, for the glory of your name; *
    deliver us and forgive us our sins, for your name's sake.

10 Why should the heathen say, "Where is their God?" *
    Let it be known among the heathen and in our sight
      that you avenge the shedding of your servants' blood.

11 Let the sorrowful sighing of the prisoners come before you,*
    and by your great might spare those who are
                   condemned to die.

12 May the revilings with which they reviled you, O Lord,*
    return seven-fold into their bosoms.

13 For we are your people and the sheep of your pasture; *
    we will give you thanks for ever
    and show forth your praise from age to age.

Gracious God, in times of sorrow and depression, when hope
itself seems lost, help us to remember the transforming power
of your steadfast love and to give thanks for that new life we
cannot now imagine. We ask this in the name of Jesus Christ
our Saviour.

# 80

1 Hear, O Shepherd of Israel, leading Joseph like a flock; *
    shine forth, you that are enthroned upon the cherubim.

2 In the presence of Ephraim, Benjamin, and Manasseh,*
    stir up your strength and come to help us.

3 Restore us, O God of hosts; *
    show the light of your countenance, and we shall be saved.

4   O Lord God of hosts,*
        how long will you be angered
        despite the prayers of your people?

5   You have fed them with the bread of tears; *
        you have given them bowls of tears to drink.

6   You have made us the derision of our neighbours,*
        and our enemies laugh us to scorn.

7   Restore us, O God of hosts; *
        show the light of your countenance, and we shall be saved.


8   You have brought a vine out of Egypt; *
        you cast out the nations and planted it.

9   You prepared the ground for it; *
        it took root and filled the land.

10  The mountains were covered by its shadow *
        and the towering cedar trees by its boughs.

11  You stretched out its tendrils to the Sea *
        and its branches to the River.

12  Why have you broken down its wall,*
        so that all who pass by pluck off its grapes?

13  The wild boar of the forest has ravaged it,*
        and the beasts of the field have grazed upon it.

14  Turn now, O God of hosts, look down from heaven;
    behold and tend this vine; *
        preserve what your right hand has planted.

15  They burn it with fire like rubbish; *
        at the rebuke of your countenance let them perish.

16  Let your hand be upon the man of your right hand,*
        the son of man you have made so strong for yourself.

17  And so will we never turn away from you; *
        give us life, that we may call upon your name.

18  Restore us, O Lord God of hosts; *
        show the light of your countenance, and we shall be saved.

Glory to you, Lord Jesus Christ, our good shepherd; you have led us to the kingdom of your Father's love. Forgive our careless indifference to your loving care for all your creatures, and remake us in the likeness of your new and risen life. We ask this in your name.

# 81

1 Sing with joy to God our strength *
    and raise a loud shout to the God of Jacob.

2 Raise a song and sound the timbrel,*
    the merry harp, and the lyre.

3 Blow the ram's-horn at the new moon,*
    and at the full moon, the day of our feast.

4 For this is a statute for Israel,*
    a law of the God of Jacob.

5 He laid it as a solemn charge upon Joseph,*
    when he came out of the land of Egypt.

6 I heard an unfamiliar voice saying,*
    "I eased his shoulder from the burden;
    his hands were set free from bearing the load."

7 You called on me in trouble, and I saved you; *
    I answered you from the secret place of thunder
    and tested you at the waters of Meribah.

8 Hear, O my people, and I will admonish you: *
    O Israel, if you would but listen to me!

9 There shall be no strange god among you; *
    you shall not worship a foreign god.

10 I am the Lord your God,
    who brought you out of the land of Egypt and said,*
    "Open your mouth wide, and I will fill it."

11 And yet my people did not hear my voice,*
    and Israel would not obey me.

12 So I gave them over to the stubbornness of their hearts,*
    to follow their own devices.

13  Oh, that my people would listen to me! *
        that Israel would walk in my ways!

14  I should soon subdue their enemies *
        and turn my hand against their foes.

15  Those who hate the Lord would cringe before him,*
        and their punishment would last for ever.

16  But Israel would I feed with the finest wheat *
        and satisfy him with honey from the rock.


Father, forgive our foolish ways, and feed us always with that
living bread which is given for the life of the world, your Son
Jesus Christ our Lord.


# 82

1  God takes his stand in the council of heaven; *
        he gives judgement in the midst of the gods:

2  "How long will you judge unjustly,*
        and show favour to the wicked?

3  Save the weak and the orphan; *
        defend the humble and needy;

4  Rescue the weak and the poor; *
        deliver them from the power of the wicked.

5  They do not know, neither do they understand;
    they go about in darkness; *
        all the foundations of the earth are shaken.

6  Now I say to you, 'You are gods,*
        and all of you children of the Most High;

7  Nevertheless, you shall die like mortals,*
        and fall like any prince.'"

8  Arise, O God, and rule the earth,*
        for you shall take all nations for your own.

Strength of the weak, Defender of the needy, Rescuer of the poor, deliver us from the power of wickedness, that we may rejoice in your justice now and forever, through Jesus Christ our Lord.

## 83

1 O God, do not be silent; *
  do not keep still nor hold your peace, O God;

2 For your enemies are in tumult,*
  and those who hate you have lifted up their heads.

3 They take secret counsel against your people *
  and plot against those whom you protect.

4 They have said, "Come, let us wipe them out from among
      the nations; *
  let the name of Israel be remembered no more."

5 They have conspired together; *
  they have made an alliance against you:

6 The tents of Edom and the Ishmaelites; *
  the Moabites and the Hagarenes;

7 Gebal, and Ammon, and Amalek; *
  the Philistines and those who dwell in Tyre.

8 The Assyrians also have joined them,*
  and have come to help the people of Lot.

9 Do to them as you did to Midian,*
  to Sisera, and to Jabin at the river of Kishon:

10 They were destroyed at Endor; *
  they became like dung upon the ground.

11 Make their leaders like Oreb and Zeëb,*
  and all their commanders like Zebah and Zalmunna,

12 Who said, "Let us take for ourselves *
  the fields of God as our possession."

13 O my God, make them like whirling dust *
  and like chaff before the wind;

14 Like fire that burns down a forest,*
  like the flame that sets mountains ablaze.

15 Drive them with your tempest *
    and terrify them with your storm;

16 Cover their faces with shame, O Lord,*
    that they may seek your name.

17 Let them be disgraced and terrified for ever; *
    let them be put to confusion and perish.

18 Let them know that you, whose name is Yahweh,*
    you alone are the Most High over all the earth.

Lord, dispel from us the error of pride and the illusions of
greatness, and help us to abandon every vice and stand in awe
of you, for you alone are the Most High over all the world now
and for ever.

# 84

1 How dear to me is your dwelling, O Lord of hosts! *
    My soul has a desire and longing for the courts of
                the Lord;
    my heart and my flesh rejoice in the living God.

2 The sparrow has found her a house
  and the swallow a nest where she may lay her young; *
    by the side of your altars, O Lord of hosts,
    my King and my God.

3 Happy are they who dwell in your house! *
    they will always be praising you.

4 Happy are the people whose strength is in you! *
    whose hearts are set on the pilgrims' way.

5 Those who go through the desolate valley will find
                it a place of springs,*
    for the early rains have covered it with pools of water.

6 They will climb from height to height,*
    and the God of gods will reveal himself in Zion.

7 Lord God of hosts, hear my prayer; *
    hearken, O God of Jacob.

8     Behold our defender, O God; *
       and look upon the face of your anointed.

9     For one day in your courts is better than
                   a thousand in my own room,*
       and to stand at the threshold of the house of my God
       than to dwell in the tents of the wicked.

10    For the Lord God is both sun and shield; *
       he will give grace and glory;

11    No good thing will the Lord withhold *
       from those who walk with integrity.

12    O Lord of hosts,*
       happy are they who put their trust in you!

God of pilgrims, teach us to recognize your dwelling-place in
the love, generosity, and support of those with whom we
share our journey, and help us to worship you in our response
to those who need our care; for all the world is your temple
and every human heart is a sign of your presence, made
known to us in Jesus Christ our Lord.

# 85

1     You have been gracious to your land, O Lord,*
       you have restored the good fortune of Jacob.

2     You have forgiven the iniquity of your people *
       and blotted out all their sins.

3     You have withdrawn all your fury *
       and turned yourself from your wrathful indignation.

4     Restore us then, O God our Saviour; *
       let your anger depart from us.

5     Will you be displeased with us for ever? *
       will you prolong your anger from age to age?

6     Will you not give us life again,*
       that your people may rejoice in you?

7 Show us your mercy, O Lord,*
  and grant us your salvation.

8 I will listen to what the Lord God is saying,*
  for he is speaking peace to his faithful people
  and to those who turn their hearts to him.

9 Truly, his salvation is very near to those who fear him,*
  that his glory may dwell in our land.

10 Mercy and truth have met together; *
  righteousness and peace have kissed each other.

11 Truth shall spring up from the earth,*
  and righteousness shall look down from heaven.

12 The Lord will indeed grant prosperity,*
  and our land will yield its increase.

13 Righteousness shall go before him,*
  and peace shall be a pathway for his feet.

God of grace, you loved the world so much that you gave your
only Son to be our Saviour. Help us to rejoice in our salvation
by showing mercy and truth, and by walking in the way of
righteousness and peace. We ask this in his name and for his sake.

# 86

1 Bow down your ear, O Lord, and answer me,*
  for I am poor and in misery.

2 Keep watch over my life, for I am faithful; *
  save your servant who puts his trust in you.

3 Be merciful to me, O Lord, for you are my God; *
  I call upon you all the day long.

4 Gladden the soul of your servant,*
  for to you, O Lord, I lift up my soul.

5 For you, O Lord, are good and forgiving,*
  and great is your love toward all who call upon you.

6     Give ear, O Lord, to my prayer,*
      and attend to the voice of my supplications.

7     In the time of my trouble I will call upon you,*
      for you will answer me.

8     Among the gods there is none like you, O Lord,*
      nor anything like your works.

9     All nations you have made will come and
                    worship you, O Lord,*
      and glorify your name.

10    For you are great;
      you do wondrous things; *
      and you alone are God.

11    Teach me your way, O Lord,
      and I will walk in your truth; *
      knit my heart to you that I may fear your name.

12    I will thank you, O Lord my God, with all my heart,*
      and glorify your name for evermore.

13    For great is your love toward me; *
      you have delivered me from the nethermost Pit.

14    The arrogant rise up against me, O God,
      and a band of violent men seeks my life; *
      they have not set you before their eyes.

15    But you, O Lord, are gracious and full of compassion,*
      slow to anger, and full of kindness and truth.

16    Turn to me and have mercy upon me; *
      give your strength to your servant;
      and save the child of your handmaid.

17    Show me a sign of your favour,
      so that those who hate me may see it and be ashamed; *
      because you, O Lord, have helped me and comforted me.

God of mercy, fill us with the love of your name, and help
us to proclaim you before the world, that all peoples may
celebrate your glory in Jesus Christ our Lord.

# 87

1   On the holy mountain stands the city he has founded; *
        the Lord loves the gates of Zion
        more than all the dwellings of Jacob.

2   Glorious things are spoken of you,*
        O city of our God.

3   I count Egypt and Babylon among those who know me; *
        behold Philistia, Tyre, and Ethiopia:
        in Zion were they born.

4   Of Zion it shall be said, "Everyone was born in her,*
        and the Most High himself shall sustain her."

5   The Lord will record as he enrolls the peoples,*
        "These also were born there."

6   The singers and the dancers will say,*
        "All my fresh springs are in you."

God of eternal light, open our eyes to the vision of your holy
city coming down from heaven; make our hearts sensitive to
your presence, and our wills eager to join in the comfort and
healing you bring to all the world. We ask this in the name of
Jesus Christ the Lord.

# 88

1   O Lord, my God, my Saviour,*
        by day and night I cry to you.

2   Let my prayer enter into your presence; *
        incline your ear to my lamentation.

3   For I am full of trouble; *
        my life is at the brink of the grave.

4   I am counted among those who go down to the Pit; *
        I have become like one who has no strength;

5   Lost among the dead,*
        like the slain who lie in the grave,

6   Whom you remember no more,*
       for they are cut off from your hand.

7   You have laid me in the depths of the Pit,*
       in dark places, and in the abyss.

8   Your anger weighs upon me heavily,*
       and all your great waves overwhelm me.

9   You have put my friends far from me;
    you have made me to be abhorred by them; *
       I am in prison and cannot get free.

10  My sight has failed me because of trouble; *
       Lord, I have called upon you daily;
       I have stretched out my hands to you.

11  Do you work wonders for the dead? *
       will those who have died stand up and give you thanks?

12  Will your loving-kindness be declared in the grave? *
       your faithfulness in the land of destruction?

13  Will your wonders be known in the dark? *
       or your righteousness in the country where all
                              is forgotten?

14  But as for me, O Lord, I cry to you for help; *
       in the morning my prayer comes before you.

15  Lord, why have you rejected me? *
       why have you hidden your face from me?

16  Ever since my youth, I have been wretched and at the
                              point of death; *
       I have borne your terrors with a troubled mind.

17  Your blazing anger has swept over me; *
       your terrors have destroyed me;

18  They surround me all day long like a flood; *
       they encompass me on every side.

19  My friend and my neighbour you have put away from me,*
       and darkness is my only companion.

O Lord, when we are plunged into the darkness of despair,
make known to us the wonders of your grace, for you alone are
God and from you comes all our help and strength. We ask this
in the name of Jesus Christ.

# 89

**Part I**

1   Your love, O Lord, for ever will I sing; *
    from age to age my mouth will proclaim your faithfulness.

2   For I am persuaded that your love is established for ever; *
    you have set your faithfulness firmly in the heavens.

3   "I have made a covenant with my chosen one; *
    I have sworn an oath to David my servant:

4   'I will establish your line for ever,*
    and preserve your throne for all generations.'"

5   The heavens bear witness to your wonders, O Lord,*
    and to your faithfulness in the assembly of the holy ones;

6   For who in the skies can be compared to the Lord? *
    who is like the Lord among the gods?

7   God is much to be feared in the council of the holy ones,*
    great and terrible to all those round about him.

8   Who is like you, Lord God of hosts? *
    O mighty Lord, your faithfulness is all around you.

9   You rule the raging of the sea *
    and still the surging of its waves.

10   You have crushed Rahab of the deep with a deadly wound; *
    you have scattered your enemies with your mighty arm.

11   Yours are the heavens; the earth also is yours; *
    you laid the foundations of the world and all that is in it.

12   You have made the north and the south; *
    Tabor and Hermon rejoice in your name.

13   You have a mighty arm; *
    strong is your hand and high is your right hand.

14 Righteousness and justice are the foundations of
your throne; *
love and truth go before your face.

15 Happy are the people who know the festal shout! *
they walk, O Lord, in the light of your presence.

16 They rejoice daily in your name; *
they are jubilant in your righteousness.

17 For you are the glory of their strength,*
and by your favour our might is exalted.

18 Truly, the Lord is our ruler; *
the Holy One of Israel is our king.

# 89

**Part II**

19 You spoke once in a vision and said to your faithful people: *
"I have set the crown upon a warrior
and have exalted one chosen out of the people.

20 I have found David my servant; *
with my holy oil have I anointed him.

21 My hand will hold him fast *
and my arm will make him strong.

22 No enemy shall deceive him,*
nor any wicked man bring him down.

23 I will crush his foes before him *
and strike down those who hate him.

24 My faithfulness and love shall be with him,*
and he shall be victorious through my name.

25 I shall make his dominion extend *
from the Great Sea to the River.

26 He will say to me, 'You are my Father,*
my God, and the rock of my salvation.'

27 I will make him my firstborn *
and higher than the kings of the earth.

28   I will keep my love for him for ever,*
        and my covenant will stand firm for him.

29   I will establish his line for ever *
        and his throne as the days of heaven.

30   If his children forsake my law *
        and do not walk according to my judgements;

31   If they break my statutes *
        and do not keep my commandments;

32   I will punish their transgressions with a rod *
        and their iniquities with the lash;

33   But I will not take my love from him,*
        nor let my faithfulness prove false.

34   I will not break my covenant,*
        nor change what has gone out of my lips.

35   Once for all I have sworn by my holiness: *
        'I will not lie to David.

36   His line shall endure for ever *
        and his throne as the sun before me;

37   It shall stand fast for evermore like the moon,*
        the abiding witness in the sky.'''

38   But you have cast off and rejected your anointed; *
        you have become enraged at him.

39   You have broken your covenant with your servant,*
        defiled his crown, and hurled it to the ground.

40   You have breached all his walls *
        and laid his strongholds in ruins.

41   All who pass by despoil him; *
        he has become the scorn of his neighbours.

42   You have exalted the right hand of his foes *
        and made all his enemies rejoice.

43   You have turned back the edge of his sword *
        and have not sustained him in battle.

44 You have put an end to his splendour *
    and cast his throne to the ground.

45 You have cut short the days of his youth *
    and have covered him with shame.

46 How long will you hide yourself, O Lord?
will you hide yourself for ever? *
    how long will your anger burn like fire?

47 Remember, Lord, how short life is,*
    how frail you have made all flesh.

48 Who can live and not see death? *
    who can save himself from the power of the grave?

49 Where, Lord, are your loving-kindnesses of old,*
    which you promised David in your faithfulness?

50 Remember, Lord, how your servant is mocked,*
    how I carry in my bosom the taunts of many peoples,

51 The taunts your enemies have hurled, O Lord,*
    which they hurled at the heels of your anointed.

52 Blessed be the Lord for evermore! *
    Amen, I say, Amen.

Remember us, gracious God, when we cannot see your way
and purpose, and renew in us the joy of your kingdom of light
and life. We ask this in the name of Jesus Christ the Lord.

**Book Four**

# 90

1 Lord, you have been our refuge *
    from one generation to another.

2 Before the mountains were brought forth,
or the land and the earth were born,*
    from age to age you are God.

3 You turn us back to the dust and say,*
    "Go back, O child of earth."

4   For a thousand years in your sight are like yesterday
                when it is past *
        and like a watch in the night.

5   You sweep us away like a dream; *
        we fade away suddenly like the grass.

6   In the morning it is green and flourishes; *
        in the evening it is dried up and withered.

7   For we consume away in your displeasure; *
        we are afraid because of your wrathful indignation.

8   Our iniquities you have set before you,*
        and our secret sins in the light of your countenance.

9   When you are angry, all our days are gone; *
        we bring our years to an end like a sigh.

10  The span of our life is seventy years,
        perhaps in strength even eighty; *
            yet the sum of them is but labour and sorrow,
            for they pass away quickly and we are gone.

11  Who regards the power of your wrath? *
        who rightly fears your indignation?

12  So teach us to number our days *
        that we may apply our hearts to wisdom.


13  Return, O Lord; how long will you tarry? *
        be gracious to your servants.

14  Satisfy us by your loving-kindness in the morning; *
        so shall we rejoice and be glad all the days of our life.

15  Make us glad by the measure of the days that you
                afflicted us *
        and the years in which we suffered adversity.

16  Show your servants your works *
        and your splendour to their children.

17  May the graciousness of the Lord our God be upon us; *
        prosper the work of our hands;
        prosper our handiwork.

Eternal Father of our mortal race, in Jesus Christ your grace has come upon us. For his sake, prosper the work of our hands until he returns to gladden our hearts forever.

# 91

1 He who dwells in the shelter of the Most High,*
    abides under the shadow of the Almighty.

2 He shall say to the Lord,
"You are my refuge and my stronghold,*
    my God in whom I put my trust."

3 He shall deliver you from the snare of the hunter *
    and from the deadly pestilence.

4 He shall cover you with his pinions,
and you shall find refuge under his wings; *
    his faithfulness shall be a shield and buckler.

5 You shall not be afraid of any terror by night,*
    nor of the arrow that flies by day;

6 Of the plague that stalks in the darkness,*
    nor of the sickness that lays waste at mid-day.

7 A thousand shall fall at your side
and ten thousand at your right hand,*
    but it shall not come near you.

8 Your eyes have only to behold *
    to see the reward of the wicked.

9 Because you have made the Lord your refuge,*
    and the Most High your habitation.

10 There shall no evil happen to you,*
    neither shall any plague come near your dwelling.

11 For he shall give his angels charge over you,*
    to keep you in all your ways.

12 They shall bear you in their hands,*
    lest you dash your foot against a stone.

13 You shall tread upon the lion and adder; *
    you shall trample the young lion and the serpent
                        under your feet.

14 Because he is bound to me in love,
    therefore will I deliver him; *
        I will protect him, because he knows my name.

15 He shall call upon me, and I will answer him; *
        I am with him in trouble;
        I will rescue him and bring him to honour.

16 With long life will I satisfy him,*
        and show him my salvation.

Gracious God, in times of anxiety and stress, teach us to wait
in quietness for your protection and defence, made known to
us in Jesus Christ our Lord.

# 92

1 It is a good thing to give thanks to the Lord,*
        and to sing praises to your name, O Most High;

2 To tell of your loving-kindness early in the morning *
        and of your faithfulness in the night season;

3 On the psaltery, and on the lyre,*
        and to the melody of the harp.

4 For you have made me glad by your acts, O Lord; *
        and I shout for joy because of the works of your hands.

5 Lord, how great are your works! *
        your thoughts are very deep.

6 The dullard does not know,
    nor does the fool understand,*
        that though the wicked grow like weeds,
        and all the workers of iniquity flourish,

7 They flourish only to be destroyed for ever; *
        but you, O Lord, are exalted for evermore.

8 For lo, your enemies, O Lord,
    lo, your enemies shall perish,*
        and all the workers of iniquity shall be scattered.

9 But my horn you have exalted like the horns of wild bulls; *
    I am anointed with fresh oil.

10 My eyes also gloat over my enemies,*
    and my ears rejoice to hear the doom of the wicked who
                rise up against me.

11 The righteous shall flourish like a palm tree,*
    and shall spread abroad like a cedar of Lebanon.

12 Those who are planted in the house of the Lord *
    shall flourish in the courts of our God;

13 They shall still bear fruit in old age; *
    they shall be green and succulent;

14 That they may show how upright the Lord is,*
    my rock, in whom there is no fault.


O Most High, at all times and in all seasons you are worthy
of our grateful praise; grant us the insight to perceive the
greatness of your works, the certainty of being founded on you
our eternal rock, and the wisdom to sing the praises of your
name, in and through Jesus Christ our Lord.


# 93

1 The Lord is king;
    he has put on splendid apparel; *
        the Lord has put on his apparel
        and girded himself with strength.

2 He has made the whole world so sure *
    that it cannot be moved;

3 Ever since the world began, your throne has
                    been established; *
    you are from everlasting.

4   The waters have lifted up, O Lord,
      the waters have lifted up their voice; *
        the waters have lifted up their pounding waves.

5   Mightier than the sound of many waters,
      mightier than the breakers of the sea,*
        mightier is the Lord who dwells on high.

6   Your testimonies are very sure,*
      and holiness adorns your house, O Lord,
        for ever and for evermore.

Blessed are you, Lord God, king of the universe; in awe and
wonder we bow before the mystery of your power and might,
for you are Lord for ever and ever.

# 94

1   O Lord God of vengeance,*
      O God of vengeance, show yourself.

2   Rise up, O Judge of the world; *
      give the arrogant their just deserts.

3   How long shall the wicked, O Lord,*
      how long shall the wicked triumph?

4   They bluster in their insolence; *
      all evildoers are full of boasting.

5   They crush your people, O Lord,*
      and afflict your chosen nation.

6   They murder the widow and the stranger *
      and put the orphans to death.

7   Yet they say, "The Lord does not see,*
      the God of Jacob takes no notice."

8   Consider well, you dullards among the people; *
      when will you fools understand?

9   He that planted the ear, does he not hear? *
      he that formed the eye, does he not see?

10    He who admonishes the nations, will he not punish? *
      he who teaches all the world, has he no knowledge?

11    The Lord knows our human thoughts; *
      how like a puff of wind they are.

12    Happy are they whom you instruct, O Lord! *
      whom you teach out of your law;

13    To give them rest in evil days,*
      until a pit is dug for the wicked.

14    For the Lord will not abandon his people,*
      nor will he forsake his own.

15    For judgement will again be just,*
      and all the true of heart will follow it.

16    Who rose up for me against the wicked? *
      who took my part against the evildoers?

17    If the Lord had not come to my help,*
      I should soon have dwelt in the land of silence.

18    As often as I said, "My foot has slipped," *
      your love, O Lord, upheld me.

19    When many cares fill my mind,*
      your consolations cheer my soul.

20    Can a corrupt tribunal have any part with you,*
      one which frames evil into law?

21    They conspire against the life of the just *
      and condemn the innocent to death.

22    But the Lord has become my stronghold,*
      and my God the rock of my trust.

23    He will turn their wickedness back upon them
and destroy them in their own malice; *
      the Lord our God will destroy them.

O just Judge of all the world, when the dark power of evil
threatens your creation, may we, through your strength within
us, maintain the sure knowledge of your love and mercy,
which we see in your Son Jesus Christ our Lord.

# 95

1　Come, let us sing to the Lord; *
　　let us shout for joy to the rock of our salvation.

2　Let us come before his presence with thanksgiving *
　　and raise a loud shout to him with psalms.

3　For the Lord is a great God,*
　　and a great king above all gods.

4　In his hand are the caverns of the earth,*
　　and the heights of the hills are his also.

5　The sea is his, for he made it,*
　　and his hands have molded the dry land.

6　Come, let us bow down, and bend the knee,*
　　and kneel before the Lord our Maker.

7　For he is our God,
　　and we are the people of his pasture and the
　　　　　　　　　　sheep of his hand.*
　　Oh, that today you would hearken to his voice!


8　Harden not your hearts,
　　as your forebears did in the wilderness,*
　　　at Meribah, and on that day at Massah,
　　　when they tempted me.

9　They put me to the test,*
　　though they had seen my works.

10　Forty years long I detested that generation and said,*
　　"This people are wayward in their hearts;
　　they do not know my ways."

11　So I swore in my wrath,*
　　"They shall not enter into my rest."


Creator of all, we give you thanks for a world full of wonder,
but above all because you have called us into a holy fellowship
with you and with each other. Guide us in the ways of this your
new creation, rooted and grounded in Jesus Christ our Lord.

# 96

1    Sing to the Lord a new song; *
     sing to the Lord, all the whole earth.

2    Sing to the Lord and bless his name; *
     proclaim the good news of his salvation from day to day.

3    Declare his glory among the nations *
     and his wonders among all peoples.

4    For great is the Lord and greatly to be praised; *
     he is more to be feared than all gods.

5    As for all the gods of the nations, they are but idols; *
     but it is the Lord who made the heavens.

6    Oh, the majesty and magnificence of his presence! *
     Oh, the power and the splendour of his sanctuary!

7    Ascribe to the Lord, you families of the peoples; *
     ascribe to the Lord honour and power.

8    Ascribe to the Lord the honour due his name; *
     bring offerings and come into his courts.

9    Worship the Lord in the beauty of holiness; *
     let the whole earth tremble before him.

10   Tell it out among the nations: "The Lord is king! *
     he has made the world so firm that it cannot be moved;
     he will judge the peoples with equity."

11   Let the heavens rejoice, and let the earth be glad;
     let the sea thunder and all that is in it; *
     let the field be joyful and all that is therein.

12   Then shall all the trees of the wood shout for joy
     before the Lord when he comes,*
     when he comes to judge the earth.

13   He will judge the world with righteousness *
     and the peoples with his truth.

We worship you, God of glory, in the beauty of holiness, and
we joyfully proclaim your just and righteous rule, established
for all, through your Son Jesus Christ the Lord.

# 97

1   The Lord is king;
    let the earth rejoice; *
        let the multitude of the isles be glad.

2   Clouds and darkness are round about him,*
        righteousness and justice are the foundations of his throne.

3   A fire goes before him *
        and burns up his enemies on every side.

4   His lightnings light up the world; *
        the earth sees it and is afraid.

5   The mountains melt like wax at the presence of the Lord,*
        at the presence of the Lord of the whole earth.

6   The heavens declare his righteousness,*
        and all the peoples see his glory.

7   Confounded be all who worship carved images
    and delight in false gods! *
        Bow down before him, all you gods.

8   Zion hears and is glad, and the cities of Judah rejoice,*
        because of your judgements, O Lord.

9   For you are the Lord,
    most high over all the earth; *
        you are exalted far above all gods.

10  The Lord loves those who hate evil; *
        he preserves the lives of his saints
        and delivers them from the hand of the wicked.

11  Light has sprung up for the righteous,*
        and joyful gladness for those who are truehearted.

12  Rejoice in the Lord, you righteous,*
        and give thanks to his holy name.


Almighty God, your whole creation declares your glory. May
we perceive you in all your works and live in the light of your
righteousness, through him who is the light of the world, Jesus
Christ our Lord.

# 98

1   Sing to the Lord a new song,*
        for he has done marvellous things.

2   With his right hand and his holy arm *
        has he won for himself the victory.

3   The Lord has made known his victory; *
        his righteousness has he openly shown in
                the sight of the nations.

4   He remembers his mercy and faithfulness to
                the house of Israel,*
        and all the ends of the earth have seen the
                victory of our God.

5   Shout with joy to the Lord, all you lands; *
        lift up your voice, rejoice, and sing.

6   Sing to the Lord with the harp,*
        with the harp and the voice of song.

7   With trumpets and the sound of the horn *
        shout with joy before the King, the Lord.

8   Let the sea make a noise and all that is in it,*
        the lands and those who dwell therein.

9   Let the rivers clap their hands,*
        and let the hills ring out with joy before the Lord,
        when he comes to judge the earth.

10  In righteousness shall he judge the world *
        and the peoples with equity.

Lord God, we see your righteous rule in all your works, and
we join our voices with the song of your whole creation in
praising you, in and through Jesus Christ our Saviour.

# 99

1 The Lord is king;
  let the people tremble; *
      he is enthroned upon the Cherubim;
      let the earth shake.

2 The Lord is great in Zion; *
      he is high above all peoples.

3 Let them confess his name, which is great and awesome; *
      he is the Holy One.

4 "O mighty King, lover of justice,
  you have established equity; *
      you have executed justice and righteousness in Jacob."

5 Proclaim the greatness of the Lord our God
  and fall down before his footstool; *
      he is the Holy One.

6 Moses and Aaron among his priests,
  and Samuel among those who call upon his name,*
      they called upon the Lord, and he answered them.

7 He spoke to them out of the pillar of cloud; *
      they kept his testimonies and the decree that he gave them.

8 "O Lord our God, you answered them indeed; *
      you were a God who forgave them,
      yet punished them for their evil deeds."

9 Proclaim the greatness of the Lord our God
  and worship him upon his holy hill; *
      for the Lord our God is the Holy One.


Lord our God, ruler of the universe, you love what is right.
Lead us in your righteousness, that we may live to praise you,
through your Son Jesus Christ our Lord.

# 100

1   Be joyful in the Lord, all you lands; *
        serve the Lord with gladness
        and come before his presence with a song.

2   Know this: The Lord himself is God; *
        he himself has made us, and we are his;
        we are his people and the sheep of his pasture.

3   Enter his gates with thanksgiving;
    go into his courts with praise; *
        give thanks to him and call upon his name.

4   For the Lord is good;
    his mercy is everlasting; *
        and his faithfulness endures from age to age.

God our Father, you have created us as your people, and you
sustain us with your hand. Help us always to give you thanks,
for you alone are worthy of thanksgiving and praise and
honour, now and for ever.

# 101

1   I will sing of mercy and justice; *
        to you, O Lord, will I sing praises.

2   I will strive to follow a blameless course;
    oh, when will you come to me? *
        I will walk with sincerity of heart within my house.

3   I will set no worthless thing before my eyes; *
        I hate the doers of evil deeds;
        they shall not remain with me.

4   A crooked heart shall be far from me; *
        I will not know evil.

5   Those who in secret slander their neighbours I will destroy; *
        those who have a haughty look and a proud
                                    heart I cannot abide.

6    My eyes are upon the faithful in the land, that they may
                    dwell with me,*
     and only those who lead a blameless life shall
                    be my servants.

7    Those who act deceitfully shall not dwell in my house,*
     and those who tell lies shall not continue in my sight.

8    I will soon destroy all the wicked in the land,*
     that I may root out all evildoers from the city of the Lord.

Loving God, help us to love what is truly perfect, so that we may
neither speak what is evil nor do what is wrong. Then bring us to
stand in your presence, to sing of your mercy and justice in the
company of all your saints, through Jesus Christ our Saviour.


# 102

1    Lord, hear my prayer, and let my cry come before you; *
     hide not your face from me in the day of my trouble.

2    Incline your ear to me; *
     when I call, make haste to answer me,

3    For my days drift away like smoke,*
     and my bones are hot as burning coals.

4    My heart is smitten like grass and withered,*
     so that I forget to eat my bread.

5    Because of the voice of my groaning *
     I am but skin and bones.

6    I have become like a vulture in the wilderness,*
     like an owl among the ruins.

7    I lie awake and groan; *
     I am like a sparrow, lonely on a house-top.

8    My enemies revile me all day long,*
     and those who scoff at me have taken an oath against me.

9    For I have eaten ashes for bread *
     and mingled my drink with weeping.

10 Because of your indignation and wrath *
     you have lifted me up and thrown me away.

11 My days pass away like a shadow,*
     and I wither like the grass.

12 But you, O Lord, endure for ever,*
     and your name from age to age.

13 You will arise and have compassion on Zion,
     for it is time to have mercy upon her; *
     indeed, the appointed time has come.

14 For your servants love her very rubble,*
     and are moved to pity even for her dust.

15 The nations shall fear your name, O Lord,*
     and all the kings of the earth your glory.

16 For the Lord will build up Zion,*
     and his glory will appear.

17 He will look with favour on the prayer of the homeless; *
     he will not despise their plea.

18 Let this be written for a future generation,*
     so that a people yet unborn may praise the Lord.

19 For the Lord looked down from his holy place on high; *
     from the heavens he beheld the earth;

20 That he might hear the groan of the captive *
     and set free those condemned to die;

21 That they may declare in Zion the name of the Lord,*
     and his praise in Jerusalem;

22 When the peoples are gathered together,*
     and the kingdoms also, to serve the Lord.

23 He has brought down my strength before my time; *
     he has shortened the number of my days;

24 And I said, "O my God,
     do not take me away in the midst of my days; *
     your years endure throughout all generations.

25     In the beginning, O Lord, you laid the foundations
                       of the earth,*
      and the heavens are the work of your hands;

26     They shall perish, but you will endure;
      they all shall wear out like a garment; *
         as clothing you will change them,
         and they shall be changed;

27     But you are always the same,*
         and your years will never end.

28     The children of your servants shall continue,*
         and their offspring shall stand fast in your sight."

God of unchanging mercy, look with compassion upon all
who suffer: the sick and the friendless, the homeless and the
captive, the weary and the depressed. Be present to them in
the power of your healing love; give them health, comfort, and
hope; and bring them to share in the life of your risen Son, our
Saviour Jesus Christ.

# 103

1     Bless the Lord, O my soul,*
      and all that is within me, bless his holy name.

2     Bless the Lord, O my soul,*
      and forget not all his benefits.

3     He forgives all your sins *
      and heals all your infirmities;

4     He redeems your life from the grave *
      and crowns you with mercy and loving-kindness;

5     He satisfies you with good things,*
      and your youth is renewed like an eagle's.

6     The Lord executes righteousness *
      and judgement for all who are oppressed.

7     He made his ways known to Moses *
      and his works to the children of Israel.

8    The Lord is full of compassion and mercy,*
         slow to anger and of great kindness.

9    He will not always accuse us,*
         nor will he keep his anger for ever.

10   He has not dealt with us according to our sins,*
         nor rewarded us according to our wickedness.

11   For as the heavens are high above the earth,*
         so is his mercy great upon those who fear him.

12   As far as the east is from the west,*
         so far has he removed our sins from us.

13   As a father cares for his children,*
         so does the Lord care for those who fear him.

14   For he himself knows whereof we are made; *
         he remembers that we are but dust.

15   Our days are like the grass; *
         we flourish like a flower of the field;

16   When the wind goes over it, it is gone,*
         and its place shall know it no more.

17   But the merciful goodness of the Lord endures for ever
                     on those who fear him,*
         and his righteousness on children's children;

18   On those who keep his covenant *
         and remember his commandments and do them.

19   The Lord has set his throne in heaven,*
         and his kingship has dominion over all.

20   Bless the Lord, you angels of his,
     you mighty ones who do his bidding,*
         and hearken to the voice of his word.

21   Bless the Lord, all you his hosts,*
         you ministers of his who do his will.

22   Bless the Lord, all you works of his,
     in all places of his dominion; *
         bless the Lord, O my soul.

God of infinite mercy and forgiveness, by the cross and resurrection of Jesus your Son, wash away our sins and deliver us from our infirmities of body and spirit, that we may live with him his risen life, to the praise and glory of your holy name.

# 104

1 Bless the Lord, O my soul; *
    O Lord my God, how excellent is your greatness!
    you are clothed with majesty and splendour.

2 You wrap yourself with light as with a cloak *
    and spread out the heavens like a curtain.

3 You lay the beams of your chambers in the waters above; *
    you make the clouds your chariot;
    you ride on the wings of the wind.

4 You make the winds your messengers *
    and flames of fire your servants.

5 You have set the earth upon its foundations,*
    so that it never shall move at any time.

6 You covered it with the deep as with a mantle; *
    the waters stood higher than the mountains.

7 At your rebuke they fled; *
    at the voice of your thunder they hastened away.

8 They went up into the hills and down to the valleys beneath,*
    to the places you had appointed for them.

9 You set the limits that they should not pass; *
    they shall not again cover the earth.

10 You send the springs into the valleys; *
    they flow between the mountains.

11 All the beasts of the field drink their fill from them,*
    and the wild asses quench their thirst.

12 Beside them the birds of the air make their nests *
    and sing among the branches.

13 You water the mountains from your dwelling on high; *
    the earth is fully satisfied by the fruit of your works.

14  You make grass grow for flocks and herds *
        and plants to serve mankind;

15  That they may bring forth food from the earth,*
        and wine to gladden our hearts,

16  Oil to make a cheerful countenance,*
        and bread to strengthen the heart.

17  The trees of the Lord are full of sap,*
        the cedars of Lebanon which he planted,

18  In which the birds build their nests,*
        and in whose tops the stork makes his dwelling.

19  The high hills are a refuge for the mountain goats,*
        and the stony cliffs for the rock badgers.

20  You appointed the moon to mark the seasons,*
        and the sun knows the time of its setting.

21  You make darkness that it may be night,*
        in which all the beasts of the forest prowl.

22  The lions roar after their prey *
        and seek their food from God.

23  The sun rises, and they slip away *
        and lay themselves down in their dens.

24  Man goes forth to his work *
        and to his labour until the evening.

25  O Lord, how manifold are your works! *
        in wisdom you have made them all;
        the earth is full of your creatures.

26  Yonder is the great and wide sea
    with its living things too many to number,*
        creatures both small and great.

27  There move the ships,
    and there is that Leviathan,*
        which you have made for the sport of it.

28  All of them look to you *
        to give them their food in due season.

29  You give it to them; they gather it; *
        you open your hand, and they are filled with good things.

30  You hide your face, and they are terrified; *
        you take away their breath,
        and they die and return to their dust.

31  You send forth your Spirit, and they are created; *
        and so you renew the face of the earth.

32  May the glory of the Lord endure for ever; *
        may the Lord rejoice in all his works.

33  He looks at the earth and it trembles; *
        he touches the mountains and they smoke.

34  I will sing to the Lord as long as I live; *
        I will praise my God while I have my being.

35  May these words of mine please him; *
        I will rejoice in the Lord.

36  Let sinners be consumed out of the earth,*
        and the wicked be no more.

37  Bless the Lord, O my soul.*
        Hallelujah!

O God of eternal light, heaven and earth are the work of your
hands, and all creation sings your praise and beauty. As in the
beginning, by your Spirit, you gave life and order to all that is,
so by the same Spirit redeem us and all things, through Christ
our Lord.

# 105

### Part I

1   Give thanks to the Lord and call upon his name; *
        make known his deeds among the peoples.

2   Sing to him, sing praises to him,*
        and speak of all his marvellous works.

3   Glory in his holy name; *
        let the hearts of those who seek the Lord rejoice.

4 Search for the Lord and his strength; *
  continually seek his face.

5 Remember the marvels he has done,*
  his wonders and the judgements of his mouth,

6 O offspring of Abraham his servant,*
  O children of Jacob his chosen.

7 He is the Lord our God; *
  his judgements prevail in all the world.

8 He has always been mindful of his covenant,*
  the promise he made for a thousand generations:

9 The covenant he made with Abraham,*
  the oath that he swore to Isaac,

10 Which he established as a statute for Jacob,*
  an everlasting covenant for Israel,

11 Saying, "To you will I give the land of Canaan *
  to be your allotted inheritance."

12 When they were few in number,*
  of little account, and sojourners in the land,

13 Wandering from nation to nation *
  and from one kingdom to another,

14 He let no one oppress them *
  and rebuked kings for their sake,

15 Saying, "Do not touch my anointed *
  and do my prophets no harm."

16 Then he called for a famine in the land *
  and destroyed the supply of bread.

17 He sent a man before them,*
  Joseph, who was sold as a slave.

18 They bruised his feet in fetters; *
  his neck they put in an iron collar.

19 Until his prediction came to pass,*
  the word of the Lord tested him.

20 The king sent and released him; *
  the ruler of the peoples set him free.

21 He set him as master over his household,*
  as a ruler over all his possessions,

22 To instruct his princes according to his will *
  and to teach his elders wisdom.

# 105

**Part II**

23 Israel came into Egypt,*
  and Jacob became a sojourner in the land of Ham.

24 The Lord made his people exceedingly fruitful; *
  he made them stronger than their enemies;

25 Whose heart he turned, so that they hated his people,*
  and dealt unjustly with his servants.

26 He sent Moses his servant,*
  and Aaron whom he had chosen.

27 They worked his signs among them,*
  and portents in the land of Ham.

28 He sent darkness, and it grew dark; *
  but the Egyptians rebelled against his words.

29 He turned their waters into blood *
  and caused their fish to die.

30 Their land was overrun by frogs,*
  in the very chambers of their kings.

31 He spoke, and there came swarms of insects *
  and gnats within all their borders.

32 He gave them hailstones instead of rain,*
  and flames of fire throughout their land.

33 He blasted their vines and their fig trees *
  and shattered every tree in their country.

34 He spoke, and the locust came,*
   and young locusts without number,

35 Which ate up all the green plants in their land *
   and devoured the fruit of their soil.

36 He struck down the firstborn of their land,*
   the firstfruits of all their strength.

37 He led out his people with silver and gold; *
   in all their tribes there was not one that stumbled.

38 Egypt was glad of their going,*
   because they were afraid of them.

39 He spread out a cloud for a covering *
   and a fire to give light in the night season.

40 They asked, and quails appeared,*
   and he satisfied them with bread from heaven.

41 He opened the rock, and water flowed,*
   so the river ran in the dry places.

42 For God remembered his holy word *
   and Abraham his servant.

43 So he led forth his people with gladness,*
   his chosen with shouts of joy.

44 He gave his people the lands of the nations,*
   and they took the fruit of others' toil,

45 That they might keep his statutes *
   and observe his laws.
   Hallelujah!

God of our salvation, through the death and resurrection of
Jesus Christ, you have fulfilled your promise to our ancestors
in the faith to redeem the world from slavery and to lead us
into the promised land. Grant us living water from the rock and
bread from heaven, that we may survive our desert pilgrimage
and praise you for ever, through Jesus Christ our Redeemer.

# 106

1 Hallelujah!
  Give thanks to the Lord, for he is good,*
    for his mercy endures for ever.

2 Who can declare the mighty acts of the Lord *
    or show forth all his praise?

3 Happy are those who act with justice *
    and always do what is right!

4 Remember me, O Lord, with the favour you have
                      for your people,*
    and visit me with your saving help;

5 That I may see the prosperity of your elect
  and be glad with the gladness of your people,*
    that I may glory with your inheritance.

6 We have sinned as our forebears did; *
    we have done wrong and dealt wickedly.

7 In Egypt they did not consider your marvellous works,
  nor remember the abundance of your love; *
    they defied the Most High at the Red Sea.

8 But he saved them for his name's sake,*
    to make his power known.

9 He rebuked the Red Sea, and it dried up,*
    and he led them through the deep as through a desert.

10 He saved them from the hand of those who hated them *
    and redeemed them from the hand of the enemy.

11 The waters covered their oppressors; *
    not one of them was left.

12 Then they believed his words *
    and sang him songs of praise.

13 But they soon forgot his deeds *
    and did not wait for his counsel.

14    A craving seized them in the wilderness,*
     and they put God to the test in the desert.

15    He gave them what they asked,*
     but sent leanness into their soul.

16    They envied Moses in the camp,*
     and Aaron, the holy one of the Lord.

17    The earth opened and swallowed Dathan *
     and covered the company of Abiram.

18    Fire blazed up against their company,*
     and flames devoured the wicked.

# 106

**Part II**

19    Israel made a bull-calf at Horeb *
     and worshipped a molten image;

20    And so they exchanged their Glory *
     for the image of an ox that feeds on grass.

21    They forgot God their saviour,*
     who had done great things in Egypt,

22    Wonderful deeds in the land of Ham,*
     and fearful things at the Red Sea.

23    So he would have destroyed them,
   had not Moses his chosen stood before him in the breach,*
     to turn away his wrath from consuming them.

24    They refused the pleasant land *
     and would not believe his promise.

25    They grumbled in their tents *
     and would not listen to the voice of the Lord.

26    So he lifted his hand against them,*
     to overthrow them in the wilderness,

27    To cast out their seed among the nations,*
     and to scatter them throughout the lands.

28 They joined themselves to Baal-Peor *
     and ate sacrifices offered to the dead.

29 They provoked him to anger with their actions,*
     and a plague broke out among them.

30 Then Phinehas stood up and interceded,*
     and the plague came to an end.

31 This was reckoned to him as righteousness *
     throughout all generations for ever.

32 Again they provoked his anger at the waters of Meribah,*
     so that he punished Moses because of them;

33 For they so embittered his spirit *
     that he spoke rash words with his lips.


34 They did not destroy the peoples *
     as the Lord had commanded them.

35 They intermingled with the heathen *
     and learned their pagan ways,

36 So that they worshipped their idols,*
     which became a snare to them.

37 They sacrificed their sons *
     and their daughters to evil spirits.

38 They shed innocent blood,
     the blood of their sons and daughters,*
          which they offered to the idols of Canaan,
          and the land was defiled with blood.

39 Thus they were polluted by their actions *
     and went whoring in their evil deeds.

40 Therefore the wrath of the Lord was kindled against
                              his people *
     and he abhorred his inheritance.

41 He gave them over to the hand of the heathen,*
     and those who hated them ruled over them.

42 Their enemies oppressed them,*
     and they were humbled under their hand.

43  Many a time did he deliver them,
      but they rebelled through their own devices,*
        and were brought down in their iniquity.

44  Nevertheless, he saw their distress,*
      when he heard their lamentation.

45  He remembered his covenant with them *
      and relented in accordance with his great mercy.

46  He caused them to be pitied *
      by those who held them captive.

47  Save us, O Lord our God,
      and gather us from among the nations,*
        that we may give thanks to your holy name
        and glory in your praise.


48  Blessed be the Lord, the God of Israel,
      from everlasting and to everlasting; *
        and let all the people say, "Amen!"
        Hallelujah!


God our Father, remembering your covenant you graciously
pardoned those who rebelled against you. Grant that where
sin abounds, grace may abound more, through Jesus Christ
our Lord.

**Book Five**

# 107

**Part I**

1  Give thanks to the Lord, for he is good,*
      and his mercy endures for ever.

2  Let all those whom the Lord has redeemed proclaim *
      that he redeemed them from the hand of the foe.

3  He gathered them out of the lands; *
      from the east and from the west,
        from the north and from the south.

4   Some wandered in desert wastes; *
        they found no way to a city where they might dwell.

5   They were hungry and thirsty; *
        their spirits languished within them.

6   Then they cried to the Lord in their trouble,*
        and he delivered them from their distress.

7   He put their feet on a straight path *
        to go to a city where they might dwell.

8   Let them give thanks to the Lord for his mercy *
        and the wonders he does for his children.

9   For he satisfies the thirsty *
        and fills the hungry with good things.

10  Some sat in darkness and deep gloom,*
        bound fast in misery and iron;

11  Because they rebelled against the words of God *
        and despised the counsel of the Most High.

12  So he humbled their spirits with hard labour; *
        they stumbled, and there was none to help.

13  Then they cried to the Lord in their trouble,*
        and he delivered them from their distress.

14  He led them out of darkness and deep gloom *
        and broke their bonds asunder.

15  Let them give thanks to the Lord for his mercy *
        and the wonders he does for his children.

16  For he shatters the doors of bronze *
        and breaks in two the iron bars.


17  Some were fools and took to rebellious ways; *
        they were afflicted because of their sins.

18  They abhorred all manner of food *
        and drew near to death's door.

19  Then they cried to the Lord in their trouble,*
        and he delivered them from their distress.

20 He sent forth his word and healed them *
 and saved them from the grave.

21 Let them give thanks to the Lord for his mercy *
 and the wonders he does for his children.

22 Let them offer a sacrifice of thanksgiving *
 and tell of his acts with shouts of joy.

23 Some went down to the sea in ships *
 and plied their trade in deep waters;

24 They beheld the works of the Lord *
 and his wonders in the deep.

25 Then he spoke, and a stormy wind arose,*
 which tossed high the waves of the sea.

26 They mounted up to the heavens and fell back to the depths; *
 their hearts melted because of their peril.

27 They reeled and staggered like drunkards *
 and were at their wits' end.

28 Then they cried to the Lord in their trouble,*
 and he delivered them from their distress.

29 He stilled the storm to a whisper *
 and quieted the waves of the sea.

30 Then were they glad because of the calm,*
 and he brought them to the harbour they were bound for.

31 Let them give thanks to the Lord for his mercy *
 and the wonders he does for his children.

32 Let them exalt him in the congregation of the people *
 and praise him in the council of the elders.

# 107

**Part II**

33 The Lord changed rivers into deserts,*
 and water-springs into thirsty ground,

34 A fruitful land into salt flats,*
 because of the wickedness of those who dwell there.

35 He changed deserts into pools of water *
 and dry land into water-springs.

36 He settled the hungry there,*
 and they founded a city to dwell in.

37 They sowed fields, and planted vineyards,*
 and brought in a fruitful harvest.

38 He blessed them, so that they increased greatly; *
 he did not let their herds decrease.

39 Yet when they were diminished and brought low,*
 through stress of adversity and sorrow,

40 (He pours contempt on princes *
 and makes them wander in trackless wastes)

41 He lifted up the poor out of misery *
 and multiplied their families like flocks of sheep.

42 The upright will see this and rejoice,*
 but all wickedness will shut its mouth.

43 Whoever is wise will ponder these things,*
 and consider well the mercies of the Lord.

O God, the divine seeker, you are light to the lost, bread to the
hungry, deliverance to the captive, healing to the sick, eternal
vision to the dying, and harbour to every soul in peril. Gather
the wanderers from every corner of the world into the
community of your mercy and grace, that we may eternally
praise you for our salvation in Jesus Christ our Lord.

# 108

1 My heart is firmly fixed, O God, my heart is fixed; *
 I will sing and make melody.

2 Wake up, my spirit;
 awake, lute and harp; *
 I myself will waken the dawn.

3 I will confess you among the peoples, O Lord; *
 I will sing praises to you among the nations.

4     For your loving-kindness is greater than the heavens,*
      and your faithfulness reaches to the clouds.

5     Exalt yourself above the heavens, O God,*
      and your glory over all the earth.

6     So that those who are dear to you may be delivered,*
      save with your right hand and answer me.


7     God spoke from his holy place and said,*
    "I will exult and parcel out Shechem;
      I will divide the valley of Succoth.

8     Gilead is mine and Manasseh is mine; *
      Ephraim is my helmet and Judah my sceptre.

9     Moab is my washbasin,
    on Edom I throw down my sandal to claim it,*
      and over Philistia will I shout in triumph."

10    Who will lead me into the strong city? *
      who will bring me into Edom?

11    Have you not cast us off, O God? *
      you no longer go out, O God, with our armies.

12    Grant us your help against the enemy,*
      for vain is the help of man.

13    With God we will do valiant deeds,*
      and he shall tread our enemies under foot.


O God, your love is wider than all the universe and your mercy greater than the heights of heaven. When we are tempted to break faith with you, put a new song of love on our lips, that we may sing your praises to all nations on earth, through your Son, our only hope and defence.

# 109

1     Hold not your tongue, O God of my praise; *
      for the mouth of the wicked,
        the mouth of the deceitful, is opened against me.

2 They speak to me with a lying tongue; *
  they encompass me with hateful words
  and fight against me without a cause.

3 Despite my love, they accuse me; *
  but as for me, I pray for them.

4 They repay evil for good,*
  and hatred for my love.

5 Set a wicked man against him,*
  and let an accuser stand at his right hand.

6 When he is judged, let him be found guilty,*
  and let his appeal be in vain.

7 Let his days be few,*
  and let another take his office.

8 Let his children be fatherless,*
  and his wife become a widow.

9 Let his children be waifs and beggars; *
  let them be driven from the ruins of their homes.

10 Let the creditor seize everything he has; *
  let strangers plunder his gains.

11 Let there be no one to show him kindness,*
  and none to pity his fatherless children.

12 Let his descendants be destroyed,*
  and his name be blotted out in the next generation.

13 Let the wickedness of his fathers be remembered before
                    the Lord,*
  and his mother's sin not be blotted out;

14 Let their sin be always before the Lord; *
  but let him root out their names from the earth;

15 Because he did not remember to show mercy,*
  but persecuted the poor and needy
  and sought to kill the brokenhearted.

16     He loved cursing,
       let it come upon him; *
         he took no delight in blessing,
          let it depart from him.

17     He put on cursing like a garment,*
         let it soak into his body like water
         and into his bones like oil;

18     Let it be to him like the cloak which he
                        wraps around himself,*
         and like the belt that he wears continually.

19     Let this be the recompense from the Lord to my accusers,*
         and to those who speak evil against me.


20     But you, O Lord my God,
       oh, deal with me according to your name; *
         for your tender mercy's sake, deliver me.

21     For I am poor and needy,*
         and my heart is wounded within me.

22     I have faded away like a shadow when it lengthens; *
         I am shaken off like a locust.

23     My knees are weak through fasting,*
         and my flesh is wasted and gaunt.

24     I have become a reproach to them; *
         they see and shake their heads.

25     Help me, O Lord my God; *
         save me for your mercy's sake.

26     Let them know that this is your hand,*
         that you, O Lord, have done it.

27     They may curse, but you will bless; *
         let those who rise up against me be put to shame,
         and your servant will rejoice.

28     Let my accusers be clothed with disgrace *
         and wrap themselves in their shame as in a cloak.

29    I will give great thanks to the Lord with my mouth; *
         in the midst of the multitude will I praise him;

30    Because he stands at the right hand of the needy,*
         to save his life from those who would condemn him.


God, source of all truth and love, the comfort and consolation
of the reproached and friendless, in your great mercy draw
near to deliver the poor, the needy, and the wounded of heart;
through the one who suffered rejection and rebuke for us all,
Jesus Christ our Lord.


# 110

1    The Lord said to my lord, "Sit at my right hand,*
         until I make your enemies your footstool."

2    The Lord will send the sceptre of your power out of Zion,*
         saying, "Rule over your enemies round about you.

3    Princely state has been yours from the day of your birth,*
         in the beauty of holiness have I begotten you,
         like dew from the womb of the morning."

4    The Lord has sworn and he will not recant: *
         "You are a priest for ever after the order of Melchizedek."

5    The Lord who is at your right hand
      will smite kings in the day of his wrath; *
         he will rule over the nations.

6    He will heap high the corpses; *
         he will smash heads over the wide earth.

7    He will drink from the brook beside the road; *
         therefore he will lift high his head.


Jesus Christ, King of kings and Lord of lords, born as a man,
exalted now on high, priest of the new covenant, judge who
will come at the end of time, glory to you for ever and ever.

# 111

1 Hallelujah!
I will give thanks to the Lord with my whole heart,*
    in the assembly of the upright, in the congregation.

2 Great are the deeds of the Lord! *
    they are studied by all who delight in them.

3 His work is full of majesty and splendour,*
    and his righteousness endures for ever.

4 He makes his marvellous works to be remembered; *
    the Lord is gracious and full of compassion.

5 He gives food to those who fear him; *
    he is ever mindful of his covenant.

6 He has shown his people the power of his works *
    in giving them the lands of the nations.

7 The works of his hands are faithfulness and justice; *
    all his commandments are sure.

8 They stand fast for ever and ever,*
    because they are done in truth and equity.

9 He sent redemption to his people;
he commanded his covenant for ever; *
    holy and awesome is his name.

10 The fear of the Lord is the beginning of wisdom; *
    those who act accordingly have a good understanding;
    his praise endures for ever.

Generous and bountiful God, give us grace always to thank
you and share your gifts with others, that the world may be
filled with the joy of our Saviour Jesus Christ.

# 112

1 Hallelujah!
Happy are they who fear the Lord *
    and have great delight in his commandments!

2     Their descendants will be mighty in the land; *
      the generation of the upright will be blessed.

3     Wealth and riches will be in their house,*
      and their righteousness will last for ever.

4     Light shines in the darkness for the upright; *
      the righteous are merciful and full of compassion.

5     It is good for them to be generous in lending *
      and to manage their affairs with justice.

6     For they will never be shaken; *
      the righteous will be kept in everlasting remembrance.

7     They will not be afraid of any evil rumours; *
      their heart is right;
      they put their trust in the Lord.

8     Their heart is established and will not shrink,*
      until they see their desire upon their enemies.

9     They have given freely to the poor,*
      and their righteousness stands fast for ever;
      they will hold up their head with honour.

10    The wicked will see it and be angry;
      they will gnash their teeth and pine away; *
      the desires of the wicked will perish.

God of light, teach us to love each other as you love us, that
we may bring peace and joy to the world, and rejoice in the
kingdom of your Son, Jesus Christ our Lord.

# 113

1     Hallelujah!
      Give praise, you servants of the Lord; *
      praise the name of the Lord.

2     Let the name of the Lord be blessed,*
      from this time forth for evermore.

3     From the rising of the sun to its going down *
      let the name of the Lord be praised.

4     The Lord is high above all nations,*
      and his glory above the heavens.

5     Who is like the Lord our God, who sits enthroned on high,*
      but stoops to behold the heavens and the earth?

6     He takes up the weak out of the dust *
      and lifts up the poor from the ashes.

7     He sets them with the princes,*
      with the princes of his people.

8     He makes the woman of a childless house *
      to be a joyful mother of children.

We magnify your name, O Lord, in all times and places. You
subdue the arrogant and raise the humble; you feed the
hungry and reveal the poverty of wealth. We give thanks for
your salvation, made known in Jesus Christ our Lord.

# 114

1     Hallelujah!
      When Israel came out of Egypt,*
      the house of Jacob from a people of strange speech,

2     Judah became God's sanctuary *
      and Israel his dominion.

3     The sea beheld it and fled; *
      Jordan turned and went back.

4     The mountains skipped like rams,*
      and the little hills like young sheep.

5     What ailed you, O sea, that you fled? *
      O Jordan, that you turned back?

6     You mountains, that you skipped like rams? *
      you little hills like young sheep?

7     Tremble, O earth, at the presence of the Lord,*
      at the presence of the God of Jacob.

8     Who turned the hard rock into a pool of water *
      and flint-stone into a flowing spring.

Source of all life, you have brought us to new being through
the waters of baptism. May your love shown in our lives
become a wonder and a beacon of hope to the whole human
family. We ask this in the name of Jesus Christ the Lord.

# 115

1   Not to us, O Lord, not to us,
    but to your name give glory; *
        because of your love and because of your faithfulness.

2   Why should the heathen say,*
    "Where then is their God?"

3   Our God is in heaven; *
        whatever he wills to do he does.

4   Their idols are silver and gold,*
        the work of human hands.

5   They have mouths, but they cannot speak; *
        eyes have they, but they cannot see;

6   They have ears, but they cannot hear; *
        noses, but they cannot smell;

7   They have hands, but they cannot feel;
    feet, but they cannot walk; *
        they make no sound with their throat.

8   Those who make them are like them,*
        and so are all who put their trust in them.

9   O Israel, trust in the Lord; *
        he is their help and their shield.

10  O house of Aaron, trust in the Lord; *
        he is their help and their shield.

11  You who fear the Lord, trust in the Lord; *
        he is their help and their shield.

12  The Lord has been mindful of us, and he will bless us; *
        he will bless the house of Israel;
        he will bless the house of Aaron;

13    He will bless those who fear the Lord,*
       both small and great together.

14    May the Lord increase you more and more,*
       you and your children after you.

15    May you be blessed by the Lord,*
       the maker of heaven and earth.

16    The heaven of heavens is the Lord's,*
       but he entrusted the earth to its peoples.

17    The dead do not praise the Lord,*
       nor all those who go down into silence;

18    But we will bless the Lord,*
       from this time forth for evermore.
       Hallelujah!

God, you delivered Israel from the worship of false gods.
Redeem, we pray, your people in every age from the pursuit
of all that is worthless and untrue in human life; through Jesus
our Saviour, who came to bring us life in all its fullness.

# 116

1    I love the Lord, because he has heard the voice of
               my supplication,*
    because he has inclined his ear to me whenever
               I called upon him.

2    The cords of death entangled me;
    the grip of the grave took hold of me; *
       I came to grief and sorrow.

3    Then I called upon the name of the Lord: *
    "O Lord, I pray you, save my life."

4    Gracious is the Lord and righteous; *
       our God is full of compassion.

5    The Lord watches over the innocent; *
       I was brought very low, and he helped me.

6 Turn again to your rest, O my soul,*
  for the Lord has treated you well.

7 For you have rescued my life from death,*
  my eyes from tears, and my feet from stumbling.

8 I will walk in the presence of the Lord *
  in the land of the living.

9 I believed, even when I said,
 "I have been brought very low." *
  In my distress I said, "No one can be trusted."

10 How shall I repay the Lord *
  for all the good things he has done for me?

11 I will lift up the cup of salvation *
  and call upon the name of the Lord.

12 I will fulfil my vows to the Lord *
  in the presence of all his people.

13 Precious in the sight of the Lord *
  is the death of his servants.

14 O Lord, I am your servant; *
  I am your servant and the child of your handmaid;
  you have freed me from my bonds.

15 I will offer you the sacrifice of thanksgiving *
  and call upon the name of the Lord.

16 I will fulfil my vows to the Lord *
  in the presence of all his people.

17 In the courts of the Lord's house,*
  in the midst of you, O Jerusalem.
  Hallelujah!

Eternal God, faithful in your tender compassion, you give us hope for our life here and hereafter through the victory of your only Son. When we share his cup of salvation, revive in us the joy of this everlasting gift. We ask this in his name.

# 117

1    Praise the Lord, all you nations; *
      laud him, all you peoples.

2    For his loving-kindness toward us is great,*
      and the faithfulness of the Lord endures for ever.
      Hallelujah!

Faithful God, your loving kindness for all people is revealed in
Jesus Christ. Let your kingdom come now in peace and justice
in all the world. We ask this in his name.

# 118

1    Give thanks to the Lord, for he is good; *
      his mercy endures for ever.

2    Let Israel now proclaim,*
      "His mercy endures for ever."

3    Let the house of Aaron now proclaim,*
      "His mercy endures for ever."

4    Let those who fear the Lord now proclaim,*
      "His mercy endures for ever."

5    I called to the Lord in my distress; *
      the Lord answered by setting me free.

6    The Lord is at my side, therefore I will not fear; *
      what can anyone do to me?

7    The Lord is at my side to help me; *
      I will triumph over those who hate me.

8    It is better to rely on the Lord *
      than to put any trust in flesh.

9    It is better to rely on the Lord *
      than to put any trust in rulers.

10    All the ungodly encompass me; *
      in the name of the Lord I will repel them.

11 They hem me in, they hem me in on every side; *
    in the name of the Lord I will repel them.

12 They swarm about me like bees;
they blaze like a fire of thorns; *
    in the name of the Lord I will repel them.

13 I was pressed so hard that I almost fell,*
    but the Lord came to my help.

14 The Lord is my strength and my song,*
    and he has become my salvation.

15 There is a sound of exultation and victory *
    in the tents of the righteous:

16 "The right hand of the Lord has triumphed! *
    the right hand of the Lord is exalted!
    the right hand of the Lord has triumphed!"

17 I shall not die, but live,*
    and declare the works of the Lord.

18 The Lord has punished me sorely,*
    but he did not hand me over to death.

19 Open for me the gates of righteousness; *
    I will enter them;
    I will offer thanks to the Lord.

20 "This is the gate of the Lord; *
    he who is righteous may enter."

21 I will give thanks to you, for you answered me *
    and have become my salvation.

22 The same stone which the builders rejected *
    has become the chief cornerstone.

23 This is the Lord's doing,*
    and it is marvellous in our eyes.

24 On this day the Lord has acted; *
    we will rejoice and be glad in it.

25    Hosannah, Lord, hosannah! *
      Lord, send us now success.

26    Blessed is he who comes in the name of the Lord; *
      we bless you from the house of the Lord.

27    God is the Lord; he has shined upon us; *
      form a procession with branches up to the
                    horns of the altar.

28    "You are my God, and I will thank you; *
      you are my God, and I will exalt you."

29    Give thanks to the Lord, for he is good; *
      his mercy endures for ever.

Holy and mighty God, your Son's triumph over sin and death
has opened to us the gate of eternal life. Purify our hearts that
we may follow where he has gone and share in the radiance of
his glory. We ask this for the sake of our risen Lord.

# 119

### Aleph

1     Happy are they whose way is blameless,*
      who walk in the law of the Lord!

2     Happy are they who observe his decrees *
      and seek him with all their hearts!

3     Who never do any wrong,*
      but always walk in his ways.

4     You laid down your commandments,*
      that we should fully keep them.

5     Oh, that my ways were made so direct *
      that I might keep your statutes!

6     Then I should not be put to shame,*
      when I regard all your commandments.

7     I will thank you with an unfeigned heart,*
      when I have learned your righteous judgements.

8    I will keep your statutes; *
        do not utterly forsake me.

**Beth**

9    How shall a young man cleanse his way? *
        By keeping to your words.

10   With my whole heart I seek you; *
        let me not stray from your commandments.

11   I treasure your promise in my heart,*
        that I may not sin against you.

12   Blessed are you, O Lord; *
        instruct me in your statutes.

13   With my lips will I recite *
        all the judgements of your mouth.

14   I have taken greater delight in the way of your decrees *
        than in all manner of riches.

15   I will meditate on your commandments *
        and give attention to your ways.

16   My delight is in your statutes; *
        I will not forget your word.

**Gimel**

17   Deal bountifully with your servant,*
        that I may live and keep your word.

18   Open my eyes, that I may see *
        the wonders of your law.

19   I am a stranger here on earth; *
        do not hide your commandments from me.

20   My soul is consumed at all times *
        with longing for your judgements.

21   You have rebuked the insolent; *
        cursed are they who stray from your commandments!

22    Turn from me shame and rebuke,*
      for I have kept your decrees.

23    Even though rulers sit and plot against me,*
      I will meditate on your statutes.

24    For your decrees are my delight,*
      and they are my counsellors.

**Daleth**

25    My soul cleaves to the dust; *
      give me life according to your word.

26    I have confessed my ways, and you answered me; *
      instruct me in your statutes.

27    Make me understand the way of your commandments,*
      that I may meditate on your marvellous works.

28    My soul melts away for sorrow; *
      strengthen me according to your word.

29    Take from me the way of lying; *
      let me find grace through your law.

30    I have chosen the way of faithfulness; *
      I have set your judgements before me.

31    I hold fast to your decrees; *
      O Lord, let me not be put to shame.

32    I will run the way of your commandments,*
      for you have set my heart at liberty.

**He**

33    Teach me, O Lord, the way of your statutes,*
      and I shall keep it to the end.

34    Give me understanding, and I shall keep your law; *
      I shall keep it with all my heart.

35    Make me go in the path of your commandments,*
      for that is my desire.

36   Incline my heart to your decrees *
     and not to unjust gain.

37   Turn my eyes from watching what is worthless; *
     give me life in your ways.

38   Fulfil your promise to your servant,*
     which you make to those who fear you.

39   Turn away the reproach which I dread,*
     because your judgements are good.

40   Behold, I long for your commandments; *
     in your righteousness preserve my life.

**Waw**

41   Let your loving-kindness come to me, O Lord,*
     and your salvation, according to your promise.

42   Then shall I have a word for those who taunt me,*
     because I trust in your words.

43   Do not take the word of truth out of my mouth,*
     for my hope is in your judgements.

44   I shall continue to keep your law; *
     I shall keep it for ever and ever.

45   I will walk at liberty,*
     because I study your commandments.

46   I will tell of your decrees before kings *
     and will not be ashamed.

47   I delight in your commandments,*
     which I have always loved.

48   I will lift up my hands to your commandments,*
     and I will meditate on your statutes.

**Zayin**

49   Remember your word to your servant,*
     because you have given me hope.

50  This is my comfort in my trouble,*
        that your promise gives me life.

51  The proud have derided me cruelly,*
        but I have not turned from your law.

52  When I remember your judgements of old,*
        O Lord, I take great comfort.

53  I am filled with a burning rage,*
        because of the wicked who forsake your law.

54  Your statutes have been like songs to me *
        wherever I have lived as a stranger.

55  I remember your name in the night, O Lord,*
        and dwell upon your law.

56  This is how it has been with me,*
        because I have kept your commandments.

**Heth**

57  You only are my portion, O Lord; *
        I have promised to keep your words.

58  I entreat you with all my heart,*
        be merciful to me according to your promise.

59  I have considered my ways *
        and turned my feet toward your decrees.

60  I hasten and do not tarry *
        to keep your commandments.

61  Though the cords of the wicked entangle me,*
        I do not forget your law.

62  At midnight I will rise to give you thanks,*
        because of your righteous judgements.

63  I am a companion of all who fear you *
        and of those who keep your commandments.

64  The earth, O Lord, is full of your love; *
        instruct me in your statutes.

### Teth

65 O Lord, you have dealt graciously with your servant,*
    according to your word.

66 Teach me discernment and knowledge,*
    for I have believed in your commandments.

67 Before I was afflicted I went astray,*
    but now I keep your word.

68 You are good and you bring forth good; *
    instruct me in your statutes.

69 The proud have smeared me with lies,*
    but I will keep your commandments with my whole heart.

70 Their heart is gross and fat,*
    but my delight is in your law.

71 It is good for me that I have been afflicted,*
    that I might learn your statutes.

72 The law of your mouth is dearer to me *
    than thousands in gold and silver.

### Yodh

73 Your hands have made me and fashioned me; *
    give me understanding, that I may learn your
            commandments.

74 Those who fear you will be glad when they see me,*
    because I trust in your word.

75 I know, O Lord, that your judgements are right *
    and that in faithfulness you have afflicted me.

76 Let your loving-kindness be my comfort *
    as you have promised to your servant.

77 Let your compassion come to me, that I may live,*
    for your law is my delight.

78 Let the arrogant be put to shame, for they wrong me
            with lies; *
    but I will meditate on your commandments.

79     Let those who fear you turn to me,*
       and also those who know your decrees.

80     Let my heart be sound in your statutes,*
       that I may not be put to shame.

**Kaph**

81     My soul has longed for your salvation; *
       I have put my hope in your word.

82     My eyes have failed from watching for your promise,*
       and I say, ''When will you comfort me?''

83     I have become like a leather flask in the smoke,*
       but I have not forgotten your statutes.

84     How much longer must I wait? *
       when will you give judgement against those who
           persecute me?

85     The proud have dug pits for me; *
       they do not keep your law.

86     All your commandments are true; *
       help me, for they persecute me with lies.

87     They had almost made an end of me on earth,*
       but I have not forsaken your commandments.

88     In your loving-kindness, revive me,*
       that I may keep the decrees of your mouth.

**Lamedh**

89     O Lord, your word is everlasting; *
       it stands firm in the heavens.

90     Your faithfulness remains from one generation to another; *
       you established the earth, and it abides.

91     By your decree these continue to this day,*
       for all things are your servants.

92     If my delight had not been in your law,*
       I should have perished in my affliction.

93 I will never forget your commandments,*
  because by them you give me life.

94 I am yours; oh, that you would save me! *
  for I study your commandments.

95 Though the wicked lie in wait for me to destroy me,*
  I will apply my mind to your decrees.

96 I see that all things come to an end,*
  but your commandment has no bounds.

**Mem**

97 Oh, how I love your law! *
  all the day long it is in my mind.

98 Your commandment has made me wiser than my enemies,*
  and it is always with me.

99 I have more understanding than all my teachers,*
  for your decrees are my study.

100 I am wiser than the elders,*
  because I observe your commandments.

101 I restrain my feet from every evil way,*
  that I may keep your word.

102 I do not shrink from your judgements,*
  because you yourself have taught me.

103 How sweet are your words to my taste! *
  they are sweeter than honey to my mouth.

104 Through your commandments I gain understanding; *
  therefore I hate every lying way.

**Nun**

105 Your word is a lantern to my feet *
  and a light upon my path.

106 I have sworn and am determined *
  to keep your righteous judgements.

107    I am deeply troubled; *
       preserve my life, O Lord, according to your word.

108    Accept, O Lord, the willing tribute of my lips,*
       and teach me your judgements.

109    My life is always in my hand,*
       yet I do not forget your law.

110    The wicked have set a trap for me,*
       but I have not strayed from your commandments.

111    Your decrees are my inheritance for ever; *
       truly, they are the joy of my heart.

112    I have applied my heart to fulfil your statutes *
       for ever and to the end.

### Samekh

113    I hate those who have a divided heart,*
       but your law do I love.

114    You are my refuge and shield; *
       my hope is in your word.

115    Away from me, you wicked! *
       I will keep the commandments of my God.

116    Sustain me according to your promise, that I may live,*
       and let me not be disappointed in my hope.

117    Hold me up, and I shall be safe,*
       and my delight shall be ever in your statutes.

118    You spurn all who stray from your statutes; *
       their deceitfulness is in vain.

119    In your sight all the wicked of the earth are but dross; *
       therefore I love your decrees.

120    My flesh trembles with dread of you; *
       I am afraid of your judgements.

### Ayin

121 I have done what is just and right; *
    do not deliver me to my oppressors.

122 Be surety for your servant's good; *
    let not the proud oppress me.

123 My eyes have failed from watching for your salvation *
    and for your righteous promise.

124 Deal with your servant according to your
                      loving-kindness *
    and teach me your statutes.

125 I am your servant; grant me understanding,*
    that I may know your decrees.

126 It is time for you to act, O Lord,*
    for they have broken your law.

127 Truly, I love your commandments *
    more than gold and precious stones.

128 I hold all your commandments to be right for me; *
    all paths of falsehood I abhor.

### Pe

129 Your decrees are wonderful; *
    therefore I obey them with all my heart.

130 When your word goes forth it gives light; *
    it gives understanding to the simple.

131 I open my mouth and pant; *
    I long for your commandments.

132 Turn to me in mercy,*
    as you always do to those who love your name.

133 Steady my footsteps in your word; *
    let no iniquity have dominion over me.

134 Rescue me from those who oppress me,*
    and I will keep your commandments.

135   Let your countenance shine upon your servant *
     and teach me your statutes.

136   My eyes shed streams of tears,*
     because people do not keep your law.

**Sadhe**

137   You are righteous, O Lord,*
     and upright are your judgements.

138   You have issued your decrees *
     with justice and in perfect faithfulness.

139   My indignation has consumed me,*
     because my enemies forget your words.

140   Your word has been tested to the uttermost,*
     and your servant holds it dear.

141   I am small and of little account,*
     yet I do not forget your commandments.

142   Your justice is an everlasting justice *
     and your law is the truth.

143   Trouble and distress have come upon me,*
     yet your commandments are my delight.

144   The righteousness of your decrees is everlasting; *
     grant me understanding, that I may live.

**Qoph**

145   I call with my whole heart; *
     answer me, O Lord, that I may keep your statutes.

146   I call to you;
     oh, that you would save me! *
     I will keep your decrees.

147   Early in the morning I cry out to you,*
     for in your word is my trust.

148   My eyes are open in the night watches,*
     that I may meditate upon your promise.

149    Hear my voice, O Lord, according to your
                    loving-kindness; *
          according to your judgements, give me life.

150    They draw near who in malice persecute me; *
          they are very far from your law.

151    You, O Lord, are near at hand,*
          and all your commandments are true.

152    Long have I known from your decrees *
          that you have established them for ever.


**Resh**

153    Behold my affliction and deliver me,*
          for I do not forget your law.

154    Plead my cause and redeem me; *
          according to your promise, give me life.

155    Deliverance is far from the wicked,*
          for they do not study your statutes.

156    Great is your compassion, O Lord; *
          preserve my life, according to your judgements.

157    There are many who persecute and oppress me,*
          yet I have not swerved from your decrees.

158    I look with loathing at the faithless,*
          for they have not kept your word.

159    See how I love your commandments! *
          O Lord, in your mercy, preserve me.

160    The heart of your word is truth; *
          all your righteous judgements endure for evermore.


**Shin**

161    Rulers have persecuted me without a cause,*
          but my heart stands in awe of your word.

162    I am as glad because of your promise *
          as one who finds great spoils.

163 As for lies, I hate and abhor them,*
    but your law is my love.

164 Seven times a day do I praise you,*
    because of your righteous judgements.

165 Great peace have they who love your law; *
    for them there is no stumbling block.

166 I have hoped for your salvation, O Lord,*
    and I have fulfilled your commandments.

167 I have kept your decrees *
    and I have loved them deeply.

168 I have kept your commandments and decrees,*
    for all my ways are before you.

**Taw**

169 Let my cry come before you, O Lord; *
    give me understanding, according to your word.

170 Let my supplication come before you; *
    deliver me, according to your promise.

171 My lips shall pour forth your praise,*
    when you teach me your statutes.

172 My tongue shall sing of your promise,*
    for all your commandments are righteous.

173 Let your hand be ready to help me,*
    for I have chosen your commandments.

174 I long for your salvation, O Lord,*
    and your law is my delight.

175 Let me live, and I will praise you,*
    and let your judgements help me.

176 I have gone astray like a sheep that is lost; *
    search for your servant,
        for I do not forget your commandments.

Lord, you are just and your commandments are eternal. Teach us to love you with all our heart and to love our neighbour as ourselves, for the sake of Jesus our Lord.

*Or*

God, as your only Son revealed you still at work in your creation, so through Christ your living Word enable us to know your love and to share it with others. We ask this in his name.

*Or*

As of old, O Lord our God, you gave commandments to make one nation just and true, so by your incarnate Word you make all peoples one in grace and in the perfect freedom of your service. We give thanks to you through Jesus Christ our Lord.

# 120

1 When I was in trouble, I called to the Lord; *
    I called to the Lord, and he answered me.

2 Deliver me, O Lord, from lying lips *
    and from the deceitful tongue.

3 What shall be done to you, and what more besides,*
    O you deceitful tongue?

4 The sharpened arrows of a warrior,*
    along with hot glowing coals.

5 How hateful it is that I must lodge in Meshech *
    and dwell among the tents of Kedar!

6 Too long have I had to live *
    among the enemies of peace.

7 I am on the side of peace,*
    but when I speak of it, they are for war.

Eternal Source of truth and peace, guard your people from the folly of rash and slanderous speech, that the words of our mouth may not cause hurt and rejection, but rather healing and unity; through Christ our Lord.

## 121

1 I lift up my eyes to the hills; *
    from where is my help to come?

2 My help comes from the Lord,*
    the maker of heaven and earth.

3 He will not let your foot be moved *
    and he who watches over you will not fall asleep.

4 Behold, he who keeps watch over Israel *
    shall neither slumber nor sleep;

5 The Lord himself watches over you; *
    the Lord is your shade at your right hand,

6 So that the sun shall not strike you by day,*
    nor the moon by night.

7 The Lord shall preserve you from all evil; *
    it is he who shall keep you safe.

8 The Lord shall watch over your going out and
                    your coming in,*
    from this time forth for evermore.

Be present, merciful God, and protect us in times of danger, so that we who are wearied by the changes and chances of this life may rest in your eternal changelessness; through Jesus Christ our Lord.

## 122

1 I was glad when they said to me,*
    "Let us go to the house of the Lord."

2 Now our feet are standing *
    within your gates, O Jerusalem.

3 Jerusalem is built as a city *
    that is at unity with itself.

4    To which the tribes go up,
the tribes of the Lord,*
    the assembly of Israel,
    to praise the name of the Lord.

5    For there are the thrones of judgement,*
    the thrones of the house of David.

6    Pray for the peace of Jerusalem: *
  "May they prosper who love you.

7    Peace be within your walls *
    and quietness within your towers.

8    For my brethren and companions' sake,*
    I pray for your prosperity.

9    Because of the house of the Lord our God,*
    I will seek to do you good."

Lord Jesus, give us the peace of the new Jerusalem. Bring all
nations into your kingdom to share your gifts, that they may
render thanks to you without end and may come to your
eternal city, where you live and reign with the Father and
the Holy Spirit, now and for ever.

# 123

1    To you I lift up my eyes,*
    to you enthroned in the heavens.

2    As the eyes of servants look to the hand of their masters,*
    and the eyes of a maid to the hand of her mistress,

3    So our eyes look to the Lord our God,*
    until he show us his mercy.

4    Have mercy upon us, O Lord, have mercy,*
    for we have had more than enough of contempt,

5    Too much of the scorn of the indolent rich,*
    and of the derision of the proud.

King of love, rule in the hearts of all people on earth through your Son Jesus Christ, that we may become one family and one kingdom serving you by serving each other. We ask this in his name.

## 124

1 If the Lord had not been on our side,*
   let Israel now say;

2 If the Lord had not been on our side,*
   when enemies rose up against us;

3 Then would they have swallowed us up alive *
   in their fierce anger toward us;

4 Then would the waters have overwhelmed us *
   and the torrent gone over us;

5 Then would the raging waters *
   have gone right over us.

6 Blessed be the Lord! *
   he has not given us over to be a prey for their teeth.

7 We have escaped like a bird from the snare of the fowler; *
   the snare is broken, and we have escaped.

8 Our help is in the name of the Lord,*
   the maker of heaven and earth.


Helper and Defender of Israel, rescue the peoples of the world from destructive anger, and set us free to love and serve each other in the peace of Christ our Lord.

## 125

1 Those who trust in the Lord are like Mount Zion,*
   which cannot be moved, but stands fast for ever.

2 The hills stand about Jerusalem; *
   so does the Lord stand round about his people,
   from this time forth for evermore.

3   The sceptre of the wicked shall not hold sway over the
                land allotted to the just,*
        so that the just shall not put their hands to evil.

4   Show your goodness, O Lord, to those who are good *
        and to those who are true of heart.

5   As for those who turn aside to crooked ways,
        the Lord will lead them away with the evildoers; *
            but peace be upon Israel.

Lord, surround your people with your presence. Do not let
us stretch out our hands to evil deeds, or be destroyed by the
snares of the enemy, but bring us to share the land prepared
for the saints in light, where you live and reign, God, now and
forever.

# 126

1   When the Lord restored the fortunes of Zion,*
        then were we like those who dream.

2   Then was our mouth filled with laughter,*
        and our tongue with shouts of joy.

3   Then they said among the nations,*
        "The Lord has done great things for them."

4   The Lord has done great things for us,*
        and we are glad indeed.

5   Restore our fortunes, O Lord,*
        like the watercourses of the Negev.

6   Those who sowed with tears *
        will reap with songs of joy.

7   Those who go out weeping, carrying the seed,*
        will come again with joy, shouldering their sheaves.

Praise to you, God of our salvation. Your generous gifts surpass
all that we can ask or imagine. You have delivered us from
the exile of sin and restored us to new life in Jesus Christ our
Saviour. Glory and honour and praise to you for ever and ever.

# 127

1    Unless the Lord builds the house,*
     their labour is in vain who build it.

2    Unless the Lord watches over the city,*
     in vain the watchman keeps his vigil.

3    It is in vain that you rise so early and go to bed so late; *
     vain, too, to eat the bread of toil,
     for he gives to his beloved sleep.

4    Children are a heritage from the Lord,*
     and the fruit of the womb is a gift.

5    Like arrows in the hand of a warrior *
     are the children of one's youth.

6    Happy is the man who has his quiver full of them! *
     he shall not be put to shame
     when he contends with his enemies in the gate.

Gracious Father, watch over the Church, built on the foundation of your love. Help us so to live and proclaim the gospel that many may find life in your Son Jesus Christ our Lord.

# 128

1    Happy are they all who fear the Lord,*
     and who follow in his ways!

2    You shall eat the fruit of your labour; *
     happiness and prosperity shall be yours.

3    Your wife shall be like a fruitful vine within your house,*
     your children like olive shoots round about your table.

4    The man who fears the Lord *
     shall thus indeed be blessed.

5    The Lord bless you from Zion,*
     and may you see the prosperity of Jerusalem all the
         days of your life.

6   May you live to see your children's children; *
      may peace be upon Israel.

Gracious God, giver of life in its fullness, you take no pleasure
in human want but intend your bounty to be shared among
your children. Lead us in the ways of justice and peace, for
Jesus Christ's sake.

# 129

1   "Greatly have they oppressed me since my youth," *
      let Israel now say;

2   "Greatly have they oppressed me since my youth,*
      but they have not prevailed against me."

3   The plowmen plowed upon my back *
      and made their furrows long.

4   The Lord, the Righteous One,*
      has cut the cords of the wicked.

5   Let them be put to shame and thrown back,*
      all those who are enemies of Zion.

6   Let them be like grass upon the housetops,*
      which withers before it can be plucked;

7   Which does not fill the hand of the reaper,*
      nor the bosom of him who binds the sheaves;

8   So that those who go by say not so much as,
"The Lord prosper you.*
      We wish you well in the name of the Lord."

Save us, gracious God, from the dark forces that threaten the
lives of your people, in nations and societies and in the human
spirit. Deliver us from cynicism and violence, from jealousy
and indifference, from fear and despair. We ask this in the
name of Jesus Christ the Lord.

# 130

1   Out of the depths have I called you, O Lord;
    Lord, hear my voice; *
        let your ears consider well the voice of my supplication.

2   If you, Lord, were to note what is done amiss,*
        O Lord, who could stand?

3   For there is forgiveness with you; *
        therefore you shall be feared.

4   I wait for the Lord; my soul waits for him; *
        in his word is my hope.

5   My soul waits for the Lord,
    more than watchmen for the morning,*
        more than watchmen for the morning.

6   O Israel, wait for the Lord,*
        for with the Lord there is mercy;

7   With him there is plenteous redemption,*
        and he shall redeem Israel from all their sins.


Rescue us, O God for whom we wait, from the depths of
depression and despair. May we trust in your mercy, know the
fullness of your redemption, and share in the glory of your
kingdom; through our Saviour Jesus Christ.

# 131

1   O Lord, I am not proud; *
        I have no haughty looks.

2   I do not occupy myself with great matters,*
        or with things that are too hard for me.

3   But I still my soul and make it quiet,
    like a child upon its mother's breast; *
        my soul is quieted within me.

4   O Israel, wait upon the Lord,*
        from this time forth for evermore.

God of earthquake, wind, and fire, may we know you also in the voice of silence. Teach us the way of quiet, that we may find our peace in your presence, in the pattern of our Saviour Jesus Christ.

## 132

1   Lord, remember David,*
       and all the hardships he endured;

2   How he swore an oath to the Lord *
       and vowed a vow to the Mighty One of Jacob:

3   "I will not come under the roof of my house,*
       nor climb up into my bed;

4   I will not allow my eyes to sleep,*
       nor let my eyelids slumber;

5   Until I find a place for the Lord,*
       a dwelling for the Mighty One of Jacob."

6   "The Ark! We heard it was in Ephratah; *
       we found it in the fields of Jearim.

7   Let us go to God's dwelling place; *
       let us fall upon our knees before his footstool."

8   Arise, O Lord, into your resting-place,*
       you and the ark of your strength.

9   Let your priests be clothed with righteousness; *
       let your faithful people sing with joy.

10  For your servant David's sake,*
       do not turn away the face of your anointed.

11  The Lord has sworn an oath to David; *
       in truth, he will not break it:

12  "A son, the fruit of your body *
       will I set upon your throne.

13  If your children keep my covenant
     and my testimonies that I shall teach them,*
       their children will sit upon your throne for evermore."

14  For the Lord has chosen Zion,*
        he has desired her for his habitation:

15  "This shall be my resting-place for ever; *
        here will I dwell, for I delight in her.

16  I will surely bless her provisions,*
        and satisfy her poor with bread.

17  I will clothe her priests with salvation,*
        and her faithful people will rejoice and sing.

18  There will I make the horn of David flourish; *
        I have prepared a lamp for my anointed.

19  As for his enemies, I will clothe them with shame; *
        but as for him, his crown will shine."

Gracious God, you have taught us in our Saviour Jesus Christ
that you are present wherever there is love, and that two or
three who gather in his name are citizens of your eternal city.
Feed us with the bread of life, that we may grow to recognize
in every human heart a sign of your presence and an
opportunity to serve you. We ask this in the name of Jesus
Christ our Lord.

# 133

1  Oh, how good and pleasant it is,*
        when brethren live together in unity!

2  It is like fine oil upon the head *
        that runs down upon the beard,

3  Upon the beard of Aaron,*
        and runs down upon the collar of his robe.

4  It is like the dew of Hermon *
        that falls upon the hills of Zion.

5  For there the Lord has ordained the blessing: *
        life for evermore.

Creator of the universe, from whom all things come, to whom
all things return, give your people such unity of heart and
mind, that all the world may grow in the life of your eternal
kingdom, through Jesus Christ our Lord.

# 134

1 Behold now, bless the Lord, all you servants of the Lord,*
   you that stand by night in the house of the Lord.

2 Lift up your hands in the holy place and bless the Lord; *
   the Lord who made heaven and earth bless
                    you out of Zion.

God our creator and redeemer, give us grateful hearts and
willing hands, that we may worthily praise your name and
build your kingdom among all people, to the glory of your
Son our Saviour Jesus Christ.

# 135

1 Hallelujah!
   Praise the name of the Lord; *
   give praise, you servants of the Lord,

2 You who stand in the house of the Lord,*
   in the courts of the house of our God.

3 Praise the Lord, for the Lord is good; *
   sing praises to his name, for it is lovely.

4 For the Lord has chosen Jacob for himself *
   and Israel for his own possession.

5 For I know that the Lord is great,*
   and that our Lord is above all gods.

6 The Lord does whatever pleases him, in heaven and
                    on earth,*
   in the seas and all the deeps.

7    He brings up rain clouds from the ends of the earth; *
     he sends out lightning with the rain,
     and brings the winds out of his storehouse.

8    It was he who struck down the firstborn of Egypt,*
     the firstborn both of man and beast.

9    He sent signs and wonders into the midst of you, O Egypt,*
     against Pharaoh and all his servants.

10    He overthrew many nations *
     and put mighty kings to death:

11    Sihon, king of the Amorites,
and Og, the king of Bashan,*
     and all the kingdoms of Canaan.

12    He gave their land to be an inheritance,*
     an inheritance for Israel his people.

13    O Lord, your name is everlasting; *
     your renown, O Lord, endures from age to age.

14    For the Lord gives his people justice *
     and shows compassion to his servants.

15    The idols of the heathen are silver and gold,*
     the work of human hands.

16    They have mouths, but they cannot speak; *
     eyes have they, but they cannot see.

17    They have ears, but they cannot hear; *
     neither is there any breath in their mouth.

18    Those who make them are like them,*
     and so are all who put their trust in them.

19    Bless the Lord, O house of Israel; *
     O house of Aaron, bless the Lord.

20    Bless the Lord, O house of Levi; *
     you who fear the Lord, bless the Lord.

21    Blessed be the Lord out of Zion,*
     who dwells in Jerusalem.
     Hallelujah!

God of freedom, you brought your people out of slavery with a mighty hand and gave them a law of love and justice. Deliver us from every temptation to be satisfied with false imitations of your will: with talk of peace that masks the face of war, and thanks for plenty that leaves the poor unfed. We pray for the coming of your kingdom, founded in Jesus Christ our Lord.

# 136

1  Give thanks to the Lord, for he is good,*
   for his mercy endures for ever.

2  Give thanks to the God of gods,*
   for his mercy endures for ever.

3  Give thanks to the Lord of lords,*
   for his mercy endures for ever.


4  Who only does great wonders,*
   for his mercy endures for ever;

5  Who by his wisdom made the heavens,*
   for his mercy endures for ever;

6  Who spread out the earth upon the waters,*
   for his mercy endures for ever;

7  Who created great lights,*
   for his mercy endures for ever;

8  The sun to rule the day,*
   for his mercy endures for ever;

9  The moon and the stars to govern the night,*
   for his mercy endures for ever.


10  Who struck down the firstborn of Egypt,*
    for his mercy endures for ever;

11  And brought out Israel from among them,*
    for his mercy endures for ever;

12  With a mighty hand and a stretched-out arm,*
    for his mercy endures for ever;

13 Who divided the Red Sea in two,*
    for his mercy endures for ever;

14 And made Israel to pass through the midst of it,*
    for his mercy endures for ever;

15 But swept Pharaoh and his army into the Red Sea,*
    for his mercy endures for ever;

16 Who led his people through the wilderness,*
    for his mercy endures for ever.

17 Who struck down great kings,*
    for his mercy endures for ever;

18 And slew mighty kings,*
    for his mercy endures for ever;

19 Sihon, king of the Amorites,*
    for his mercy endures for ever;

20 And Og, the king of Bashan,*
    for his mercy endures for ever;

21 And gave away their lands for an inheritance,*
    for his mercy endures for ever;

22 An inheritance for Israel his servant,*
    for his mercy endures for ever.

23 Who remembered us in our low estate,*
    for his mercy endures for ever;

24 And delivered us from our enemies,*
    for his mercy endures for ever;

25 Who gives food to all creatures,*
    for his mercy endures for ever;

26 Give thanks to the God of heaven,*
    for his mercy endures for ever.

Maker and Sustainer of all things, Source of all life and goodness,
help us always to love and serve one another, and to worship
you with joy and gladness, through Jesus Christ our Lord.

# 137

1   By the waters of Babylon we sat down and wept,*
    when we remembered you, O Zion.

2   As for our harps, we hung them up *
    on the trees in the midst of that land.

3   For those who led us away captive asked us for a song,
    and our oppressors called for mirth: *
     "Sing us one of the songs of Zion."

4   How shall we sing the Lord's song *
    upon an alien soil?

5   If I forget you, O Jerusalem,*
    let my right hand forget its skill.

6   Let my tongue cleave to the roof of my mouth
    if I do not remember you,*
     if I do not set Jerusalem above my highest joy.

7   Remember the day of Jerusalem, O Lord,
    against the people of Edom,*
     who said, "Down with it! down with it!
     even to the ground!"

8   O Daughter of Babylon, doomed to destruction,*
    happy the one who pays you back
    for what you have done to us!

9   Happy shall he be who takes your little ones,*
    and dashes them against the rock!

God of courage and compassion, comfort the exiled and
oppressed, strengthen the faith of your people, and bring us all
to our true home, the kingdom of our Lord and Saviour Jesus
Christ.

# 138

1   I will give thanks to you, O Lord, with my whole heart; *
    before the gods I will sing your praise.

2   I will bow down toward your holy temple
and praise your name,*
> because of your love and faithfulness;

3   For you have glorified your name *
> and your word above all things.

4   When I called, you answered me; *
> you increased my strength within me.

5   All the kings of the earth will praise you, O Lord,*
> when they have heard the words of your mouth.

6   They will sing of the ways of the Lord,*
> that great is the glory of the Lord.

7   Though the Lord be high, he cares for the lowly; *
> he perceives the haughty from afar.

8   Though I walk in the midst of trouble, you keep me safe; *
> you stretch forth your hand against the
> > fury of my enemies;
> your right hand shall save me.

9   The Lord will make good his purpose for me; *
> O Lord, your love endures for ever;
> do not abandon the works of your hands.

God of creation and fulfilment, help us to seek and discover
your purposes, that we may become willing instruments of
your grace, and that all the world may come to love and praise
your name, in the kingdom of your Son Jesus Christ our Lord.

# 139

1   Lord, you have searched me out and known me; *
> you know my sitting down and my rising up;
> you discern my thoughts from afar.

2   You trace my journeys and my resting-places *
> and are acquainted with all my ways.

3   Indeed, there is not a word on my lips,*
> but you, O Lord, know it altogether.

4 You press upon me behind and before *
  and lay your hand upon me.

5 Such knowledge is too wonderful for me; *
  it is so high that I cannot attain to it.

6 Where can I go then from your Spirit? *
  where can I flee from your presence?

7 If I climb up to heaven, you are there; *
  if I make the grave my bed, you are there also.

8 If I take the wings of the morning *
  and dwell in the uttermost parts of the sea,

9 Even there your hand will lead me *
  and your right hand hold me fast.

10 If I say, "Surely the darkness will cover me,*
  and the light around me turn to night,"

11 Darkness is not dark to you;
 the night is as bright as the day; *
  darkness and light to you are both alike.

12 For you yourself created my inmost parts; *
  you knit me together in my mother's womb.

13 I will thank you because I am marvellously made; *
  your works are wonderful, and I know it well.

14 My body was not hidden from you,*
  while I was being made in secret
  and woven in the depths of the earth.

15 Your eyes beheld my limbs, yet unfinished in the womb;
 all of them were written in your book; *
  they were fashioned day by day,
  when as yet there was none of them.

16 How deep I find your thoughts, O God! *
  how great is the sum of them!

17 If I were to count them, they would be more in number
     than the sand; *
  to count them all, my life span would need to
     be like yours.

18    Oh, that you would slay the wicked, O God! *
     You that thirst for blood, depart from me.

19    They speak despitefully against you; *
     your enemies take your name in vain.

20    Do I not hate those, O Lord, who hate you? *
     and do I not loathe those who rise up against you?

21    I hate them with a perfect hatred; *
     they have become my own enemies.

22    Search me out, O God, and know my heart; *
     try me and know my restless thoughts.

23    Look well whether there be any wickedness in me *
     and lead me in the way that is everlasting.

God of mystery and power, even our minds and hearts are the
veils and signs of your presence. We come in silent wonder to
learn the way of simplicity, the eternal road that leads to love
for you and for your whole creation. We come as your Son
Jesus Christ taught us, and in his name.

# 140

1    Deliver me, O Lord, from evildoers; *
     protect me from the violent,

2    Who devise evil in their hearts *
     and stir up strife all day long.

3    They have sharpened their tongues like a serpent; *
     adder's poison is under their lips.

4    Keep me, O Lord, from the hands of the wicked; *
     protect me from the violent,
     who are determined to trip me up.

5    The proud have hidden a snare for me
and stretched out a net of cords; *
     they have set traps for me along the path.

6    I have said to the Lord, "You are my God; *
     listen, O Lord, to my supplication.

7   O Lord God, the strength of my salvation,*
      you have covered my head in the day of battle.

8   Do not grant the desires of the wicked, O Lord,*
      nor let their evil plans prosper.

9   Let not those who surround me lift up their heads; *
      let the evil of their lips overwhelm them.

10  Let hot burning coals fall upon them; *
      let them be cast into the mire, never to rise up again."

11  A slanderer shall not be established on the earth,*
      and evil shall hunt down the lawless.

12  I know that the Lord will maintain the cause of the poor *
      and render justice to the needy.

13  Surely, the righteous will give thanks to your name,*
      and the upright shall continue in your sight.


Save us, Lord, from all terror and oppression; strengthen us to
maintain the cause of the poor, that justice may roll down like
waters and righteousness like an ever-flowing stream. We ask
this in the name of Jesus Christ the Lord.

# 141

1   O Lord, I call to you; come to me quickly; *
      hear my voice when I cry to you.

2   Let my prayer be set forth in your sight as incense,*
      the lifting up of my hands as the evening sacrifice.

3   Set a watch before my mouth, O Lord,
      and guard the door of my lips; *
      let not my heart incline to any evil thing.

4   Let me not be occupied in wickedness with evildoers,*
      nor eat of their choice foods.

5   Let the righteous smite me in friendly rebuke;
      let not the oil of the unrighteous anoint my head; *
      for my prayer is continually against their wicked deeds.

6   Let their rulers be overthrown in stony places,*
        that they may know my words are true.

7   As when a plowman turns over the earth in furrows,*
        let their bones be scattered at the mouth of the grave.

8   But my eyes are turned to you, Lord God; *
        in you I take refuge;
        do not strip me of my life.

9   Protect me from the snare which they have laid for me *
        and from the traps of the evildoers.

10  Let the wicked fall into their own nets,*
        while I myself escape.

God our protector and guide, incline our hearts to turn from
evil and do good, that our lives may be a prayer for the coming
of your kingdom, through Jesus Christ our Lord.

# 142

1   I cry to the Lord with my voice; *
        to the Lord I make loud supplication.

2   I pour out my complaint before him *
        and tell him all my trouble.

3   When my spirit languishes within me, you know my path; *
        in the way wherein I walk they have hidden a trap for me.

4   I look to my right hand and find no one who knows me; *
        I have no place to flee to, and no one cares for me.

5   I cry out to you, O Lord; *
        I say, "You are my refuge,
        my portion in the land of the living."

6   Listen to my cry for help, for I have been brought very low; *
        save me from those who pursue me,
        for they are too strong for me.

7   Bring me out of prison, that I may give thanks to your name; *
        when you have dealt bountifully with me,
        the righteous will gather around me.

God our consoler and redeemer, save your people coerced and made captive by the powers of evil, and bring us into the way of freedom and liberty prepared by the sacrifice of your Son our Saviour Jesus Christ.

# 143

1 Lord, hear my prayer,
and in your faithfulness heed my supplications; *
   answer me in your righteousness.

2 Enter not into judgement with your servant,*
   for in your sight shall no one living be justified.

3 For my enemy has sought my life;
he has crushed me to the ground; *
   he has made me live in dark places like those who
       are long dead.

4 My spirit faints within me; *
   my heart within me is desolate.

5 I remember the time past;
I muse upon all your deeds; *
   I consider the works of your hands.

6 I spread out my hands to you; *
   my soul gasps to you like a thirsty land.

7 O Lord, make haste to answer me; my spirit fails me; *
   do not hide your face from me
   or I shall be like those who go down to the Pit.

8 Let me hear of your loving-kindness in the morning,
for I put my trust in you; *
   show me the road that I must walk,
   for I lift up my soul to you.

9 Deliver me from my enemies, O Lord,*
   for I flee to you for refuge.

10 Teach me to do what pleases you, for you are my God; *
   let your good Spirit lead me on level ground.

11 Revive me, O Lord, for your name's sake; *
   for your righteousness' sake, bring me out of trouble.

12   Of your goodness, destroy my enemies
and bring all my foes to naught,*
     for truly I am your servant.

God of our hope, when we are distracted by care and sickness,
help us to recognize your image in ourselves and others, that
we may be made whole and the world become the kingdom of
our Lord and Saviour Jesus Christ.

# 144

1   Blessed be the Lord my rock! *
     who trains my hands to fight and my fingers to battle;

2   My help and my fortress, my stronghold and my deliverer,*
     my shield in whom I trust,
     who subdues the peoples under me.

3   O Lord, what are we that you should care for us? *
     mere mortals that you should think of us?

4   We are like a puff of wind; *
     our days are like a passing shadow.

5   Bow your heavens, O Lord, and come down; *
     touch the mountains, and they shall smoke.

6   Hurl the lightning and scatter them; *
     shoot out your arrows and rout them.

7   Stretch out your hand from on high; *
     rescue me and deliver me from the great waters,
     from the hand of foreign peoples,

8   Whose mouths speak deceitfully *
     and whose right hand is raised in falsehood.

9   O God, I will sing to you a new song; *
     I will play to you on a ten-stringed lyre.

10   You give victory to kings *
     and have rescued David your servant.

11  Rescue me from the hurtful sword *
        and deliver me from the hand of foreign peoples,

12  Whose mouths speak deceitfully *
        and whose right hand is raised in falsehood.

13  May our sons be like plants well nurtured from their youth,*
        and our daughters like sculptured corners of a palace.

14  May our barns be filled to overflowing with all
                            manner of crops; *
        may the flocks in our pastures increase by thousands
                            and tens of thousands;
        may our cattle be fat and sleek.

15  May there be no breaching of the walls, no going into exile,*
        no wailing in the public squares.

16  Happy are the people of whom this is so! *
        happy are the people whose God is the Lord!

Generous and bountiful God, give compassion to the
prosperous and comfort to the needy, that all people may
come to love and praise you, through Jesus Christ our Lord.

# 145

1  I will exalt you, O God my King,*
        and bless your name for ever and ever.

2  Every day will I bless you *
        and praise your name for ever and ever.

3  Great is the Lord and greatly to be praised; *
        there is no end to his greatness.

4  One generation shall praise your works to another *
        and shall declare your power.

5  I will ponder the glorious splendour of your majesty *
        and all your marvellous works.

6  They shall speak of the might of your wondrous acts,*
        and I will tell of your greatness.

7   They shall publish the remembrance of your
                    great goodness; *
      they shall sing of your righteous deeds.

8   The Lord is gracious and full of compassion,
      slow to anger and of great kindness.

9   The Lord is loving to everyone *
      and his compassion is over all his works.

10  All your works praise you, O Lord,*
      and your faithful servants bless you.

11  They make known the glory of your kingdom *
      and speak of your power;

12  That the peoples may know of your power *
      and the glorious splendour of your kingdom.

13  Your kingdom is an everlasting kingdom; *
      your dominion endures throughout all ages.

14  The Lord is faithful in all his words *
      and merciful in all his deeds.

15  The Lord upholds all those who fall; *
      he lifts up those who are bowed down.

16  The eyes of all wait upon you, O Lord,*
      and you give them their food in due season.

17  You open wide your hand *
      and satisfy the needs of every living creature.

18  The Lord is righteous in all his ways *
      and loving in all his works.

19  The Lord is near to those who call upon him,*
      to all who call upon him faithfully.

20  He fulfils the desire of those who fear him,*
      he hears their cry and helps them.

21  The Lord preserves all those who love him,*
      but he destroys all the wicked.

22  My mouth shall speak the praise of the Lord; *
      let all flesh bless his holy name for ever and ever.

Almighty God, give us grace to know you more and more, that knowing we may love and loving we may praise, that the whole world may hear your name and worship you, through Jesus Christ our Lord.

# 146

1  Hallelujah!
Praise the Lord, O my soul! *
  I will praise the Lord as long as I live;
  I will sing praises to my God while I have my being.

2  Put not your trust in rulers, nor in any child of earth,*
  for there is no help in them.

3  When they breathe their last, they return to earth,*
  and in that day their thoughts perish.

4  Happy are they who have the God of Jacob for their help! *
  whose hope is in the Lord their God;

5  Who made heaven and earth, the seas, and all that
            is in them; *
  who keeps his promise for ever;

6  Who gives justice to those who are oppressed,*
  and food to those who hunger.

7  The Lord sets the prisoners free;
the Lord opens the eyes of the blind; *
  the Lord lifts up those who are bowed down;

8  The Lord loves the righteous;
the Lord cares for the stranger; *
  he sustains the orphan and widow,
  but frustrates the way of the wicked.

9  The Lord shall reign for ever,*
  your God, O Zion, throughout all generations.
  Hallelujah!

God our creator and redeemer, inspire your people, in prosperity or adversity, to turn always to you, eternal source of life, health, and goodness; through Jesus Christ our Lord.

# 147

1 Hallelujah!
How good it is to sing praises to our God! *
   how pleasant it is to honour him with praise!

2 The Lord rebuilds Jerusalem; *
   he gathers the exiles of Israel.

3 He heals the brokenhearted *
   and binds up their wounds.

4 He counts the number of the stars *
   and calls them all by their names.

5 Great is our Lord and mighty in power; *
   there is no limit to his wisdom.

6 The Lord lifts up the lowly,*
   but casts the wicked to the ground.

7 Sing to the Lord with thanksgiving; *
   make music to our God upon the harp.

8 He covers the heavens with clouds *
   and prepares rain for the earth;

9 He makes grass to grow upon the mountains *
   and green plants to serve mankind.

10 He provides food for flocks and herds *
   and for the young ravens when they cry.

11 He is not impressed by the might of a horse,*
   he has no pleasure in the strength of a man;

12 But the Lord has pleasure in those who fear him,*
   in those who await his gracious favour.

13 Worship the Lord, O Jerusalem; *
   praise your God, O Zion;

14 For he has strengthened the bars of your gates; *
   he has blessed your children within you.

15 He has established peace on your borders; *
   he satisfies you with the finest wheat.

16 He sends out his command to the earth,*
   and his word runs very swiftly.

17 He gives snow like wool; *
   he scatters hoarfrost like ashes.

18 He scatters his hail like bread crumbs; *
   who can stand against his cold?

19 He sends forth his word and melts them; *
   he blows with his wind, and the waters flow.

20 He declares his word to Jacob,*
   his statutes and his judgements to Israel.

21 He has not done so to any other nation; *
   to them he has not revealed his judgements.
   Hallelujah!

God of the universe, Lord of life, give us grace to see you in all
your works, in all creatures, all people, and in our hearts, that
we may faithfully serve you and worthily praise your holy
name, through Jesus Christ our Lord.

# 148

1 Hallelujah!
Praise the Lord from the heavens; *
   praise him in the heights.

2 Praise him, all you angels of his; *
   praise him, all his host.

3 Praise him, sun and moon; *
   praise him, all you shining stars.

4 Praise him, heaven of heavens,*
   and you waters above the heavens.

5 Let them praise the name of the Lord; *
   for he commanded, and they were created.

6 He made them stand fast for ever and ever; *
   he gave them a law which shall not pass away.

7 Praise the Lord from the earth,*
   you sea-monsters and all deeps;

8    Fire and hail, snow and fog,*
         tempestuous wind, doing his will;

9    Mountains and all hills,*
         fruit trees and all cedars;

10   Wild beasts and all cattle,*
         creeping things and wingèd birds;

11   Kings of the earth and all peoples,*
         princes and all rulers of the world;

12   Young men and maidens,*
         old and young together.

13   Let them praise the name of the Lord,*
         for his name only is exalted,
         his splendour is over earth and heaven.

14   He has raised up strength for his people
     and praise for all his loyal servants,*
         the children of Israel, a people who are near him.
         Hallelujah!

Blessed are you, Lord our God, creator of heaven and earth;
you open our eyes to see the wonders around us, and our
hearts and mouths to praise you. Now give us strength for
loving service, through Jesus Christ our Lord.

# 149

1    Hallelujah!
     Sing to the Lord a new song; *
         sing his praise in the congregation of the faithful.

2    Let Israel rejoice in his maker; *
         let the children of Zion be joyful in their king.

3    Let them praise his name in the dance; *
         let them sing praise to him with timbrel and harp.

4    For the Lord takes pleasure in his people *
         and adorns the poor with victory.

5    Let the faithful rejoice in triumph; *
         let them be joyful on their beds.

6    Let the praises of God be in their throat *
        and a two-edged sword in their hand;

7    To wreak vengeance on the nations *
        and punishment on the peoples;

8    To bind their kings in chains *
        and their nobles with links of iron;

9    To inflict on them the judgement decreed; *
        this is glory for all his faithful people.
        Hallelujah!

Accept our praise, God of justice, defender of the oppressed.
Give us grace to join in this your holy work, that all the world
may see your glory, through Jesus Christ our Lord.


# 150

1    Hallelujah!
     Praise God in his holy temple; *
        praise him in the firmament of his power.

2    Praise him for his mighty acts; *
        praise him for his excellent greatness.

3    Praise him with the blast of the ram's-horn; *
        praise him with lyre and harp.

4    Praise him with timbrel and dance; *
        praise him with strings and pipe.

5    Praise him with resounding cymbals; *
        praise him with loud-clanging cymbals.

6    Let everything that has breath *
        praise the Lord.
        Hallelujah!

Maker of the universe, Source of all life, give us grace to serve
you with our whole heart, that we may faithfully perform your
will and joyfully participate in your creation, to the praise and
glory of your name, through Jesus Christ our Lord.

# Music

## Morning Prayer 1

*Either or both of the following responses may be used.*

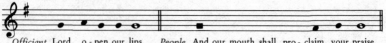

Officiant Lord, o-pen our lips.    People And our mouth shall pro-claim your praise.

Officiant O God, make speed to save us.    People O Lord, make haste to help us.

All Glory to the Father, and to the Son, and to the Holy Spir-it:

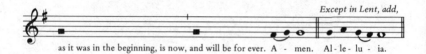

*Except in Lent, add,*

as it was in the beginning, is now, and will be for ever. A - men. Al-le-lu-ia.


## Morning Prayer 2    *Tones by Norman Mealy*

*Either or both of the following responses may be used.*

Officiant Lord, o-pen our lips.    People And our mouth shall pro-claim your praise.

Officiant O God, make speed to save us.    People O Lord, make haste to help us.

All Glory to the Father, and to the Son, and to the Ho-ly Spir-it:

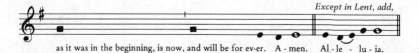

*Except in Lent, add,*

as it was in the beginning, is now, and will be for ev-er. A - men. Al-le-lu-ia.

**Evening Prayer 1**

Officiant  O Lord, I call to you; come to me quick-ly;    People  Hear my voice when I cry to you.

Officiant  Let my prayer be set forth in your sight as in-cense,

People  The lifting up of my hands as the evening sac-ri-fice.

All  Glory to the Father, and to the Son, and to the Holy Spir-it:

*Except in Lent, add,*

as it was in the beginning, is now, and will be for ever. A - men. Al-le-lu-ia.

**Evening Prayer 2**    *Tones by Norman Mealy*

Officiant  O Lord, I call to you; come to me quick-ly.  People  Hear my voice when I cry to you.

Officiant  Let my prayer be set forth in your sight as in-cense,

People  The lifting up of my hands as the eve-ning sac-ri-fice.

All  Glory to the Father, and to the Son, and to the Ho-ly Spir-it:

*Except in Lent, add,*

as it was in the beginning, is now, and will be for ev-er. A - men. Al-le-lu-ia.

**Late Evening 1**

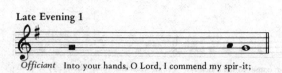

*Officiant*  Into your hands, O Lord, I commend my spir-it;

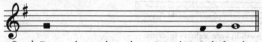

*People* For you have redeemed me, O Lord, O God of truth.

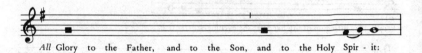

*All* Glory to the Father, and to the Son, and to the Holy Spir - it:

*Except in Lent, add,*

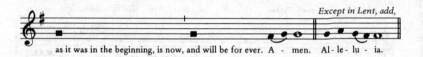

as it was in the beginning, is now, and will be for ever. A - men. Al - le - lu - ia.

**Late Evening 2**   *Tones by Norman Mealy*

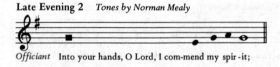

*Officiant*  Into your hands, O Lord, I com-mend my spir-it;

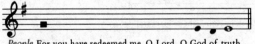

*People* For you have redeemed me, O Lord, O God of truth.

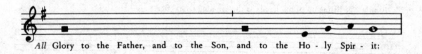

*All* Glory to the Father, and to the Son, and to the Ho - ly Spir - it:

*Except in Lent, add,*

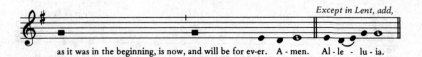

as it was in the beginning, is now, and will be for ev-er.   A - men.   Al - le - lu - ia.

# Litany Responses

*In the litanies, the response may be changed to a similar appropriate expression. The suffrages may be changed to make them fit with another response.*

*When the litanies are sung, they may be introduced by a cantor singing the response, which is repeated by all before the first petition. The response is then sung by all after each suffrage.*

*These responses may be sung at any suitable pitch, preferably without accompaniment. When the last note is tied to the next bar, it is possible to continue humming the last note as an accompaniment to the next suffrage. In Response No. 1, the people may begin their response simultaneously with the end of the leader's bidding, so that the two overlap and both leader and people sing the word Lord together.*

*Suggested tones are provided for the suffrages. When the tone has two parts and the words are divided into two main clauses, both parts of the tone are used. When the words form a single clause, either part of the tone may be used. The last accented syllable of the words is sung to the note marked with an accent. The tones may be expanded, contracted, altered, or replaced by others. What is important is that it be clear when the people's part is to follow.*

**1**

Cantor Lord, have mer-cy. *All* Lord, have mer-cy.
To you, O Lord.

...let us pray to the Lord.

**2**

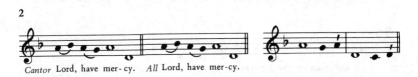

Cantor Lord, have mer-cy. *All* Lord, have mer-cy.

**3**

Cantor Ky-ri-e e - le-i-son. *All* Ky-ri-e e - le-i-son.

**4**

Cantor Lord, hear our prayer. *All* Lord, hear our prayer.

**5**

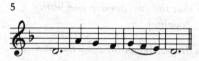

Cantor Lord, hear and have mer - cy.

*All* Lord, hear and have mer - cy.

**6 Late Evening** *Tones by Norman Mealy*

Cantor Keep us, O Lord, as the apple of your eye. *All* Hide us under the shadow of your wings.

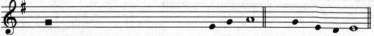

Cantor For the peace of the whole world, we pray to you, Lord. *All* Lord, have mer -cy....

Cantor ... and asleep we may rest in peace. *All* A - men.

## 7 Advent

*Cantor* Lord Je-sus, come soon! *All* Lord Je-sus, come soon!

## 8 Easter

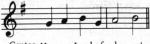

*Cantor* Hear us, Lord of glo - ry!

*All* Hear us, Lord of glo - ry!

... let us pray to the Lord.

## 9 Thanksgiving Litany

*Cantor* We thank you, Lord. *All* We thank you, Lord.

# The Lord's Prayer 1

Office

*Officiant* Gathering our prayers and praises in-to one, let us pray as our Sa-viour taught us.

Prayers at Mid-day

*Officiant* Lord, re - mem- ber us in your king-dom, and teach us to pray,

Eucharist

*Celebrant* As our Sa-viour taught us, let us pray,

Funeral Liturgy

*Celebrant* Gathering all our cares in - to one, let us pray as our Sa-viour taught us,

*Music by McNeil Robinson*

*All* Our Fa-ther in heav-en, hal-lowed be your name, your king-dom come,

your will be done, on earth as in heav-en. Give us to-day our dai - ly bread,

For-give us our sins as we for-give those who sin a-gainst us.

Save us from the time of trial, and de-liv-er us from e - vil. For the king-dom,

the pow-er, and the glo-ry are yours, now and for ev - er. A - men.

# The Lord's Prayer 2

Office

*Officiant* Ga-thering our prayers and praises into one, let us pray as our Sa-viour taught us,

Prayers at Mid-day

*Officiant* Lord, re-mem-ber us in your king-dom, and teach us to pray,

Eucharist

*Celebrant* As our Sa-viour taught us, let us pray,

Funeral Liturgy

*Celebrant* Ga-thering all our cares into one. let us pray as our Sa-viour taught us,

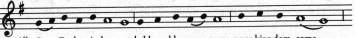

*All* Our Fa-ther in heav-en, hal-lowed be your name, your king-dom come,

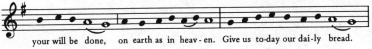

your will be done, on earth as in heav-en. Give us to-day our dai-ly bread.

For-give us our sins as we for-give those who sin a-gainst us.

Save us from the time of tri-al and de-liv-er us from e-vil. For the king-dom,

the pow'r, and the glo-ry are yours, now and for ev-er. A-men.

## The Gospel

*Reader*  The Lord be with you  *People*  And also with you.

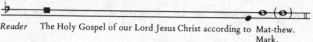

*Reader*  The Holy Gospel of our Lord Jesus Christ according to  Mat-thew.
Mark.
Luke.
John.

*People*  Glory to you, Lord Je - sus Christ.

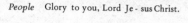

*Reader*  The Gos-pel of Christ.  *People*  Praise to you, Lord Je - sus Christ.

## The Peace

*Celebrant*  The peace of the Lord be al - ways with you.  *People*  And al - so with you.

## The Great Thanksgiving 1

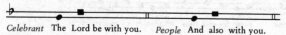

*Celebrant*  The Lord be with you.  *People*  And also with you.

*Celebrant*  Lift up your hearts.  *People*  We lift them to the Lord.

*Celebrant*  Let us give thanks to the Lord our God. *People*  It is right to give our thanks and praise.

## The Great Thanksgiving 2

*The quilisma ( ∿ ) implies both that the note before it is to be lengthened slightly and that the three notes slurred together are to be sung with a crescendo.*

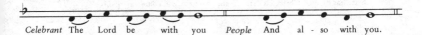

Celebrant The Lord be with you People And al - so with you.

Celebrant Lift up your hearts. People We lift them to the Lord.

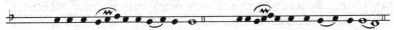

Celebrant Let us give thanks to the Lord our God. People It is right to give our thanks and praise.

Conclusion

Celebrant ... for ev - er. People A - men.

### Christ Our Passover

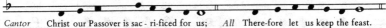

Cantor Christ our Passover is sac - ri-ficed for us; All There-fore let us keep the feast.

### Christ Our Passover *with Alleluias*

Cantor Al - le - lu-ia! Christ our Passover is sac - ri - ficed for us;

All There-fore let us keep the feast. Al - le - lu - ia!

## Eucharistic Prayer 1

### Acclamation 1 *two settings*

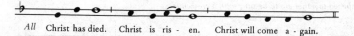

*All* Christ has died. Christ is ris - en. Christ will come a - gain.

*This acclamation may be sung first by a cantor and then repeated by all.*

Christ has died. Christ is ris - en. Christ will come a - gain.

### Acclamation 2

*This acclamation may be sung first by a cantor and then repeated by all.*

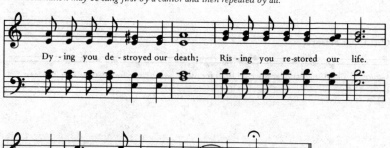

Dy - ing you de - stroyed our death; Ris - ing you re - stored our life.

Lord Je - sus, come in glo - ry.

**Eucharistic Prayer 3**  Anamnesis

*Celebrant* There-fore, Father, according to his com-mand,

*All* we re-mem-ber his death, we pro-claim his re-sur-rec-tion, we a-wait his com-ing in glo - ry;

**Eucharistic Prayers 4 and 5**  Acclamations *two settings*

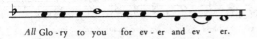

*All* Glo -ry to you for ev - er and ev - er.

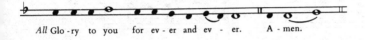

*All* Glo -ry to you for ev - er and ev - er. A - men.

*All* Glo - ry to you for ev - er and ev - er.

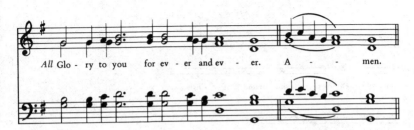

*All* Glo - ry to you for ev - er and ev - er. A - - - men.

**Eucharistic Prayer 6** Acclamation *Plainsong*

*All* We praise you, we bless you, we give thanks to you, and we pray to you Lord our God.

*In the Language of the Book of Common Prayer 1962*

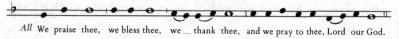

*All* We praise thee, we bless thee, we __ thank thee, and we pray to thee, Lord our God.

**Eucharistic Prayer 6** Acclamation *Byzantine*

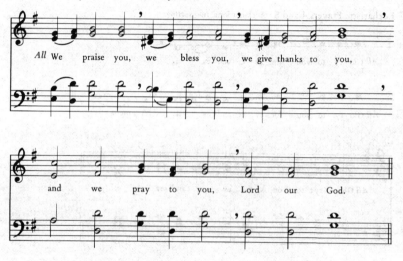

*All* We praise you, we bless you, we give thanks to you,

and we pray to you, Lord our God.

**Dismissal**

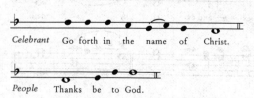

*Celebrant* Go forth in the name of Christ.

*People* Thanks be to God.

# Acknowledgements

Portions of this book are taken from *The Book of Common Prayer* (1979) of the Episcopal Church of the United States of America, and other portions have been adapted from that book with approval.

A portion of scripture quotation is from the Revised Standard Version of the Bible copyrighted 1946, 1952, © 1971, 1973 by the Division of Christian Education of the National Council of the Churches of Christ in the U.S.A., and used by permission.

English translation of the *Lord's Prayer, Apostles' Creed, Nicene Creed* (adapted), *Kyrie, Gloria in Excelsis, Sursum Corda* (adapted), *Sanctus and Benedictus, Gloria Patri, Benedictus, Te Deum, Magnificat,* and *Nunc Dimittis,* © by the International Consultation on English Texts.

Introductory Response No. 6 on p. 98 is reprinted from Contemporary Worship 5—*Services of the Word,* copyright © 1972, by permission of the publishers for the Inter-Lutheran Commission on Worship, representing the copyright holders.

Excerpts from *Praise God in Song,* copyright © 1979 by G.I.A. Publications, Inc., Chicago, Illinois. All rights reserved.

The canticle "Bless'd be the God of Israel" on p. 89, © 1969, James Quinn, SJ, printed by permission of Geoffrey Chapman, a division of Cassell Ltd.

The canticle "Jesus Christ is Lord" on p. 91, the Lent Responsory on pp. 106–107, the Advent Litany on pp. 119–120, the Prayer for Guidance on pp. 130–131, and the Prayer for Grace and Faith on p. 131, have been adapted from *Praise in all our Days (Praise God),* copyright © (1977), Oxford University Press, New York, N.Y.

Timothy Dudley-Smith, hymn: "Tell Out, My Soul." Copyright © 1965 by Hope Publishing Co., Carol Stream, IL 60188. All Rights Reserved. Used by Permission.

The Collect for Peace on p. 130 is adapted from the *Book of Common Prayer* of the Church of England, and the prayer commencing "Gracious God . . ." on p. 214 is based on a prayer in *The Alternative Service Book* 1980. Both are reproduced with permission.

"A Prayer for Strength" on p. 130 is based on a prayer in *The Daily Office*, Ronald C.D. Jasper, ed., SPCK and The Epworth Press, London 1968, © The Joint Liturgical Group, 1968. Adapted with permission of SPCK.

The second eucharistic prayer is based on a number of sources, including the English translation of the *Eucharistic Prayer of Hippolytus* and notes for this translation, © 1983, International Committee on English in the Liturgy, Inc. All rights reserved. Altered and adapted with permission.

The proper prefaces for the Epiphany, Trinity Sunday, the Reign of Christ, and Ordinations, and the blessings for Advent and the Incarnation are based on forms in *The Roman Missal*, © 1973, International Committee on English in the Liturgy, Inc. All rights reserved. Altered and adapted with permission.

Some of the prayers in the Proper Sentences, Readings, and Prayers, and Psalm Prayer 70, are based on prayers in *The Roman Missal*, © 1973, International Committee on English in the Liturgy, Inc. All rights reserved. Altered and adapted with permission.

Anthem 1, on pp. 314–316, is excerpted from *From Ashes to Fire*, Supplemental Worship Resource 8. Copyright © 1979 by Abingdon. Reprinted by permission.

The prayer beginning, "God of grace and glory," on pp. 602–603 is adapted from "For a Dead Person" from *Your Word is Near* by Huub Oosterhuis. © 1968 by the Missionary Society of St Paul the Apostle in the State of New York. Used by permission of Paulist Press.

No. 7 in Occasional Prayers, "For Home and Family," from David Mace, *Whom God Hath Joined*, © The Epworth Press, London, 1953 and 1975.

No. 19 in Occasional Prayers, "For Fisheries." Excerpt from *A Book of Blessings*, copyright © Concacan Inc., 1981. Reproduced with permission of the Canadian Conference of Catholic Bishops, Ottawa.

No. 21 in Occasional Prayers, "For the Neighbourhood," is reprinted from the *Lutheran Book of Worship*, copyright © 1978, by permission of the publishers and the copyright holders.

No. 26 in Occasional Prayers, "For those in Affliction," is reprinted from the *Service Book and Hymnal*, © 1958, The Board of Publication, Lutheran Church in America. Reprinted and adapted with permission.

F. Bland Tucker, hymns: "All praise to thee, for thou, O King divine," and "O Gracious Light." Used by permission, from *The Hymnal 1982*, copyright The Church Pension Fund.

The prayer, "A Thanksgiving," on p. 697 is reprinted from *Contemporary Parish Prayers* by Frank Colquhoun, Hodder & Stoughton, London, 1975. Copyright © 1967 by Frank Colquhoun.

Psalm Prayers 54, 59, 62, 63, 64, 65, 86, 90, 99, 100, 105, 106, 119, 122 and 125, from the English translation of *The Liturgy of the Hours*, © 1974 International Committee on English in the Liturgy, Inc., were adapted for the *Lutheran Book of Worship*, copyright © 1978, and are used by permission of the International Commission on English in the Liturgy and the Board of Publication of the Lutheran Church in America.

Tones for the introductory responses Morning Prayer I, Morning Prayer II, Evening Prayer I, Evening Prayer II, Late Evening I, Late Evening II, and for the litany for Late Evening, are from *The Book of Canticles*, copyright © 1979, The Church Pension Fund, New York. Used by permission.

Tones for the eucharistic dialogue (solemn form), the Peace (two forms), Christ our Passover, and Christ our Passover with Alleluias on p. 921, are from *The Holy Eucharist, Altar Edition*, copyright © 1977, Church Hymnal Corporation. Used by permission.

Tones for the eucharistic dialogue (simple form), are from *Songs for Liturgy*, copyright © 1971, Walton Music Corporation, Chapel Hill, N.C.

McNeil Robinson, setting of the Lord's Prayer, © 1979, Theodore Presser Co. Used by permission.

If, through inadvertence, anything has been printed without permission, the publishers ask that the omission be excused and agree to make proper acknowledgement in future printings after notice has been received.

The use of capitals in English sentences (except in the opening word) has diminished steadily during recent centuries, not least in words of sacred reference where the process has accelerated in the last few decades. In a compilation such as this, which draws on a number of sources representing different stages of linguistic development, some inconsistencies may appear. In general the following standards apply: the names of rites are not capitalized except in their titles and in references to their titles; in liturgical texts appropriate words in the titles of sections of liturgies are capitalized, but the functions they contain are not; *Word* is capitalized when it refers to Christ as the incarnate *Logos*, but usually not otherwise; traditional titles of Christ are capitalized, but metaphors applied to God, either as titles or attributes, usually are not, except in forms of address. Spelling in the Psalter has been adapted to the standard of the *Concise Oxford Dictionary*.